Louise Wells

The Greek language of healing from Homer to New Testament times

W DE G

Beihefte zur Zeitschrift für die neutestamentliche Wissenschaft

und die Kunde der älteren Kirche

Herausgegeben von
Erich Gräßer

Band 83

Walter de Gruyter · Berlin · New York
1998

Louise Wells

The Greek language of healing from Homer to New Testament times

Walter de Gruyter · Berlin · New York
1998

∞ Printed on acid-free which falls within the guidelines of the ANSI
to ensure permanence and durability.

Die Deutsche Bibliothek – Cataloging-in-Publication Data

[Zeitschrift für die neutestamentliche Wissenschaft und die Kunde der älteren Kirche / Beihefte]
Beihefte zur Zeitschrift für die neutestamentliche Wissenschaft und die Kunde der älteren Kirche. – Berlin ; New York : de Gruyter
Früher Schriftenreihe
Reihe Beihefte zu: Zeitschrift für die neutestamentliche Wissenschaft und die Kunde der älteren Kirche
Bd. 83. Wells, Louise: The Greek language of healing from Homer to New Testament times. – 1998

Wells, Louise:
The Greek language of healing from Homer to New Testament times / Louise Wells. – Berlin ; New York : de Gruyter, 1998
(Beihefte zur Zeitschrift für die neutestamentliche Wissenschaft und die Kunde der älteren Kirche ; Bd. 83)
Zugl.: Diss., 1993
ISBN 3-11-015389-0

ISSN 0171-6441

Printed in Germany
Printing: Werner Hildebrand, Berlin
Binding: Lüderitz & Bauer-GmbH, Berlin

For my family

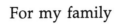

Preface

The problem of suffering has preoccupied mankind since the earliest times. From the time of Homer to the present day humans have constantly searched for a solution to their suffering and an understanding of it. This study focuses on two expressions of this search through a study of the Greek language of healing: the healing cult of Asklepios, which flourished in the Mediterranean world from the fifth century BC to the fourth century AD, and that of Jesus of Nazareth, whose healing ministry began in the first century AD, supplanted that of Asklepios in the fourth century AD, and is still in existence today. The investigation does not consider whether physical healings actually occurred; rather it is an exploration of the meaning of the general terms used to describe the healings recorded.

The study is in two parts: Part One contains the argument, Part Two the texts and translations (or analysis of texts) on which the argument is based. Usually only the primary texts in which language has been discussed are cited in the bibliography, otherwise reference to primary sources is made by the usual method in footnotes.

Part One is in two sections: Section One begins with the use of healing language in the work of Homer, and traces the development of this semantic field through a study of the language surrounding the cult of Asklepios at Epidauros, Athens, Kos and Pergamon. These four centres were chosen because they illustrate the differing nature of the cult over the period of its existence. Epidauros was a major colonising sanctuary, and remained a major centre of pilgrimage throughout its existence; Athens became a state cult and so illustrates a parochial and familial quality; Kos was the centre of a major medical school; and Pergamon was both the cult focus of a major hellenistic monarchy, and the site where the great Galen practised medicine. Thus a focus on these four centres allows a study of a breadth of sources, from before the time of Hippokrates until the time of Galen. Naturally the study of sources is not exhaustive. A selection was made from as wide a field as possible to illustrate the use of general healing terms in inscriptions and literature over the longest possible timespan.

After a bridging survey of the Jewish use of this semantic field in the Septuagint, together with complementary material from Philo of Alexandria, and Josephus, Section Two focuses on the meaning of the same semantic field in the New Testament. A linguistic survey of Hebrew and Aramaic documents is excluded, as being outside the scope of the topic, in terms of both space and relevance.

Central to this study are the human concepts of health and wholeness, and of the relationship of mind and body, spirit and soul, and the language used to express these concepts and relationships. Especially significant are the forms and usage of θεραπεύω, ἰάομαι, ὑγιαίνω, σῴζω, and their derivatives. It will be seen that θεραπεύω and ἰάομαι, while overlapping slightly in meaning, are not synonymous in a healing context, and that there is an aspectual quality implicit in each that is important for our understanding of them. As well, from its first appearance in cognate form in the work of Homer, the verb θεραπεύω over time burgeons in meaning to include emotional, physical, spiritual, and psychological factors (although these factors are foreshadowed in the characteristics of the Homeric θεράπων), until, in a teaching context, its focus is primarily spiritual. In contrast, the meaning of the other verb groups remains reasonably static. Thus these characteristics, noted in Section One, reflected in the healing language of the Septuagint, and corroborated by contemporary Jewish authors writing in Greek, are important for our understanding of the appearance of these word groups in the New Testament.

I owe acknowledgement to those who have made the research for this book possible: the Commonwealth of Australia for the award of a postgraduate scholarship; the Tasmanian Friends of the Australian Archaeological Institute at Athens for a scholarship which enabled me to travel to Greece, stay at the Institute Hostel in Athens for three months and read at the libraries of the foreign schools there; the Classics Department of the University of Tasmania for the award of a Dunbabin Scholarship which enabled me to travel to the archaeological sites of asklepieia in Greece and Turkey; the staff of the museums at Athens, Bergama, Epidauros, Korinth, Kos, and Piraeus for permission to photograph exhibits; and the staff of the Epigraphical Museum at Athens for permission to work there and to photograph some of the stones. The debt I owe to Ludwig and Emma Edelstein will also become obvious. Their collection of testimonies concerning the cult of Asklepios has been an invaluable resource for this study.

I would also like to thank the staff of Walter de Gruyter & Co. for their interest and patience. I have appreciated their goodwill and assistance.

There are a number of special people who in one way or another have greatly enriched my life, and my work, and whom I would like to name. Of my teachers: Professors Russel Ward, Portia Robinson, Raoul Mortley, Max Wilcox, and Paul Weaver. Others whom I would like to mention for support of differing kinds are Barbara Chisholm, John Bishop, Mary Bagnall, Marnie Yeates, Ted Nixon, Frank Clarke, Janice Crowley, Robert Barnes, Greg Horsley, Michael Lattke, Frank Moloney, Iain Lonie, Hermann Kienast, Martin Schäfer, George Cresswell, Rudy Quadfasel, Andy Heron, Nancy Bookidis, Stuart Godfrey, Ellen Malm, Robert Wesley-Smith, Barbara Johnson, Warwick Cuthbertson, Owen Dowling, Jenny Day, Patsy Graham, Beatrice Newton, and Jocelyn and Bill Windeyer. To them all my grateful thanks.

Last and most of all I would like to thank my family, particularly my husband and children, for their continuing support and encouragement. My especial thanks to my husband Graham, who not only encouraged my postgraduate studies, but also toiled over my drawings to reproduce the maps in Appendices 1:1 and 1:2, and supervised the type-setting of the entire work for publication.

All mistakes are, of course, my own.

Louise Wells 17 September, 1997

Table of Contents

Preface vii
Table of Contents xi
List of illustrations xvii
Abbreviations xviii
Plates xix

Part One: Argument

Section One

The language of healing in the Greek world

1. *In the beginning* 1
2. *Asklepios at Epidauros* 13
   2.1. Sources 16
   2.2. Epidauros 18
   2.3. Epigraphical evidence 21
   2.4. Patient profile 22
   2.5. Healing methods 25
   2.6. Healing language 31
   2.6.1. ὑγιής 31
   2.6.2. ἰάομαι 33
   2.7. Conclusion 36

3. Asklepios at Athens 40

3.1. Healing methods 43
3.2. Healing language in inscriptions 46
3.3. Literary evidence 50
3.3.1. Thucydides (Xenophon) 50
3.3.2. Isocrates (Aeschylus, Sophocles, Euripides) 52
3.3.3. Epicurus 57
3.3.4. Marinos, Suidas 59
3.4. Conclusion 61

4. Asklepios at Kos 62

4.1. History 63
4.2. The asklepieion at Kos - Herodas 66
4.3. The Hippokratic Corpus 71
4.3.1. θεραπεύω 73
4.3.2. ἰάομαι 77
4.4. Inscriptions 79
4.5. Conclusion 81

5. Asklepios at Pergamon 83

5.1. Inscriptions 84
5.2. Galen 85
5.3. Marcus Aurelius 89
5.4. Aelius Aristides 93
5.4.1. σῴζω 96
5.4.2. ὑγιής 96
5.4.3. ἰάομαι 97
5.4.4. θεραπεύω 98
5.5. Conclusion 100

Section Two

The language of healing in the New Testament

6. Jewish use of Greek healing language in the Septuagint, Philo of Alexandria, and Josephus 103

6.1. Septuagint 103

6.2. Philo 112

6.3. Josephus 115

6.4. Conclusion 119

7. The synoptic gospels: θεραπεύω 120

7.1. The importance of healing in the synoptic gospels 120

7.2. Mark 125

7.3. Matthew 130

7.4. Luke 132

7.5. θεραπεύω 134

7.5.1. θεραπεύω in general healing episodes 136
7.5.2. θεραπεύω in specific healing stories 143
7.5.3. The use of θεραπεύω in thought or conversation 146

7.6. Conclusion 154

8. The New Testament use of ἰάομαι 155

8.1. Mark 156

8.2. Matthew 156

8.3. Luke-Acts 159

8.3.1. The Lukan use of ἰάομαι in general healing episodes 160
8.3.2. The Lukan use of ἰάομαι in specific healing episodes 162

8.4. John 172

8.5. The use of ἰάομαι in the epistles of the New testament . 174

8.5.1. Hebrews 174
8.5.2. 1 Peter 175
8.5.3. James 175
8.5.4. 1 Corinthians 176

8.6. Conclusion 177

9. Other New Testament healing words: σῴζω καθαίρω ἅπτομαι ὑγιαίνω 179

9.1. διασῴζω σῴζω 180

9.1.1. διασῴζω σῴζω in general healing episodes 180
9.1.2. διασῴζω σῴζω in specific healing episodes 181

9.2. καθαίρω 191

9.3. Jesus' method of healing 195

9.3.1. ἅπτομαι in general healing episodes 196
9.3.2. ἅπτομαι in specific healing episodes 196
9.3.3. κρατέω 200
9.3.4. ἐπιτίθημι (τὰς χεῖρας) 202

9.4. ὑγιαίνω ὑγιής 203

9.4.1. ὑγιής -ές 203
9.4.2. The participial use of the verb ὑγιαίνω 205

10. Commands and commissions 209

11. Conclusion 219

11.1. ἰάομαι 219

11.2. ὑγιαίνω 221

11.3. σῴζω 221

11.4. θεραπεύω 222

Bibliography 231

Part Two: Appendices

Section One

The language of healing in the Greek world

1:1 Map of Greece and the Aegean 251
1:2 Map of Greece 252

2:1 *Inscriptiones Graecae* IV^2 1, no. 121 [2nd half of 4th c. BC] 253
2:2 *Inscriptiones Graecae* IV^2 1, no. 122 [2nd half of 4th c. BC] 265
2:3 *Inscriptiones Graecae* IV^2 1, no. 125 [3rd c. BC] 275
2:4 *Inscriptiones Graecae* IV^2 1, no. 126 [ca. 160 AD] 276
2:5 *Inscriptiones Graecae* IV^2 1, no. 126 [ca. 160 AD] 278
2:6 *Inscriptiones Graecae* IV^2 1, no. 127 [224 AD] 279

3:1 Votive reliefs 280
3:2 The language of healing in inscriptions at Athens 288
3:3 *Inscriptiones Graecae* II^2, no. 4514 [2nd c. AD] 293
3:4 Suidas, Lexicon, *s.v.* Δομνῖνος 294
3:5 Epicurus 295
3:6 *Inscriptiones Graecae* VII, no. 235 299

4:1 Hippokrates 300
4:2 Decree conferring a gold crown on a physician, Xenotimos 308
4:3 Decree of Knossos in honour of a doctor from Kos 309
4:4 Herodas IV 310
4:5 *Inscriptiones Creticae* IV, no. 168 312

5:1 *Inscriptio Pergamena* [ed. R. Herzog, *Berl. Sitzber.*, 1934, pp. 753ff.] 313
5:2 *Inscriptio Pergamena* [ed. M. Fränkel, *Inschriften von Pergamon*, II, 1895, no. 264] 314
5:3 *Inscriptio Pergamena* [ed. M. Fränkel, *Inschriften von Pergamon*, II, 1895, no. 251] 315
5:4 Oribasius, *Collectiones Medicae* XLV, 30.10-14 318
5:5 Galen 319
5:6 Aelius Aristides 323
5:7 Marcus Aurelius 336

Section Two

The language of healing in the New Testament

6:1 Greek healing language in the Septuagint: θεραπεύω and ἰάομαι 339
6:2 Josephus 354
6:3 Philo 361

7:1 The language of healing in the synoptic gospels: *Matthew* 364
7:2 The language of healing in the synoptic gospels: *Mark* 369
7:3 The language of healing in the synoptic gospels: *Luke* 376
7:4 Peter's declaration 389
7:5 The incidence of healing in the synoptic gospels 390
7:6 Gender differentiation of specific healings 391
7:7 The synoptic portrayal of issues and antagonists 392
7:8 New Testament healing words: θεραπεύω θεραπεία θεράπων 402
7:9 Incidence of θεραπεύω in the New Testament according to tense, voice and mood 415
7:10 New Testament healing words : διασῴζω σῴζω 419
7:11 Incidence of διασῴζω σῴζω in New Testament healing stories according to tense, voice and mood 426
7:12 Incidence of ἅπτομαι in New Testament healing stories according to tense, voice and mood 430
7:13 Incidence of ἅπτομαι κρατέω ἐπιτίθημι τᾶς χεῖρας ἐπιτιμάω ἐμβριμάομαι σπλαγχνίζομαι in synoptic healing stories 433

8:1 The language of healing in *Acts* 440
8:2 The language of punishment in *Acts* 452
8:3 New Testament healing words : ἰάομαι ἴασις ἴαμα ἰατρός 459
8:4 Incidence of ἰάομαι in the New Testament according to tense, voice and mood 472

9:1 The language of healing in the gospel according to John 477
9:2 New Testament healing words : ὑγιαίνω ὑγιής 481

Acknowledgements............485

Index 487

List of illustrations

Part One

Plate 1: Statue of Asklepios (Athens, N.M. 263) xix
Plate 2: Votive relief of Asklepios (Athens, N.M. 173) xx
Plate 3: Asklepios of Mounychia (Athens, N.M. 258) xxi
Plate 4: Votive relief of an Athenian family (Athens, N.M. 1384) xxii
Plate 5: Statue of Hippokrates (Kos Museum 32) xxiii
Plate 6: Headless statue of Asklepios (Kos Museum 101) xxiv
Plate 7: Head of a statue of Hygieia (Athens, N.M. 3602) xxv

Part Two

Appendix 1:1 Map of Greece and the Aegean 251
Appendix 1:2 Map of Greece 252
Appendix 3:1
Plate 1: Relief of Asklepios and his family (Athens, N.M. 1402) 280
Plate 2: The relief of the doctors (Athens, N.M. 1332) 280
Plate 3: Relief of Archinos to Amphiaraos (Athens, N.M. 3369) 281
Plate 4: Relief of Asklepios in the act of healing (Piraeus Museum 405) 281
Plate 5: Relief of Asklepios in the act of healing (Athens, N.M. 1841) 282
Plate 6: Relief of healing activity (Athens, N.M. 2373) 282
Plate 7: Relief of Asklepios seated (Athens, N.M. 1352) 283
Plate 8: Relief of woman giving a patient a footbath (Athens, N.M. 1914) 283
Plate 9: Relief of an Athenian family (Athens, N.M. 1384) 284
Plate 10: Relief of an Athenian family (Athens, N.M. 1408) 284
Plate 11: Relief of an Athenian family (Athens, N.M. 1345) 285
Plate 12: Relief of Asklepios, Hygieia, and offering (Athens, N.M. 1335) 285
Plate 13: Relief of suppliants with sacrificial ox (Athens, N.M. 1429) 286
Plate 14: Relief of suppliants with sacrificial ram (Athens, N.M. 1333) 286
Plate 15: Anatomical votives (Korinth Museum) 287
Plate 16: Relief depicting a varicose vein (Athens, N.M. 3526) 287

Abbreviations

App.	Appendix
Apps	Appendices
ANRW	*Aufstieg und Niedergang der römischen Welt*
BETL	Bibliotheca Ephemeridum Theologicarum Lovaniensium
GT	Gospel of Thomas
JBL	*Journal of Biblical Literature*
Jn	The gospel according to John
JSNT	*Journal for the Study of the New Testament*
Kittel *et al.*	*Theological Dictionary of the New Testament*
Lk	The gospel according to Luke
LXX	Septuagint
Mk	The gospel according to Mark
Mt	The gospel according to Matthew
New Docs	*New Documents illustrating Early Christianity*
NHL	Nag Hammadi Library
NT	New Testament
NTS	*New Testament Studies*
RSV	Revised Standard Version
Suddhoffs Archiv	*Suddhoffs Archiv für Geschichte der Medizin und der Naturwissenschaften*

κρεῖσσον δὲ νοσεῖν ἢ θεραπεύειν·
τὸ μέν ἐστιν ἁπλοῦν, τῷ δὲ συνάπτει
λύπη τε φρενῶν χερσίν τε πόνος.

Euripides, *Hippolytos* 186-8

Καὶ περιῆγεν ἐν ὅλῃ τῇ Γαλιλαίᾳ,
διδάσκων ἐν ταῖς συναγωγαῖς αὐτῶν
καὶ κηρύσσων τὸ εὐαγγέλιον τῆς βασιλείας
καὶ θεραπεύων πᾶσαν νόσον καὶ πᾶσαν μαλακίαν ἐν τῷ λαῷ

Matthew 4.23

PLATE 1

Statue of Asklepios from Epidauros (4th century BC) (Athens, N.M. 263)

PLATE 2

Votive relief from the Temple of Asklepios at Epidauros representing Asklepios seated on a throne, arm raised in greeting. (Probably the type of cult statue of Asklepios placed in the interior of the temple) (4th century BC) (Athens, N.M. 173)

PLATE 3

The "Asklepios of Mounychia." The expression of the face shows suffering and passion (Found in Piraeus) (Athens, N.M. 258)

PLATE 4

Votive relief from the asklepieion at Athens depicting an Athenian family (Athens, N.M. 1384)

PLATE 5

Portrait statue probably dated to the late Hellenistic period, after a classical prototype. It was found in the Odeum and was believed by the excavator to be a statue of Hippokrates (Kos Museum 32)

PLATE 6

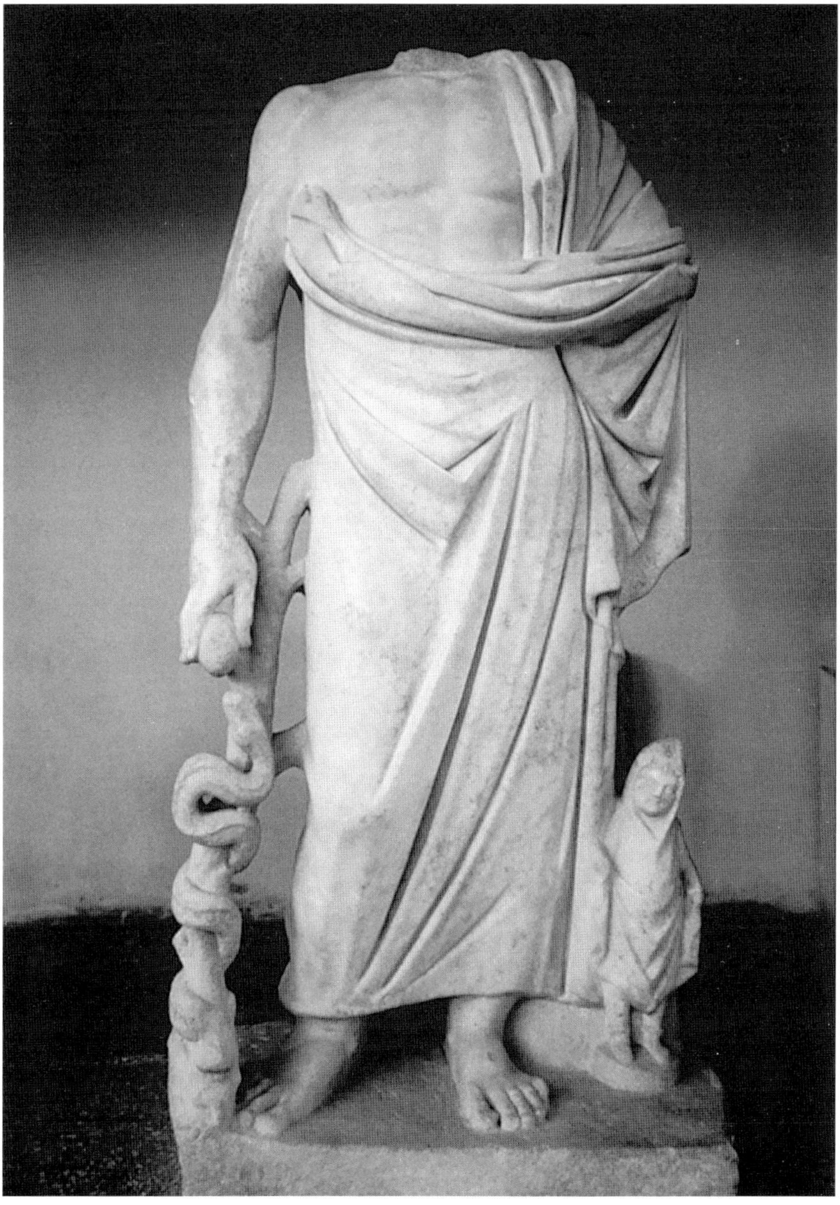

Headless statue of Asklepios: by his feet the figure of Telesphoros (Second half of the 2nd century AD) (Kos Museum 101)

PLATE 7

Head of a statue of the goddess Hygieia from Tegea, commonly attributed to the sculptor Scopas (Middle of the 4th century BC) (Athens, N.M. 3602)

Part One
Argument

Section One

The language of healing in the Greek world

1. *In the beginning*

"In the beginning was the Word"[1] and the 'Word', for the Greeks, was embodied in Homer's[2] *Iliad*.[3] In this mighty epic the Greek understanding of the Cosmos was outlined. The nature of the gods, their role in the Cosmos, and their relationship with mankind, as portrayed in the *Iliad*, formed the way in which the gods were imagined. Several themes at once emerge that are pertinent to this study. These are the concepts of good and evil, and the understanding of their source, the role of destiny in the life of mankind, and the gods' administration of justice.

Even at this early stage in Greek thought,[4] Asklepios and his sons are linked with healing, although it is the god, Apollo, who is seen as the cause of both sickness and health. The *Iliad* makes it clear that Zeus is the source of both evil and good:

> There are two urns that stand on the doorsill of Zeus. They are unlike
> for the gifts they bestow: an urn of evils (κακῶν), an urn of blessings (ἑάων).
> If Zeus who delights in thunder mingles these and bestows them
> on man, he shifts, and moves now in evil (κακῷ) again in good fortune (ἐσθλῷ)
> But when Zeus bestows from the urn of sorrows (λυγρῶν), he makes a failure

---

1 Jn 1.1

2 A discussion of the controversy surrounding the Homeric question is not relevant to this study. For information on this issue see Kirk (1962); Young (1967); and on the *Iliad* and *Odyssey* as literature, see Bowra (1930); Clarke (1967); Mueller (1984); and Murnaghan (1987).

3 All translations of the *Iliad* are by Richmond Lattimore, in Homer (1961). The Greek text is that found in Homer (1978) and (1984), ed M. M. Willcock. References are based on Lattimore's translation in Homer (1961) as the line numbering in the Greek text and Lattimore's translation occasionally varies by one line.

4 Approximately the middle of the eighth century BC.

of man, and the evil hunger drives him over the shining
earth, and he wanders respected (τετιμένος) neither of gods nor mortals.[5]

Thus Achilleus explains the suffering of mankind in general, and his own and Priam's in particular, in the final book of the *Iliad*. It is an interesting explanation. Evil (κακός) here is used in the more general sense of sorrows or suffering, and Achilleus catalogues the worst woes he can think of: homelessness, childlessness, grinding poverty, disgrace, and, the very worst of all evils: to be without respect. Zeus' administration of justice appears to be quite arbitrary - he dabbles in evils and blessings seemingly without thought, or reason. What is most interesting, however, is that Achilleus accepts this arbitrariness without question, as does Priam. Their acceptance of good or ill as the work of the gods is typical of the characters in the *Iliad,* and can be explained by their concept of destiny.[6] Elsewhere evil is synonymous with death, or the series of events leading to death. Zeus is again described as the source of this evil:

And the son of Kronos
drove down the evil turmoil upon them, and from aloft cast
down dews dripping blood from the sky, since he was minded
to hurl down a multitude of strong heads to the house of Hades.[7]

The events leading up to Patroklos' death are described as "...the beginning of his evil (κακοῦ)...."(11.603). And this evil was begun by the gods, as Thetis makes clear, when trying to comfort Achilleus after Patroklos' death:

My child, now, though we grieve for him, we must let this man lie
dead, in the way he first was killed through the gods' designing.[8]

Thetis already knows that "...death and powerful destiny stand closely above..."(24.132) her son Achilleus. It is impossible for man to escape his destiny, i.e. his death, and not even Thetis attempts this on behalf of her son, even though she makes Zeus give him glory in the manner of it (the *raison d'être* of the whole plot of the *Iliad*). That it is impossible for a man to escape his destiny is shown by the life and death of Lykaon, a son of Priam. He thought he had escaped his destiny, when, having been sold as a slave in Lemnos

5 *Iliad* 24.527-533
6 See below, 2-3.
7 *Iliad* 11.52-55
8 *Iliad* 19.9-10

by Achilleus, he was later ransomed. However, he again faces Achilleus before Troy (21.34-135). Lykaon,

> in terror came near him
> in an agony to catch at his knees, and the wish in his heart was
> to get away from the evil death and the dark fate.[9]

He bewailed the fact that "...Now again cursed destiny has put me in your hands;..."(21.82-83), and knew that:

> This time
> the evil shall be mine in this place, since I do not think
> I shall escape your hands, since divinity drove me against them.[10]

Thus the manner of a man's life, but especially of his death, is fore-ordained by his destiny. So Hecabe weeps for her son Hektor:

> and the way at the first strong Destiny
> spun with his life line when he was born,[11]

for Hektor was born to die by the hand of Achilleus while defending Troy.

The role of destiny is central to the plot of the *Iliad* and seems to be accepted by both mortals and gods. The inevitability of death for mortals is seen as part of life; the struggle is not so much to escape destiny (death), as it is to win glory in the manner of one's destiny. So Zeus inclines his head to Thetis' request for glory for her son Achilleus (1.524), but does not prevent his death (19.409-417). Thus the purpose of life in the *Iliad* is to attain glory, to win renown,[12] and to leave behind sons who will follow in their father's footsteps (24.538-539). All this is in the gods' hands, and so it is vital to ensure that the gods are on one's own side. To this end man prays, sings, and makes sacrifices to win the gods' favour.[13]

The gods also administer justice. Zeus is portrayed as the source of natural disaster, as explained in Homeric simile:[14]

---

9 *Iliad* 21.64-66

10 *Iliad* 21.91-93

11 *Iliad* 24.209-210

12 Note the punishment given to Thamyris the Thracian (2.594-600) who is "forgotten" (ἐκλέλαθον) as a singer.

13 See 1.450-479 where the Danaans try to appease Apollo's wrath (after restoring Chryseis to her father) by sacrifice, prayer and singing - to good effect (1.479). However, some sacrifices are more effective than others (10.45-46).

14 Willcock in Homer (1984) 249, commenting on this simile, asserts that the "...attribution of storm damage to punishment inflicted by Zeus on human

As underneath the hurricane all the black earth is burdened
on an autumn day, when Zeus sends down the most violent waters
in deep rage against mortals after they stir him to anger
because in violent assembly they pass decrees that are crooked,
and drive righteousness from among them and care nothing for what the gods think,
and all the rivers of these men swell current to full spate
and in the ravines of their water-courses rip all the hillsides
and dash whirling in huge noise down to the blue sea, out of
the mountains headlong, so that the works of men are diminished;
so huge rose the noise from the horses of Troy in their running.[15]

This passage gives us a clue to man's notion of the god's integrity. Zeus shows anger at unjust laws (σκολιὰς...θέμιστας), at loss of righteousness (δίκην), and especially for not heeding the vengeance of the gods (θεῶν ὄπιν οὐκ ἀλέγοντες). So we see the concept of right behaviour promoted, i.e. just laws passed in assembly without violence (βίῃ), a pursuit of righteousness, and careful nurturing of the goodwill of the gods. This notion of the god's integrity is evident elsewhere in the *Iliad*. Agamemnon exhorts his men on the basis that Zeus will not give aid to liars (4.235); i.e. he believes that his cause against the Trojans is a just one, and, as such, is duly blessed by Zeus.

Disregard of and disrespect for a priest of Apollo are also reason enough for Apollo himself to dispense his version of just punishment and so set in motion all the events of the *Iliad*. Apollo,

---

wickedness is unique in the *Iliad*,..." but, in my opinion, the strength to do so is implicit in his attributes, and his role as chief dispenser of justice, however arbitrary that justice may be, perhaps demands this. See also Dodds (1951) 32, who argues that this simile is, "...a reflex of later conditions which, by an inadvertence common in Homer, has been allowed to slip into a simile....". He bases his argument on the fact that he has found "...no indication in the narrative of the *Iliad* that Zeus is concerned with justice as such...." See also Grube (1951) 69, who disagrees. According to Grube (78, n.25) "...We might declare at least 386-387 a later interpolation, but that way lies chaos. While we are not told that punishment always follows crooked judgments (which it obviously does not), the implication that crooked judgments are punished by Zeus is there, even if the punishment is rather indiscriminate. The sentiments are closely parallel in Hesiod, *Works and Days* 219-264. It is wiser to let this passage remind us that we are not dealing with static ideas about the gods. Human rewards for the best judgment are found in *Il.* 18.507-508...."

15 *Iliad* 16.384-393

> in anger at the king drove
> the foul pestilence (νοῦσον ... κακήν) along the host, and the people
> perished,[16]

the reason being that Agamemnon had dishonoured (ἠτίμασεν) Chryses, his priest. So, as in Sophocles' *Oedipus Tyrannus*,[17] Apollo is depicted as the source of men suffering disease and death, in the form of a plague.

The Muses, too, punish a mortal in anger:

> the Muses
> encountering Thamyris the Thracian stopped him from singing
> ...for he boasted that he would surpass, if the very Muses,
> daughters of Zeus who holds the aegis, were singing against him,
> and these in their anger struck him maimed (πηρὸν), and the voice of
> wonder they took away, and made him a singer without memory.
> (ἐκλέλαθον)[18]

Here the punishment seems very severe - not death (as Zeus and Apollo), but a living death: Thamyris forced to live his life disfigured, disabled, and unknown. He exemplifies Achilleus' catalogue of woes.[19] These cameos of the gods' justice stress that if mortals wish to succeed and flourish they must give due honour to the gods and their representatives. And if we take the Homeric simile about Zeus' punishment seriously, then mortals are also required to live upright lives in their dealings with other mortals.

Nevertheless, mortals can, and do, blame the gods for their own bad behaviour. So Agamemnon explains away his actions[20] to Achilleus:

> yet I am not responsible
> but Zeus is, and Destiny, and Erinys the mist-walking
> who in assembly caught my heart in the savage delusion
> on that day I myself stripped from him the prize of Achilleus.
> Yet what could I do? It is the god who accomplishes all things.
> Delusion is the elder daughter of Zeus, the accursed
> who deludes all; her feet are delicate and they step not

---

16 *Iliad* 1.9-10

17 Oedipus also acknowledges Apollo as the author of his 'evil' and suffering (*OT* 1329-1330). Thucydides too notes that some of his contemporaries attributed the plague that devastated Athens in the early years of the Peloponnesian War to Apollo (2.54; cf. 1.118).

18 *Iliad* 2.594-595, 597-600

19 See above, 1-2.

20 See Dodds (1951) 1-27.

> on the firm earth, but she walks the air above men's heads
> and leads them astray. She has entangled others before me.[21]

Thus a man may rejoice that the gods favour him, or weep that the gods are against him, and so absolve himself of all responsibility for his actions.[22] Even though he may attempt to make reparation for wrongdoing, he does not suffer from guilt for actions and events that he sees as ultimately beyond his control. So he rationalises his situation. In this way his actions and behaviour are in the gods' hands, just as a man's life and death are foreordained, and therefore beyond his control. This thought even extends to a man's prowess in battle, or in athletic contest. So Aias recognises that Athene "...made me slip on my feet..." (23.782), so that she could answer Odysseus' silent prayer (23.768-771). This explanation of his defeat is readily understood and accepted by his peers (23.784).

Given the role of destiny, does man have any control at all over his life? Can he make the gods intervene on his behalf, and if so, how?

The answer, of course, is affirmative. Although ultimately Zeus decrees that destiny must be satisfied,[23] man can gather strength,[24] win glory,[25] and bring suffering on others,[26] by means of prayer. Prayer is an effective weapon in man's armory, both spoken and silent. We have already seen how Odysseus' silent prayer to Athene was effective (23.763-783); and Apollo's wrath in action, in answer to the fervent prayer of his priest, Chryses (1.35-43). Zeus also hears the twofold prayer of Achilleus, although he grants only one:

> So he spoke in prayer, and Zeus of the counsels heard him.
> The father granted him one prayer, and denied him the other.
> That Patroklos should beat back the fighting assault on the vessels
> he allowed, but refused to let him come back safe out of the fighting.[27]

Zeus also hears, and answers, the prayer of Aias (17.645-650).

---

21 *Iliad* 19.86-94
22 Note the different role given to Oedipus by Sophocles in this regard (*OT* 1331f.).
23 *Iliad* 8.469-477; 15.47-77
24 *Iliad* 5.114-132; 16.523-532; 23.763-783
25 *Iliad* 7.200-312; 10.277-514
26 *Iliad* 1.35-100, 380-382
27 *Iliad* 16.249-252

But in relation to this study, it is man's conception of Apollo that is the most significant of all the portraits of the gods. He is the god who is most directly and continuously linked with man's physical well-being. Apollo's wrath causes the plague: he inflicts sickness, suffering and death on Chryses' enemies, in answer to Chryses' urgent prayer (1.8-100). Thus he is the source of disease, and death as a result of disease. He is also the source of healing, again as a result of prayer. Glaukos (16.508-531) in battle, beseeches Apollo to heal him:

> 'Hear me, my lord...wherever you are you can listen
> to a man in pain (ἀνέρι κηδομένῳ) as now this pain has descended on me
> (ὡς νῦν ἐμὲ κῆδος ἱκάνει)....
> make well this strong wound (τόδε καρτερὸν ἕλκος ἄκεσσαι)
> and put the pains to sleep, (κοίμησον δ' ὀδύνας,) give me strength, (δὸς δὲ κράτος,)'[28]

so that he may defend Sarpedon's body, and instil confidence in his companions. Apollo hears, and immediately grants his prayer:

> So he spoke in prayer, and Phoibos Apollo heard him.
> At once he made the pains stop, and dried away from the hard wound
> the dark running of blood, and put strength (μένος) into his spirit (θυμῷ).
> And Glaukos knew in his heart what was done, and was happy
> that the great god had listened to his prayer.[29]

Thus Apollo is both the source of disease and healing,[30] and, prompted by mortal prayer, he can, and does, prescribe both. His role in the *Iliad* is curious. He favours the Trojans (4.507-513), especially Hektor (11.349-366; 15.254-257;[31] 20.440-445). Achilleus calls him the "most malignant (ὀλοώτατε) of all gods" (22.15) when he thwarts his plans. He is capable of foul play, as when in anger he dashes the shining whip from the hands of Diomedes (23.383-384), and leaves him defenceless. (It is fortunate for Diomedes that Athene comes to his rescue, and restores his whip 23.387-390). He has links with Pergamon, whence he watches the battle (4.507-508, *et al.*), and whither he spirits the wounded Aineias:

> away from the onslaught, and set him
> in the sacred keep of Pergamos where was built his own temple.

28 *Iliad* 16.514-516, 523-524
29 *Iliad* 16.527-532
30 The God of the Septuagint fulfils a similar role (see App. 6:1, **9**, **36**, **57** and **64**).
31 In this example, he has been sent by Zeus to help Hektor.

There Artemis of the showering arrows and Leto within
the great and secret chamber healed his wound and cared for him.
(ἀκέοντό τε κύδαινόν τε·)[32]

Thus Apollo, from the very earliest times in Greek memory, was associated with Pergamon, and healing. Pergamon later became one of the great healing centres of the ancient world.[33]

Other figures also heal in the *Iliad.* When the goddess Dione recounts the suffering and endurance of the gods (5.381-415) to the wounded goddess Aphrodite, she tells how Paiëon healed Hades of an arrow wound, when "his spirit was suffering (κῆδε δὲ θυμόν)" (5.400):

But Paiëon, scattering medicines that still pain (ὀδυνήφατα φάρμακα πάσσων),
healed him (ἠκέσατ'·), since he was not made to be one of the mortals.[34]

That the gods themselves quarrel (over giving favour to mortals), and hurt each other in the process, is illustrated by Ares' encounter with Athene (5.825-909).[35] Again it is Paiëon who heals, this time at the command of Zeus (ἀνώγειν ἰήσασθαι) (5.899). The language used to describe Paiëon's act (5.900-901) is the same as that cited above (5.401-402), and so assumes the form of an epithet, to describe Paiëon's character and behaviour. The language used to describe Dione's healing of Aphrodite is different. She heals by touch:

with both hands stroked away from her arm the ichor,
so that the arm was made whole again and the strong pains rested.
(ἢ ῥα καὶ ἀμφοτέρῃσιν ἀπ' ἰχῶ χειρὸς ὀμόργνυ·
ἄλθετο χείρ, ὀδύναι δὲ κατηπιόωντο βαρεῖαι.)[36]

Amongst mortals, Agamede,

32 *Iliad* 5.445-448
33 See below, chapter five.
34 *Iliad* 5.401-402
35 In this incident Ares assumes that Zeus will be angry at their "acts of violence (καρτερὰ ἔργα)" (5.873). This echoes Zeus' displeasure at the simile discussed above (n.14), illustrating the human notion that Zeus expected right behaviour from gods as well as men. Hera echoes this sentiment (5.757-759).
36 *Iliad* 5.416-417

> knew of all the medicines that are grown in the broad earth[37]

but in the *Iliad* it is the brothers Podaleirios and Machaon who are represented as healers, and blameless physicians. In the catalogue of ships we are told that the leaders of Trikka, Ithome and Oichalia, were the:

> two sons of Asklepios,
> good healers (ἰητῆρ' ἀγαθώ) both themselves, Podaleirios and Machaon,[38]

who commanded thirty vessels. But it is Machaon who is given greater stature as a healer, and who is summoned to tend Agamemnon:

> and he stood in the midst of them, a man godlike,
> straightway he pulled the arrow forth from the joining of the war belt,
> and as it was pulled out the sharp barbs were broken backwards....
> But when he saw the wound where the bitter arrow was driven,
> he sucked the blood and in skill laid healing medicines on it
> (ἐπ' ἄρ' ἤπια φάρμακα εἰδὼς πάσσε)
> that Cheiron in friendship long ago had given his father.[39]

From this we gain some insight into battlefield medicine,[40] and add to our knowledge of the skills and background of Machaon and his family. Removal of the foreign body, clearing of poison,[41] and the application of healing medicines are still common medical practice today.

Cheiron is mentioned several times in the *Iliad* as provider of medicines and weapons. In this way his character, like that of Apollo, is inherently paradoxical - they are both agents of healing and death.[42] He is first mentioned as having given healing medicines to Asklepios (4.219). We are told that he was the "most righteous (δικαιότατος) of the Centaurs" (11.831) and had also told Achilleus of kind (ἤπια) and good (ἐσθλά) medicines (11.829, 830), and given a Pelian ash spear to his father, Peleus, "to be death for

---

37 *Iliad* 11.740

38 *Iliad* 2.731-732

39 *Iliad* 4.212-214, 217-219

40 Wounds are described in great detail, and show a marked knowledge of anatomy. For example, see: 5.305-310 (Aineias); 8.325-328 (Teukros); 14.463-468 (Archelochos); 14.493-499 (Ilioneus).

41 Until recently the same method (sucking) was recommended by *First Aid* manuals for clearing poison in cases of snake bite.

42 Does this reflect the natural dichotomy in human nature, i.e. the potential for both good and evil?

fighters" (16.144; 19.391). Asklepios, although mentioned as a blameless physician (ἀμύμονος ἰητῆρος) (11.518), only figures as the recipient of Cheiron's teaching, and the father of Podaleirios and Machaon in the *Iliad*. Machaon himself is wounded in battle and immediately taken to the shelter of the ships, since:

> A healer is worth many men in his knowledge
> of cutting out arrows and putting kindly medicines on wounds.[43]

This is an Homeric ploy to open the way for Achilleus to involve Patroklos in battle, and is thus the beginning of Patroklos' evil.[44] It is odd that although Podaleirios and Machaon are represented as the active blameless healers in the *Iliad*, and although Machaon treats Agamemnon's wound, and is wounded himself, it is Patroklos who stands out as the man of compassion and healing (11.822-848; 15.390-404). It is Patroklos who answers Eurypylos' plea for help and healing (11.828-831).[45] He has been taught the healing art by Achilleus (who had it from Cheiron), and it is his treatment of Eurypylos' wound that is recounted in most detail (11.843-847).

He performs surgery, cutting the arrow out of his thigh with a knife; washes the wound with warm water and clears the blood; and applies a pain-killing plant, after pounding it. His efforts succeed in drying the wound and stemming the blood. After treating the wound in this way he provides post-operative care by remaining with Eurypylos: he sits with him, entertains him, and repeatedly applies pain-killing medicines to his wound (15.390-394). He does not leave his patient until circumstances dictate that he must; even then he leaves Eurypylos in the care of his henchman (θεράπων) (15.401-402).

Thus Patroklos fits much more the modern image of a holistic healer: he heeds the cry for help, he treats the wound, and remains to comfort and care for his patient. Machaon, in comparison, is more aloof. Homer describes him as "god-like" (ἰσόθεος) (4.212). He is summoned to treat Agamemnon, does so, and with spectacular results, for Agamemnon immediately goes back into battle. Machaon is efficient and effective, but lacking in warmth. He fulfils his role speedily, with the minimum of fuss. In this way he

43 *Iliad* 11.514-515

44 See above, 2.

45 Machaon, suffering a battle wound is himself out of the action at this time, while Podaleirios is engaged in battle (11.832-835).

prefigures the Hippokratic physician, as portrayed in *Epidemics 1* and *3*.[46]

Several words emerge in Homer's *Iliad* that continue to be an important part of the language of healing throughout Greek literature, and are later incorporated into the healing vocabulary of the *New Testament*. In the healing episode where Patroklos treats Eurypylos, Eurypylos uses the verb σῴζω in its imperative form σάωσον to entreat Patroklos' help. Σῴζω is a most significant verb in the language of healing. Here it is used to mean *rescue and treat*, and Eurypolos gives detailed instructions to Patroklos in a string of imperatives: save (by leading) σάωσον (ἄγων), cut ἔκταμ', wash νίζ', and apply πάσσε. Obviously he too knew how to practise battlefield medicine. Patroklos follows precisely these instructions.[47]

Another word that continues to be important in the language of healing, and is given prominence in the *Iliad*, is ἰάομαι. This verb is used by Zeus when instructing Paiëon to heal Ares (5.899), and is also used to describe Patroklos' care of Eurypylos (12.2). ἀκέομαι is also used to describe the act of healing, by Paiëon (5.402, 901) and in Glaukos' request to Apollo (16.523). The verb θεραπεύω appears in the *Iliad* in its noun form θεράπων to mean henchman, or companion in arms, as Patroklos was to Achilleus.[48] So Patroklos leaves Eurypylos in the care of his θεράπων after treating his wounds. It does not figure in the language of healing in the *Iliad*, but in its connotation of "caring for" one can readily see how it later achieved such prominence in a general sense in the language of healing.

In the *Odyssey* [49] ἰάομαι is the most prominent word in the language of healing. It is used by the Cyclops (9.520) when he

---

46 Hippokrates (1972)

47 *Iliad* 11.827-847

48 For a discussion of the meaning of this term, see Finley (1954) 54-55: "Just what it meant, in terms of customary or legal obligation and in a man's own familial life, to be a permanent but free member of the *oikos* of another is by no means clear. Negatively it meant considerable loss of freedom of choice and mobility. Yet these men were neither slaves nor serfs nor bondsmen. They were retainers ... exchanging their service for a proper place in the basic social unit, the household - a vicarious membership, no doubt, but one that gave them both material security and the psychological values and satisfactions that went with belonging.... The hierarchy of retainers, it should be added, reached very high indeed. As a child Patroclus was forced to flee his home. Peleus received him in his palace and 'named him retainer' of young Achilles...."

49 There is not as much emphasis on healing in the *Odyssey*. Odysseus' companions do not survive his ordeals. However, there are interesting digressions:

expresses the hope that his father Poseidon will heal him, and in Odysseus' reply (9.525), ridiculing this notion. It is also used (εὖ ἰησάμενοι) to describe the result of the treatment of Odysseus' boar wound by the sons of Autolycus (19.460). Otherwise its noun form ἰητρός is used to describe the physician; by Helen (4.231), and by Eumaeus(17.384). It is interesting here to note that the Homeric world knew the physician as one who gave public service, not attached to one master, but who worked for the people in general. Eumaeus describes the physician as being welcome the world over, and includes seers, carpenters and bards in the same category. Heralds are added later (19.135). As in the *Iliad*, θεραπεύω is used in its cognate form in the *Odyssey* to describe personal attendants of noblemen (18.297).

So Homer portrays healers as a useful and necessary part of the Homeric world. Asklepios is already famous as a healer in this world, and his sons, Podaleirios and Machaon, continue to practise the healing craft. Other mortals, such as Agamede, are especially skilled in the use of healing herbs. But perhaps all warriors were supposed to have some knowledge of war wounds and how to treat them. For example, Eurypylos gives detailed instructions to Patroklos concerning his wound, and although Patroklos is depicted as having superior knowledge (through Achilleus and Cheiron), he nevertheless follows Eurypylos' instructions. No doubt this is a stylistic device; repetition is one of the outstanding motifs of the *Iliad*. However, when Patroklos tells Achilleus of the wounded Achaeans (16.20-27), listing four outstanding warriors (Diomedes, Odysseus, Agamemnon and Eurypylos), he adds:

> And over these the healers skilled in medicine are working
> to cure their wounds.[50]

This implies that there are healers, other than those already mentioned.

In this way mortals heal each other (but with knowledge from other than mortals), and Paiëon heals gods (wounded by gods). It is only Apollo who both hurts, and heals, mortals.

---

describing Egyptian medicine and an unknown drug (opium?) (4.219-237); and the successful use of an incantation to stem Odysseus' flow of blood (19.455-466, especially 457-458). Compare Sophocles, *Ajax* 581-582. For other magical uses of song and poetry, see 13.2 and 11.334.

50 *Iliad* 16.28-29

We have already seen that the gods' justice, as portrayed in the *Iliad*, appears to be quite arbitrary: it depends on which mortal the god is listening to at that time. For example, Apollo, the "most deadly of all gods" (22.15) seems uncaring about the effects his "justice" has on the enemies of those he loves (1.10, 43-52). His "justice" is generally depicted as the result of his anger (1.9). So man tries to avert his wrath by making propitiation in the form of offerings (1.66-67, 458-479). Other gods are also placated in this way (6.86-98, 115), at times without effect (2.419-420; 6.304-311). Even so, humans deem it important to give the gods their "due gifts" (24.425-428).

And so several important themes emerge from the *Iliad* that are pertinent to this study. The gods exist, and become personally involved in the lives of individuals. Moreover, the father of the gods, Zeus, is seen to be the author of good and evil, and his son, Apollo, the author of sickness and health. Ultimately, Zeus is seen to be the author of destiny. Both Apollo and Zeus dispense their version of justice, a justice which may not conform to human desire.[51] Thus humans are very much at the mercy of the gods.

Where then could humans turn who wanted help in their suffering and a cure for their wounds and diseases? As we shall see the Greek world increasingly turned towards a new healing cult and a new god; a god who made his first appearance in heroic form in Homer's *Iliad*. This healing cult arose out of the deep human desire for a consistently benevolent deity, a deity to whom humans could turn in trust and hope at any time of crisis in their lives.

Several words have appeared in the Homeric language of healing: ἀκέομαι, ἤπια (φάρμακα) (*Iliad* 11.829), θεραπεύω, ἰάομαι, and σῴζω, words which it will be profitable to trace in meaning and form as they appear in the language of healing used to describe the cult of Asklepios, the hero who became the Greek healing god.

2. *Asklepios at Epidauros*

Originally a Greek hero[52] known as "the blameless physician" (*Iliad* 11. 518), whose sons[53] took part in the Trojan War, Asklepios

---

51 *Iliad* 2.411-420

52 Homer, *Iliad* 2.729-733. For a discussion of the heroic status of Asklepios, see Edelstein (1945) 2: 1-64.

53 Podaleirios and Machaon (Homer, *Iliad* 2.729-733). See above, chapter one.

became the Greek god of medicine.[54] His healing cult flourished in the Mediterranean world from the fifth century BC to the fourth century AD, and was so widespread that some early Christians regarded the god Asklepios, and his healing cult, as Christianity's greatest rival.[55]

Asklepios, like Jesus of Nazareth, is represented by all legends as being the son of a god (the healing god Apollo), and a mortal woman (Arsinoë, Coronis).[56] From the very beginning his interest and effectiveness in the healing art was stressed.[57] Even his birth was unusual from a medical point of view: he is represented as being brought into the world by Apollo, out of the dead body of his mother.[58] Thus Apollo used his medical knowledge to deliver him, and then gave him into the care of Cheiron the centaur,[59] the sage skilled in medical knowledge.[60] It is an impeccable background for a healing hero who was later to be deified as the healing god of the Mediterranean world.[61]

We first hear of Asklepios in the *Iliad*. He is described as an aristocrat, the father of Podaleirios and Machaon, who were the

---

54 Theodoretus, *Graecarum Affectionum Curatio* 3.24-28; Minucius Felix, *Octavius* 23.7; Hyginus, *Fabulae* 224.5; Cicero, *De Natura Deorum* 2.24.62, 3.18.45; Porphyrius, *Epistula ad Marcellam* 7; Origen, *In Jeremiam Homilia* 5.3; Xenophon, *Cynegeticus* 1.6; Celsus, *De Medicina, Prooemium* 2; Galen, *Protrepticus* 9.22; Apuleius, *De Deo Socratis* 15.153

55 Justin, *Apologia* 54.10, 22.6; *Dialogus* 69.3; Origen, *Contra Celsum* 3.25

56 Legends disagree concerning the identity of the mother of Asklepios. For Coronis: Pindar, *Pythiae* 3.8-37; Ovid, *Metamorphoses* 2.542-648; Diodorus, *Bibliotheca Historica* 4.71.1-4; Cyrillus, *Contra Julianum* 6.805B-808B; Eustathius, *Commentarii ad Homeri Iliadem* 2.729; Homer, *Hymni* 16.1-5; *IG* IV^2 I, no. 128, iv, 40-50 [Isyllus; *ca* 300 BC]. For both accounts: Apollodorus, *Bibliotheca* 3.10, 3, 5-4, 1; Pausanias, *Descriptio Graeciae* 2.26.7; Theodoretus, *Graecarum Affectionum Curatio* 8.19-23; Scholia in Pindar, *Ad Pythias* 3.14. For Arsinoë: Pausanias, *Descriptio Graeciae* 3.26.4, 4.3.1-2. For other contenders (Epione, Xanthe): Scholia in Homerum, *Ad Iliadem* 4.195.

57 Homer, *Iliad* 4.219; Pindar, *Pythiae* 3.7, 47-53

58 Pindar, *Pythiae* 3.44; Ovid, *Metamorphoses* 2.628-630; Servius, *Commentarii in Aeneidem* 7.761, 10.316; Hyginus, *Fabulae* 202.1-2

59 Homer, *Iliad* 4.218-219; Pindar, *Nemeae* 3.54-56; Scholia in Pindarum, *Ad Nemeas* 3.92, *Ad Pythias* 3.9, 79, 102b; Xenophon, *Cynegeticus* 1.1-6; Philostratus, *Heroicus* 9; Justin, *De Monarchia* 6.23

60 According to Pindar (*Pythiae* 3.45-46)Apollo gave Asklepios to the centaur specifically so that the centaur could "teach him how to heal mortal men of painful maladies" (καί ῥά νιν Μάγνητι φέρων πόρε Κενταύρῳ διδάξαι πολυπήμονας ἀνθρώποισιν ἰᾶσθαι νόσους). See also Heraclitus, *Quaestiones Homericae* 15.

61 For a discussion of Asklepios' deification see Edelstein, (1945) 2:65-138.

leaders of the Greek contingent from Trikka in the Trojan War.[62] However, neither Podaleirios nor Machaon excel at the normal heroic arts.[63] Instead they are valued for their medical expertise,[64] expertise which they had inherited from their father, Asklepios.[65] Of Asklepios' "heroic" life virtually nothing is known, except that he was supposed to have been numbered among the Argonauts, and to have hunted the Calydonian boar, ventures which did not win him any outstanding individual glory.[66] Thus he was not renowned as a warrior hero in the Homeric sense, but as a medical man, interested only in conquering disease[67] and death.[68] This last was his undoing. According to legend he was struck by a thunderbolt from Zeus when he dared to restore a mortal to life.[69] However, through his own death he achieved immortality, returning as a god to help suffering mankind.[70] As the healing god of the Mediterranean world Asklepios welcomed any who came to his sanctuaries for help, regardless of race, age, or status. Thus he became the only god to whom any person could turn for help, regardless of the nature of his problem, or his background. As such Asklepios was unique among the Greek gods for his constant benevolence towards mankind, for his constant availability to mankind, and the constant morality of his personal relationships.[71] The parallels with the life and work of the man Jesus of

---

62 Homer, *Iliad* 2.729-733

63 Diodorus, *Bibliotheca Historica* 4.71 states that "they were exempted from the dangers of battle and from other duties because of their exceeding usefulness in the art of healing".

64 Homer, *Iliad* 4.192-219, 11.504-520; Scholia in Homerum, *Ad Iliadem* 11.515

65 Eustathius, *Commentarii ad Homeri Iliadem* 11.517

66 Clement of Alexandria (*Stromateis* 1.21.105) cites Apollonius of Rhodes as his authority when he states that Asklepios and the Dioscuri sailed with the Argonauts. Hyginus (*Fabulae* 14.21) also mentions Asklepios as being among the assembly of the Argonauts. Hyginus also states that Asklepios was amongst those who went to hunt the Calydonian boar (*Fabulae* 173.1).

67 Pindar, *Pythiae* 3.1-53

68 Pindar, *Pythiae* 3.54-60; Aeschylus, *Agamemnon* 1022-1023; Euripides, *Alcestis* 122-129; Libanius, *Orationes* 20.8; Sextus Empiricus, *Adversus Mathematicos* 1.260-262; Ovid, *Fasti* 6.743-762

69 See n.61 above, and, in addition, Pindar, *Pythiae* 3.54-58; Vergil, *Aeneis* 7.765-773; Hyginus, *Fabulae* 49.1; Hesiod, Fr. 125; Euripides, *Alcestis* 1-7.

70 Xenophon, *Cynegeticus* 1.6; Theodoretus, *Graecarum Affectionum Curatio* 3.24-28; Minucius Felix, *Octavius* 23.7; Hyginus, *Fabulae* 251.2, 224.5; Cicero, *De Natura Deorum* 2.24.62, 3.18.45; *De Legibus* 2.8.19; Origen, *In Jeremiam Homilia* 5.3; Celsus, *De Medicina, Prooemium* 2

71 As a god Asklepios was faithful to his wife, and raised a large family who continued his interest in the healing art.

Nazareth, and with the post-resurrection nature of the Christian Jesus, are obvious.[72]

An important area of difference, however, is in the families of the two healers. Where Jesus collected a small band of disciples, and trained them, Asklepios and his family became the focus of the healing cult, and practising physicians claimed the title of Asklepiadae. The most important member of his family was his daughter, Hygieia, but his sons, Podaleirios and Machaon, and other daughters, Akeso, Iaso and Panakeia, together with his wife, Epione, are also represented as being involved in healing activities. The women are all personifications of healing attributes: Hygieia (ὑγίεια, health), Akeso (ἄκεσις, cure), Iaso (ἴασις, cure), Panakeia (πανάκεια, universal cure), Epione (ἤπιος, mild). There has been much conjecture over the origin and meaning of Asklepios' name, but the most likely explanation seems to be that it is based on ἤπιος with a prefix.[73]

2.1. Sources

There are three main sources of information concerning Asklepios: literary, epigraphical, and archaeological. The literary sources[74] are many and varied, ranging from the ancient Greek literary giants like Homer, Hesiod, Pindar, Aristophanes and Plato, through to early Christian apologists like Origen. As well, epigraphical remains have been found in all major asklepieia, and these range from inscriptions recording miraculous cures, to inventories of votives given as thank offerings for restored health, as well as inventories of building costs, and records of the people who held priestly and administrative positions in the healing cult.[75]

---

72 These similarities were recognised by early Christian apologists who struggled to find differences. See Justin, *Apologia* 22.6: ᾧι δὲ λέγομεν χωλοὺς καὶ παραλυτικοὺς καὶ ἐκ γενετῆς πονηροὺς ὑγιεῖς πεποιηκέναι αὐτὸν καὶ νεκροὺς ἀνεγεῖραι, ὅμοια τοῖς ὑπὸ 'Ασκληπιοῦ γεγενῆσθαι λεγομένοις καὶ ταὐτὰ φάσκειν δόξομεν. See also Justin, *Dialogus* 69.3; Origen, *Contra Celsum* 3.23; Ambrose, *De Virginibus* 3.176.7.

73 Some philologists argue that the name Asklepios is connected with the Greek word ἀσκάλαβος (a kind of lizard), and so developed from the serpent. For a discussion see Schouten (1967) 223.

74 For a collection of literary sources, including some inscriptions, see Edelstein (1945) vol. 1.

75 See *IC* I, *ID*, *IG* II-III^1 1-2, *IG* II-III^3 1-2, *IG* IV^2 1, *IG* VII; Aleshire (1989); Burford (1969); Edelstein (1945) vol. 1; Paton and Hicks (1891); Rouse (1976); and van Straten (1981) 65-151.

Archaeological remains too, such as votive reliefs depicting scenes of worship and healing, images of Asklepios himself, and of his family,[76] and the remains of the asklepieia buildings,[77] all provide information about this healing cult.

Thus a logical point of reference for the study of the Greek language of healing is the literary evidence surrounding the Greek god of healing, Asklepios. That the literary evidence survives in such a variety of forms (poetry, prose, inscriptions), from such a variety of sources (famous poets to anonymous priests and unknown patients), and over such a long period of time (fifth century BC to fourth/fifth century AD) is fortunate because, as much as is possible, the whole spectrum of humanity is reflected in the literary remains, rather than the thoughts of a few erudite (and perhaps atypical) minds. The literary evidence then is an exciting field of study.

Since the wealth of material is so great,[78] it would be impossible to study every literary source in detail. Therefore a study will be made of a selection of sources from four differing asklepieia: those at Epidauros, Athens, Kos and Pergamon. These four sites have been chosen because they differed in nature and function,[79] and because their literary yield enables a study of the language of literature (both poetry and prose), and the language of inscriptions, over a period of time. This makes it possible to study the changing nature of Asklepios the healing god in the perception of the people, and also to compare the language chosen to describe that perception, with the language chosen to describe the perception of

---

76 At the National Archaeological Museum at Athens, and the museums at Epidauros, Kos, and Bergama. See App. 3:1 for plates of reliefs and votives from these museums.

77 The sites at Epidauros, Athens, Kos and Pergamon have all been excavated, and work continues at Epidauros (under the direction of V. Lambrinoudhakis) and Pergamon (under the direction of Wolfgang Radt).

78 There were more than three hundred asklepieia in the Mediterranean world (see Merriam [1885] 358; and Walton [1894] 95). See also Apuleius, *De Deo Socratis* 15.153: Aesculapius ubique; Aristides, *Oratio* 38.21: ὁσαχοῖ δὲ Ἀσκληπιῷ εἴσοδοι ... πανταχοῦ γῆς. Many have yielded literary evidence of some kind.

79 The sanctuary at Epidauros was an international sanctuary which colonised all over the Mediterranean world (see below, 18-39); the sanctuary at Athens was local and later became a state cult (see below, chapter three); the sanctuary at Kos a medical school (see below, chapter four); and the sanctuary at Pergamon the cult focus of a major hellenistic monarchy (see below, chapter five).

Jesus of Nazareth, the ultimate supplanter of Asklepios in the Mediterranean world.

2.2. Epidauros

The asklepieion at Epidauros is the oldest of the four sites chosen for study. Despite the Homeric evidence for Trikka in Thessaly as the birthplace of Asklepios,[80] later legend credits Epidauros as the origin of the healing cult.[81] Certainly the asklepieion at Epidauros became the major centre of pilgrimage in the Greek world, and the major colonising asklepieion. It was from Epidauros, for example, that the asklepieia at Athens,[82] Pergamon,[83] and Rome[84] were later established. The sanctuary was founded in a small valley[85]

80 See *Iliad* 2.729-733, and 4.202-203. There is still debate concerning this. For a discussion, see Edelstein (1945) 2: 17-22. Current excavation at Trikka should yield answers regarding the age of the sanctuary there, and so supplement the literary evidence. See Theodoretus, *Graecarum Affectionum Curatio* 8.19, (cf. Apollodorus Atheniensis, Fr. 138 [Jacoby]) which states that "In Trikka first and in Epidauros he gave proof of his art (ἐν Τρίκκῃ δὲ πρῶτον καὶ Ἐπιδαύρῳ δοῦναι πεῖραν τῆς τέχνης)". Strabo, *Geographica* 14.1.39, and Hyginus, *Fabulae* 14.21, both cite Trikka as Asklepios' place of origin. Strabo, *Geographica* 9.5.17 also states that Trikka has "the earliest and most famous temple of Asklepios." Eusebius, *Praeparatio Evangelica* 3.14.6, quotes Asklepios himself as citing "holy Trikka" as his place of origin, and that his mother bore him in wedlock to Apollo. However, Pausanias (*Descriptio Graeciae* 4.3.1-2), cites the Messenian belief that Asklepios was the son of Arsinoë, not Coronis, and that the Trikka referred to in the *Iliad* was, in fact, a desolate spot in Messenia. Thus the Messenians believed that the sons of Asklepios who went to Troy were Messenians.

81 See Pausanias, *Descriptio Graeciae* 2.26.7, where Pausanias states his belief that the story that Asklepios was the son of Arsinoë was "a fiction invented by Hesiod, or by one of Hesiod's interpolators, just to please the Messenians". As evidence Pausanias cites the answer, that Asklepios was born of Coronis in Epidauros, which the Pythian priestess at Delphi gave to Apollophanes, an Arcadian, when he asked about Asklepios' origin and birthplace.

82 See below, chapter three. See also, *SEG* 25.226 (the Telemachos Monument), and for a discussion of this monument, and a survey of the published scholarship concerning it, see Aleshire (1989) 6-13, and 6, n.3. See also Pausanias, *Descriptio Graeciae* 2.26.8; Philostratus, *Vita Apollonii* 4.18.

83 See below, chapter five. See also Aristides, *Oratio* 39.5; Pausanias, *Descriptio Graeciae* 2.26.8.

84 In 292 BC, in response to the plague. See Livy, *Periocha* 11; *Ab Urbe Condita* 29.11.1; Valerius Maximus, *Facta et Dicta Memorabilia* 1.8.2; Anonymous, *De Viris Illustribus* 22.1-3; Ovid, *Metamorphoses* 15.622-744; Claudianus, *De Consulatu Stilichonis* 3.171-173

85 Pausanias, *Descriptio Graeciae* 2.27.1-7

about two days' journey from the port of Epidauros, at about the end of the sixth century BC.[86] At Epidauros Asklepios was regarded as healing in conjunction with his father Apollo.[87] This is verified by inscriptions dedicated to both Apollo and Asklepios.[88] Excavations have revealed a sanctuary to Apollo Maleatas on Mt. Kynortion, where Apollo had been worshipped since prehistoric times.[89] The asklepieion at Epidauros reached its peak in the fifth and fourth centuries BC, when it was a major centre for festivals and pan-hellenic games.[90] The festivals, known as the

---

86 Excavations have established that an altar and a sacred building for Asklepios were erected at the end of the sixth century BC. The asklepieion was excavated by P. Kavvadias 1879-1928, and more thoroughly in 1881-1889 (see Kavvadias [1891]); by the French School of Archaeology in 1942; and by J. Papadimitriou (1948-1951), who did additional research on the sanctuary of Maleatas; and by V. Lambrinoudhakis in recent years.

87 The Epidaurian sanctuary was built in the valley below the site of the ancient sanctuary of Apollo Maleatas, which was situated beyond the theatre, on the summit of Mt. Kynortion. Thus worship of Apollo at Epidauros started on Mt. Kynortion, continuing there until Roman times. The Roman senator, Antoninus, renovated this ancient sanctuary in the second century AD (Pausanias, *Descriptio Graeciae* 2.27.7). At the same time he renovated the Asklepieion and "built a temple to Health, as well as to Asklepios, and Apollo, with the surname 'Egyptians'" (Pausanias, *Descriptio Graeciae* 2.27.6). The surname "Egyptians" reflects a hellenistic influence, an influence also visible at Pergamon at this time (see below, chapter five). The association of Asklepios with Apollo is not unusual. Other asklepieia were established over or near old Apollo temples, for example, (i) at Korinth (see Lang (1977) 3-4, who states (4) that "it seems likely that Asklepios joined Apollo first in a perhaps junior capacity ... perhaps [in] the 5th century B.C."; and (ii) Pergamon is mentioned in the *Iliad* (4.507-508, 5.445-448) as the site of one of Apollo's temples, and yet later became a major sanctuary of the healing cult. Nor is the medical association of Asklepios with Apollo unusual, given their relationship, and Apollo's arrangement for Asklepios' tutelage under Cheiron.

88 See, for example, *IG* IV^2 1, nos. 121-122 [2nd half of 4th c. BC], inscriptions of cures at Epidauros under the title of: Θεός Τύχα [ἀγ]αθά | [Ἰά]ματα τοῦ Ἀπόλλωνος καὶ τοῦ Ἀσκλαπιοῦ; and *IG* IV^2 1, no. 127 [224AD]: Ἀπόλλωνι Μαλεάτᾳ καὶ Σωτῆρι Ἀσκληπιῷ.

89 See n.87 above, and for a discussion of the connection between Apollo Maleatas and Asklepios, see Edelstein (1945) 2: 99, and 99 notes 30, 31, and 32. Whether Maleatas was originally an independent iatric hero (Wilamowitz-Moellendorff [1931-1932] 393f.), or a specific form of Apollo (Farnell [1907] 235f.; cf. Kerényi [1959] 28-32), Apollo Maleatas is connected with Asklepios: at Athens (*IG* II^2, no. 4962 [beginning 4th c. BC, {but dated 355-354 BC by Pritchett and Meritt}]), and Trikka (*IG* IV^2 1, no. 128, iii, 27-31 [Isyllos, *ca.* 333 BC]), as well as at Epidauros (*IG* IV^2 1, no. 127 [224 AD]).

90 *IG* IV^2 1, no. 40 [*ca.* 400BC], no. 41 [*ca.* 400BC]

Asklepieia,[91] were held four-yearly, nine days after the Isthmia, between April and June.[92] Musical and dramatic contests were also held from the fifth century BC.[93] Liturgical music too had its place in the life of the cult, certainly in the Imperial period, and possibly well before.[94] The sanctuary was visited by Aemilius Paulus in 167 BC after the Battle of Pydna, who found "a splendid temple of Asklepios ... rich in offerings...".[95] Sulla was the first to loot the sanctuary, seizing "ex votos" (as at Delphi and Olympia) in 86 BC,[96] a practice that was continued by Cilician pirates.[97] However the sanctuary continued to survive as a place of pilgrimage. Strabo found the temple at Epidauros "full of the sick".[98] Festivals were reintroduced in the Imperial period, and the sanctuary was renovated in the second century AD, through the generosity of the Roman senator Antoninus.[99] In AD 395 the Goths of Alarich invaded, and in AD 426 the sanctuary was closed, along with other pagan sanctuaries, when worship was forbidden by Theodosius II. Disused, the sanctuary finally fell into a state of disrepair, following the earthquakes of AD 522 and AD 551. By this time it had enjoyed a special place in the hearts of pilgrims for almost one thousand years.

---

91 Scholia in Pindarum, *Ad Nemeas* 5.94b

92 Scholia in Pindarum, *Ad Nemeas* 3.147

93 Plato, *Ion* 530A; *IG* IV^2 1, no. 128, iii, 32-iv, 56 [*ca.* 300 BC]

94 Suzanne Bonefas (1989) 62 writes concerning *SEG* 30.390, excavated at Epidauros in July 1977, that "however the music of this fragment is interpreted, its importance not only for Greek music but also for Greek religion should not be underestimated. The linking of *SEG* XXX 390 with *IG* IV^2 1, no. 135 yields a third set of hymns from the sanctuary at Epidauros. The presence of musical notation provides concrete evidence for the performance of liturgical hymns and so gives a glimpse of the workings of cult ritual in the Imperial period. The existence of a means of musical abbreviation suggests that sacred music was probably standardized in this period. The apparently archaic features of this notation perhaps indicate that such a process of standardization had already begun before the Imperial period."

95 Livy, *Ab Urbe Condita* 45.28.3. Livy also states that the sanctuary in his time was "now rich in traces of broken votives".

96 Diodorus, *Bibliotheca Historica* 38.7; Plutarch, *Sulla* 12.3; Pausanias, *Descriptio Graeciae* 9.7.5; Appianus, *Historia Romana* 12.54. But cf. Polyaenus, *Strategemata* 5.2.19; Cicero, *Verrinae Orationes* 4.57.127-128

97 Plutarch, *Pompeius* 24.6

98 *Geographica* 8.6.15: καὶ τὸ ἱερὸν πλῆρες ἔχοντος ἀεὶ τῶν τε καμνόντων καὶ τῶν ἀνακειμένων πινάκων.

99 Pausanias, *Descriptio Graeciae* 2.27.6-7

2.3. Epigraphical evidence

Pausanias, describing the sanctuary at Epidauros, commented on the six stelae, still standing in his day, which recorded miraculous cures.[100] Some of these stelae were excavated by Kavvadias, who published their inscriptions.[101] They are temple records, testifying to miraculous healings, placed in the sanctuary so that all who visited the sanctuary might see and read them. They are thus an explicit temple proclamation of Asklepios' healing power, that is, propaganda for the healing cult.[102] It is to a consideration of the nature of their healing language that we shall first turn. Of these, only a selection with sufficient text to support a study of this nature will be considered.[103] For this purpose the inscriptions known as *Inscriptiones Graecae* IV^2 1, nos. 121-122 [2nd half of 4th c. BC] have been chosen. They describe forty-three healing incidents associated with the asklepieion at Epidauros.[104]

As temple propaganda these inscriptions should reveal something of the nature of temple medicine: that is, the running of the sanctuary itself, the sort of medical problems physicians were unable to treat effectively, healing methods, the origin and background of the people who came for healing, and, finally, they should provide a clue as to the meaning of general healing terms like ὑγιής, ἰάομαι and θεραπεύω.

The inscriptions are dedicated to "God" (θεός) and "Good Fortune" (Τύχα [ἀγ]αθά), and are described as cures ([Ἰά]ματα) of both Apollo and Asklepios,[105] implying that both Apollo and Asklepios played an equal part in effecting the cures. However, Apollo is not mentioned specifically by name in the inscriptions, whereas Asklepios is specifically mentioned on eleven occasions.[106] However,

---

100 *Descriptio Graeciae*, 2.27.3: στῆλαι δὲ εἱστήκεσαν ἐντὸς τοῦ περιβόλου τὸ μὲν ἀρχαῖον καὶ πλέονες, ἐπ' ἐμοῦ δὲ ἓξ λοιπαί. ταύταις ἐγγεγραμμένα καὶ ἀνδρῶν καὶ γυναικῶν ἐστιν ὀνόματα ἀκεσθέντων ὑπὸ τοῦ Ἀσκληπιοῦ, προσέτι δὲ καὶ νόσημα ὅ τι ἕκαστος ἐνόσησε, καὶ ὅπως ἰάθη. γέγραπται δὲ φωνῇ τῇ Δωρίδι." See also 2.36.1.

101 See (1891) and (1900).

102 Do they differ very much from the purpose and proclamation of the gospels in the New Testament?

103 The inscriptions now known as *Inscriptiones Graecae* IV^2 1, nos. 121-122 [2nd half of 4th c. BC]. Edelstein (1945) 1: 221-237, includes the Greek text, with an English translation. See also Herzog (1931)145-147.

104 See Apps 2:1 and 2:2.

105 See App. 2:1, Title.

106 Including the two times the sanctuary of Asklepios is mentioned in *IG* IV^2 1, no. 122: 33.

forms of the indeterminate θεός occur forty-nine times, thirty of these occurring in two distinct formulae.[107] Three of the remaining nineteen occur in inscriptions where Asklepios is specifically mentioned,[108] while nine of the formulae occur in "Asklepios" inscriptions.[109] Thus it seems that the use of both names in the dedication is also a formula,[110] but that it is to Asklepios that individuals turn for practical help, given that Apollo does not play an explicit role in the healing episodes.

The first inscription shows a basic pattern of four steps: it states (i) the identity of the patient and the nature of the complaint, (ii) that the patient slept in the abaton, (iii) the result, and (iv) describes the patient's votive offering.[111] This pattern forms the basis, with variations, for recording most of the inscriptions, so is a convenient way to analyse the data presented.

2.4. Patient profile

Of the forty-three inscriptions, thirty-one describe male patients (twenty-six adults and five boys), males thus representing 72% of those who approach the god for help. Of the remainder, eleven describe adult female patients, and one describes the restoration of a broken goblet. Patients come from all over the Greek world, testifying to the sanctuary at Epidauros being the focus of pilgrims at this early date. For example, Hermodikos came from Lampsakos,[112] Heraieus from Mytilene,[113] Antikrates from Knidos,[114] Hermon from Thasos,[115] Pandaros and Echedoros from Thessaly,[116] Sostrata from Pherae,[117] Kleinatas from Thebes,[118] and an

---

107 Variations of: (i) ὄψιν εἶδε· ἐδόκει οἱ ὁ θεὸς occur twenty-five times; and (ii) variations of ποὶ τὸν θεὸν ἱκέτας occur five times.

108 *IG* IV^2 1, no. 121: 10; *IG* IV^2 1, no. 122: 25, 33

109 *IG* IV^2 1, no. 121: 2; *IG* IV^2 1, no. 122: 23, 24, 27, 35, 37

110 See also *IG* IV^2 1, no. 127 [224 AD]: Ἀπόλλωνι Μαλεάτᾳ καὶ Σωτῆρι Ἀσκληπιῷ.

111 For an outline of the inscriptions, based on these four steps, see Apps 2:1 and 2:2. Hereinafter reference will be made to the number of the inscription as recorded in these appendices for ease of reference.

112 App. 2:1, **15**

113 App. 2:1, **19**

114 App. 2:2, **32**

115 App. 2:2, **22**

116 App. 2:1, **6** and **7**

117 App. 2:2, **25**

118 App. 2:2, **28**

unnamed man from Torone.[119] Athens,[120] Aegina,[121] Keos,[122] Kios,[123] Herakleia,[124] Epeiros,[125] and Kirrha,[126] are also represented.[127] More locally, the Peloponnese is represented by patients from Halieis,[128] Hermione,[129] Pellene,[130] Sparta,[131] Troezen,[132] Argos,[133] Kaphyiae,[134] Messene,[135] and Epidauros itself.[136] Korinth is notable for its absence, but that is not surprising as its own asklepieion was flourishing at this stage.[137]

The diseases specified vary. Blindness, either from disease or injury, is the most common complaint, accounting for eight inscriptions, and common to both sexes.[138] Paralysis is an adult male

---

119 App. 2:1, **13**
120 App. 2:1, **4**
121 App. 2:2, **26**
122 App. 2:2, **39**
123 App. 2:2, **43**
124 App. 2:2, **30**. But it is not clear which Herakleia. See App. 1:1.
125 App. 2:2, **31**
126 App. 2:2, **38**
127 See Apps 1:1 and 1:2 for maps showing the locations of the asklepieia, and the cities of origin of the patients represented in the inscriptions.
128 App. 2:1, **18**;App. 2:2, **24** and **33**. Inscription 33 describes the establishment of an asklepieion at Halieis, which is not surprising, given the demand from there for the services of the asklepieion, in comparison with other places. It is interesting for an account of the procedure followed: the (unexpected) arrival of a sacred serpent at Halieis after the patient had seen no vision at Epidauros, the curing of Thersandros, and the inquiry of the Delphic oracle by the people of the city as to the correct course of action concerning the return of the serpent to Epidauros, and the oracle's direction to establish a sanctuary in that place. This inscription also illustrates the colonising activity of the asklepieion at Epidauros at this time.
129 App. 2:1, **20**
130 App. 2:1, **2**
131 App. 2:2, **21**
132 App. 2:2, **34**. But note that the incident described in inscription **23** took place at the sanctuary at Troezen, and that Asklepios was summoned from Epidauros to perform a healing which his children were unable to accomplish. (Cf. the synoptic account of the healing of the epileptic boy: Mt 17.14-20; Mk 9.14-29; Lk 9.37-43.)
133 App. 2:2, **37**
134 App. 2:2, **41**
135 App. 2:2, **42**
136 App. 2:1, **8**; App. 2:2, **35**
137 See Lang (1977).
138 App. 2:1, **4**: an Athenian woman, blind in one eye, who was incredulous of the reported cures; **9**: a man so blind that one of his eyeballs was missing, and others laughed at him for believing that he could be cured; **11**: a man injured in a fall at the sanctuary; **18**: a blind man who first sees trees, after the god

complaint, affecting the fingers,[139] body,[140] and knees,[141] as is lameness.[142] Battle wounds are also a male complaint, as is to be expected.[143] Other male problems specified are stigmata,[144] stone,[145] lack of voice,[146] leeches,[147] sores,[148]consumption,[149] internal abscess,[150] lice,[151] baldness,[152] external tumour,[153] insomnia from headaches,[154] and gout.[155] A father also approaches the

---

opens his eyes with his fingers (cf. Mk 8.22-26); **20**: a blind boy treated by one of the temple dogs; **22**: Hermon of Thasos who was cured of blindness, omitted to bring thank-offerings, was blinded again as punishment, but cured when he again approached the god; **32**: a battle wound causing blindness; **40**: a battle wound which presumably caused blindness as the god treated his eye.

139 App. 2:1, **3**

140 App. 2:1, **15**, and see also App. 2:3; App. 2:2, **37**.

141 App. 2:2, **38**

142 App. 2:1, **16**; App. 2:2, **35** and **36**. Inscription 36 describes lameness inflicted by the god as punishment for disbelief and derision. When the patient is suitably remorseful he is healed.

143 App. 2:1, **12**: a spear point embedded in the jaw; App. 2:2, **30**: arrow wound in the lung; **32**: spear wound in both eyes causing blindness; **40**: spear wound under the eye, causing blindness (?).

144 App. 2:1, **6** and **7**. Inscription 7 gives the only account of punishment by the god that is not reversed. Echedoros is punished for failing to deliver the thank-offerings entrusted to him by his friend Pandaros (**6**), lying about them to the god, and making (empty?) promises about his own thank-offering.

145 App. 2:1, **8** and **14**

146 App. 2:1, **5**

147 App. 2:1, **13**. This occurrence of δεμελέας is the only citation of this word in Liddell and Scott (1968). The cause of his illness is attributed to his swallowing the leeches, having been tricked by his stepmother who had thrown them into a potion which he drank. Is this the first appearance of the wicked stepmother (ματρυιᾶς) in healing inscriptions?

148 App. 2:1, **17**. This is an unusual inscription. The healing agent is a serpent, outside the abaton, in the daytime. The man's vision does not agree with the healing report. Cf. the Archinos relief, Athens, N.M. 3369 (App. 3:1, **3**).

149 App. 2:2, **33**. See above, n.128.

150 App. 2:2, **27**

151 App. 2:2, **28**

152 App. 2:1, **19**

153 App. 2:2, **26**. This boy was treated by one of the temple dogs while he was awake (cf. App. 2:1, **20**).

154 App. 2:2, **29**. The god gives gymnastic instruction in this inscription, to great effect. Hagestratos won the pancratium at the Nemean games not long afterwards! For similar activities by the god at Pergamon, cf. Aelius Aristides, *Or.* 42.11 (App. 5:6, **16**).

155 App. 2:2, **43**. This man is cured by a goose while wide awake. The goose bit his feet and made them bleed.

god on behalf of his missing son.[156] Problems relating to conception and childbearing are the main female complaints, accounting for over half (54.5%) of the female maladies.[157] Otherwise worms[158] are the major female complaint. Blindness,[159] and dropsy[160] account for the remaining female problems. A broken goblet[161] is also restored, showing that the god was not only concerned with treating human health, but was anxious to alleviate any human distress.

2.5. Healing methods

Healing methods are usually recounted as the patient's vision while he/she is sleeping, and occur in a regular formula: the patient slept "and saw a vision/dream. And it seemed to him/her that the god ...".[162] Dream visions include conversations between the patient and the god, commands from the god, or actions by the god and his helpers, such as touching, surgery, application of drugs, or other (sometimes bizarre)[163] behaviour.

Conversations between the god and his patients occur frequently. They reveal a god who has a sense of humour, as when Ithmonika was told she would get pregnant with a daughter, and was asked if

---

156 App. 2:2, **24**

157 App. 2:1, **1**: a 5-year pregnancy; **2**: (i) conception, and (ii) a 3-year pregnancy. App. 2:2, **31**: conception; **34**: conception; **39**: conception; **42**: conception.

158 App. 2:2, **33**: a tapeworm; **25**: worms (two basins full); **41**: pregnant with worms.

159 App. 2:1, **4**: see above, n.138.

160 App. 2:2, **21**: in this inscription the mother slept in the temple on behalf of her daughter, who remained in Sparta, but saw the same dream. On her return the mother found her daughter in good health (ὑγιαίνουσαν). Cf. the NT story of the centurion's servant, particularly Luke 7.10, where the present participle of ὑγιαίνω occurs as the final description of the boy's health when the centurion returns home. App. 2:2, **24** also reports a parent approaching the god on behalf of a child. The child, in this case, is missing.

161 App. 2:1, **10**. This is a most interesting inscription. It is the only occasion in *IG* IV^2 1, 121-122, where an inanimate object is restored so that it is sound. The same word (ὑγιής) is used to describe the restoration of the goblet as is used in formulae to describe the restoration of people. For a discussion of the significance of this, see below, 31-33, 38-39.

162 Variations of the formula " ὄψιν εἶδε· ἐδόκει οἱ ὁ θεὸς " occur as an introduction to accounts of healing methods twenty-five times. See above, n.107.

163 See *IG* IV^2 1, no. 122: 38 (App. 2:2, **38**), where the god drove his horses and chariot around a patient suffering from paralysis of the knees, and trampled on him with his horses. The patient instantly gained control of his knees!

she desired anything else. She replied negatively, and so was compelled to approach the god again after a three-year pregnancy in order to give birth.[164] Perhaps this inscription inspired patients to be specific in their requests. Conversations also reveal a god who has an ability to relate to all ages, as when the boy, Euphanes, promised to give the god ten dice if he would cure him. We are told that the god laughed, and agreed.[165] The god laughs on another occasion, as well as showing anger.[166]

Many conversations, like the one with Euphanes, concern the giving of votive offerings. Ambrosia of Athens is asked to give the temple a silver pig as a memorial of her ignorance in disbelieving the cures,[167] Pandaros is told to dedicate his headband[168], Echedoros is questioned about votive offerings and punished for his untruthful replies,[169] Hermodikos is ordered to bring to the temple as large a stone as he could,[170] and Sostrata is told to send thank-offerings to Epidauros.[171]

Conversations between the god and his patients also deal with patient incredulity, as when a man who had expressed incredulity is told that his name in future would be "Incredulous" (Ἄπιστος).[172] Incredulity is prominent in a number of inscriptions. Patient incredulity is expressed and dealt with,[173] as is bystander incredulity,[174] and Kaphisias, who laughed at the cures is actually punished with an injury, although healed when he is suitably humble and remorseful.[175] These inscriptions show that contemporary Greeks were sceptical enough of the temple cures to warrant temple propaganda of this sort.

Inscriptions relate that the god healed with action as well as conversation. He performed surgery on battle wounds, extracting parts of weapons which were embedded in patients' bodies. Euhippos had the point of a spear extracted from his jaw after it had been embedded there for six years,[176] Gorgias had an arrow

164 App. 2:1, **2**
165 App. 2:1, **8**
166 App. 2:2, **35**
167 App. 2:1, **4**
168 App. 2:1, **6**
169 App. 2:1, **7**
170 App. 2:1, **15**. See also App. 2:3.
171 App. 2:2, **25**
172 App. 2:1, **3**
173 App. 2:1, **3** and **4**
174 App. 2:1, **9** and **10**
175 App. 2:2, **36**
176 App. 2:1, **12**

point extracted from his lung. It had been there for a year and a half, and had suppurated so badly he had filled sixty-seven basins with pus.[177] The man from Torone had leeches surgically removed from his chest.[178] Arata dreamt that a lot of fluid matter drained out of her daughter after the god cut off her daughter's head and hung up her body in such a way that her throat was turned downwards.[179] Aristagora[180] also dreamt that she had her head cut off. She slept in the temple at Troezen, and was attended in her dream by the sons of the god. They were unable to put her head back on, so sent to Epidauros for Asklepios. The following night Asklepios reattached her head to her neck, cut open her stomach, removed the tapeworm, and stitched her up again. This inscription shows that Asklepios is superior in healing power to his sons, and that the sanctuary at Epidauros is superior to the sanctuary at Troezen. In this case Asklepios' sons were guilty of making an incorrect diagnosis, and an inability to complete their treatment successfully.[181] One wonders how much competition there was between neighbouring asklepieia. The inscription notes that the priest saw the evidence of mismanagement, 'proof' that the story is true.

Two other patients had surgery performed on their stomachs by Asklepios: a man with an abscess in his abdomen had it surgically removed, leaving the abaton floor covered with blood;[182] and Sostrata had worms which filled two washbasins surgically removed from her stomach.[183] At the time she was undertaking her homeward journey and was unaware that it was Asklepios who was the surgeon, until after the outcome was successful.[184]

---

177 App. 2:2, **30**

178 App. 2:1, **13**

179 App. 2:2, **21**

180 App. 2:2, **23**

181 Compare the disciples' inability to heal a patient in the synoptic account of the healing of the epileptic boy (Mt 17.14-20; Mk 9.14-29; Lk 9.37-43).

182 App. 2:2, **27**

183 App. 2:2, **25**

184 This seems an extraordinary thing to allow a stranger to do. Sostrata is an unusual case: she comes from further away than any other female patient, so was obviously in great distress to even think of undertaking a journey of this nature. She must also have possessed the financial resources to be able to do so, explaining Asklepios' command to send thank-offerings to Epidauros. She is also unusual in that she had no vision while at Epidauros (like Thersandros of Halieis, **33**), but had unexpected treatment on the road. We are told that "a man of fine appearance seemed to come upon her and her companions" (αὐτᾶι καὶ τοῖς ἑ[πομέ]νοις ἔδοξε τὰν ὄψιν εὐπρεπὴς ἀνήρ). As in the accounts of dream visions the verb δοκέω implies a subjective experience.

Asklepios also healed with drugs. He cut Ambrosia's diseased eyeball and poured in a drug,[185] poured a drug into the sockets of the man who had no eyeball,[186] and rubbed down a herb and poured it into an eye injured by a spear wound.[187] He anointed the head of a bald man with a drug, and made the hair grow,[188] and gave a drug to Erasippe to drink which induced vomiting.[189]

Asklepios also healed with his fingers,[190] and by touch.[191] He led a father to the place where his missing son could be found,[192] stretched out the paralysed fingers of a man while he was playing at dice,[193] swept the lice from a man's body with a broom,[194] and taught another how to lunge.[195] He expected his instructions to be obeyed, no matter how bizarre they might have seemed, and did not easily tolerate cowards. When Kleimenes complained that a lake was too cold for a bath, Asklepios said he would not heal the cowardly, but only those who approached him with hope and trust.[196] He broke the crutch of a lame man and ordered him to get a ladder and climb as high as he could. When the man gave up, Asklepios was angry, and then laughed at him for being a coward. The man fulfilled his task in daylight.[197]

All these healing methods are recounted as the patient's perception of the healing process that occurred in the patient's dream vision. However one inscription makes it obvious that a dream vision might not correspond to reality, although the end result is the same.[198] It is true that this vision and cure occurred in unusual circumstances: in the sanctuary grounds in the daytime, rather than within the abaton or temple at night. Thus, it would be unwise to generalise too much from this one inscription. However, there is certainly scope for suspecting that, while the cure is

185 App. 2:1, **4**
186 App. 2:1, **9**
187 App. 2:2, **40**
188 App. 2:1, **19**
189 App. 2:2, **41**
190 App. 2:1, **18**
191 App. 2:2, **31**. The verb used to describe this touch is ἅπτομαι, the synoptic word for describing the healing touch of Jesus. See below, Section Two, chapter nine, and Apps 7:12 and 7:13.
192 App. 2:2, **24**
193 App. 2:1, **3**
194 App. 2:2, **28**
195 App. 2:2, **29**
196 App. 2:2, **37**
197 App. 2:2, **35**
198 App. 2:1, **17**

real enough, the inscriptions recounting dream visions might not even pretend to be a factual account of actual healing methods, but rather might be only a personal rationalisation and interpretation of a particular patient's healing experience. In this inscription the man fell asleep outside the temple on a seat. A snake came out of the temple and healed his toe with its tongue, but the man reported a vision of a beautiful youth anointing his toe with a drug.[199] Thus the difference between dream and reality is publicly acknowledged in this inscription.[200]

Patients can also be healed by temple serpents, temple dogs, or in one case, by a goose.[201] Serpents are instrumental in the healing process on four occasions. We have already noted the inscription that states that a serpent healed a man's toe with its tongue, while the man dreamed of a beautiful youth anointing his toe with a drug,[202] and the case of Thersandros, who was healed by a temple serpent after he returned home.[203] Serpents are also instrumental in fulfilling the desire of two women to become pregnant. Aga-

---

199 Cf. the Archinos relief, Athens, N.M. 3369 (App. 3:1, **3**). For a discussion of the meaning of this relief, see Mitropoulou (1976a) 35-40. According to her (36) "the three human figures represent one person, Archinos, who came to the Asklepieion seeking a cure. As he was sleeping in the temple, the snake licked him and he dreamt that the god came and performed an operation...". Although this votive relief is dedicated to Amphiaraos, a healing hero, and not to Asklepios, it is a good illustration of the difference between vision and reality, a difference that was portrayed publicly in this relief, as the dif-ference is acknowledged publicly in inscription **17** (App. 2:1).

200 Cf. however, Kerényi (1959) 33-34, who gives a different interpretation. According to him (34) this episode "is a kind of dream within a dream, an amplification reaching out for a still deeper meaning - the immediate experience of the divine in the natural miracle of healing."

201 The serpent was one of the attributes of Asklepios, and appears wound around his staff in statues and reliefs (see Plate 1; Athens, N.M. 1345; and the statuettes, Athens, N.M. 265 and 266). The serpent is also depicted in many votive reliefs coiled under his chair (see App. 3:1, **7**; and the votive relief, Athens, N.M. 1330); and around trees (see App. 3:1, **12**). At Kos Museum a snake appears coiled around the shoulders of a statue of Hygieia (Kos Museum, 98); as well as wound around the staff of Asklepios (Plate 6). Asklepios was thought to take on the guise of a serpent: this is the form in which he arrived at Athens (*IG* II^2, no. 4960a; *SEG* 25.226), and Rome (Livy, *Periocha* 11, *Ab Urbe Condita* 29.11.1), and, of course, Halieis (App. 2:2, **33**). For a discussion of the role of animals in the healing cult, see Schouten (1967) 37-44.

202 App. 2:1, **17**. See above 28, and n.148. The verb used to describe the serpent's action is *ἰάομαι*, while *ὑγιής* occurs in the final formula. For a discussion of the use of these words see below, 31-39.

203 App. 2:2, **33**. Again the verb chosen to describe the serpent's action is *ἰάομαι*.

mede of Keos dreamt that a serpent lay on her stomach, and afterwards she gave birth to five children,[204] and Nikasibula of Messene dreamt that the god approached her with a snake creeping behind him. She had intercourse with the snake, and within a year gave birth to two sons.[205]

Dogs also healed on two occasions, and both times their patients were boys who were wide-awake. Lyson of Hermione was blind, but one of the dogs in the temple treated him (licked his eyes?) and he went away healthy.[206] Similarly, a boy from Aegina who had a growth on his neck was treated by one of the temple dogs. The dog licked him (the growth?) and made him healthy.[207]

A goose also healed a man who was suffering from gout. While he was wide-awake the goose bit his feet, and by making them bleed, made him healthy.[208] Thus animals assume an important healing role in temple medicine. Indeed these inscriptions imply that they were more successful than Asklepios' sons.[209]

Several themes emerge from a study of healing methods and dream visions: the importance of votive offerings,[210] and the importance of honesty[211] and humility, hope and trust when approaching the healing god.[212] Obedience was also required.[213] Where votive offerings do not figure prominently in the inscrip-

---

204 App. 2:2, **39**. The inscription doesn't specify whether this was a multiple birth, or a series of multiple births, or five single births over a period of years.

205 App. 2:2, **42**: presumably twins?

206 App. 2:1, **20**. The verb chosen to describe the dog's treatment is θεραπεύω, and ὑγιής occurs in the final formula. For a discussion of the use of these words see below, 31-39. The curative properties of canine saliva are discussed in Reinach (1884) 129.

207 App. 2:2, **26**. Again the verb describing the dog's treatment is θεραπεύω, although ἰάομαι occurs in this account, as well as ὑγιής in the final formula.

208 App. 2:2, **43**

209 See Schouten (1967) 37-44 for a discussion of the role of animals in the healing cult (cf. Kérenyi [1959] 32).

210 Votive offerings were vital to the survival and growth of the asklepieion, in whatever form they were given. Monetary assistance (as promised by Pandaros, **6** and **7**) maintained the asklepieion, while votive offerings testified to the god's healing power and ensured a continuing flow of clients. Punishment is inflicted for failure to bring votive offerings as promised. (See Apps 2:1, **7** and 2:2, **22**. Cf. Acts 5.1-11.)

211 Dishonesty is permanently punished (App. 2:1, **7**).

212 The motif of patient disbelief is introduced and dealt with at the beginning of the stele (App. 2:1, **3** and **4**), and bystander derision of a trusting patient, whose trust is vindicated (App. 2:1, 9). Hope and trust is emphasised (App. 2:2, **37**).

213 App. 2:2, **27**, **35**, **37**

tions, other tangible evidence of the god's healing power is offered: blood on the abaton floor[214], a dress full of vomit,[215] basins full of worms,[216] victory at the Nemean Games,[217] an arrow point,[218] a spear point,[219] leeches,[220] a sanctuary established,[221] babies are born.[222] Bystanders are used to verify stories[223] or marvel at miracles.[224]

2.6. The healing language of inscriptions

2.6.1. ὑγιής

The results of these healing episodes, despite their diverse nature and treatment, are described in surprisingly uniform language. Of the forty-three inscriptions, forty-two[225] record a healing episode of some sort, and, of these, twenty-nine record the wholeness of the person (or object) when they departed from the sanctuary with some form of ὑγιής. Otherwise their cure (or punishment) is precise: babies were born;[226] stigmata vanished[227] or were increased;[228] a man who arrived blind, and with only one eyeball,

214 App. 2:2, **27**
215 App. 2:2, **41**
216 App. 2:2, **25**
217 App. 2:2, **29**
218 App. 2:2, **30**
219 App. 2:1, **12**
220 App. 2:1, **13**
221 App. 2:2, **33**
222 App. 2:1, 2;App. 2:2, **34, 39, 42**
223 App. 2:2, **23**. The priest "sees" (ὁρῆι) the state of the woman.
224 App. 2:1, **5**. This inscription, concerning a voiceless unidentified boy, provides extra information about preliminary sacrifices, rites and the duties of temple servants. The boy is accompanied by his father, who is asked by a temple servant to bring the thank-offering within one year, if his son is cured. The boy replies in the affirmative, startling his father (ἐκπλήσσω). This healing occurred *before* a temple sleep. The role of the bystander exhibiting amazement is also important in New Testament stories, and in accounts of Vespasian's healing miracles (Tacitus, *Histories* 4.81).
225 There is only one inscription which describes a permanent punishment (App. 2:1, **7**). Otherwise, those who are punished are later healed, after they have shown suitable remorse (App. 2:2, **22, 36**).
226 A daughter (App. 2:1, **2**), a son (App. 2:2, **31, 34**), five children (App. 2:2, **39**), two sons (twins?) (App. 2:2, **42**).
227 App. 2:1, **6**
228 App. 2:1, **7**

departed seeing with both eyes;[229] a man left holding his (genital?) stone;[230] a bald man's hair grew again;[231] a missing child was found;[232] a sanctuary was established;[233] and a lame man walked unaided and unhurt.[234] The word ὑγιής is thus a general healing term, and covers a surprising range of restorations. But what precisely does it mean?

ὑγιής regularly occurs in one of two formulae: (i) "at daybreak he/she departed sound" (ἁμέρας δὲ γενομένας ὑγιὴς ἐξῆλθε),[235] and (ii) "and (out of this) he/she became sound" (καὶ (ἐκ τούτου) ὑγιὴς ἐγένετο).[236] Sometimes both formulae overlap.[237] Otherwise ὑγιής occurs in variations of "the god made him/her sound".[238] Similarly Hermon was restored to health,[239] while another man woke up and was healthy.[240] A dog made a boy sound,[241] as a goose made the man with gout sound,[242] and another boy departed sound after being treated by a dog.[243]

---

229 App. 2:1, **9**
230 App. 2:1, **14**
231 App. 2:1, **19**
232 App. 2:2, **24**
233 App. 2:2, **33**
234 App. 2:2, **35**
235 See part (iii) of *Words* in App. 2:1, **3**, **4**, **8**, **12**, **13**, **18**; and App. 2:2, **28**, **29**, **30**, **32**, **38**.
236 See part (iii) of *Words* in App. 2:1, **5**, **11**, **13**, **16**; and App. 2:2, **23**, **27**, **40**, **41**.
237 As in App. 2:1, **13**: ἁμέρας δὲ γενομένας ἐξῆλθε τὰ θηρία ἐν ταῖς χερσὶν ἔχων | καὶ ὑγιὴς ἐγένετο.
238 App. 2:1, **1**: καί μιν ἔθηκε ὑγιῆ. App. 2:2, **25**: καὶ ποήσας ὑ[γιῆ] | τὰν γυναῖκα; **36**: αὐτὸν ὁ θεὸς ὑγιῆ ἐπόησε.
239 App. 2:2, **22**: ὑγι]ῆ κατέστασε.
240 App. 2:1, **17**: ἐξεγερθεὶς δὲ ὡς ἦς ὑγιής.
241 App. 2:2, **26**: ἀφικόμενο[ν] | δ' αὐτὸν ποὶ τ[ὸν] θε[ὸ]ν κύων τῶν ἱαρῶν ὑ[παρτ]ᾶι γλώσσαι ἐθεράπευσε | καὶ ὑγιῆ ἐπόη[σ]ε.
242 App. 2:2, **43**: ὑγιῆ ἐπόη[σε]. I have been unable to find another healing incident involving a goose. This incident appears to be unique.
243 App. 2:1, **20**: ὑπὸ κυνὸς τῶν | κατὰ τὸ ἱαρὸν θε[ραπ]ευόμενος τοὺς ὀπτίλλους ὑγ[ιὴ]ς ἀπῆλθε. Dogs play an important role in the healing cult, and are often depicted on votive reliefs, either sitting at Asklepios' feet, or under his chair, or frisking about other members of his family. See, for example, the votive relief from Epidauros (Athens, N.M. 1426) which depicts Asklepios, his two sons Podaleirios and Machaon, who are accompanied by dogs, three goddesses and two worshippers. According to Kerényi (1959) 32, there "is a striking equivalence of dog and snake in the Greek mythology of the underworld; their forms merge and their meanings as well ... both animals may express the same psychic content."

Asklepios uses the word in the conversation of dream visions, to the boy who made him laugh,[244] and to his reluctant patient, Kleimenes.[245] Echedoros too tells the god what votive offering he would set up if the god would make him well.[246] When Arata returned to Sparta she found her daughter healthy.[247]

Finally, a bystander tells a dispirited porter that not even Asklepios in Epidauros could make his broken goblet sound again,[248] only to be proved wrong when the porter lifts it out of the bag and finds it sound.[249] This last incident provides a clue as to the meaning of the word ὑγιής. As the goblet was restored to its former unbroken and useful state, so patients must be restored to the health they had enjoyed prior to the onset of the specific problem about which they consulted Asklepios. Thus the word ὑγιής implies the restoration of a person or object to their original undamaged state of health or usefulness.

2.6.2. ἰάομαι

The verb ἰάομαι also occurs as a general healing term, but only in eight inscriptions,[250] and, of these eight inscriptions, ἰάομαι appears in six of them in conjunction with ὑγιής.[251] None of the patients were surgical patients. The two inscriptions which contain only ἰάομαι are those concerning Hermodikos of Lampsakos,[252] and Thersandros of Halieis.[253] Both stories have as their end result tangible proof of their validity. Hermodikos inscribed and erected a very large votive to the god as evidence of his healing power,[254] while an asklepieion was erected at Halieis, at the direction of the Delphic oracle.[255]

---

244 App. 2:1, **8**: 'τί μοι δωσεῖς, αἴ τυ|κα ὑγιῆ ποιήσω;'

245 App. 2:2, **37**: ὑγιῆ ἀποπ[εμψοῖ.

246 App. 2:1, **7**: ἀλλ' αἴ κα ὑγιῆ νιν ποήσαι.

247 App. 2:2, **21**: θυγατέρα ὑγιαίνουσαν.

248 App. 2:1, **10**: τοῦτον γὰρ οὐδέ κα ὁ ἐν Ἐπιδαύ|ρωι Ἀσκλαπιὸς ὑγιῆ ποῆσαι δύναιτο.

249 App. 2:1, **10**: ἀνῶιξε τὸγ γυλιὸν καὶ ἐξαιρεῖ ὑγιῆ τὸγ κώθωνα γεγενημέ|νον.

250 App. 2:1, **15** and **17**; App. 2:2, **22**, **26**, **29**, **23**, [**36**] and [**37**]

251 App. 2:1, **17**; App. 2:2, **22**, **29**, **23**, [**36**] and [**37**]

252 App. 2:1, **15**

253 App. 2:2, **33**

254 See *IG* IV^2 1, no. 125 [3rd c. BC], (App. 2:3).

255 Thus the Delphic oracle instigated the colonising activity of the cult.

The incident at Halieis has one thing in common with another inscription, in that they share the same healing agent. A serpent[256] (ὁ δράκων) was the healing agent at Halieis, while a serpent (ὁ ὄφις . . . δράκων) also healed the man who slept outside the temple in the daytime.[257] In this last story, the man was put on the seat where he fell asleep by the temple attendants (τῶν θε‖ραπόντων), the serpent healed him with its tongue (ἰάσατο τᾶι γλώσσαι), and he woke up healthy (ὑγιής).

A dog is the healing agent in another inscription where the three general healing terms, ἰάομαι, θεραπεύω and ὑγιής, occur.[258] In this inscription we are told that a dog healed the boy from Aegina (Κύων ἰά|σατο παῖδα Αἰ[γιν]άταν). It treated him with its tongue while he was awake and made him healthy (γλώσσαι ἐθεράπευσε | καὶ ὑγιῆ ἐπόη[σ]ε).

The remaining four inscriptions detail actions of the god, including two punishments, gymnastic instruction and psychological counselling, as well as healing in each case. Asklepios healed (ἰάσατο) Hermon of Thasos who had come to him because he was blind.[259] When Hermon failed to bring votive offerings the god punished him by making him blind again (ἐπόησε τυφλὸν αὖθις), but restored his health (ὑγι]ῆ κατέστασε) when Hermon slept in the temple a second time. Unlike Echedoros,[260] Hermon is given a second chance. Presumably he brought thank-offerings on the second occasion. It is curious that the inscription omits the details.

Kaphisias[261] is also punished by the god, but his sin is not one of omission, as in Hermon's case, but disbelief and derision at Asklepios' treatments (θεραπεύμασιν). The verb ἰάομαι occurs twice, in comments attributed to Kaphisias, belittling the cures. The number of times ἰάομαι is used in this inscription is unusual. Both occurrences are supplied by Herzog,[262] as is the final (common) formula containing ὑγιῆ.

---

256 Serpents appear in only four inscriptions (App. 2:1, **17**; App. 2:2, **33**, **39**, **42**). The last two aid conception in female patients.

257 App. 2:1, **17**

258 App. 2:2, **26**

259 App. 2:2, **22**

260 App. 2:1, **7**. Echedoros committed the (unpardonable?) sin of lying to the god.

261 App. 2:2, **36**

262 (1931): Καφισί[ας – – – τὸμ πόδα. οὗτος τοῖς τοῦ Ἀσ]‖κλαπιοῦ θεραπεύμασιν ἐπ[ιγελῶν 'χωλούς,' ἔφα, 'ἰάσασθαι ὁ θεὸς ψεύ]‖δεται λέγων· ὡς, εἰ δύναμιν ε[ἶχε, τί οὐ τὸν Ἅφαιστον ἰάσατο'; ὁ δὲ θεὸς] | τᾶς ὕβριος ποινὰς λαμβάνω[ν οὐκ ἔλαθε·. . ὁ θεὸς ὑγιῆ ἐπόησε.] This is the only occasion the infinitive of ἰάομαι appears in these inscriptions, here in its

Hagestratos[263] approached the god suffering from insomnia, caused by headaches. The god healed (ἰασάμενος) his headaches, and taught him the lunge used in the pancratium. The treatment was effective, for Hagestratos departed healthy (ὑγιής), and not long afterwards won in the pancratium at the Nemean games.

The final inscription to be considered is that relating to Kleimenes of Argos.[264] Again ἰάομαι in this inscription is supplied by Herzog.[265] It occurs in the conversation which took place between Asklepios and Kleimenes in Kleimenes' dream vision.

Thus ἰάομαι is the verb chosen to describe the result of actions performed by Asklepios, and the result of actions performed by him in his manifestation as a serpent. This verb is also chosen to describe the results of the actions of a temple dog and a goose.

In comparison, the verb θεραπεύω is used in a highly technical and specific sense. It only occurs in two inscriptions,[266] and both times describes the treatment given by temple dogs to boys who are awake. While it is explicitly stated in only one inscription that the dog licked the boy,[267] the inference is that this was the form of treatment on both occasions. Thus the verb seems to describe treatment, rather than cure, the cure in each case being described by ὑγιής, with ἰάομαι included as well in one inscription.[268]

The healing touch of Asklepios is described on only one occasion, when the god touched Andromache with his hand (μετὰ δὲ τοῦτο τὸν θεὸν ἅψασθαί οὑ τᾶι [χη]ρί).[269] She had approached the god concerning children, and we are told that later a son was born to her. The verb ἅπτομαι is also the most frequently used synoptic word to describe the healing touch of Jesus.[270]

So what does the language of these fourth century BC inscriptions reveal about the healing cult, about the nature of the healing

---

aorist form. But ἰάομαι also appears twice in App. 2:1, **17**: ἰάθη ... ἰάσατο, in narrative rather than conversation.

263 App. 2:2, **29**

264 App. 2:2, **37**

265 (1931)

266 App. 2:1, **20** and App. 2:2, **26**

267 App. 2:2, **26**

268 App. 2:2, **26**. But relatives of the verb θεραπεύω: τῶν θε||ραπόντων and τοῖς τοῦ 'Ασ||κλαπιοῦ θεραπεύμασιν occur once each, respectively describing the temple attendants and the treatments of Asklepios. (App. 2:1, **17** and App. 2:2, **36**)

269 App. 2:2, **31**

270 See below, Section Two, chapter nine, and Apps 7:12 and 7:13.

god, Asklepios, about the people of the time, and about the use of general healing terms?

2.7. Conclusion

The inscriptions reveal that the sanctuary at Epidauros offered treatment to pilgrims with a wide variety of problems from all over the Greek world.[271] As males are reported as making the longest journeys and account for 72% of the patients it can be concluded that males enjoyed far greater mobility at the end of the fourth century BC than females. This is hardly surprising. The case of Sostrata however is surprising. She made a long and expensive journey,[272] leading one to presume that she was both desperate, and wealthy. Her case shows that Asklepios is not confined to Epidauros, or even to a sanctuary. He can appear unexpectedly to patients anywhere and effectively practise his healing art.

The inscriptions also reveal that, to flourish, the sanctuary relied on monetary support from grateful patients, and that, if promised support did not eventuate, the patient could expect to be punished (usually only temporarily) with an appropriate disease or injury.[273]

---

271 This sanctuary does not seem to specialise in any one area of treatment. Cf. the asklepieion at Korinth, where a large number of votive offerings of body parts, particularly hands and feet have been found, as well as male genitals and female breasts, leading one to suppose that the asklepieion there specialised in treating problems of locomotion and fertility (see App. 3:1, **15**). But perhaps it is to be expected that people with problems of locomotion would patronise their local (and most accessible) asklepieion, and also that the local asklepieion would be more accessible to women (see, for example, Herodas 4, below, 66-70, and App. 4:4). However, where eye trouble is the most frequently attested problem at Epidauros, and Athens (see below, chapter three), surprisingly few votive offerings of eyes have been found at Korinth. Perhaps different localities experienced different health problems. For an account of the votives excavated at Korinth, see Lang (1977) 15-27.

272 She was carried on a litter, which means that the trip would have been slow, that her companions would have been numerous: she needed those to carry the litter as well as others to take care of supplies. As she was so sick, her own supplies would have been extensive, and obviously included such cumbersome articles as washbasins. She must have been wealthy.

273 Cf. the stories of Ananias and Sapphira in Acts 5.1-11. The punishment of Echedoros seems light by comparison, and both Hermon and Kaphisios are given a second chance. Is the perception of Asklepios in the 4th c. BC of a more forgiving god than the perception of his Christian counterpart in the 1st c. AD?

Nevertheless, Asklepios is not portrayed as a vengeful god, but as an approachable and forgiving god, as well as being capable of the human emotions of frustration, anger, and amusement. Even sceptical patients approach him with hope and trust, not fear. And Asklepios does not disappoint them. His treatment may seem bizarre at times, but it is always effective.

One would expect that only patients with particularly difficult problems would make the long trip to Epidauros, but the people represented reflect universal human desires: women want to bear children, the lame and paralysed wish to walk, the blind to see, the wounded to be healed, and distressed parents approach the god on behalf of their children. Patients include the sceptical, the credulous, the greedy, the timid, and the sensitive; parents, children, servants and war veterans. All were suffering in some way, whether physically or emotionally, and all turned to Asklepios for help.

The language and form of the inscriptions is uniform: the name and origin of the patient is cited, the problem identified and a case history given.[274] Healing methods and treatment are usually described as part of the patient's dream vision. Several words emerge as the general healing descriptive terms of these inscriptions. ὑγιής is the favourite word used to describe the patient's return to their former (undamaged) state. However, the verb ἰάομαι also occurs as a description of the results of the actions of the god, serpents, a dog and a goose. In contrast, the verb θεραπεύω is used sparingly, and only describes the treatment given by dogs to

274 Several themes emerge in the inscriptions, and inscriptions can be grouped, or paired, according to theme. For example, there are four accounts of war veterans with battle wounds: two undergo surgery and depart holding the offending piece of weapon in their hands (App. 2:2, **12**; 2:2, **30**), while the other two both suffer eye trouble from a spear wound (App. 2:2, **32** and **40**). Two boys are treated by dogs while awake (App. 2:1, **20** and 2:2, **26**). Parents approach the god on behalf of their children: a mother for her daughter (App. 2:2, **21**); and a father for his son (App. 2:2, **24**). Bystanders play an important role, expressing scorn and disbelief (App. 2:1, **9** and **10**), amazement (App. 2:1, **5**), and amusement (App. 2:1, **19**). Failure to bring votive offerings features as the motive for punishment (App. 2:1, **7** and 2:2, **22**), as does disbelief and derision (App. 2:2, **36**). Patients depart holding tangible evidence of treatment in their hands (App. 2:1, **13** and **14**), clothing (App. 2:2, **41**), or left behind on the floor (App. 2:2, **27**). Cures are enacted offsite (App. 2:2, **25** and **33**). Women are treated for extended pregnancies (App. 2:1, **1** and **2**), infertility (by the god, App. 2:2, **31** and **34**; and by serpents App. 2:2, **39** and **42**), and worms (App. 2:2, **23**, **25** and **41**).

juvenile patients who are awake. The healing touch of the god is described only once, with the verb ἅπτομαι.

But do these words occur in later descriptions of cures at Epidauros, and, if so, is their meaning the same?

An inscription from over four centuries later which has survived in very good condition is that of the attestation of Marcus Julius Apellas, known as *Inscriptiones Graecae* IV^2 1, no. 126 [ca. 160 AD].[275] It illustrates both a change in medical technique and patient introspection not noticeable in the fourth century BC inscriptions, but exhibited in both inscriptions (as here) as well as the literature of the second century AD.[276]

The form of the inscription follows a similar pattern to the earlier inscriptions: the patient is identified by name and origin, and a short case history given. He has come a long way - from Mylasa[277] - at the command of the god, suffering from chronic ill health and dyspepsia. On his way he visited the asklepieion at Aegina.[278] His treatment at Epidauros, (undertaken as the result of conversations with the god), is described in much greater detail than the earlier inscriptions, and is more Hippokratic in content,[279] requiring changes in diet,[280] exercise,[281] personal hygiene,[282] and temperament.[283] Instructions from the priest concerning votive offerings

---

275 For the text and translation, see App. 2:4, and for an analysis, App. 2:5.

276 Although this inscription does not specifically mention a dream vision, a vision could be implied in the lines following ᾤμην (end of line 17, App. 2:4). Apellas exhibits striking similarities with his contemporary Aelius Aristides (see below, chapter five).

277 Mylasa is inland from Miletus (see App. 1:1), so this patient has the time and wealth to make a pilgrimage of this nature. Since he could have gone to the asklepieion at Pergamon, we must assume that he had a specific "call" to Epidauros. Thus the sanctuary at Epidauros is still the focus of pilgrims from afar at this date.

278 It is to this asklepieion that Bdelykleon, in desperation, takes his father, Philokleon, in Aristophanes *Wasps* (122-123). See below, n.286. Thus this asklepieion had been active for at least six centuries by the time Apellas visited it.

279 See below, 71-79, and App. 4:1.

280 To eat cheese and bread, celery and lettuce, to take milk with honey, and to use dill with olive oil for headaches.

281 To press against the wall in the bath (similar to modern hydrotherapy?), to walk in the upper portico, to take passive exercise, to walk around barefoot, to practise running.

282 To bathe without help.

283 The god tells him not to be so irritable, and on two occasions to bathe without help (as well as to give an Attic drachma to the bath attendant).

are noted,[284] and fulfilled, and the result is that the patient departed well (ὑγιής).

Apellas illustrates a different sort of patient to the ones we have seen earlier: instead of a quick-fix he undergoes extended treatment, requiring time, effort and follow-up consultations with the god. He seems to be a wealthy hypochondriac. The priest has to tell him when he is better and the time has come to pay up!

The healing language of the inscription is similar to earlier inscriptions in that the same words occur. The inscription ends with the words "Full of gratitude and having become healthy I departed" (χάριν εἰδὼς καὶ ὑγιὴς γενόμενος ἀπηλλάγην), echoing the language of earlier final formulae. When the patient's blistered hand recovers its former soundness, it is described in the same terms: "the hand became sound" (ὑγιὴς ἡ χεὶρ ἐγένετο).[285] When the god touches the patient, his touch is again described with a form of ἅπτομαι (ἥψατο). However, the word translated as "cured" in the priest's saying "You are cured, and must now pay up the thank offerings" (τεθεράπευσαι, χρὴ δὲ ἀποδιδόναι τὰ ἴατρα) is the perfect passive form of θεραπεύω, a particularly appropriate word, and tense, to describe the result of the extensive treatment (both physical and emotional) that the patient has undergone.

Thus, while again ὑγιής describes the restoration of a patient, or a limb, to a former functioning state of health, θεραπεύω now describes the result of extensive treatment, treatment that has been both physical and psychological. In this way θεραπεύω, while still retaining the idea of nurturing and caring treatment so obvious in the θεράπων of Homeric times, and the idea of physical treatment exemplified above by the treatment of the temple dogs, now seems to include a psychological dimension. This is an important addition in meaning, and a difference that seems to have occurred in the intervening centuries between the two inscriptions.

But does the healing language of other asklepieia echo that of Epidauros, in form and meaning?

---

284 These instructions could be part of a "vision", following ᾤμην (end line 17, App. 2:4).

285 This adjective (ὑγιής) also appears as a predicative adjective in Matthew's account of the sabbath healing of the man with the withered hand (Mt 12.13), describing the restoration of the man's hand to its original state: "it was restored whole, like the other" (καὶ ἀπεκατεστάθη ὑγιὴς ὡς ἡ ἄλλη). Thus the use of ὑγιής in *Matthew*, and in this inscription reflect each other, in form and meaning. For a discussion of the use of ὑγιής in the New Testament, see below, Section Two, chapter nine.

3. *Asklepios at Athens*

The god Asklepios arrived at Athens from Epidauros in the late fifth century, probably in the year 420/419 BC,[286] and took up residence on the southern slopes of the acropolis.[287] At first the asklepieion was private in nature, but about the middle of the fourth century BC it became a state cult.[288] Thus the asklepieion at Athens differed in both nature and function from the asklepieion at Epidauros, in that it was a sanctuary that catered primarily for the local population, and was administered by the people of Athens for most of its existence.[289]

There are three important sources of information for the activities of this asklepieion that survive in a quantity sufficient to show the nature of the patients who patronised this asklepieion, and the duration of its popularity. These are, firstly, the epigraphical evidence, which includes inscriptions of decrees,[290] inventories of votive offerings,[291] and the contract and specifications for the construction of a building;[292] secondly, the archaeological evidence

---

286 It is unlikely that the journey to the Peloponnese to fetch the god could have been made during the early years of the Archidamian War, and Aristophanes, in *Wasps* (122-123), makes Philokleon take his father Bdelykleon to Aegina to sleep in the temple of Asklepios there, as a last attempt to cure him of his litigious mania. This suggests that there was no Athenian asklepieion at the time the play was performed in 422 BC. Since the Telemachos Monument (*SEG* 25.226) records that Telemachos, a private citizen, founded a sanctuary of Asklepios before 419-418 BC, and conditions would have improved after the Peace of Nikias, the year 420-419 BC seems the most probable date for the founding of the sanctuary. For a thorough discussion of the recent scholarship concerning this monument, see Aleshire (1989) 7, n.3.

287 Most of the fragments of the Telemachos Monument were found in this area, which argues for Telemachos having founded the city asklepieion.

288 Aleshire (1989) 14, n.3, defines a state cult as "one where the Athenian demos and boule, either directly or through their agents, exercise some supervision over the presence and disposition of the votives dedicated in a sanctuary." For a discussion, see Aleshire (1989) 14-15.

289 The dates of the inscriptions from the asklepieion range from the end of the fifth century BC to the end of the third century AD, while a literary source (Marinos, *Vita Procli* 29) makes it obvious that the asklepieion was still active in the fifth century AD. Thus the asklepieion survived as an active sanctuary for over eight centuries.

290 For a selection of these decrees, with plates and commentary, see Hubbe (1959) 169-201, and App. 3:2.

291 See (i) Aleshire (1989) 112-369, for a reproduction of inventories, with translation and commentary; and (ii) van Straten (1981) 65-151.

292 See *IG* II^2, no. 1685 [300-299 BC].

which includes the site itself,[293] and a very interesting collection of reliefs,[294] and, thirdly, references to the asklepieion at Athens in literature.[295] All three sources of information will be drawn on in this chapter, in an effort to try to understand the role of Asklepios in a local setting. For a study of the vocabulary of healing language at Athens, healing terms which appear in the epigraphical and literary evidence relating to the asklepieion will be noted, and their use by other Athenian authors will be discussed.[296]

It is at once obvious that the asklepieion at Athens was patronised by families. Votive reliefs of family groups approaching the god abound,[297] as do inscriptions erected on behalf of children.[298] Thus this asklepieion immediately exudes a particularly local and familial quality.[299] The "family", as depicted on reliefs, generally includes both parents, several children, and a servant.[300]

---

293 See Aleshire (1989) 7-36 for a discussion of the history and topography of the site.

294 See the collection in the National Archaeological Museum, Athens, and App. 3:1. For a list of the published work concerning them, see Aleshire (1989) 6, n.1.

295 This is slight, but continuous. See, for example, Aristophanes, *Ploutos* 620-621, and Scholia in Aristophanem, *Ad Plutum* 621; Xenophon, *Memorabilia* 3.13.3; Pliny, *Natural History* 2.103(106).225; Pausanias, *Descriptio Graeciae* 1.21.4-5; Lucian, *Piscator* 42; Aelian, *De Natura Animalium* 7.13; Marinos, *Vita Procli* 29.

296 Terms that appear in the epigraphical and literary evidence concerning the asklepieion, forming the bones, as it were, of a skeleton, can thus be fleshed out by reference to their use by contemporary Athenian authors.

297 For example, the votive reliefs from the asklepieion in the National Archaeological Museum, Athens, especially 1331, 1333, 1334, 1345, 1377, 1384, 1407, 1408, and 1503 (1331 and 1334 are both good examples of Christian mutilation). See App. 3:1, **9-11**.

298 See, for example, *IG* II^2 , nos. 4403, 4412, 4429, 4474.

299 See Aleshire (1989) 52-71, for a prosographic analysis of the people connected with the asklepieion. Her study shows that there were certain Athenian families who (63) "had a tradition of participation in the cult of Asklepios".

300 See n.297 above, and especially, (i) Athens, N.M. 1408: a poignant family scene, which shows a mother, kneeling in front of Asklepios, pleading with him, a father with his hand raised in greeting, three children, and a servant with a basket of goodies (see App. 3:1, **10**); and (ii), Athens, N.M. 1384: a father giving something to a temple attendant, accompanied by his wife, three children, and a servant with a basket of goodies. This is a very realistic family scene: the older child, standing behind the mother, strains forward, watching intently, while the two younger children fidget, and chat to each other (see Plate 4; and App. 3:1, **9**).

The illnesses suffered by these people can perhaps be best illustrated by an analysis of the inventories of the dedications.[301] These show that body parts formed the largest class of dedication, and that, while all parts of the body were represented, the dedication of eyes far outnumbered other parts of the body.[302] Thus, although, as we have seen, eye problems accounted for the greatest number of patients at Epidauros, it is possible to speculate that eye problems were even more prevalent at Athens, although these problems may have been specific to the middle of the third century BC.[303] Otherwise fingers, feet, heads, abdomens, chests, breasts, and genitalia were dedicated, possibly reflecting health problems similar to those cited on the stelae at Epidauros.[304] However, some votive body parts - a bladder, back, hearts, hips, jaws, mouth and neck - are peculiar to Athens.[305] Coins,[306] typoi,[307] crowns,[308] cult equipment,[309] medical equipment[310] and jewellery[311] were also

301 For the inventories from the asklepieion, with a translation, commentary, and analysis, see Aleshire (1989) an excellent work, on which the following general comments concerning the inventories are based.

302 Rouse (1902) 212, and, more recently van Straten (1981) 149-150, have assumed that this points to the asklepieion at Athens successfully specialising in eye problems. However, Aleshire (1989) 42, has pointed out that the numbers of eyes as votive offerings are concentrated in Inventory 5, thus preventing generalisations of this nature. She offers two possible explanations: (i) that eyes being small dedications had been liquidated, and were therefore absent from the other inventories; or (ii), that "visual problems were for some reason especially prevalent in Athens ca. 250B.C." The Hippokratic treatise *Airs, Waters, Places* in Hippokrates (1972) emphasises the local (and seasonal) nature of disease in the ancient world, an argument that would support the notion that eye disease at Athens was both particular (in time) and local (in extent). But see Grmek (1989), for a fascinating study of diseases in the ancient Greek world from a medical and philological standpoint.

303 But note the case of Ambrosia from Athens, who made the pilgrimage to Epidauros, suffering from blindness in one eye. See App. 2:1, **4**.

304 It is dangerous to generalise, however, as these votives could signify disease, injury, or, in the cases of the breasts and genitalia, a desire for children.

305 See Aleshire (1989) 41, and van Straten (1981) 110-112, especially 'f', 'g-h', 'j', and 'p-q'. But van Straten notes that the hearts and bladder "are the only internal organs mentioned in the inscriptions from the Athenian Asklepieion" (111: 'p-q').

306 See Aleshire (1989) 43.

307 ibid. 43

308 ibid. 43-44

309 ibid. 44

310 ibid.

311 ibid.

dedicated, but these give no clue as to the nature of the patients' diseases. Names of dedicants, however, preserved in the inventories, do yield information concerning the gender,[312] and sometimes even the social class of the dedicant.[313] Female dedicants outnumber male, in sharp contrast to the inscriptional evidence from Epidauros,[314] but since the discrepancy between dedications on a gender basis only varies between less than two per cent to less than thirteen percent, patronage of the asklepieion reflects a healthy gender balance.[315] The greater patronage of women at Athens, compared with Epidauros, probably reflects the easier accessibility of the local asklepieion, and its familial nature.

3.1. Healing methods

Since the epigraphical evidence has not yielded anything like the detail of the accounts of temple healing at Epidauros it is to the playwright Aristophanes, and to the archaeological evidence in the form of votive reliefs that we must turn for evidence of Asklepios' healing methods at Athens. A relief from the Athenian asklepieion shows Asklepios in the act of healing, although it is not obvious what his healing action entails.[316] Another relief, from the Piraeus asklepieion, is far more explicit. It shows Asklepios touching his patient, and it is obvious from his stance and muscle tone that the touch is not a mere pat, but involves some physical effort.[317] Yet another relief shows two people lifting a patient onto a bed while Asklepios leans forward, presumably to touch the

312 ibid. 45-46

313 ibid. 52-71

314 See above, 21-39, and Apps. 2:1 and 2:2.

315 See Aleshire (1989) 45-46.

316 See Athens, N.M. 1841 (App. 3:1, **5**). This relief is dated to the end of the 5th century BC. Hippokrates (1990) 68 (Letter 15) describes how "the god stretched out his hand to me (ἔπειτα ὤρεξέ μοι τὴν χεῖρα ὁ θεός)", a gesture consistently portrayed in reliefs. See Plate 2; and App. 3:1, **5**. The orator Aelius Aristides (*Or.* 42.10 [App. 5:6. **15**]) also reports how the god stretched out his hand (ὁ θεὸς χεῖρα ὤρεξεν) to people in danger at sea.

317 See Piraeus Archaeological Museum, 405 (App. 3:1, **4**). The patient is lying on a couch, her family (two men, a woman and a child) watch while Asklepios massages (or manipulates?) her neck or shoulder. Hygieia stands behind Asklepios, watching.

patient.[318] Thus, as at Epidauros, Asklepios heals by touch in some cases.[319]

Another relief shows a woman giving a man a footbath, while Hygieia watches.[320] Bathing may have been part of his medical treatment, or part of the required ritual prior to incubation, noted in Aristophanes' *Ploutos*.[321] In *Ploutos*, Aristophanes depicts an incubation scene at an asklepieion.[322] Since the description comes out of the mouth of the slave, Carion, and his function is to provide comic relief in the play, his description must be treated with caution. Nevertheless, it must be genuine enough to be credible to his audience and is therefore useful as an early account of incubation, and the healing methods of Asklepios.[323]

Carion describes (633-747) the healing of Wealth thus: he bathed, went to the temple, made an offering on the altar of honey-cakes and bakemeats,[324] and then, with his companions, and many other sick people, lay down in the temple to sleep. The temple servant put out the lights and told the people to go to sleep. Carion, unable to sleep, saw the priest removing food from the altars;[325] he also saw Asklepios' daughters, Iaso and Panakeia, and he saw Asklepios doing his rounds,[326] accompanied by a servant who carried a stone

---

318 Unfortunately the top half of this relief is missing, so it is not certain just what is happening. See Athens, N.M. 2373 (App. 3:1, **6**).

319 The word chosen to describe Asklepios' touch is ἅπτομαι (Aristophanes, *Ploutos* 728), as at Epidauros (Apps 2:2, **31**, and 2:4; and above, 38-39).

320 See Athens, N.M. 1914 (App. 3:1, **8**).

321 See Aristophanes, *Ploutos* 656-658. Pausanias, *Descriptio Graeciae* 5.13.3 also notes that patients may not go to the temple of Asklepios before they have bathed.

322 There is some ambiguity about the identity of this asklepieion. The scholia identifies it thus: εἰς 'Ἀσκληπιοῦ· τὸν ἐν ἄστει λέγει 'Ἀσκληπιόν· δύο γάρ εἰσιν, ὁ μὲν ἐν ἄστει, ὁ δὲ ἐν Πειραιεῖ. However, see Aleshire (1989) 13, for a discussion of the problem. See also App. 3:2, 11 (ii), lines 5-6, 17.

323 *Ploutos* was produced in 388 BC.

324 For an illustration of this from the asklepieion at Athens, see the votive relief, Athens, N.M. 1335 (App. 3:1, **12**). Dated ca. 330 BC, it shows a family sacrificing to Asklepios: in the background, the goddess Hygieia, and a serpent descending a tree; on the altar, fruit and cakes.

325 See van Straten (1981) 86, for a discussion of the legal right of the priest to collect sacrificial cakes and fruit, as illustrated in the votive relief Athens, N.M. 1335 (see n.324 above, and App. 3:1, **12**), and described here by Aristophanes.

326 μετὰ ταῦτ' ἐγὼ μὲν εὐθὺς ἐνεκαλυψάμην | δείσας, ἐκεῖνος δ' ἐν κύκλῳ τὰ νοσήματα | σκοπῶν περιήει πάντα κοσμίως πάνυ. | ἔπειτα παῖς αὐτῷ λίθινον θυείδιον | παρέθηκε καὶ δοίδυκα καὶ κιβώτιον. (707-711)
The verb σκοπέω occurs in an intensified form, ἐπισκοπουμένην, in Aeschylus' *Agamemnon*, 13, as the start of a medical metaphor, which culminates in

pestle and mortar, and medicine box.[327] Carion describes how Asklepios mixed and applied medicines to the other patients in the asklepieion.[328] All these events Carion describes as reality, not vision.[329] However, his account of the healing of Wealth is reported as a vision: Wealth was healed by two serpents (summoned by Asklepios) who licked his eyes.[330]

The similarities of this account with the inscriptional evidence of temple healings at Epidauros recorded as dream visions, is striking. It is interesting too, that, except for his description of the actions of the serpents, Carion does not claim that he saw a vision, but that he saw reality.[331]

While Aristophanes' play *Ploutos* is helpful for an account of Asklepios' healing methods, and for an account of temple incubation (albeit for comic effect), he does not choose general healing terms to describe these events. Instead he prefers to play on the meanings associated with blindness and sight.[332] Apollo is both a physician and a prophet (ἰατρὸς ὢν καὶ μάντις)[333] who instructs Chremylos to follow the first man he sees, a man who happens to be blind! When Wealth is cured, his cure is described in terms of sight, not with a general healing term.[334]

---

line 17: ἐντέμνων ἄκος (incising a cure). Cf. ἐπισκοπεῖσθαι meaning to *watch over the sick bed* (Demosthenes, *Against Neaera* 56): τὰ πρόσφορα τῇ νόσῳ φέρουσαι καὶ ἐπισκοπούμεναι.

327 Hippokrates (1990) 68 (Letter 15) also describes Asklepios, serpents, and associates carrying boxes of drugs (φαρμάκων).

328 This reflects healing practices as related by the inscriptions at Epidauros. See *IG* IV^2 1, nos. 121 and 122 (Apps. 2:1 and 2:2, especially **4**, **19**, **40**).

329 Carion does not introduce his account with δοκέω, (cf. Apps 2:1 and 2:2, and for a discussion of dream "visions"see above, chapter two) and when he is questioned as to his ability to see what was going on, he claims that he watched through the holes in his cloak (713-715).

330 Here Carion does describe the serpents' actions with a disclaimer in the form of δοκέω: ὥς γ' ἐμοὶ δοκεῖ· (736).

331 See n.329, and n.330, above.

332 It is the 'blind' who really 'see' (δῆλον ὁτιὴ καὶ τυφλῷ | γνῶναι δοκεῖ τοῦθ', ὡς σφόδρ' ἐστὶ συμφέρον | τὸ μηδὲν ἀσκεῖν ὑγιὲς ἐν τῷ νῦν χρόνῳ [48-50]). This is a common motif, exemplified in the inscriptions at Epidauros (see App. 2:1, **9**), here, and in Sophocles' *Oedipus Tyrannus*. 'Blindness' and 'sight' is also a common motif in the healing stories of the New Testament.

333 *Ploutos* 11. Cf. the description of Apollo's healing power in Aeschylus' *The Eumenides* (62): ἰατρόμαντις.

334 ἐγὼ δ' ἐπήνουν τὸν θεὸν πάνυ σφόδρα, | ὅτι βλέπειν ἐποίησε τὸν Πλοῦτον ταχύ, | τὸν δὲ Νεοκλείδην μᾶλλον ἐποίησεν τυφλόν (745-747). However, the term θεράπων appears twice (at *Ploutos* 3 and 5), as Carion's description of himself as the servant of his master. Otherwise the term used

3.2. Healing language in inscriptions

Inscriptional evidence is somewhat more helpful. Healing terms which appear in Homer also appear in Athenian inscriptions, but as the personifications of Asklepios' family.[335] Other healing terms appear in the language of votive dedications and state decrees.

An inscription from the middle of the third century BC, a decree by the demos, notes that it was an ancestral custom of physicians in the service of the state to sacrifice to Asklepios and to Hygieia twice a year on behalf of themselves and of the people whom they had healed.[336] This tells us not only that there were public physicians

---

for *healer* to describe Asklepios is the epithet παιών, (see, for example, Ἀσκληπιοῦ παιῶνος, 636), an epithet we have already met (see above, chapter one). This epithet also appears in inscriptions from the Athenian asklepieion (for example, *IG* II^2, no. 4514, line 22; App. 3:3).

335 See above, 16. And see, for example, *IG* II^2, no. 4388: Ἀκεσώ Ἰασώ Πανάκεια Ἠ[πιόνη] (App. 3:2, **1**); and *IG* II^2, no. 4473. Most dedications however include Hygieia with Asklepios, and incorporate the rest of his family (and other gods) into the general phrase "and to all the other gods", as in *IG* II^2, no. 4486: Ἀσκληπιῷ καὶ Ὑγείᾳ | καὶ τοῖς ἄλλοις θεοῖς | πᾶσι καὶ πάσαις κατὰ ὄ|νειρον (see App. 3:2, **2**; and *IG* II^2, no. 976, App. 3:2, **14**).
The noun ἄκος is used frequently by Aeschylus in the *Oresteia* to mean a cure, or means of a cure, to preserve the health of a dynasty, the state, and the body or mind of an individual. The first occurrence of ἄκος in *Agamemnon* is in the medical metaphor (see n.326 above) ἐντέμνων ἄκος (17), literally "incising a cure", a "condensed expression for 'curing by means of incision'" (Denniston and Page in Aeschylus [1960] 68, *re* line 17). It usually means *cure*, as here, and in 1169, but can also mean *medicine*, as in ἄκος δὲ πᾶν μάταιον (387). Here Aeschylus' use of the word requires some comment. It occurs in a passage which discusses the role of the gods in the life of humankind (351f.). Aeschylus states that there is no means of a cure, no antidote, no remedy or medicine, which can thwart the design of Zeus, when he determines to punish wrongdoing. As in the Homeric poems, humans are utterly helpless when faced with the designs of the gods. In *The Libation Bearers*, ἄκος occurs first in a doomladen pronouncement by the Chorus, who state that there is no cure (atonement?) for one who has incurred blood-guilt by violating the marriage bond with murder (71-72). Later, it is the members of the Chorus who again use this word when they realise that a cure may be possible (472); and finally when they describe Clytaemestra's actions (539). Here (539), ἄκος is linked with hope. Finally, in *The Eumenides*, it is the Chorus which uses ἄκος in a gnomic statement about the treatment for the prevention of civil war (στάσις), their prescription being grace for grace, and love and hatred with a common will: χάρματα δ' ἀντιδιδοῖεν | κοινοφιλεῖ διανοίᾳ, | καὶ στυγεῖν μιᾷ φρενί· | πολλῶν γὰρ τόδ' ἐν βροτοῖς ἄκος (984-987).

336 *IG* II^2, no. 772 [ca. 252-251 BC] (but dated 270-269 BC by Pritchett and Meritt). See App. 3:2, **3**.

in Athens at this time, but also that their relationship with the healing god was both cordial and expected.[337] The verb chosen to describe the physical healing of the physicians' patients is ἰάομαι.[338] This verb is also the verb chosen to describe Asklepios' healing in inscriptions from the Athenian asklepieion,[339] and occurs three times in one inscription from the second century AD, illustrating both a continuity and specificity of use during the lifespan of the asklepieion.[340]

The noun ὑγιεία occurs as part of a formula in the decrees of the demos, concerning "the health and safety of the boule and the demos",[341] and "the health and safety of the boule and the demos and children and wives...".[342] Thus the concept of ὑγιεία in Athenian decrees relating to the asklepieion embraces the whole state, which includes the well-being of the organs of government,

---

337 The role of public physicians is outside the scope of this discussion, and has been competently addressed already. See Cohn-Haft (1956). Another inscription, the dedicatory relief *IG* II^2, no. 4359 (Athens, N.M. 1332; App. 3:1, **2**), has also been associated with public physicians. For a discussion, and the conclusion that this is an erroneous assumption, see Aleshire (1989) 94-95.

338 "... ὑπέρ τε αὐτῶν καὶ τῶν σωμάτων ὧν ἕ|καστοι ἰάσαντο ..." See App. 3:2, **3**.

339 See, for example, *IG* II^2, no. 4475a (ἰαθέντα), (App. 3:2, **5**).

340 *IG* II^2, no. 4514 (see App. 3:3). This is a most interesting inscription for its use of ἰάομαι in different forms. The verb appears twice in the aorist middle participial form ἰασάμενος (and once in this form coupled with the imperative σῶσόν), and once in the aorist passive participial form [ἰα]θεὶς. It also appears in adjectival form with an alpha privative - ἀνίατον - qualifying ἕλκος, meaning "incurable". The dedicant had suffered from painful gout (ποδάγραν κακήν). This inscription does not end with the final formula so common to the inscriptions from Epidauros, but is far more specific. The dedicant has become ἀρτίπος - "sound of foot", rather than ὑγιής.

341 *IG* II^2, no. 354 [328-327 BC] (see App. 3:2, **8**). According to the restoration of Hubbe (1959) 172, lines 43-44: [ὁ ἱερεὺς γεγονέναι ἐν τοῖς] ἱεροῖς ἐ[φ' ὑγιεί][αι καὶ σωτηρίαι τῆς βουλῆς κ]αὶ τοῦ [δήμου.] Hubbe's commentary (174) on these lines: "The restoration is complicated by a final letter in line 43 not recorded in the Editio Minor. It is most naturally read as *tau*, with its vertical stroke somewhat left of center and its horizontal stroke tipped slightly upward. Since no satisfactory restoration with *tau* has been found, however, it seems best to read the letter as *epsilon*; what appeared to be the top bar of *tau* must then be a scratch. We can now retain the restoration in the Editio Minor, but must again place *iota* as an extra letter at the end of line 43."

342 *IG* II^2, no. 775 [244-243 BC] (see App. 3:2, **9**). Again according to Hubbe's restoration, (1959) 175, lines 14-15 read: "τοῖς ἱεροῖς ἐφ' ὑγιείαι κα[ὶ σωτηρίαι τῆς βουλῆς καὶ] | τοῦ δήμου καὶ παίδων καὶ γ[υναικῶν ⟦καὶ τοῦ βασιλέως⟧". See also *IG* II^2, no. 950, line 8 (App. 3:2, **11**); and *IG* II^2, no. 975 + 1061, lines 8-10, (App. 3:2, **13**).

the boule and the demos, (Athenian males), and their wives and children. It is a universal, rather than a particular term, and certainly illustrates the fact that the function of the asklepieion at Athens was to focus on the health of the Athenian state,[343] the family, and the individual, in that order.[344]

In contrast, the verb θεραπεύω is notable for its absence in a healing context, although the noun θεραπεία does appear twice in *IG* II^2, no. 1019,[345] referring to the care of sacred property. This noun is also restored in *IG* II^2, no. 974,[346] but the meaning is slightly dif-

343 Healing language in Athenian literature also encompasses the well-being of family and state, as well as individual human health. For example, the opposite of *health* (ὑγιεία) is *disease* (νόσος), and these terms can refer to human health in a physical, emotional or mental sense, or to the health (or disease) of the state. Aeschylus is fond of using medical metaphors when prescribing treatment for the well-being of the state (see above, n.335). For example (*Agamemnon* 844-850): λέγω. τὰ δ' ἄλλα πρὸς πόλιν τε καὶ θεούς | κοινοὺς ἀγῶνας θέντες ἐν πανηγύρει | βουλευσόμεσθα· καὶ τὸ μὲν καλῶς ἔχον | ὅπως χρονίζον εὖ μενεῖ βουλευτέον· | ὅτῳ δὲ καὶ δεῖ φαρμάκων παιωνίων, | ἤτοι κέαντες ἢ τεμόντες εὐφρόνως | πειρασόμεσθα πῆμ' ἀποστρέψαι νόσου. ("Now in the business of the city and the gods | we must ordain full conclave of all the citizens | and take our counsel. We shall see what element | is strong, and plan that it shall keep its virtue still. | But that which must be healed - we must use medicine, | or burn, or amputate, with kind intention, take | all means at hand that might beat down corruption's pain." Translation by Richmond Lattimore, in Aeschylus [1964]).

344 Unless the safety of the state was assured families and individuals could not prosper. One wonders to what extent the 'Athenian' character of the asklepieion was a product of the outcome of the Peloponnesian War, and the decline in Athenian influence and prosperity in the following centuries.

345 Dated 138-137 BC. The term appears twice: at lines 14 and 18, and refers to the care of sacred property. (For a commentary, and a restoration of lines 13-14, based on lines 25-26 of *IG* II^2, no. 974 [137-136 BC] see Hubbe (1959) 188: "[ὁ ἱερεὺ]ς τοῦ 'Ασκληπιοῦ Λεωνίδη[ς Νικοκράτου | Φλυεὺς ἐμφανίζει τό τε τέμενος καὶ τὸν ναὸν καὶ πάντα τὰ ἐ]ν αὐτῷι θεραπείας καὶ ἐπι[σκευῆς δεό|μενα]. The Editio Minor shows [ἐ]ν αὐτεῖ. The letter read as *epsilon* has a central horizontal bar; but in place of the lower bar one sees only two dots, such as might be expected at the feet of *omega*, while there is also a fine line that might be the right vertical stroke of the rectangular *omega* common on this stone. A reading of *eta* is not excluded." For a discussion of the decree, see 187-188.) See App. 3:2, **4**.

346 Dated 137-136 BC. For a commentary, and a discussion of this decree, see Hubbe (1959) 188-194. Lines 22-26 are restored thus: " . . . καταστήσας] | δὲ καὶ τὸν ὑὸν Δῖον κλειδοῦχον κα[ὶ πυρφόρον ἐπὶ ἁπάσας τὰς] | [κ]αθ' ἑκάστην ἡμέραν γινομένας θε[ραπείας ἐν αἷς τοῖς θύουσιν] | [τ]ῶι θεῶι κεχορήγηκεν ἐκτενῶς, τοῦ τ[ε τεμένους τοῦ 'Ασκληπιοῦ] | [καὶ] τῆς 'Υγιείας καὶ τοῦ ναοῦ καὶ τῶν ἐν [αὐτοῖς . . . ". Of θε[ραπείας] Hubbe says (193-194): "In line 24, θε[ραπείας] was restored already by Koehler in the older Corpus. The word could refer to divine cures, but since this is not

ferent. It is most unlikely that it refers to cures in this context, given the rarity of θεραπεύω and its related word group in the healing language of inscriptions from this asklepieion, so Hubbe[347] is probably correct when he takes the word to mean *worship*. However, the noun θεραπεία does occur in an inscription where its probable meaning is *treatment*.[348] Unfortunately the inscription is fragmentary, but it seems to be have been dedicated to Asklepios by a person who, through the treatment of a disease revealed in a vision, was delivered from a severe illness. The operative verb is σῴζω, a word that often occurs in healing inscriptions to describe deliverance from suffering (and possible death).[349] The adjectival form of σῴζω is also chosen to describe the welfare of the state in decrees.[350]

---

specifically stated, we are probably meant to understand it in the more general sense of *worship*. The worship took place daily, according to the text, apparently being that of visitors who came to the sanctuary each day, whether to pray for health in general, or to be cured, or to ask for the cure of others, or to offer sacrifices of thanksgiving."

347 See above, n.346.

348 θεραπίᾳ: see *IG* II[2], no. 4538 (App 3:2, **12**). This is an interesting inscription, both in content and language. The dedicant (the aorist passive participle of σῴζω is feminine [σωθεῖσα]), erected it along with physicians (μετὰ τῶν ἰα[τρῶν]), and it mentions a vision (ὄναρ), and a severe illness (μεγάλη(ς) νόσο(υ)).

349 See *IG* II[2], no. 4514 (App. 3:3), line 13.

350 See, for example, *IG* II[2], no. 950, line 9 (App. 3:2, **11**); *IG* II[2], no. 354 (App. 3:2, 8); and *IG* II[2], no. 775 (App. 3:2, **9**).
The verb σῴζω and its related forms is also prominent in Athenian literature. As we have already seen the Homeric use of the word means *rescue and preserve* (see above, chapter one). This concept of σῴζω continues. Aeschylus uses it to mean *safety from death*. The cognate form σωτήρ, prominent in later inscriptions (see, for example, *IG* IV[2] 1, no. 127 [224AD], line 5: Σωτῆρι 'Ασκληπιῷ, App. 2:6) and literature as an epithet of Asklepios, is linked in the *Agamemnon* with παίων, when the herald greets his homeland and his gods. The herald addresses Apollo, and begs him to be again the Achaeans' saviour and healer (νῦν δ' αὖτε σωτὴρ ἴσθι καὶ παιώνιος, | ἄναξ Ἄπολλον· [512–513]). He uses the term σωτήρ again when describing the return of the Achaeans from Ilium (646), with their message of "glad tidings of deliverance" (σωτηρίων δὲ πραγμάτων εὐάγγελον), only to be confronted by a storm at sea. They were saved by "life-giving fortune" (τύχη δὲ σωτὴρ ναῦν θέλουσ' ἐφέζετο [664]). The word is used again in a nautical metaphor, when Clytaemestra describes Agamemnon as "the stay that keeps the ship alive" (σωτῆρα ναὸς πρότονον [897]). (Cf. *New Docs* 4 [1987] 113, #26 [b], for the use of σῴζω by a Jew in a nautical context: Θεοῦ εὐλογία· | Θευόδοτος Δωρίωνος | 'Ιουδαῖος σωθεὶς ἐκ πε-|λ<άγ>ους. See also *New Docs* 3 [1983] 58-59 for examples of σωθεὶς ἐγ μεγάλου κινδύνου in a similar

Thus the epigraphical evidence for general healing terms at Athens, although not evident in great quantity, does provide a skeletal framework, and the meaning of these terms can be fleshed out from an analysis of the use of these terms by Athenian authors.[351]

3.3. Literary evidence

3.3.1. Thucydides (Xenophon)

It is helpful here to turn to the historian Thucydides, and to his account of the plague that devastated Athens in the early years of the Peloponnesian War.[352] Thucydides' account is most useful for a study of the language of healing, and the study of the effect on human nature of the indiscriminate appearance of disease. It is probably no accident that the asklepieion at Athens was established within ten years of this disaster.[353]

---

context; and *New Docs* 6 [1992] 82-86 for evidence that storms at sea were viewed as acts of god [τι βίαιον ἐκ θεοῦ or θεοῦ βία] for insurance purposes. Cf. also the significance of this for the New Testament story of the stilling of the storm [Mt 8.27; Mk 4.41; Lk 8.25]).

In *The Libation Bearers* Orestes begs Hermes to be his saviour and ally, that is, to keep him safe (σωτὴρ γενοῦ μοι ξύμμαχός τ' αἰτουμένῳ· [2]), when he embarks on the dangerous task of avenging his father's brutal murder. Later, Elektra refers to Orestes as the darling of their father's house, its hope of saving seed (ἐλπὶς σπέρματος σωτηρίου [236]), expressing the hope that Orestes will finally put the curse to rest, and Agamemnon's family be saved from extinction.

Euripides also uses the verb σῴζω to mean *safety from death*. In *Hippolytos*, for example, the verb σῴζω appears four times in the sense of saving life. It is used three times by the nurse (497, 501, 705), and each time she is conniving to save Phaedra's life, a life she refers to as a great prize (νῦν δ' ἀγὼν μέγας | σῶσαι βίον σόν [496–497]). Hippolytos also uses the term, when he tells Phaedra that it is his piety that continues to preserve her way of life (εὖ δ' ἴσθι, τοὐμόν σ' εὐσεβὲς σῴζει, γύναι [656]).

351 An analysis of the use of these terms has been restricted to their occurrence in a medical, a philosophical, or a theological context.

352 2.47-55

353 The citizens of Athens had desperate need of the healing god during these early years of the war, but it was not until after the Peace of Nikias that the journey to the Peloponnese could have been made in safety. See above, n.286. The asklepieion at Rome was established in 292 BC in response to a plague (See above, chapter two, n.84).

One expression that occurred frequently in the Epidaurian inscriptions is also present in Thucydides' account of the plague. The adjective ὑγιής is used by Thucydides to describe people who were in good health before being struck down by disease (ὑγιεῖς ὄντας 2.49.2). In this way his use of ὑγιής echoes the language of the Epidaurian inscriptions, in that ὑγιής describes the original (good) health of an individual.

Thucydides' language is precise: he does not use a general term like ἰάομαι to describe those who recover from the plague. Instead the verbs ἀνίστημι (2.49.8) and διαφεύγω (2.49.8; 2.51.6) are chosen. In fact the verb ἰάομαι does not occur, and only its related forms ἰατρός (2.47.4; 2.49.3), meaning *physician*, and ἴαμα (2.51.2), meaning a *remedy* appear. This is not surprising, as physicians were ineffective (2.47.4), and no one remedy could be found (2.51.2). Even the fortunate few who recovered bore permanent reminders of their suffering (2.49.7-8).

However, the verb θεραπεύω does appear, and in a quite precise sense. It includes the Homeric sense of *caring for*, and the Epidaurian sense of *treatment*, but these occurrences focus quite precisely on *the nursing of those who are sick*. It applies equally to physicians and ordinary citizens, any who fulfil the role of caring for the sick. Nowhere is it used by Thucydides to describe healing, in the sense of curing, but rather to describe nursing treatment which may, or may not, be successful.

At first physicians (ἰατροί) were treating the disease in ignorance (θεραπεύοντες ἀγνοίᾳ) (2.47.4). People died, despite careful nursing (πάνυ θεραπευόμενοι) (2.51.2), and despite being nursed with all medical care (τὰ πάσῃ διαίτῃ θεραπευόμενα) (2.51.3). They became infected by nursing one another, and died like sheep (καὶ ὅτι ἕτερος ἀφ' ἑτέρου θεραπείας ἀναπιμπλάμενοι ὥσπερ τὰ πρόβατα ἔθνῃσκον) (2.51.4), so that there was a shortage of those to do the nursing (τοῦ θεραπεύσοντος) (2.51.5).

In every case of the use of this verb, continuity of action is stressed. Either the present participle is used (2.47.4; 2.51.2; 2.51.3), or the cognate form (2.51.4), or the future participle (2.51.5). Thus the Thucydidean use of θεραπεύω, in relation to illness and suffering, is quite precise, meaning medical treatment in the form of continuous nursing; treatment that may, or may not, be successful in its outcome.

Like Thucydides, the historian Xenophon uses this verb in a medical context to mean nursing, in the sense of providing medical treatment. In his description of Cyrus' freeing of prisoners, Xenophon recounts how Cyrus "sent for physicians and ordered

them to give medical treatment to the wounded men (τοὺς δὲ τετρωμένους ἰατροὺς καλέσας θεραπεύειν ἐκέλευσεν)."[354] Xenophon extends this sense of θεραπεύω when he uses the verb to describe the actions of the gods, rather than humans. In *Memorabilia* (4.3) Socrates, in trying to teach Euthydemus the value of prudence, tries first to encourage him to be of sound mind (σώφρων) concerning the gods. In so doing Socrates lists all the gifts that exemplify the care of the gods: light, darkness, food, water, fire, the seasons, and so on, to which Euthydemus replies (4.3.9) that he doubts whether the gods are occupied in any other work than the nurture of mankind (ἐγὼ μέν, ἔφη ὁ Εὐθύδημος, ἤδη τοῦτο σκοπῶ, εἰ ἄρα τί ἐστι τοῖς θεοῖς ἔργον ἢ ἀνθρώπους θεραπεύειν·). Thus the sense of continuous, nurturing, and selfless action in θεραπεύω, implied by Thucydides' use of the word, is emphasised.

3.3.2. Isocrates (Aeschylus, Sophocles, Euripides)

However, it is in the work of the Athenian orator Isocrates that we get a detailed exposition of the verb θεραπεύω. In *Aegineticus*, a speech written in the first decade of the fourth century BC,[355] Isocrates presents the case for a claim to an inheritance. One of his arguments rests on the fact that his client (the defendant) was the only person to nurse the testator through the long and difficult illness which resulted in his death.[356] Thus we see θεραπεύω used in a medical context akin to the Thucydidean use of the term in his description of the plague. In both cases, death was the result. Isocrates' use of the term is instructive, for he also uses the terms νοσηλεύω, and ἐπιμέλεια in his account, so that it becomes possible to detect the subtle differences in meaning between words of a similar sense content. The verb ἰάομαι does not occur. As in the Thucydidean account of the plague, this is not surprising, since the testator's disease was considered to be terminal.

It becomes immediately obvious that the verb θεραπεύω is used to describe the selfless comforting care of the physical (however disgusting the symptoms), and emotional (however irascible and difficult) welfare of the patient. In the beginning, the defendant says that he nursed his friend with unremitting care and devotion because he was so completely destitute of companionship (μετὰ

---

354 *Cyropaedia* 3.2.12 (my translation).

355 The exact date of the speech is uncertain, but ##18-20 show that it must not be long after 394 BC. See van Hook in Isocrates (1968) 299.

356 See Isocrates (1968) *Aegineticus* 11, and 20-33, but especially 20-29.

τοσαύτης ἐρημίας γενόμενον οὕτως ἐπιπόνως καὶ καλῶς αὐτὸν ἐθεράπευσα).[357] Thus the concept of emotional support is immediately implicit in θεραπεύω. The defendant claims that he nursed him with a care such as no one else he knew had ever bestowed on another (οὕτως αὐτὸν ἐθεράπευσα ὡς οὐκ οἶδ' ὅστις πώποθ' ἕτερος ἕτερον).[358] This involved him in drudgery (τῶν ταλαιπωριῶν),[359] hardship (τοὺς πόνους), exile (τὴν φυγὴν) and isolation (τὴν ἐρημίαν).[360] His duties in nursing (ἐν τῇ θεραπείᾳ) his friend were not easy to describe (οὐκ εὐδιήγητ'), but required the utmost diligence (πλείστης ἐπιμελείας) over a long period of time (τοσοῦτον χρόνον) and involved the most severe (τὰ χαλεπώτατα), most offensive (δυσχερέστατα), and most disgusting labours (πόνους ἀηδεστάτους).[361]

In every instance this practical devotion is described by θεραπεύω. The only occasion another verb is used is when the defendant states that no one shared the nursing with him, except a slave boy (ἐνοσήλευον).[362] Since such a distinction is made it is obvious that the slave boy only provided menial nursing support (under duress?) for none of the domestics could stand it (οὐδὲ γὰρ τῶν οἰκετῶν οὐδεὶς ὑπέμεινεν).[363] Some of these difficulties are explained: although able to get about the patient was ill for a long time, until, filled with pus,[364] he became bedridden for six months before he died.[365] As well, as his physical health declined his naturally irascible temperament became even more difficult.[366] Nobody visited, except his mother and sister, who made the defendant's task even more difficult as they were sick themselves, and in need of care (θεραπείας).[367] It is a sorry picture, and quite obvious that θεραπεύω does indeed involve "vexation for the mind and hard work for the hands" as the Athenian playwright Euripides points out in *Hippolytos* :

---

357 ibid. 11
358 ibid. 24
359 ibid. 25
360 ibid. 27
361 ibid. 28
362 ibid. 25
363 ibid. 26
364 ibid. 26-27: ὃς ἔμπυος μὲν ἦν πολὺν χρόνον, ἐκ δὲ τῆς κλίνης οὐκ ἠδύνατο κινεῖσθαι.
365 ibid. 24
366 ibid. 26: καὶ γὰρ φύσει χαλεπὸς ὢν ἔτι δυσκολώτερον διὰ τὴν νόσον διέκειτο.
367 ibid. 25

κρεῖσσον δὲ νοσεῖν ἢ θεραπεύειν·
τὸ μέν ἐστιν ἁπλοῦν, τῷ δὲ συνάπτει
λύπη τε φρενῶν χερσίν τε πόνος.
πᾶς δ' ὀδυνηρὸς βίος ἀνθρώπων,
κοὐκ ἔστι πόνων ἀνάπαυσις. (186-191)[368]

There is no doubt that θεραπεύειν in this context means continuous mental and physical toil, (note the present infinitive), and certainly denotes *caring for* rather than *curing*, echoing both Thucydides' and Isocrates' use of the verb θεραπεύω.

However, Isocrates, as well as emphasising the physical drudgery implicit in the meaning of θεραπεύω, also emphasises the selfless and nurturing nature of that care, so that it seems that while anybody can nurse a patient in the sense of νοσηλεύω, only those who have the physical, emotional, and spiritual welfare of their patient at heart are capable of giving the care implied by θεραπεύω. Thus θεραπεύω does not involve a quick-fix, but long-term devoted care, which incorporates the physical care implied in νοσηλεύω, and the painstaking attention implied in ἐπιμέλεια,[369] as well as requiring the love of selfless service. It thus describes the holistic care given to meet the needs of those who are suffering.

The problem of suffering is inexorably present in any study of health and healing. It exists as the dark side of human experience, a dark side that humans have ever sought to understand and to explain. The Greek word chosen to signify that suffering is πάσχω. It is used to describe physical, emotional and mental suffering in inscriptions and literature, suffering that has either been intense, or has occurred continuously over a period of time.

---

368 "It's better to be sick than nurse the sick. | Sickness is single trouble for the sufferer: | but nursing means vexation of the mind, | and hard work for the hands besides. | The life of man entire is misery: | he finds no resting place, no haven from calamity." (186-191) Translation by David Grene, in Euripides (1955) 171.

369 The verb ἐπιμελέομαι is the verb used to describe the actions of the Samaritan in Jesus' parable of the good Samaritan (Lk 10.34,35). In this New Testament story the verb ἐπιμελέομαι describes the painstaking attention that the noun ἐπιμέλεια describes in Isocrates' 4th century BC account. However, as in Isocrates' account, the nature of the care described by ἐπιμελέομαι in the New Testament story should be distinguished from the nature of the care described by θεραπεύω elsewhere in the New Testament. For a discussion, see below, chapter seven. Note also that ἐπιμελέομαι and its related forms in Athenian inscriptions from the asklepieion refers to the order and maintenance of the sanctuary, its belongings, and the surrounding area. See *IG* II^2, no. 354 (App. 3:2, **8**); *IG* II^2, no. 950 (App. 3:2, **11**); and *IG* II^2, no. 976 (App. 3:2, **14**).

Thus Isocrates uses the verb πάσχω in the imperfect continuous tense when he describes the suffering endured by the testator.[370] Thucydides twice chooses the same verb to describe the sufferings of those who were ill with the plague:[371] firstly, where he tells us that he had the disease himself and saw others suffering from it (αὐτος τε νοσήσας καὶ αὐτὸς ἰδὼν ἄλλους πάσχοντας 2.48.3); and secondly, where he comments that men's recollections conform to their sufferings (οἱ γὰρ ἄνθρωποι πρὸς ἃ ἔπασχον τὴν μνήμην ἐποιοῦντο 2.54.3). It is a strong verb, and intended to describe intense and continuous suffering, so Thucydides uses the present participle, and the imperfect tense. He does not use it of himself, and elsewhere he uses the more clinical verb ἀναπίμπλημι (2.51.4) to describe those infected, and πονέομαι (2.51.6) to describe those who are sick. It is significant that he also uses an intensified form of this verb (κακοπαθέω) on two occasions to sum up the sufferings endured by the Athenian prisoners in the stone quarries at Syracuse (7.87.2, 6), using the aorist tense in both places.[372] The cognate form of πάσχω appears only once, at 2.54.1, where Thucydides sums up the history of the plague. Here τό πάθος is synonymous with ἡ νόσος.

In early Athenian tragedy the concept of the efficacy of suffering is central to Greek ideas on human happiness. It figures in Aeschylus' solution to the problem of suffering: that Zeus ordained that through suffering would come human wisdom. This idea is first presented in the *Agamemnon*,[373] and is reinforced at regular intervals throughout the play. It is bound up with Aeschylus' idea of justice,[374] and the further idea that the sins of the father will be

---

370 ibid. 27: τοιαῦτα δ' ἔπασχεν ὥσθ' ἡμᾶς μηδεμίαν ἡμέραν ἀδακρύτους διάγειν.

371 It is a strong verb, intended to convey intense suffering, so it is rarely used, and only in conjunction with a detailed exposition of those sufferings (as in the case of Isocrates' *Aegineticus*, and here). Its use is also rare in the New Testament, see below, chapter seven.

372 As usual, Thucydides is precise (cf. 1.1.1) in his use of tense. In this case the sufferings of the prisoners had ended with their death, after one intense period of sustained suffering.

373 176-178: "Zeus, who guided men to think, who has laid it down that wisdom comes alone through suffering (τὸν φρονεῖν βροτοὺς ὁδώ|σαντα, τὸν πάθει μάθος | θέντα κυρίως ἔχειν)."

374 249-251: "Justice so moves that those only learn who suffer; and the future you shall know when it has come; before then, forget it (Δίκα δὲ τοῖς μὲν παθοῦ|σιν μαθεῖν ἐπιρρέπει· τὸ μέλλον [δ'] | ἐπεὶ γένοιτ' ἂν κλύοις· πρὸ χαιρέτω)."

visited on his children.[375] Suffering does not necessarily denote physical disease, but a relentless and continuous deprivation of human happiness.[376] Cities too can suffer in the same way as individuals,[377] and this suffering, in Aeschylus' view, is ordained by the gods. It is in *The Libation Bearers* that the image of πάθος as continuous and burgeoning misery is most powerfully drawn:

μίμνοντι δὲ καὶ πάθος ἀνθεῖ. (1009)[378]

Sophocles also uses τό πάθος to mean *suffering*, incorporating physical, mental, emotional, and spiritual anguish, and including a sense of loss. In Sophocles' *Oedipus Tyrannus* Oedipus sums up his sufferings with the word παθέα,[379] and Sophocles concludes the play with the word παθών.[380]

---

375 1560-1566: "Here is anger for anger. Between them who shall judge lightly? The spoiler is robbed; he killed, he has paid. The truth stands ever beside God's throne eternal: he who has wrought shall pay; that is the law. Then who shall tear the curse from their blood? (ὄνειδος ἥκει τόδ' ἀντ' ὀνείδους, | δύσμαχα δ' ἐστὶ κρῖναι· | φέρει φέροντ' , ἐκτίνει δ' ὁ καίνων· | μίμνει δὲ μίμνοντος ἐν θρόνῳ Διὸς | παθεῖν τὸν ἔρξαντα· θέσμιον γάρ. | τίς ἂν γονὰν ἀραῖον ἐκβάλοι δόμων; | κεκόλληται γένος πρὸς ἄτᾳ.)." This idea of inherited guilt/punishment is echoed in Old Testament thought (see Deuteronomy 28.58-61).

376 See *The Libation Bearers* 313: δράσαντι παθεῖν. See also a fragment attributed to Aeschylus - δράσαντι γάρ τοι καὶ παθεῖν ὀφείλεται - in Aeschylus (1971) 506, Fragment 236 (456). The editor notes that this fragment is "probably from Sophocles (Fragment 229 Jebb-Pearson)", but has been ascribed to Aeschylus because of *The Libation Bearers* 313.

377 See *Agamemnon* 1169-1171: " ἄκος δ' | οὐδὲν ἐπήρκεσαν | τὸ μὴ πόλιν μὲν ὥσπερ οὖν ἐχρῆν παθεῖν·." The aorist infinitive also occurs at 1658, after a corrupt text (see Aeschylus [1960] 222, commentary to lines 1657-1658).

378 *The Libation Bearers* 1009. For Orestes, the one surviving, suffering blossoms. It is a powerful image. And Orestes' reaction is grief; grief for the deed (the murder of his father: πάθη [1070]), grief for the suffering, and grief for the whole race. Thus the reality of suffering is inexorably present in the process of living.
The noun πάθος also denotes the suffering of the fleet on its journey home from Ilium (*Agamemnon* 669); and Cassandra's suffering and imminent death (*Agamemnon* 1137); while the plural πάθη denotes Agamemnon's imagined wounds (*Agamemnon* 893).

379 'Απόλλων τάδ' ἦν, 'Απόλλων, φίλοι, | ὁ κακὰ κακὰ τελῶν ἐμὰ τάδ' ἐμὰ παθέα (1329–1330); "It was Apollo, friends, Apollo who brought my evil evils, my sufferings to completion" (my translation).

380 In the famous maxim: ὥστε θνητὸν ὄντ' ἐκείνην τὴν τελευταίαν ἰδεῖν | ἡμέραν ἐπισκοποῦντα μηδέν' ὀλβίζειν, πρὶν ἂν | τέρμα τοῦ βίου περάσῃ μηδὲν ἀλγεινὸν παθών (1528-1530); "Look upon that last day always. Count

Euripides also uses πάσχω in various forms to denote mental suffering, suffering which usually includes a sense of loss.[381]

3.3.3. Epicurus

All these terms - θεραπεύω, ὑγιαίνω, πάθος, ἰατρικὴ - occur in the writings of the Athenian philosopher Epicurus.[382] This is helpful, for Diogenes Laertius says of Epicurus that his style was lucid, and that the terms he used for things were 'ordinary' terms.[383] Therefore Epicurus' use of healing language should reflect contemporary usage.[384]

---

no mortal happy till he has passed the final limit of his life secure from pain." (Translation by David Grene in Sophocles [1954].)

381 The nurse asks Phaedra "τί πάσχεις..." (*Hippolytos* 340) when trying to ascertain the source of her anguish; the members of the chorus cry of πάθεα with a sense of impending doom and loss, when they overhear Phaedra's 'confession' (*Hippolytos* 363). The nurse speaks of πέπονθας when trying to whitewash Phaedra's 'trouble', and diminish its importance (*Hippolytos* 438). However, it is in Phaedra's use of πάσχω in various forms; as παθημάτων, (*Hippolytos* 570) πημάτων, (*Hippolytos* 600) and πάθος, (*Hippolytos* 677, echoing her cry of despair at 570) that the quality of loss implicit in this word group becomes most obvious. Phaedra has lost her self respect. She can no longer function in her female world of husband and children. The only solution is to take her own life: death is her only cure (*Hippolytos* 600. This is the only occurrence of ἄκος in the play, and means *cure* in the sense of *relief from suffering*). This sense of loss in πάσχω is echoed by Theseus' "ἔπαθον" (*Hippolytos* 817) when he learns of Phaedra's death and his loss of his wife, and by Hippolytus, when he cries "οἷα πάσχομεν κακά" (*Hippolytos* 1079), when he realises that he has unjustly lost his father's love and respect.

382 The son of Neocles and Chaerestrate, of the deme Gargettus, and the family Philaidae, Epicurus (341-271 BC) was brought up at Samos after the Athenians sent settlers there, and came to Athens at the age of eighteen. When Alexander of Macedon died and settlers were expelled from Samos by Perdiccas, Epicurus left Athens for Colophon, but returned to Athens in 307-306 BC, and later established a philosophical school. See Diogenes Laertius (1970) 10.

383 (1970) 10.13: κέχρηται δὲ λέξει κυρίᾳ κατὰ τῶν πραγμάτων.

384 For a collection, see App. 3:5. The text for Epicurus is based on Epicurus (1973). References in App. 3:5, and in the notes, are numbered by numeral, and then as in the edition cited, together with the page number of that edition, and the source.

Epicurus uses the verb θεραπεύω to mean *heal*,[385] *give service/pay homage*,[386] and *find comfort*.[387] Thus his use includes the range of meaning already noticed in the use of θεραπεύω. He uses the noun θεραπεία to mean *care*,[388] in a similar sense to the care implied in the stewardship of property in inscriptions from the asklepieion.[389] Where Epicurus uses the verb θεραπεύω to mean *heal*, the healing agent is the teaching (λόγος) of the philosopher.[390] It is by this λόγος that the anguish of humankind is healed (πάθος ἀνθρώπου θεραπεύεται), and this λόγος that banishes the anguish of the soul (τὸ τῆς ψυχῆς ἐκβάλλει πάθος).[391] This use makes explicit the psychological dimension of the healing implicit in θεραπεύω, a psychological dimension manifest in the behaviour of Patroklos,[392] in the behaviour of Isocrates' defendant,[393] and in the account of the healing of Marcus Julius Apellas at Epidauros.[394]

Thus Epicurus uses the verb θεραπεύω to describe the healing action of teaching, teaching that banishes psychological suffering,[395] and the noun πάθος to name this emotional anguish. He also uses the verb πάσχω to denote the suffering brought about by error.[396] However, Epicurus not only uses πάθος to denote mental and emotional anguish, he also uses the noun πάθος to refer to physical suffering, the τῶν τοῦ σωματίου παθῶν, that he endured when he was ill.[397]

---

385 App. 3:5, **1**: **[247]** (570, #64) Porphyrius (Pötscher) *ad Marcellam* 31 34 10

386 App. 3:5, **2**: **[1] 121** b (29) *Vita Epicuri cum testamento*

387 App. 3:5, **4**: **[6] 55** (151) *Gnomologium Vaticanum*

388 App. 3:5, **3**: **[54]** (428) *Epistularum fragmenta* Plutarch *ad. Coloten* 1117d-e

389 *IG* II^2, no. 1019 [138-137 BC], App. 3:2, **10**

390 App. 3:5, **1**: **[247]** (570, #64) Porphyrius (Pötscher) *ad Marcellam* 31 34 10

391 Cf. the New Testament exorcism stories, and particularly Matthew's description of Jesus' behaviour (καὶ ἐξέβαλεν τὰ πνεύματα λόγῳ, καὶ πάντας τοὺς κακῶς ἔχοντας ἐθεράπευσεν· [Mt 8.16]). For a discussion of the use of ἐκβάλλω in exorcism stories in the New Testament, see below, Section Two, chapter nine, n.643.

392 Patroklos stayed with Eurypylos as long as he could, offering comfort, and talking with him (*Iliad* 15.390-404). See above, chapter one.

393 Isocrates (1968) *Aegineticus* 11, 20-33; and see above, 52-55.

394 *IG* IV^2 1, no. 126 [ca. 160 AD], App. 2:5; and see above, 38-39.

395 It should be noted that this teaching requires a positive response on the part of the student, in that the λόγος must produce a discernible effect: freedom from pain and fear, which is the final end of the blessed life (τοῦτο τοῦ μακαρίως ζῆν ἐστι τέλος [App. 3:5, **15**: **[4] 128** (111) *Epistula ad Menoeceum* 128]).

396 App. 3:5, **11**: **[6] 63** (153) *Gnomologium Vaticanum*

397 App. 3:5, **9**: **[259]** (672) Marcus Aurelius 9.41

Epicurus uses other healing terms to describe the curative effectiveness of the pursuit of philosophy as a way of life. In his letter to Menoeceus, Epicurus states that the study of philosophy is necessary for the well-being (τὸ ὑγιαῖνον) of the soul.[398] In personal letters he stresses his own and his friends' "health" (ὑγιαίνοντες . . . ὑγ[ι]αίνοντας),[399] and expresses the wish that the recipient also be in good health (ὑγιαίνεις).[400] According to Diogenes Laertius (10.14) these greetings in personal letters referred to his friends' way of living as well as their physical health. Indeed physical health is inextricably linked with the health of the soul in Epicurus' thought, in that pain is a distraction, an evil which ruins the soul and makes it weak,[401] whereas pleasure (freedom from pain and fear)[402] saves the soul.[403] Thus Epicurus advocates the choosing of virtues on account of pleasure, not for their own sake, but as medicine for the sake of health.[404] And to be truly healthy, without pain or fear, is the ultimate aim of his philosophy.

It is significant, although it comes as no surprise, that ἰάομαι does not feature in Epicurus' healing language, for the pursuit of the philosophical life is a process, a way of life, requiring an active and continuous response in the student. Thus the λόγος of the philosopher heals (θεραπεύει), it is a treatment that requires the ignition of a continuing spark of recognition in the student to be effective, and this recognition-process continues throughout life. In this way the philosopher's λόγος produces a new way of living among those who heed his teaching, a way of life that banishes the πάθος of mankind. Thus the continuous notions of work, comfort, care and service are combined in the verb θεραπεύω.

3.3.4. Marinos, Suidas

It is appropriate that this discussion of healing language conclude with two of the last literary witnesses to the contemporary efficacy and popularity of Asklepios at Athens. In both the majority

398 App. 3:5, **6**: **[4] 122** (107) *Epistula ad Menoeceum*
399 App. 3:5, **8**: **[261]** (679) *Pap. Herc.* 176 5 XXIII Vo.
400 ibid.
401 App. 3:5, **10**: **[6] 37** (147) *Gnomologium Vaticanum*
402 App. 3:5, **15**: **[4] 128** (111) *Epistula ad Menoeceum*
403 App. 3:5, **10**: **[6] 37** (147) *Gnomologium Vaticanum*
404 App. 3:5, **14**: **[1] 138** (31) Vita Epicuri cum testamento: διὰ δὲ τὴν ἡδονὴν καὶ τὰς ἀρετὰς αἱρεῖσθαι, οὐ δι' αὑτάς, ὥσπερ τὴν ἰατρικὴν διὰ τὴν ὑγίειαν

of the terms encountered in the general language of healing are present.

The story of the miraculous healing of a young maiden called Asclepigenia in Marinos' *Vita Procli*,[405] illustrates the power of the prayer of a righteous man,[406] the well-being of the asklepieion at Athens,[407] the importance of maintaining the family line,[408] and the fact that the normal procedure in cases of illness was to seek the help of physicians first, and only when they despaired of help to turn elsewhere.[409] In it the terms ἰάσασθαι (meaning to *cure /heal*, referring to physicians), ἰᾶτο (meaning *healed*, referring to Asklepios), παθῶν (referring to the physical suffering of the patient), and ὑγιεινῇ (referring to the patient's return to health), occur.

A young maiden, Asclepigenia, was stricken with a grievous illness, which the physicians were unable to cure (νόσῳ χαλεπῇ κατείχετο καὶ τοῖς ἰατροῖς ἰάσασθαι ἀδυνάτῳ). Her father turned to the philosopher Proclus and asked him to pray for his daughter. Proclus' prayer was effective, for after going to the asklepieion, and while he was praying (in the more ancient fashion), a change came over the girl and she suddenly found relief (εὐχομένου δὲ αὐτοῦ τὸν ἀρχαιότερον τρόπον, ἀθρόα μεταβολὴ περὶ τὴν κόρην ἐφαίνετο καὶ ῥᾳστώνη ἐξαίφνης ἐγίγνετο·). The explanation given is that the

---

405 *Vita Procli* 29. According to Armstrong (1965) 199, Proclus, the Platonic Successor at Athens, (410-485 AD) was "the greatest of the later Neo-Platonists". For a discussion of his thought and influence, see Armstrong (1965) 199-204.

406 Cf., for example, James 5.15-16 (*re* the prayer of a righteous man) in the New Testament; and the Babylonian Talmud (Berakhoth 34b) *re* the Jewish *ḥasid* Hanina ben Dosa (for a discussion see Vermes [1983] 72-76). Thus this story echoes earlier thought on the value of prayer, and the power of the holy man.

407 "For the city still enjoyed the god's presence at that time and still held the temple of the Saviour unravaged (καὶ γὰρ ηὐτύχει τούτου ἡ πόλις τότε, καὶ εἶχεν ἔτι ἀπόρθητον τὸ τοῦ Σωτῆρος ἱερόν)" i.e. in the 5th century AD.

408 This desire is probably not peculiar to Athens, but a universal desire, eloquently expressed by Athenian authors. It figures in lawsuits as a (supposedly) persuasive argument for justifying action. For example, this was the reason given in Isocrates (1968) (*Aegineticus* 12, 13, 34) for his client's adoption, and here it accounts for the father's despair: "Since Archiades rested all his hopes for his family line on her alone, he was grieved and greatly distressed, as was natural (ὁ δὲ Ἀρχιάδας ἐπ' αὐτῇ μόνῃ τὰς ἐλπίδας ἔχων τοῦ γένους, ἤσχαλλε καὶ ὀδυνηρῶς διέκειτο, ὥσπερ ἦν εἰκός)."

409 Marinos, *Vita Procli* 29

"Saviour"[410] (Asklepios), because he was a god, easily healed her (ῥεῖα γὰρ ὁ Σωτήρ, ὥστε θεός, ἰᾶτο). When Proclus left the asklepieion and visited Asclepigenia he found her relieved of her bodily suffering (τὸ σῶμα λελυμένην παθῶν), and in a healthy state (ἐν ὑγιεινῇ δὲ καταστάσει διάγουσαν).

This story, although later in time, shows a continuity in the meaning of healing language. The verb ἰάομαι, as in earlier inscriptions, still refers to the miraculous healing wrought by Asklepios, but also describes the actions of physicians.[411] Similarly πάθος continues to refer to suffering, but, in this case the suffering is specifically defined as being physical in nature, and ὑγιεινή continues to refer to a restoration to a former state of health.

Suidas,[412] although he is writing much later,[413] relates the story of the healing of Domninus (a philosopher of the 5th century AD) and Plutarch the Athenian (*ca.* AD 400).[414] His account is interesting for several reasons: it shows an understanding of and a sympathy for the Jewish religion (in particular Jewish abstention from eating pork); it shows a patient questioning a prescribed cure, and Asklepios' ability to offer an acceptable alternative; it implies that Jewish people could (and did?) go to Asklepios for healing help; and it uses the terms ἴασις (meaning *cure*), νόσος (meaning *disease*), ὑγιεία (meaning *a return to former health*), θεραπεία (meaning prescribed *treatment*), and πάθος (meaning *illness*, or *physical suffering*).

3.4. Conclusion

Thus it can be seen that the literary evidence at Athens, comprising the language of inscriptions, poetry, history, oratory and philosophy, during the life span of the asklepieion there, shows

---

410 Cf. the designation of Asklepios as "Saviour" in (i) inscriptions (see above, n.350); and (ii) literature (Aelius Aristides, *Or.* 50.9, and see below, chapter five; Hippokrates [1990] 88, Letter 17.9; Aelian, *De Natura Animalium* 10.49).

411 Of Asklepios, see *IG* II^2, no. 4514 [2nd c. AD], (App. 3:3); of physicians, see *IG* II^2, no. 772 [ca. 252-251 BC {but dated 270-269 BC by Pritchett and Meritt}].

412 Lexicon, *s. v.* Δομνῖνος.

413 Suidas was writing in the 10th century AD.

414 App. 3:4

definite trends in the meaning of healing words. The verb ὑγιαίνω, and its related forms, continues to indicate a return to former (good) health, and to indicate the maintenance of a healthy way of life. It is generally used in a holistic sense to indicate the general well-being and effective functioning of the state, family or individual, both in inscriptions and literature. In contrast, the verb πάσχω, and its related forms, continues to indicate suffering, whether it be mental anguish or physical pain. The verbs θεραπεύω, ἰάομαι and σῴζω, and their related forms, although overlapping slightly in their meaning on occasion, in that each can mean *preserve*, show a distinct difference in meaning and usage. The verb θεραπεύω is noticeably absent from the language of inscriptions and the literature surrounding activities at the asklepieion. It is clear that where divine intervention is required or expected the verbs ἰάομαι and σῴζω are preferred. Both can provide a permanent quick-fix. Successful healing by physicians (where the patients recover!) is also reported with the verb ἰάομαι. In contrast, the verb θεραπεύω is reserved for the description of the long and arduous nursing of the terminally ill, or the ascetic lifestyle of the true philosopher. Both are continuous in that nursing involves much "vexation of the mind and hard work for the hands" while the true pursuit of philosophy involves a life-long commitment, and both emphasise the value of providing psychological comfort and care.

But is this difference in meaning reflected in the medical writings of the Hippokratic Corpus?

4. *Asklepios at Kos*

Ancient opinion was divided as to whether the origin of the Koan Asklepios was Trikka in Thessaly, or Epidauros.[415] Modern opinion favours Trikka,[416] although the issue is still controver-

---

415 Herodotos 7.99 states that the colonists of Kos were Dorian, from Epidauros; Tacitus, *Ann.* 12.61 states that Asklepios came to Kos from Argos (meaning Epidauros? Furneaux in Tacitus [1961] 138, n.7, basing his ideas on this passage in Tacitus, also assumes that Epidauros was the original seat of Asklepios, and the origin of the asklepieion at Kos); Pausanias 3.23.7 implies that Epidauros and Kos had close ties; and Julian, *Contra Galilaeos* 200 A-B agrees. However Herodas 2.97 states that Asklepios came to Kos from Trikka.

416 Sherwin-White (1978) 335-340

sial.[417] As well, the discipline of archaeology, which should have contributed much to settle the issue, has not yielded as much information as might have been hoped. Indeed, the history of archaeology on the island has not been a happy one.[418] Nevertheless, it is still possible to sketch an outline of the history of the asklepieion there, and, whatever the gaps in our knowledge of the history and functioning of the asklepieion, or of its relationship to the Hippokratic medical school, the writings of the Hippokratic Corpus,[419] local inscriptions,[420] and the mimes of Herodas[421] provide an immensely rich and varied field for a study of healing language in the classical and hellenistic eras.

4.1. History[422]

Kos appears in Homer's catalogue of ships,[423] contributing (together with the islands Nisyros, Krapathos, Kasos and the Kalydnian group) a contingent of thirty ships to the Greek cause. These ships were under the leadership of Pheidippos and Antiphos, "sons both of Thessalos who was born to the lord Herakles".[424] Thus the Dorian ancestry of the Koans, alluded to

---

417 Wilamowitz-Moellendorff (1886) 49f. favoured Thessaly; Hicks (in Paton and Hicks [1891] xv) Epidauros; Paton (in Paton and Hicks [1891] 347) Knidos; while Edelstein (1945) 2: 238-240, concluded that the asklepieion at Kos originated from Epidauros. Sherwin-White, (1978) 335-340, discusses the evidence for both Trikka and Epidauros and concludes that Trikka was "probably" the origin of the Koan cult. However, Jackson (1988) 143 favours Epidauros.

418 For a discussion of the problems, see Cohn-Haft (1956) 61-63; van Straten (1981) 129-132.

419 The text and translation is that of the Loeb Classical Library edition of *Hippocrates*, vols 1-6 (1968-1988). See App. 4:1.

420 The text used is that found in *Inscriptiones Creticae* I (1935), (see App. 4:3); and Paton and Hicks (1891), (see App. 4:2).

421 The text used is that found in Herodas (1904), (see App. 4:4).

422 It is not proposed, nor is it appropriate, to give a detailed history of Kos here, but rather to sketch an historical outline within which the language of healing manifest in the Hippokratic Corpus, local inscriptions, and the mimes of Herodas can be discussed. For a history of the island, see Sherwin-White (1978).

423 *Iliad* 2.676-680

424 The *Iliad* twice mentions a storm sent by Hera, which swept Herakles off course to Kos on his return journey from Troy (14.249-255; 15.26-28). Herodas 2.96 refers to this, when he mentions Thessalos, the son of Herakles by Chalkiope, daughter of Eurypylos, king of Kos.

here in the *Iliad*, was, according to Herodotos, further strengthened by later colonisation from Epidauros.[425]

Herodotos also tells us that Kos, which had been ruled by Skythes, but whose son Kadmos had abdicated in favour of the people,[426] was, in the fifth century, included in the satrapy of the Karian queen Artemisia, and, with three other states (Halikarnassos, Nisyra, and Kalydna) contributed five ships to Xerxes' navy.[427] Later in the fifth century Kos was a tribute-paying ally of Athens,[428] and, at the beginning of the Peloponnesian War was numbered among the allies of Athens.[429] In 413 BC the island suffered a major earthquake, which destroyed a large part of the town of Kos, and in 412 BC the Spartan admiral, Astyochus, invaded and sacked what was left of the city and overran the country.[430] Alkibiades fortified Kos for use as a base the following year and appointed a governor there.[431] Thus Kos suffered at the hands of both the Spartans and the Athenians during the final years of the Peloponnesian War because of its usefulness as a naval base.

In 366, as a result of faction fighting, all Koans became citizens of one city named Kos,[432] the towns of the island being δῆμοι. After this centralisation the city grew in wealth and power.[433] Kos joined the second Athenian Alliance, but revolted in 357 (with Khios, and Rhodes, supported by Byzantium and Mausolus of Caria) which resulted in the Social War of 357-355BC.[434] Finally, the inde-

425 Herodotos 7.99

426 7.164

427 7.99: "They were the most famous in the fleet, after the contingent from Sidon." Cf. Hippokrates (1990) 114-117.

428 See Meritt, Wade-Gery, McGregor (1950) 213.

429 Thucydides 2.9

430 ibid. 8.41

431 ibid. 8.108

432 Strabo 14.2.19: "on account of a sedition, they changed their abode to the present city ... and changed the name to Kos, the same as that of the island. Now the city is not large, but is the most beautifully settled of all, and is most pleasing to behold as one sails from the high sea to its shore." Strabo goes on to describe the wealth of the island, and its famous citizens. (Loeb 6, translated by H. L. Jones.)

433 Dio. Sic. 15.76: "the Coans transferred their abode to the city they now inhabit and made it a notable place (ἀξιόλογον); for a large population was gathered into it, and costly walls and a considerable harbour were constructed. From this time on its public revenues and private wealth constantly increased, so much so that it became in a word a rival of the leading cities of Greece." (Loeb 7, translated by C. L. Sherman.)

434 Dio. Sic. 16.7.21

pendence of the islands Kos, Khios and Rhodes, and the city of Byzantium was recognised by Athens in the peace of 354BC.

During the campaigns of Alexander the island was subdued by Alexander's generals.[435] Some of Alexander's doctors came from Kos.[436] On Alexander's death in 323 the island passed to the Ptolemies.

In 309BC Ptolemy I brought Queen Berenike to Kos and their son Ptolemy II Philadelphos was born there in that year. Kos enjoyed special privileges under the Ptolemies: it had its own mint, and became a literary centre for Alexandrian writers.[437] The painter, Apelles of Ephesus,[438] who flourished at this time, and whose works of art adorned the Kos asklepieion,[439] lived for many years at Kos.[440]

Indeed, the Koans seem to have enjoyed remarkable foresight in choosing powerful benefactors. They early supported Roman interests,[441] resisted those who would have led them to desert Rome,[442] and helped Rome prosecute the Mithridatic Wars.[443] They sheltered Roman citizens in the temple of Asklepios, when Mithridates VI was on the rampage.[444] For these reasons, and because his own physician, Xenophon, was a Koan, the emperor Claudius exempted Kos from taxation.[445] Pliny described Kos as a "very famous and powerful island".[446] Pliny also mentions inscriptions in the temple that described cures, and which Hip-

---

435 Ptolemaeus and Asandros (Arrian 2.5.7), and Amphoteros (Arrian 3.2.6).

436 According to Arrian 6.11.1, it was either Kritodemos, a Koan physician, or Perdiccas, who removed a potentially fatal arrow from Alexander.

437 Literary activity there is described by Theokritos (*Idyll* 7). The Koan poet, Philetas, was tutor of Ptolemy II when he was crown prince (295-292BC), and Ptolemy II Philadelphos seems to have maintained strong links with the island. For a discussion, see Nairn in Herodas (1904) xx-xxi.

438 Both Strabo (14.1.25), and Herodas (4.72), state that Apelles was from Ephesus.

439 Herodas 4.72-78; Strabo 14.2.19

440 Pliny, *Natural History* 35.36.79 describes him as a Koan, probably because he lived there for so long, and his works of art adorned the asklepieion there.

441 Livy 37.16.2

442 Polybius 30.7, 9

443 Plutarch, *Lucullus* 3.3

444 Tacitus, *Ann.* 4.4

445 ibid. 12.61. Xenophon, who had acquired Roman citizenship, and practised medicine in Rome, was later credited with poisoning Claudius (Tacitus, *Ann.* 12.67). Xenophon maintained strong links with Kos (see below, n.574).

446 *Natural History* 29.2.4

pokrates was supposed to have copied.[447] These have not been found. However, it is because of its asklepieion and the Hippokratic school of medicine that Kos is chiefly remembered today.

4.2. The asklepieion at Kos - Herodas

Both Strabo[448] and Aristides[449] described the asklepieion at Kos, but the best extant description of the asklepieion at Kos occurs in the fourth mime of Herodas.[450] This mime describes the early morning visit of two women to the asklepieion, their offering, and their subsequent examination of and commentary on the works of art there. Since the mime "is a piece depicting actual life, generally the life of the common people, and employing their language",[451] this description paints a remarkable picture of the asklepieion at Kos in the third century BC.[452]

The mime is only ninety-five lines long, and is structured thus: the women salute Asklepios and his family, and offer their sacrifice and dedication.[453] Then, while the νεωκόρος[454] attends to the sacrifice, the women tour the asklepieion, commenting on the

---

447 ibid. See also 20.100.264, where Pliny reproduces a prescription supposed to counteract the poison of venomous animals, which was carved in verse on a stone in the temple of Asklepios at Kos. King Antiochus the Great was said to have used the preparation as an antidote for the poison af all venomous creatures except the asp.

448 14.2.19: "a temple exceedingly famous and full of numerous votive offerings, among which is the Antigonus of Apelles." Strabo also mentions votive tablets recording cures at 8.6.15, none of which have been found.

449 38.15. This is only a fleeting mention in a speech about the sons of Asklepios: according to Aristides they didn't settle in the suburbs of Kos but filled every place with their medicine. However, Aristides (38.12) does say that the Asklepiads "cured" (ἰάσαντο) Kos and made it accessible to all, both Greek and barbarian (App. 5:6, **4**).

450 See App. 4:4.

451 Nairn in Herodas (1904) xxii

452 The date of the mime has been placed between 270BC and 260BC. See Nairn in Herodas (1904) 44.

453 Lines 1-20 (App. 4:4, **1-2**)

454 The νεωκόρος seems to perform the function of a sacristan here: he attends to the sacrifice, reports on the omens (lines 79-80), and presumably is responsible for the opening of the doors (lines 55-56). The duties of a νεωκόρος at a healing sanctuary are clearly delineated in an inscription from the amphiaraon at Oropis in Boeotia. See *IG* VII, no. 235 (App. 3:6).

works of art.[455] After the νεωκόρος returns with favourable news, the women depart.[456]

The first twenty lines of the mime are rich in detail concerning Asklepios and his family, and the rite of sacrifice at the asklepieion. The mime begins with Kynno's salutation: she hails Asklepios as "Lord Paiëon,[457] ruler of Trikka, who lives at sweet Kos and Epidauros,"[458] and continues by recounting Asklepios' lineage,[459] and naming the members of Asklepios' family.[460] As usual, Hygieia enjoys pride of place,[461] but Panake, Epio, and Iaso are named as having altars dedicated to them in the Kos asklepieion.[462] Asklepios' sons, Podaleirios and Machaon, are described as "healers of savage sicknesses".[463]

After these salutations, Kynno asks Asklepios and his family to accept their sacrifice of a cock, apologising that they are not wealthy enough to afford to sacrifice an ox or a stuffed pig.[464] This is interesting, for it implies that the cock was the poor man's offering.[465] They also offer a votive tablet, a pinax,[466] before ogling the

---

455 Lines 20-78

456 Lines 79-95 (App. 4:4, **3-4**)

457 Asklepios is addressed as ἄναξ Παίηον (1), πάτερ Παίηον (11), and Παίηον (81, 82, 85); and referred to as ὁ Παιὼν (26). For the use of this term in Homer, see above, chapter one.

458 Herodas 4, 1-2 (App. 4:4, **1**). Herodas thus implies that Trikka was the origin of the asklepieions at both Epidauros and Kos, and that, at this time, these three sites were the most important of the asklepieions in the Greek world.

459 Herodas 4.3 names Koronis and Apollo as the parents of Asklepios (App. 4:4, **1**).

460 4.5-9: Hygieia, Panake, Epio, Iaso, Podaleirios and Machaon (App. 4:4, **1**). Cf. Hippokrates, *Oath* (App. 4:1, **4**); and see App. 3:1, **1** (Athens, N.M. 1402), for a pictorial representation of Asklepios and his family.

461 The woman, Kynno, describes Asklepios touching Hygieia with his right hand at 4.4. (App. 4:4, **1**). It appears that Kynno is describing a sculpted group of Asklepios and his family. Hygieia's close proximity to Asklepios in the group is consistent with portrayals of Asklepios and his family (particularly Hygieia) on reliefs from the Athenian asklepieion (see App. 3:1, **7** [Athens, N.M. 1352]; **11** [Athens, N.M. 1345]; **12** [Athens, N.M. 1335] and **14** [Athens, N.M. 1333]); and, from the Piraeus asklepieion (see App. 3:1, **4** [Piraeus Museum 405]).

462 4.5-6 (App. 4:4, **1**)

463 4.8: ἰητῆρες ἀγρίων νούσων

464 4.14-16 (App. 4:4, **1**). For a pictorial representation of sacrificial offerings, see App. 3:1, **12-14** (Athens, N.M. 1335, 1429, 1333).

465 So Nairn in Herodas (1904) 46, *re* line 12; but cf. Edelstein (1945) 2: 190: "The cock was indeed the most common sacrifice; the phrase 'a cock to Asclepius' was almost proverbial, not only on account of Socrates' offering" (*Phaedo*

works of art: statues, some sculpted by the sons of Praxiteles,[467] and paintings by Apelles of Ephesus.[468] The paintings and sculptures are described in detail,[469] and give a vivid picture of the adornment and atmosphere of the asklepieion. It was a popular place, at daylight Kynno complains about the crush of people.[470]

When the women have completed their tour the νεωκόρος returns with a favourable report on their sacrifice,[471] and the women leave, after Kynno has given instructions concerning the carving up of the cock: the νεωκόρος is to receive the leg, the snake the clotted blood and cakes of ground barley with honey,[472] and the remainder the women will take home to eat.[473] The mime concludes with the νεωκόρος complaining about his share.[474]

Thus the fourth mime of Herodas is a comic sketch of the patrons of and the ritual at the asklepieion at Kos. However, while it provides valuable insight into the nature of both patrons and ritual, it also provides a mental picture of the beauty of the sanctuary, by describing the works of art in detail, and naming some of

---

118a). See also 190 n.23, where Edelstein maintains that the cock may have been of importance because it was the herald of the dawn, or because of a belief in its apotropaic nature. The sacrifice to Asklepios of a cock is mentioned in *IG* IV^2 1, no. 41 [ca. 400 BC]; and by Artemidorus, *Onirocritica* 5.9.

466 Nairn in Herodas (1904) 47, *re* line 19, describes τὸν πίνακα as "a votive tablet of painted terra-cotta, with a picture of the diseased limb, &c., upon it". See App. 3:1, **15**, for examples of votive offerings of this type found at the asklepieion at Korinth.

467 4.23

468 4.72-78

469 A girl looking up at an apple (27-29), a boy strangling a goose (30-33), a statue of Batale (35-38), a naked boy so life-like his flesh throbs with life (59-62), a silver toasting-iron (62-65), an ox and its leader, and attendants (66-71). For a pictorial representation of an ox with its attendants from the asklepieion at Athens, see App. 3:1, **13** (Athens, N.M. 1429).

470 4.54-56

471 4.79-86 (App. 4:4, **3**)

472 91-92: τὸν πελανὸν . . . καὶ ψαιστὰ (see App. 4:4, **4**). Cf. Aristophanes, *Ploutos* 138 and 1115, for the use of these cakes in sacrifices, and App. 3:1, **12** (Athens, N.M. 1335) for a pictorial representation of such a sacrifice. See also App. 5:3, lines12-15, an inscription from Pergamon, in which the Council and Demos at Pergamon decreed that the priest should take as a perquisite the right leg and the skin of all the sacrificial animals offered in the temple, and all the other offerings dedicated on the holy table: λαμβάνειν δὲ | καὶ γέρα τῶν θυομένων ἱερείων ἐν τῶι ἱερῶι | πάντων σκέλος δεξιὸν καὶ τὰ δέρματα καὶ τἆλλ[α | τραπεζώματα πάντα τὰ παρατιθέμεν[α.

473 4.88-93 (see App. 4:4, **4**)

474 4.93-95

the artists. Nor is this all. Information in the mime confirms other reports of the origin of the asklepieion, and of Asklepios' lineage and family, and the language echoes other healing language and practices.

We have already met the word Paiëon, both as a title, and as an epithet.[475] In the mime it is used exclusively of Asklepios, although the language of the *νεωκόρος*[476] echoes the Homeric *Hymn to Apollo*.[477] It is, as Nairn suggests, probably part of a liturgical formula.

Healing method appears to be one of touch. Kynno thanks Asklepios for wiping away their diseases by laying his gentle hands on them.[478] It is an image we have met before, both in inscriptions,[479] and portrayed on archaeological reliefs.[480] Indeed the image of Asklepios with his hand stretched out towards his patients is a common one on reliefs.[481] There is no evidence in the mime that Hippokratic medicine was practised at the Kos asklepieion,[482] although Herzog has surmised that it was, based on the type of votives, and medical instruments, that he excavated.[483]

---

475 See above, chapter one.

476 See lines 82 and 85. Nairn in Herodas (1904) 56, *re* line 81, points out that lines 82-85 are probably part of a formula used regularly by the priest or *νεωκόρος*. See App. 4:4, **3**.

477 517: *ἰὴ Παίηον*

478 16-19: *ἴητρα | νούσων ἐποιεύμεσθα τὰς ἀπέψησας | ἐπ' ἠπίας σὺ χεῖρας, ὦ ἄναξ, τείνας*

479 See, for example, *IG* IV^2 1, no. 122:31 (App. 2:2, **31**); *IG* IV^2 1, no. 126 (Apps. 2:4 and 2:5).

480 See, for example, Piraeus Museum 405 (App. 3:1, **4**) and Athens, N. M. 1841 (App. 3:1, **5**) and Athens, N. M. 2373 (App. 3:1, **6**). For a discussion, see above, chapter three.

481 See Plate 2 (Athens, N.M. 173); and App. 3:1, **5** (Athens, N.M. 1841), **7** (Athens, N.M. 1352), and **10** (Athens, N.M. 1408).

482 For a discussion of whether Hippokratic medicine was practised at the asklepieion, and Herzog's opinion regarding this, see Cohn-Haft (1956) 63, n.40.

483 But cf. (i) Cohn-Haft (1956) 63, n.40, where Cohn-Haft chastises Herzog for "his arbitrary remarks on the relations between the Coan medical school and the asklepieion ... [and] his reiterated claims for the rational medicine practised at the Coan asklepieion, claims apparently based ultimately upon an act of will rather than upon any evidence", and (ii) van Straten (1981) 65-151, who, while expressing doubt about their authenticity, nevertheless lists the votives in the Meyer-Steineg collection from the Kos asklepieion (129-132), noting that some of them betray (131) "considerable anatomical knowledge".

The evidence of Pliny would also seem to support Herzog's thesis.[484]

It is perhaps significant that women are represented as the patrons of the asklepieion in this mime. As at Athens,[485] the asklepieion at Kos was more accessible to local women, than the asklepieion at Epidauros.[486] As well, they have timed their visit before the public day begins,[487] perhaps to fit in with their own daily schedule. And, as at Athens, their prayer is that they will return in full health (with larger offerings), bringing their husbands and children with them.[488] As expected by now, the word used to denote health is ὑγιής, here qualified by the adjective πολλή.[489]

Modern archaeological excavations, conducted by Herzog in 1902, discovered the asklepieion on a hill slope two miles west of the town of Kos, and revealed that the main constructions there were no earlier than the fourth century BC.[490] Thus the temple revealed is that visited by the women. Near the altar are bases of statues dedicated to Asklepios which are referred to in the fourth mime of Herodas.[491] The asklepieion was built on three terraces, cut one above the other into the hill slope. It is still a magnificent site, commanding a fine view to the coast of modern Turkey.[492]

---

484 *Natural History* 20.100.264. See above, n.447.

485 Women were represented more frequently in the votive offerings, see Aleshire (1989) 45-46.

486 The distance from the ancient port at Epidauros to the sanctuary was far greater. See above, chapter two.

487 Kynno comments on the time of day, the opening of the door, and the growing crush of people (lines 54-56).

488 εἴη γάρ, ὦ μέγιστε, κὐγίῃ πολλῇ | ἔλθοιμεν αὖτις μέζον' ἴρ' ἀγινεῦσαι | σὺν ἀνδράσιν καὶ παισί (lines 86-88). Thus, in this mime, it is the local and familial concerns of the women that are represented: a reflection of the decrees (App. 3:2), and the marble reliefs from the asklepieion at Athens (App. 3:1, **9-11** [Athens, N.M. 1384, 1408, 1345]); and a marble relief from the Piraeus asklepieion (App. 3;1, **4** [Piraeus Museum 405]).

489 86: κὐγίῃ πολλῇ

490 Herzog (1932). For a discussion of the evidence and a description of the site and its buildings, see Sherwin-White (1978) 340-346.

491 Lines 20-22f.

492 From the upper terrace one can see the town of Kos surrounded by orchards and gardens, the harbour, and, across the sea the peninsula of Knidos and the promontory of Bodrum flanking the gulf of Kos, and, to the NW the islands of Kalymnos and Pserimos.

4.3. The Hippokratic Corpus

Kos forms a convenient centre for the study of the healing language of the body of medical writings known as the Hippokratic Corpus, for it was out of the teachings of the Kos medical school that they originated.[493] The Koan medical school was founded by Hippokrates in the fifth century BC.[494] Very little is known about his life, but, according to his biographers, he was born in or around 460BC,[495] and was a member of the Asklepiads, a family who claimed to be descended from Asklepios.[496] The close link between the Hippokratic school of medicine and the healing god Asklepios, and his family, is illustrated by the Hippokratic Oath, in which the physician swears by "Apollo Physician, by Asklepios, by Health, by Panakeia, and all the gods and goddesses ".[497]

Hippokrates taught medicine for a fee,[498] and was known to both Plato[499] and Aristotle.[500] His biographers stated that Hippokrates travelled widely, and was consulted by Perdiccas of Macedon. Artaxerxes of Persia wanted Hippokrates at his court,[501] and, upon his refusal,[502] asked the Koans to give him up.[503] The Koans refused.[504] He is said to have been in Athens at the time of the

493 Not all the treatises are Koan, however. Some are Knidian. On this issue, see Lonie (1965b) 1-30. It seems probable that the Corpus is a collection of medical treatises from varying schools, gathered together to form the library of the medical school at Kos, and attributed to Hippokrates because he was the founder of the school there. See Phillips (1973) 34, who concludes that "Hippocrates may have written some or none of the books which we have".

494 Plato, *Protagoras* 311b

495 See Jones in Hippokrates (1972) xlii-xlvi for a survey of the literature surrounding Hippokrates' life. Three biographies exist: those of Suidas, Tzetzes and Soranus. They favour 460BC as Hippokrates' birth date, but Aulus Gellius 17.21, states that Hippokrates was older than Sokrates, which places his birth prior to 470 BC.

496 Plato, *Protagoras* 311b. See Jones in Hippokrates (1972) xliv-xlvi, and Temkin (1991) 5, 80-81. See also Smith in Hippokrates (1990) 1-18.

497 *Oath* (App. 4:1, **4**). Cf. Kynno's opening salutation in the fourth mime of Herodas, 1-11.

498 Plato, *Protagoras* 311 b-c

499 *Phaedrus* 270c, *Protagoras* 311 b-c

500 *Politics* 1326^{a} 14 f.

501 Hippokrates (1990) 50-51, Letter 3

502 ibid. 52-53, Letters 5, 5a, 6, 6a

503 ibid. 54-55, Letter 8

504 ibid. 54-55, Letter 9. For a discussion of these letters, 18-19. Later Koan physicians were consulted by eastern royalty (Pliny, *Natural History* 20.

Great Plague, and to have treated those suffering from it.[505] He is thought to have died at Larissa in Thessaly.[506]

It is not known for certain whether Hippokrates was the author of any of the writings that bear his name.[507] However that may be, his fame and influence grew over succeeding generations until it was his name that became synonymous with the foundation of scientific medicine,[508] a reputation entrenched and perpetuated for all time by the great second century physician Galen.[509]

The Hippokratic Corpus consists of approximately seventy works of varying age and authorship.[510] All are anonymous. Scholars have commented on the treatises and tried since antiquity to ascribe authorship to some of them, with differing degrees of success.[511] Opinion, style and medical attitude varies within the Corpus.[512] Despite this, the use of general healing terms within the Corpus remains surprisingly constant.[513]

100.264), Greek cities (e.g. Gortyn, see App. 4:3), and Roman emperors (e.g. Claudius, Tacitus, *Ann.* 12.61, 67).

505 See Jones in Hippokrates (1972) xliii, and Pinault (1986) 52-75.

506 The supposed grave of Hippokrates is there, and Suidas believed this to be the case. But see Phillips (1973) 186-188, for a discussion of the biographical tradition surrounding Hippokrates.

507 For a discussion of this problem see Edelstein (1967) 133-144; Lloyd (1975) 171-192; and, more recently, Temkin (1991) 5, 39f.

508 Seneca, *Epistulae* 95.20: Maximus ille medicorum et huius scientiae conditor. Celsus (*De Medicina, Prooemium* 6-8), also says that Hippokrates was the first to separate medicine from philosophy. Interest in Hippokrates, and Hippokratic medicine, is illustrated by the work of Erotian, a Greek lexicographer of the first century AD, who listed works ascribed to Hippokrates, and early commentators of them. For a list of works known to Erotian, see Jones in Hippokrates (1972) xxxviii-xxxix.

509 See Temkin (1973) 32-33, 58.

510 For a list, see Jones in Hippokrates (1972) xxxviii-xxxix.

511 In antiquity: Herophilus, Bacchius, Heraclides of Tarentum, Erotian, and Galen, to name a few. See Jones in Hippokrates (1972) xxxv-xlii. See also Edelstein (1967) 133-144; Phillips (1973) 28-37; and Lloyd (1975) 171-192.

512 See Lloyd (1975) 171-192; and Lonie (1965b) 1-30.

513 See App. 4:1 for a selection of references which illustrate the uses of the verbs θεραπεύω, ὑγιαίνω, ἰάομαι, and πάσχω in the Corpus.

4.3.1. θεραπεύω

It is at once obvious that the verb θεραπεύω is used consistently to refer to medical treatment.[514] This use is startlingly clear in *Aphorisms* where the pronouncement:

> It is better to give no treatment (μὴ θεραπεύειν) in cases of hidden cancer; treatment (θεραπευόμενοι) causes speedy death, but to omit treatment (μὴ θεραπευόμενοι) is to prolong life[515]

makes it self-evident that the verb θεραπεύω does not include any idea of *cure* in its meaning. It is, simply, the course of action prescribed in an attempt to improve the health or well-being of the patient. Thus θεραπεύω implies an active process, an active and continuous attempt to change an undesirable state of health for a better one. And, in some cases, interference of any sort can have an undesirable effect.

Another aphorism[516] states that vomiting (without fever) can be cured (σωτήριον), but implies that vomiting with fever is difficult to cure (κακόν). The verb used to prescribe treatment is θεραπεύω.[517] Thus this aphorism also makes a clear distinction between treatment (θεραπεύειν) and cure (σωτήριον). Similarly, the treatise *Ancient Medicine*, thought to have been written in the early years of the Peloponnesian War,[518] discusses the proper treatment of patients in terms of θεραπεύω.[519]

This meaning of θεραπεύω is further illustrated in the treatise *The Art*, a treatise thought to have been written at the end of the fifth century BC by a sophist who was not a physician, one who was interested not in science, but in "subtle reasonings and in literary

514 See App. 4:1.

515 *Aphorisms* 6.38 (App. 4:1, **5**). This can be shown to be true in contemporary medical treatment, where surgery on patients with terminal cancer has been shown to hasten the multiplication of cancer cells.

516 7.37. See App. 4:1, **6**.

517 ibid. Note that θεραπεύω appears in the present active infinitive, implying continuous treatment.

518 Jones in Hippokrates (1972) 5, places the date of composition as between 430 and 420 BC. Jones suggests that the writer was "either Hippocrates or a very capable supporter of the medical school of which Hippocrates was a contemporary member". However, Lloyd (1975) 171-179, discusses the authorship of this treatise (and others) based on external and internal evidence, concluding (178) that "None of the evidences . . . can be said to establish with a reasonable degree of probability, let alone with certainty, the authenticity of any treatise in the Hippocratic Corpus."

519 See App. 4:1, **1**, **2**, and **3**.

style".[520] Thus this treatise should be particularly valuable for a pedantic and classical use of language in a medical context.[521] Again, a clear distinction is made between the notions of *treat* and *cure*:

> It is conceded that of those treated by medicine (τῶν θεραπευομένων ὑπὸ ἰητρικῆς) some are healed (ἐξυγιαίνονται).[522]

Indeed, treatment is undertaken to prevent diseases growing worse[523] and there are differing degrees of treatment: while some patients are treated well, others are treated badly (κακῶς θεραπευομένοισι). However, by employing the art of "good" medical treatment, patients can recover (ὑγιάσθησαν).[524] The verb chosen to designate those who escape disease is ἀποφεύγω,[525] while those who recover are described in terms of ὑγιαίνω,[526] σῴζω,[527] and ἀπαλλάττω.[528] Medical attendants, i.e. those who do the nursing, are designated as οἱ θεραπεύοντες.[529] Patients are designated τῶν

520 Jones in Hippokrates (1981) 186. Jones favours Plato's Hippias (*Protagoras* 337c-338b) as the author, basing his opinion on Hippias' style as depicted in the *Protagoras*, and comparing it with the style of *The Art* (186-189). This treatise appears in Erotian's list. See above, n.508.

521 For a selection of passages, see App. 4:1, **7**, **8**, **9** and **10**.

522 *The Art* 4. See App. 4:1, **7**.

523 *The Art* 11 (App. 4:1, **10**) : τῆς γὰρ αὐτῆς συνέσιός ἐστιν ἧσπερ τὸ εἰδέναι τῶν νούσων τὰ αἴτια καὶ τὸ θεραπεύειν αὐτας ἐπίστασθαι πάσῃσι τῇσι θεραπείῃσιν αἳ κωλύουσι τὰ νοσήματα μεγαλύνεσθαι (for the same intelligence is required to know the causes of diseases as to understand how to treat them with all the treatment that prevents illnesses from growing worse).

524 ibid.

525 Thucydides 2.51 uses οἱ διαπεφευγότες to designate those who recovered from the plague. For a discussion of healing language in Thucydides' account of the plague, see above, chapter three.

526 *The Art* 4: ὑγιασθεῖσιν . . . ὑγιάσθησαν (App. 4:1, **7**); *The Art* 5: ὑγιάσθησαν (App. 4:1, **8**); *The Art* 11: ὑγιανθῆναι (App. 4:1, **10**). ὑγιαίνω is also the verb chosen in *The Art* 7 to describe those who are healthy in mind (ὑγιαινούσῃ γνώμῃ), and in body (ὑγιαίνοντος σώματος). See App. 4:1, **9**.

527 *The Art* 5 : σῳζόμενοι. See App. 4:1, **8**.

528 *The Art* 7 : ἀπήλλαξαν. See App. 4:1, **9**. This is a very precise word meaning to *get off free*, or *escape*.

529 That this is a continuous exercise is illustrated by the choice of tense: the present participle here, and again - τοῖσι θεραπεύουσιν - in the same passage (*The Art* 11, App. 4:1, **10**).

καμνόντων[530] and their sufferings described with the present tense of πάσχω.[531]

Perhaps the clearest use of the meaning of θεραπεύω is illustrated in the treatises known as *Regimen II-IV*,[532] which are concerned with the early detection and treatment of health problems.[533] In them the author discusses the beneficial use of certain foods and drinks, in conjunction with exercise, and gives advice on what course of action to undertake in the event of overindulgence in either food, or exercise, or both. This author finds dreams a significant indicator of impending illness.[534] Prescribed treatment has a very modern ring: attention to diet, (including the advice to eat less), bathing, and regular exercise in the form of walking - after dinner, in the morning, and after exercise - is constantly recommended.[535] Massage too is a regular feature.[536] Prayer is also recommended.[537] All these measures are active and deliberate changes in lifestyle, designed to produce a change for the better in the patient's general health. Treatment continues until the patient has recovered, and even then permanent changes in lifestyle are recommended. The verb used to designate these treatments is θεραπεύω.[538] Recovery, using the prescribed treatment, may be slow, or rapid.[539] Thus the verb θεραπεύω signifies a method whereby human health can be restored and maintained.

530 ibid. Cf. James 5.15, where the person who is sick is designated as τὸν κάμνοντα.

531 ibid.: πάσχουσιν. For a discussion of the use of this verb by Athenian authors, see above, chapter three.

532 See Jones in Hippokrates (1979) for text and translation, and xlix-lv for a discussion. For excerpts, see App. 4:1, **12-20**.

533 As Jones points out (see above note), this is preventative medicine, a marked departure from the attitude of other treatises where the course of a disease is thought to be inexorable, and the author is interested only in prognosis (as in, for example, *Epidemics I* and *III*, and *Prognostic*).

534 *Regimen IV*

535 For example: gentle walks (II.66 [App. 4:1, **13**]), plenty of early-morning walks, but only short ones after dinner (III.75 [App. 4:1, **15**]), long walks (III.78 [App. 4:1, **17**]; IV.88 [App. 4:1, **19**]).

536 See, for example, *Regimen* III.78; and note the use of oil in *Regimen* II.66.41-42 (App. 4:1, **13**). The verb used to describe the anointing with oil is here ἀλείφω, and is used in a purely physical sense. Cf. James 5.15.

537 *Regimen* IV.90. (App. 4:1, **20**). Jones notes here that the "Christian" corrector of ms. θ struck out the words Γῇ . . . ἥρωσιν".

538 See App. 4:1, **12-19**.

539 *Regimen* III.75 (App. 4:1, **15**)

A much later treatise, *Decorum*,[540] further illustrates this meaning of θεραπεύω, despite being "written in a quaint and obscure manner".[541] Disagreeable drinks are denoted θεραπευόμενοι,[542] while the author notes that disease can sometimes be cured (ἰώμενα) by surgery, or relieved (βοηθεόμενα)[543] either through treatment (θεραπευόμενα), or regimen (διαιτώμενα).[544] It is obvious that θεραπεύω still denotes the method of medical treatment, which may be successful in varying degrees, while ἰάομαι retains the notion of *cure*[545] that is completely foreign to θεραπεύω.

The treatise *On Fractures*, of which E.T. Withington says that "nothing in the *Corpus* has a better claim to be by Hippocrates himself",[546] also uses the verb θεραπεύω to denote prolonged and repeated treatment for chronic conditions.[547]

But perhaps most interesting of all is the use of the noun θεραπεία in the confidentiality clause of the *Oath*,[548] a Hippokratic writing which is so well known even in contemporary society:

> I swear . . . whatsoever I shall see or hear in the course of my profession (ἐν θεραπείῃ), as well as outside my profession (ἄνευ θεραπείης) in my intercourse with men, if it be what should not be published abroad, I will never divulge, holding such things to be holy secrets.[549]

Here, the idea of a vocation, of a calling which provides continuous and confidential service at the most vulnerable times of life, is meant by θεραπεία. In this way θεραπεία is more than an occupa-

---

540 See Jones in Hippokrates (1981) 269-277, and (1979) xi-xii.

541 Jones in Hippokrates (1981) 270, n.1. Jones comments (270) on its "general tortuousness of ... style". For a discussion, see 269-277.

542 *Decorum* 14 (App. 4:1, **21**)

543 Cf. the use of the cognate form of this verb in a decree from Kos (App. 4:2, line 12: τὰν βο[άθειαν), and also in the New Testament, where βοήθει μοι are the words used in Matthew's account of the Canaanite woman's request of Jesus (Mt 15.25).

544 *Decorum* 6 (App. 4:1, **22**)

545 Surgery implies a cure of a more instantaneous nature than the relief brought about by a method of extended treatment, or change in regimen. There is in these verbs (θεραπεύω and ἰάομαι) an implicit notion of aspect, that is important for an understanding of them.

546 Hippokrates (1968) 85. Withington bases his conclusion on internal evidence and ancient testimony (84-85).

547 *On Fractures* 11 (App. 4:1, **23**)

548 See Jones in Hippokrates (1972) 291-297 for a discussion of the problems of authorship and content. Edelstein (1967) 3-63 detects a Pythagorean influence in *Oath*.

549 See App. 4:1, **4**.

tion, the term implies availability, succour, understanding of and compassion for humanity.

Thus there is in the verb θεραπεύω and its cognate form the idea of continuous service, service performed with the express purpose of improving the health, and therefore the happiness, of the patient. It implies selfless and persevering care on an individual level, but does not, in and of itself, guarantee a cure.[550] The verb usually reserved for the notion of cure is ἰάομαι, or σῴζω, and for a restoration of health ὑγιαίνω.[551]

4.3.2. ἰάομαι

The language of the treatise *The Sacred Disease* is different.[552] The author of this treatise is sparing in his use of the verb θεραπεύω.[553] Instead he is fond of the verb ἰάομαι and its cognate forms, while reserving ὑγιαίνω to denote a restoration of health.[554]

The Sacred Disease is an early work. It was known to Bacchius,[555] and Galen,[556] and appears in Erotian's list of the genuine works of Hippokrates.[557] Its authorship and date remains controversial.[558] It has definite parallels with the treatise *Airs, Waters, Places*,[559] causing some scholars to assume identical authorship.[560] Jones, however, favours the notion that the author was a student of the author of *Airs, Waters, Places*, and assumes that he was a younger contemporary of Sokrates.[561] If this is so the treatise was composed at the end of the fifth century, or the beginning of the fourth century.

---

550 Cf. Isocrates, *Aegineticus*, above, chapter three.

551 Cf. chapters two and three, above, and *Aphorisms* 7.37 (App. 4:1, **6**); *The Art* 4, 5, 7 and 11 (App. 4:1, **7-10**).

552 See App. 4:1, **24**.

553 See App. 4:1, **24**:3 (ὑπὸ θεραπείης) and App. 4:1, **25**:11 (μὴ θεραπευθῶσι). Perhaps this is because he considers contemporary treatments (καθαρμοῖσί . . . καὶ ἐπαοιδῆσιν [1]) to be of a magical (μαγείης [21]) rather than a medical nature.

554 See App. 4:1, **24**:2.

555 Bacchius lived early in the third century BC.

556 See Jones in Hippokrates (1981) 129.

557 See Jones in Hippokrates (1972) xxxviii.

558 For a survey of modern scholarship, see Jones in Hippokrates (1981) 129.

559 ibid. 130-131, where Jones sets these out in parallel passages.

560 ibid. 129, 132

561 ibid. 132

This author favours the cognate forms of ἰάομαι to describe the current "cure" for the disease about which he writes. So ἡ ἴησις consists of purifications and incantations (καθαρμοὺς προσφέροντες καὶ ἐπαοιδάς).[562] Familiar therapeutic practices such as bathing and certain foods are forbidden, and, instead, bizarre instructions such as the prohibition against wearing black, lying on or wearing goatskin, putting foot on foot or hand on hand are prescribed.[563] Thus the author explains that "having given nothing to eat or drink, and not having steeped their patients in baths",[564] the practitioners cannot be blamed if the "cure" is ineffective. But the "cure" the author describes is not Hippokratic in character: it does not involve the active interference on the part of the physician described, for example, in *Regimen*, nor the active cooperation of the patient in participating in long-term changes in diet and exercise. It is not surprising then that the author is sparing in his use of the verb θεραπεύω. In his single use of the verb, the author warns that the disease will be nourished and grow with the patient, unless appropriate treatments (μὴ θεραπευθῶσι) be used.[565] These appropriate treatments have not been discovered. Current treatment (ὑπὸ θεραπείης)[566] is described in a disparaging tone and the author chooses ἰάομαι to describe attempts to cure the disease by such magical means.[567] However he does imply that, if it were to be discovered how to cause in men moist or dry, hot or cold, the disease could be permanently cured (ἰῷτο).[568]

Therefore, there is a distinct difference in meaning between the verbs ἰάομαι and θεραπεύω in the treatise *The Sacred Disease*. The verb ἰάομαι retains the notion of a quick and complete cure, while θεραπεύω continues to imply extended treatment, treatment that is Hippokratic in character. This idea of a cure, a quick-fix, implicit in the verb ἰάομαι in Hippokratic writings, is neatly summed up in *Aphorisms*:

> Those diseases that medicines do not cure (οὐκ ἰῆται) are cured (ἰῆται) by the knife. Those that the knife does not cure (οὐκ ἰῆται)

---

562 *The Sacred Disease* 2

563 ibid.

564 ibid.

565 See App. 4:1, **25**:16.

566 The only time the author chooses the word in preference to ἡ ἴησις. See App. 4:1, **24**:3.

567 *The Sacred Disease* 3: "Accordingly I hold that those who attempt in this manner to cure (ἰῆσθαι) these diseases . . . " (App. 4:1, **24**:3).

568 ibid. 21 (App. 4:1, **25**:21)

are cured (ἰῆται) by fire. Those that fire does not cure (οὐκ ἰῆται) must be considered incurable (ἀνίατα).[569]

Thus, as in the healing language at Epidauros, and at Athens, at Kos ἰάομαι denotes a cure, while θεραπεύω describes treatment. In all centres ὑγιαίνω describes a restoration to health.

What then of those who were trained in the principles of Hippokratic medicine at Kos? For information in this regard it is necessary to turn to the evidence available in inscriptions.

4.4. Inscriptions

The medical school at Kos gained distinction in the Mediterranean world, particularly in the hellenistic period, for training the citizens of Kos as physicians.[570] Their excellence is demonstrated by the numbers of Koan physicians honoured in decrees.[571] Indeed, many public physicians throughout the Greek world were of Koan origin, and inscriptions show that cities made formal requests to Kos for the recommendation and service of physicians who would live and practise in their cities.[572] If they were successful they were honoured in decrees, copies of which were sent back to Kos.[573] In this way physicians could build a successful reputation.[574]

Koan physicians were honoured by their own cities, as illustrated by the case of Xenotimos, who performed services above and beyond the call of duty during an epidemic in Kos.[575] This inscription also shows that Kos had more than one public physician, presumably practising in different demes.[576] Koan physicians were

---

569 *Aphorisms* 7.87 (App. 4:1, **26**)

570 For example, Alexander took a Koan physician on campaign (Arrian 6.11.1). For a discussion of the role of the physician in the Greek world, see Cohn-Haft (1956), and for the role of Kos in particular, 61-67. For the special difficulties in gaining access to Koan archaeological material, 61-62.

571 Paton and Hicks (1891), and, as examples, Apps 4:2 and 4:3.

572 For example, *IC* I, **7** (App. 4:3), lines 2-5.

573 For example, the decree honouring Hermias, App. 4:3. For other examples, see Cohn-Haft (1956) 66, n.54.

574 Note too the case of the successful Koan physician, Xenophon, personal physician to the emperor Claudius (Tacitus, *Ann.* 12.61, 67), whose name was inscribed at the Kos asklepieion (ἥρωι τῷ τᾶς πατρίδος εὐεργέτᾳ), and who carried out extensive renovations there (Furneaux in Tacitus [1961] 139, note to 12.61).

575 App. 4:2

576 App. 4:2, lines 7-10

also honoured by other Greek cities where they practised, as illustrated by the Koan doctor, Hermias, who was honoured by the people of Knossos for his outstanding help during a revolution in Crete.[577]

These two decrees, although describing entirely different situations - an epidemic and battle wounds - use similar language. Both use the verb διασῴζω to describe the saving action of both physicians: Xenotimos saved many because of his zeal,[578] and worked zealously for the safety of those who were ill;[579] while Hermias saved the wounded from great dangers.[580] However, there the similarity ends. Their "saving" methods are described in different language.

Xenotimos is lauded for his painstaking care (τὰν ἐπιμέλειαν).[581] He brought help (τὰν | βο[άθειαν)[582] and a cure (τὰν ἄ]κ[εσι]ν)[583] to the afflicted (τῶν καμνό[ντων])[584]. The description of the sufferings (τὰς [κ]α[κο]παθίας)[585] of those who were ill is reminiscent of Thucydides' description of the plague at Athens.[586] The decree, which confers a gold crown on Xenotimos[587] for his services during the epidemic, begins and ends by praising the medical skill of Xenotimos,[588] exemplified by his attention to detail,[589] and the zeal

---

577 App. 4:3. Hermias' services were requested by the people of Gortyn, but, during a revolution he worked willingly for all the wounded, even those from allied cities (lines 6-21). See also App. 4:5.

578 τὰ]ς πολί[τ]ας [σπουδ]άζων διέσωσε πολλούς (App. 4:2, lines 14-15)

579 εἰς | τὰν σωτηρίαν τῶν νοσεύντ[ων (App. 4:2, lines 4-5)

580 διέσωσε αὐτο[ὺς ἐγ | μεγάλων κινδύνων (App. 4:3, lines 12-13)

581 App. 4:2, lines 2, 9, 18 and 23

582 App. 4:2, line 12. Cf. App. 4:1, **21**, for the use of this word in the Hippokratic treatise *Decorum*, and above, n.543.

583 App. 4:2, line 13

584 App. 4:2, line 10. Cf. the Hippokratic use of this word above, and its use in the New Testament by the author of *James* (5.15).

585 App. 4:2, line 8

586 And of the sufferings of the Athenians at Syracuse. See above, chapter two.

587 App. 4:2, line 17

588 κατὰ τὰν τέ[χ]ναν τὰν | ἰατρικὰν (App. 4:2, lines 3-4, 24)

589 ἐπιμελείας (App. 4:2, lines 2, 23). This word can be translated either as *painstaking care* or *attention to detail*. The same word is used in the New Testament parable of the Good Samaritan (Luke 10.34). The Samaritan gave medical attention to the wounded man, and then made arrangements for him to be nursed by somebody else until he had recovered. The word ἐπιμελείας does not imply long-term continuous nursing like θεραπεύω (see above, chapter two, for a discussion of this differentiation of meaning in Isocrates' *Aegineticus*). Indeed, Xenotimos would have been too busy to have provided such care in an epidemic. Rather, he must have visited many of the citizens, leaving effective instructions for those who did the nursing.

with which he undertook his task. The verb θεραπεύω, and its cognate forms, does not appear. From this we must assume that Xenotimos did not undertake the nursing of those who were ill, but visited numbers of them frequently and regularly, leaving effective medical instructions for their care.

In contrast, Hermias displayed all his zeal in looking after (ταῖς θεραπείαις) the wounded,[590] and constantly gave assistance without stint to those who called upon him.[591] The scene is somewhat different. In a battle situation those who were wounded were probably placed in locations near to one another. One can then imagine the physician not only issuing orders for their care, and supervising that care, but probably carrying the major burden of that care, providing surgical, bandaging and pharmacological treatment. One assumes from the decree that, when the people of Gortyn applied to Kos for a physician, their city of Gortyn was without any physician at all.[592] Thus Hermias found himself in the unenviable situation of being the only man in a war zone with a reputation for medical expertise.[593] It follows that Hippokratic treatments - surgery, and treatment of wounds - would have been carried out by him alone. Normal arrangements for nursing (family, friends)[594] would not have existed. Family and friends would either have been absent, or busy. It is not surprising then that Hermias' therapeutic method is described by the noun θεραπεία.

4.5. Conclusion

What then does the use of healing language from Kos - in inscriptions, the Hippokratic Corpus, and the fourth mime of Herodas - reveal about the meaning of healing words? Is there a difference in meaning exhibited at Kos, from the healing language used at Epidauros, and at Athens?

The answer of course is negative. In fact, healing terms in literature and in inscriptions is surprisingly uniform in meaning. The

---

590 App. 4:3, line 18

591 ἀπροφα[σίστ]‖ως διετέλει συναντῶν τοῖς παρακαλοῦσι [αὐτό]‖ν (App. 4:3, lines 13-15)

592 App. 4:3, lines 2-3. See also Cohn-Haft (1956) 64.

593 The situation is reminiscent of that in which Patroklos found himself in the *Iliad*, where he answered Eurypylos' pleas for help (11.828-831), attended to his wounds (11.844-848), and stayed to comfort and care for him (15.390-394). See above, chapter one.

594 As implied in Isocrates, *Aegineticus* 25-26.

verb σῴζω continues to mean *rescue and preserve*, as we saw in Homer,[595] and as it was used by Athenian authors.[596] In a healing situation, the verb σῴζω means to rescue and preserve from the danger of imminent death.[597] It is generally used in an aoristic aspectual sense. Patients are "saved" on a particular occasion.[598]

Similarly the verb ἰάομαι is generally used in an aoristic aspectual sense,[599] and so is the verb that is most commonly used in a miraculous situation.[600] It seems to be reserved for a quick-fix, that is complete.

Most common, however, is some form of ὑγιαίνω, signalling a restoration of former health, illustrated in inscriptions from Epidauros,[601] in decrees at Athens,[602] and in the Hippokratic Corpus.[603]

By far the most interesting, however, is the verb θεραπεύω and its cognate forms. It too has an aspectual aspect, but in contrast to both σῴζω and ἰάομαι, the aspect of θεραπεύω is imperfect. This is usually signalled by the use of tense,[604] or, in its cognate forms, by a description of the frequency and duration of the treatments described.[605] It is rarely used in the aorist tense,[606] and if it appears in the perfect tense it usually describes a present state achieved by long and regular therapies.[607] It embraces physical,[608] emotion-

595 *Iliad* 11.828-831

596 See above, chapter three, n.350.

597 See Apps. 4:2 and 4:3.

598 Thus escaping death as the result of a war wound (App. 4:3), or as the result of a virulent disease (App. 4:2).

599 See App. 4:1, **24**, 3.

600 See App. 4:1, **24**, 3; and cf. inscriptional evidence from both Epidauros and Athens.

601 See Apps. 2:1 and 2:2.

602 See Apps. 3:2 and 3:3.

603 See App. 4:1, **7-10**.

604 For example, θεραπεύω in the present tense: App. 4:1, **2**, **5**, **6**, **7**, **11**, **13**, **17**, **19**, **21**.

605 See, for example, App. 4:1, **12**, **13**, **15**.

606 For example, App. 4:1, **8** (*The Art* 5) and App. 4:1, **25** (*The Sacred Disease* 16).

607 As in the inscription of Apellas (Apps. 2:4 and 2:5).

608 *IG* IV² 1, no. 121:20 (App. 2:1, **20**); *IG* IV² 1, no. 122:26 (App. 2:2, **26**); *IG* IV² 1, no. 126 (Apps. 2:4 and 2:5) embraces physical, emotional, and psychological therapy; Isocrates, *Aegineticus* 24-28 (see above, chapter two); and Hippokrates (see App. 4:1).

al,[609] spiritual[610] and psychological[611] therapies, and generally implies a permanent change in a person's way of life.[612]

But is there a change in the use of healing language at the asklepieion at Pergamon in the hellenistic and early Christian eras?

5. *Asklepios at Pergamon*

Asklepios arrived at Pergamon from Epidauros during the fourth century BC,[613] a healing site earlier associated with his father, Apollo.[614] The sanctuary to Asklepios was established in a little valley, outside the city, below the acropolis. According to Wolfgang Radt, the present Director of Excavations there, the sanctuary was continually being expanded from the beginning:

> In the pre-Roman period alone the excavators have distinguished 18 building phases. The presently visible state of the sanctuary, however, belongs chiefly to a large-scale reorganization and extension carried out during the time of the emperor Hadrian (117-138).[615]

It was during this century that the asklepieion reached its zenith and became the focus of pilgrims from all over the world.[616] It boasted a library, a theatre, temples, an underground passage, an elaborate water system, and flushing latrines.[617]

The asklepieion at Pergamon is rich in sources of information for a study of treatment at an asklepieion, and for the use of healing language in the Graeco-Roman world. Inscriptions, literary and medical works survive in a quantity that necessitates selection. Ac-

---

609 Isocrates, *Aegineticus* 11

610 Epicurus (App. 3:5, **1**)

611 *IG* IV^2 1, no. 126 (Apps. 2:4 and 2:5)

612 *IG* IV^2 1, no. 126 (Apps. 2:4 and 2:5); Epicurus (see above, chapter three, and App. 3:5); Hippokrates (App. 4:1)

613 Pausanias 2.26.8 states that Archias, the son of Aristaechmus, brought the god to Pergamon. This gives a probable date of 350 BC for the founding of the sanctuary.

614 It was from the acropolis at Pergamon that Apollo watched battles in the Trojan War (*Iliad* 4.507-508), and it was to this place that he spirited the wounded Aineias for healing (*Iliad* 5.445-448). See above, chapter one.

615 (1984) 28

616 For Pergamon as a major centre, App. 5:6, **9**. For the patronage of Greeks and barbarians alike, App. 5:6, **27**.

617 For diagrams, see Radt (1984) 35, 37.

cordingly, this chapter will focus on a selection of inscriptions,[618] the works of the second century physician Galen,[619] and his patient, the emperor, Marcus Aurelius,[620] and the literary works of the orator Aristides.[621]

5.1. Inscriptions

Inscriptions from Pergamon reveal a similarity of practice at the asklepieion there with other asklepieia in the Greek world. One, thought to be from the second century BC, is a decree concerning the duties of and the benefits to a priest of Asklepios.[622] It complements information from other sources. Here the priesthood is hereditary in perpetuity.[623] The priest is entitled to the right leg and skin of all sacrificial animals, and all the other offerings dedicated on the holy table.[624] He is also entitled to exemption from all the obligations the city is entitled to impose,[625] and to a front seat at all the games.[626] As well, the priest is responsible for good conduct within the sanctuary,[627] and has power over the temple servants.[628] These regulations were to be enforced for all time to come (εἰς ἅπαντα τὸν χρόνον).[629]

Another inscription from Pergamon[630] details the ritual required at the temple of Asklepios. The inscription mentions a period of ten days, bathing, purification, and incubation. Pure white sacrificial victims are to be garlanded with olive shoots, and

618 Apps. 5:1, 5:2, and 5:3
619 App. 5:5
620 App. 5:7
621 App. 5:6
622 App. 5:3
623 Lines 7-11, App. 5:3. Cf. Aleshire (1989) 72-86 concerning the priesthood of the asklepieion at Athens.
624 Cf. Aristophanes *Ploutos* , 676-678; Herodas 4.88-90; and App. 3:1, **12**
625 Cf. the struggle of Aristides to be exempt from such obligations (*Or.* 50.63-104).
626 Cf. *IG* II², no. 5045 [time of Hadrian]: Ἱερέως | Ἀσκληπιοῦ | Π[αί]ω(ν)ος ? [inscribed on front seat in the theatre of Dionysus at Athens].
627 Cf. the inscriptions from the asklepieion at Athens (App. 3:2). The same language is used: ἐπιμελεῖσθαι δὲ καὶ τῆς εὐκοσμίας τῆς κατὰ τὸ ἱερ[ὸν | πάσης τὸν ἱερέ[α] ὡς ἂν αὐτῶι δοκῆ[ι | καλῶς ἔχειν καὶ ὁσίως (lines 24-26).
628 Here: τῶν ἱερῶν παίδων (line 26).
629 App. 5:3, lines 19 and 43
630 App. 5:2

the suppliant[631] is to wear neither seal-ring nor belt, but to enter barefoot.

A third inscription is a hymn of praise to Asklepios.[632] It is interesting for its use of the verb σῴζω in a nautical context,[633] and for its similarity with the gospel stories of the calming of the storm.[634] In it Asklepios is addressed as Saviour (σωτήρ), and his attendance upon request, his protection at sea, his calming of the winds and power over the waves are praised. The parallels with the nature and attributes of the New Testament Jesus are striking.[635]

As at Athens and Kos, physicians were also among those who patronised the asklepieion at Pergamon, and prayed to the healing god Asklepios. The most notable at this time was the great Galen himself.

5.2. Galen

Galen was born in Pergamon around the year AD 130, during the reign of the emperor Hadrian, and died at the end of the century in the time of Septimius Severus.[636] His early education at Pergamon was at a time when the library there was second only to that of Alexandria, and when the asklepieion was flourishing. It was a time (in that area) of relative peace and order, where paganism was the norm, and the ideals of classical Greece were valued.

At the age of seventeen, after studying philosophy, Galen began medical studies, studies which took him from Pergamon to Smyrna, Korinth, Alexandria, and Rome.[637] He became highly respected as a physician, and, at Rome, numbered the Roman emperor Marcus Aurelius and his son Commodus amongst his patients.[638]

Galen's early study of philosophy had instilled in him a quest for "truth and knowledge".[639] As a result his pursuit of philosophical

---

631 I assume that the person specified is a suppliant, rather than a priest.

632 App. 5:1. Herzog attributes this hymn to the orator Aristides, however this is doubted by Behr in Aristides (1973) xvi, n. 'b'.

633 App. 5:1, line 13; and cf. chapter three, n.350.

634 Mt 8.23-27. Cf. Mk 4.35-41; Lk 8.22-25

635 ibid.

636 For a brief account of Galen's life and work, see the introduction by Brock to Galen (1979) xvif.; and for a discussion of the problems pertaining to his biography, Temkin (1973) 3-9.

637 This was in answer to a dream sent to his father by Asklepios. For a discussion of this and his early medical training, see Smith (1979) 62-77.

638 Brock in Galen (1979) xvii-xviii

639 *De methodo medendi* 7.1

truth and his vision of medical knowledge were closely intertwined in his literary works. It was in the Hippokratic writings that Galen found his ideal.[640] Thus, in his medical practice and in his literary works Galen promoted his understanding of Hippokratic medicine.[641] This understanding included severe criticism of his fellow physicians.[642] His literary output ensured that he not only influenced contemporary thought, but also influenced subsequent medical thought,[643] an influence that is still discernible today.[644]

It is obvious from Galen's writings that he both esteemed and sought the healing aid of the god Asklepios. He mentions the construction of the temple of Zeus Asklepios,[645] and how it was a common practice for people in their everyday-life to swear by the name of "Asklepios in Pergamon".[646] Indeed he even prayed to the god on behalf of the emperor,[647] and himself. He declared himself a servant (θεραπευτήν) of Asklepios because Asklepios had saved (διέσωσε) him from the deadly condition of an abscess. Galen reports his declaration of servitude in the imperfect tense (ἀπέφαινον), signalling that his service to Asklepios was continuous.[648]

Galen also used his association with Asklepios to lend credibility to the medical successes he claimed as his own. For example, he states that he had made healthy (ὑγιεινοὺς ἀπεδείξαμεν) men who had been ill for many years by correcting the disproportion of their emotions, a practice advocated by Asklepios. He then lists the composition of odes, comical mimes, and songs, as well as the pursuit of hunting, horse riding and exercising in arms, as among the god's successful prescriptions, describing the precise instructions

---

640 Temkin (1991) 47-50. For a discussion of Galen's interpretation of Hippokratic writings see Smith (1979), especially 72-74, 83.

641 This was largely unquestioned in antiquity. It was not until the time of Paracelsus (1493-1541), that Galen's understanding of the ideas of Hippokrates was questioned. For a discussion, see Smith (1979) 13-18, 72-74, 83; and Temkin (1991) 46-50.

642 For example, a scathing attack on Asclepiades (App. 5:5, **9** and **10**).

643 Temkin (1973) 1-133; Smith (1979) 13-44

644 Temkin (1973) 135f.

645 App. 5:5, **1**

646 App. 5:5, **2**

647 App. 5:5, **3**

648 App. 5:5, **4**. In contradiction to this, Smith (1979) 63, states that Galen, although called by the god, was not in service to him. Certainly Galen's medicine seems secular, but then many of the prescriptions of the god are also secular in nature (for example those involving moderate exercise and a restrained diet).

issued by Asklepios in relation to the kind of hunting, the type of armour, and the duration and difficulty of the exercise to be undertaken.[649] Another source, the orator Aelius Aristides, attests to and thus corroborates very specific directions like these.[650]

Galen also notes the remarkable obedience with which the patients at the asklepieion followed bizarre directions of the god simply because they believed that the result would be of benefit to them, whereas they refused to follow the same instructions from physicians.[651] He thus acknowledges the importance of positive thinking in the therapeutic process. He cites an instruction given by the god, which forbade the patient to drink for fifteen days - a rather difficult (and dangerous?) prescription to follow. Those undergoing this long and arduous treatment are denoted τοὺς θεραπευομένους.

Another extended treatment for an unnamed disease, presumably a skin condition of some sort, advocated by the god in a dream, and described by Galen, concerned the drinking of a drug and anointment of the body every day. Galen notes that the

> disease after a few days turned into leprosy (εἰς λέπραν); and this disease, in turn, was cured (ἐθεραπεύθη) by the drugs which the god commanded.[652]

Again θεραπεύω refers to the outcome of extended treatment.[653] Thus Galen's use of healing language in association with the asklepieion at Pergamon in the second century AD reflects earlier healing language at other asklepieia. He addresses the god as Παιών,[654] describes himself as a servant of the god with a cognate form of the verb θεραπεύω (θεραπευτήν),[655] and chooses the verb σῴζω to describe his salvation from a life-threatening abscess.[656] He describes those undergoing extended treatment as τοὺς θεραπευομένους,[657] and cures brought about by extended treatment with

649 App. 5:5, **6**
650 App. 5:6, **14**
651 App. 5:5, **7**
652 App. 5:5, **8**
653 Galen's use of θεραπεύω reflects its use by the Hippokratic authors (see chapter four, and App. 4:1), and the contemporary inscription *IG* IV^2 1, no. 126 (App. 2:4) from Epidauros.
654 Reflecting the language at Epidauros, Athens and Kos. See App. 5:5, **3**.
655 App. 5:5, **4**
656 ibid. This use of σῴζω also conforms to the pattern of its usage in other centres: it is used here of an escape from a life-threatening disease on a particular occasion.
657 App. 5:5, **7**

the verb θεραπεύω,[658] but reserves the verb ἰάομαι to describe the miraculous healing of a man who had swelled so excessively it was impossible for him to move himself (ἀλλὰ τοῦτον μὲν ὁ Ἀσκληπιὸς ἰάσατο).[659] The restoration of health he describes with ὑγιεινός.[660]

But is this use of healing language consistent with his other works that do not refer to treatment at the asklepieion? In his treatise *On the natural faculties*, a treatise called by one of its translators the crystallisation of Galenic thought,[661] Galen uses the verb θεραπεύω three times in a critical context.[662] In a vitriolic attack on the opinions of the physician Asklepiades, Galen asks how Asklepiades' opinions profited his treatment (εἰς τὰς θεραπείας), and answers that he was unable to treat (δύνασθαι θεραπεῦσαι) various diseases.[663] After noting that Asklepiades must be "either mad, or entirely unacquainted with practical medicine"[664] Galen details his own successful treatment of jaundice. He notes that after treating the liver condition (μετὰ τὸ θεραπεῦσαι) he has then removed the disease (ἀπηλλάξαμεν τοῦ παθήματος) by a single purgation.[665] This use of the verb makes it clear that θεραπεύω denotes preliminary treatment which forms the necessary basis for further treatment that can lead to a cure.

Galen's final use of this verb occurs in a passage criticising the ideas of the Erasistrateans, where he stresses the importance of understanding the causes of bodily function, in this case digestion. For, he says, if we know the cause, we should be able to treat the failures of function (τὰ σφάλματα θεραπεύσαιμεν).[666]

Here the verb θεραπεύω occurs in the optative aorist in the apodosis of a conditional clause which allows a degree of doubt (however small) as to the outcome of a hypothetical situation. That is, the treatment should be successful, but may not be (depending on the correct diagnosis of the cause of the problem). Thus Galen is consistent in his use of θεραπεύω to describe medical treatment, usually of an extended nature, that should be successful (but may not be successful in some circumstances). In this his use of θεραπεύω

658 App. 5:5, **8**
659 App. 5:5, **5**
660 App. 5:5, **6**
661 Brock in Galen (1979) xxv, says of this work: "If Galen be looked on as a crystallisation of Greek medicine, then this book may be looked on as a crystallisation of Galen".
662 App. 5:5, **9**, **10** and **11**
663 App. 5:5, **9**
664 App. 5:5, **10**
665 ibid.
666 App. 5:5, **11**

reflects common usage, and lends credence to Galen's assertion that, since he was convinced that the chief merit of language was clarity, so, rather than using unfamiliar terms he chose to employ in his works terms that were in common use at that time.[667]

As Galen was unquestionably the most famous physician at Pergamon,[668] so his most famous patient was the Roman emperor, Marcus Aurelius. In a study of the use of healing language in the Graeco-Roman world it is instructive to look at the writing of this articulate man to see how a Roman mind understood and used the verb θεραπεύω at that time.

5.3. Marcus Aurelius

Marcus Aurelius Antoninus (AD 121-180), was born at Rome, educated and adopted by his guardian and uncle, the Emperor T. Antoninus Pius. Herodes Atticus and M. Cornelius Fronto were among his tutors. He was converted to Stoicism by Diognetus, and strongly influenced by Epictetus.[669] His writings "to himself" reveal a man of sincerity and dignity.

Marcus Aurelius uses the verb θεραπεύω six times in his writings, meaning *to give service* (2.13), *to give treatment* (3.13; 6.55), *to cure*

---

667 *On the natural faculties*, 1.1. Galen's assertion, and his usage, rather detracts from the thesis of Hobart (1882) 1, that the New Testament author known as Luke was a physician, because he used the technical and medical language favoured by Galen.

668 Another notable physician associated with the asklepieion at Pergamon was Rufus of Ephesus, who practised in the first century AD. In a medical work, taken from Rufus (see App. 5:4) which refers to a cure (ἴαμα) for epilepsy prescribed at the asklepieion, the verb θεραπεύω is used in the reported conversation of a patient with Asklepios (cf. the reported conversations between patient and god at Epidauros [chapter two, and Apps 2:1, 2:2, 2:3, 2:4]; and between patient and god at Athens [App. 3:4]). In this conversation Asklepios offers the patient an alternative sickness to that of epilepsy, on the grounds that "it would be easier and . . . would cure him more plainly than anything else (ἄλλου σαφέστερον θεραπεύσειν)". The patient agreed, as long as the disease was no worse than his present condition. Freed from epilepsy, he was attacked thereafter by a quartan fever. Thus θεραπεύω in this context does not refer to a complete return to health, but long-term future treatment. In this way Rufus too assumes the continuous aspect of this verb in a healing context. (For a discussion of the work and importance of Rufus of Ephesus see Smith [1979] 240-246.)

669 For a brief outline of his life see Haines in Marcus Aurelius (1979) xi-xv.

(5.28; 12.16), and *to fulfil one's duty* (6.12).[670] The first occurs in a prescription for human contentment:

> [a man] needs but to associate himself with the divine 'genius' in his bosom, and to serve it truly (γνησίως θεραπεύειν). And service (θεραπεία) of it is to keep it pure from passion and aimlessness and discontent with anything that proceeds from Gods or men.[671]

Here, the verb θεραπεύω demands an introspection and a knowledge of self (and god), and a commitment to a life of action governed by that knowledge. It is thus a call to a way of living. The concept of duty is implicit in this call to service. At another place Marcus cites as an example of fulfilling one's duty the due service (ἐθεράπευες) one should give to one's stepmother, even if one's natural mother were alive.[672]

The other four instances of the verb θεραπεύω occur in a more overtly medical context, although the ideas of service and duty still appear. In a medical simile comparing the behaviour of physicians with other men, Marcus advises how to carry out any human duty well, no matter how trivial.[673] On another occasion Marcus posits the question:

> If the sailors spoke ill of a steersman or the sick of a physician, what else would they have in mind but how the man should best effect the safety (τὸ σωτήριον) of the crew or the health of his patients (τὸ τοῖς θεραπευομένοις ὑγιεινόν)?[674]

Here it is quite obvious that θεραπεύω stands for *those whom the doctor was treating at that time*. Again the context includes the notion of doing all in one's power to bring about the best possible result. Thus, so far, the verb θεραπεύω includes the notions of giving service, of living life in the best possible way, and of always trying to achieve a beneficial outcome in whatever one undertakes. The continuous aspect of the verb is self-evident.

Marcus chooses θεραπεύω two more times, and on both occasions the verb means *cure*. However the method on both occasions is not medical, but didactic in nature.[675] In both passages an example of an 'illness' is given. In the first, the 'illnesses' from which the patient suffers are the personal problems of smelly armpits and

---

670 App. 5:7, **1-6**
671 App. 5:7, **1**
672 App. 5:7, **4**
673 App. 5:7, **2**
674 App. 5:7, **5**
675 App. 5:7, **3** and **6**

foul breath. Marcus denies the productivity of anger in such a case, but advises talking with the person concerned (καὶ σὺ λόγον ἔχεις):

> By a rational attitude (λογικῇ), then, in thyself evoke a rational attitude in him, enlighten him, admonish him. If he listen, thou shalt cure him (θεραπεύσεις), and have no need of anger.[676]

Thus it is that the λόγος is the healing agent, and this λόγος requires an active response in the listener. It is this active response to the λόγος that effects the 'cure'.[677] There is then an element of persuasion implicit in the verb θεραπεύω when it occurs in a teaching context. The illness cited is a curious example, and one that appears in Galen's work, referring to an actual person, a physician who suffered from this problem, and on that account was failing to attract patients.[678] One wonders whether this was a common problem, or whether the association between Marcus Aurelius and Galen prompted philosophical discussion between them on such issues.

Marcus also uses the verb θεραπεύω in the context of treating those who do wrong (τὸν φαῦλον ἁμαρτάνειν). For, he says, such actions stem from a certain sort of disposition. His advice:

> If then it chafes thee, cure the disposition (εἰ οὖν γοργὸς εἶ, ταύτην θεράπευσον).[679]

---

676 App. 5:7, **3**

677 Cf. Epicurus, App. 3:5, **1**

678 Galen, *Comm.* 4.9, *Epid.* 6 [17.B.151]: ἕτερον δ' ἰατρὸν ἐπὶ τῆς ἡμετέρας Ἀσίας οἶδα δυσώδεις ἔχοντα τὰς μάλας ὡς διὰ τοῦτο μὴ φέρειν αὐτοῦ τὴν εἴσοδον ἄνθρωπον νοσοῦντα μηδένα καθάριον. ἐχρῆν οὖν αὐτὸν ἑαυτοῦ πρῶτον ἰᾶσθαι τὸ σύμπτωμα καὶ οὕτως ἐπιχειρεῖν ἑτέρους θεραπεύειν. This is a notable example for Galen uses ἰᾶσθαι to mean *heal/ cure*, in contrast to θεραπεύειν, which seems in this context to mean *treat medically* rather than *cure*. θεραπεύειν is also linked with the verb ἐπιχειρεῖν, a verb which means *to endeavour to..., to make an attempt...* thus involving the idea of a process which requires effort, effort which may be either successful or unsuccessful in its outcome. This particular passage is cited by Hobart (1882) 1, to support his theory that the author of the third gospel was a physician, but, as we can see here, the same illustration occurs in the writings of Marcus Aurelius, and the same language is used.

679 App. 5:7, **6.** It is interesting that the verb is here used in the aorist imperative (cf. Lk 4.23), implying a completed action (a change in attitude?). Again the λόγος is the healing agent, and the clientele are those who ἁμαρτάνειν.

Obviously this is not a quick process, but one that requires instruction, and a response to a call to a different way of living.[680] It is again the λόγος that is the healing agent.

Thus the work of Marcus Aurelius illustrates several meanings of the verb θεραπεύω that are reflected in contemporary and earlier thought, including the ideas of giving service,[681] fulfilling one's duty,[682] providing medical treatment,[683] and curing through teaching.[684] In all instances the idea of a continuing process is explicit. This long-term continuous aspect of θεραπεία is also evident where Marcus acknowledges his debt to Rusticus, through whom he became

> aware of the fact that I needed amendment and training for my character (τὸ λαβεῖν φαντασίαν τοῦ χρῄζειν διορθώσεως καὶ θεραπείας τοῦ ἤθους·).[685]

Marcus also uses other terms found in the language of healing: he chooses the verb ὑγιαίνω when he admits to being cured of his amatory passions (ἀλλὰ καὶ ὕστερον ἐν ἐρωτικοῖς πάθεσι γενόμενον ὑγιᾶναι).[686] When he talks of taking watchful care over himself he chooses ἐπιμέλεια (πρὸς ἐπιμέλειαν ἐμαυτοῦ).[687] He also acknowledges the significance of dreams.[688] Thus the usage of healing terms in the writings of Marcus Aurelius reflects the healing language of his time. And like the inscription from Epidauros of the cure of Marcus Julius Apellas, the verb θεραπεύω includes a

680 The aorist active imperative singular form of θεραπεύω occurs only once in the New Testament, at Luke 4.23, in Jesus' curious saying "Ἰατρέ, θεράπευσον σεαυτόν·". It is in an attempt to explain the meaning of this saying that Hobart (1882) 1, cites Galen (see above, n.678). Hobart wanted to prove that 'Luke' was a physician, by showing this to be a medical proverb. The parallel in the work of Marcus Aurelius I find more telling, although Marcus' work would not have supported Hobart's thesis.

681 For example, the Homeric θεράπων (see chapter one).

682 Isocrates, *Aegineticus* (see chapter three).

683 Hippokrates (App. 4:1, **3**, **5**, **8**, **9**, **10**, **16**, **17**); and Isocrates, *Aegineticus* (see chapter three).

684 Epicurus (App. 3:1, **1**)

685 App. 5:7, **8**

686 App. 5:7, **10**

687 App. 5:7, **9**. Cf. inscriptional use of this word at Athens (chapter three, and App. 3:2) meaning *care of property, meticulous attention to detail*, and *responsibility for public order*.

688 App. 5:7, **11**

psychological element, and requires a degree of introspection on the part of the patient.[689]

This introspection is also exhibited in the works of his contemporary, the orator Aelius Aristides.

5.4. Aelius Aristides

Publius Aelius Aristides was born in Mysia in AD 117. His father was a citizen of Smyrna, a wealthy landholder, and a priest of the Temple of Zeus Olympius, who, in AD 123 was given Roman citizenship by the emperor Hadrian. He was thus in a position to give his son the finest education available. Aristides studied under Alexander of Cotiaeum (who was later to be tutor to Marcus Aurelius) and other leading sophists in Smyrna, Pergamon and Athens. He chose to become an orator and travelled extensively in the eastern Mediterranean, visiting Kos, Knidos, Rhodes, Alexandria and Egypt, before setting out to try his art in Rome.[690] On the journey he became so ill that he was unable to practise his art and returned home, still ailing, where he received his first revelation from Asklepios. This revelation, and his subsequent relationship with Asklepios, were to have a permanent effect on his life and thought.

Aristides spent two years at the asklepieion at Pergamon as an incubant,[691] a time when he was utterly immersed in contemplating his own health and spiritual life. He is an invaluable source for a study of the Graeco-Roman understanding of the history of Asklepios and his family and their place and role in the universe, of healing practices at the asklepieion, of the relationship between the healing god and his patients, and for a study of healing language.

According to Aristides the sons of Asklepios, Podaleirios and Machaon, played their part in history, healing the ills of cities,[692] saving their subjects,[693] and even causing the fall of Troy.[694] In their involvement in history the sons of Asklepios show similarities with the Old Testament god Yahweh. However, unlike the

---

689 *IG* IV^2 1, no. 126 (App. 2:4)

690 For a brief outline of his life and education see Behr in Aelius Aristides (1973) vii-xiii.

691 AD 145-147

692 App. 5:6, **2**

693 ibid.

694 App. 5:6, **3**

Old Testament god, who showed divine favour to his chosen people of Israel, the healing Asklepiads were available to all, both Greek and barbarian.[695] Indeed their deified father, Asklepios, had a definite role and function within Aristides' cosmos. This role shows definite affinities with the place and role of the New Testament Jesus. For Asklepios himself, and his father Apollo, like the Old Testament Yahweh, and the New Testament Jesus, formed part of a trinity. Asklepios was

> he who saves that which already exists and that which is in a state of becoming . . . the son of Apollo, and the third from Zeus . . . the father and maker of everything.[696]

Indeed, Asklepios having all powers (πάσας δὲ ἔχων ὁ θεὸς τὰς δυνάμεις) had chosen to be men's benefactor in every respect, establishing healing places (ἰατρεῖα) in their midst, where he ever sought to bring cheer to whosoever was in need.[697] Here, he raised (ἀναστῆναι) people from the dead,[698] restored (γενέσθαι σφίσι) the damaged limbs of men and women,[699] and delivered innumerable people from sufferings and distresses.[700] He even stretched forth his hand (ὁ θεὸς χεῖρα ὤρεξεν) to those at sea in the midst of a storm,[701] and advised people on how to settle their affairs.[702] Aristides deems Asklepios the gentlest and most manloving of the gods (ὁ δὲ θεὸς καὶ θεῶν ὁ πραότατός τε καὶ φιλανθρωπότατος),[703] as the great miracle-worker who does everything for the salvation of men (οὕτω τοῦ μεγάλου θαυματοποιοῦ καὶ πάντα ἐπὶ σωτηρίᾳ πράττοντος ἀνθρώπων).[704] It is no wonder that early Christian apologists thought of Asklepios as a threat to the infant church,[705] and that the New Testament author of *Revelation* alluded to Pergamon as "the seat of Satan".[706]

---

695 App. 5:6, **4**, and App. 5:6, **27**. Cf. also the patrons at Epidauros (chapter two), and Athens (App. 3:4).

696 App. 5:6, **10**. Cf. the language of the creeds of the early Christians in Bettenson (1963) 33-37.

697 App. 5:6, **11**. Cf. Mt 11.5; Lk 7.18-35

698 App. 5:6, **12**. Cf. Jn 11.1-57

699 App. 5:6, **13**. Cf. Mt 8.5-13; Mk 3.1-6; Lk 5.17-26; Jn 5.1-15

700 ibid. Cf. the general healing episodes in the New Testament, for example, Mt 4.24; Lk 6.17-19; and Jn 6.2.

701 App. 5:6, **15**. Cf. Mt 14.31: Ἰησοῦς ἐκτείνας τὴν χεῖρα

702 ibid. Cf. Mt 5-7

703 App. 5:6, **18**

704 App. 5:6, **20**

705 Justin, *Apologia* 54.10, 22.6; *Dialogus* 69.3; Origen, *Contra Celsum* 3.25

706 Revelation 2.13

Aristides reports extensively on healing practices prescribed by Asklepios. These include the taking of drugs, cold ablutions in rivers and the sea, extensive exercise, purgings, fasting, and the instruction to continue speaking and writing. Aristides chooses the verb ἰάομαι (ἰώμενος) and its cognate form (τοῖς ἰάμασι) to describe these cures, and θεραπεύω to summarise the various treatments (θεραπευθεῖσιν) in which the patients participated.[707]

Dreams also form a central part of the healing experience, as at other asklepieia in the Greek world.[708] Accounts of dream experiences not only describe healing prescriptions and practices, and explain miraculous cures, they are also a strong force motivating action. Thus Aristides can explain his action and motivation to his audience:

> 'Listen friends, a dream came to me, a vision sent from the gods,' said the dream itself . . . . May the dream then become waking reality, and the actual performance be like the prediction.[709]

Indeed dreams are a means of salvation for mankind (ῆ τὸ θεοὺς ἀνθρώπων κήδεσθαι ποιεῖ καὶ δι' ὀνειράτων ἀνθρώπους σῴζεσθαι;).[710] They tell patients what they must do to be saved (σωθῆναι).[711] Similarly dreams play an important part in salvific action in both the Old and New Testaments.[712]

Aristides' use of language is elegant and precise, so is particularly instructive for the study of the Greek language of healing.[713] What does his use of language reveal about the meaning of healing words like θεραπεύω, ἰάομαι, ὑγιής and σῴζω?

---

707 App. 5:6, **14**. Edelstein (1945) translates this occurrence of θεραπεύω as "healed", where a much better translation would be "treatments".

708 Dreams were significant as a means of communication between the gods and men. For the ideas of Marcus Aurelius on the significance of dreams, see App. 5:7, **11**.

709 App. 5:6, **1**

710 App. 5:6, **28**

711 ibid.

712 For example, in the Old Testament, the story of Joseph as told in Genesis 37-50; and in the New Testament, Mt 2.13-15, where Joseph is told in a dream how to save the infant Jesus from Herod. Cf. also God's visit to Solomon in a dream, and their conversation (1 Kings 3.3-14) and the angel's command to Joseph in a dream to marry Mary (Mt 1.20-25).

713 Behr in Aelius Aristides, (1973) xiv, says that he was "justly famous for the precision of his style. His efforts to conform to the highest canons of Atticism earned him the title 'divine' among posterity and commended him as a model to the theorists on composition." The influence of Plato, Demosthenes, and Isocrates is obvious in his work.

5.4.1. σῴζω

The verb σῴζω is consistently used meaning *to rescue or preserve from danger*. The original Asklepiads saved their subjects from both bodily ailments and political ills (ἀπ' ἀμφοῖν σῴζοντες τοὺς ὑπηκόους).[714] Asklepios is denoted as the saviour (σωτήρ) of the whole universe, as the one who saves that which already exists and that which is in a state of becoming (σῴζων τά τε ὄντα ἀεὶ καὶ τὰ γιγνόμενα).[715] It is in a nautical metaphor that the notion of safety inherent in the verb σῴζω and its cognate forms is most clearly expressed:

> Therefore no one would say that these regions have no harbor, but most correctly and justly is it said that this is the most secure and steadfast of all ports, receiving the greatest number of people and affording the most in tranquillity. Here, the stern-cable of salvation for all is anchored in Asklepios (οὐκοῦν οὐδὲ ἀλίμενα φῆσαι τις ἂν εἶναι τὰ τῆδε, ἀλλ' ἐκεῖνο ὀρθότατον καὶ δικαιότατον λέγειν, ὡς ἄρα οὗτος λιμένων ἁπάντων ὀχυρώτατος καὶ βεβαιότατος καὶ πλείστους δεχόμενος καὶ γαλήνῃ πλεῖστον προέχων, ἐν ᾧ πᾶσιν ἐξ 'Ασκληπιοῦ τὰ ἐπίγυια τῆς σωτηρίας ἤρτηται).[716]

Asklepios is the god who has no leisure to do anything except to save men (ἐκεῖνος ἄγει σχολὴν ἄλλο τι πράττειν ἢ σῴζειν ἀνθρώπους).[717] He is a great miracle-worker who does everything for the salvation of men (οὕτω τοῦ μεγάλου θαυματοποιοῦ καὶ πάντα ἐπὶ σωτηρίᾳ πράττοντος ἀνθρώπων).[718] The means of gaining this salvation is communicated through dreams.[719]

5.4.2. ὑγιής

Prayer is an important part of healing ritual in the life of Aristides. When he prays for health he chooses a cognate form of the verb ὑγιαίνω:

---

714 App. 5:6, **2**

715 App. 5:6, **10**. Here the influence of Platonic terminology is clearly evident, as it is in Jn 1.

716 App. 5:6, **9**. Cf. the verb σῴζω in a nautical context above, 85, and chapter three, n.350. Cf. Mt 8.23-27

717 App. 5:6, **19**

718 App. 5:6, **20**

719 App. 5:6, **28**. Cf. above, n.712

> . . . relieve me of my disease and grant me as much health as is necessary in order that the body may obey that which the soul wishes . . . (τῆς τε νόσου παύετε καὶ διδοίητε ὑγιείας τε ὅσον οἷς ἡ ψυχὴ βούλεται τὸ σῶμα ὑπακούειν).[720]

Indeed health (τῇ ὑγιείᾳ χρώμενος) is the means by which a remedy is found for all pains and troubles,[721] and, while the art of doctors exists for no other purpose than to cure (ποιεῖν ὑγιεῖς), many of the sick are cured without doctors and art (πολλοὶ τῶν καμνόντων ὑγιεῖς γίγνονται χωρὶς ἰατρῶν καὶ τέχνης).[722] Thus ὑγιής continues to refer to a restoration to a healthy state by human and divine means.[723]

5.4.3. ἰάομαι

In a healing context, the verb ἰάομαι occurs when describing the successful intervention of the god, or other members of his family, in the lives of humans. When the sons of Asklepios, Podaleirios and Machaon, dwelt among men they went about healing (ἰώμενοι) the ills of cities,[724] and healed (ἰάσαντο) Philoktetes, even though his ailment was thought to be incurable (ἀνίατον).[725] Similarly they cured (ἰάσαντο), and made accessible to all, the island of Kos.[726] Places of healing (ἰατρεῖα)[727] were established, where the healing (ἰώμενος) god[728] prescribed his cures (τοῖς ἰάμασι).[729] Many were cured (ἰάθησαν) by the water from the sacred well at the asklepieion at Pergamon.[730] Indeed, in contrast to Asklepios, physicians were many times not only unable to cure (ἰάσασθαι) as the god could, but were even unable to identify Aristides' complaints![731]

Aristides also uses the verb ἰάομαι in a political context to denote the healing that unification, brought about by a common purpose,

---

720 App. 5:6, **6**
721 App. 5:6, **11**
722 App. 5:6, **26**
723 Cf. the inscriptions at Epidauros (chapter two, and Apps 2:1, 2:2, 2:4), Athens (App. 3:2), and the Hippokratic writings (chapter four, and App. 4:1).
724 App. 5:6, **2**
725 App. 5:6, **3**
726 App. 5:6, **4**. Cf. Septuagint, App. 6:1, **12**
727 App. 5:6, **11**
728 App. 5:6, **14**. Cf. Septuagint, App. 6:1, **2**, **26**, **28**
729 App. 5:6, **14**
730 App. 5:6, **21**. Cf. Septuagint, App. 6:1, **13**
731 App. 5:6, **27**

can bring;[732] and in a military context to denote Pharnabazus' attempt to retrieve a military situation.[733]

Does Aristides use the verb θεραπεύω in a different context?

5.4.4. θεραπεύω

We have already seen how Aristides sums up the various treatments prescribed by Asklepios with the verb θεραπεύω.[734] He also describes himself as one of the servants of Asklepios (τοῖς τούτου θεράπουσιν).[735] Otherwise the verb is noticeably absent from literature concerning Asklepios.[736] Perhaps this should not be surprising. We have already seen how the verb was absent from the literature surrounding the asklepieion at Athens. So in what context does Aristides choose to use the verb θεραπεύω?

A survey of two orations[737] reveals that Aristides consistently uses the verb to denote a form of *service*. The cognate form θεραπεία occurs referring to the service of the body,[738] and, in the same passage, the verb is used to describe how medicine and gymnastics, justice and legislation "ever serve aiming at the best (καὶ ἀεὶ πρὸς τὸ βέλτιστον θεραπευουσῶν)" for the body and soul of humankind. The verb θεραπεύω also includes the idea of *nurture*. For, he says, as to nurture (θεραπεῦσαι) belongs to art, so art is the maid (θεραπαίνης) to nature (φύσις).[739] Conversely, the negated form of θεραπεύω (ἀθεραπευσίαν) means *neglect*.[740]

The verb also includes the idea of *medical treatment*, a meaning with which we are already familiar. Medical treatment is, of course, a form of service. Aristides differentiates between human and divine healing thus:

> For many of the sick become well, some by human art, some by a divine portion. Those by human art, being treated by physicians; those by a divine portion, desire leads to what will profit them (πολλοὶ γὰρ καὶ τῶν καμνόντων ὑγιεῖς γίγνονται οἱ μὲν ἀνθρωπίνῃ

---

732 App. 5:6, **44**: ἰάθη; and **45**: ἰάσατο

733 App. 5:6, **43**: ἰωμένου

734 See above, n.707, and App. 5:6, **14**: θεραπευθεῖσιν, in a passage which describes Asklepios as ἰώμενος, and his cures as τοῖς ἰάμασι.

735 App. 5:6, **18**

736 The literature surveyed is that included in Edelstein (1945) vol. 1.

737 *Or.* 1 and 2. See App. 5:6, **24-47**

738 App. 5:6, **24**

739 App. 5:6, **29**

740 App. 5:6, **39**

(τέχνῃ), οἱ δὲ θείᾳ μοίρᾳ. ὅσοι μὲν οὖν ἀνθρωπίνῃ τέχνῃ, ὑπὸ ἰατρῶν θεραπευόμενοι, ὅσοι δὲ θείᾳ μοίρᾳ, ἐπιθυμία αὐτοὺς ἄγει ἐπὶ τὸ ὀνῆσον·).[741]

Again, those who become well are ὑγιεῖς γίγνονται, either by divine or human means.[742] Those undergoing human treatment are designated θεραπευόμενοι, while for those who become well by divine means it is desire (ἐπιθυμία) that is the motivating force. Aristides further elaborates on human medical treatment in a passage commenting on the art of the physician who is called upon to treat patients whom he has never seen before:

> Indeed, a doctor's art commands him to treat (θεραπεύειν) whatever chance person has requested his aid, even if someone has just now come from the ends of the earth. What of necessity is left, other than conjecture? If he will not know all men and will treat (θεραπεύσει) whoever approaches him, . . . [743]

Here, the medical treatment is obviously one of trial and error.

Aristides also advocates the addition of oratory to a physician's medical art, as a preliminary treatment (προθεραπεύειν), before touching the instruments of medicine. Indeed, he deems oratory the "wisest of drugs (τῷ σοφωτάτῳ τῶν φαρμάκων)."[744]

Here it is the power to persuade that is the healing agent.[745] Thus θεραπεύω in a 'teaching' context implies the ability to have an effect on the hearer that will, in turn, produce a voluntary change in the hearer's attitude and/or life-style.

The idea of *service* in the verb θεραπεύω and its cognate forms frequently appears in a discussion about the role of oratory in serving the will of the people in Aristides' second oration.[746] Aristides asks the question:

---

741 App. 5:6, **25**. My translation differs slightly from the Loeb translation here. I think the present passive participle θεραπευόμενοι requires a present tense translation, rather than the past and completed "cured" of the Loeb translation.

742 Cf. The inscriptions from the asklepieion at Epidauros, and the writings of the Hippokratic Corpus.

743 App. 5:6, **31**

744 App. 5:6, **40**. Cf. Aeschylus, *Prometheus* 379-380; Plato, *Critias* 106B; Seneca, *Epistles* 75; Tertullian, *Pall.* 6

745 Cf. the λόγος of the philosopher (Epicurus, App. 3:5, **1**), and of the rational man (Marcus Aurelius, App. 5:8, **3**).

746 Perhaps this is not surprising in *Or.* 2 (*To Plato: In defence of oratory*). See App. 5:6, **32-38**.

> What method can be contrived to know and continuously serve (θεραπεῦσαι διὰ τέλους) the will of the people?[747]

He asserts that orators do not serve pleasures (ἡδονὰς θεραπεύουσιν), but chastise desires (ἐπιθυμίας σωφρονίζουσιν),[748] and, while he denotes flatterers as servants (θεραπευταί) of tyrants, in the same passage he also says of tyrants that it is impossible to get any moderate treatment from them, to say nothing of service beyond their duty (τῆς ὑπὲρ τὸ προσῆκον θεραπείας).[749] Service beyond one's duty is a meaning of θεραπεύω we have already encountered in the writings of Marcus Aurelius.[750]

The art of oratory is not always successful of course. It did not persuade the Greek allies to fight at Salamis, instead they had to be forced into it, and undergo "treatment" (θεραπείᾳ), a treatment that was successful.[751]

Thus the verb θεραπεύω includes the ideas of medical treatment, service, nurture and persuasion in its meanings as used by Aristides. It implies a positive attitude on the part of the agent, and a receptive and active response on the part of the recipient. For both parties the association endures for some time. In this way the aspect of θεραπεύω and its cognate forms remains continuous.

5.5. Conclusion

A survey of a selection of inscriptions from Pergamon, and of a selection of the works of those who had some connection with the asklepieion there shows a remarkable degree of consistency in the use of healing language by authors as diverse as the orator Aristides, the Roman emperor Marcus Aurelius, and the physician Galen. As well, their use of healing language mirrors that of other asklepieia, in differing locations and at earlier times.

So what can we conclude from a study of healing language at four major asklepieia in the Mediterranean world? The most obvious result seems to be the static nature of the meaning and contextual use of words such as σῴζω, ἰάομαι and ὑγιαίνω. The verb σῴζω continues to mean the rescuing from the possibility of im-

---

747 App. 5:6, **35**. Cf. Epictetus 1.19; Josephus (App. 6:2); and Philo (App. 6:3, **1**, **2**, **12**)

748 App. 5:6, **34**

749 App. 5:6, **38**

750 See above, 89-93.

751 App. 5:6, **42**

minent death on particular occasions, ἰάομαι continues to denote (successful) medical treatment, and is the verb used to describe the intervention of the god and miraculous healing, while the verb ὑγιαίνω continues to imply a restoration to a previous state of (good) health.

However, the most interesting word is the verb θεραπεύω and its associated forms, for rather than remaining static, it burgeons in meaning from the loving and loyal service required of the Homeric θεράπων to include the notions of medical treatment,[752] medical nursing (involving physical drudgery and emotional support),[753] persuasive teaching that brings about a change in a person's way of life,[754] a vocation of service,[755] fulfilling one's duty,[756] and worship.[757] All these ideas are of course expressed through loving service. But it is the continuous nature of the verb θεραπεύω and its cognate forms that demands attention. That the verb also requires a degree of introspection by the time of the New Testament is evident from its use by such diverse characters as the supplicant Marcus Julius Apellas,[758] the emperor Marcus Aurelius,[759] and the orator Aelius Aristides.[760]

That there were similarities between the nature and attributes of the pagan god, Asklepios, and the New Testament Jesus has also been noted. It is in the literary works of the orator Aristides that these similarities are most obvious.

It is important to ask then whether healing language as exemplified by its use at asklepieia in the Greek world can contribute anything to our understanding of the Greek language of healing as used by the New Testament authors.

752 Hippokrates (App. 4:1); Galen (App. 5:5, **7**)
753 Thucydides 2.47.4; 2.51.2-3, 5; Isocrates, *Aegineticus* (see chapter three).
754 Epicurus (App. 3:5, **1**); Marcus Aurelius (App. 5:7, **3**, **6**); Aelius Aristides (App. 5:6, **40**)
755 Hippokrates (App. 4:1, **4**); Galen (App. 5:5, **4**)
756 Marcus Aurelius (App. 5:7, **4**); a decree (App. 4:3)
757 *IG* II^2, no. 974, line 24; *IG* VII, no. 235, lines 21-22
758 *IG* IV^2 1, no. 126 (App. 2:4)
759 App. 5:7
760 App. 5:6

Section Two

The language of healing in the New Testament

6. Jewish use of Greek healing language in the Septuagint, Philo of Alexandria, and Josephus

Before attempting a detailed study of the healing language of the New Testament, it is important to analyse the Jewish use of Greek healing language in the Septuagint,[1] and in a selection of the writings of Philo[2] and Josephus,[3] to ascertain whether there are any particularly Jewish connotations in Greek verbs such as θεραπεύω and ἰάομαι that might have a bearing on their use in the New Testament, and to ascertain how far the use of these verbs reflects their use in the healing language of the Greek world, as outlined in Section One.

6.1. Septuagint

It is at once obvious that ἰάομαι is the verb chosen to describe the healing activity of the Septuagint god,[4] while θεραπεύω describes the

1 For the incidence of the verbs θεραπεύω and ἰάομαι in the Septuagint, based on the list given in Hatch and Redpath (1897) 648, 668, see App. 6:1.

2 Space does not allow a survey of all Philo's treatises, so a selection of four of his works was made. For the incidence of the verb θεραπεύω in these four treatises, see App. 6:3.

3 Similarly, space does not allow a survey of all Josephus' works. For the incidence of the verb θεραπεύω in *The Life*, *The Jewish War*, and in *Jewish Antiquities*, books 5-11, see App. 6:2.

4 Choosing a name for the Septuagint god poses a dilemma: the "Septuagint god" is clumsy, "the Lord", although more popular in the Septuagint as a title, open to ambiguity (particularly in New Testament discussions below), and "Yahweh" inappropriate, as we are dealing with Greek texts. Therefore, in the interests of a smooth text, the Septuagint god will be denoted hereafter simply as "God" in the sense of a proper noun, as "Asklepios" in Section One. Similarly, for convenience, the masculine personal pronoun will be used to refer to the Septuagint god, without in any way excluding the

activity of humans,[5] except on one rare and extremely important occasion. In *Wisdom* it is God's healing λόγος which healed (ἐθεράπευσεν) all humankind, rather than the human use of herbs or poultices.[6] This is an unusual use of θεραπεύω and will be discussed below.[7] The verb ἰάομαι is the more popular verb, occurring almost three times as frequently as θεραπεύω.[8]

Like Apollo in the Greek world, God in the Jewish world is the source of both suffering and healing.[9] And, like Apollo, God also answers prayer.[10] And as Apollo's epithet is Paiëon,[11] so God is known as the healing god, the verb ἰάομαι forming an epithet.[12] When humans pray to God for healing, they do so using the verb ἰάομαι,[13] while God speaks of healing using the same verb.[14]

Problems in need of healing vary. They range from individual human emotional, spiritual and physical illnesses, and collective

---

possibility that the Septuagint god may have had androgynous characteristics. App. 6:1 illustrates the problem of naming the Septuagint god: for example, θεός (**1**, **5**), κύριος (**2**, **5**, **6**, **8**, and so on), and Ὑψίστου (**43**). While recognising that the use of titles has figured in the attribution of Hebrew texts to a Priestly, Yahwist or Elohist source (see Campbell [1989] 116-121), a discussion of the origin of Hebrew texts is outside the scope of this enquiry.

5 See App. 6:1. This reflects the use of ἰάομαι in Asklepiadic literature discussed in Section One.

6 App. 6:1, **40**

7 See below, 107-109, and n.69.

8 Forms of ἰάομαι occur sixty-three times, θεραπεύω twenty-four times. Of these occurrences, ἰάομαι appears ten times in *Isaiah*, eight times in *Jeremiah*, seven times in *Psalms*, five times each in *Hosea* and *1-4 Kings*, four times each in *Tobit* and *Deuteronomy*, three times each in *Proverbs* and *Chronicles*, twice each in *Wisdom*, *Job* and *Leviticus*, and once each in *Genesis*, *Exodus*, *Numbers*, *Ecclesiastes*, *Sirach*, *Zechariah*, *Lamentations* and *4 Maccabees*. Forms of θεραπεύω occur four times in *Tobit*, three times each in *Sirach*, *Esther* and *Proverbs*, twice each in *Wisdom*, *1-4 Kings*, *Esdras* and the *Letter of Jeremiah*, and once each in *Judith*, *Isaiah* and *Daniel*. See App. 6:1. Again this reflects the incidence of ἰάομαι and θεραπεύω in the Asklepiadic literature discussed in Section One.

9 App. 6:1, **9**, **36**, **57**, and **64**. For the actions of Apollo, see above, Section One, chapter one.

10 App. 6:1, **1**, **15**, **18**, **19**, **23**, **44**. Cf. Section One, chapter one.

11 See above, Section One, chapter one. Asklepios also receives this epithet (App. 3:2, **6**).

12 App. 6:1, **2** and **28**: ὁ ἰώμενός; **26**: τὸν ἰώμενον. Cf. *IG* II^2, no. 4533, line 30 (App. 3:2, **6**) of Telesphoros. Cf. also Aristides (App. 5:6, **14**) of Asklepios. Cf. also the Lukan use at Acts 10.38.

13 App. 6:1, **5**, **22**, **24**, **73**

14 App. 6:1, **2**, **9**, **15**, **18**, **58**, **59**, **60**, **62**, **63**, **68**

human spiritual ills, to the dysfunction of things necessary for the maintenance of human life, such as the water supply, and the land itself.

At this stage, then, it is important to ask questions about the healing nature and activity of God. Why does God heal? What are his healing methods? Who are his patients? Is there any clue in the answers to these questions to the meaning of general healing terms like ὑγιής, ἰάομαι and θεραπεύω in Jewish usage?

As we have already seen, the Septuagint god heals in answer to prayer.[15] In fact, the Septuagint god seems to have acute hearing, and this is just as well, for his people expect him to hear them![16] He also has an intimate knowledge of human emotions,[17] and human actions. When his people err, he is moved to healing action by their repentance.[18] He is a serious god, who expects to be obeyed.[19] He is capable of anger,[20] but also displays other emotions common to humans, such as love,[21] and compassion,[22] and can feel pain.[23] Thus the Septuagint portrays God as a being interested in the affairs of humankind, ready to intervene in history for the ultimate good of his people.[24]

What problems does God heal? Individual human problems reflect universal human desires, as at Epidauros.[25] The desire for children,[26] the need to be free from disease and thus able to function as part of the community,[27] the desires for freedom of movement,[28] for sight,[29] and indeed to be free from all ills,[30] feature in the Septuagint stories. As well, emotional trauma[31] and spiritual

---

15 See above, n.10.
16 App. 6:1, **1**, **15**, **17**, **18**, **19**, **23**, **44**, **64**
17 App. 6:1, **17**
18 App. 6:1, **18**, **24**, **57**, **70**
19 The Septuagint god does not display the humour of the Greek healing god Asklepios (see App. 2:1, **2**, **8**), although Asklepios too expects obedience from those who approach him for healing help (see App. 2:2, **35**, **37**).
20 App. 6:1, **6**, **7**, **60**, **63**, **74**
21 App. 6:1, **59**, **60**
22 App. 6:1, **8**, **15**, **18**, **22**, **24**, **39**
23 App. 6:1, **66**
24 For a discussion of the intervention of God in history, see Campbell (1989) 316f.
25 See above, Section One, chapter two, and Apps 2:1, 2:2.
26 App. 6:1, **1**
27 App. 6:1, **3**, **4**
28 App. 6:1, **22**
29 App. 6:1, **51**, **52**, **55**, **69**
30 App. 6:1, **26**: πάσας τὰς νόσους
31 App. 6:1, **28** and **69**: τοὺς συντετριμμένους τὴν καρδίαν

pain[32] demand the attention of the healing God. However, the healing God does not only attend to individual personal distress. Collective distress,[33] and distress caused by failures of function in the water supply,[34] and the land,[35] move God to take action.

Can anyone other than God heal? It appears that only God or his agents are capable of the healing expressed by the verb ἰάομαι. It is mostly used of the action of God himself,[36] although his agent Elijah repaired (ἰάσατο) the altar,[37] and Elisha treated the water supply with salt, acknowledging the result as the work of God.[38] Raphael, the angel of God, also heals, having been sent on a mission specifically for this purpose.[39]

In contrast, erring humans are unable to heal in the same way. For example, the king of Assyria was "unable to heal" (οὐκ ἠδυνάσθη ἰάσασθαι) or relieve pain.[40] The negated form of ἰάομαι also occurs denoting laziness,[41] and dissatisfaction[42] in humans, as well as the incurable nature of disease sent by God.[43] When human agents do "heal" there is always some qualification. For example, although the people of Jerusalem "heal" (ἰῶντο) the wounds of the people, they do so superficially (ἐξουθενοῦντες), mouthing the word "Peace" without there being true peace (εἰρήνη).[44] Thus their word is impotent. Indeed the healing "word" and the concept of "peace" are integral to the notion of health and healing in the Septuagint, "peace" being particularly prominent in *Isaiah*,[45] *Jeremiah*,[46] and *Sirach* in a healing context.[47] In *Sirach* εἰρήνη appears upon the face of the earth as the result of God's healing work through the agency

---

32 App. 6:1, **8**, **23**, **24**, **66**
33 App. 6:1, **19**, **37**, **58**
34 App. 6:1, **13**. Cf. Aelius Aristides, App. 5:6, **19**, **21**
35 App. 6:1, **18**, **25**
36 This action is mostly positive, but it can be brutally negative too. See App. 6:1, **6**, **7**, **61**, **74**, and **75**.
37 App. 6:1, **12**
38 App. 6:1, **13**
39 App. 6:1, **51**, **52**, **53** and **55**. For a discussion, see below, 109-110.
40 App. 6:1, **56**
41 App. 6:1, **31**
42 App. 6:1, **80**
43 App. 6:1, **6**, **7**. The parallel with the nature of an angry Apollo in the nature of God is here evident, in contrast to the benevolent natures of the New Testament Jesus, and the Greek Asklepios.
44 App. 6:1, **71**. Perhaps there is a link in meaning here with the Markan report of Jesus' words to the haemorrhaging woman (Mk 5.34).
45 App. 6:1, **66**, **68**
46 App. 6:1, **71**
47 App. 6:1, **43**

of physicians.[48] "Peace" in this sense appears to be akin to holistic health with a spiritual emphasis, and so the Greek word εἰρήνη is used in preference to the Greek word ὑγιής.

How then does God heal? Information is rather sparse on this point. Like Asklepios, he is represented as communicating in conversation,[49] although his audience appears to be more selective than the audience of Asklepios.[50] It is through a selected group of agents that God delivers a message for all his people, a message that is usually spiritual in nature. His primary concern appears to be the spiritual health of his people. As a result, while physical ailments do attract his attention, he is also depicted as healing "mistakes".[51] This healing is dependent on a change in living, on a rearrangement of priorities, on undoing past and avoiding future "mistakes".[52] God's healing method is rarely described, and when it is, it is usually in a metaphorical sense. For example, he binds up emotional wounds,[53] and heals with his hands.[54] His mercy also heals.[55] Where physical healing is concerned usually only the result is noted. For example, Abimelech "was healed", and his wife and female slaves bore children.[56] However, on several occasions we are told that it is the λόγος of God which heals:

> [God] sent forth his word and healed them (ἀπέστειλεν τὸν λόγον αὐτοῦ καὶ ἰάσατο αὐτούς),[57]

and,

> For neither herb nor poultice healed them, but your healing word, O Lord, healed all people (καὶ γὰρ οὔτε βοτάνη οὔτε μάλαγμα ἐθεράπευσεν αὐτους, ἀλλὰ ὁ σός, Κύριε, λόγος ὁ πάντα ἰώμενος).[58]

---

48 App. 6:1, **43**, v. 8

49 App. 6:1, **2**, **9**, **13**, **15**, **18**, **59**, **60**, **63**, **67**, **68**. Cf. Asklepios at Epidauros (Apps 2:1, 2:2, 2:3, 2:4); Athens (App. 3:4); and Pergamon (Apps 5:4, 5:6).

50 The great men and women in Jewish history: Abraham, Moses, Samuel, Elisha, Elijah, Saul, David, Solomon, the prophets, Sarah, Judith, and so on. Unfortunately we do not have evidence such as the inscriptional evidence of Epidauros for the common Jewish man and woman.

51 App. 6:1, **8**: τὰς ἁμαρτίας, usually translated as "sins". See also App. 6:1, **18**, **24**, **44**. Cf. Marcus Aurelius (App. 5:7, **6**) and Section One, chapter five, n.679.

52 App. 6:1, **18**, **57**, **62**, **64**

53 App. 6:1, **28**

54 App. 6:1, **36**

55 App. 6:1, **39**

56 App. 6:1, **1**

57 App. 6:1, **27**

58 App. 6:1, **40**

Human "word" too can heal, as we are told in *Proverbs*, but it can also injure:[59]

> There are those whose words injure like swords, but the tongues of the wise bring healing (εἰσὶν οἳ λέγοντες τιτρώσκουσιν μάχαιραι, γλῶσσαι δὲ σοφῶν ἰῶνται).[60]

Here it is only wise human word that can heal, and the word must be heard to be effective. Similarly God's word must be heard, and also understood, and obeyed, for healing to occur: humans are rewarded according to the ways of their hearts,[61] they are healed if they pray and seek God, and turn from their wicked ways,[62] and if they pray and give up their faults, directing their hands aright.[63] If they return to God they will be healed and will live, and understand.[64] In this way "life" and "knowledge" appear to be part of God's healing. However, it is possible for humans to be unaware of God's healing presence, a watchful presence that brings comfort (καὶ ἔσομαι αὐτοῖς ὡς ῥαπίζων ἄνθρωπος ἐπὶ τὰς σιαγόνας αὐτοῦ) and power (δυνήσομαι αὐτῷ) in love (ἀγαπήσεώς μου).[65] Awareness - seeing with their eyes and hearing with their ears - is an important component of the human-God relationship as portrayed in the Septuagint.[66] But ultimately it is God who is portrayed as being responsible for the nurturing of the health of the people, a health that is expressed by the Greek word εἰρήνη.[67]

Thus the verb ἰάομαι in the Septuagint denotes the activity and nature of the Septuagint God, and on occasion, of his agents. It is the preferred verb in a healing context, and is the verb that is put into God's mouth when he speaks of healing.[68] In this incidence and use it reflects the language of healing in the Greek world. In contrast the adjective ὑγιής, chosen in the Greek world to describe health, is not favoured as much as the Greek word εἰρήνη in the Septuagint, which includes a strong spiritual emphasis in its notion of health. But what of the verb θεραπεύω?

---

59 Cf. App. 6:1, **29, 33**

60 App. 6:1, **33**

61 App. 6:1, **17**

62 App. 6:1, **18**

63 App. 6:1, **44**

64 App. 6:1, **57**

65 App. 6:1, **59**

66 App. 6:1, **62** Cf. the saying "He who has ears to hear, let him hear" (Mt 11.15).

67 App. 6:1, **66**

68 App. 6:1, **9,15, 18, 58, 60, 62, 63, 68, 70**

In contrast to the verb ἰάομαι, the verb θεραπεύω is not put into God's mouth, nor does it describe divine healing, except when it refers to the healing λόγος of God.[69] Instead the verb θεραπεύω describes the activity of humans as they repair,[70] flatter,[71] pay attention to personal presentation,[72] or give service.[73] In a medical context θεραπεύω describes medical treatment akin to modern medical nursing,[74] or is linked with the healing properties of herbs and medicines.[75]

That there is a distinct difference in the quality of physical healing denoted by ἰάομαι and θεραπεύω in the Septuagint is most clearly seen in the story of the healing of Tobit.[76] Tobit was partially blind, and went to the physicians to be treated (πρὸς τοὺς ἰατροὺς θεραπευθῆναι). The treatment was unsuccessful, for his eyesight deteriorated in proportion with the drugs (τὰ φάρμακα) he was given, until he was completely blind.[77] Thus, as in the Hippokratic writings, the use of θεραπεύω does not necessarily imply a successful outcome, but a course of treatment, which may or may not, be successful in its outcome.[78] In this story God intervened and sent the angel Raphael to heal (ἰάσασθαι) Tobit.[79] Tobit was amazed that a stranger wished to speak with him, for he described himself as a man who was living in death (ζῶν ἐγὼ ἐν νεκροῖς εἰμι), unable to see the light of heaven. His words imply that his physical affliction denied him social intercourse, placing him outside the community. Raphael told him to have confidence (θάρσει) that he would

69 Wisdom 16.12 (App. 6:1, **40**) According to Arndt and Gingrich (1957) 359 θεραπεύω is here used in the "one isolated instance: of God".

70 App. 6:1, **21**

71 App. 6:1, **30**, **32**, **34**

72 App. 6:1, **11**

73 App. 6:1, **20**, **38**, **42**, **45**, **46**, **47**, **48**, **49**, **67**, **77**, **78**, **79**

74 App. 6:1, **14**. Cf. Thucydides 2.47.4, 2.51.2-3, 5; Isocrates, *Aegineticus* (see chapter three).

75 App. 6:1, **40**, **43**, **50**

76 App. 6:1, **49-55**

77 App. 6:1, **50**

78 See above, Section One, chapter four.

79 App. 6:1, **51**. Raphael was also sent to heal Sarah, the daughter of Raguel. In order for her to be healed, Raphael had to bind (δῆσαι) the evil demon, Asmodeus. The method has a magical ring: smoke made from the heart and liver of a fish before a person troubled by an evil spirit was supposed to ensure that the spirit never troubled that person again (Tobit 6.7-8). Cf. the treatment given to a man possessed by an evil demon by Eleazar, a contemporary of Josephus (App. 6:2, **27**).

soon be healed by God (ἐγγὺς παρὰ τῷ θεῷ ἰάσασθαί σε).[80] But when Tobit's son, Tobias, talks about his father's subsequent healing, he uses the verb θεραπεύω.[81] At this stage of the story, Tobias still believes Raphael to be a human friend, who knew the appropriate treatment for his father's condition. The treatment prescribed by Raphael was to anoint Tobit's eyes with the gall of a fish, in order to remove the white films from his eyes.[82] While Raphael consistently uses ἰάομαι in this context, Tobias understands him to be prescribing 'medical' treatment, and therefore describes his treatment with the verb θεραπεύω. When Raphael later explains that God sent him to heal Tobit, he again uses the verb ἰάομαι.[83]

This story illustrates a consistent pattern of usage in the Septuagint: divine healing is described by the verb ἰάομαι, whereas human healing treatment is described by the verb θεραπεύω. For the most part this human healing involves the use of herbs (βοτάνη)[84] or drugs (φάρμακα).[85] However it can also include the notion of nurturing care invoved in preventive medicine:

> before you fall ill, take care of your health (καὶ πρὸ ἀρρωστείας θεραπεύου),[86]

as well as the care given in nursing the sick or wounded. King Joram was nursed (ἐθεραπεύετο)[87] for arrow wounds, recovered sufficiently to leave his sick bed, only to be killed soon after.[88]

What then does the Septuagint have to say about physicians and their profession?

It is in *Sirach* that the Septuagint gives advice concerning physicians and comments on their place in God's plan for health (εἰρήνη) upon the face of the earth. According to *Sirach* God created physi-

80 App. 6:1, **52**. Cf. Jesus' words on the water when he tells the disciples to have confidence (Mt 14.27; Mk 6.50).

81 App. 6:1, **54**

82 App. 6:1, **53**. The ms. ℵ prefers the verb ὑγιαίνω here, in the present tense, and describes the restoration of eyes with this disease to their former functioning state of health, a meaning reflected in the Greek Asklepiadic texts discussed in Section One. The verb ὑγιαίνω also appears at 5.20 and 5.21, signifying Tobias' safe and healthy return to his father. Luke uses the same language in his parable of the prodigal son, when describing his safe return to his father (Lk 15.27).

83 App. 6:1, **55**

84 App. 6:1, **40**

85 App. 6:1, **43**, **50**

86 App. 6:1, **41**

87 App. 6:1, **14**

88 4 Kings 9

cians, and they are therefore worthy of honour. For although healing (ἴασις) comes from God, he gave skill (ἐπιστήμην) and medicines (φάρμακα) to men, to heal (θεραπεύω) and to take away pain (ἦρεν τὸν πόνον).[89] However, if anyone is sick and prays, God will heal (ἰάσεταί) that person, and, similarly, if physicians also pray, God will grant them success and gracious healing (ἴασιν χάριν). The passage ends with the rather daunting advice:

> He who sins before his Maker, may he fall into the hands of a physician (ὁ ἁμαρτάνων ἔναντι τοῦ ποιήσαντος αὐτὸν ἐμπέσοι εἰς χεῖρας ἰατροῦ)![90]

Again this passage makes it clear that θεραπεύω in a healing context refers to human treatment (albeit using resources provided by God), while ἰάομαι refers to divine healing.

However, the verb θεραπεύω only appears seven times in a healing context.[91] It appears more often in the context of giving service: to God,[92] to Wisdom (σοφία),[93] to the people of Israel,[94] to King Artaxerxes,[95] to idols,[96] and in Daniel's vision.[97] This idea of giving service is carried to its extreme in a pejorative sense in *Proverbs*, where θεραπεύω appears on three occasions in the sense of *to flatter*.[98] The verb also appears in the first book of *Esdras* in the context of making repairs to the market places and walls of Jerusalem.[99] In its negated form the verb θεραπεύω describes a state of unkemptness: Saul's son had not dressed his feet (οὐκ ἐθεράπευσεν τοὺς πόδας).[100]

Thus it can be seen that the verb θεραπεύω appears with a range of meanings in the Septuagint, meanings which include *serve, give medical care to, flatter* and *repair*. All of these meanings refer to

---

89 App. 6:1, **43**
90 App. 6:1, **44**
91 Sirach 18.19 (App. 6:1, **41**) 38.7 (App. 6:1, **43**); Tobit 2.10 (**א**) (App. 6:1, **50**), twice in 12.3 (+**א**) (App. 6:1, **54**); 4 Kings 9. 16 (App. 6:1, **14**); and Wisdom 16.12 (App. 6:1, **40**)
92 App. 6:1, **42, 48, 49, 67**
93 App. 6:1, **38**
94 App. 6:1, **20**
95 App. 6:1, **45, 46, 47**
96 App. 6:1, **77, 78**
97 App. 6:1, **79**
98 App. 6:1, **30, 32, 34**. Cf. Epictetus 1.19
99 App. 6:1, **21**
100 App. 6:1, **11**. Cf. Aelius Aristides (App. 5:6, **39**)

the activity of humans, with one notable exception: when θεραπεύω describes the effect of God's healing word (λόγος . . . ἰώμενος).[101]

We have already seen how the Septuagint god communicates with his people by word, as well as action. Indeed it is his word that usually guides his people towards a right way of living, and therefore a right relationship with him. The end result of this right relationship - between humans, between humans and God, and between humans, God and the land - is εἰρήνη, a concept that is usually translated either by *health* or *peace*, in a holistic sense. Thus God's λόγος, when it is heard and acted upon, produces holistic health. In this way God's λόγος and the verb θεραπεύω have a special relationship. This relationship has implications for the significance of the use of θεραπεύω in the New Testament.[102]

But what of Jewish authors whose works were closer in time to the writings of the New Testament? Since the verb θεραπεύω appears to have acquired a specialised meaning in a Jewish spiritual and teaching context, it is important to ask whether Jewish writers of the first century use θεραπεύω in the same way as the Septuagint, or whether there is a trend in their work towards using the verb in a more medical sense. For this purpose the Jewish authors Philo and Josephus have been chosen.

6.2. Philo

Philo of Alexandria, generally known as Philo Judaeus, was born about 20 BC and lived until after AD 40.[103] He was thus a contemporary of Jesus of Nazareth, although there is no evidence that he was aware of his existence. Philo, a citizen of Alexandria, the city which was both the major centre of the Jewish Dispersion and the centre of Hellenic culture, was steeped in both Jewish religion and Greek philosophy. He wrote in Greek, but with a thorough knowledge of the Pentateuch as written in the Septuagint,[104] so his work is invaluable for a study of the use of Greek healing language, by a Jew, who was living at the time of the events portrayed in the New Testament.

---

101 App. 6:1, **40**

102 See below, chapter seven.

103 Philo, *Leg. ad Gaium* 31 refers to himself as having been an old man at the time of the embassy to Caligula (AD 39-40), which implies that he was born sometime around 20 BC.

104 Most of Philo's quotations come from the Pentateuch. See Philo (1971) xxviii-xxxiv.

Since Philo's writings were so voluminous, a study of his use of the verb θεραπεύω will be restricted to four of his treatises.[105] In *Every good man is free* the verb θεραπεύω appears three times, meaning *to court*[106] and *to worship*.[107] The noun θεραπευτής also appears, meaning *a servant* (of God). In his description of the Essenes, Philo remarks that:

> they have shown themselves especially devout in the service of God, not by offering sacrifices of animals, but by resolving to sanctify their minds (ἐπειδὴ κἀν τοῖς μάλιστα θεραπευταὶ θεοῦ γεγόνοσιν, οὐ ζῷα καταθύοντες, ἀλλ' ἱεροπρεπεῖς τὰς ἑαυτῶν διανοίας κατασκευάζειν ἀξιοῦντες).[108]

So devout service, in Philo's opinion, is not signalled by outward attention to ritual, but inner holiness.

This meaning becomes more evident in Philo's treatise *The Contemplative Life*, a description of a group of people known to him who called themselves the *Therapeutae* and *Therapeutrides*. Philo, discussing the significance of their name, explains that it was derived from the meaning of the verb θεραπεύω, either in its sense of *cure*, or in its sense of *worship*. He explains that his reason for attributing the sense of *cure* to the meaning is:

> because they profess an art of healing better than that current in the cities which cures only the bodies, while theirs treats also souls oppressed with grievous and well-nigh incurable diseases, inflicted by pleasures and desires and griefs and fears, by acts of covetousness, folly and injustice and the countless host of the other passions and vices (ἤτοι παρόσον ἰατρικὴν ἐπαγγέλλονται κρείσσονα τῆς κατὰ πόλεις—ἡ μὲν γὰρ σώματα θεραπεύει μόνον, ἐκείνη δὲ καὶ ψυχὰς νόσοις κεκρατημένας χαλεπαῖς τε καὶ δυσιάτοις, ἃς ἐγκατέσκηψαν ἡδοναὶ καὶ ἐπιθυμίαι καὶ λῦπαι καὶ φόβοι πλεονεξίαι τε καὶ ἀφροσύναι καὶ ἀδικίαι καὶ τὸ τῶν ἄλλων παθῶν καὶ κακιῶν ἀνήνυτον πλῆθος).[109]

Here *to cure* in the sense of θεραπεύω involves healing the soul as well as the body, incorporating spiritual, mental, emotional and physical healing. Indeed, while not excluding the importance of physical health, the spiritual, emotional and mental health of a person appears to be more important in Philo's definition of θεραπεύω. Thus *to cure* in the sense of θεραπεύω is to strive for holis-

---

105 See App. 6:3.
106 App. 6:3, **1, 2**
107 App. 6:3, **3**
108 App. 6:3, **4**
109 App. 6:3, **5**

tic health. How do the Therapeutae do this? The answer lies in their life of worship, the other meaning attributed by Philo to θεραπεύω. Philo gives a detailed description of the way the community lived and worshipped, particularly admiring their piety.[110]

In this way Philo makes it clear that holistic health and spiritual worship are inextricably entwined in the notion of θεραπεύω. This is further explained by Philo's definition of an incurable (ἀθεράπευτοι) disease, loss of sight. He explains that:

> And by this I do not mean the sight of the body but of the soul, the sight which alone gives a knowledge of truth and falsehood (λέγω δὲ οὐ τὴν σώματος, ἀλλὰ τὴν ψυχῆς, ᾗ τὸ ἀληθὲς καὶ τὸ ψεῦδος μόνῃ γνωρίζεται).[111]

Indeed physical and spiritual blindness is an important motif in both Greek[112] and Jewish[113] literature. This has important implications for the motifs of blindness and sight in the New Testament healing miracles.

The community of the Therapeutae consisted of both men and women.[114] They lived and worshipped in harmony, sharing their contemplative life, and forming a single choir.[115] Philo states that their chief aim was piety,[116] and concludes that they lived in the soul alone.[117]

If we admit that Philo's definition of θεραπεύω is relevant to a study of healing language, then it is obvious that in a healing context in a spiritual work, θεραπεύω should never be understood in a purely physical sense. Indeed, Philo makes it clear that it should be understood in a primarily spiritual sense, and this spiritual sense is intensified when θεραπεύω is placed in a teaching or contemplative context.

---

110 ibid.

111 App. 6:3, **6**

112 For example, Sophocles, *Oedipus Tyrannus*, where Teiresias the blind prophet is the one who 'sees' the truth, and Oedipus, who cannot bear to physically see once he 'sees' the truth.

113 For example, Tobit in the Septuagint (App. 6:1, **52-55**), and Paul in the New Testament (App. 8:1, Acts 9.1-22).

114 For a discussion of the role of the women in this community, see Kraemer (1992) 113-117, 126-127. She concludes (127) that their "form of asceticism . . . did not so much change the rules for all women as it simply redefined Therapeutic women as men". Cf. *GT*114 (Robinson [1978] 130)

115 App. 6:3, **8**.

116 ibid.

117 App. 6:3, **9**

This is borne out in Philo's other uses of θεραπεύω.[118] In *Flaccus*, an historical rather than a spiritual work, the verb θεραπεύω appears meaning to *be devoted*,[119] and to *flatter*,[120] and, as we have seen, it is only in a spiritual context in *Every good man is free* that the verb means to *worship*,[121] rather than to *court*.[122]

Even this limited survey of Philo's use of θεραπεύω shows that the verb has not acquired any great medical significance by his time, but that in a healing and teaching context it refers primarily to spiritual health and healing, while incorporating emotional, mental and some physical aspects. What then of the later Jewish writer, Josephus?

6.3. Josephus

Josephus was born in Palestine of an eminent family in the year AD 37-38,[123] after the recall of Pontius Pilate from Judaea, and in the year Caligula became Emperor. As part of his education, Josephus studied the tenets of the Sadducees, the Essenes and the Pharisees, then spent three years in the wilderness as the disciple of Bannus. He became a Pharisee, visited Rome in AD 64, and on his return attempted, without success, to prevent revolt against Rome.[124] He became responsible for affairs in Galilee, and after the troubles there, was captured by the Romans in AD 67.[125] After Vespasian's accession, Josephus was freed, and returned to Jerusalem with Titus until it fell in AD 70.[126] He spent the rest of his life at Rome, writing his *History of the Jewish War*, and *Jewish Antiquities*. He was thus a Jewish priest, soldier, statesman, Roman citizen[127] and author. How does Josephus use the verb θεραπεύω?

A survey of *The Life*, *The Jewish War*, and books 5-11 of *Jewish Antiquities*, shows that Josephus mostly uses the verb θεραπεύω to

118 In *The eternity of the world*, a treatise thought by some to be non-Philonic, the negated adjectival form of θεραπεύω is "a fatal delusion (ἀθεραπεύτῳ μανίᾳ)". See App. 6:3, **10**.

119 App. 6:3, **11**

120 App. 6:3, **12**

121 App. 6:3, **3**. Cf. **4**

122 App. 6:3, **1**, **2**

123 *Life* 1-6

124 ibid. 7-19

125 ibid. 414

126 ibid. 416-422

127 ibid. 423

mean to *court* or to *flatter*.[128] He uses it in the context of bribery,[129] political alliances,[130] favouritism to cities,[131] winning support,[132] and flattery.[133] However θεραπεύω can also mean to tend humans;[134] and, in a religious context, to tend objects,[135] to worship God,[136] and to serve God.[137]

In a medical context, the verb θεραπεύω appears eight times in the works surveyed.[138] In five of these the patients die,[139] despite, or perhaps even because of,[140] the treatment given, so Josephus definitely does not use the verb in the sense of *cure*. One concerns a physician, who, called in to treat (θεραπεῦσαι) the patient Phasael, injected him with noxious drugs and so killed him. This particular use of θεραπεύω is cited by Arndt and Gingrich as an example of the verb meaning to *restore*,[141] a curious example, given the context. In six of the other occurrences Josephus uses the verb θεραπεύω to mean *nursing treatment*. He tells us that Herod recovered (σώζεται),[142] and that, not long after, he affectionately nursed (συμπαθῶς ἐθεράπευεν) Pheroras, a display of greater humanity (εὑρίσκετο δὲ Ἡρώδης μετριώτερος) than he had hitherto shown. However, Pheroras died after a few days. Thus θεραπεύω is invested by Josephus with an emotional quality we have witnessed before in a similar nursing context in the work of Isocrates.[143] Moreover,

---

128 The verb θεραπεύω occurs thirty-three times in the works surveyed. Of these occurrences the broad meaning of *to court* or *flatter* appears nineteen times. See App. 6:2, **1, 2, 3, 5, 6, 7, 9, 10, 11, 13, 17, 18, 19, 20, 21, 22, 23, 25, 28.**

129 App. 6:2, **2, 3, 6, 25**

130 App. 6:2, **1, 5, 9, 10, 11, 18, 22, 23**

131 App. 6:2, **13**

132 App. 6:2, **17, 19**

133 App. 6:2, **7, 20, 28**

134 In the sense of fulfilling a servant's duties: App. 6:2, **14.**

135 In this case the ark: App. 6:2, **26**. Cf. IG II^2, no. 1019 (App. 3:2, **10**) *re* the care of sacred property at the asklepieion at Athens.

136 App. 6:2, **24, 32**

137 App. 6:2, **8**

138 App. 6:2, **4, 12, 15, 16, 30, 31, 33**, and **34**. It also occurs at **27**, which would make its occurrence nine times in a medical context. However, as the text has been questioned, this occurrence will be discussed separately. See below, 117-118.

139 App. 6:2, **4, 15, 16, 31, 34**

140 App. 6:2, **4**

141 (1957)

142 This use of the verb σῴζω reflects Greek usage (see above, 61, 81-82, 100-101) and is also present in the New Testament (Apps 7:10, 7:11).

143 *Aegineticus*. See above, Section One, chapter three.

θεραπεύω in this case also denotes a virtuous quality in the character of the carer.[144]

Later, when recounting the events surrounding Herod's death, Josephus denotes those doing the nursing, as τῶν θεραπευόντων, and Herod's different modes of treatment as θεραπεία.[145] Similarly, Joram's medical nursing care, when he was being treated for arrow wounds is described by the imperfect passive of θεραπεύω, ἐθεραπεύετο.[146] In this usage Josephus is faithful to the language of the Septuagint,[147] and also reflects Greek usage.[148]

Patients can recover because of their nursing treatment, or die in spite of it. Ochozias, despite receiving treatment (θεραπευόμενος), died from his wound soon after.[149] Similarly, two of Josephus' friends, taken down from Roman crucifixion at the order of Titus, died while being nursed (οἱ μὲν δύο τελευτῶσιν θεραπευόμενοι), despite the most careful treatment (θεραπείας ἐπιμελεστάτης), while a third lived (ὁ δὲ τρίτος ἔζησεν) because of it.[150] Josephus himself, after receiving medical attention (θεραπευθείς), later recovered.[151] Thus, for Josephus, the verb θεραπεύω in a medical context refers to nursing treatment, treatment which may or may not, be successful.[152] The one example in the works surveyed where the verb could be used in a spiritual healing context occurs in a doubtful text.[153] Here the text:

> Nay, be ye righteous and, casting out wickedness from your souls and purging them, turn with all your hearts to the Deity and persevere in honouring Him (ἀλλὰ γίνεσθε δίκαιοι, καὶ τὴν πονηρίαν ἐκβαλόντες τῶν ψυχῶν καὶ θεραπεύοντες αὐτάς, ὅλαις ταῖς διανοίαις προστρέπεσθε τὸ θεῖον καὶ τιμῶντες διατελεῖτε·),

according to Thackeray and Marcus,[154] is doubtful, and an emendation, ἀρετήν in place of αὐτάς, has been proposed, so that the text would then read 'and cultivating virtue' instead of 'and purging

144 App. 6:2, **15**
145 App. 6:2, **16**
146 App. 6:2, **30**, and above, n.74.
147 App. 6:1, **14**
148 Cf. Thucydides 2.47-55; Isocrates, *Aegineticus* (Section One, chapter three); and the Hippokratic Corpus (Section One, chapter four).
149 App. 6:2, **31**
150 App. 6:2, **34**
151 App. 6:2, **33**
152 Cf. the use of the verb in the Hippokratic Corpus (App. 4:1), and at Pergamon (Apps 5:4, 5:5).
153 App. 6:2, **27**
154 Josephus (1977) 175, n. *d*

them'. While this emendation seems sensible, given Josephus' consistent use of θεραπεύω in the sense of 'to cultivate' in all its senses, and his rare use of the verb in a medical sense to signify anything other than nursing attention, it is possible that Josephus is using the word in the spiritual sense we have noticed in Philo's use of the verb. The text as it stands would then make perfect sense, and a better translation would be 'and (spiritually) nurturing them'. Given the context, this seems a better solution to the problem. One must be cautious, however. If Josephus is using the verb θεραπεύω in this sense, it is the only occurrence of this type in the works of Josephus that have been surveyed.

There remains one passage that is important in its use of the noun θεραπεία in a healing context. It is where Josephus discusses the practice of exorcism, a practice of ancient origin, that was still undertaken by his contemporaries.[155] The purpose of the passage was to glorify the wisdom of Solomon, who had left behind prescriptions for successful exorcisms. Josephus claims to have been present at such an event, carried out by one of his countrymen, Eleazar. Josephus bolsters the credibility of his account by appealing to the witness of important bystanders: no less than "Vespasian, his sons, tribunes and a number of other soldiers". The treatment prescribed, and the incantation hinted at, is reminiscent of incantations for exorcism found in the magical papyri.[156] The prescription (θεραπεία), details procedural instructions which include the use of a ring containing a herb, and the recitation of potent words. 'Proof' that the procedure has been successful is given by the mysterious overturning of a basin of water, at the exorcist's command (προστάσσω). Clearly the procedure entails a magical element, an element that was acceptable to Josephus' audience. It is significant that the gospels of the New Testament do not recount exorcism in either the same language, or using the same magical props. In the New Testament it is generally the word of command that leads to a successful outcome.[157]

155 App. 6:2, **29**

156 *PGM* XCIV.17-21 contains the words "depart" and "Solomon". See Betz (1986) 304. Another, *PGM* IV.1227-1264, (Betz [1986] 62), gives an "excellent rite for driving out demons": it uses olive branches, placed and used a special way, a formula, and an inscribed phylactery to be worn by the patient afterwards. The formula, to be spoken over the patient's head, hails the "God of Abraham, Isaac, Jacob, Jesus Chrestus (Chrestus here being the excellent rather than the anointed) the Holy Spirit and Son of the Father". This spell doesn't leave anything to chance! Cf. Tobit 6.16-18

157 See Mk 1.25; Mk 9.14-29. Cf. Mk 5.1-20; Mk 7.24-30

6.4. Conclusion

What then has a survey of the use of the language of healing in the Septuagint, and of the verb θεραπεύω in a selection of the writings of Philo and Josephus, revealed about the Jewish use of Greek healing language?

The use of the verb ἰάομαι seems straightforward, and reflects its use in the healing language of the Greek world, as outlined in Section One. It is the God-word in the Septuagint, describing divine healing and clothing God's healing promises. This is consistent with the use of ἰάομαι to describe divine healing at Greek asklepieia.

The adjective ὑγιής also describes physical health (and therefore safety) in the Septuagint, as it does in the Greek world, as well as a restoration to a former state of physical health. However, when the Septuagint wishes to speak of health in a holistic sense, or with a spiritual emphasis, it uses the Greek word εἰρήνη to express this concept. In this way Jewish use differs from Greek usage.

In contrast with the verb ἰάομαι the verb θεραπεύω describes human activity in the Septuagint, except where it refers to the healing λόγος of God. This use of θεραπεύω reflects Greek use of the verb in describing human treatment, or extended treatment carried out at the command of the Greek healing god, Asklepios, but Greek usage also refers to the healing λόγος of the human philosopher.[158] The Jewish authors, Philo and Josephus, further illustrate that the use of θεραπεύω in a secular context differs greatly from its use in a spiritual context. In a spiritual and teaching context the verb θεραπεύω refers primarily to the health and well-being of the soul, and the nurturing of the God-human relationship. In this sense the verb θεραπεύω is both active and passive. When passive it describes the result of God's healing λόγος, but this result demands an active and ongoing response in the life of the hearer of the word. Thus humans can be both healed and themselves take an active part in the healing process. Jewish use of the verb θεραπεύω then can differ from Greek usage, although it generally retains its imperfect aspect when referring to human activity, whether in a spiritual or secular context.

In a spiritual or teaching context then, Jewish use of the verb θεραπεύω should be understood primarily in a spiritual sense. What significance does this have for the use of Greek healing language in the New Testament?

---

158 Epicurus (App. 3:5, **1**)

7. The synoptic gospels: θεραπεύω

The synoptic authors chose to present Jesus of Nazareth as a healer *par excellence*. As Koine Greek was the lingua franca of the time it was by this medium the synoptists proclaimed their message. Thus we are bound, as they were, by the semantic networks of meaning of the Koine Greek of the first century of our era.[159] As well, we must be alert for any essentially Jewish connotations that may colour the meaning of Greek terms.[160] Therefore it is to a consideration of semantics that we must turn if we are to understand the essence of the synoptists' message. But before an analysis of the New Testament language of healing, it is important to discuss the synoptists' portrayal of the place and importance of Jesus' healing ministry in their gospels.

7.1. The place and importance of healing in the synoptic gospels

Teaching (διδάσκων), preaching (κηρύσσων), and healing (θεραπεύων),[161] were the three components of the ministry of Jesus of Nazareth. His authority (ἐξουσία) to teach and preach, and the credibility of his ministry rested on his ability to perform miracles, mostly of healing. More than any other of his deeds or words while living, Jesus' healing ministry was presented by the synoptists as evidence of the divine nature of his commission. Indeed, Matthew[162] reports that Jesus himself, when asked by messengers from John the Baptist whether he was "ὁ ἐρχόμενος,"[163] listed his response to suffering in the world as his credentials:

159 Which is why an understanding of Greek healing language as outlined in Section One is both a relevant and necessary background for an understanding of the thought of the NT authors.

160 Such as that already noted in the healing language of the Septuagint, and contemporary Jewish authors, such as Philo and Josephus.

161 Mt 4.23

162 It is not my intention to imply that "Matthew" was the author of the gospel commonly known by his name, nor that "Mark" is the author of *Mark*, nor that "Luke" is the author of *Luke-Acts*, nor that "John" is the author of *John*. It is merely for convenience that I refer to these works in this traditional way.

163 The term "ὁ ἐρχόμενος," while probably alluding to the Messiah, does not imply divinity in Jewish thought, but a divinely appointed "king", i.e. a second David, or a second Moses/liberator. It is because of this second Moses/second liberator aspect that the Messiah, in Jewish thought, was expected to perform σημεῖα καὶ τέρατα καὶ δυνάμεις as the first

And in reply Jesus said to them, 'When you have made the journey back tell John what you see and hear: the blind see and the lame walk, lepers are cleansed and the deaf hear, the dead are raised up and the poor have good news preached to them; and blessed is he who takes no offence at me' (καὶ ἀποκριθεὶς ὁ Ἰησοῦς εἶπεν αὐτοῖς, Πορευθέντες ἀπαγγείλατε Ἰωάννῃ ἃ ἀκούετε καὶ βλέπετε· τυφλοὶ ἀναβλέπουσιν καὶ χωλοὶ περιπατοῦσιν, λεπροὶ καθαρίζονται καὶ κωφοὶ ἀκούουσιν, καὶ νεκροὶ ἐγείρονται καὶ πτωχοὶ εὐαγγελίζονται· καὶ μακάριός ἐστιν ὃς ἐὰν μὴ σκανδαλισθῇ ἐν ἐμοί).[164]

This is a most interesting reply. It is typical of Matthew[165] that he has Jesus quote the Old Testament - here the Septuagint version of Isaiah 35.5-6 and 61.1,[166] a passage highly charged with symbolism. Taken in a metaphorical sense it is indicative of the synoptists' portrayal of Jesus' mission: i.e. to open the eyes and ears of all people so that they could understand his message; to produce action (the lame walk); to sanctify (lepers are cleansed); to give new life (the dead are raised up); and to give hope to the hopeless (πτωχοί: the poor in spirit);[167] with the result that those who hear and understand the message are indeed blessed (μακάριος).[168]

Luke recounts a similar story,[169] while Mark, typically, prefers to portray Jesus in action. However, all three synoptists focus on Jesus' healing ministry, and its place in his struggle against evil.

The synoptists present Jesus as acknowledging evil as a present, terrifying and powerful force, as interfering with God's plan for the perfection of creation. They depict his life as the ultimate struggle against evil, in whatever form it chose to manifest itself. Jesus saw

---

Moses/first liberator did in Egypt and in the Wilderness. (For example, cf. the feedings of the 4,000 [Mt 15.32-39; Mk 8.1-10] and 5,000 [Mt 14.13-21; Mk 6.30-44; Lk 9.10-17; Jn 6.1-14] with the feedings in the wilderness [Exodus 16.1-36; Numbers 11.1-35].)

164 Mt 11.4-6

165 See Hawkins (1909) 154-158; Barclay (1976) 161-164; Beare (1981) 5-49.

166 These passages in the Hebrew Bible are known to have been interpreted of the Messiah in Jewish thought. See Wilcox (1979a) 231-243.

167 Cf. Mt 5.3

168 For a discussion of the meaning of this word see de Heer (1968).

169 Lk 7.18-35. Luke's context is different: he places this story straight after Jesus has raised the widow of Nain's son from the dead. Luke also uses Isaiah 61.1-2 in his story of Jesus reading in the synagogue at Nazareth. There it is a prelude to Jesus' explanation that his message is worthy for gentiles too, which is the catalyst for his rejection by the people of Nazareth. Thus, just in this example, we can see the synoptists' use of the same material in different contexts, and for different purposes.

evil as always producing some kind of suffering - and he sought actively to overcome and bind it. His ministry, without the healing component, would have been impotent. Therefore the synoptists devoted more than one third of their narrative space to the description of Jesus' healing activity. If we compare each gospel we find that Mark devoted 40% of his narrative, Matthew 40% and Luke 35% to accounts of Jesus' healing ministry.[170]

The gospels of Matthew and Luke are both longer than Mark's, and both include more healing stories (twenty-five[171] each, cf. Mark: nineteen).[172] Matthew records eleven general healing episodes and fourteen specific cases.[173] He does not record any successful healings by the disciples, despite their having been given the commission and authority to do so. Luke, in contrast, cites seven healing episodes and eighteen specific cases.[174] He also records healing activity by the disciples, although not in as much detail as Mark.[175]

Luke generally gives more precise information about diseases than Matthew, sometimes more than Mark,[176] and tells of a greater number of female patients. He shares the stories of Peter's mother-in-law, Jairus' daughter, the haemorrhaging woman, and the healing of the man with the withered hand with Matthew and Mark, but gives the extra detail that Peter's mother-in-law had a high fever,[177] and that it was the man's right hand which was

---

170 For an analysis see Wilkinson (1980) 18-19. It is curious that Luke, who is thought to have been especially interested in events of a medical nature, actually devotes proportionally less narrative space to these events than Matthew or Mark.

171 For a discussion of the importance of the number five, and three, seven, and ten, and multiples of them, particularly in *Matthew*, see Hawkins (1909) 163-167.

172 See Apps 7:1, 7:2, 7:3, 7:4, and 7:5.

173 See Apps 7:1 and 7:5.

174 See Apps 7:3 and 7:5.

175 For a discussion, see below, 127-130.

176 But note the instances where Mark gives a fuller account of healing miracles: 7.31-37, 9.14-29; and a fuller account of medical practices: 6.13, 7.31-37, 8.22-26.

177 Lk 4.38-39. Hobart (1882) 4, notes that Galen stated that it was usual for ancient physicians to distinguish degrees of fever in this way (*De different. febrium* 1.1 [7.275 Kühn]; *Cur. per Ven. Sect.* 6 [11.270 Kühn]), but Cadbury (1969) 51, n.1, disagrees: "Galen does not say that physicians make a technical distinction between big fevers and small ones, but - in two places - that 'big fever' is an inaccurate expression (since the nature of a fever is not defined in quantitative terms), though common among physicians", citing *De comp. medic. per genera* 3.2 (13.572 Kühn); and *De different. febrium* 1.1

withered.[178] Two cases peculiar to his gospel are those of the bent woman,[179] and of Mary, Joanna and Susanna, who are not only named, but also described as "... some women who had been healed of evil spirits and infirmities...", with the added information that Joanna was the wife of Chuza, a steward of Herod Antipas, and that these women (and others) "provided for them (i.e. Jesus and his disciples) out of their means".[180] In this way Luke provides important sociological and economic information. He also emphasises Jesus' compassion,[181] and the sabbath healings.[182] It is Luke who has Jesus refer to himself as a physician,[183] and who has Jesus tell the parable of the Good Samaritan, which is significant in its account of healing practices.[184] So Luke, although using material found in both *Mark* (and *Matthew*) for many of his healing stories, provides more social information and sometimes more medical detail, uses a wider healing vocabulary and includes more healing stories.

Matthew also uses material found in *Mark*, but his language is highly stylised, following a systematic pattern: a formula for general healing (θεραπεύω plus a general statement);[185] and a formula for specific healings in response to a request made in faith: (i) *in absentia* (ἰάομαι);[186] (ii) through the touch of the patient (ἅπτομαι ...

(7.275 Kühn). Cadbury is anxious to refute Hobart's claims that Luke's language was medical, and therefore indicative of his belonging to the medical profession (vi). However, in this case, it could also have been an attempt to heighten the element of miracle in the story.

178 Lk 6.6-11. Hobart (1882) 7, assumes that it is Luke's medical background that makes him distinguish which hand was withered, especially as this detail is omitted by both other synoptists. However, if we assume that the man was right-handed, this information would have elicited more sympathy from Luke's audience. Cf. other details in Lukan healing stories designed to elicit sympathy: the only daughter of Jairus (8.42); the only son of the widow of Nain (7.12).

179 Lk 13.10-17

180 Lk 8.2-3

181 For example, for the widow at Nain (7.11-18).

182 Where Mark (3.1-6) and Matthew (12.9-14) only cite the man with the withered hand, Luke includes this healing (6.6-11), but adds the stories of the bent woman (13.10-17) and the man with dropsy (14.1-6).

183 Lk 4.23. For a full discussion of this incident, see below, 147-149.

184 Lk 10.25-37. See below, 128-129.

185 See below, 136, 138-139.

186 See below, chapter eight; and Apps 8:3 and 8:4.

σῴζω);[187] and (iii) through Jesus' touch (ἅπτομαι, κρατέω).[188] For particular healings of a similar nature his choice of words is deliberate and uniform (ἰάομαι, σῴζω, καθαρίζω). For general accounts of healing Matthew uses θεραπεύω in the active voice followed by general formulae which are vague as to the nature and extent of the healings performed. These formulae, through repetition, stress the magnitude of the healings and Jesus' role as a wonder-worker.[189] In this sense, like Homeric formulae, they become extensions of personality and assume the role of epithets, so that, for the reader, healing becomes an expected part of Jesus' behaviour.[190]

The synoptic gospels make it clear that Jesus' healing, preaching and teaching ministries formed an indissoluble unity. They went together. Each part was the logical extension of the other. Jesus was concerned with the whole man: with the health of his spirit and soul, body and mind. Mental distress, bodily pain, poverty and hunger all moved him with compassion. He saw all suffering, whatever its form, as the manifestation of evil. He saw his role as a struggle against suffering and evil. It is the combination of his perception of evil,[191] his holistic approach to the health of humankind,[192] and his compassion[193] that set him apart from all other wonder-workers.[194] In this he exhibits a completely new

---

187 See below, chapter nine; and Apps 7:10, 7:11 and 7:12.

188 See below, chapter nine; and App. 7:13.

189 For a discussion of Jewish wonder-workers see Vermes (1983) 58-82.

190 In the terms of contemporary narrative critical study, the 'implied author' manipulates the expectation of the 'implied reader'. (For a discussion, and an explanation of contemporary narrative critical study, see Moloney [1991], and [1992] 19-42.)

191 There is no concept of this in the literature surrounding Asklepios.

192 However, it is obvious from the works of Aristides especially (see App. 5:6), and even from the inscription of Marcus Julius Apellas at Epidauros (see App. 2:4), that treatment at asklepieia by the first and second centuries AD was holistic, including psychological, spiritual, mental and physical prescriptions.

193 Asklepios is not recorded as having been moved by the emotions implicit in the term σπλαγχνίζομαι, as Jesus was (see Section One).

194 Other wonder-workers were common enough to attract literature surrounding their amazing feats. See, for example, Philostratus, *Life of Apollonius* (esp. 4.45); and Lucian, *Philopseudes* (esp. 11). In the healing sphere, exorcists were common in Syria and Palestine (Lucian, *Philopseudes* 16; and Josephus, *Ant.* 8.45-49 [App. 6:2, **29**]); and the Roman emperor, Vespasian, is reported to have healed a blind man and a maimed man (Tacitus, *Hist.* 4.81; Suetonius, *Vespasian* 7; Dio 45.8.1).

approach to medicine and to humankind, and reveals a new perception of God.

7.2. Mark

Mark, as the earliest canonical gospel,[195] and including much of the material presented by Matthew and Luke,[196] must have priority in any analysis of Jesus' healing ministry. For it is in Mark's account that one comes closest in time to the historical Jesus,[197] and closest to an unidealised account of his actions.[198]

Several interesting features at once emerge. For Mark, Jesus' healing power is proof of Jesus' identity. There are no miraculous birth stories, as in *Matthew* and *Luke*, nor is there any lengthy genealogy. Mark, in contrast, begins his gospel with the highly theological statement:

> The beginning of the good news of Jesus Christ [the Son of God] (Ἀρχὴ τοῦ εὐαγγελίου Ἰησοῦ Χριστοῦ [υἱοῦ θεοῦ])[199]

and then, in the first chapter alone, reports 25% of his healing miracles - as proof of Jesus' identity and the arrival of the "king-

195 There is still debate concerning the dating of *Mark*. Recent scholarship suggests that it could be as early as AD 41 (see Hengel [1985] 2), although Hengel himself favours AD 69 as the earliest date for *Mark*. But see also Robinson (1985) who argues for an earlier dating for parts of John's gospel than *Mark*.

196 It is not proposed here to go into what has become known as the Synoptic Problem, or the relative merits of Source, Form or Redaction Criticism. It is sufficient to note that until the late 1960s scholars favoured the idea that *Mark* was the earliest canonical gospel, and that both Matthew and Luke used *Mark* and another source, known as Q, to compose their gospels, and that Matthew and Luke had access to further material exclusive to each of them. Since then other theories have been advanced, and no one solution has found universal approbation. See Hawkins (1909); Streeter (1930); Dibelius (1935); Bultmann (1963); Farmer (1964); Perrin (1969); Goulder (1974); Stoldt (1980); Farmer (1983); Sanders and Davies (1989). While a study of the synoptic use of the language of healing does not provide a simple solution, it does support the idea of the priority of *Mark*, and also that *Mark* (or some form of *Mark*) was known to the authors of both *Matthew* and *Luke*.

197 For the historical Jesus, see Schweitzer (1948); McCown (1940); Wrede (1971); Robinson (1983); Sanders and Davies (1989).

198 For a discussion, with examples, of passages in *Mark* supposedly altered or omitted by Matthew and Luke, see Hawkins (1909) 117-125.

199 Mk 1.1

dom".[200] As well, seventeen of the nineteen cases of healing reported by Mark occur in the first eight chapters of his gospel, prior to Peter's recognition and declaration of Jesus as the Messiah (8.29).[201] Therefore Mark's placing of the healing miracles is no accident, for, to him, Jesus himself is proof of his own identity, manifest in action. Mark uses Jesus' healing miracles to force his audience to the same conclusion.

There is a sense of urgency in Mark's account. Events move at speed (καὶ εὐθὺς), and are often portrayed in the perfect tense, creating a vivid atmosphere of present time, of a breathless, eye-witness account.[202] Mark is also fond of the imperfect tense in unusual places, to stress continuing action.[203]

Mark stresses the demonic nature of illness, and the *a priori* recognition of Jesus' identity by the demon world. Three[204] of the six general healing episodes[205] noted in *Mark* describe people cured of demonic possession. Four of the thirteen specific healing cases describe the activity of the spirit world, one case described as a demonic unclean spirit,[206] the other three as unclean spirits.[207] In this way illness, as in *Matthew* and *Luke*, is portrayed as the manifestation of evil, and Jesus' healing ministry is the logical outcome of his desire to combat and overcome the forces of evil at work in the world. It is significant that Jesus' identity is first recognised, and proclaimed, by an unclean spirit:

---

200 From the outset Mark's gospel is unashamedly polemical. It is a mistake to underestimate both the purpose and the craft of the author of this gospel.

201 See App. 7:4.

202 (i) Mark's penchant for the historic present tense has long been noted by scholars. See e.g. Hawkins (1909) 143, 214; Barclay (1976) 88, 130; Sanders and Davies (1989) 266.
(ii) A discussion of the authorship of *Mark* is outside the scope of this work at this stage. It is sufficient to note that many believe that Mark is the John Mark of Acts 12.12, 25; 15.37. In antiquity both Papias and Irenaeus suggested that Mark was Peter's interpreter (Eusebius, *Ecclesiastical History* 3.39.15, citing Papias; and 5.8.3, citing Irenaeus). The rather breathless style of the gospel supports this idea of an eye-witness account. However, the gospel could also be the product of an excellent raconteur, attempting to place his reader in the middle of the action.

203 See below, 130. Mark's use of the imperfect tense has not hitherto been given much attention.

204 Mk 1.32-34; 1.39; 6.13

205 Mk 1.32-34; 1.39; 3.10; 6.1-6; 6.13; 6.53-56

206 Mk 7.24-30

207 Mk 1.23-28; 5.1-20; 9.14-29

> What have you to do with us, Jesus of Nazareth? Have you come to destroy us? I know who you are: the holy one of God (Τί ἡμῖν καὶ σοί, Ἰησοῦ Ναζαρενέ; ἦλθες ἀπολέσαι ἡμᾶς; οἶδά σε τίς εἶ, ὁ ἅγιος τοῦ θεοῦ).[208]

In this way, Mark, at the outset, presents a dualistic understanding of the cosmos, of Good versus Evil, with Jesus as the agent of Good, with authority (ἐξουσία) over the agents of Evil.[209] Jesus is portrayed as bringing to fulfilment Judaistic eschatological hopes, as inaugurating the kingdom of God. Jesus' authority to heal, and particularly to triumph in his battle against demonic power is, to Mark, proof of his identity.

The battle with demonic power is given prominence in *Mark*. It figures in many of the healing miracles, in Jesus' motives for choosing the twelve, and in their commission. Mark gives three reasons for Jesus' choosing of the twelve:

> And he appointed twelve [whom also he named apostles] so that they might be with him, and that he might send them out to preach and to have authority to cast out demons (καὶ ἐποίησεν δώδεκα, [οὓς καὶ ἀποστόλους ὠνόμασεν,] ἵνα ὦσιν μετ' αὐτοῦ καὶ ἵνα ἀποστέλλῃ αὐτοὺς κηρύσσειν καὶ ἔχειν ἐξουσίαν ἐκβάλλειν τὰ δαιμόνια·).[210]

Thus companionship is to produce a mission - a mission of two equal parts - preaching and casting out demons. Later Jesus gives the twelve authority over unclean spirits:

> and he gave them authority over unclean spirits (καὶ ἐδίδου αὐτοῖς ἐξουσίαν τῶν πνευμάτων τῶν ἀκαθάρτων·)[211]

and sends them out two by two. Their mission was successful in this respect, for Mark reports:

> And after going out they preached that people should repent, and they began casting out many demons, and used to anoint with oil many who were ill and began healing [them] (καὶ ἐξελθόντες ἐκήρυξαν

---

208 Mk 1.24

209 In Jewish thought the "evil" power is not independent of God, but also created by him, so that there is no 'ontological' dualism: at most an 'ethical' dualism. However, when reading the gospels the synoptist portrayal of evil assumes an almost ontological nature. One wonders then how much the synoptists and their contemporaries were influenced by the dualistic thought inherent in the Persian religions.

210 Mk 3.14-15

211 Mk 6.7

> ἵνα μετανοῶσιν, καὶ δαιμόνια πολλὰ ἐξέβαλλον, καὶ ἤλειφον ἐλαίῳ πολλοὺς ἀρρώστους καὶ ἐθεράπευον).[212]

This is a most significant passage. There is no parallel in Matthew's gospel, and Luke only records in very general language that:

> and going out they began travelling through the villages, preaching the gospel and healing everywhere (ἐξερχόμενοι δὲ διήρχοντο κατὰ τὰς κώμας εὐαγγελιζόμενοι καὶ θεραπεύοντες πανταχοῦ).[213]

It is the only account in *Mark* of the success of the disciples' healing practices, and the only occasion in *Mark* where anointing with oil is mentioned as a therapeutic practice.

Anointing with olive oil was a common therapeutic practice in the ancient world.[214] It had several functions. If the skin was broken it served as an antiseptic by providing an effective barrier against harmful bacteria, and as an emollient, preventing bandages sticking to the wound.[215] As well, it was used extensively to treat skin disorders, and as the emollient agent for massage, particularly in the treatment of muscular complaints and bruising.[216] Matthew does not mention this practice, while Luke only mentions it in his account of Jesus' parable of the Good Samaritan.[217] No gospel writer records that Jesus himself ever used it as a therapeutic technique. However, it is unlikely that the disciples would have employed methods of which Jesus did not approve, and far more likely that they would have emulated his actions in every possible way. It is interesting to note that the Good Samaritan, when attending to the wounded man, poured on to his wounds a mixture

---

212 Mk 6.12-13

213 Lk 9.6

214 Hobart (1882) 28-29, cites Hippokrates, *Morb. Mul.* 656, *Affect.* 526, *Artic.* 829, *Ulcer.* 881, *Epid.* 1157; Aretaeus, *Cur. Acut. Morb.* 98; Dioscorides, *Mat. Med* 2.205, *Medic. Parab.* 2I.128; Galen, *Comp. Med.* 5.1 (12.815 Kühn), *Antid.* 2.17 (14.201 Kühn). See also App. 4:1, **13**.

215 Hippokrates, *In the Surgery* 12, and see also Withington in Hippokrates (1968) xx-xxi.

216 (i) Celsus, *De Medicina* 2.14.4: "... For it is desirable that even in acute and recent diseases the body should be anointed and then gently stroked, but only during remissions and before food...." See also Pliny, *Nat. Hist.* 15.5 and 23.39-40.
(ii) Wilkinson (1980) 152-154

217 Lk 10.25-37

of olive oil and wine, a treatment advocated by Hippokrates.[218] In *Luke*, the operative word is ἐπιχέω, not found elsewhere in the New Testament in the language of healing.[219]

The only other mention the practice of anointing with oil receives in the New Testament, in connection with healing, is in the letter of James[220] where James gives procedural advice, to be followed in cases of sickness:

> Is anyone among you ill? Let him call for the elders of the church, and let them pray over him, after anointing him with oil in the name of the Lord (ἀσθενεῖ τις ἐν ὑμῖν; προσκαλεσάσθω τοὺς πρεσβυτέρους τῆς ἐκκλησίας, καὶ προσευξάσθωσαν ἐπ' αὐτὸν ἀλείψαντες (αὐτὸν) ἐλαίῳ ἐν τῷ ὀνόματι τοῦ κυρίου·).[221]

Here it is possible that the act of anointing with oil might have a sacramental function either instead of, or as well as, a physical function. But, given the medical context of contemporary medical practice, James is probably endorsing the use of current medical knowledge in conjunction with prayer. The verb ἀλείφω does not normally carry any other than a physical connotation.[222]

Whatever their meaning and purpose, these three references do show that the practice of anointing with oil was implemented by the disciples in response to their healing commission, that it was part of their therapeutic technique, and that the early church continued to use it as part of its healing ministry.

---

218 Hippokrates, *Morb. Mul.* 656: ἢν δὲ αἱ μῆτραι ἐξίσχωσι, περινίψας αὐτὰς ὕδατι χλιερῷ καὶ ἀλείψας ἐλαίῳ καὶ οἴνῳ.

219 Hobart (1882) 28, citing Hippokrates, Dioscorides and Galen, concludes that "ἐπιχέειν, peculiar to St. Luke, is of frequent occurrence in the medical writers, and often, too, used in conjunction with ἔλαιον or οἶνος, or both together."

220 Sidebottom (1986) 61, notes that oil was used as a healing agent amongst the Hebrews, and that oil was a symbol of joy. See Psalm 45.7: "ἔλαιον ἀγαλλιάσεως" (LXX: ΨΑΛΜΟΙ ΜΔ 44 [45] 8). But see also Isaiah 1.5-6: "πᾶσα κεφαλὴ εἰς πόνον καὶ πᾶσα καρδία εἰς λύπην. ἀπὸ ποδῶν ἕως κεφαλῆς οὔτε τραῦμα οὔτε μώλωψ οὔτε πληγὴ φλεγμαίνουσα, οὐκ ἔστιν μάλαγμα ἐπιθεῖναι οὔτε ἔλαιον οὔτε καταδέσμους" (LXX).

221 James 5.14

222 This is the verb used at Mark 6.13 to describe the disciples' therapeutic technique, and at Mark 16.1 to describe the women's intention to anoint the body of Jesus with spices. It is also the verb used to describe the behaviour of the woman who anointed Jesus' feet with perfume (Luke 7.38). Luke puts this verb into the mouth of Jesus (7.46). See Trench (1961) 129: "ἀλείφειν is the mundane and profane, χρίειν the sacred and religious, word." Cf. Hippokrates, *Regimen* II.66 (App. 4:1, **13**) where ἀλείφω is used in a therapeutic context. See above, Section One, chapter four, n.536.

Mark's use of the imperfect tense to account for the healing ministry of the disciples is also significant:

> And they began casting out many demons, and used to anoint with olive oil many who were weak, and they began healing them.[223]

In contrast to the completed action of preaching, healing by the disciples is represented as an ongoing affair, as the beginning of a process. The nature of the healing ministry of the disciples is not characterised by instant cures and completed actions as is Jesus' ministry.

Mark has often been criticised for his use of Greek tense. However, it would appear that Mark was more discriminating in his choice of tense than at first sight seems obvious. Indeed, Mark's choice of tense appears to be deliberate, designed to convey a distinct difference between the disciples' and Jesus' healing ministries, and a distinct difference between the disciples' preaching and healing activities.

Mark's choice of language is varied. It is not as highly stylised as Matthew's, nor like Luke's,[224] but it does appear more spontaneous. Where Matthew carefully groups different sorts of healing, and is consistent in his use of language to describe them, Mark's language is more varied. In this way Matthew appears to have carefully categorised the healing stories in his gospel that are parallel to those found in *Mark*, and described each category in uniform language. Thus Mark's and Matthew's selection and treatment of healing language must be another argument in favour of the priority of Mark's gospel; an argument, to my knowledge, not hitherto discussed.[225]

7.3. Matthew

An analysis of the way Matthew portrays the authors of healing, their methods of treatment, and the illnesses of the patients treated, through the language used to describe these events, reveals

223 Mk 6.12-13

224 For a discussion of Luke's healing language, see below, especially chapter eight.

225 See also App. 7:7 for an analysis of Matthew's and Mark's presentation of controversial issues.

certain patterns: patterns of behaviour, patterns of treatment, and patterns of language.[226]

Matthew lists twenty-five[227] separate occasions when Jesus healed people. According to Matthew only Jesus was capable of healing,[228] despite giving his disciples the authority,[229] and the command[230] to do so. Healing usually occurred after a period of withdrawal, in response to compassion on the part of Jesus,[231] or faith in his power on the part of the patient,[232] and was by word or touch.[233] Healing involved an effort of will by Jesus and an active response by the patient.

The illnesses treated varied. Those specifically cited possibly reflect the prevalent medical problems of the time: four instances of blindness,[234] three instances of paralysis,[235] two maimed,[236] epilepsy,[237] leprosy,[238] fever,[239] haemorrhaging,[240] deafness,[241]

---

226 It also raises several questions. What was the purpose of Jesus' healing ministry, in his mind, in the minds of his disciples, and in the minds of the early Christians? If the answers to these questions differ, why is this so?

227 Fourteen specific, and eleven general (see Apps 7:1 and 7:5). I cannot accept 13.58 as does Wilkinson (1980) 22. The word δυνάμεις is ambiguous. However, I would divide the Galilean tour, described in 4.23-25 into two (or more) general healing episodes. Note the general description here, and for a discussion of Matthew's use of healing language to describe general healing episodes, and the epithetical nature of his descriptions, see below, 136, 138-139.

228 Mt 17.14-20

229 Mt 10.1

230 Mt 10.8

231 Mt 14.14; 20.34. The feeding of the 4,000 (15.32-39) was also in response to compassion felt by Jesus (15.32). The verb used is σπλαγχνίζομαι. For the use of this verb in a healing context see App. 7:13.

232 The centurion's "boy" (8.5-13); the Canaanite woman's daughter (15.21-28); the haemorrhaging woman (9.20-22).

233 Three verbs occur in healing accounts which describe the 'touch' of Jesus: ἅπτομαι, κρατέω and ἐπιτίθημι (τὰς χεῖρας). ἅπτομαι is the most common, but occurs only in synoptic stories, and only in the middle voice. See Apps 7:12, 7:13, and below, chapter nine. For a discussion of Jesus' rare use of saliva, see below, chapter nine, n.674.

234 Mt 9.27-28; 15.30-31; 20.30; 21.14 (App. 7:1)

235 Mt 4.24; 8.6; 9.2 (App. 7:1)

236 Mt 15.30-31; 21.14 (App. 7:1)

237 Mt 4.24 (App. 7:1)

238 Mt 8.2 (App. 7:1)

239 Mt 8.14 (App. 7:1)

240 Mt 9.20 (App. 7:1)

241 Mt 15.30-31 (App. 7:1)

crippleness,[242] a withered hand,[243] and death itself.[244] However, of those illnesses specifically cited, people suffering from demonic possession greatly outnumbered those suffering from all other illnesses.[245]

In seven instances Jesus healed people "possessed": on two occasions the patients being simply demonic,[246] on five occasions their "possession" being compounded by intensity,[247] blindness and deafness,[248] dumbness,[249] and epilepsy.[250]

As well as illnesses specifically cited, Jesus healed disorders in bulk on nine occasions; on ten, if the blind and maimed in the temple are included.[251] The language used to decribe these is imprecise and all embracing. It is not possible to ascertain the nature and extent of these healings. It is possible to ascertain that, in Matthew, the verb θεραπεύω in the active voice, followed by a general number, becomes a repetitive formula in the language of healing, a refrain used to sum up Jesus' behaviour with people, particularly crowds.[252]

7.4. Luke

Luke has the same number of healing stories as Matthew (twenty-five),[253] but is far more specific in his accounts of them. Where Matthew has eleven general healing episodes and Mark five, Luke

---

242 Mt 15.30 (App. 7:1)

243 Mt 12.10 (App. 7:1)

244 Mt 9.18, 23-26 (App. 7:1). The blind, lame, paralysed and maimed are also mentioned in inscriptions from Epidauros (see above, Section One, chapter two; and Apps 2:1 and 2:2).

245 Demonic possession is notably absent from the literature surrounding the asklepieia, but present in Jewish material. In the Septuagint, the book of Tobit deals with demon possession (see App. 6:1, **51**); while Josephus also describes Jewish exorcism (see App. 6:2, **29**). Exorcism, exhibiting a Jewish influence, also features in the magical papyri (see *PGM* 4.1227-1264 in Betz [1986] 62, and *PGM* 94.17-21 in Betz [1986] 304.

246 Mt 4.24, 8.16: δαιμονιζομένους

247 Mt 8.28: δύο δαιμονιζόμενοι ... χαλεποὶ λίαν ; 15.22: κακῶς δαιμονίζεται

248 Mt 12.22: δαιμονιζόμενος τυφλὸς καὶ κωφός

249 Mt 9.32: κωφὸν δαιμονιζόμενον

250 Mt 17.14-20

251 Mt 21.14

252 For a discussion of the significance of the use of this verb in general healing episodes, see below, 136-143; and for a detailed analysis of the verb itself, see Apps 7:8 and 7:9.

253 App. 7:3

has seven,[254] and even gives specific information in these. For example, Luke describes the disciples' healing activity (9.6); and names Joanna (wife of Chuza), Susanna and Mary as companions and women who had been healed (8.1-3). As well he gives details of seventeen other specific healing episodes (Mark thirteen, Matthew fourteen) performed by Jesus. Of these, five patients are women (Mark and Matthew four each).[255] Luke's interest in women is reflected in the rest of his gospel: it is Luke who tells the stories of Elizabeth, and Anna the prophetess,[256] of Martha and Mary; and it is Luke who describes Jesus' compassion for the widow of Nain, and the subsequent "healing" of her son.[257] Luke is also more interested in the poor, and the outcast. Therefore his purpose appears to be to appeal to people of all stations in life, and of both sexes. His is a gospel for all humankind.

Luke is also more explicit in his analogies between health or wholeness, and righteousness. It is Luke who has Jesus refer to himself as a physician at Nazareth in a pejorative tone,[258] and it is Luke who has Jesus explain:

> The healthy have no need of a physician, only those who are ill; I am not here to call the righteous, but sinners [irreligious people],[259] to repentance[260] (Οὐ χρείαν ἔχουσιν οἱ ὑγιαίνοντες ἰατροῦ ἀλλὰ

---

254 App. 7:5

255 App. 7:6

256 These two stories are parts of the first two chapters of Luke, which contain material unparalleled in other gospels. As well, Luke's gospel has a second preface at the beginning of chapter 3. This has led some scholars to suppose that Luke adapted this material, and inserted it as a new beginning to his gospel (see Ropes [1960] 69). However, Moloney (1992) 105, n.12 presumes "that Luke 1-2 form the prologue to the Gospel of Luke." Certainly the theological interests and issues raised in the first two chapters of *Luke* are reflected in the rest of the gospel, as Moloney, 101-130, shows. Luke's interest in women, and compassion for mothers, is also reflected in his choice of healing stories in the later chapters of the gospel.

257 Lk 7.1-11

258 Lk 4.23. For a discussion of this saying see below, 147-149.

259 Arndt and Gingrich (1957) 43, cite the use of ἁμαρτωλὸς in Lk 5.30 as meaning *"irreligious, unobservant people,* of those who did not observe the law in detail". Here, this saying occurs in the same context (a dispute with the Pharisees and their scribes concerning the keeping of the law, especially with regard to table-fellowship).

260 The Greek verb μετανοέω and its cognate forms are generally used in the gospels in the same sense as the Hebrew *shûb,* which means to *turn back* or *return* (to God). See Cranfield (1959) 43-46.

οἱ κακῶς ἔχοντες· οὐκ ἐλήλυθα καλέσαι δικαίους ἀλλὰ ἁμαρτωλοὺς εἰς μετάνοιαν).[261]

So the synoptists portray Jesus' mission as a mission to heal humankind, and the physical healings exemplify this. To illustrate this Luke includes a cross-section of society amongst those who were healed: sons,[262] a daughter,[263] a mother-in-law,[264] a state slave,[265] a temple slave,[266] a beggar,[267] the outcast (lepers);[268] and those from "acceptable" society.[269] Luke also includes a range of diseases: those demonic,[270] feverish,[271] weak,[272] leprous (unclean),[273] maimed,[274] paralysed,[275] haemorrhaging (unclean),[276] epileptic,[277] dumb,[278] blind[279] and wounded.[280]

Like Matthew and Mark, Luke portrays illness and disease as the manifestation of evil, as the work of Satan.[281]

But what are the terms the synoptists use to describe the healing activity of Jesus, and what do they mean? Are these terms reflected in John's gospel, and other New Testament writings?

7.5. θεραπεύω

It is to a consideration of the verb θεραπεύω and its family of words[282] that we must turn first, as this family of words is by far the most popular in the New Testament language of healing. At

261 Lk 5.31-32
262 Lk 7.11-18; 9.37-43 (App. 7:3)
263 Lk 8.40-42, 49-56 (App. 7:3)
264 Lk 4.38-39 (App. 7:3)
265 Lk 7.1-10 (App. 7:3)
266 Lk 22.49-51 (App. 7:3)
267 Lk 18.35-43 (App. 7:3)
268 Lk 5.12-14; 17.11-19 (App. 7:3)
269 Lk 4.38-39; 5.17-26; 8.2-3 (App. 7:3)
270 Lk 4.31-38; 4.41; 6.17-19; 7.21; 8.2-3; 8.26-39; 9.37-43; 11.14-16 (App. 7:3)
271 Lk 4.38-39 (App. 7:3)
272 Lk 4.40; 5.15-16; 8.2-3; 13.10-17 (App. 7:3)
273 Lk 5.12-14 (App. 7:3)
274 Lk 6.6-11 (App. 7:3)
275 Lk 5.17-26 (App. 7:3)
276 Lk 8.43-48 (App. 7:3)
277 Lk 9.37-43 (App. 7:3)
278 Lk 11.14-16 (App. 7:3)
279 Lk 7.21; 18.35-43 (App. 7:3)
280 Lk 22.49-51 (App. 7:3)
281 See especially Lk 13.10-17 (App. 7:3).
282 See Apps 7:8 and 7:9.

first sight this is surprising, as it is completely contrary to the incidence of the verb in healing language surrounding the Greek asklepieia,[283] and the incidence of the verb in the Septuagint in a healing context.[284] θεραπεύω occurs in verbal form forty-three times in the New Testament, thirty-five times in the synoptic gospels.[285] It appears once in John's gospel,[286] five times in *Acts*[287] and twice in *Revelation*.[288] θεραπεύω occurs almost twice as frequently as the other medical healing verb ἰάομαι, which only occurs in verbal form twenty-six times.[289] The very popularity of θεραπεύω seems to have led to its neglect in semantic studies, scholars consistently having studied words that appear infrequently, while taking for granted the meaning of words which appear frequently and in similar contexts.[290] It is time then to redress this imbalance, and

---

283 See Section One: chapter two, and Apps 2:1 and 2:2; chapter three, and App. 3:2; chapter five.

284 See chapter six, and App. 6:1.

285 It is at once obvious that Luke is most at home with the Greek language. He uses θεραπεύω in a variety of forms (thirteen in his gospel, and a further three in *Acts*), whereas Matthew only uses seven different forms, and of his sixteen usages the same form occurs eight times. Mark, although only using θεραπεύω five times, uses it in three different forms, and is carefully selective in his use of tense. See Apps 7:8 and 7:9.

286 John 5.10. See App. 7:8.

287 Acts 4.14; 5.16; 8.7; 17.25; 28.9. See App. 7:8.

288 Revelation 3.3, 12

289 See Apps 8:3 and 8:4. ἰάομαι in cognate form occurs thirteen times, seven times denoting a physician, three times referring to the gifts of healing, and three times as the noun "healing". See App. 8:3.

290 So Hawkins (1909), although stating (2) that it is "much more important to examine words which are used more frequently, though it may not be exclusively" does not consider the role of θεραπεύω in its own right. As his object is to contribute to the study of the Synoptic Problem, this is perhaps understandable. However, less easily understood is the complete absence of θεραπεύω in the works of Hobart (1882), and Cadbury (1969), for, even though Hobart chose to focus on words that were peculiar to Luke, some comment on Luke's use of θεραπεύω in a discussion of healing language would surely have been justified. That the meaning of θεραπεύω in the New Testament is far from certain is illustrated by comparing Beyer in Kittel *et al.* (1965) 129: "θεραπεύω is used ... in the sense of 'to heal,' and always in such a way that the reference is not to medical treatment, which might fail, but to real healing" with Moulton and Milligan (1930) 289: "... θεραπεύω, used as a medical term, means strictly 'treat medically' rather than 'heal' ...". Arndt and Gingrich (1957) 359, cite both meanings, i.e. to "treat" (medically) and to "heal". As well, there is an imbalance in terms of the space devoted to each word group, especially in Kittel *et al.* (1965): 4 pages (128-132) for the θεραπεύω word group; 21 pages (194-215) for the ἰάομαι word group.

analyse the use and meaning of this verb. In order to do this θεραπεύω will be considered in three different contexts in the synoptic gospels: as it appears in general healing episodes, in specific healing episodes, and in thought and conversation.[291]

7.5.1. θεραπεύω in general healing episodes

In Section One we saw how θεραπεύω in a medical context meant *to give medical treatment* and was used to describe a process, and that in a teaching context it meant *to change one's way of life*. In meaning its aspect was generally continuous. So it is interesting to find that this imperfect aspect of the verb also appears in the New Testament. According to Matthew, when Jesus began his ministry he was:

> θεραπεύων πᾶσαν νόσον καὶ πᾶσαν μαλακίαν.[292]

This θεραπεύων behaviour is linked to the activities of διδάσκων and κηρύσσων. It is the first of two instances of Matthew using the present participle of θεραπεύω, the second occurring at 9.35 in identical language. Both usages occur in general healing episodes, describing Jesus' behaviour while travelling. No other New Testament author uses θεραπεύω in this form to describe Jesus' behaviour.[293] Thus θεραπεύω in the form of a present participle in *Matthew* is part of a formula used to describe Jesus' behaviour while travelling. These two instances form a doublet. Both occur immediately prior to collections of Jesus' sayings, in chapters 5-7 and 10. Several suggestions have been put forward to account for this doublet,[294] but as Luke also uses a present participle to describe the disciples' healing behaviour while travelling (9.6), behaviour exhibited in response to their commission (9.1-2), it seems most probable that Matthew's use of the formula is to describe Jesus' habitual behaviour while travelling from village to village.[295]

---

291 For the occurrence of θεραπεύω in commands and commissions see below, chapter ten.

292 Mt 4.23

293 Although Luke uses a present participle to describe the disciples' healing behaviour while travelling at 9.6.

294 See Hawkins (1909) 92-93.

295 This could be a description of Jesus' sabbath behaviour. It was his custom (Luke 4.16) to teach and preach in the local synagogue, if there was one, and this behaviour usually included a healing component: διδάσκων ἐν ταῖς συναγωγαῖς αὐτῶν καὶ κηρύσσων τὸ εὐαγγέλιον τῆς βασιλείας καὶ

And, just as Jesus' teaching and preaching was habitual behaviour, either reported by the use of a present participle (as in both these instances), or introduced by a verb in the imperfect tense, as ἐδίδασκεν αὐτοὺς λέγων (5.2), so it is perfectly normal for Matthew to emphasise this behaviour by repeating his description.

θεραπεύω also appears in the active indicative imperfect tense. We have already noted in some detail Mark's use of the imperfect tense to describe the disciples' healing behaviour in response to their commission.[296] Luke also uses the imperfect tense[297] to describe Jesus' behaviour in a crowd situation (4.40), where "having laid his hands upon each one of them,[298] he began healing them." Does this imply that θεραπεύω in a crowd situation in the imperfect means one-by-one in *Luke*? Or is the healing therapy the beginning of a process? It is surprising that a possible answer to this question is found in the synoptic use of θεραπεύω in the 3rd person singular active indicative aorist, ἐθεράπευσεν.

Mark uses ἐθεράπευσεν three times in his gospel,[299] each time describing Jesus' behaviour in a crowd situation. In the first episode (1.34) the patients are described as πολλοὺς κακῶς ἔχοντας ποικίλαις νόσοις. These patients were "brought" to Jesus, at sundown, i.e. after the sabbath had ended. Mark reports that "the whole city (Capernaum?) was gathered together about the door." The second episode (3.10) is also a general healing episode in a very large crowd situation. Here the crowd "followed" Jesus, and were so anxious to touch him that he was in danger of being crushed - the reason being that he had healed many (πολλοὺς γὰρ ἐθεράπευσεν), so that as many as suffered (εἶχον μάστιγας) were anxious to touch him (αὐτοῦ ἅψωνται). This healing behaviour makes unclean spirits recognise him and proclaim his identity (3.11), although Jesus commands them to secrecy (ἐπετίμα), as in the first healing episode recorded by Mark.[300] Thus these two instances of θεραπεύω in the 3rd person singular aorist describe

---

θεραπεύων πᾶσαν νόσον καὶ πᾶσαν μαλακίαν ἐν τῷ λαῷ (teaching in their synagogues and preaching the good news of the Kingdom and healing/ treating every disease and every weakness among the people [Mt 4.23]).

296 See above, 129-130.

297 Another Lukan usage (in the present tense) describes the scribes' and Pharisees' perception of Jesus' sabbath behaviour in the story of the man with the withered hand (6.7), a usage of θεραπεύω that is entirely in keeping with the use of all four gospel authors. For a full discussion, see below, 146-151.

298 For the language, see App. 7:13, and for a discussion, below, chapter nine.

299 Mk 1.34, 3.10, 6.5

300 Mk 1.21-28

Jesus' behaviour in a crowd situation, with people who "follow" or are "brought" to him. Both episodes follow accounts of Jesus' teaching in the synagogues.[301]

Mark's final use of this form of θεραπεύω occurs in his description of Jesus' activities at Nazareth.[302] Again it describes a general healing episode in a crowd situation. Mark reports that Jesus was unable to do any mighty works there except that he laid his hands on a few who were ill and healed them (καὶ οὐκ ἐδύνατο ἐκεῖ ποιῆσαι οὐδεμίαν δύναμιν, εἰ μὴ ὀλίγοις ἀρρώστοις ἐπιθεὶς τὰς χεῖρας ἐθεράπευσεν).[303] Neither Matthew nor Luke describe this episode in these terms. Matthew (13.58) states that "he did not do many mighty works there because of their unbelief" (καὶ οὐκ ἐποίησεν ἐκεῖ δυνάμεις πολλὰς διὰ τὴν ἀπιστίαν αὐτῶν), while Luke does not report any mighty works at all.[304] Can it be, then, that the prerequisite for Jesus to exhibit θεραπεύων behaviour is the willingness of the people present to listen to his message? Perhaps *Matthew* can provide the answer.

Although Matthew chooses to omit θεραπεύω from his account of the episode at Nazareth, he is fond of the 3rd person singular aorist indicative of this verb to describe Jesus' behaviour. This form of θεραπεύω accounts for half of Matthew's use of this verb and in every instance it describes Jesus' behaviour in a crowd situation (as in *Mark*), when people either "follow" him, or are "brought" to him. In seven of the eight instances[305] the language used to describe the maladies of the people who "follow", or are "brought" is vague and generalised:

> πάντας τοὺς κακῶς ἔχοντας ... ἐθεράπευσεν (4.24; 8.16)

with the added information at 4.24:

> ποικίλαις νόσοις καὶ βασάνοις συνεχομένους.

Similarly:

> [ὄχλοι] πολλοί, καὶ ἐθεράπευσεν αὐτοὺς πάντας (12.15),

---

301 Mk 1.21f.; 3.1-6

302 Mk 6.1-6

303 Mark describes the laying on of hands in healing episodes more frequently than either Matthew (who doesn't use it at all) or Luke. See App. 7:13.

304 Lk 4.16-30. This is odd, and must be deliberate, for Luke likes to record wondrous things.

305 Cf. 12.22: a specific healing in a crowd situation. For a discussion, see below, 143-144.

ἐθεράπευσεν τοὺς ἀρρώστους αὐτῶν (14.14),

ἑτέρους πολλούς ... καὶ ἐθεράπευσεν αὐτούς (15.30),

ὄχλοι πολλοί, καὶ ἐθεράπευσεν αὐτοὺς (19.2),

τυφλοὶ καὶ χωλοὶ ... ἐθεράπευσεν (21.14).

It is not possible to ascertain the nature and extent of these episodes. It is possible to ascertain that ἐθεράπευσεν followed by a general number becomes a repetitive formula in Matthew's language of healing, a refrain used to sum up Jesus' behaviour with people, particularly crowds, and, in every instance this behaviour is accompanied by the activities of preaching and teaching. Indeed, Matthew even substitutes the verb θεραπεύω for διδάσκω, when using the same material as Mark.[306] Thus Matthew uses θεραπεύω in the 3rd person singular aorist as a gnomic aorist, describing the habitual action of Jesus, and the usual result of his preaching and teaching. Since Matthew places all these instances in a teaching context, the inference is that θεραπεύω refers to spiritual, rather than physical, healing.

Luke also uses this form of θεραπεύω in a general healing episode, to describe the treatment of diseases (νόσων), illnesses/chronic irritations (μαστίγων) and evil spirits (πνευμάτων πονηρῶν). The context is significant. This episode occurs between the question from John the Baptist concerning Jesus' identity, and Jesus' answer to him. That the aorist ἐθεράπευσεν describes completed action is emphasised by Luke's use of ἐν ἐκείνῃ τῇ ὥρᾳ. The stress on the instantaneous and the miraculous is typical of Luke. However, in this case, one cannot help wondering if the instantaneous nature of the "cure" can be explained by conversion.[307]

Luke also likes to use the passive voice of θεραπεύω. In fact, θεραπεύω in the passive voice only occurs fourteen times in the New Testament, and, of these fourteen, ten are peculiar to Luke.[308] Luke is the only New Testament author to use θεραπεύω in the passive voice in the present and imperfect tenses, and all occur in general healing episodes. The present passive infinitive of θεραπεύω, θεραπεύεσθαι, occurs only once, at Luke 5.15, in a narrative passage. Jesus is in a crowd situation and we are told that the people came "to listen and to be healed of their infirmities (ἀσθενειῶν)." Luke is

306 Cf. Mk 10.1; Mt 19.2

307 Lk 7.21

308 *Luke* five, *Acts* five. The other four are found in *Matthew* (17.18), *John* (5.10), and *Revelation* (13.3, 12). See App. 7:9.

fond of the broad term "ἀσθενειῶν" and uses it often in accounts of general healing episodes in conjunction with θεραπεύω.[309] One wonders what sort of infirmities they were: mental? emotional? spiritual? physical? or a combination of some or all of them? The inference here is that it is Jesus' "message" that heals, and that this is a process. Hence the use of the present infinitives: ἀκούειν and θεραπεύεσθαι. His audience were "great crowds" (ὄχλοι πολλοὶ) who came to "hear" (an active infinitive requiring an active response by the listener) and "be healed" (by an unnamed agent). Luke does not mention any physical contact by Jesus, such as his laying his hands on them, as at 4.40. The therapy in this case seems to be not only listening, but also hearing (and understanding) Jesus' message. Here θεραπεύεσθαι is very much linked to the idea of the arrival of the kingdom (an awareness of God's presence), and the change in thinking (μετάνοιαν, 5.32) that this brings in their lives, and the resultant sense of community belongingness that this engenders. Again, the primary emphasis of θεραπεύω appears to be spiritual, and its aspect continuous.

Luke uses the 3rd person plural passive imperfect ἐθεραπεύοντο on three occasions, once in his gospel, and twice in *Acts* .[310] All three episodes are general healing episodes, the main characters being Jesus, Peter and Paul respectively. In the gospel episode Luke is careful to use θεραπεύω and ἰάομαι contiguously.[311] It is, as one would expect by now, a crowd situation. The people came to listen/hear (ἀκοῦσαι), and be healed (ἰαθῆναι). It was those who were troubled by unclean spirits who ἐθεραπεύοντο. Again, the therapy appears to be the "message" of Jesus.

The context of the next occurrence of ἐθεραπεύοντο is so atypical that one wonders whether most of the episode,[312] or indeed the entire context[313] could be an interpolation. Certainly θεραπεύω is used in a crowd situation, in a general healing episode, and those healed were "brought" to Peter. The patients were the weak (τοὺς ἀσθενεῖς), and those afflicted by unclean spirits (ὀχλουμένους ὑπὸ πνευμάτων ἀκαθάρτων). This is all perfectly in keeping with other usages of θεραπεύω. The healing agent is unspecified, again a perfectly normal Lukan practice. But the context is unnatural.

---

309 Lk 4.40, 5.15, 8.2, 10.9, 13.10-17; Acts 5.16, 28.9. But cf. Mt 10.8. Mark prefers the term ἄρρωστος in conjunction with θεραπεύω (6.13).

310 Lk 6.18; Acts 5.16, 28.9

311 Luke likes to use θεραπεύω and ἰάομαι contiguously. For a full discussion of the significance of this see below, and chapters eight and ten.

312 Acts 5.12-15 (App. 8:1)

313 Acts 5.1-15, 19-26 (App. 8:1)

There is no mention of teaching, which is most unusual. The context is also unnatural: the episode is sandwiched between the account of the deaths of Ananias and Sapphira,[314] and the apostles' imprisonment by the Sadducees and their miraculous release by an angel.[315] It is appropriate that the episode is introduced by the vague general statement:

> many signs and wonders (σημεῖα καὶ τέρατα πολλὰ) were done among the people by the hands of the apostles.

The preceding episode is characterised by greed and violence, injecting an atmosphere of fear, this episode by magic,[316] and the following by violence.[317] The language of the actual verse in which ἐθεραπεύοντο appears is entirely predictable, it is the context which is unnatural. Jesus' gospel teaching, motivated by compassion[318] and focusing on love[319] and forgiveness,[320] is replaced by fear-inspiring signs and wonders. Perhaps this is the strongest argument yet for the verb θεραπεύω implying conversion. Certainly these fearful events caused the number of believers to grow mightily.[321] The whole chapter appears highly hellenised.

The final occurrence of ἐθεραπεύοντο occurs at Acts 28.9, in a general healing episode on the island of Malta, and Paul is the central figure. It follows the specific healing episode where Paul visited Publius' father and prayed, and putting his hands on him healed him (ἐπιθεὶς τὰς χεῖρας αὐτῷ ἰάσατο αὐτόν).[322] He had been sick with dysentery and fever (πυρετοῖς καὶ δυσεντερίῳ). Publius fulfilled the hospitality requirements laid down by Jesus as a prerequisite for healing.[323] Paul also fulfilled the instructions Jesus gave to the disciples.[324] Luke chooses ἰάομαι to describe this

---

314 Acts 5.1-11 (App. 8:2)

315 Acts 5.17-21

316 Peter's shadow: 5.15

317 It may be significant that this is not a "we" passage, and that, in fact, no punitive miracles occur in "we" passages (see Apps 8:1 and 8:2).

318 See Mt 9.36; and cf. Mt 14.14, 20.34; Mk. 1.41, 9.22; Lk 7.11-18. Luke also has the verb σπλαγχνίζομαι motivating the actions of the Good Samaritan (10.33).

319 Mk 12.28-34; Mt 22.34-40; Lk 10.25-28; Jn 13.34-35

320 Lk 5.17-26

321 Acts 9.31, 9.35, 9.42, 12.24, 19.20 (see Apps 8:1 and 8:2)

322 Acts 28.7-8 (App.8:1)

323 Mt 10.8-14; Lk 9.4-5

324 Lk 10.1-12. Similar requirements and instructions are noted at *GT* #14 in Robinson (1978) 119.

healing.[325] The very next verse describes the healing of a crowd of weak people (οἱ λοιποὶ οἱ ἐν τῇ νήσῳ ἔχοντες ἀσθενείας) who came and were healed (προσήρχοντο καὶ ἐθεραπεύοντο). This is a far happier context for this form of θεραπεύω than that described above.[326] But, as with Peter, no agent is specified, the Lukan and Jewish way of signalling that "God" was the source of healing treatment. And, as with Peter, the catalyst for the gathering of the crowd is an event, rather than teaching. As well, an element of magic was introduced in the episode prior to the healing of Publius' father, where Paul was bitten by a viper without ill effect. It seems that the editor of *Acts* was most anxious to balance all features of the stories concerning Peter and Paul,[327] and to set the scene for a miraculous event. Thus it becomes obvious that both audience and setting have important effects on editorial comment.

Luke also uses θεραπεύω in the third person aorist passive at Acts 8.7, in a general healing episode in Samaria, with Philip as the central character. The people there "gave heed to what was said by Philip, when they heard him (ἐν τῷ ἀκούειν) and saw the signs (τὰ σημεῖα) which he did." The illnesses cited are more specific than is usual with a form of θεραπεύω: the lame and the paralysed (πολλοὶ δὲ παραλελυμένοι καὶ χωλοὶ), rather than the infirm. However, there are crowds of people (οἱ ὄχλοι), and θεραπεύω is used in conjunction with preaching (8.4). As with the passive use of this verb with Peter (5.16) and Paul (28.9) as the central characters, no agent is specified, the inference being that again "God" was the source of healing. As in the gospels, people are healed when they hear and understand Philip's message, and are conscious of the presence of the kingdom.

Luke describes another general healing episode with the pluperfect passive of θεραπεύω at Luke 8.2.[328] Here it is part of a general healing that contains some specific information. The use of the feminine participle, and the following very specific information concerning three of the women, including their

---

325 This is significant. The form is the aorist middle: ἰάσατο, elsewhere used only of Jesus. See App. 8:4.

326 The account of the healing of Publius' father, and the following crowd episode, both occur in a "we" passage.

327 Peter's shadow (5.15), Paul's immunity (28.3-6), Paul's aprons (19.12). However, only Paul has his actions described with the aorist middle of ἰάομαι, a tense only used elsewhere by Luke of Jesus (see App. 8:4).

328 The only occurrence of the pluperfect passive of θεραπεύω in the New Testament (see App. 7:9).

names, is typical of Lukan precision concerning identity.[329] Luke provides the important sociological and economic information that the women contributed to the support of Jesus and his disciples out of their means. They had been healed of evil spirits and infirmities (πνευμάτων πονηρῶν καὶ ἀσθενειῶν). The result was that they were included in the new community and travelled with Jesus (on this occasion at least). Their "cure" was discipleship, i.e. listening, understanding, and acting on Jesus' message. In short, they were τεθεραπευμέναι.[330]

Thus, in general healing episodes, θεραπεύω is the preferred synoptic word to describe the effect of Jesus' (or Peter's, Philip's or Paul's) presence, and in the gospels it is always linked with preaching and teaching.

7.5.2. θεραπεύω in specific healing stories

In contrast to the wealth of occurrences of θεραπεύω in general healing episodes in the synoptic gospels, θεραπεύω occurs relatively few times in specific healing episodes. We have already noted that Matthew only uses the 3rd singular aorist ἐθεράπευσεν once in a specific healing episode (12.22), and then it is in a crowd situation, in an episode that forcefully links healing activity with teaching and preaching. As with other instances of this form of θεραπεύω, the man, who was δαιμονιζόμενος τυφλὸς καὶ κωφός, was brought to Jesus by unnamed persons. This incident is used by Matthew as a catalyst for Jesus' teaching (12. 23-50). It is obvious that his audience is both blind and dumb to the significance of his person and message. Therefore this healing takes on a symbolic significance. Jesus healed the blind and dumb demoniac so that he could speak and see; Jesus treated his audience by preaching and teaching. Their therapy was to "hear" and "see" (i.e. understand) his message. It is not surprising that the man is also characterised

329 Cf. the information given concerning the identity of the victims of punishment miracles in *Acts* (App. 8:2).

330 Cf. the case of Marcus Julius Apellas (*IG* IV^2 1, no. 126; Apps 2:4, 2:5 and chapter two), who was told by the priest of Asklepios at Epidauros that he was healed (τεθεράπευσαι), and the time had come for him to pay up. Presumably those were also his marching orders: it was time for him to rejoin his community and get on with his life. For him, and also for the Lukan women, to be healed involved an active response. Cf. Moulton and Milligan (1930) 289, who translate this inscription thus: "treatment has been prescribed for you, and you must pay the physician's fee", with the comment that "the actual treatment is to follow".

as a demoniac: to be unable to "hear" and "see" Jesus' message is, in synoptist thought, to be separated from God, i.e. in the grip of "evil". It is interesting that Matthew reports that it was specifically the Pharisees who misunderstood Jesus' teaching and healing actions on this occasion, and who cited the source of his power as Beelzebul. Later Jesus was to call them "blind" guides.[331] As in general healing episodes Matthew again uses the active form of θεραπεύω in a teaching context.

Matthew's use of θεραπεύω in the passive voice is quite different. Indeed, while forms of θεραπεύω occur fourteen times in *Matthew*,[332] θεραπεύω occurs only once in the passive voice,[333] in an episode that is significant for its unusual language, context, and content. As well as being the only occasion in *Matthew* where θεραπεύω appears in the passive voice, it is also the only occasion where πάσχω appears in Matthew's language of healing, and the only occasion where ἐπιτιμάω occurs in the act of healing.

The condition of the patient, the son of the man requesting the cure, is described as:

> σεληνιάζεται καὶ κακῶς πάσχει.[334]

Jesus' treatment is recorded thus:

> καὶ ἐπετίμησεν αὐτῷ ὁ Ἰησοῦς, καὶ ἐξῆλθεν ἀπ' αὐτοῦ τὸ δαιμόνιον· καὶ ἐθεραπεύθη ὁ παῖς ἀπὸ τῆς ὥρας ἐκείνης.[335]

This is the only occasion in *Matthew* where a δαιμόνιον is specifically linked with epilepsy. And here, despite Jesus' previously giving the twelve authority (10.1) to "heal", and the command (10.8) to do so, they were unable to do so in this case (17.16), much to Jesus' chagrin (17.17). When the disciples ask Jesus privately why they were unable to "heal", the reply is:

331 See below for a discussion of the significance of the verb θεραπεύω in Pharisaic thought and conversation.

332 Mt 4.23, 24; 8.7, 16; 9.35; 10.1, 8; 12.15, 22; 14.14; 15.30; 17.18; 19.2; 21.14

333 Mt 17.18

334 Mt 17.15. One would expect ἔχει, in keeping with Matthew's normal usage. But note the manuscript variation. Metzger (1975) 43, *re* 17.15 πάσχει {C}: "The reading κακῶς ἔχει appears to have been substituted for κακῶς πάσχει, either as a more idiomatic Greek expression or because κακῶς πάσχει was thought to be pleonastic."

335 Mt 17.18

διὰ τὴν ὀλιγοπιστίαν ὑμῶν.[336]

Then follows the famous saying about faith the size of a mustard seed.

In this story, Jesus cured by command, with authority and anger (ἐπετίμησεν). As has been noted, this is the only occasion in *Matthew* that ἐπιτιμάω occurs in the act of healing.[337] However, the use of this verb to describe Jesus' behaviour on another occasion is worth noting. At 8.26 Jesus ἐπετίμησεν the winds and the sea, and then, just as at 17.20, chided the disciples for their ὀλιγοπιστίαν. The similarity in usage, and the combination of terminology, are too striking to ignore. The linking of ἐπιτιμάω and ὀλιγοπιστία in both stories highlights Jesus' immense ἐξουσία, over the forces of nature,[338] and over the forces of evil.[339] Both episodes attempt to measure success or failure in terms of faith. The disciples, guilty of ὀλιγοπιστία in chapter eight, nevertheless are given authority to "heal" (10.1) by Jesus. However, they remain guilty of ὀλιγοπιστία (17.20), and therefore of failure. Faith therefore, for Matthew, both of the person requesting the healing, and of the person performing the healing, is of enormous importance to the outcome.[340] This particular healing, in common with other healings specifically cited by Matthew[341] is a healing performed in response to a parental request, made in faith. However, through his choice of language, Matthew highlights the immense significance of this particular healing story.

Howard Clark Kee,[342] attempting to isolate the meaning of ἐπιτιμάω in Mark's exorcism stories, has noted that it is equivalent to a Semitic root found in several of the Qumran texts.[343]

He has pointed out that the common translation of ἐπιτιμάω as "rebuked", does not do it justice, but rather that the use of ἐπιτιμάω describes:

---

336 Mt 17.20

337 But see 12.16, where it occurs after a healing episode. See also App. 7:13 for the use of this verb in the context of other healing stories in the New Testament.

338 Mt 8

339 Mt 17. But the sea was associated with evil in the Old Testament, so that, in both episodes, Jesus is depicted as overcoming the power of evil. (See, for example, Isaiah 27.1)

340 Note the episode in Nazareth, where the people were without faith (13.58).

341 See below, chapter eight.

342 (1968) 232-246

343 ibid. 232

> the word of command that brought ... hostile powers under control.[344]

Therefore this story contains several interesting features, described in unusual language. Matthew's single usage of ἐπετίμησεν to describe the act of healing, and the single usage of πάσχει and ἐθεραπεύθη, all combine to signal the uniqueness of the episode. Not least of these is the use of θεραπεύω in the passive voice, describing the intervention and activity of God.[345] On other occasions when the passive voice of a healing verb is required to describe a healing episode, Matthew chooses to use ἰάομαι, σῴζω and καθαίρω.[346] The context of this story is also significant: it is the first healing episode after Peter's declaration of Jesus' identity.[347] This story is designed to provide further 'proof' of the veracity of Peter's declaration, should the reader require it.

7.5.3. The use of θεραπεύω in thought or conversation

Jesus is reported by the synoptists as using θεραπεύω in direct speech on five occasions.[348] Matthew reports that Jesus used θεραπεύω in the future tense (θεραπεύσω), describing his intention, in reply to the centurion's request to heal his son,[349] although the centurion uses forms of ἰάομαι when making his request.[350] The second time in *Matthew* that Jesus uses θεραπεύω in direct speech is when he commissions his disciples, and commands them to "θεραπεύετε"

---

344 ibid. 246

345 The other two instances of this form of θεραπεύω occur in *Revelation* (13.3,12), in a description of the vision of the first beast. It had seemed to have a mortal wound on one of its heads, but the wound had been healed. The inference is that the scarring is visible, so that the state of the beast, while healed, is different to its original state. This usage of θεραπεύω is in keeping with the Lukan usages of θεραπεύω, and that of the author of the gospel of John: the third person passive is the Jewish way of describing the activity of God without mentioning the divine name. For example, the passive voice is also used in this way in Matthew's account of the Beatitudes (5.3-10). See Wilcox (1965) 127-128; Beare (1981) 129; Wilcox (1984) 1017.

346 See Apps 8:3, 8:4, 7:10, 7:11, 7:13.

347 See App. 7:4.

348 Mt 8.7, 10.8; Lk 4.23, 10.9, 14.3

349 Mt 8.7, the only occasion Matthew uses θεραπεύω in the future tense (see App. 7:9).

350 Mt 8.8: ἰαθήσεται. See App. 8:4.

(10.8). Luke also reports this command to the disciples using the same form of θεραπεύω (10.9).[351]

An interesting form of θεραπεύω occurs at Luke 4.23, where Luke has Jesus recount the proverb "Ἰατρέ, θεράπευσον σεαυτόν·" referring to himself, the only use of the aorist active imperative of θεραπεύω in the New Testament. What does this proverb (παραβολή) mean?

Although many explanations, ranging from physical to behavioural abnormalities, have been attempted,[352] no one explanation has been completely satisfying. Therefore we must seek some answer from the context in which this saying occurs. Jesus (according to Luke) had only just begun his ministry prior to

---

351 For a discussion of the language of commands and commissions, see below, chapter ten.

352 Hobart (1882) 1, says of this saying: "there would seem to have been somewhat similar sayings used in the [medical] profession". However, Hobart, contrary to his usual practice, only cites the following example (Galen, *Comm.* 4.9, *Epid.* 6. [17. B. 151]): ἕτερον δ' ἰατρὸν ἐπὶ τῆς ἡμετέρας Ἀσίας οἶδα δυσώδεις ἔχοντα τὰς μάλας ὡς διὰ τοῦτο μὴ φέρειν αὐτοῦ τὴν εἴσοδον ἄνθρωπον νοσοῦντα μηδένα καθάριον. ἐχρῆν οὖν αὐτὸν ἑαυτοῦ πρῶτον ἰᾶσθαι τὸ σύμπτωμα καὶ οὕτως ἐπιχειρεῖν ἑτέρους θεραπεύειν. This is a notable example, for Galen uses ἰᾶσθαι to mean *heal/cure*, in contrast to θεραπεύειν, which seems in this context to mean *treat medically* rather than *cure*. θεραπεύειν is also linked with the verb ἐπιχειρεῖν, a verb which means *to endeavour to, to make an attempt* thus involving the idea of a process which requires effort, effort which may be either successful or unsuccessful in its outcome. As far as the physician himself was concerned, his disability was of a physically repellant nature - δυσώδεις ἔχοντα τὰς μάλας - and that Jesus himself was physically repellant in some way has been suggested by those seeking to find a meaning for Jesus' use of this proverb concerning himself. This may have a factual foundation. Certainly there seems to be some evidence that Jesus was physically unattractive, for Origen, *Contra Celsum* 6.75 reports Celsus as saying that Jesus' body was, "as they say, small and ugly and undistinguished". However, Morton Smith (1978) 32, suggests that abnormal behaviour on Jesus' part led others to assume he was demonic and therefore insane (Jn 7.20, 8.52, 10.20) and so, in the eyes of others, in need of medical treatment himself. This explanation of the meaning of Luke 4.23 is unsatisfactory. Luke has not mentioned any exorcisms prior to Jesus' saying. To make any sense, the answer must lie in Luke's preceding material, not in unrelated incidents in other gospels. Cf. the use of this form of θεραπεύω in the writings of Marcus Aurelius (App. 5:7, **6**), and for a discussion, see above, Section One, chapter five. Cf. also the use of θεραπεύω in the Septuagint (App. 6:1), Josephus (App. 6:2) and Philo especially (App. 6:3), where in a teaching and spiritual context (and Luke certainly places this story in a teaching and spiritual context) θεραπεύω refers primarily to the health and well-being of the soul, and the nurturing of the God-human relationship.

this episode at Nazareth. Following his baptism,[353] and the temptation in the wilderness,[354] Jesus, in the power of the spirit, returned to Galilee. As a result of this a report was circulated concerning him, and he began teaching (ἐδίδασκεν) in their synagogues, being glorified by all.[355] So, all we know of his behaviour[356] (and all that he could expect the people of Nazareth to know of his current behaviour prior to his visit there - after all we do not know how long he had been away from Nazareth) was that he was a gifted teacher, whose custom was to go to the synagogue on the sabbath (4.16). He is described only as being "in the power of the spirit" (whatever that may mean) and being glorified because of his teaching. So Luke has given us only a location (Galilee), and an example of his behaviour there: teaching. When Jesus arrived at Nazareth he continued this behaviour by attending the synagogue there on the sabbath, reading and interpreting scripture.[357] The scripture chosen is significant. It is a proclamation of Jesus' mission, but although those present speak well of him, and wonder, Jesus does not expect to be accepted. He is defensive when he talks to them, and then, it seems, deliberately offensive when he recounts those whom God has helped in the past - a widow and a Syrian leper - while ignoring the Israelites. Matthew and Mark do not record Jesus' reading from scripture or his interpretation of it at Nazareth.[358] The only comment the three synoptists share is that concerning a prophet being without honour in his own country. Why does Luke include these sayings, and at this point?

After reading the scripture and announcing its fulfilment, Luke reports that Jesus said, "Doubtless you will quote to me this proverb, 'Physician, heal yourself; what we have heard you did at Capernaum, do here also in your own country."[359] This is the first we have heard of Jesus' actions at Capernaum, apart from his teaching and being "in the power of the spirit" in Galilee. Luke does not record any healing miracles until Jesus' next visit to Capernaum,[360] and only one of these, a general healing episode,

353 Lk 3.21-22
354 Lk 4.1-13
355 Lk 4.14-15
356 The role of reader in the narrative is important here. See above, n.190.
357 Lk 4.18-21
358 Although both place him in the synagogue, teaching. See Mt 13.53-58; Mk 6.1-6.
359 Lk 4.23 (Apps 7:3, 7:8)
360 Lk 4.31-41 (App. 7:3)

contains the word θεραπεύω.[361] θεραπεύω then, must have more than a physical connotation. It must have a spiritual dimension, that is the product of spiritual teaching.[362] So, it would seem that Jesus is commenting on his own spiritual relationship with God, which would be a perfectly normal thing to do in his home town, after the extraordinary spiritual claims he has just made in his interpretation of scripture. It is possible that Jesus was referring to a physical shortcoming[363] as well, but it is far more likely that he was attempting to overcome the genuine and natural disbelief that could be expected to be shown by those who had watched him grow up, in the light of the extraordinary claim he has just made.

Jesus' final use of θεραπεύω in conversation occurs at Luke 14.3, where Jesus asks the lawyers and Pharisees whether it is lawful to heal/treat people on the sabbath. Indeed θεραπεύω is always the healing verb chosen by the synoptists[364] when Jews, especially Pharisees, wonder and talk about Jesus' healing activities. Thus do the Pharisees wonder whether Jesus will heal on the sabbath,[365] the ruler of the synagogue commands people to come and be healed/treated on any other day but the sabbath,[366] the Pharisees perceive Jesus' behaviour in Luke's account of the sabbath healing of the man with the withered hand.[367] Finally, it is used to describe the perception of the man lame from birth, whom Peter had caused to walk, in the Lukan account in *Acts*, by the rulers, elders and scribes, and the high priest and all who were of high-priestly family.[368] It is the only occurrence of the verb θεραπεύω in this (very long) story. Luke chooses specific language to describe the healing itself: the man's feet and ankles were made strong (ἐστερεώθησαν), so that, jumping up, he stood and began walking about (ἐξαλλόμενος ἔστη καὶ περιεπάτει), walking about and praising God (περιπατῶν καὶ ἁλλόμενος καὶ αἰνῶν τὸν θεόν). Peter later (3.16) describes the man as made strong (ἐστερέωσεν), and in perfect health (ὁλοκληρίαν); and when describing him to all the rulers, noted above, who saw him as τὸν τεθεραπευμένον (4.14), Peter

361 Lk 4.40
362 See above, chapter six, and n.352 above, for a discussion of the meaning of θεραπεύω in a spiritual and teaching context. Cf. also Epicurus (App. 3:5, **1**).
363 See above, n.352.
364 But note that John also (5.10), in his only use of θεραπεύω, uses it to describe the man who had been healed by Jesus on the sabbath, when the Jews addressed him. (Cf. John 9.1-41)
365 Mk 3.2
366 Lk 13.13
367 Lk 6.6-11; cf. Mt. 12.9-14; Mk. 3.1-6
368 Acts 4.14. See Acts 3.1-26, 4.1-22.

describes him (4.9) as a man who has been saved (σέσωται). Later (4.22), Luke describes the incident as: τὸ σημεῖον τοῦτο τῆς ἰάσεως. As in the three synoptic gospels, θεραπεύω is chosen to describe a person perceived as a patient by Jewish elders. Elsewhere the healing language is clinical (the miracle itself), or other words are chosen (σῴζω, ἰάομαι).

In the synoptic accounts all healings where the verb θεραπεύω is used to describe authoritative thought in a controversial sense occur on the sabbath. When the Pharisees wonder what Jesus will "do", they do so in terms of θεραπεύω. Does this have any significance for the meaning of θεραπεύω?

All three synoptic gospels contain parallel accounts of the sabbath healing of the man with the withered hand.[369] Mark notes that they (the Pharisees) watched him (Jesus), to see if he would heal (θεραπεύσει) the man. Luke's account is similar: he adds that the scribes were there as well, and he changes Mark's future tense θεραπεύσει to the present θεραπεύει. Both Mark and Luke frame Jesus' question about the legality of his actions around the words "to save life" (ψυχὴν σῶσαι), while Matthew prefers to illustrate the point with an example of conditions under which it was permissible to break the sabbath law,[370] also a story about saving life. Luke adopts this method of illustration in the sabbath healings peculiar to his gospel.[371] The important point to note here is that Jesus equates all these healings with saving life. Pharisaic law allowed the sabbath to be broken where there was a "threat to life".[372] This explains why, when Jesus spoke in terms of saving life, the Pharisees were unable to openly accuse Jesus of wrongdoing. Jesus' form of questioning was normal rabbinical practice, where points of law were disputed. So, it appears that implicit in the meaning of θεραπεύω is the concept of saving life. However, Luke tells us (6.6) that when Jesus healed the man with the withered hand, his primary purpose in going to the synagogue had been to teach (διδάσκειν). Similarly, in the case of the bent woman (13.10), Jesus was in the synagogue, teaching (διδάσκων). Thus the healings, clothed in the question-and-answer rabbinical teaching technique, illustrate Jesus' teaching. But they also exemplify "work". All stories, put into Jesus' mouth as examples

369 Mk 3.1-5; Mt 12. 9-14; Lk 6.6-11
370 Mt 12.11-12
371 Lk 13.15, 14.5
372 Wilcox (1982) 176. See especially 176-177, and n.247, for a discussion of Pharisaic law and practice regarding the sabbath.

of saving life, involve work.[373] Indeed, in the story of the bent woman, the ruler of the synagogue,

> indignant because Jesus had healed (ἐθεράπευσεν) on the sabbath, said to the people, 'There are six days on which work ought to be done (δεῖ ἐργάζεσθαι); come on those days and be healed (θεραπεύεσθε), and not on the sabbath day.'[374]

He obviously understands healing treatment to be work (ἐργάζεσθαι).[375] That a Jewish ruler understands the meaning of θεραπεύω in this way is entirely consistent with the use of the term by all other New Testament authors.[376] Luke's description of the healing itself is clinical. Jesus

> said to her, 'Woman, you are freed from your weakness.'[377] And he laid his hands upon her, and immediately she was made straight, and she began glorifying God (καὶ εἶπεν αὐτῇ, Γύναι, ἀπολέλυσαι τῆς ἀσθενείας σου, καὶ ἐπέθηκεν αὐτῇ τὰς χεῖρας· καὶ παραχρῆμα ἀνωρθώθη, καὶ ἐδόξαζεν τὸν θεόν).[378]

Luke does not leave the reader in any doubt as to the physical symptoms of the patient (καὶ ἦν συγκύπτουσα καὶ μὴ δυναμένη ἀνακύψαι εἰς τὸ παντελές), the length of her illness (ἔτη δεκαοκτώ), or her physical state after the healing (παραχρῆμα ἀνωρθώθη). Nor does Luke leave the reader in any doubt as to his understanding of Jesus' perception of the cause of her illness: she was separated from God (i.e. in the grip of Satan). This story makes it clear that θεραπεύω is a theological rather than a technical healing term. (No other general descriptive healing term occurs in this story.) It is a description of the process which occurs when the gap between the patient and "God" is closed, when an individual's sense of alienation and separation is destroyed. In this way θεραπεύω is used in the New Testament in the sense of the Hebrew "shalom", particularly by the synoptists.

Thus the notion of θεραπεύω in Pharisaic thought in the synoptic gospels involves the idea of sabbath-breaking work. This idea is also found in the gospel of John, where, in the context of a controversial sabbath healing, Jesus says:

---

373 Mt 12.11-12; Lk 13.15; 14.5

374 Lk 13.14

375 Cf. Jn 5.1-15

376 See below, 152.

377 Luke (13.11) describes her as having had a spirit of "weakness" (ἀσθενείας) for eighteen years.

378 Lk 13.12-13 (App. 7:3)

'Ὁ πατήρ μου ἕως ἄρτι ἐργάζεται, κἀγὼ ἐργάζομαι.'[379]

The patient in this case had been sick for thirty-eight years. Jesus chose to heal him, one of many who were ill, on the sabbath. John's only use of θεραπεύω occurs in this story, as a description of the man - τῷ τεθεραπευμένῳ - when the Jews addressed him.[380] John explains (5.16) that "this was why the Jews persecuted Jesus, because he did this on the sabbath." Thus Jesus' answer (5.17): "My Father is working (ἐργάζεται) still, and I also am working (ἐργάζομαι)" is significant. So it seems when the Pharisees wonder what Jesus will do, and they think in terms of θεραπεύω, that θεραπεύω for them involves the notion of work in a sense that the other components of Jesus' ministry - preaching and teaching - do not. And yet the gospel authors continually link the word θεραπεύω with Jesus' teaching, and preaching. Perhaps this is why the three words go together as an indissoluble unity to describe Jesus' ministry - θεραπεύω is the visible effect of teaching and preaching, the 'action' product of the message.

So, following a study of θεραπεύω as it occurs in thought and conversation, it becomes apparent that θεραπεύω is consistently used by Jews, and particularly Pharisees, in the context of Sabbath teaching and healing. When not used in thought or conversation[381] the verb θεραπεύω is used in a descriptive sense: to describe Jesus' behaviour, the disciples' behaviour, and crowd response to the behaviour of Jesus, Peter, Philip, and Paul.[382] But what of the meaning and usage of the cognate forms of θεραπεύω?

---

379 Jn 5.17: "My father is working still, and I also am working." See Jn 5.1-18.

380 John prefers to use ὑγιής to describe Jesus' language to the patient, and to describe the state of the man after Jesus had spoken to him. See below, chapter nine, and Apps 9:1 and 9:2.

381 There are two other occasions when θεραπεύω is used in direct speech in the New Testament by people other than Jesus, and the Jewish hierarchy. The first occurs at Matthew 17.16 when the father of the epileptic boy explains to Jesus that the disciples were unable to heal his son (see above, 144-146); and the second is a Lukan usage at Acts 17.25, occurring in a speech of Paul's at Athens about the nature of God: "nor is he cared for (θεραπεύεται) by human hands, as though he needed anything, since he himself gives life and breath and everything to all." It is significant that Paul, an ex-Pharisee, should be quoted as using this word in this context. Here the notion implied in θεραπεύω is definitely one of "nurturing", embracing the continuous ideas of serving, looking after, diagnosing and attending to needs.

382 It also describes the healed beast (Revelation 13.3, 12).

The noun θεραπεία occurs three times in the New Testament, twice in Luke's gospel, and once in *Revelation*.[383] Luke uses the genitive singular form (θεραπείας) twice, the first occurring in a general healing episode, immediately prior to his account of the feeding of the 5,000.

> After he (Jesus) welcomed them (the crowd) he began speaking to them of the kingdom of God, and those in need of treatment he began healing (καὶ τοὺς χρείαν ἔχοντας θεραπείας ἰᾶτο)[384]

Again, in keeping with the verbal use of θεραπεύω in crowd scenes, the therapy appears to be Jesus' message about the kingdom of God. This is a striking example of Luke's use of θεραπεύω and ἰάομαι side-by-side, and it is obvious that Luke is investing both words with a primarily spiritual meaning. His use of the imperfect tense of ἰάομαι also introduces the notion of process to the event, perhaps implying treatment of individuals both one-by-one, and by degree, the degree of healing being dependent on the degree of listening to (ἀκούω) and understanding of Jesus' message.

Luke's second use of θεραπείας occurs in his account of Jesus' reply to Peter, concerning the wise and faithful servant, "whom his master will set over his household (θεραπείας), to give them their portion of food (σιτομέτριον) at the proper time."[385] In this context θεραπείας means "household," (i.e. the individuals living in the house under the jurisdiction of the master, who, in this instance, is responsible for providing their life-sustaining food), rather than "treatment". However, the sense of nurturing is common to both uses of the word.[386] Elsewhere the gospel authors portray Jesus as equating food with spiritual teaching, both in word,[387] and deed.[388]

---

383 The accusative singular θεραπείαν occurs at *Revelation* 22.2 in a description of the tree of life, where the leaves of the tree are described as being for the healing treatment of the nations (καὶ τὰ φύλλα τοῦ ξύλου εἰς θεραπείαν τῶν ἐθνῶν). Wilcox (1977) 85, states that ξύλου here "refers to the 'tree of life,' recalling Gen. 2:9b; 3: 22,24 (and also passages found in certain of the apocalyptic books)", such as *1 Enoch* 24:4; 25:1-6; *T. Levi* 18:11; 4 Ezra 8:52; 1QH 8:5.

384 Lk 9.11. See below, chapter eight, for a discussion of Luke's use of forms of θεραπεύω and ἰάομαι in close proximity.

385 Lk 12.42

386 Cf. Mt 24.45, where Matthew uses οἰκετείας in a parallel saying.

387 Mt 4.4 (Deut. 8.3); Mk 6.52; Jn 4.31-34; 6.25-27, 34, 35, 48-51

388 Mk 6.34-44; 8.1-10; Mt 14.13-21; 15.32-39; Lk 9.11-17; Jn 6.1-14

The cognate form θεράπων occurs only once in the New Testament.[389] It is used to describe Moses' relationship with God, as faithful servant (θεράπων), in contrast to Jesus' relationship with God as son (υἱός). So θεράπων faithfully reflects its Homeric meaning and usage,[390] when used to describe Patroklos' relationship to Achilleus, by Achilleus (*Iliad* 16.244), and by Patroklos (*Iliad* 23.89-90). Thus the notions of love and loyalty, nurture and service, are implicit in both Homeric and New Testament usage.

7.6. Conclusion

Following our investigation of the incidence of all forms of θεραπεύω in the New Testament are we then any closer to an understanding of the meaning of this family of words?

So far we have established:

(i) that it is consistently used by the synoptists to describe the effect of Jesus' presence in crowd situations, and that this effect is linked with preaching and teaching,

(ii) that Matthew can even substitute it for the verb διδάσκω in material with a Markan parallel,[391] which implies that, for him, the activities of teaching and healing were similar,

(iii) that it is invariably the Jewish, and especially Pharisaic, word for sabbath healing, and that there is implicit in its meaning the notion of "work" in the Jewish and Pharisaic understanding of the term,

(iv) that it was part of Jesus' ongoing commission to his disciples, and their response to this commission was reported by the synoptists in the imperfect tense and linked with the activities of preaching and teaching,

(v) that discipleship seems to be the result of many θεραπεύω episodes.

Thus θεραπεύω seems to be a description of a process which occurs when the gap between a human and God is closed, i.e. when an individual's sense of alienation and separation from God is destroyed, and that individual becomes aware of the presence of the kingdom (i.e. "God"), and inclusion in a new spiritual community. In this way θεραπεύω is primarily a spiritual term, but

389 Hebrews 3.5 (App. 7:8)
390 See above, Section One, chapter one.
391 Cf. Mk 10.1; Mt 19.2

it can have a holistic effect, affecting the physical, mental, and emotional state of a person, as well as a person's spiritual state. But perhaps the meaning of θεραπεύω will become clearer still after a study of the other general healing terms the New Testament authors chose to use in their narratives. The next important term to consider in this context is ἰάομαι.

8. The New Testament use of ἰάομαι

ἰάομαι occurs twenty-six times in verbal form in the New Testament.[392] Of these twenty-six, fifteen are Lukan usages (gospel eleven,[393]*Acts* four[394]). Matthew uses ἰάομαι four times,[395] John three times,[396] and Mark once.[397] ἰάομαι also appears once in *Hebrews*,[398] and in the letters of Peter[399] and James.[400]

It is again obvious that Luke is most at home with the Greek language. He uses ἰάομαι in a variety of forms, in differing tenses, and voices. He is the only author to use ἰάομαι in the present and imperfect tenses in the middle voice (six times), always describing the activities of Jesus, although he designates Peter as the channel in one instance (Acts 9.34).[401] Luke chooses the aorist tense of the middle voice only to describe the activities of Jesus and Paul (Acts 28.8).[402] Indeed, the only other authors to use the middle voice are Matthew (quoting the Septuagint), and John (once quoting the Septuagint, and once in reported speech). All other instances of the verb ἰάομαι appear in the passive voice, a typically Jewish way of describing the activity of God.[403]

---

392 See Apps 8:3 and 8:4.

393 Lk 5.17, 6.18, 6.19, 7.7, 8.47, 9.2, 9.11, 9.42, 14.4, 17.15, 22.51 (App. 8:3)

394 Acts 9.34, 10.38, 28.8, 28.27 (App. 8:3)

395 Mt 8.8, 8.13, 13.15, 15.28 (App. 8:3)

396 Jn 4.47, 5.13, 12.40 (App. 8:3)

397 Mk 5.29 (App. 8:3)

398 Hebrews 12.13 (App. 8:3)

399 1 Peter 2.24 (App. 8:3)

400 James 5.16 (App. 8:3)

401 See App. 8:4.

402 See Apps 7:3, 8:1, 8:3 and 8:4.

403 As noted above (chapter seven), the third person passive is the Jewish way of describing the activity of God without mentioning the divine name. See Wilcox (1965) 127-128; Beare (1981) 129, 133; Wilcox (1984) 1017.

8.1. Mark

The only use of the perfect tense of ἰάομαι in the New Testament occurs, not unexpectedly, in Mark's gospel.[404] It is his only use of the verb, and appears in the third person singular indicative, in a passive sense, in his story of the haemorrhaging woman in her thoughts concerning the state of her body, after she had touched Jesus' cloak (καὶ ἔγνω τῷ σώματι ὅτι ἴαται ἀπὸ τῆς μάστιγος (5.29)). The woman thinks in terms of σῴζω and ἰάομαι; Mark reports Jesus as using the terms σῴζω and ὑγιής. Mark's use of the perfect form makes it perfectly clear that, in this case, the woman is experiencing a present state, following a completed action. No more treatment is necessary. Jesus too makes it obvious that the action is completed: he knew that power had gone out from him (τὴν ἐξ αὐτοῦ δύναμιν ἐξελθοῦσαν (5.30)). Thus ἰάομαι in *Mark* describes instantaneous healing, as a result of faith, faith so great it causes Jesus to comment. Mark chooses this verb for the healing of an "unclean" woman. Matthew does not follow suit, only choosing ἰάομαι to describe gentile healings. Matthew concludes his description of this healing with a passive form of σῴζω, while Luke, in contrast, is quite happy to conclude his narrative account with a passive form of ἰάομαι,[405] although, like Mark, he has Jesus issue a command after his statement "Daughter, your faith has saved you (θυγάτηρ, ἡ πίστις σου σέσωκέν σε)".[406] Mark adds ὕπαγε εἰς εἰρήνην, καὶ ἴσθι ὑγιὴς ἀπὸ τῆς μάστιγός σου, which Luke reduces to πορεύου εἰς εἰρήνην.[407] However, all three synoptists focus on the link between σῴζω and πίστις in this healing story.[408]

8.2. Matthew

Matthew uses the aorist passive[409] third person singular of ἰάομαι on two occasions, to describe two healings: those of the centurion's

---

404 Mark likes the perfect tense. See above, chapter seven, n.202(i). It is possible that that this may reflect the Aramaic/Hebrew perfect(ive) form.

405 Lk 8.47: ἰάθη. Cf. Mt 9.22

406 Mt 9.22; Mk 5.34; Lk 8.48

407 Lk 8.48. See above, chapter six, for a discussion of the use of εἰρήνη and ὑγιής in the Septuagint (App. 6:1, **43**, **66**, **68**, **71**); and below, chapter nine.

408 See below, chapter nine, for a discussion of the frequent linking of these two word groups.

409 The aorist passive of ἰάομαι occurs ten times in the New Testament, accounting for 83% of the use of this verb in the passive voice. As one would expect, Luke uses it the most - four times in his gospel - Matthew twice, and John

boy (8.13), and the Canaanite woman's daughter (15.28). Both occasions record Jesus' ability to heal *in absentia*, in answer to a "parental" request.[410] On both occasions the faith of the "parent" in Jesus' power is noted by Jesus, and healing is in response to this faith:

Ὕπαγε, ὡς ἐπίστευσας γενηθήτω σοι (8.13)

Ὦ γύναι, μεγάλη σου ἡ πίστις· γενηθήτω σοι ὡς θέλεις (15.28).

On both occasions, like the ἐθεραπεύθη episode discussed above,[411] the healing occurred from the very hour Jesus had spoken to the "parents":

καὶ ἰάθη ὁ παῖς (αὐτοῦ) ἐν τῇ ὥρᾳ ἐκείνῃ (8.13)

καὶ ἰάθη ἡ θυγάτηρ αὐτῆς ἀπὸ τῆς ὥρας ἐκείνης (15.28).

Therefore ἰάομαι in *Matthew* only records specific healings which are performed *in absentia*, are in answer to the faith of a "parent" in Jesus' ἐξουσία, and are instantaneous. The use of the passive voice also signals that Matthew is justifying these healings by appealing to a higher power. The use of the third person passive in Jewish thought describes the action of God, and accounts for the instantaneous nature of these cures (and of the cure of the epileptic boy, which Matthew described with the passive voice of the verb θεραπεύω).[412]

It is significant that Matthew chooses ἰάομαι to recount these gentile healing stories. In the first story, the centurion, a member of the Roman occupying forces,[413] would have been seen as an outsider by the Jewish people, as a particularly loathsome gentile.

---

once. Other examples of the aorist passive occur once each in *James* and *1 Peter*, and once in *Hebrews*. See App. 8:4.

410 The centurion's paralytic παῖς (8.5-13), and the Canaanite woman's badly demonic daughter (15.21-28). The Greek term παῖς is ambiguous, but whether a slave, servant or son, the centurion had an emotional, legal, and financial investment in his well-being. Whatever his status, the centurion was acting *in loco parentis* for him, and therefore with parental authority.

411 See above, chapter seven, 144-146.

412 ibid. Also see above, n.403.

413 Despite the comments in Sanders and Davies (1989) 307 to the contrary, it was normal practice for client princes to second Roman officers, so this man could easily have been a Roman centurion as both Matthew and Luke understood him to be.

In the second story, the mother is a Canaanite, and therefore not only a member of a gentile nation, but a gentile nation with a long history of inciting Jewish enmity.[414] The mother's importunity is the catalyst for a conversation between the mother and Jesus concerning the relative claims of the Jews and the gentiles on Jesus. Jesus is reluctant to act: he ignores her, and then questions her about her rights. When she asks only for scraps (i.e. what the Jews themselves did not want) Jesus makes it clear that it is only her exceptional faith that causes the healing of her daughter.

Therefore, in both instances of gentile healing - the centurion's boy, and the Canaanite woman's daughter - Matthew takes pains to make the healing action intelligible and acceptable to his Jewish audience. It is significant that in this story he appears to have reworked Mark's version,[415] using different language to describe the healing itself (Mark does not use ἰάομαι), and also to describe the mother. (Mark defines her as a Syro-Phoenician, the more common gentile, rather than Jewish, word for people of that region.)[416]

Therefore Matthew's choice of language is a conscious decision, a decision that can only be explained if ἰάομαι has a gentile connotation to Matthew and does not involve any ongoing treatment or association between Jesus and the patient. This explains why he chooses to use θεραπεύω in his account of the healing of the epileptic boy, a boy with whom both he (and his disciples) had direct contact.[417] There isn't any teaching associated with the healings described by ἰάομαι, nor is there any physical contact. Instead, Matthew uses a Greek verb that has enjoyed a long history in the language of healing in the gentile world[418] to describe healings of two extraordinarily gentile people - is there a more genuine gentile than a soldier of a foreign occupying army, or a Canaanite woman? - but he stresses the extraordinary faith of each to explain God's intervention to his Jewish readers.

414 Mt 15.21-28

415 Mk 7.24-30

416 Thus the healing language of this story would support the theory, put forward by Ross Saunders (1991) 6, that "... Jesus came to bring the kingdom of God especially to the Jews, and only to those gentiles who showed outstanding faith...."

417 Mt 17.18

418 We have seen how ἰάομαι was already in use as part of the language of healing in the *Iliad* (see above, Section One, chapter one). But it is also important to note that ἰάομαι described the intervention of God in the Septuagint (see App. 6:1, and chapter six), as well as the healing action of Asklepios at Epidauros, Athens and Pergamon.

Matthew also uses ἰάομαι when quoting the Septuagint.[419] ἰάσομαι is part of a most significant passage, linking healing with seeing and hearing (and therefore understanding) God's message. It is Jesus' message that causes the blind to see, the deaf to hear, and that ultimately brings healing. In *Matthew* it is obvious that Jesus is referring to spiritual sight, spiritual hearing, and spiritual health. For he explains (13.16) that the eyes and ears of the disciples are blessed (μακάριοι), because they see and hear what many prophets and righteous men before them had longed to see and hear, but had not.[420]

8.3. Luke-Acts

The author of *Luke-Acts* does not use the verb ἰάομαι in the same way as the authors of *Matthew* and *Mark*, or indeed in the same way as the author of *John*.[421] However, as in *Mark* and *Matthew*, ἰάομαι in the passive is used to describe the intervention of God. It is Luke's use of the middle voice that differentiates his work from the other gospel authors.[422] As we have seen, both Mark and

419 The future indicative first person singular of ἰάομαι occurs three times in the New Testament, at Matthew 13.15, John 12.40, and Acts 28.27, in parallel quotations of the Septuagint. John quotes Isaiah 6.10 (see App. 6:1, **62**) in a passage explaining why people did not recognise Jesus' identity. A more accurate version of the longer passage (Isaiah 6.9-10) appears in *Matthew* and *Acts*.

420 At Acts 28.27, Paul uses this quotation as the final justification for his mission to the gentiles. Here healing is spiritual healing, incorporating spiritual understanding and perception, which, according to Paul, is the "salvation of God" (τὸ σωτήριον τοῦ θεοῦ (28.28)). Luke ends *Luke/Acts* by noting (28.31) that Paul continued "preaching the kingdom of God and teaching about the Lord Jesus Christ... (κηρύσσων τὴν βασιλείαν τοῦ θεοῦ καὶ διδάσκων τὰ περὶ τοῦ κυρίου Ἰησοῦ Χριστοῦ). It is a fitting quotation to use at the end of his story about the preaching, teaching and healing message.

421 Thus the implication in the words of Oerke in Kittel *et al.* (1965) 204, that: "All the Gospels use ἰᾶσθαι of the work of Jesus, especially Luke" is questionable. Luke does use ἰᾶσθαι of the work of Jesus (and, surprisingly, of Paul, see below, 163-164), but his use of this verb is quite different from the other gospel authors.

422 Fourteen forms of ἰάομαι in the middle voice occur in the New Testament. Of these fourteen, eleven are Lukan, while two appear in the gospel of John (one quoting the Septuagint [12.40, see above, n.419], and one [the aorist subjunctive] in the reported speech of the official who asks Jesus to heal his son [4.47]), and one in Matthew's gospel (in a parallel quotation from the Septuagint [13.15, see above, n.419]). Of the eleven Lukan forms, five occur in the

Matthew only choose ἰάομαι in specific healing episodes, and then in the passive voice.[423] In contrast, Luke uses both the middle and passive voice of ἰάομαι in both general and specific healing episodes.

8.3.1. The Lukan use of ἰάομαι in general healing episodes

Both Lukan usages of the imperfect middle of ἰάομαι occur in his gospel, and describe the behaviour of Jesus in a crowd situation.[424] Both are also linked to his preaching and teaching, and both appear in close proximity to a form of θεραπεύω. It is at once obvious that, for Luke, it is important to establish a link in meaning between ἰάομαι and θεραπεύω.[425] In the first episode (6.19) Luke chooses θεραπεύω for those in the crowd who were troubled by unclean spirits (οἱ ἐνοχλούμενοι ἀπὸ πνευμάτων ἀκαθάρτων ἐθεραπεύοντο), whereas ἰάομαι is reserved for those of the crowd seeking to touch Jesus (καὶ πᾶς ὁ ὄχλος ἐζήτουν ἅπτεσθαι αὐτοῦ, ὅτι δύναμις παρ' αὐτοῦ ἐξήρχετο καὶ ἰᾶτο πάντας). Luke also differentiates in the voice of the verbs, although being careful to keep both in the imperfect tense. ἐθεραπεύοντο is in the third person plural passive, implying intervention by "God", whereas ἰᾶτο, in the third person singular middle, describes Jesus' behaviour. "Healing" in the imperfect tense and the middle voice is not instantaneous, but rather a process, especially in crowd situations. The language of this whole episode is immensely important for an understanding of Luke's message:

> They came to hear him and to be healed from their illnesses; and those troubled with unclean spirits began being healed. And all the crowd were seeking to touch him, because power was radiating from him and he began healing them all (οἳ ἦλθον ἀκοῦσαι αὐτοῦ καὶ ἰαθῆναι ἀπὸ τῶν νόσων αὐτῶν· καὶ οἱ ἐνοχλούμενοι ἀπὸ πνευμάτων ἀκαθάρτων ἐθεραπεύοντο. καὶ πᾶς ὁ ὄχλος ἐζήτουν

---

present tense, one in the imperfect, one in the future (in the parallel quotation from the Septuagint [28.27, see above, n.419]), and four in the aorist. See App. 8:4.

423 Except when quoting the Septuagint. This is true also of John (see App. 8:4).

424 See App. 8:4, ἰᾶτο.

425 That there is a difference in meaning is obvious from Luke's use of both verbs. Perhaps each verb has a different meaning for different audiences. Is Luke's choice of healing language governed by his intended audience?

ἅπτεσθαι αὐτοῦ, ὅτι δύναμις παρ' αὐτοῦ ἐξήρχετο καὶ ἰᾶτο πάντας).[426]

For Luke (as for Mark and Matthew), healing by God or Jesus, is dependent on hearing (ἀκοῦσαι), and understanding, the message. It is this awareness of God's presence (the arrival of the kingdom) that brings spiritual healing (a process of understanding the message? inner peace? inclusion in the spiritual community?), and Jesus' touch that brings holistic health. This episode is immediately prior to Luke's account of Jesus' teaching about those who are blessed (μακάριοι).

Luke's use of the aorist passive infinitive ἰαθῆναι in the same passage deserves comment here. This is its only occurrence in the New Testament,[427] and describes a crowd of people who came to hear Jesus and to be healed of their diseases (οἳ ἦλθον ἀκοῦσαι αὐτοῦ καὶ ἰαθῆναι ἀπὸ τῶν νόσων αὐτῶν). Here healing is obviously dependent on hearing the message, and the use of the aorist passive infinitive implies that this is an instantaneous conversion experience. Luke immediately contrasts this with θεραπεύω[428] in the 3rd person plural imperfect passive, for "those troubled by unclean spirits" (6.19), and ἰάομαι in the 3rd person singular imperfect middle for a description of Jesus' effect on all those whom he touched.[429] Thus Luke invests ἰάομαι with the spiritual notion of the perception of God's presence (i.e. an awareness of the presence of the kingdom), and the physical notion of a healing process, inherent in Jesus' touch. In this way, the Greek medical "curing" verb assumes a theological dimension, and Luke also draws a parallel between the healing powers of God, and of Jesus.

Luke's second use of the imperfect middle form of ἰάομαι is immediately prior to his account of the feeding of the 5,000:

> after he [Jesus] welcomed them [the crowd] he began speaking to them of the kingdom of God, and those in need of treatment he began healing (καὶ ἀποδεξάμενος αὐτοὺς ἐλάλει αὐτοῖς περὶ τῆς βασιλείας τοῦ θεοῦ, καὶ τοὺς χρείαν ἔχοντας θεραπείας ἰᾶτο).[430]

Again Luke uses a sense form of θεραπεύω and ἰάομαι in close proximity so that both his Jewish and his gentile audience are alerted to his meaning. Their linking so closely with the message

---

426 Lk 6.18-19
427 Lk 6.18. See App. 8:4, ἰαθῆναι.
428 See above, 140.
429 See above, 160.
430 Lk 9.11. See Apps 8:3 and 8:4.

of the kingdom of God implies healing that is primarily spiritual in nature, but, as we have seen, this spiritual healing is holistic in effect, affecting the emotional, mental and physical state of a person as well. It is no accident that this episode is immediately prior to the feeding of the 5,000.

8.3.2. The Lukan use of ἰάομαι in specific healing episodes

All four uses of the third person singular middle aorist form of ἰάομαι in the New Testament are Lukan.[431] Luke only uses this form to describe the activities of Jesus (on three occasions) and Paul (on one occasion).

The first (9.42) is a description of Jesus' action in Luke's version of the healing of the epileptic boy.[432] All synoptic gospels emphasise the significance of this healing by placing it after Peter's declaration of Jesus' identity,[433] and his transfiguration. Luke is curiously condensed in his account; it is Mark who gives the more clinical case history.[434] All three synoptists use this healing to portray Jesus' chagrin at the disciples' lack of faith. Luke is the only synoptist to choose ἰάομαι to describe the result of Jesus' action, action described by the verb ἐπιτιμάω.[435] As we have seen, Matthew signals the importance of this episode by using the verb ἐπιτιμάω and the passive voice of θεραπεύω, whereas Mark describes the whole episode in precise language reminiscent of the Hippokratic description of an epileptic seizure.[436]

Luke's second use of this form occurs in his description of Jesus' action, when he heals the man with dropsy, on the sabbath.[437] Luke again uses forms of θεραπεύω and ἰάομαι in the one healing story. This is the only sabbath healing story recorded in the synoptic gospels that includes ἰάομαι in its healing language. The

---

431 Lk 9.42, 14.4, 22.51; Acts 28.8 (see App. 8:4, ἰάσατο).

432 Lk 9.37-43

433 See App. 7:4.

434 Mk 9.14-27

435 But note that this verb is also found in the Lukan story of the healing of Peter's mother-in-law (App. 7:13). It is curious that Luke, who is generally thought to have belonged to the medical profession, should choose to use ἐπιτιμάω in a story where the illness was a fever.

436 Thus, in medical terms, Mark's story contains a fine piece of medical history, in contrast to the stories in both *Matthew* and *Luke*. Cf. Hippokrates, *The Sacred Disease*, 10. If Luke is supposed to have been a physician, what does this make Mark?

437 Lk 14.1-6

reason is that it is a story peculiar to Luke, and the only sabbath healing to take place outside a synagogue. Nevertheless, it occurs in the house of a leading Pharisee, so Luke is still careful to retain θεραπεύω when recounting conversation with the Pharisees. Thus he puts θεραπεύω into the mouth of Jesus, when Jesus asks the Pharisees whether it is lawful to heal (θεραπεῦσαι) on the sabbath.[438] All that Luke says of the actual event is that Jesus, "took him, healed him, and let him go (καὶ ἐπιλαβόμενος ἰάσατο αὐτὸν καὶ ἀπέλυσεν)", a most unsatisfactory description of a specific healing episode. The focus of the story is a controversy between Jesus and the Pharisees.[439] The man with dropsy is just a convenient prop in a dramatic altercation concerning the law, and the law, for the Pharisees and Jesus, concerned the meaning of θεραπεύω.[440] Luke, however, chooses to describe the event with ἰάομαι, a word aimed at his gentile audience.

Luke's final gospel use of ἰάσατο describes Jesus' action when he heals the severed right ear of the high priest's slave at the Mount of Olives.[441] There is no synoptic parallel to this healing, Mark only noting that the man's ear was severed,[442] while Matthew, typically, expands Mark's sayings in an effort to explain Jesus' betrayal.[443] It would seem then that an unhealed slave was incompatible with Luke's conception of Jesus, and incompatible with the message he wanted to convey.[444]

Luke's fourth and final use of ἰάσατο describes Paul's behaviour, and its effect on Publius' father at Malta.[445] This episode occurs in the final "we" passage of *Acts*. Paul, after praying (προσευξάμενος), "placed his hands on him and healed him (ἐπιθεὶς τὰς χεῖρας αὐτῷ

---

438 See above, 149.

439 Indeed Luke is fascinated by Jesus-Pharisaic controversies. For an analysis of Pharisaic issues raised by the synoptists, and a comparison of their treatment of them, see App. 7:7.

440 So Jesus argues for an extension to the Pharisaic rule that the sabbath should be broken if there was a threat to life. See above, 149, *re* θεραπεύσει (Mk 3.2); *re* θεραπεύει (Lk 6.6,9); and Jesus' examples of "saving" life: Mt 12.11; Lk 13.15; 14.5. See also Wilcox (1982) 176.

441 Lk 22.51

442 Mk 14.43-50

443 Mt 26.47-56

444 The institution of slavery was a normal and accepted part of the culture of the Graeco-Roman world. It is interesting that Luke, in the story of the healing of the centurion's "boy" is the only author to designate him as a δοῦλος (7.3), although he does later designate him as παῖς (7.7), as does Matthew (8.5); while John designates him as υἱός (4.46).

445 Acts 28.8

ἰάσατο αὐτόν)". Publius had fulfilled the hospitality requirements laid down by Jesus,[446] with the effect that Paul healed (completed action) Publius' father of specific ailments (fever and dysentery).[447] As in the gospels this healing brought the weak (ἔχοντες ἀσθενείας) of the rest of the population to Paul, and they began being healed (ἐθεραπεύοντο). Luke contrasts the aspect of the two healing episodes by using the aorist tense of ἰάομαι for the healing of Publius' father, and the imperfect passive of θεραπεύω for the rest of the population. It is curious that Luke does not mention Paul preaching the gospel during this general healing episode.[448]

Two other Lukan uses of ἰάομαι in the middle voice occur in *Acts*. Both instances occur in speeches given by Peter, and both are in the present tense. Luke is the only author to use the present tense of ἰάομαι in the middle voice in a healing context.[449] The present participle (nominative singular masculine), only appears once in the New Testament,[450] in a speech given by Peter to the centurion Cornelius, and Cornelius' kinsmen and close friends as a description of Jesus' activity. It occurs in a chapter redolent of Homeric repetition of visions and orders. It is a crucial chapter for Luke's message that it was God's will that the gentiles receive the gospel. Peter describes to Cornelius how God sent the word (τὸν λόγον) to Israel, preaching good news of peace (εὐαγγελιζόμενος εἰρήνην) by Jesus,[451] who:

> went about doing good and healing all that were oppressed by the devil, for God was with him (ὃς διῆλθεν εὐεργετῶν καὶ ἰώμενος πάντας τοὺς καταδυναστευομένους ὑπὸ τοῦ διαβόλου, ὅτι ὁ θεὸς ἦν μετ' αὐτοῦ).[452]

---

446 Mt 10.11-14; Mk 6.8-11; Lk 9.1-6, 10.4-9, especially 10.8-9; *GT* #14.

447 This is a puzzling Lukan use of ἰάομαι. Certainly, Luke also uses the middle voice for the words of Peter (Acts 9.34), but in the present tense, and in a conversion context. That this use (Acts 28.8) appears in a "we" passage, and the Peter episode does not, is perhaps significant. As well, the deliberate use of the aorist tense and middle voice (only used elsewhere of Jesus) is striking.

448 However, it is tempting to conclude that this is a "conversion" scene, in keeping with the gospels' use of θεραπεύω, and in keeping with the effect on the surrounding population of other specific healings recorded in *Acts* (see App. 8:1, Acts 9.32-35, and 36-43).

449 See Apps 8:3 and 8:4.

450 Acts 10.38

451 Acts 10.36

452 Acts 10.38

Here, Luke is obviously using ἰώμενος in the gospel sense of θεραπεύων, a word more familiar to his gentile audience[453] in its healing connotation, and yet he is careful to define those receiving this healing as those who were spiritually oppressed or separated from God. Thus ἰάομαι is invested with a spiritual dimension.

The other instance of ἰάομαι in the middle voice occurs in Peter's speech to the bedridden Aeneas: "Jesus Christ heals you..." (ἰᾶταί σε Ἰησοῦς Χριστός).[454] This healing is important as a catalyst for mass conversion: all the residents of Lydda and Sharon turned to the Lord (πάντες ... ἐπέστρεψαν ἐπὶ τὸν κύριον).[455] We are not told why Peter chose Aeneas. The story appears only as an explanation for mass conversion. It is part of a conversion account, sandwiched between the conversion of Saul, and the raising of Dorcas (which also led to mass conversion). Luke appears to be trying to appeal to a hellenistic audience. He is certainly narrating events taking place in the hellenistic world, a world which seems far removed from the world of Jesus. Perhaps this accounts for the difference in healing accounts in the gospel and *Acts*, and Luke's need to stress signs and wonders in *Acts*, rather than the message of the gospel, which is love in action in the form of Jesus.[456]

This is noticeable when we compare these instances with the Lukan gospel usage of this verb. A good example, where Luke chooses the present infinitive of ἰάομαι in the middle voice,[457]

---

453 ἰάομαι had enjoyed a long history in the Greek language of healing, in the sense of "curing", and also described the healing intervention of "God", both in Asklepiadic literature (Section One), and in the Septuagint (App. 6:1); whereas θεραπεύω in the Greek language of healing contained the ongoing notions of service, nurture, caring for, and medical treatment (nursing). See above, Section One. This particular use of ἰάομαι is very interesting, for it reflects the language of Wisdom 16.12 (App. 6:1, **40**): καὶ γὰρ οὔτε βοτάνη οὔτε μάλαγμα ἐθεράπευσεν αὐτους, ἀλλὰ ὁ σός, Κύριε, λόγος ὁ πάντα ἰώμενος.

454 Acts 9.34 (see App. 8:4).

455 Acts 9.35

456 Indeed, one is conscious of a definite change, of a sense of loss, once the human Jesus disappears from New Testament healing narrative. See App. 8:1, and especially App. 8:2. Note also that the New Testament healing vocabulary changes after the gospels and *Acts*, referring to doctrine rather than people. This is most noticeable with the verbs ἰάομαι and ὑγιαίνω and their derivatives (see Apps 8:3, 8:4, 9:2). However, as we have seen, even θεραπεύω occurs in different contexts in *Acts* .

457 Although the perfect infinitive of ἰάομαι would appear in the same form - ἰᾶσθαι - it is certain that a present infinitive is intended at Luke 9.2, where Jesus commissions the disciples with a string of present infinitives, and it is probable that a present infinitive is intended at Luke 5.17 also. These are

occurs in an introductory statement to the story of the healing of the paralytic who was let down through the roof by his friends.[458] Luke notes (5.17) that the power of the Lord was to heal (καὶ δύναμις κυρίου ἦν εἰς τὸ ἰᾶσθαι αὐτόν). However, this healing allows Jesus to discuss his mission to forgive sins (heal) with the Pharisees and the teachers of the law, which is the spiritual focus of the story. Again Luke is investing ἰάομαι with a spiritual dimension. Neither Mark,[459] nor Matthew,[460] use ἰάομαι in this story.

Like Matthew, Luke also uses the aorist passive twice in his gospel,[461] but in two different healing stories. The first occurs in Luke's version of the story of the haemorrhaging woman, when she declares how she had been immediately healed (ὡς ἰάθη παραχρῆμα) after she touched the fringe of Jesus' cloak.[462] Luke had previously explained that although the woman had spent all her livelihood on physicians she was unable to be treated (θεραπευθῆναι). While he does follow Mark, as does Matthew, in focusing on the link between σῴζω and πίστις, Luke is the only one to combine θεραπεύω and ἰάομαι in his story. By now, this does not surprise us. It is significant that he chooses the passive form of both verbs in this story. As a haemorrhaging woman, this woman would have been classed as ritually "unclean" by her Jewish contemporaries, and therefore would have been excluded from participating in the religious life of her community. Mark records that she had been ill for twelve years,[463] thus her sense of isolation and alienation must have been unbearably acute. Both Mark[464] and Luke[465] report Jesus as instructing her to "Go in peace", both choosing present imperatives (Mark: ὕπαγε; Luke: πορεύου). The idea of a life journey in a continuing state of peace (εἰρήνην), as a result of a faith (πίστις) action which saved (σέσωκέν) is thus

---

the only two occurrences of this form of ἰάομαι in the New Testament (see App. 8:4). For a discussion of Luke's use of ἰᾶσθαι at 9.2, see below, chapter ten.

458 Lk 5.17-26

459 Mk 2.1-12

460 Mt 9.1-8

461 In the aorist passive indicative 3rd person singular. See App. 8:4, ἰάθη.

462 Lk 8.47

463 Mk 5.25. Jairus' daughter, whose story is closely linked with this one, is also, according to Mark (5.42), twelve years old. Obviously the number twelve is of religious significance.

464 Mk 5.34

465 Lk 8.48

introduced. In this way it becomes obvious that the woman's physical health is only a guide to a much deeper spiritual message.

We have already seen how the synoptists consistently use θεραπεύω to describe the active effect of Jesus' proclamation of the presence of the kingdom, and how this effect produces a change in thinking (μετάνοια) and includes those who experience it in a new spiritual community, a spiritual community that is aware of the presence of God. These people experience shalom. The nearest Greek word to this Hebrew word is εἰρήνη, the word chosen by Mark as Jesus' command, and retained by Luke.[466] For twelve years this woman had been excluded from her spiritual community. Now, as the result of her action, and the intervention of God (passive verbs), she is restored not only to physical health, but to membership of her community. Thus the primary focus of this story is the restoration of this woman to full participation in her spiritual community.

Luke's other use of this form of ἰάομαι has a similar focus. It occurs in Luke's story of the ten lepers who were cleansed (ἐκαθαρίσθησαν).[467] One of them, a Samaritan, seeing that he was healed (ἰδὼν ὅτι ἰάθη), returned to thank Jesus, praising God. Thus ἰάθη describes the man's perception of himself. This story closely parallels Luke's story of the haemorrhaging woman, who has the same perception of herself (8.47), and to whom Jesus is reported as making the same comment: "Your faith has saved you (ἡ πίστις σου σέσωκέν σε)."[468] Both these people, the woman and the leper, would have been isolated from full participation in their communities because of their physical ailments. Both were ritually "unclean". Both suffered further social disabilities through no fault of their own: one on the basis of gender, the other of race. Luke's language makes it clear that Jesus' primary healing activity was holistic, restoring people to the fullest possible participation in their spiritual communities.[469]

Luke, like Matthew, also uses ἰάομαι in the speech of the centurion who asks Jesus:

---

466 Cf. the use of εἰρήνη in the Septuagint (and see App. 6:1, **43**, **66**, **68**, **71**). Cf. also Acts 10.36.

467 Lk 17.11-19

468 Lk 8.48; 17.19

469 It is perhaps worth noting that Luke does not use θεραπεύω in the story of the Samaritan leper (or, for that matter, in the parable of the good Samaritan).

> But say the word, and let my boy be healed (ἀλλὰ εἰπὲ λόγῳ, καὶ ἰαθήτω ὁ παῖς μου)![470]

Earlier he had asked that Jesus might come and save (διασώσῃ) his slave.[471] There is a significant manuscript variation, citing the Matthaean ἰαθήσεται here.[472] It is notable that both variations occur in the 3rd person passive, both synoptists preferring the passive voice to describe an *in absentia* healing. Luke sums up the boy's return to health as ὑγιαίνοντα.[473]

The synoptic authors also use cognate forms of ἰάομαι, especially the noun ἰατρός. Forms of ἰατρός, the Greek word for "doctor/ physician", occur seven times in the New Testament, six times in the synoptic gospels,[474] and once in *Colossians*.[475]

---

470 Lk 7.7. The aorist passive imperative 3rd person singular, ἰαθήτω, occurs only here in the New Testament (see App. 8:4).

471 Lk 7.3

472 See Metzger (1975) 142.

473 Lk 7.10. Cf. *IG* IV^2 1, 122: 21 (App. 2:2, **21**), where Arata of Lacedaemon, after visiting the asklepieion at Epidauros on behalf of her daughter, returned home to find her daughter ὑγιαίνουσαν. Cf. also Lk 15.27, where a slave tells of a father's joy because his estranged son returned home ὑγιαίνοντα. Cf. also Tobit 6.9 (א) andTobit 12.3 (א). See App. 6:1, **53**, **54**.

474 Mt 9.12; Mk 2.17, 5.26; Lk 4.23, 5.31, 8.43 (see App. 8:3). The genitive plural ἰατρῶν (Mark 5.26) and the dative plural ἰατροῖς (Luke 8.43) of the noun ἰατρός occur in parallel accounts of the story of the haemorrhaging woman (Mark 5.21-43; Luke 8.40-56). This story has already been discussed at length, (see above, 156, 166-167) but it is important to note here that Matthew omits any reference to doctors in his account (9.18-26), in contrast to Mark, who tells us that "she had suffered much under many physicians (καὶ πολλὰ παθοῦσα ὑπὸ πολλῶν ἰατρῶν), and had spent all that she had" (5.26). Luke omits the reference to her suffering at the hands of physicians, but states (in a disputed text) that she had spent all her living upon them. (Metzger (1975) 145, states that the evidence for the shorter text is "well-nigh compelling". But the language of the longer text looks remarkably Lukan. Accordingly, I have included ἰατροῖς in the incidence of forms, but will not discuss it at length, as it does look "like a digest of Mk 5.26.") Mark's choice of πάσχω emphasises the woman's sufferings (cf. Mt 17.15, the only use of this word in a healing context in Matthew's gospel [see above, 144-145]), and emphasises the contrast in his portrait of Jesus as a physician with other physicians.

475 In the phrase Λουκᾶς ὁ ἰατρός, at Colossians 4.14. The author not only designates Luke as ἰατρὸς, he also designates him as ἀγαπητὸς, thus measuring his esteem for Luke, as well as identifying him by his profession. It has been widely assumed that this Luke is the author of *Luke-Acts*, an assumption of which I am not altogether convinced. However, the question of authorship is outside the scope of this study.

The genitive singular ἰατροῦ occurs three times, once each in *Matthew, Mark,* and *Luke,* in parallel sayings of Jesus.[476] In each case Jesus is replying to a question of the Pharisees (Matthew), the scribes of the Pharisees (Mark), the Pharisees and their scribes (Luke), concerning his choice of those with whom he shared table-fellowship. Mark, and Matthew both report Jesus as saying:

> Those who are well have no need of a physician, but those who are ill (οὐ χρείαν ἔχουσιν οἱ ἰσχύοντες ἰατροῦ ἀλλ' οἱ κακῶς ἔχοντες)[477]

while Luke substitutes ὑγιαίνοντες for ἰσχύοντες, a word that implies holistic health rather than just physical well-being.[478] Luke has several other differences, but, overall, he reflects Mark more faithfully than Matthew in this story, inserting slivers rather than chunks.[479] Matthew adds material, amongst which is a quotation from the Septuagint.[480] He refers to this quotation again (12.7), in the context of another Pharisaic controversy.[481] Luke's differences are important however: where Mark says that Levi rose and followed Jesus, Luke adds that *he left everything,* and rose and followed him. Mark does not describe the food, but Luke tells us that Levi made him *a great feast.* Perhaps Luke's most important addition is that of εἰς μετάνοιαν to Mark's and Matthew's version of Jesus' final saying:

---

476 Mk 2.17 = Mt 9.12 = Lk 5.31

477 ἔχω κακῶς does not always mean "feeling poorly" in a physical sense only: it can apply to mental and emotional distress as well. Here the present participle implies the notion of the duration of time. These people are in an on-going state of "feeling poorly", whether physically, emotionally, mentally, or spiritually.

478 Cadbury (1969) 183 states that ὑγιαίνοντες is "a good Greek word", replacing what he calls "perhaps another Latinism in Mark's use of ἰσχύω = *valeo.*" But ἰσχύω has a long history in the "best" Greek literature meaning *bodily strength,* see: Sophocles, *Trachiniae* 234; Sophocles, *Ajax* 502; Xenophon, *Cyropaedia* 6.1.24: ὅπως ὑγιαίνοιεν καὶ ἰσχύοιεν, where ἰσχύω is used of bodily strength, and ὑγιαίνω in a more holistic sense; Xenophon, *Memorabilia* 2.7.7; Aristophanes, *Vespae* 357; meaning *to be powerful, to prevail,* see: Aeschylus, *Prometheus Vinctus* 510; Euripides, *Hecuba* 1188; Aristophanes, *Aves* 1607.

479 Cf. Mt 9.9-13; Mk 2.13-17; Lk 5.27-32

480 Hosea 6.6

481 See App. 7:7. For a discussion of the significance of this quotation, see Beare (1981) 227-228.

> I have not come to call the righteous but sinners (οὐ γὰρ ἐλήλυθα καλέσαι δικαίους ἀλλὰ ἁμαρτωλοὺς)[482]

so that Jesus' final saying on the question of his companions is

> I have not come to call the righteous but sinners (literally: those who have missed the mark) to repentance (literally: a change in thinking; i.e. a going back [to God][483] (οὐκ ἐλήλυθα καλέσαι δικαίους ἀλλὰ ἁμαρτωλοὺς εἰς μετάνοιαν).[484]

Jesus' concept of his work as a physician is couched in purely spiritual terms: he states his mission as an intention to change a person's way of life, by changing that person's attitude to life itself. Thus a change in thinking is to produce a new way of living. Now, it has been noted by scholars that while gospel authors may change the context and interpretation of Jesus' sayings, there is surprising agreement between them on the actual words that Jesus is supposed to have said,[485] which makes Luke's addition here all the more important. While the English word "repentance" contains the negative connotations of misgiving and regret, Luke seems to be also stressing a looking forward, anticipation as well as regret. It is a statement of challenge that looks forward to a positive change, a change that Jesus hopes to bring about in the lives of those people who have been alienated from God.

The vocative Ἰατρέ occurs only once in the New Testament, in Luke's gospel (4.23) out of the mouth of Jesus, in reference to himself. This saying has already been discussed at length.[486] It is obvious that Luke wished to portray Jesus as a spiritual physician.

All three occurrences of the noun ἴασις in the New Testament are Lukan, one appearing in his gospel,[487] and two in *Acts*.[488] The gospel usage occurs in a Lukan saying of Jesus, in answer to the Pharisees' warning to him that Herod wanted to kill him. Luke is far more interested than the other synoptists in recounting Jesus'

482 Mk 2.17; Mt 9.13

483 The Greek verb μετανοέω and its cognate forms are generally used in the New Testament as the equivalent of the Hebrew *shûb*, which means to *turn back* or *return* (to God). See Cranfield (1959) 43-46.

484 Lk 5.32

485 See Cadbury (1933) 416; (1958) 188; Wilcox (1975) 209.

486 See above, 147-149.

487 Lk 13.32

488 Acts 4.22, 4.30

relationship with the Pharisees.[489] Here, their warning to Jesus is recounted only by Luke, as is Jesus' reply:

> Go and tell that fox, 'Behold, I cast out demons and bring healings to completion (ἰάσεις ἀποτελῶ) today and tomorrow, and on the third day I finish my course....'

It is appropriate that Luke chooses the present tense for all three verbs (ἐκβάλλω, ἀποτελῶ, τελειοῦμαι), and that this passage occurs in a teaching passage,[490] between the sabbath healings of the bent woman,[491] and the man with dropsy,[492] both sabbath healings peculiar to Luke. Again Luke focuses on the effect of Jesus' teaching: healing. Again healing is inextricably bound up with Jesus' message.

In *Acts*, the genitive singular ἰάσεως of the noun ἴασις occurs as the summing up - this sign of healing (τὸ σημεῖον τοῦτο τῆς ἰάσεως) - of the first healing episode recorded in *Acts*.[493] The actual account is described in clinical language: πιάζω is used to describe Peter's grip on the man; στερεόω to describe the state of his feet and ankles, after Peter had spoken to and touched him.[494] His condition is given in the terms of a clinical case history: he was over forty,[495] and had been lame from birth.[496] Immediately he was able to jump up (ἐξάλλομαι), and walk about (περιπατέω).[497] Peter describes him as being in perfect health (τὴν ὁλοκληρίαν),[498] and as "saved" (σέσωται).[499] The Pharisees (4.14) see him as the man who had been treated/healed (τὸν τεθεραπευμένον), the Pharisaic word for healing.[500]

---

489 In Luke's gospel Jesus appears to know many Pharisees well, and to be on good terms with them. He is often in their homes, as a guest (7.36-50; 11.37-12.3; 14.1-6). Luke includes the same controversial issues as Matthew and Mark, but places their final issue (the great commandment) as a central issue in his work, and includes his own special material. See App. 7:7.

490 Lk 13.22-35

491 Lk 13.10-17

492 Lk 14.1-6

493 Acts 3.1-4.31 (see above, 149-150; and Apps 8:1, 8:3).

494 Acts 3.7

495 Acts 4.22

496 Acts 3.2

497 Acts 3.8

498 Acts 3.16

499 Acts 4.9

500 Acts 4.14. See above, 149-150. Luke does not explicitly state that this healing was performed on the sabbath, but perhaps the fact that "Peter and

Luke's final use of ἴασις occurs in the same chapter of *Acts*[501] in a corporate prayer that describes the place and function of Jesus in the history of creation.[502] Again the "word" and healing are linked:

> grant to thy servants *to speak thy word* (λαλεῖν τὸν λόγον σου) with all boldness, *while thou stretchest out thy hand to heal* (ἐν τῷ τὴν χεῖρά [σου] ἐκτείνειν σε εἰς ἴασιν), and signs and wonders are performed through the name of thy holy servant Jesus (καὶ σημεῖα καὶ τέρατα γίνεσθαι διὰ τοῦ ὀνόματος τοῦ ἁγίου παιδός σου Ἰησοῦ).[503]

As the message (word) of Jesus was linked with θεραπεύω in a Jewish context in *Matthew*, and with ἰάομαι to describe the intervention of God in gentile healings in his gospel, so Luke links the "word" (τὸν λόγον) with "healing" (ἴασιν) and "signs and wonders" (σημεῖα καὶ τέρατα) in an account dedicated to a gentile reader.[504]

8.4. John

It is perhaps appropriate that we move from "signs and wonders" in *Acts* to a consideration of the use of ἰάομαι in the gospel of John. John chooses to use ἰάομαι three times in his gospel, in two healing stories,[505] and in a quotation from the Septuagint.[506] The third person singular aorist subjunctive of ἰάομαι occurs only once in the New Testament, in John's account of the reported speech of the official (βασιλικός) who asked Jesus to heal his son (καὶ ἠρώτα ἵνα καταβῇ καὶ ἰάσηται αὐτοῦ τὸν υἱόν).[507] This is the first healing reported in *John*, and the second sign (σημεῖον).[508] It appears at the

John were going up to the temple at the hour of prayer, the ninth hour" implies this.

501 Acts 4.30

502 Acts 4.24-30

503 Acts 4.29-30. Cf. Aelius Aristides (App. 5:6, **15**) where Asklepios stretched forth his hand to save people in a storm at sea.

504 Lk 1.1-4; Acts 1.1

505 Jn 4.46-54; 5.1-15 (see Apps 8:3, 9:1).

506 Jn 12.40 (cf. Mt 13.15; Acts 28.27; Isaiah 6.10 [App. 6:1, **62**]).

507 Jn 4.47. Cf. Mt 8.5-13; Lk 7.1-10

508 John uses ring composition to record his selection of healing miracles. There are five healings: four specific and one general. The general episode occurs in the middle (6.2). The first (4.46-54) and last (11.1-57) specific episodes both deal with death, and are in response to a family request, made in faith. The

end of a 'gentile' chapter: after the story of the Samaritan woman at the well, Jesus' declaration of identity,[509] and the belief of the Samaritans. The boy's fever left him at the seventh hour,[510] the hour at which the father spoke to Jesus. It is an *in absentia* instantaneous healing - Jesus does not touch the patient, or the father.[511] It is instructive to compare John's treatment of this story with Matthew's and Luke's treatment of the same story.[512] In John's account the man requesting Jesus' help is a βασιλικός, in both *Matthew* and *Luke* he is a ἑκατόνταρχος; in *John* the patient is the man's υἱός, in *Matthew* his παῖς, and in *Luke* his δοῦλος (although Luke later designates him a παῖς).[513] The boy's condition in *John* is ἠσθένει, in *Matthew* παραλυτικός, δεινῶς βασανιζόμενος, in *Luke* κακῶς ἔχων ἤμελλεν τελευτᾶν. In *John* the man asks that Jesus ἰάσηται his son, in *Luke* that he διασώσῃ his slave. In *Matthew* Jesus says θεραπεύσω in reply, in *Luke* he doesn't say anything but goes with him, while in *John* Jesus says "Unless you see signs and wonders you will not believe"! In *Matthew* and *Luke* the man tells Jesus to say the word, and the boy will be healed (Matthew: ἰαθήσεται; Luke: ἰαθήτω, but some manuscripts cite ἰαθήσεται), which allows Jesus to comment on the man's faith, faith he had not found in Israel. Matthew chooses the passive aorist of ἰάομαι to describe the boy's recovered state, whereas Luke uses the present participle of ὑγιαίνω. In John's account Jesus uses the verb ζάω to describe the boy's return to health, and John comments that the man and his whole household believed (ἐπίστευσεν αὐτὸς καὶ ἡ οἰκία αὐτοῦ ὅλη).[514] In this way John stresses the consequence of the healing: i.e. group conversion. The language used by each author reflects a deliberate choice. As we have already noticed, Matthew reserves the verb ἰάομαι to describe only gentile healings,

---

second (5.1-15) and fourth (9.1-41) specific healings are both of patients chosen by Jesus, on the sabbath, and are highly symbolic. Both represent spiritual ignorance. See App. 9:1.

509 Jn 4.26

510 The number seven has symbolic significance for John. For a discussion of the importance of particular numbers, see Hawkins (1909) 163-167.

511 See Robinson (1985) 69, n.158, for an interesting discussion concerning the identity of the father.

512 Is this story from a 'Q' source?

513 Lk 7.7 (see above, 167-168).

514 Jn 4.53. Cf. the stories in *Acts* (9.36-43; 20.7-12) where the participial form of ζάω is chosen to describe the revived condition of both Dorcas and Eutychus (see App. 8:1). The result of the healing of Dorcas had the same effect: many believed (Acts 9.42).

Mark the self-perception of an 'unclean' woman, while Luke is fond of the word, and John uses it in conjunction with other words like ζάω, θεραπεύω, and ὑγιής to convey an impression of holistic healing.[515]

John also uses ἰάομαι in his account of the healing of the man who was by the Bethzatha pool, in Jerusalem, on the sabbath.[516] John uses both θεραπεύω (5.10) and ἰάομαι (5.13) to describe the man in his narrative, both in the passive voice, while in direct speech Jesus uses ὑγιής (5.6), as does the man himself in reported speech (5.15). This healing is highly symbolic and John has chosen all three healing words to encompass the spiritual, emotional, mental and physical aspects of this man's "cure".[517]

8.5. The use of ἰάομαι in the epistles of the New Testament

The verb ἰάομαι only occurs in three other New Testament texts: *Hebrews*, *1 Peter*, and *James*; and, on each occasion, in a form not used by any other New Testament authors.[518]

8.5.1. Hebrews

In *Hebrews* the verb appears in a passage extolling the benefits of God's discipline.[519] Here the author of *Hebrews* is definitely referring to spiritual healing:

> Therefore lift your drooping hands and strengthen your weak knees, and make straight paths for your feet, so that what is lame may not be put out of joint, but rather be healed (ἵνα μὴ τὸ χωλὸν ἐκτραπῇ, ἰαθῇ δὲ μᾶλλον).[520]

---

515 Thus although John does choose to use ἰάομαι, there is not the same indication of the gentile-Jewish controversy in John's account, that is evident in *Matthew*.

516 The aorist passive participle (nominative singular masculine) ἰαθείς, occurs only once in the New Testament, in John's gospel (5.13), as a description of this man (see App. 9:1, 8:4).

517 On the basis of the language it is tempting to conclude that the man might be symbolic of Israel: he had been ill for thirty-eight years, the same time as the people of Israel wandered in the wilderness.

518 See Apps 8:3 and 8:4.

519 Hebrews 12.13: the aorist passive subjunctive 3rd person singular ἰαθῇ (see App. 8:4).

520 Hebrews 12.12-13

This is typical of the use of healing words by New Testament authors other than the gospel authors. As the early Christian movement focused on Christian behaviour and church doctrine, so the healing vocabulary came more and more to refer to spiritual health which was the result of right doctrine.[521]

8.5.2. 1 Peter

In *1 Peter* the verb appears in the author's call to the Jewish exiles of the Dispersion to be submissive, even as Christ was.[522] He argues that "by his wounds you have been healed (οὗ τῷ μώλωπι ἰάθητε)". As at *Hebrews* 12.13 this use of ἰάομαι refers to spiritual healing, and appears in the context of teaching about correct Christian conduct.

8.5.3. James

In *James* ἰάομαι occurs in a passage giving advice as to procedure in the case of suffering (κακοπαθεῖ), for which the author advocates prayer; happiness (εὐθυμεῖ), for which he advocates praise; and infirmity (ἀσθενεῖ), for which he advocates prayer by church elders and anointing with oil in the name of the Lord.[523] James stresses the role of the prayer of faith, which, he says, will save (σώσει) the sick man (τὸν κάμνοντα)[524] whom the Lord will raise up (ἐγερεῖ). James also stresses the spiritual nature of this healing, saying that if the weak person has committed sins he will be forgiven. So the instruction is:

---

521 See Apps 8:3 and 9:2.

522 1 Peter 2.24: the aorist passive indicative 2nd person plural, ἰάθητε (see App 8:4).

523 James 5.16: the aorist passive subjunctive 2nd person plural, ἰαθῆτε, (see App. 8:4). See above, 128-129, for a discussion of the therapeutic use of oil in the ancient world.

524 The use of κάμνω, among other things, is cited as an example of the superior use of Greek by the author of *James*. See Davids (1982) 58, who claims that "the writer of the epistle is an able master of literary Koine." Dibelius (1981) 252 interprets this whole procedure as an exorcism. Davids (1982) 194 disagrees. He states that it is "not a magical rite, nor an exorcism". Dibelius (1981) 252 also states that the use of oil was a remedy from folk medicine. He draws a parallel with the use of oil by the disciples at Mark 6.13. However, as we have seen (above, 128-129), oil was used in Hippokratic medicine. See App. 4:1, **13**.

> to pray for one another, that you may be healed (ὅπως ἰαθῆτε), [for] the prayer of a righteous man (δικαίου) has great power in its effects.[525]

However, it would be incorrect to assume that James is speaking primarily of physical weakness here, as he designates the illness as ἀσθενεῖ, a word used by the gospel authors most frequently to denote those who were healed in general healing episodes in a teaching context by hearing the message of Jesus, i.e. by conversion.[526] James is writing to Jews of the Dispersion (1.1), Jews scattered throughout the Graeco-Roman world, so it is appropriate that he, like Luke, should use the more common Greek medical verb ἰάομαι to describe healing.[527] However, like Luke, he too uses it with a spiritual dimension in its meaning. James is also anxious to establish rules for correct Christian procedure in certain circumstances, so, again, this is an example of the Christian use of healing language to promote behaviour that the author thought to be theologically correct.

8.5.4. 1 Corinthians

The cognate form of ἰάομαι, ἴαμα, also appears three times in *1 Corinthians*.[528] In each case ἴαμα refers to the spiritual gifts of healing (χαρίσματα ἰαμάτων), in this chapter entirely devoted to an exposition of spiritual gifts, and their place and function within the Christian community.

What then does the verb ἰάομαι mean in the New Testament? Has any pattern of usage emerged, or do different authors use the verb in completely different ways? Are we now in a better position to comment on the meaning of ἰάομαι?

A study of the use of ἰάομαι has established that:

(i) Each synoptist uses ἰάομαι in different ways. Both Mark and Matthew use it rarely, and then only in the passive voice to signify

525 James 5.16. Cf. the Babylonian Talmud (Berakhoth 34b) *re* the Jewish *ḥasid* Hanina ben Dosa (for a discussion see Vermes [1983] 72-76); and Marinos, *Vita Procli* 29 (above, 59-61) for similar ideas about the effectiveness of the prayer of the righteous man.

526 Particularly Luke (see above, 139-140).

527 James is also expecting prayer to effect the intervention of God here, so ἰάομαι reflects its use in Asklepiadic literature.

528 1 Corinthians 12. 9, 28, 30: in the genitive plural ἰαμάτων, (see App. 8:3).

the intervention of God.[529] Mark only uses it once, for a woman's self-perception,[530] while Matthew reserves it for accounts of instantaneous *in absentia* gentile healings, performed as a result of parental requests made in faith.[531] In contrast, Luke is fond of the verb, and uses it contiguously with θεραπεύω in healing accounts, in both the middle and passive voice.[532] Luke invests ἰάομαι with a spiritual dimension, using ἰάομαι and θεραπεύω in close proximity to each other, while faithfully reserving θεραπεύω for Jewish thought and conversation, and as the subject of Pharisaic controversy. Thus audience is critical for Luke (as for Matthew), and this becomes most obvious in their different uses and selection of ἰάομαι and θεραπεύω.

(ii) John uses ἰάομαι sparingly in healing accounts,[533] preferring a range of healing words that are holistic in effect, and which emphasise the symbolic nature of his healing stories.

(iii) Other New Testament authors use the verb in a teaching context, referring to right doctrine, or correct Christian practice.[534]

How then does our understanding of the use of the verbs ἰάομαι and θεραπεύω affect our understanding of the New Testament portrayal of Jesus' healing ministry?

8.6. Conclusion

An analysis and comparison of the usage of θεραπεύω and ἰάομαι has established:

1. The priority of Mark's gospel.[535]

---

529 Reflecting the use and meaning of ἰάομαι in both Asklepiadic literature (see Section One) and the Septuagint (see App. 6:1). In this way both Mark and Matthew justify the healings they describe (Mark: an 'unclean' woman; Matthew: gentiles) by appealing to a higher power. There is in their use of ἰάομαι a clue as to the identity of their readers: Matthew's audience must be of Jewish origin. (Dare one posit a predominantly male audience for Mark?)

530 Mk 5.29 (see App. 8:3).

531 Mt 8.8, 8.13, 15.28 (see App. 8:3).

532 That Luke feels constrained to use both verbs contiguously so consistently, points to a difference in meaning for different readers, and thus implies an audience of differing cultural and social origins.

533 Jn 4.47, 5.13

534 Hebrews 12.13; 1Peter 2.24; James 5.16

535 That Mark is prior to Matthew is obvious from their healing language; and that Mark is prior to both Matthew and Luke is also obvious from their selection and treatment of controversial Pharisaic issues (see App. 7:7).

2. That Matthew wrote for a primarily Jewish audience,[536] and Luke for a gentile audience that included Jewish people.[537]

3. That Luke had an intense interest in Pharisaic issues. While all three synoptists portray Jesus as spending leisure time in Pharisaic houses, discussing points of law, Luke focuses on Pharisaic issues and Pharisaic companionship more than Mark, or Matthew.[538] However, all four gospel authors agree in portraying Jews (including Jesus), and particularly Pharisees, as using the verb θεραπεύω to denote sabbath healing.[539] From this it would appear that Jesus himself was a Pharisee, a Pharisee that had discovered a new way of thinking, a way of thinking that contradicted contemporary Pharisaic thought and practice.[540] Hence the gospel interest in and portrayal of Pharisaic opposition to Jesus' ministry.

4. That θεραπεύω does not primarily denote physical healing, but is primarily a spiritual term denoting spiritual healing, while including the holistic effects of mental, emotional and physical health. Indeed θεραπεύω often describes conversion (i.e. a change in thinking), especially in general healing episodes describing crowd events. Conversion involves active participation in and experience of the kingdom of God, inclusion in the spiritual community. It is the active response of teaching and preaching (ἀκούω), the

536 See above, 156-159, for a discussion of Matthew's use of ἰάομαι to describe the intervention of God in gentile healings.

537 See especially Luke's use of the verb ἰάομαι.

538 See App. 7:7. This may be either because of his association with Paul, an ex-Pharisee, or it may indicate that he was especially anxious to explain Jesus' departure from accepted Pharisaic law.

539 See above, 146-152. (But cf. John 9.1-41)

540 Wilcox(1982) 131-195 argues that Jesus was a Pharisee, and concludes (185) that "No other known movement in First Century Judaism provides us with as close a 'fit' to Jesus and his movement as does Pharisaism, and the tension between him and the Pharisees thus probably arises out of his very nearness to them, its intensity reflecting the fact that he was viewed as representing one strand - a non-conforming one - within it. This enables us to make sense of the motif of Pharisees 'testing' or 'observing' Jesus or his disciples: his teaching and practice - or theirs - is under scrutiny to see whether or not it is in conformity with expected Pharisaic guidelines in such matters. Thus the questions in the main concern table-fellowship, Sabbath-keeping, purity, and other points of law. He is not an *'am ha-'aretz*, who is careless about the rules, but resembles rather a ḥasid, a pious man whose emphasis in matters of *halakhah* is more stringent in duty to fellow man and less so in questions of 'purity' and table-fellowship than is the case with acceptable Pharisaic norms. His healing and other miracle-working activities fit the same pattern...." Wilcox reaches this conclusion by studying Jesus in the light of his Jewish environment. A study of the gospel depiction of the Pharisaic use of θεραπεύω and Pharisaic disputes supports his conclusion.

active effect of διδάσκω, which involves saving service (ἐργάζομαι). Thus θεραπεύω provides a practical meaning for Jesus' command to love one another. In this sense the aspect of θεραπεύω is continuous.

5. That Luke introduces ἰάομαι in conjunction with θεραπεύω, and substitutes it for θεραπεύω in gentile settings, because the word is more intelligible to his gentile audience. As we have seen in Section One, θεραπεύω in a medical context refers to medical treatment in the Greek world (i.e. nursing care), and in a teaching/oratorical context it implies persuasion. It seems that Luke didn't want to dispense with either the notion of 'nurture' or 'persuasion' implicit in θεραπεύω. However he did want to introduce a word that could imply both a 'cure' and 'divine intervention' in its meaning. As we have seen in Section One, both notions are present in the Greek world for ἰάομαι. So Luke chooses to use both word groups contiguously. Thus audience has a great effect on the gospel message.

6. That to translate both words as "heal" is misleading, as, in our modern secular society, readers understand this term in a purely physical sense, a sense not intended by the New Testament authors.

But what of other important terms that appear in healing stories? Does their use shed any light on the meaning and purpose of Jesus' healing ministry?

9. Other New Testament healing words: *σῴζω καθαίρω ἅπτομαι ὑγιαίνω*

There are several other general healing terms that appear in the New Testament language of healing and, of these, ὑγιαίνω and σῴζω are the most important. Forms of the ὑγιαίνω ὑγιής family of words occur twenty-two times in the New Testament,[541] while forms of διασῴζω σῴζω also occur twenty-two times in healing stories.[542] As

541 See App. 9:2.

542 Forms of these verbs have been restricted to healing stories that appear to have a physical element, as this family of "salvation" words appears so often in the New Testament, in differing contexts. See Apps 7:10 and 7:11. The twenty-two cited are: Mt 9.21, 9.22, 9.22, 14.36; Mk 3.4, 5.23, 5.28, 5.34, 6.56, 10.52; Lk 6.9, 7.3, 8.36, 8.48, 8.50, 17.19, 18.42; Jn 11.12; Acts 4.9, 4.12, 14.9; James 5.15. Also relevant are Acts 4.12 (σωτηρία); Acts 16.17 (ὁδὸν σωτηρίας); Acts 16.30 (σωθῶ); Acts 16.31 (σωθήσῃ); and Acts 28.28 (τοῦτο τὸ

well, a study of the synoptic use of καθαίρω[543] and ἅπτομαι[544] in healing stories reveals much about the reporting method of each synoptist, and about Jesus' healing methods. Thus each word group will be considered in turn. It is to a consideration of the διασῴζω σῴζω family of words that we shall turn first, and, as with θεραπεύω and ἰάομαι, we shall consider the synoptic use of this word group as it appears in general and specific healing episodes.

9.1. διασῴζω σῴζω

9.1.1. διασῴζω σῴζω in general healing episodes

This verb group appears twice, in parallel synoptic episodes, in the passive voice. The third person plural imperfect passive indicative ἐσῴζοντο occurs only once in a healing context in the New Testament. It is, not surprisingly,[545] in Mark's gospel (6.56), and occurs in an account of general healing episodes in the region of Gennesaret. Mark reports that the people there began bringing sick people (τοὺς κακῶς ἔχοντας ... τοὺς ἀσθενοῦντας) to any place where they heard Jesus was (villages, cities, or country), and they asked him whether they might touch the hem of his cloak (ἵνα κἂν τοῦ κρασπέδου τοῦ ἱματίου αὐτοῦ ἅψωνται). And as many as touched him were healed on each occasion (καὶ ὅσοι ἂν ἥψαντο αὐτοῦ ἐσῴζοντο). Mark's choice of the imperfect tense, implying continuous action over a period of time, is supported by his description of Jesus' movements. Mark links σῴζω with ἅπτομαι. Matthew has a similar story (14.36). Luke does not use this verb in a general healing episode,[546] and this is the only general healing episode in

---

σωτήριον τοῦ θεοῦ) because they appear in close proximity to healing stories (or language).

543 See App. 7:13, "Other".

544 See Apps 7:12 and 7:13.

545 See above, 130, for a discussion of Mark's use of the imperfect tense.

546 Hobart (1882) 8-9 compares these passages with Luke 6.19, an important general healing episode discussed above (160-161). He states (9) that "Luke uses a term strictly medical (i.e. ἰᾶτο), the other writers one less precise". However, we have seen that Luke uses ἰάομαι in a holistic sense, but with a spiritual emphasis (see chapter eight), especially in crowd scenes. Mark and Matthew may be doing the same thing here with διασῴζω and σῴζω.

Mark[547] that does not include a form of θεραπεύω. We are not told what specific weaknesses the people suffered, only the very vague τοὺς κακῶς ἔχοντας ... τοὺς ἀσθενοῦντας. In all other healings in *Mark* where σῴζω occurs we are told the physical nature of the problem,[548] whereas here the description of the ailments is so vague and generalised that it is impossible to determine anything other than that a positive result occurred in the lives of those who reached out and touched (ἥψαντο) Jesus.

Matthew chooses the aorist passive indicative to report the general healing episode at Gennesaret.[549] In his account the men of the region brought all those feeling poorly (πάντας τοὺς κακῶς ἔχοντας) to Jesus. Again σῴζω is linked with ἅπτομαι:

> They began asking him if they might only touch the hem of his cloak (καὶ παρεκάλουν αὐτὸν ἵνα μόνον ἅψωνται τοῦ κρασπέδου τοῦ ἱματίου αὐτοῦ), and as many as touched (it) were healed (καὶ ὅσοι ἥψαντο διεσώθησαν).

As in *Mark*, the passive voice of the verb is chosen, although (typically) Matthew has chosen the aorist tense, signifying a single completed action. As in *Mark*, this is the only general healing episode in *Matthew* that does not include a form of θεραπεύω, but includes forms of ἅπτομαι. When the people "reach out" in faith they are "healed".

9.1.2. διασῴζω σῴζω in specific healing episodes

An interesting feature of the use of this word group is that Jesus is portrayed as the only person to use σῴζω in direct speech in specific healing episodes.[550] Jesus uses σῴζω when discussing the legality of

547 Matthew's parallel account, at 14.36, is also the only general healing episode in *Matthew* that does not include a form of θεραπεύω. Neither passage mentions teaching, and perhaps this is why θεραπεύω does not appear. The choice of σῴζω in the passive voice implies the intervention of God.

548 A withered hand (3.4); Jairus' daughter: dying (5.23); the haemorrhaging woman (5.28, 34); and blind Bartimaeus (10.52).

549 The only occurrence of this form: διεσώθησαν, in the NT. Cf. Mk 6.56. See App. 7:11.

550 However, the verb does appear in indirect speech in the active voice. The active aorist subjunctive third person singular of διασῴζω occurs only once in a healing context, in the reported speech of Jewish elders, in Luke's account of the healing of the centurion's servant. Matthew (8.5-13) does not use διασῴζω in this story, while John (4.47) chooses ἰάσηται. Luke makes Jesus comment on the centurion's faith (πίστιν 7.9), and then (7.10) chooses ὑγιαίνοντα to

healing on the Sabbath with the Pharisees, and in the healing of the haemorrhaging woman, a blind man, and in the Lukan story of the ten lepers.

Both occurrences of the aorist active infinitive of σῴζω in New Testament healing stories come out of Jesus' mouth in the parallel accounts of the sabbath healing of the man with the withered hand.[551] While all three synoptists preserve this story,[552] only Luke retains Mark's form of σῴζω in the question that Jesus puts to the Pharisees,[553] while choosing to make other substitutions. In *Mark*, Jesus asks whether it is lawful on the sabbath to do good or to do harm (ἀγαθὸν ποιῆσαι ἢ κακοποιῆσαι), to save life or to kill (ψυχὴν σῶσαι ἢ ἀποκτεῖναι). Luke "improves" Mark's Greek by framing Jesus' question thus: ἀγαθοποιῆσαι ἢ κακοποιῆσαι, ψυχὴν σῶσαι ἢ ἀπολέσαι, while Matthew prefers to give an illustration of "saving" life, rather than retaining the question in these words.[554] The use of σῴζω is significant. Jesus equates this healing with "saving" life.[555] Since Pharisaic law did allow the sabbath to be broken where there was a "threat to life"[556] Jesus' question is a quite legitimate example of Pharisees engaging in disputes concerning matters of *halakhah*.[557] But what did Jesus mean by his question? The man was not in danger of dying, in a physical sense. However, Jesus obviously felt that his life was threatened in some way. Certainly a physical disability of this nature would prevent the man from leading a normal life, it would also exclude him from full participation in the religious life of his community.[558] So, in restoring the man's hand, Jesus was not only physically

---

describe the servant's condition when the centurion returns home (cf. *IG* IV[2] 1, 122, 21 [App. 2:2, **21**]). See App. 7:11, διασώσῃ.

551 Mk 3.4; Lk 6.9 (see App. 7:10; and App. 7:11, σῶσαι).

552 Mk 3.1-6; Lk 6.6-11; Mt 12.9-14

553 In *Mark* Jesus puts the question to the Pharisees; in *Luke* he puts it to the Pharisees and scribes.

554 Mt 12.11-12

555 But note that the word for 'life' is ψυχή.

556 See Wilcox (1982) 176-177, and n.247, for a discussion of this issue. Cf. Hull (1974) 1, who claims that: "The Jewish objection to the healings on the sabbath was ... not the sabbath activity itself but the magical techniques used by Jesus." However the language used by the gospel authors would seem to question this interpretation. See above, 150-152, for the link between θεραπεύω and ἐργάζομαι.

557 However, all three synoptic authors record that the Pharisees thought of this sabbath healing in terms of θεραπεύω. See above, chapter seven.

558 See Leviticus 13.46

healing the man, he was giving him the opportunity for full spiritual participation in his community. Thus, in this way, σῴζω as it is used here is holistic in meaning.

On other occasions when Jesus uses the verb σῴζω in healing stories, he does so in the active perfect tense.[559] This form appears six times in New Testament healing stories, in all three synoptic gospels. On all occasions it comes out of the mouth of Jesus to a person who has been healed in the saying "Your faith has saved you (ἡ πίστις σου σέσωκέν σε)." It occurs in all three synoptic accounts of the healing of the haemorrhaging woman.[560] As well, all three synoptists choose the verb ἅπτομαι to describe the woman's touch, a verb that is often chosen to describe the touch of those who reach out in faith,[561] and is linked with σῴζω.

The second parallel account that features this saying is the account of the healing of the blind man near Jericho.[562] Both Mark and Luke state that discipleship is the result of this man's healing, Mark stating: "and immediately he saw, and began following him on the way (καὶ εὐθὺς ἀνέβλεψεν, καὶ ἠκολούθει αὐτῷ ἐν τῇ ὁδῷ (10.52))", while Luke (καὶ παραχρῆμα ἀνέβλεψεν, καὶ ἠκολούθει αὐτῷ) adds: "praising God. And all the people, when they saw it, gave praise to God (δοξάζων τὸν θεόν. καὶ πᾶς ὁ λαὸς ἰδὼν ἔδωκεν αἶνον τῷ θεῷ (18.43))". Mark gives the blind man's name as Bartimaeus, in contrast to Luke, who makes him an anonymous beggar. This seems an unusual practice for Luke, if we assume that he was working from Mark's account.[563] In other places Luke provides precise personal details.[564] This is the only specific Lukan account of the healing of blindness, apart from that of Paul in *Acts*.[565] Both

559 The active perfect indicative third person singular σέσωκεν: see App. 7:11.

560 Mt 9.22; Mk 5.34; Lk 8.48

561 See below, 185f.

562 Mk 10.52; Lk 18.42; cf. Mt 20.29-34

563 So some have thought that the name was added to Mark's account after Luke made use of it (see Sanders and Davies [1989] 172).

564 For example, the names of Mary, Joanna, and Susanna (8.2-3) in a passage peculiar to Luke. He also retains the identities of Peter's mother-in-law (4.38-39), and Jairus (8.40-42); and in *Acts* names Aeneas (9.32-35), Dorcas (9.36-43), Eutychus (20.7-12), and Publius' father (28.7-9) and, of course, Saul (9.1-22), in his twelve healing episodes; and carefully identifies each of the seven victims of punishment in *Acts* either by name or parentage, and gives their location, history, and occupation as well. (See Apps 7:3, 8:1 and 8:2) It is curious that he would omit Bartimaeus' name, in a parallel account, supposedly based on *Mark*. The language used certainly presupposes a parallel account.

565 Acts 9.1-22. But see the general healing episode at Luke 7.21, and 139-140, above.

accounts are conversion accounts and result in active discipleship: the blind man follows Jesus, praising God, and all those nearby also praise God; Paul began preaching (ἐκήρυσσεν (9.20)) and converting others. Thus physical blindness in Lukan writings is used as a motif denoting spiritual blindness. Certainly the use of σῴζω in both synoptic accounts invests this healing with a spiritual dimension. Matthew records a similar episode which also includes discipleship as the result,[566] but Matthew features *two* blind men.[567] He also omits Jesus' saying, and therefore σῴζω, but includes ἅπτομαι to describe Jesus' touch.[568]

The third episode in which this saying of Jesus appears occurs in a story peculiar to Luke (17.11-19). On the way to Jerusalem, between Samaria and Galilee, ten lepers asked Jesus to have mercy on them. All found they were cleansed when they followed Jesus' instructions to show themselves to the priests. One, a Samaritan, a foreigner (ἀλλογενής), returned to praise God and thank Jesus. Jesus told him his faith had "saved" him. This story links several words that appear frequently in healing stories: ἐλεάω,[569] καθαίρω,[570] ἰάομαι,[571] πίστις, and σῴζω.

The author of the epistle *James* also links ἰάομαι and πίστις with the verb σῴζω.[572] It appears in a passage in *James* giving advice as to procedure in the case of suffering. James advises prayer, for "the prayer of faith will save the man laid low[573] (ἡ εὐχὴ τῆς

566 Mt 20.29-34

567 See Jeremias (1975) 86f. where he discusses the tendency of the author of *Matthew* to heighten the element of miracle by exaggerating numbers cited in *Mark*.

568 Matthew also features ἅπτομαι in his other account of the healing of two blind men (9.27-31), an account thought to be a duplicate of this account (Mt 20.29-34). See Sanders and Davies (1989) 172.

569 The blind men also attract Jesus' attention with this word. See Mk 10.47; Lk 18.38; Mt 20.30.

570 See below, 191-195.

571 See above, chapter eight.

572 James 5.15: σώσει (see App. 7:11). The future active indicative third person singular of σῴζω only occurs once in a healing context.

573 The use of κάμνω, among other things, is cited as an example of the superior use of Greek by the author of *James*. See Davids (1982) 58, who claims that "the writer of the epistle is an able master of literary Koine." Dibelius (1981) 252 interprets this whole procedure as an exorcism. Davids (1982) 194 disagrees. He states that it is "not a magical rite, nor an exorcism". Dibelius (1981) 252 also states that the use of oil was a remedy from folk medicine. He draws a parallel with the use of oil by the disciples at Mark 6.13. However, as we have seen (above, 128-129), oil was used in Hippokratic medicine (see

πίστεως σώσει τὸν κάμνοντα)". As in the gospel healing stories σῴζω is linked with πίστις.

Several interesting patterns emerge from a study of the use of σῴζω in the active voice in New Testament healing stories.

1. σῴζω appears ten times in the active voice in a healing context. Of these ten, eight appear in direct speech, always out of the mouth of Jesus. Thus only Jesus uses σῴζω in direct speech in the active voice in a healing context.

2. Furthermore, where Jesus says "ἡ πίστις σου σέσωκέν σε", in each case, there is a strong spiritual emphasis. The blind men all "followed" Jesus, as soon as they could "see"; the haemorrhaging woman, and the leper, both having been excluded from full participation in their communities because of "uncleanness", were told to continue their life journey,[574] having been saved by faith. Thus σῴζω, like θεραπεύω and ἰάομαι, includes the notion of discipleship in its meaning.

3. σῴζω likes to appear in close proximity to a form of πίστις, and/or ἅπτομαι.

In the passive voice the verb σῴζω appears in differing forms in six specific healing episodes: the accounts of the haemorrhaging woman, the accounts of the healing of Jairus' daughter, and the raising of Lazarus; and the Lukan stories of the healing of the Gerasene demoniac, and of both the lame men in *Acts*.

σῴζω appears in two forms in the parallel accounts of the healing of the haemorrhaging woman: in the thought of the woman,[575] and as a concluding description of her healed state.[576] In both *Matthew* and *Mark*, healing (σωθήσομαι) is here thought of by the haemorrhaging woman as being conditional on her touching (ἅψωμαι) Jesus' cloak. Matthew also uses σῴζω to conclude his account of the healing of the haemorrhaging woman: καὶ ἐσώθη ἡ γυνὴ ἀπὸ ὥρας ἐκείνης. Indeed, Matthew uses a combination of forms of σῴζω, ἅπτομαι and πίστις in this story. Neither Mark nor Luke uses this form in their parallel accounts. It is significant that

---

App. 4:1, 13). κάμνω appears frequently in the Hippokratic Corpus identifying those who were patients (see App. 4:1).

574 See above, 166-167, and App. 8:4: ἰάθη.

575 Twice in the first person future passive indicative of σῴζω in the parallel accounts of *Mark* (5.28) and *Matthew* (9.21). See App. 7:11, σωθήσομαι.

576 The third person singular aorist passive indicative ἐσώθη occurs as Matthew's final description of the woman (9.22); and also in the Lukan account of the healing of the Gerasene demoniac (8.36). See Apps 7:10 and 7:11.

Matthew describes this healing, that of an "unclean" woman, with a passive verb, implying the intervention of God.[577]

σῴζω also appears in the accounts of the healing of Jairus' daughter, in both *Mark* and *Luke*, occurring in direct speech between Jairus and Jesus. In Mark's account, Jairus uses the verb in his request that Jesus come and lay hands on his daughter (ἵνα ἐλθὼν ἐπιθῇς τὰς χεῖρας αὐτῇ), in order that she might be healed and might live (ἵνα σωθῇ καὶ ζήσῃ).[578] Later, when he is told that his daughter has died, Jesus tells him: "Do not be afraid, only keep on believing (μὴ φοβοῦ, μόνον πίστευε (5.36))." Thus again πίστις is linked to σῴζω.[579] In Luke's parallel account of this story Luke expands Jesus' Markan saying to "Don't be afraid. Only believe, and she will be saved (μὴ φοβοῦ, μόνον πίστευσον, καὶ σωθήσεται)."[580]

Similarly, σωθήσεται comes out of the mouths of the disciples to Jesus, in the Johannine story of the raising of Lazarus (11.12), after Jesus had told the disciples that Lazarus was sleeping (εἰ κεκοίμηται σωθήσεται). Both stories deal with death/sleep, and both link a form of σῴζω with a form of πιστεύω. Indeed, John makes Jesus claim that he did not go to Lazarus earlier "in order that you (disciples) might believe (ἵνα πιστεύσητε (11.15))". John uses this story to stress Jesus' identity, and the link between belief and life:

> Jesus said to her (Martha), 'I am the resurrection and the life (ἡ ἀνάστασις καὶ ἡ ζωή); he who believes in me (ὁ πιστεύων εἰς ἐμὲ), though he die, yet shall he live (κἂν ἀποθάνῃ ζήσεται), and whoever lives and believes in me shall never die (καὶ πᾶς ὁ ζῶν καὶ πιστεύων εἰς ἐμὲ οὐ μὴ ἀποθάνῃ εἰς τὸν αἰῶνα·). Do you believe this? (πιστεύεις τοῦτο;)' She said to him, 'Yes, Lord; I believe (ἐγὼ πεπίστευκα) that you are the Christ (ὁ Χριστὸς), the Son of God (ὁ υἱὸς τοῦ θεοῦ), he who is coming (ὁ ἐρχόμενος) into the world.[581]

Later Jesus uses πιστεύω twice, once to Martha (ἐὰν πιστεύσῃς (11.40)), and once in prayer (ἵνα πιστεύσωσιν (11.41)). πιστεύω also appears in the narrative. The result of Lazarus' restoration was, pre-

577 As does Mark, in his only use of the verb ἰάομαι (see above, 156).

578 Mk 5.23: the third person aorist passive subjunctive σωθῇ only occurs once in the New Testament in a healing context (see App. 7:11, σωθῇ).

579 ἅπτομαι does not appear in this story however, rather κρατέω is used to describe Jesus' touch (5.41), as in the parallel accounts in *Luke* (8.54), and *Matthew* (9.25). κρατέω is a strong verb. It implies a more overpowering touch than ἅπτομαι (see below, 196-201).

580 Lk 8.50: the third person singular future passive indicative, σωθήσεται, appears twice in a healing context, here and at John 11.12.

581 Jn 11.25-27

dictably, that "many of the Jews ... believed (ἐπίστευσαν)",[582] so that the chief priests and the Pharisees wonder what to do about him, saying,

> If we let him go on thus, everyone will believe in him (πάντες πιστεύσουσιν εἰς αὐτόν), and the Romans will come and destroy both our (holy?) place (τὸν τόπον) and our nation.[583]

Thus the verb πιστεύω occurs nine times in this story, six times out of the mouth of Jesus,[584] once in narrative describing result,[585] once out of Martha's mouth affirming her belief,[586] and once expressing the fear of the chief priests and Pharisees.[587] It is linked with the verb ζάω, a verb that appears in six of ten New Testament stories dealing with death (sleep).[588]

In the Lukan story of the healing of the Gerasene demoniac Luke puts σῴζω into the mouths of bystanders who explain how the Gerasene demoniac was healed: πῶς ἐσώθη ὁ δαιμονισθείς.[589] The result in the life of this man (as in the lives of the blind beggar, and the Samaritan leper) was discipleship. People found the man "sitting at the feet of Jesus, clothed and in his right mind (καθήμενον ... ἱματισμένον καὶ σωφρονοῦντα παρὰ τοὺς πόδας τοῦ Ἰησοῦ)".[590] However, when the man begged "that he might be with him (εἶναι σὺν αὐτῷ)", Jesus "sent him away[591] (ἀπέλυσεν δὲ αὐτὸν)", with instructions to "return home and declare how much God has done for you".[592] This story does not exhibit the secrecy motif that is so prominent in many other healing stories.[593]

The verb σῴζω also appears in two Lukan healing stories in *Acts* in the same form. The aorist passive infinitive σωθῆναι occurs in both accounts of the healing of different lame men.[594] The first

---

582 Jn 11.45
583 Jn 11.48
584 Jn 11.15, 25, 26, 27, 40, 41
585 Jn 11.45
586 Jn 11.27
587 Jn 11.48
588 Mk 5.23; Mt 9.18; Jn 4.50ff.; Jn 11.25ff.; Acts 9.40; Acts 20.12
589 Lk 8.36: the third person singular aorist passive indicative ἐσώθη. Cf. Mt 9.22, and see Apps 7:10 and 7:11.
590 Lk 8.35
591 Lk 8.38 (see Vermes [1983] 49).
592 Lk 8.39
593 Mark 5.19 contains the same command, but cf. Mk 1.44 = Lk 5.14 = Mt 8.4; Lk 8.56 = Mk 5.43; Mk 7.36; Mk 8.26; Mt 9.30. See also Wrede (1971).
594 The first where Peter (and John?) is the agent (Acts 3.1-26, 4.1-31); the second where Paul is the agent (Acts 14.8-11). See App. 8:1.

comes out of Peter's mouth in his speech to the Council, explaining the healing of the lame man at the temple gate.[595] Although Luke uses a range of healing words in this story: σῴζω, θεραπεύω, ὑγιής, ἴασις, ὁλοκληρία, (δύναμις, σημεῖον), Peter's speech revolves around the importance of faith (πίστις) in Jesus' name (3.16), and he explains how the man was healed (σέσωται)[596] in the name of Jesus (4.9-10), and that there isn't any salvation (ἡ σωτηρία) in anyone/anything else (4.12), for there is no other name by which we must be saved (ᾧ δεῖ σωθῆναι ἡμᾶς (4.12)). Thus it was πίστις which led to the ὁλοκληρίαν (3.16) of the man who was lame. The result in the behaviour of the man was (as with the blind beggar at Luke 18.43) that he began praising God (3.8), and soon "everybody began praising God" (4.21). His restoration became this "sign of healing (τὸ σημεῖον τοῦτο τῆς ἰάσεως)",[597] a catalyst for mass conversion.

The second appearance of σωθῆναι occurs in the Lukan account of Paul's healing of the man lame from birth.[598] Paul saw that "he had faith to be made well (καὶ ἰδὼν ὅτι ἔχει πίστιν τοῦ σωθῆναι)." Again σῴζω depends on πίστις.

What then of the use of the σῴζω διασῴζω family of words in New Testament healing stories?

Matthew uses forms of σῴζω διασῴζω four times in two healing stories.[599] Both incidents record the healing of those who touched Jesus' clothes, in faith. Jesus claims that it was the faith of the haemorrhaging woman which saved her: "ἡ πίστις σου σέσωκέν σε".[600] The faith of those at Gennesaret is also noted: "καὶ παρεκάλουν αὐτον ἵνα μόνον ἅψωνται τοῦ κρασπέδου τοῦ ἱματίου αὐτοῦ καὶ ὅσοι ἥψαντο διεσώθησαν".[601] The thoughts of the haemorrhaging woman: "ἔλεγεν γὰρ ἐν ἑαυτῇ, Ἐὰν μόνον ἅψωμαι τοῦ ἱματίου αὐτοῦ σωθήσομαι",[602] echo the description of the crowd, in content and language. And like the man's demonic epileptic son,[603] the centurion's "boy",[604] and the Canaanite woman's daughter,[605] the haemorrhaging woman was healed from the hour

595 Acts 4.12

596 Acts 4.9: the third person singular perfect passive indicative σέσωται occurs only once in the New Testament in a healing context (see Apps 7:10 and 7:11).

597 Acts 4.22

598 Acts 14.9

599 Mt 9.21, 22, 22; 14.36 (see Apps 7:10 and 7:11).

600 Mt 9.22

601 Mt 14.36

602 Mt 9.21

603 Mt 17.18

604 Mt 8.13

605 Mt 15.28

that Jesus spoke to her: "καὶ ἐσώθη ἡ γυνὴ ἀπὸ τῆς ὥρας ἐκείνης".[606] σῴζω and διασῴζω then, in *Matthew*, record instantaneous healing of those who touched Jesus' clothes in faith. The verb chosen to describe that touch on each occasion is ἅπτομαι. In *Matthew* it is only Jesus who uses σῴζω in the active voice.

Mark uses σῴζω on more occasions than Matthew. However, as in *Matthew* σῴζω is linked with ἅπτομαι in the story of the haemorrhaging woman, in (almost) identical language: "ἐὰν ἅψωμαι κἂν τῶν ἱματίων αὐτοῦ σωθήσομαι".[607] Jesus' saying is identical: "ἡ πίστις σου σέσωκέν σε".[608] Like Matthew, Mark also uses σῴζω with ἅπτομαι to report the healing of crowds of people at Gennesaret,[609] but he chooses the imperfect, rather than the aorist, to describe these events, implying a series of episodes over a period of time. Mark uses σῴζω on two other occasions, occasions where Matthew chooses to omit σῴζω. The first is in Mark's story of the sabbath healing of the man with the withered hand,[610] where Jesus asks the Pharisees whether it is lawful on the sabbath to save life (ψυχὴν σῶσαι), or to kill, wording that is retained by Luke.[611] Mark also has Jesus repeat the saying, "ἡ πίστις σου σέσωκέν σε" to Bartimaeus,[612] a saying preserved by Luke.[613] Thus, in *Mark*, as in *Matthew*, it is only Jesus who uses σῴζω in the active voice in direct speech.

Luke chooses to use σῴζω more than Mark, in more healing stories. As in *Mark*, Luke retains σῶσαι in the story of the sabbath healing of the man with the withered hand.[614] Luke also retains Jesus' saying, "ἡ πίστις σου σέσωκέν σε", in the stories of the haemorrhaging woman,[615] and the healing of the blind beggar near Jericho.[616] However Luke also puts this saying into the mouth of Jesus, when he addresses the Samaritan leper, who returned to thank him for his health.[617] Jewish elders also use διασῴζω, when they request Jesus' help on behalf of the

606 Mt 9.22
607 Mk 5.28
608 Mk 5.34
609 Mk 6.56
610 Mk 3.4
611 Mk 6.9
612 Mk 10.52
613 Lk 18.42
614 Lk 6.9
615 Lk 8.48
616 Lk 18.42
617 Lk 17.19

centurion,[618] and by-standers explain how the Gerasene demoniac was healed in terms of σῴζω.[619] Finally, Luke puts σωθήσεται into the mouth of Jesus, when he tells Jairus not to fear, only believe, and his daughter will be saved.[620] This same form of σῴζω comes out of the mouths of the disciples in John's only use of this word in a healing story, the raising of Lazarus.[621] It is interesting that the same form is used by both Luke and John, in stories concerning "sleep" and "death", and that in both stories the link between "belief" and "salvation" is stressed.

Other Lukan uses of σῴζω in healing stories occur in two stories in *Acts*.[622] The first three forms come out of Peter's mouth in the Lukan account of the healing of the lame man,[623] a story which emphasises the man's faith.[624] The second story is the Lukan account of Paul's healing of the man lame from birth.[625] Again faith is linked with σῴζω. Thus the exploits of Peter and Paul are balanced, in deed, and word.

The only other New Testament use of σῴζω in a (physical?) healing context, is at James 5.15, where James says that the prayer of faith will save the man laid low (ἡ εὐχὴ τῆς πίστεως σώσει τὸν κάμνοντα). Again πίστις is linked with σῴζω.

Thus the use of σῴζω and διασῴζω in healing stories denotes far more than physical healing. Like θεραπεύω and the Lukan use of ἰάομαι the σῴζω διασῴζω family of words in healing stories is primarily spiritual in meaning. Those that are "saved/healed" are

618 Lk 7.3

619 Lk 8.36

620 Lk 8.50

621 Jn 11.12

622 Acts 3.1-26, 4.1-31 and 14.8-11. But forms of σῴζω also occur in the story that is the result of the healing of the slave girl who had a spirit of divination (16.30, 31). The girl herself had shouted (16.17) that Paul and his companions were proclaiming the way of salvation (ὁδὸν σωτηρίας). As a result of her healing Paul and Silas were imprisoned. There the gaoler asked them "What must I do to be saved? (τί με δεῖ ποιεῖν ἵνα σωθῶ;)" (16.30). Paul's and Silas' answer to the gaoler's question: "Believe in the Lord Jesus, and you will be saved, you and your household (Πίστευσον ..., καὶ σωθήσῃ σὺ καὶ ὁ οἶκός σου)." The result was that he believed (πεπιστευκὼς τῷ θεῷ (16.34)), and he and his family were baptised. Again πιστεύω is linked with σῴζω. This is obviously a conversion account, and is not supposed to describe physical healing. But that this combination of terminology appears so often in "healing" stories is too striking to ignore. Discipleship must be part of the healing/saving process.

623 Acts 4.9, 12, 12

624 Acts 3.16

625 Acts 14.9

those who reach out to Jesus in faith. Faith is emphasised and some form of discipleship is the usual result. Thus there is a strong element of conversion in healing stories that feature σῴζω or διασῴζω in their healing language. And, unless it comes out of the mouth of Jesus, the verb usually appears in the passive voice.

There are other important healing words in the New Testament healing narrative. Indeed, a study of one generally leads to a network of associated others. One of these is the verb καθαίρω.

9.2. καθαίρω

καθαίρω occurs in two healing stories in the synoptic gospels: the synoptic parallel account of the leper's cleansing,[626] and the Lukan story of the ten lepers.[627] It also occurs in Matthew's account of Jesus' command to the disciples,[628] and in the Matthaean and Lukan account of Jesus' reply to the messengers of John the Baptist who question his identity.[629]

A study of the synoptic use of καθαίρω reveals a pattern of treatment concerning the same healing story. In the parallel accounts of the leper's cleansing the request of the leper is reported in (almost) identical language,[630] Jesus' reply is reported in

626 Mk 1.40-45; Mt 8.1-3; Lk 5.12-13

627 Lk 17.11-19. See above, 167, 184.

628 Mt 10.8. The second person plural present active imperative καθαρίζετε occurs only once, out of the mouth of Jesus. This instruction, to "cleanse lepers" (λεπροὺς καθαρίζετε) appears in a long list of instructions to the newly commissioned disciples of where to go (and where not to go), what to say, what to do, and what to take with them. Cf. Mk 3.13-19, 6.7-13; Lk 6.12-16, 9. 1-6; and *GT* #14. For a discussion of this use, see below, chapter ten.

629 Mt 11.5; Lk 7.22. The third person plural present passive indicative καθαρίζονται occurs twice, in the Lukan and Matthaean accounts of Jesus' reply to the messengers from John the Baptist. Both replies are based on the Septuagint version of Isaiah 35.5-6, 42.18 and 61.1. However, Isaiah does not mention the cleansing of lepers, (nor the raising of the dead), and so καθαίρω does not appear in the promises of Isaiah. This raises the question of the origin, significance, and purpose of this saying.

630 The aorist active infinitive καθαρίσαι appears three times in the parallel synoptic accounts of the leper's cleansing (Mk 1.40; Mt 8.2; Lk 5.12). On each occasion it comes out of the mouth of the leper, when he addresses Jesus with the words: "If you want to, you can make me clean (ἐὰν θέλῃς δύνασαί με καθαρίσαι)". The request is framed in identical language in the three accounts, except that both Matthew and Luke preface the leper's request with the vocative κύριε.

identical language,[631] Jesus' action is reported with the same verb (ἅπτομαι),[632] and Jesus' instruction to the leper to show himself to the priest and fulfil the requirements of the law is also reported in very similar language in each account. Similarly, Jesus' request for secrecy is also reported in identical language[633] by all three synoptists. Thus all three synoptists report Jesus' speech in identical language, and are very similar in their reporting of indirect speech.

However, for all these similarities, there are significant differences in their accounts. The location of each incident is different. Mark does not specify a location, but places Jesus somewhere in Galilee (1.39), while Matthew says that Jesus had come down from the mountain (where he had been teaching) and that great crowds had followed him (8.1). Luke places Jesus in an (anonymous) city (5.12). Both Mark and Matthew describe the man as a λεπρός, while Luke says he was πλήρης λέπρας.[634] And while all three report Jesus' secrecy instruction, and his command to go to the priest and offer the gift that Moses commanded,[635] the sequel is entirely different in each gospel. Matthew launches straight into the account of the healing of the centurion's servant (8.5-13), while Mark reports that the leper disobeyed Jesus' demand for secrecy, and spread the news so much that Jesus could no longer openly enter a town but was out in the wilderness, where people were coming to him from all the surrounding area (1.45). Luke does not ascribe the lack of secrecy to the leper himself, but just states that

631 The aorist passive second singular imperative καθαρίσθητι occurs three times, in the parallel synoptic accounts of Jesus' saying to the leper: θέλω, καθαρίσθητι. Jesus' saying is reported in identical language in each gospel.

632 The result is reported in different language however. The aorist passive third person singular indicative ἐκαθαρίσθη occurs twice, as a narrative summation of the story of the leper's cleansing in the Markan and Matthaean accounts. Mark (1.42) describes the result thus: "καὶ εὐθὺς ἀπῆλθεν ἀπ' αὐτοῦ ἡ λέπρα, καὶ ἐκαθαρίσθη". Matthew (8.3) reduces this to: "καὶ εὐθέως ἐκαθαρίσθη αὐτοῦ ἡ λέπρα", while Luke (5.13) prefers: "καὶ εὐθέως ἡ λέπρα ἀπῆλθεν ἀπ' αὐτοῦ". This difference shows that while the synoptists are comfortable changing the language of narration, they are far less likely to tamper with direct speech.

633 Matthew and Luke omit Mark's μηδὲν.

634 Lk 5.12. Hobart (1882) 5-6, sees this as an indication of Luke's medical profession. However Jeremias (1975) 86 sees details like this as an indication of Luke's wish to heighten the element of the miraculous. Luke also makes the leper "fall on his face" (πεσὼν ἐπὶ πρόσωπον), whereas Mark (γονυπετῶν) and Matthew (προσεκύνει αὐτῷ) make him "kneel".

635 See Leviticus, chapters 13 and 14 for the law regarding leprosy. The rite that the priest had to perform has a strong element of magic in it: see especially Leviticus 14.2-32.

the report concerning Jesus circulated, with the result that great crowds gathered to listen to him, and θεραπεύεσθαι ἀπὸ τῶν ἀσθενειῶν (a mass conversion?)[636] after which Jesus withdrew to the wilderness and prayed.[637] Thus the synoptists, while not tampering with the words of Jesus, are quite happy to alter location, audience, and effect.

There is one other striking difference in this story. Mark reports Jesus' compassion (1.41) and anger (1.43), details that both Matthew and Luke choose to omit. The language is difficult. While σπλαγχνισθείς (1.41) has a doubtful attestation[638] (ὀργισθείς being the variant reading),[639] it occurs in other places in the gospels as the motive for healing,[640] and does give a credible reason for Jesus' touching an unclean person (a touch which rendered him ritually unclean).[641] However, the verse in *Mark* (1.43): καὶ ἐμβριμησάμενος αὐτῷ εὐθὺς ἐξέβαλεν αὐτὸν is puzzling. Just what does this verse mean? While ἐμβριμάομαι does appear in one other place in a healing story,[642] ἐκβάλλω normally appears in *Mark* (in a healing con-

636 See above, chapter seven.

637 Lk 5.15-16

638 σπλαγχνισθεὶς is the reading preferred to ὀργισθείς, but with a high level of doubt, and therefore designated category {D}. See New Testament (1975) 123, and Metzger (1975) 76-77.

639 Schweizer (1981) 58, prefers ὀργισθείς because of "the horror of the misery which accompanied the disease"; however, Metzger (1975) 76, states that the "character of the external evidence in support of ὀργισθείς is less impressive than the diversity and character of evidence that supports σπλαγχνισθεὶς." He suggests (77) "that the reading ὀργισθείς either (a) was suggested by ἐμβριμησάμενος of ver. 43, or (b) arose from confusion between similar words in Aramaic...".

640 It is not specifically given as the motive for healing in any episode in *Mark*, although it does occur as a possible motive in the request of the epileptic boy's father, when he asks Jesus to help his son (9.22). However, Matthew uses this form (20.34) to explain Jesus' healing of the two blind men, and twice uses ἐσπλαγχνίσθη (9.36; 14.14), firstly to describe Jesus' emotion at seeing the crowds "harassed and helpless" (9.36), and secondly, as his motive for healing the weak among the crowd (καὶ ἐσπλαγχνίσθη ἐπ' αὐτοῖς καὶ ἐθεράπευσεν τοὺς ἀρρώστους αὐτῶν), before the feeding of the 5,000 (14.14). Luke also uses ἐσπλαγχνίσθη as the motive for Jesus' healing of the only son of the widow of Nain (7.13).

641 See Leviticus ch.13, ch.14. Jesus also touched (ἥψατο) the bier of the son of the widow of Nain (Luke 7.14).

642 Not in *Mark*. He prefers ἐπιτιμάω (1.25, 9.25), διαστέλλομαι (5.43, 7.36), and ἐπιτιμάω when commanding the disciples to secrecy (8.30). However, Matthew reports that Jesus ἐνεβριμήθη αὐτοῖς (9.30), in his first story of the healing of two blind men, when he demands that they keep their healing secret, a request that was disobeyed (9.31). But, when a similar request for

text) in stories related to exorcism.[643] It certainly seems inappropriate in this instance. Some commentators have taken the view that Mark views this entire episode as an exorcism, and that Jesus is here addressing the demon rather than the man.[644] However, Mark does use this term in another healing story (that of Jairus' daughter (5.40)) to describe the physical expulsion of people,[645] a story that also contains a touching verb (κρατήσας [5.41]). It is most unlikely that this story could in any way be regarded as an exorcism, when Mark has stated explicitly that Jesus touched (ἥψατο) the man.[646] Therefore ἐκβάλλω must refer to bodily expulsion.

The Lukan story of the ten lepers corresponds in some details to the synoptic story of the man with leprosy. Again Jesus is ap-

---

secrecy is made in a general healing episode in *Matthew*, Matthew chooses to use the verb ἐπιτιμάω (12.16). Jeremias (1975) 92 says of ἐμβριμάομαι that it "presumably paraphrases the oriental sign-language for a command to be silent", and, given the context of its appearance in both these healing stories, this would make sense. However, if we compare the context of John's use of this word in the story of the raising of Lazarus (11. 33, 38), this meaning does not make any sense at all.

643 But it is not as popular as one might think. Mark describes Jesus' activity thus only in general healing episodes (1.34, 1.39) and that of the disciples (6.13). He also puts this word into the mouth of the Syro-Phoenician woman (7.26), and the disciples (9.28). However, in the story of the healing of Jairus' daughter, Mark (5.40) describes Jesus' action when he banishes the people from the sick room in terms of ἐκβάλλω (ἐκβαλών). Similarly, Matthew reports that Jesus banished the crowd (ἐξεβλήθη ὁ ὄχλος) in his account of the same story (9.25). Luke (8.51) prefers to describe Jesus' action thus: "he permitted no one to enter with him, except Peter and John and James, and the father and mother of the child". Matthew uses ἐκβάλλω in exorcism stories to describe Jesus' behaviour (8.16), and its result (9.33); and also puts this word into the mouth of demons (8.31), the Pharisees (9.34, 12.24), and the disciples (17.19). Luke uses the word sparingly. He describes Jesus' behaviour (11.14), and puts this word into the mouth of John (9.49), and "some" of Jesus' critics (11.15). Similarly, he omits it from his account of Jesus' commission to his disciples (Luke 9.1), while both Matthew and Mark choose to use it in their accounts of Jesus' commission to the disciples (Mt 10.1, 10.8; Mk 3.15. See below, chapter ten).

644 Beare (1981) 204, takes this view, and also prefers the reading ὀργισθείς to that of σπλαγχνισθείς. However, Mark's other uses of ἐκβάλλω do not support this interpretation. It is not used to describe Jesus' behaviour in the specific demonic episode (1.23-28), only to voice the request of the Syro-Phoenician mother (7.26), and the question of the disciples (9.28). In general healing episodes it appears at 1.34, 1.39, and 6.13.

645 See above, n.643.

646 Mk 1.41. But cf. Mark's story of the epileptic boy (9.14-29). Jesus touches (κρατήσας) the boy after his "cure".

proached by the "patients" (17.12-13). This time, however, Jesus does not touch them, but, as on the other occasion, instructs them to show themselves to the priests (17.14). On the way they were cleansed (ἐκαθαρίσθησαν).[647] Only one of them, seeing that he had been healed (ἰάθη)[648] turned with a loud voice praising God (17.15), and "fell on his face" at Jesus' feet, thanking him. He was a Samaritan, an ἀλλογενής (17.16,18). Jesus comments on the absence of the other nine (17.17-18), and instructs the man to get up and go on, for his faith has saved him (17.19). One wonders what happened to the other nine! Certainly the inference is that they have not experienced the same faith (πίστις) as the Samaritan leper, and are therefore excluded from the same salvation (σῴζω).[649]

9.3. Jesus' method of healing

As has been noted, Jesus' method of healing involved either word or touch, or a combination of both. Three verbs occur in healing accounts which describe the "touch" of Jesus:[650] ἅπτομαι, κρατέω and ἐπιτίθημι (τὰς χεῖρας).[651] ἅπτομαι is the most common, but occurs only in synoptic stories, and only in the middle voice.[652] (It does not feature in healing stories in either *John* or *Acts*.) It appears twenty-five times in synoptic healing stories, and in four other significant places.[653] It appears in both general and specific healing episodes.

---

647 The aorist passive third person plural indicative ἐκαθαρίσθησαν occurs twice in the Lukan account of the healing of the ten lepers. One occurs in a narrative description: "καὶ ἐγένετο ἐν τῷ ὑπάγειν αὐτοὺς ἐκαθαρίσθησαν" (17.14), while the other comes out of the mouth of Jesus: "Οὐχὶ οἱ δέκα ἐκαθαρίσθησαν;" (17.17).

648 See above, 167, and App. 8:4: ἰάθη.

649 See above, 181f.

650 See below n.674 for a discussion of Jesus' rare use of saliva. Cf. Vespasian's use of saliva (Tacitus, *Hist.* 4.81), and see Jeremias (1975) 88-89.

651 Hobart (1882) does not consider any of these expressions.

652 See App. 7:12. It is odd that ἅπτομαι does not appear in Kittel *et al.* (1964).

653 Twice in the Markan and Lukan parallel report that they brought children to Jesus in order that he might touch them (Mk 10.13: ἅψηται; Lk 18.15: ἅπτηται); describing Jesus' touch when he allayed the disciples' fear after the Transfiguration (Mt 17.7: ἁψάμενος); and where the Pharisees discuss the woman who anointed Jesus, and describe her touch in the present tense (Lk 7.39: ἅπτεται).

9.3.1. ἅπτομαι in general healing episodes

Luke uses ἅπτομαι in a general healing episode following the words ἀκοῦσαι ... ἰαθῆναι ... ἐθεραπεύοντο.[654] Luke reports that "the entire crowd were seeking to touch (and keep on touching) Jesus, because power was radiating from him and healing them all (καὶ πᾶς ὁ ὄχλος ἐζήτουν ἅπτεσθαι αὐτοῦ, ὅτι δύναμις παρ' αὐτοῦ ἐξήρχετο καὶ ἰᾶτο πάντας)". Luke is the only author to use the present tense in this context, but his account could be a parallel report to the general healing episodes at Gennesaret described by both Matthew and Mark.

Both Mark and Matthew choose a combination of two forms of the aorist tense of ἅπτομαι in parallel accounts of the general healing episode at Gennesaret.[655] In both accounts the people reached out to touch Jesus, and in both accounts Mark and Matthew choose to use a combination of the verbs ἅπτομαι and σῴζω.[656] The language of this account mirrors the language used in the synoptic parallel accounts of the healing of the haemorrhaging woman.[657]

9.3.2. ἅπτομαι in specific healing episodes

The verb ἅπτομαι appears in nine specific healing episodes: the parallel accounts of the haemorrhaging woman and the leper; in the Markan stories of the man who was both deaf and dumb, and the blind man; in the Matthaean accounts of the healing of Peter's mother-in-law, and both his accounts of the blind men; and the Lukan stories of the widow's son and the temple slave.[658]

The most popular form of ἅπτομαι is the aorist third person singular middle indicative ἥψατο, which occurs fifteen times in seven synoptic healing stories, eight times describing Jesus' touch (in six stories), and seven times in the combined parallel accounts of the

654 Lk 6.18-19. The present infinitive ἅπτεσθαι occurs only once, in this Lukan general healing episode.

655 ἥψαντο ... ἅψωνται Mk 6.56; Mt 14.36.

656 See above 180-181, and below, 196-200.

657 The aorist middle subjunctive first person singular, ἅψωμαι, occurs twice, in the Markan and Matthaean parallel account of the the thought of the haemorrhaging woman (Mk 5.28 = Mt 9.21). In her mind, salvation (rescue/ healing?: σῴζω), is dependent on her being able to touch Jesus (ἅψωμαι). Thus the language chosen by the synoptists Mark and Matthew here mirrors the language in their parallel account of the general healing episode at Gennesaret (Mk 6.56; Mt 14.36).

658 Lk 22.51: ἁψαμενός, in a story peculiar to Luke (see above, 163).

healing of the haemorrhaging woman, describing her touch,[659] Jesus' question,[660] the disciples' question,[661] and the woman's confession.[662] Forms of both πίστις and σῴζω[663] appear in the three synoptic accounts of this story.

Elsewhere this form only describes Jesus' touch in healing stories. The first, the synoptic parallel account of the healing of the leper,[664] is interesting because all synoptists are happy to agree that Jesus "touched" the leper, a touch that would have made him ritually unclean.[665] And yet, in the same story, all three synoptists are careful to point out that Jesus commanded the man to show himself to the priest, and fulfil the requirements commanded by Moses.[666] Thus, in the one story, Jesus shows disregard for the law concerning himself, and yet concern that the leper should exactly fulfil legal requirements.[667]

The form ἥψατο also occurs in Luke's story of the son of the widow of Nain, describing Jesus' touching of the bier (7.14). This touch would have rendered Jesus ritually unclean,[668] as did his touching the leper. Thus again Jesus shows disregard for his own ritual purity.

Matthew chooses ἥψατο to describe Jesus' touch when healing Peter's mother-in-law,[669] and chooses the same form to describe Jesus' touch in both his accounts of the healings of the two blind

---

659 Mk 5.27 = Mt 9.20 = Lk 8.44. The woman's touch would have rendered Jesus unclean: see Leviticus 15.19-30.

660 Mk 5.30 = Lk 8.46. Jesus also uses another form of ἅπτομαι in Luke's account of Jesus' questioning: the aorist middle participle, ἁψαμενός, (nominative masculine singular) at 8.45. Here Luke has chosen it in preference to the repeated Markan form ἥψατο (5.31).

661 Mk 5.31

662 Lk 8.47

663 See above, 185-186.

664 Mk 1.41 = Mt 8.3 = Lk 5.13

665 See Leviticus, chapters 13 and 14.

666 Cf. Mk 1.40-45; Mt 8.1-4; Lk 5.12-16. The requirements are set out in Leviticus 14.1-32. The priest and the cleansed leper perform a highly magical ritual, which, when performed, signals the leper's purification, and his right to re-enter society.

667 This acts as a 'proof' that the miracle has taken place. 'Proof' of the miracle by means of tangible evidence is also a common feature of healings at Epidauros (see Apps 2:1 and 2:2).

668 See Leviticus 22.4-6: "...Whoever touches anything that is unclean through contact with the dead ... shall be unclean ...".

669 Mt 8.15. Mark (1.31) chooses κρατήσας to describe this touch, while Luke prefers to make Jesus "rebuke" (ἐπετίμησεν) the fever (4.39). See Sanders and Davies (1989) 279.

men.[670] In both these incidents the patients approach Jesus and attract his attention.[671] In the first incident Jesus touched their eyes (ἥψατο τῶν ὀφθαλμῶν), and issued the command "Let it be to you according to your faith (κατὰ τὴν πίστιν ὑμῶν γενηθήτω ὑμῖν)" (9.29), echoing the language used to the centurion (8.13), and the Canaanite woman (15.28). This is the only story where Matthew chooses to use ἐμβριμάομαι in a secrecy command, a command which was disregarded.[672] In the case of the second incident involving two blind men, Jesus, overcome by compassion (σπλαγχνισθείς 20.34), touched their eyes (ἥψατο τῶν ὀμμάτων). In both cases the cure was instantaneous.[673]

Mark chooses ἅπτομαι in two of his most controversial healings.[674] He chooses ἥψατο to describe Jesus' touch in the story of the healing of the deaf and dumb man, a healing story peculiar to his gospel.[675] "Touching" figures prominently in this healing. Jesus is requested (7.32) to lay his hand on him (ἐπιθῇ αὐτῷ τὴν χεῖρα) by the crowd, but his touch is described thus:

670 Mt 9.29; 20.34
671 Mt 9.27; 20.30
672 Mt 9.30-31. See above, n.642.
673 Mt 9.30; 20.30
674 Mk 7.31-37: the deaf and dumb man; Mk 8.22-26: the blind man. Hull (1974) 76, 82f., uses these two healings as examples of his theory that Jesus used magical techniques, and cites as evidence Jesus' touching of the afflicted parts, the use of saliva, and a foreign command (7.31-37); and the protracted nature of the cure with the use of saliva, and frequent touching (8.22-26). If we compare healing methods at Epidauros, the 'touch' of the god (*IG* IV^2 1, 122, 31: ἅπτομαι), his use of his fingers (*IG* IV^2 1, 121, 18), and the use of saliva by temple dogs (*IG* IV^2 1, 121, 20 and 122, 26) are well documented (see Section One, chapter two, and Apps 2:1 and 2:2). A more telling example is the witness of Jesus' contemporary, Pliny the Elder, who records that human saliva was thought to have healing properties, especially for the treatment of lichens, leprous sores, ophthalmia, carcinomata, pains in the neck, and even to expel insects from the ear canal. In some cases the saliva had to be from a fasting human being (*Natural History* 28.37-8). Thus, far from recording techniques that he considered to be magical, Mark could be reflecting current medical thought in the portrayal of Jesus' use of touch and saliva. Saliva was also used in a magical fashion at that time, as Pliny's account also shows, and yet the instances specifically recorded by Mark are those which were used in medical, not magical, practice. The physician Galen also comments on the healing properties of saliva (*On the natural faculties* 3.7.163).
675 Mk 7.31-37

he put his fingers in his ears (ἔβαλεν τοὺς δακτύλους αὐτοῦ εἰς τὰ ὦτα αὐτοῦ), and he spat and touched his tongue (καὶ πτύσας ἥψατο τῆς γλώσσης αὐτοῦ).[676]

In the Markan story of the protracted healing of the blind man, ἅπτομαι occurs only once, in the reported speech of the people who brought the blind man to Jesus, and begged that Jesus might touch him.[677] This healing is unusual for its description of Jesus' touch, and its protracted nature.[678] Jesus' does touch the man, and his touch is described thus: ἐπιλαβόμενος τῆς χειρὸς ... ἐπιθεὶς τὰς χεῖρας (8.23) ... πάλιν ἐπέθηκεν τὰς χεῖρας (8.25). The only other healing story in *Mark* where Jesus' actions are described ἐπιθεὶς τὰς χεῖρας is in his account of the general healing episode at Nazareth (6.5). Elsewhere this expression in *Mark* occurs only in healing requests.[679]

Thus ἅπτομαι is a primary synoptic healing word. It describes either Jesus' touch,[680] or the touch of those wishing to be healed,[681] or figures in the requests of those who ask for healing on behalf of others.[682] It occurs in at least nine,[683] and possibly eleven,[684] synoptic healing episodes. It appears in fairly exclusive company. For

---

676 Mk 7.33

677 Mk 8.22: the aorist middle subjunctive third person singular, ἅψηται.

678 Mk 8.22-26. The man at first saw men that looked like trees walking (8.24), but later saw everything clearly (8.25). Cf. *IG* IV^2 1, 121, 18 (App. 2:1, **18**) where Alketas of Halieis who was blind approached Asklepios at Epidauros and "the god came up to him and with his fingers opened his eyes, and ... he first saw the trees in the sanctuary (ὁ θεὸς ποτελθὼν τοῖς δα|κτύλοις διάγειν τὰ ὄμματα καὶ ἰδεῖν τὰ δένδρη πρᾶτον τὰ ἐν τῶι ἱαρῶι)".

679 Mk 5.23; 7.32

680 Nine times in seven stories: the parallel accounts of the healing of the leper, the Matthaean account of the healing of Peter's mother-in-law, the Markan deaf-mute, both Matthaean stories of the two blind men, the Lukan account of the bier at Nain, and the Lukan account of the temple slave.

681 All three synoptic accounts of the haemorrhaging woman, the Markan and Matthaean crowds at Gennesaret, and the Lukan crowd (a parallel story?).

682 On behalf of the Markan blind man (8.22).

683 The synoptic account of the leper (Mk 1.40-45; Mt 8.2-4; Lk 5.12-14), the Matthaean account of Peter's mother-in-law (8.14-15), the synoptic account of the haemorrhaging woman (Mk 5.24-34; Mt 9.20-22; Lk 8.42-48), the Matthaean blind men (9.27-31; 20.29-34), the Lukan widow's son (7.11-18), the Markan blind man (8.22-26), the Markan deaf and dumb man (7.31-37), the Lukan temple slave (22.49-51), and the crowd scenes in *Matthew* (14.35-36), *Mark* (6.53-56), and *Luke* (6.17-19).

684 If Matthew's blind men (9.27-31; 20.29-34) are taken as separate healing stories, and if the Lukan crowd scene (6.17-19) is separated from the Markan and Matthaean crowd scenes at Gennesaret (Mk 6.53-56; Mt 14.35-36).

example, both occurrences of ἐμβριμάομαι in synoptic healing stories occur in company with ἅπτομαι;[685] and σπλάγχνίζομαι also always occurs in "touching" healing stories,[686] three times with ἅπτομαι,[687] and once with κρατέω.[688]

9.3.3. κρατέω

κρατέω appears five times in synoptic healing stories, describing three specific healing episodes. Mark chooses κρατέω to describe Jesus' touch in three healing stories:[689] Peter's mother-in-law (1.31), Jairus' daughter (5.41), and the epileptic boy (9.27). Both Matthew and Luke retain this verb in only one story - that of Jairus' daughter.[690] It has already been noted that in the story of Peter's mother-in-law Matthew preferred to substitute ἅπτομαι for κράτεω, while Luke preferred to say that Jesus "rebuked the fever (ἐπετίμησεν τῷ πυρετῷ)".[691] In Mark's other story containing κράτεω, that of the epileptic boy,[692] Matthew does not allow Jesus to touch the boy,[693] nor Luke, although one wonders then how Jesus "gave him back to his father"![694] However all three synoptists agree that Jesus "rebuked" (ἐπετίμησεν) the demon, only Mark adding the verb ἐπιτάσσω in this story, a verb that he includes with ἐπιτιμάω in

685 The Markan leper, 1.43; and the Matthaean blind men, 9.30. But note the appearance of ἐμβριμάομαι in John's story of the raising of Lazarus (11.1-57), in the expressions ἐνεβριμήσατο τῷ πνεύματι (11.33), and ἐμβριμώμενος ἐν ἑαυτῷ (11.38). Here Jesus' distress is limited by the phrases τῷ πνεύματι and ἐν ἑαυτῷ, rather than directed elsewhere, as in the synoptic accounts.

686 Otherwise σπλάγχνίζομαι occurs in crowd scenes in *Matthew* (9.36; 14.14).

687 Mk 1.41; Mt 20.34; Lk 7.13

688 Mk 9.22

689 Mark always uses κρατέω in the same form: the aorist active participial nominative masculine singular κρατήσας (see App. 7:13).

690 Luke (8.54) chooses the same participial form as Mark (κρατήσας τῆς χειρός), while Matthew (9.25) chooses the aorist indicative (ἐκράτησεν τῆς χειρός). Perhaps it is appropriate that Matthew and Luke should only choose to retain κρατέω in a story describing Jesus' overpowering of death. κρατέω is a "stronger" verb than ἅπτομαι, and generally implies some form of resistance.

691 Lk 4.39

692 Mk 9.14-29. However Jesus does not touch the boy until after his 'cure' when the boy was "like a corpse". (A period of utter exhaustion is a typical aftermath of a grandmal epileptic seizure.)

693 Mt 17.14-20

694 Lk 9.42. Matthew's and Luke's reason for omitting Jesus' touch from this story must be that they view this episode as primarily an exorcism.

his first healing story, that of the man in the synagogue who had an unclean spirit.[695] Luke uses ἐπιτιμάω and ἐπιτάσσω in his parallel account of the man in the synagogue who had an unclean spirit,[696] and also uses ἐπιτιμάω in a general demonic healing episode to command silence.[697] It has already been noted that Howard Clark Kee,[698] discussing the terminology of Mark's exorcism stories, has pointed out that ἐπιτιμάω describes,

> the word of command that brought ... hostile powers under control....[699]

That Mark reserves it to describe Jesus' actions in two healing stories only,[700] both dealing with a "demon", is significant. Both Matthew and Luke are sparing in their use of the term, Matthew using it to describe Jesus' actions in his story of the epileptic boy (17.18), and in a secrecy command following a general healing episode (12.16),[701] while Luke uses it in his account of the healing of Peter's mother-in-law (4.39), as well as the two demonic episodes, parallel to the Markan episodes already noted (4.34, 9.42), and in a secrecy request, following a demonic general healing episode (4.41). Thus there is a definite synoptic pattern in the use of this word.

Luke also chooses κρατέω in a different context in a healing story in *Acts* (3.11), to describe the behaviour of the lame man after his healing at the temple gate: he was clinging (κρατοῦντος δὲ αὐτοῦ) to Peter and John, after jumping about and praising God.[702] The verb Luke chooses to describe Peter's touch in this healing story is πιάζω (3.7).

695 Mk 1.23-38
696 Lk 4.31-38
697 Lk 4.41
698 Kee (1968) 232-246. (See above, 145-146.)
699 ibid. 246.
700 Although note that Mark uses this word to describe the crowds' rebuking of blind Bartimaeus' importunity (10.48); and to describe Jesus' secrecy command to the disciples (8.30).
701 Matthew also notes that the crowd "rebuked" (ἐπετίμησεν) the two blind men for their importunity (20.31), as do Luke (ἐπετίμων: 18.39), and Mark (ἐπετίμων: 10.48) in their parallel episodes.
702 To cling to both men at once was a rather difficult feat! Was he exhausted, or grateful? Was the healing of long duration?

9.3.4. ἐπιτίθημι (τὰς χεῖρας)

The expression ἐπιτίθημι (τὰς χεῖρας) to describe Jesus' actions is surprisingly infrequent in the synoptic healing stories.[703] It occurs in requests, in the parallel accounts of the healing of Jairus' daughter,[704] and the Markan story of the deaf and dumb man;[705] and as a description of Jesus' behaviour in four stories: (i) the Markan story of the protracted healing of the blind man;[706] (ii) the Markan story of the general healing episode at Nazareth;[707] (iii) a Lukan general healing episode;[708] and in the Lukan story of the bent woman.[709] It also occurs in two healing stories in *Acts*:[710] (i) in instructions to Ananias and a description of his subsequent action with Paul;[711] and (ii), as a description of Paul's behaviour with Publius' father, on the island of Malta.[712] Thus, in all, this expression only appears in eight healing stories in the gospels and *Acts*. It is not recommended in the instructional passage in *James*.[713]

Thus of the touching verbs, ἅπτομαι is the most popular, especially to describe Jesus' healing touch. This reflects the use of this verb to describe the healing touch of Asklepios. Clearly, the image of a "god" who would stretch out a healing hand to help humans in distress seems to have had universal appeal in the ancient world, a universal appeal which has continued to the present day.

703 The incidence of this word group does not support the conclusion of Theissen (1983) 62: that the healing touch "usually takes place as the laying on of hands ... probably also where the text has only ἅπτεσθαι". He has probably based this assumption on the linking of these two 'touching' word groups in Mark's story of the protracted healing of the blind man (8.22-26). It is dangerous to generalise on the basis of this story. That there has been strong temptation to assume that this was the way the healing touch was performed is illustrated by the fact that the laying-on-of-hands has become standard practice in healing services in the contemporary Western Christian church.

704 Mk 5.23; Mt 9.18

705 Mk 7.32

706 Mk 8.23; 8.25

707 Mk 6.5

708 Lk 4.40

709 Lk 13.13

710 In *Acts* it also occurs as a means of commissioning (6.6, 13.3); and in stories relating the transmission of the Holy Spirit (8.19, 19.6).

711 Acts 9.12, 17

712 Acts 28.8

713 James 5.13-18

9.4. ὑγιαίνω ὑγιής

The last family of words to be considered in this study is the ὑγιαίνω ὑγιής family of words, words that were extremely popular in the Greek world to describe the result of the intervention of Asklepios.[714]

Of the twenty-two occurrences of this family of words in the New Testament, nineteen are adjectival.[715] Forms occur six times in the synoptic gospels,[716] six times in *John*,[717] once in *Acts*,[718] and nine times in the epistles of Timothy,[719] Titus,[720] and John.[721] Since the majority of New Testament authors choose to use this family of words in an adjectival way (as in the inscriptions at Epidauros) we shall consider their adjectival role first.

9.4.1. ὑγιής -ές

The two termination adjective ὑγιής -ές occurs eleven times in the New Testament, once in *Mark*, twice in *Matthew*, six times in *John*, once in *Acts*, and once in *Titus*.[722]

ὑγιής occurs out of the mouth of Jesus, in Mark's account of the healing of the haemorrhaging woman.[723] It is part of a command from Jesus, following a statement from him that the woman's faith had saved her: Θυγάτηρ, ἡ πίστις σου σέσωκέν σε· ὕπαγε εἰς εἰρήνην καὶ ἴσθι ὑγιὴς ἀπὸ τῆς μάστιγός σου. The word ὑγιής implies more than physical health. It builds on the concept of εἰρήνη, implying emotional, mental, and spiritual health as well.[724] Thus Jesus' command to her: "Go (and keep going) in peace, and be (always) healthy (whole) from your suffering" is a life-journey command, emphasised by Mark's use of present imperatives. The

714 See *IG* IV^2 1, 121 and 122 (Apps 2:1 and 2:2) and App. 3:2.
715 See App. 9:2.
716 Mt 12.13, 15.31; Mk 5.34; Lk 5.31, 7.10, 15.27
717 Jn 5.6, 9, 11, 14, 15, in the one healing story. ὑγιής also occurs at Jn 5.4, in the same healing story, but, according to Metzger (1975) 209, verse 4 is a gloss, category {A}. Therefore it will be disregarded in this study.
718 Acts 4.10
719 1 Timothy 1.10, 6.3; 2 Timothy 1.13, 4.3
720 Titus 1.9, 1.13, 2.1, 2.8
721 3 John 2
722 ὑγιής: Mt 12.13; Mk 5.34; Jn 5.6, 5.9, 5.14; Acts 4.10; ὑγιεῖς: Mt 15.31; ὑγιῆ: Jn 5.11, 5.15, 7.23; Titus 2.8
723 Mk 5.34: in its nominative singular feminine form (see App. 9:2).
724 See chapter six, and App. 6:1.

concept of εἰρήνη and its relationship with the Hebrew shalom has been discussed above.[725] The call to spiritual health (discipleship? an awareness of the presence of God?) is explicit in Jesus' command.

Matthew also uses this form in his account of the sabbath healing of the man with the withered hand, after Jesus had spoken to him.[726] Matthew uses ἀποκαθίστημι in the passive voice as a copulative verb to describe what happened: "it was restored whole, like the other (καὶ ἀπεκατεστάθη ὑγιὴς ὡς ἡ ἄλλη)". The use of the passive voice signifies the intervention of God here, as in other healing episodes, while ὑγιής carries the physical meaning of "sound" or "healthy". Matthew also uses ὑγιής as an attributive adjective, in a general healing episode, qualifying κυλλούς (the maimed/crippled).[727] Matthew is consistent in his use of this word: he chooses to use it only in a physical sense, to describe sound limbs, which had formerly been maimed (12.13, 15.31). In this use Matthew mirrors the meaning and use of ὑγιής in Greek inscriptions at Epidauros.[728]

The author of *John* is fond of the adjective ὑγιής and uses it six times in one healing story: that of the man beside the Bethzatha pool in Jerusalem.[729] All six forms are predicative adjectives, four occurring in direct speech, one in reported speech, and the other as a description. Three occurrences of direct speech come out of the mouth of Jesus, twice when talking to the sick man, and once when talking to the Jews. He questions the sick man: "Do you want to be healthy/whole? (θέλεις ὑγιὴς γενέσθαι;)" (5.6), and then exclaims (5.14): "Behold! You are whole! (ἴδε ὑγιὴς γέγονας)". Finally he asks the Jews (7.23): "Are you angry with me because I made a man wholly healthy on the sabbath? (ἐμοὶ χολᾶτε ὅτι ὅλον ἄνθρωπον ὑγιῆ ἐποίσα ἐν σαββάτῳ;)" There is no mention of healing in relation to the body only.[730] Rather, the language stresses that the whole man is ὑγιής. This stress is unusual. Jesus uses it to point out the right judgment (τὴν δικαίαν κρίσιν) of his action to his accusers.[731]

---

725 See above, 166-167.

726 Mt 12.13: as a predicative adjective (see App. 9:2).

727 Mt 15.31

728 See Section One: chapter two.

729 Jn 5.6-23

730 Cf. the RSV translation: "... are you angry with me because on the sabbath I made a man's whole body well?" (7.23)

731 Jn 7.24

John also puts ὑγιής into the mouth of the man who had been healed, as he describes to the Jews what had happened to him, and why he was carrying his pallett on the sabbath. He described Jesus as "the man who made me whole (ὁ ποιήσας με ὑγιῆ)"(5.11). The second (5.15) occurs in his reported speech, when he identifies Jesus to the Jews as the man who made him healthy/whole (ὅτι Ἰησοῦς ἐστιν ὁ ποιήσας αὐτόν ὑγιῆ).

ὑγιής also appears in the narrative as a description of the man after Jesus had commanded him to get up and pick up his pallet (καὶ εὐθέως ἐγένετο ὑγιὴς ὁ ἄνθρωπος).

That Jesus sought out this particular healing, and this particular confrontation, seems obvious. It is significant that Jesus chose the sabbath to perform this healing - his justification that he was working just as his father was still working (ὁ πατήρ μου ἕως ἄρτι ἐργάζεται, κἀγὼ ἐργάζομαι (5.17)). John emphasises the symbolic significance of this healing by reserving his use of ὑγιής for this healing alone. Furthermore, of its six occurrences, John puts three into the mouth of Jesus. ὑγιής as John uses it, must, in common with its use in *Mark*, and the Septuagint, describe holistic health, i.e. total mental, emotional, physical and spiritual well-being.

Luke also uses the nominative form of ὑγιής, at Acts 4.10, in Peter's reply to the rulers, elders, scribes, and those of high-priestly family, concerning the healing of the man lame from birth (Acts 3.1-26, 4.1-31). In this speech (4.8-12) Peter describes the man in terms of σῴζω, and ὑγιής. Earlier (3.16), Peter had described him as enjoying perfect health (τὴν ὁλοκληρίαν). All these words convey holistic health.

The final use of ὑγιής in the New Testament occurs in the letter of Titus in the expression: "sound argument that cannot be censured (λόγον ὑγιῆ ἀκατάγνωστον)".[732] It appears in the context of a catalogue of the qualities of good teaching. Thus, to the writer, ὑγιής implies soundness, i.e. truth that springs out of faith.

9.4.2. The participial use of the verb ὑγιαίνω

As the participial use of the verb ὑγιαίνω is the most popular use of this verb in the New Testament, it is to that use we now turn. ὑγιαίνω in participial form occurs nine times, three times in Luke's

732 Titus 2.8: the accusative masculine singular form ὑγιῆ, as an attributive adjective (see App. 9:2).

gospel, four times in the letters of *Timothy*, and twice in *Titus*, always occurring in the active voice of the present tense.

Luke first uses the present participle of ὑγιαίνω as a noun with the article οἱ in a saying which Luke attributes to Jesus:

> Those who are whole/healthy have no need of a physician, but those who are suffering. I have not come to call the righteous, but sinners (those who have missed the mark) to a different way of thinking (repentance) (οὐ χρείαν ἔχουσιν οἱ ὑγιαίνοντες ἰατροῦ ἀλλὰ οἱ κακῶς ἔχοντες· οὐκ ἐλήλυθα καλέσαι δικαίους ἀλλὰ ἁμαρτωλοὺς εἰς μετάνοιαν).[733]

This saying occurs in Jesus' reply to a question from the scribes and the Pharisees concerning his eating companions. All three synoptic gospels report this controversy,[734] and all three record Jesus' reply.[735] The wording of Jesus' reply is identical in *Mark* and *Matthew*, but Luke changes the wording of his reply, substituting ὑγιαίνοντες for Mark's and Matthew's ἰσχύοντες, and adding εἰς μετάνοιαν to Mark's and Matthew's version of Jesus' final saying. Elsewhere the synoptists show reluctance to change the actual wording of Jesus' sayings,[736] while being quite happy to change the context,[737] and even the characters.[738] Thus Luke's substitution and addition is important. The verb ὑγιαίνω has a far wider meaning than the verb ἰσχύω, ὑγιαίνω implying holistic health and, sometimes, the notion of safety,[739] while ἰσχύω generally denotes physical strength. As well, the contrast of οἱ ὑγιαίνοντες with δικαίους, and οἱ κακῶς ἔχοντες with ἁμαρτωλούς underlines the spiritual emphasis of this saying. Thus Jesus implies that his task is that of a spiritual physician (ἰατροῦ), bringing a change in thinking (μετάνοιαν) that will offer wholeness (ὑγιαίνοντες) to those who continually miss the mark (ἁμαρτωλούς). This saying indicates the Lukan idea of the nature of Jesus' mission.

---

733 Lk 5.31

734 See App. 7:7.

735 Mt 9.12, Mk 2.17. (Cf. Mt 9.9-13, Mk 2.13-17, Lk 5.27-32, and see above, 169-170.)

736 For example the synoptic parallel account of the healing of the leper (Mk 1.40-45; Mt 8.1-3; Lk 5.12-13).

737 ibid. and the incident at Nazareth (Mk 6.1-6; Mt 13.53-58; Lk 4.16-30).

738 For example the people reported to have been with Jesus, in the synoptic parallel account of the healing of Jairus' daughter (Mk 5.37; Mt 9.25; Lk 8.51).

739 See, for example, the Lukan use of ὑγιαίνοντα in his parable of the lost son (Lk 15.27).

Luke also uses a participle of ὑγιαίνω as the final description of the state of the centurion's slave.[740] The earlier healing words are spoken by the centurion. He uses διασῴζω, when asking the Jewish elders to request Jesus' help, and later ἰάομαι, in a message sent through his friends. Jesus does not take any action, other than to marvel at the man's faith, faith that he had not found in Israel. However, those sent out to talk to Jesus find the slave ὑγιαίνοντα when they return to the house.[741] The slave had been ill, and about to die (κακῶς ἔχων ἤμελλεν τελευτᾶν (7.2)).

Luke's final use of this form is found in the parable of the lost son.[742] There, a slave tells of the father's joy because he has received his son ὑγιαίνοντα, i.e. safe and sound. Later, the father attempts to explain his joy to his other son, explaining that his brother who was dead (νεκρός) and lost (ἀπολωλώς), has become alive (ἔζησεν), and been found (εὑρέθη). ζάω and νεκρός are similarly contrasted in the Lukan story of Paul's treatment of Eutychus in *Acts*.[743]

Elsewhere in the New Testament, ὑγιαίνω in participial form occurs adjectivally, four times qualifying διδασκαλία,[744] twice

---

740 Lk 7.10: the accusative singular masculine present active participle ὑγιαίνοντα. See App. 9:2.

741 Cf. *IG* IV^2 1, 122, 21 (App. 2:2, **21**).

742 Lk 15.27

743 Acts 20.7-12

744 1 Timothy 1.10; 2 Timothy 4.3; Titus 1.9; Titus 2.1: (i) The dative singular feminine present active participle of ὑγιαίνω occurs three times in the New Testament, each time as an adjectival participle qualifying διδασκαλία. At 1 Timothy 1.10, it appears in an explanatory exposition on the use of the law, i.e. that the law is laid down for anything contrary to sound doctrine (τῇ ὑγιαινούσῃ διδασκαλίᾳ), according to the glorious gospel of the blessed God (κατὰ τὸ εὐαγγέλιον τῆς δόξης τοῦ μακαρίου θεοῦ). At Titus 1.9, the writer is expounding the qualities necessary in a bishop (ἐπίσκοπον): "He must hold firm to the believing word (πιστοῦ λόγου), as taught, so that he may be able to speak words of encouragement in sound teaching (ἵνα δυνατὸς ᾖ καὶ παρακαλεῖν ἐν τῇ διδασκαλίᾳ τῇ ὑγιαινούσῃ), and refute those who contradict it." And, again, at Titus 2.1, the writer commands Titus to "utter what befits sound teaching" (Σὺ δὲ λάλει ἃ πρέπει τῇ ὑγιαινούσῃ διδασκαλίᾳ).
(ii) The genitive feminine singular present active participle occurs only once, as an adjectival participle qualifying διδασκαλίας, at 2 Timothy 4.3. In this, the final use of ὑγιαίνω in *1* and *2 Timothy*, the writer warns that the time is coming when people will not endure sound teaching (τῆς ὑγιαινούσης διδασκαλίας), but will turn away from listening to the truth (τῆς ἀληθείας τὴν ἀκοὴν), and wander into myths (τοὺς μύθους). Thus ὑγιαίνω, used as an adjectival participle in *1* and *2 Timothy*, implies pious teaching, teaching

λόγος,[745] always referring to sound doctrine. Sound doctrine was supposed to produce sound faith, and the present tense of ὑγιαίνω is chosen by the author of Titus to express this idea.[746]

Finally, the present active infinitive ὑγιαίνειν occurs only once, in the opening salutation of the third letter of John to Gaius:

> Beloved, I pray concerning all things that you are prospering and healthy, just as your soul prospers.[747]

In this use of ὑγιαίνω the author reflects Greek usage of this verb in personal letters.[748]

Thus of the twenty-two occurrences of the ὑγιαίνω ὑγιής family of words in the New Testament, nineteen are adjectival. Matthew uses ὑγιής in a physical sense, to describe sound limbs, which had formerly been maimed,[749] while Mark uses it only once, in a holistic sense, in Jesus' command to the haemorrhaging woman.[750] Luke uses ὑγιαίνω three times in his gospel, in participial form, to mean holistic health;[751] and ὑγιής once in *Acts* in a holistic sense.[752] John uses ὑγιής six times, in a holistic sense, in one healing story.[753] The present infinitive is also used in a holistic sense

---

that is in accordance with the writer's interpretation of Jesus' gospel. This involves listening in faith (ἤκουσας ἐν πίστει (2 Tim. 1.13)).

745 (i) The dative plural masculine present active participle occurs only once, at 1 Timothy 6.3, as an adjectival participle qualifying λόγοις, words attributed to Jesus, and linked to teaching which is pious (τῇ κατ' εὐσέβειαν διδασκαλίᾳ). Thus ὑγιαίνω as an adjectival participle in *1 Timothy* implies "pious" teaching, i.e. teaching which is thought to be in accordance with the teaching of Jesus.
(ii) The genitive plural masculine present active participle occurs only once, at 2 Timothy 1.13, as an adjectival participle qualifying λόγων in a command from Paul to Timothy to "keep the example of sound words which you have heard from me in faith (ὧν παρ' ἐμοῦ ἤκουσας ἐν πίστει) and in the love (ἀγάπῃ) which is in Christ Jesus".

746 The present subjunctive third person plural occurs once, in a final clause expressing purpose, at Titus 1.13. The writer orders Titus to "rebuke them sharply, that they may be sound in the faith" (δι' ἣν αἰτίαν ἔλεγχε αὐτοὺς ἀποτόμως, ἵνα ὑγιαίνωσιν ἐν τῇ πίστει). Again ὑγιαίνω and πίστις are linked, as at Titus 1.9, and 2 Timothy 1.13.

747 3 John 2

748 For example, Epicurus. See App. 3:5, 7 and 8.

749 Mt 12.13; 15.31; reflecting Greek usage in Asklepiadic literature.

750 Mk 5.34

751 Lk 5.31; 7.10; 15.27

752 Acts 4.10

753 Jn 5.6-23

by the author of *3 John*.[754] Elsewhere forms of ὑγιαίνω always refer to sound teaching, sound doctrine, and sound faith, reflecting the doctrinal debate of the infant church.[755]

What then is the significance of a study of the language of healing for understanding the nature of the gospel portrayal of Jesus' commands and commissions?

10. Commands and commissions

All four gospel authors portray Jesus as commanding his disciples to undertake certain tasks.[756] The three synoptists report specific instructions as to how to go about their tasks,[757] and both Mark and Luke comment on the success of their venture.[758]

Matthew, Mark and Luke choose a string of present infinitives to record Jesus' commissioning of the disciples: ἐκβάλλειν... θεραπεύειν;[759] κηρύσσειν ... ἐκβάλλειν;[760] θεραπεύειν ... κηρύσσειν ... ἰᾶσθαι [τοὺς ἀσθενεῖς]).[761] The use of present infinitives by all three synoptists is significant. Jesus commands habitual action by the disciples, action that includes preaching, casting out unclean

---

754 3 John 2

755 1 Timothy 1.10; 6.3; 2 Timothy 1.13; 4.3; Titus 1.9; 1.13; 2.8. This is not the place to discuss the doctrinal debate of the infant church, or the "heresies" that were part of its growth. It is noticeable, however, that healing language was commandeered by the orthodox to its detriment, so that words like ὑγιαίνω and its derivatives, instead of referring to holistic health and thus promising life and hope, instead refer to doctrine and teaching, and the human element is lost.

756 Mk 3.14-15; Mt 10.1, 5-8; Lk 9.1-2, 10.1. Cf. [Mk 16.14-18]; Mt 28.16-20; Lk 24.36-49; and Jn 20.19-23. Cf. also Mk 12.28-34; Mt 22.34-36; Lk 10.27 (10.25-37); and Jn 13.34-35

757 Mk 6.8-11; Mt 10.8-14; Lk 9.3-5, 10.4-12. Cf. *GT* #14

758 Mk 6.12-13; Lk 9.6, 10.17

759 Mt 10.1

760 Mk 3.14-15

761 Lk 9.1-2: note that the presence of τοὺς ἀσθενεῖς is disputed. However, it is integral to the Lukan use of ἰάομαι in conjunction with θεραπεύω; and ἰάομαι in *Luke*, in the middle voice, always has a direct object. ℵ A D L Ξ Ψ f^1 *et al.* all support the inclusion of τοὺς ἀσθενεῖς. While there is an argument for supporting the shorter text (based on B and $syr^{c,s}$) Luke's use of ἰάομαι, and his obvious intention to link it in meaning with θεραπεύω (which is usually accompanied by τοὺς ἀσθενεῖς [see above, 139-140, and n.309]), all argue for the inclusion of τοὺς ἀσθενεῖς. See Metzger (1975) 146-147.

spirits, nurturing and loving service, and healing. Mark also includes the idea of companionship in his account.[762]

Luke is the only synoptist to include ἰάομαι in the disciples' mission. His use of ἰᾶσθαι occurs in conjunction with preaching (κηρύσσειν), after the disciples have been given authority and power (δύναμιν καὶ ἐξουσίαν) over all demons, and to treat diseases (νόσους θεραπεύειν). However, although Luke reports that Jesus sent the disciples out to ἰᾶσθαι, they are not reported as doing so in his gospel.[763] Thus his introduction of the verb here does not have a bearing on his gospel record of the disciples' ministry, but is important for the story of Peter's and Paul's gentile mission in *Acts*.[764] Luke is introducing a term that he wishes to use later in a gentile context, and he needs the reader to understand that the command for this later activity came from Jesus himself. Audience once again becomes a critical factor in the compilation of the gospel story. The choice of the present tense by all three synoptists signifies an ongoing commission.

All three synoptists report that Jesus gave his disciples extensive instructions concerning their commission.[765] These commands included instructions of what to do, where to go, what to take with them, where to stay, and how to behave.

Mark simply reports again that Jesus gave the twelve authority over unclean spirits, and that he sent them out two by two;[766] Matthew and Luke extend these instructions by detailing the subject-matter of preaching (the imminence of the kingdom of heaven/God),[767] and Matthew has Jesus command the disciples to heal the sick,[768] raise the dead,[769] cleanse lepers,[770] and cast out demons.[771] Luke adds to the number of those to take part in the mission in his second account,[772] and records that Jesus told them to heal the sick in the towns that welcomed them, and to preach that the kingdom of God was near.[773]

---

762 Mk 3.14: ἵνα ὦσιν μετ' αὐτοῦ

763 Luke chooses θεραπεύω to describe the disciples' 'healing' activities (9.6).

764 See below, n.803, and App. 8:4.

765 Mk 6.6-11; Mt 10.5-15; Lk 9.3-5; Lk 10. 4-12

766 Mk 6.7

767 Mt 10.7: ἡ βασιλεία τῶν οὐρανῶν; Lk 10.9: ἡ βασιλεία τοῦ θεοῦ

768 Mt 10.8: ἀσθενοῦντας θεραπεύετε

769 Mt 10.8: νεκροὺς ἐγείρετε

770 Mt 10.8: λεπροὺς καθαρίζετε

771 Mt 10.8: δαιμόνια ἐκβάλλετε

772 Lk 10.1: seventy (-two)

773 Lk 10.8-9

The verb θεραπεύω occurs in the present imperative (2nd plural) in both *Matthew* and *Luke*, in these instructions.[774] In both instances the disciples are instructed to heal/treat the weak.[775] ἰάομαι is not included in either set of instructions, for different reasons. Matthew only uses ἰάομαι on specific occasions (out of the mouth of a gentile, to report gentile healings, or to quote the Septuagint),[776] whereas Luke is fond of the word, but careful where he uses it. In this instance its omission is significant. The Jewish Jesus is speaking to his Jewish disciples about their Jewish mission. While it is Matthew, not Luke, who records Jesus' instruction in his parallel passage that the disciples were not to go to the gentiles, nor any towns in Samaria, but only to the lost sheep of the house of Israel,[777] Luke's omission of ἰάομαι makes it clear that this is a Jewish mission, even though his sending of those appointed ahead to every town and place where he was about to come leaves the question of destination ambiguous.[778]

It is interesting to compare the detailed instructions recorded in each account. Luke sends the twelve out, leaving their destination unspecified,[779] Mark sends the twelve two-by-two, also to unspecified destinations,[780] Matthew sends the twelve only to the lost sheep of Israel;[781] while Luke, in his second account, sends the seventy-two ahead of Jesus.[782] All three synoptists state that Jesus gave authority to the twelve, but Luke does not mention this in his account of the appointment of the seventy-two.[783]

Jesus is also reported as telling the disciples what to wear and what to take with them. In *Mark* they are to take nothing except the tunic they are wearing, sandals, and a staff.[784] Luke doesn't mention sandals, but forbids a staff in his instructions to the twelve,[785] and forbids sandals in his account of the instructions to the seventy-two,[786] while Matthew forbids both sandals and a

---

774 Mt.10.8; Lk 10.9

775 Mt 10.8: ἀσθενοῦντας θεραπεύετε; Lk 10.9: καὶ θεραπεύετε τοὺς ἐν αὐτῇ ἀσθενεῖς.

776 See above, chapter eight, and Apps 8:3 and 8:4.

777 Mt 10.5

778 Lk 10.1

779 Lk 9.2

780 Mk 6.7

781 Mt 10.5

782 Lk 10.1

783 Mk 6.7; Mt 10.1; and Lk 9.1: ἐξουσία. Cf. Lk 10.1

784 Mk 6.8-9

785 Lk 9.3

786 Lk 10.4

staff![787] All synoptists agree that the disciples were instructed not to take any bread, spare clothing, a bag or any money.[788] Both Matthew and Luke give the same reason: that the labourer deserves his food/wages.[789]

The mission presupposes an activity (which might take time, and certainly required effort) and a result. The activity included preaching, the expulsion of demons, and healing; the result, a change in the people encountered. However, of the proposed activities, preaching was to come first. For if any place did not welcome them,[790] and listen to them,[791] then the disciples were not to stay, but to shake the dust of that place off their feet when they left it, as a testimony against it.[792] Thus healing (and any other labouring activity) is dependent on the people being prepared to offer hospitality to the disciples, and on their being open to and hearing the message.

Mark has little to say about the type of hospitality to be offered, nor has Luke in his parallel account.[793] However, Matthew's instructions (and the instructions in Luke's second account) are more elaborate.[794] All three synoptists agree that when the disciples enter a place they should stay in the one place until they depart.[795] Matthew adds that, after entering any place they should first find out who is worthy in that place, and stay with that worthy person until they depart.[796] Luke is more prosaic: he instructs those sent out to remain in the same house, eating and drinking whatever is provided![797] Both Matthew and Luke record sayings about the greetings to be offered and received, and comment on the 'peace' (εἰρήνη) to be bestowed (or withheld, as the case may be) upon the places they enter.[798] Both Matthew and Luke add the

787 Mt 10.10
788 Mk 6.8-9; Mt 10.9-10; Lk 9.3; cf. Lk 10.4
789 Mt 10.10: ἄξιος γὰρ ὁ ἐργάτης τῆς τροφῆς αὐτοῦ; cf. Lk 10.7: ἄξιος γὰρ ὁ ἐργάτης τοῦ μισθοῦ αὐτοῦ. This implies that their mission activities will be recognised as 'work' by their hosts.
790 Mk 6.11; Mt 10.14; Lk 9.5
791 Mk 6.11; Mt 10.14
792 Mk 6.11; Mt 10.14; Lk 9.5; Lk 10.11
793 Mk 6.7-13; Lk 9.1-6
794 Mt 10.5-15; Lk 10.1-12. Thus it becomes obvious that of Luke's two accounts, the first (9.1-6) is parallel to Mk 6.7-13; while the second (10.1-12) is parallel to Mt 10.5-15.
795 Mk 6.10; Mt 10.11; Lk 9.4; Lk 10.7
796 Mt 10.11
797 Lk 10.7
798 Lk 10. 4-6; Mt 10.12-13

warning about Sodom (and Gomorrah) upon those who do not welcome the disciples.[799]

Only Mark and Luke record the results of the disciples' venture. Luke chooses two present participles to describe the response of the twelve: εὐαγγελιζόμενοι καὶ θεραπεύοντες πανταχοῦ;[800] and the present tense to describe the the exclamation of the seventy-two: καὶ τὰ δαιμόνια ὑποτάσσεται ἡμῖν ἐν τῷ ὀνόματί σου![801] Mark chooses the imperfect tense to describe the disciples' healing activity:

> And after going out they preached that people should repent, and they began casting out many demons, and used to anoint with oil many who were weak and began healing [them] (καὶ ἐξελθόντες ἐκήρυξαν ἵνα μετανοῶσιν, καὶ δαιμόνια πολλὰ ἐξέβαλλον, καὶ ἤλειφον ἐλαίῳ πολλοὺς ἀρρώστους καὶ ἐθεράπευον.)[802]

Matthew is silent on this point. It is noteworthy that Luke chooses to describe the disciples' healing activities in terms of θεραπεύω, when they were commissioned to both θεραπεύειν and ἰᾶσθαι. His omission of ἰάομαι when describing the disciples' response is significant. It is an accurate use of the word, for the disciples were ministering only to Jewish people at this stage.[803] Luke, in other places, when describing the activity of Jesus,[804] is careful to use θεραπεύω and ἰάομαι contiguously, so that both the Jewish and the gentile members of his audience would understand his portrait of the healing Jesus.

Thus there is substantial agreement in the synoptic account of Jesus' commission and instructions to the disciples: they were to preach (κηρύσσω), heal (θεραπεύω) and exorcise (ἐκβάλλω), probably only among the Jews. That these activities are time-consuming is also explicit. Luke comments that the harvest is plentiful, but the labourers few,[805] Matthew that the labourer deserves his food,[806] while Luke notes that a labourer deserves his wages.[807] There is

---

799 Mt 10.15 (Matthew adds Gomorrah); Lk 10.12

800 Lk 9.6

801 Lk 10.17

802 Mk 6.12-13. See above, 127-130.

803 The only occasions Luke chooses ἰάομαι to report healing activity by 'disciples' of Jesus is in *Acts*, where he reports the activity of both Peter (Acts 9.34) and Paul (Acts 28.8) in a gentile context. However, only Paul shares the same verbal form with Jesus. See App. 8:4.

804 Luke 6.17-19; 8.43-48; 9.11; 14.1-6

805 Lk 10.2

806 Mt 10.10

807 Lk 10.7

the notion of 'work' in these instructions, a notion that we have already noticed, and which the author of John makes explicit.[808]

What commands does John record Jesus as having given? The author of John sums up Jesus' commands in a 'new' commandment:

> I give to you a new commandment, that you love one another; even as I have loved you, that you also love one another. By this everyone will know that you are my disciples, if you have love for one another. (ἐντολὴν καινὴν δίδωμι ὑμῖν, ἵνα ἀγαπᾶτε ἀλλήλους· καθὼς ἠγάπησα ὑμᾶς ἵνα καὶ ὑμεῖς ἀγαπᾶτε ἀλλήλους. ἐν τούτῳ γνώσονται πάντες ὅτι ἐμοὶ μαθηταί ἐστε, ἐὰν ἀγάπην ἔχητε ἐν ἀλλήλοις).[809]

This command follows the example of loving service that Jesus gave the disciples when he washed their feet.[810] Here the notion of selfless service is implicit in ἀγαπάω, and, as in the synoptic gospels, John chooses the present imperative (an ongoing commission) to record this command.

The synoptists also present their version of this command. Both Mark and Matthew choose to present it as their final issue between Jesus and the authorities, while Luke makes it a central issue in his gospel, and illustrates it with the parable of the Good Samaritan.[811] In Mark's and Matthew's account of this incident Jesus is asked what he considers to be the most important commandment,[812] while in Luke's account Jesus is asked what should be done to inherit eternal life.[813] In each gospel the question is presented as an issue, in *Mark* the antagonist being a scribe, in *Matthew* a lawyer who was also a Pharisee, and in *Luke* a lawyer.[814] The command is presented as a command to love God with all one's heart, mind, soul and strength, and one's neighbour as oneself.[815] It is Luke who includes the parable of the Good Samaritan as an example of love in action, and an example of the type of recipient (neighbour). The omission of θεραπεύω from this story makes it

---

808 Jn 5.17; 9.4: ἐργάζομαι (see above, 150-152).

809 Jn 13.34-5. Cf. Mt 22.34-46; 25.35-6; Mk 12.28-34; Lk 10.25-37

810 Jn 13.1-20

811 Mk 12.28-34; Mt 22.34-40; Lk 10.25-37. See App. 7:7 for an analysis of the synoptic portrayal of issues and antagonists: issue 13 in *Mark* and *Matthew*; issue 7 in *Luke*.

812 Mk 12.28: the 'first' (ἐντολὴ πρώτη); Mt 22.36: the 'great' (ἐντολὴ μεγάλη).

813 Lk 10.25: τί ποιήσας ζωὴν αἰώνιον κληρονομήσω;

814 Mk 12.28; Mt 22.35: [νομικός]; Lk 10.25. It probably goes without saying that a lawyer is a Pharisee!

815 Mk 12.30-31; Mt 22.37-9; Lk 10.27

obvious that the verb does not only describe medical treatment. Instead of θεραπεύω Luke chooses ἐπιμελέομαι to describe the care and attention the Samaritan gave to the wounded man.[816] The Samaritan provided medical care by pouring onto his wounds a mixture of oil and wine, a treatment advocated by Hippokrates,[817] and then made arrangements for his convalescent costs and physical care. The Samaritan provided excellent physical care for the man, but did not provide long-term emotional or spiritual care. This is not surprising. Luke chose an unlikely candidate for the role of protagonist in this story to emphasise that the concept of 'neighbour' should not be limited by prejudice of any sort. However, it would have been unthinkable that this man could also provide spiritual support in a Jewish context, hence the absence of spiritual terms in the story. Luke concludes the story with Jesus' command to the lawyer to: "Go and do likewise (πορεύου καὶ σὺ ποίει ὁμοίως)!"[818] The present imperatives command habitual action.[819]

Mark does not illustrate this command although he does make Jesus tell the scribe that he is not far from the kingdom of God (οὐ μακρὰν εἶ ἀπὸ τῆς βασιλείας τοῦ θεοῦ),[820] echoing Luke's instruction to the seventy-two to heal (θεραπεύετε) the sick where they were given hospitality, and to tell their hosts that the kingdom of God had come near to them.[821] Thus there is a link between θεραπεύων and ἀγαπῶν behaviour, in that both involve the propinquity of the kingdom.

---

816 Lk 10.34. See Isocrates, *Aegineticus* 11, 20-33, where a distinction is made between different types of nursing care, and above, Section One, chapter three, 52-54, for a discussion. Overall long-term emotional, physical and psychological care is described by θεραπεύω, the physical attention to detail inherent in this by ἐπιμελεία (28). Here, while the Samaritan shows great attention to physical detail, and to initial medical treatment, he provides for the man's convalescent care to be carried out by others (10.35).

817 Hippokrates, *Morb. Mul.* 656. This would have the effect of cleaning the wounds, providing a barrier against infection, and preventing bandaging from sticking to the wounds. See above, chapter seven, 128-129.

818 Lk 10.37

819 The command πορεύου is the same as the command given to the haemorrhaging woman (Lk 8.48: πορεύου εἰς εἰρήνην), and is reminiscent of the Old Testament commands (Deuteronomy 10.12-13) to fear the Lord God, and to walk in all his ways (πορεύεσθαι ἐν πάσαις ταῖς ὁδοῖς), to love him (ἀγαπᾷν αὐτόν), and to serve (λατρεύειν) the Lord God out of one's whole heart (ἐξ ὅλης τῆς καρδίας) and whole soul (ὅλης τῆς ψυχῆς). See Septuagint (1887) 364 for the text, and Campbell (1989) 39-41 for a discussion.

820 Mk 12.34

821 Lk 10.9

Like Mark, Matthew does not illustrate the command, but he does (later) make Jesus describe the sort of behaviour of those who would inherit a place in the kingdom. His description has parallels with the behaviour exhibited by Luke's Samaritan: providing food for the hungry, drink for the thirsty, a welcome for strangers, clothing for the naked, and visiting those who are sick or in prison,[822] i.e. love in action.

By the end of each gospel, the synoptists envisage a different mission. Matthew's mission now consists of teaching and baptising and includes all nations, who are to be made disciples;[823] Luke's mission is to preach repentance and forgiveness to all nations in Jesus' name.[824] Mark's longer (spurious) ending also features preaching.[825] The verb θεραπεύω is notably absent from these commands.

It is a valuable exercise at this point to consider the positive commands that are recorded in the *Gospel of Thomas*, a gnostic text that has aroused considerable interest because of its similarities and differences in form and content when compared with the canonical gospels.[826] In the *Gospel of Thomas* the instances where Jesus recommends behaviour in a positive sense are extremely rare. Most instructions are given in a negative manner - "Do not " - and these are continually reinforced by the message to deny the world and "Become passers-by!"[827] However, comfort is offered in a positive way:

> Come unto me, for my Yoke is easy and my Lordship is mild, and you will find repose for yourselves.[828]

Given then the negative nature of the instructions in the *Gospel of Thomas*, those given in a positive way gain significance:

---

822 Mt 25.35-40

823 Mt 28.16-20

824 Lk 24.36-49

825 Mk 16.14-18

826 The *Gospel of Thomas* is a collection of unrelated sayings of Jesus, many of which have parallels in the synoptic gospels. Thus the *Gospel of Thomas* appears similar to the sayings source proposed by scholars as a common source for material found in *Matthew* and *Luke*, and known as 'Q'. See Montefiore (1960-1961); Walls (1960-1961); Koester in Robinson (1981) 117; and Pagels (1981) xiii-xvi.

827 *GT* #42

828 *GT* #90

> When you go into any land and walk about in the districts, if they receive you, eat what they set before you, and heal (θεραπεύειν) the sick among them...,[829]

> Love your brother like your soul (ψυχή), guard (τηρεῖν) him like the pupil of your eye...,[830] and,

> Preach from your housetops that which you hear in your ear....[831]

The emphasis, as in the canonical gospels, is on healing and loving and preaching. The destination is an indeterminate "any land". But what does θεραπεύω mean in this context? It is most unlikely that the term refers only to physical healing, if it has any physical connotation at all, for, in common with many other gnostic texts, the *Gospel of Thomas* shows a definite revulsion for the flesh, and, by implication, bodily needs and function.[832] Indeed, amazement is expressed that spirit, potentially so beautiful, should be housed in such poverty:

> If the flesh came into being because of spirit, it is a wonder. But if spirit came into being because of the body, it is a wonder of wonders. Indeed, I am amazed at how this great wealth has made its home in this poverty.[833]

There is revulsion and disgust expressed for the body, the same revulsion as is expressed for the contamination of worldly matter.[834] In contrast, there is a constant call to recognise the spark of divinity within (spirit/soul) and to nurture its growth.[835] Thus the

---

829 *GT* #14. All Greek references are from the *Gospel of Thomas* in New Testament (1988) 517-530.

830 *GT* #25

831 *GT* #33

832 See, for example, *GT* #87: "Wretched is the body that is dependent on a body, and wretched is the soul that is dependent on these two"; and *GT* #112: "Woe to the flesh that depends on the soul, woe to the soul that depends on the flesh".

833 *GT* #29

834 For example, *GT* #27: "If you do not fast as regards the world, you will not find the Kingdom"; and *GT* #56: "Whoever has come to understand the world has found (only) a corpse, and whoever has found a corpse is superior to the world".

835 For example, *GT* #89: "Why do you wash the outside of the cup? Do you not realise that he who made the inside is the same who made the outside?" and *GT* #24: "There is light within a man of light, and he (or it) lights up

focus in this text is spiritual. And we have seen how θεραπεύω in a spiritual and teaching context refers to a change in thinking (conversion) in the canonical gospels, particularly in a Jewish setting. But that the *Gospel of Thomas* was not written for an exclusively Jewish audience seems obvious, for in reply to the question, "Is circumcision beneficial or not?" Jesus replied,

> If it were beneficial, their father would beget them already circumcised from their mother. Rather, the true circumcision in spirit has become completely profitable.[836]

It is interesting that the question should have come up at all, and that it is answered in this way is significant. The emphasis is again on the spirit, on the excision of worldly matter (the foreskin) in a spiritual sense only. As well, this instruction refers to "any land" and θεραπεύειν is dependent, as in the canonical gospels, on the welcome and hospitality of the inhabitants. That this is most likely to happen among strangers is indicated by the saying:

> No prophet is accepted in his own village; no physician heals (θεραπεύειν) those who know him.[837]

Thus the verb θεραπεύω in this document, a document which focuses on spiritual enlightenment, and in which affairs of the world and the flesh are constantly denigrated, must be understood to imply conversion to a different way of thinking, a way of thinking that will bring repose for the soul. In this it reflects the use of θεραπεύω in the canonical gospels in a teaching context, and also the use of θεραπεύω by authors such as Epicurus[838] and Marcus Aurelius.[839]

So what can we conclude about the use of Greek healing language in an early Christian context?

---

the whole world"; and *GT* #49: "Blessed are the solitary and elect, for you will find the Kingdom. For you are from it, and to it you will return".

836 *GT* #53

837 *GT* #31

838 App. 3:5, **1**

839 App. 5:7, **3**, **6**

11. *Conclusion*

A study of the use of Greek healing language in the New Testament shows that the gospel authors use the verbs *ἰάομαι*, *ὑγιαίνω*, *σῴζω*, θεραπεύω and their derivatives in a variety of ways to depict the healing ministry of Jesus of Nazareth.

11.1 *ἰάομαι*

ἰάομαι only occurs twenty-six times in the New Testament in verbal form, and of these twenty-six, fifteen are Lukan usages.[840] Matthew only uses *ἰάομαι* four times, once quoting the Septuagint,[841] and three other times in two healing stories, always in the passive voice, and always to describe instantaneous *in absentia* healings of gentiles, which occurred as a result of 'parental' requests made in faith.[842] Mark only uses *ἰάομαι* once, to describe the self-perception of the haemorrhaging woman, but, like Matthew's stories of the centurion's 'boy' and the Canaanite woman's daughter, *ἰάομαι* describes instantaneous healing as a result of the intervention of God, intervention brought about by faith so great it causes Jesus to comment.[843] Thus the Markan and Matthaean use of *ἰάομαι* mirrors its use in the healing language of the Greek world and the Septuagint, in that both gospel authors choose it to describe the intervention of God.[844]

The Lukan use of *ἰάομαι* is different.[845] Luke needed the notion of 'cure' in a healing word, and θεραπεύω in the Greek world (and in the Septuagint and the writings of Josephus) referred to human

840 See Apps 8:3 and 8:4.

841 Mt 13.15 (cf. App. 6:1, **62**)

842 Mt 8.8, 8.13; 15.28

843 Mk 5.29. It may be significant that the Markan woman (Mk 5.25-34), the centurion's 'boy' (Mt 8.5-13) and the Canaanite woman's daughter (Mt 15.21-8) were all outsiders: the woman because she was 'unclean', the others because they were not Jewish. Matthew chooses the third person passive; the Jewish way of describing the activity of God without mentioning the divine name (see Wilcox [1965] 127-128; Beare [1981] 129; Wilcox [1984] 1017). Mark uses the third person perfect indicative middle in a passive sense. See App. 8:4.

844 See App. 6:1, and chapter six for the use of *ἰάομαι* in the Septuagint; and Section One for the use of *ἰάομαι* in the healing language surrounding Greek asklepieia.

845 See Apps 7:3, 8:1, 8:2, 8:3 and 8:4.

treatment which might or might not be successful.[846] As we have seen, ἰάομαι is the God-word in the Septuagint,[847] and also describes the intervention of Asklepios at Greek healing centres.[848] It includes the notion of 'cure' in its meaning, and hints at the source: in both the Septuagint and at asklepieia healing was of divine origin. However, the verb ἰάομαι does not include the notion of 'service', so vital to the gospel message. Luke, because his audience was of differing cultural and social origins, needed to use words which were both familiar to his audience and also conveyed the meaning he intended. Thus the nature of Luke's audience dictated his use of ἰάομαι. Because he needed the notion of 'cure' but also needed the notion of 'service' and wanted to invest both with a spiritual meaning, Luke chose to use ἰάομαι and θεραπεύω contiguously.[849] And although he reports that Jesus gave authority to his disciples to both θεραπεύειν and ἰᾶσθαι, the only 'disciples' to ἰᾶσθαι were Peter and Paul in a gentile context,[850] while the disciples' actions in a Jewish context are reported by the verb θεραπεύω.[851] In a Jewish context it is only the activity of Jesus that is described by both verbs, and then Luke is careful to use them contiguously.[852] Thus audience dictates the language of the gospel message. Audience also dictates the nature of the message. As Luke uses the God-word in his portrait of the healing Jesus, so also he stresses the importance of 'signs' and 'wonders' and their results: amazement, fear and mass conversion.[853]

John is sparing with his use of ἰάομαι, using it only twice in healing stories, and once to quote the Septuagint.[854] Elsewhere the verb refers to right doctrine or correct Christian practice.[855] Thus

---

846 For the Greek world: App.4:1, **1-10**, **13-24**; Thucydides 2.47-55; Isocrates, *Aegineticus* 11, 20-29; the Septuagint: App. 6:1; Josephus: App. 6:2, **15**, **31**, **34**.

847 See App. 6:1.

848 See Apps 2:1, 2:2, and 3:2, **5**.

849 See Apps 7:3, 8:1.

850 Luke needed the God-word to explain the healing of Aeneas, but Peter is careful to explain the spiritual context (Acts 9.32-35); similarly, Luke needed the God-word to explain the healing of Publius' father (Acts 28.7-8: but note that Publius had fulfilled all hospitality requirements [Mt 10.11-14; Mk 6.8-11; Lk 9.1-6, 10.4-9; *GT* #14], and that Luke is careful to choose θεραπεύω to describe the following general healing episode [Acts 28.9]).

851 Lk 9.6

852 Lk 6.17-19; 8.43-48; 9.11; 14.1-6

853 Acts 3.1-4.31; 4.30; 5.12-16; 8.6-8; 9.32-35; 9.36-43; 16.16-18 (see Apps 8:1 and 8:2).

854 In healing stories: Jn 4.47; 5.13. To quote the Septuagint: Jn 12.40 (cf. Mt 13.15; Acts 28.27, and Isaiah 6.10 [App. 6:1, **62**]).

855 Hebrews 12.13; James 5.16; 1 Peter 2.24. See Apps 8:3 and 8:4.

the verb becomes sterile as soon as it is removed from the gospel story.

11.2. ὑγιαίνω

The use of the verb ὑγιαίνω and its derivatives is similar in that gospel and epistle usage differs dramatically.[856] In *Matthew* the adjectival form faithfully reflects its use and meaning as illustrated in inscriptions from the asklepieia in the Greek world,[857] while in *Mark* it appears in a parting command to the haemorrhaging woman out of the mouth of Jesus.[858] Here too it reflects the closing formulae of Greek inscriptions.[859] Luke also chooses it in a remarkably similar context to an inscription from Epidauros.[860] John uses it six times in one highly symbolic story.[861] Elsewhere in the New Testament, ὑγιαίνω suffers the same fate as ἰάομαι: it becomes sterile, describing doctrine and teaching.[862]

11.3. σῴζω

The verb σῴζω appears in many different contexts in the New Testament: in a nautical context as in Greek literature,[863] in a theological context,[864] and in healing stories.[865] It is only with the last that we have been concerned. Here it retains the Homeric

856 See App. 9:2.
857 Mt 12.13; 15.31. Cf. Apps 2:1, **3** and 2:2, **36, 37** and **38** where ὑγιής refers to the restoration of crippled or paralysed body parts.
858 Mk 5.34
859 See especially Apps 2:1 and 2:2.
860 Lk 7.10: cf. App. 2:2, **21**. (Cf. also Lk 15.27)
861 Jn 5.4-15; 7.23
862 1 Timothy 1.10, 6.3; 2 Timothy 1.13, 4.3; Titus 1.9, 13; 2.1, 8. However, the verb is used in a holistic sense by the author of 3 John 2. See App. 9:2.
863 Mt 8.25: σῶσον out of the mouths of the disciples, in Matthew's account of Jesus' calming of the storm at sea (8.23-27). Neither Mark (4.35-41) nor Luke (8.22-25) use σῴζω in this story. Matthew also puts this form into Peter's mouth (14.30), addressing Jesus, when he tries to walk on water. In both these episodes σῴζω means to *rescue and preserve*, a meaning of σῴζω explicit in Homer, Aeschylus, Sophocles and Euripides (see Section One: chapters one and three; and chapter three, n. 350). Cf. Acts 27.43,44 where Luke also uses διασῴζω in a nautical context.
864 See Foerster and Fohrer in Kittel *et al.* (1971) 965-1024.
865 There is naturally some overlapping in these categories, but see Apps 7:10 and 7:11.

notion of rescue and successful treatment.[866] Mark uses it to describe incidents which involve patients who reach out and touch Jesus in faith,[867] or to record Jesus' words linking salvation and faith in a healing context.[868] He also uses it in the story of Jairus' daughter,[869] and introduces it in the language of the controversial sabbath healings.[870] Matthew only chooses σῴζω to describe patients who reach out and touch Jesus in faith,[871] and to record Jesus' words linking salvation and faith in one incident.[872] Luke introduces this saying - ἡ πίστις σου σέσωκέν σε - in more stories in his gospel,[873] retains σῴζω in the sabbath controversy,[874] as well as introducing it into healing stories in *Acts*.[875] An outstanding feature of this word group is the company it keeps. It usually appears with forms of πίστις and/or ἅπτομαι.[876]

Indeed ἅπτομαι is the most popular 'touching' verb in healing stories, and describes the touch of those who reach out in faith, and also the healing touch of Jesus.[877] In this its use reflects the language used to describe the healing touch of Asklepios.[878]

11.4. θεραπεύω

However, the most interesting verb in this study is θεραπεύω, which has emerged from the cognate form found in Homer, to include all the characteristics of the Homeric θεράπων in its verbal meaning. Thus it includes the ideas of selfless service,[879] loyalty,[880] love,[881] and nurture[882] in its meaning, and, depending on its context, can

866 From danger and imminent death (see Apps 7:10 and 7:11).
867 The haemorrhaging woman: Mk 5.28-34; the crowd at Gennesaret: Mk 6.56
868 To the haemorrhaging woman: Mk 5.34; to blind Bartimaeus: Mk 10.52
869 Mk 5.23
870 Mk 3.4
871 The haemorrhaging woman: Mt 9.20-22; the crowd at Gennesaret: 14.36
872 To the haemorrhaging woman: Mt 9.22
873 Like Matthew and Mark, Luke uses σῴζω in Jesus' saying to the haemorrhaging woman (Lk 8.48); but also to the blind beggar (Lk 18.42: parallel to Mk 10.52); and to the leper (Lk 17.19).
874 Lk 6.9
875 Acts 4.9, 12; 14.9
876 See Apps 7:10 and 7:11.
877 See Apps 7:12 and 7:13.
878 For example, see App 2:2, **31**; App. 2:4, line 23.
879 Thucydides 2.47-55; Isocrates, *Aegineticus* 11, 20-29
880 Isocrates, *Aegineticus* 11, 20-29
881 ibid.
882 Aristides (App. 5:6, **29**)

range in meaning from medical treatment[883] to persuasion.[884] Context is the crucial factor. Always therapeutic behaviour is active in that it is designed to bring about a change in either circumstances or behaviour,[885] and because of its nature its aspect is continuous.[886]

The verb θεραπεύω occurs forty-three times in verbal form in the New Testament, making it the most popular verb in a healing context.[887] In this it differs from the incidence of its use in Asklepiadic literature.[888] It is a synoptic word in that it occurs thirty-five times in the synoptic gospels, and five times in *Acts*. Elsewhere it occurs only once in *John*, and twice in *Revelation*. In the gospels it describes the activity of both Jesus and the disciples.[889] This reflects its use in the Septuagint where it is the human-word, in contrast to ἰάομαι which is the God-word.[890]

All three synoptists consistently designate Jesus' behaviour as preaching, teaching and θεραπεύων-behaviour,[891] and in controversial sabbath healings the authorities are invariably depicted as thinking of healing in terms of θεραπεύω.[892] Therefore θεραπεύων-behaviour must involve 'work'.[893] But this is the description often given to Jesus' behaviour in crowds, and is usually linked with the activities of preaching and teaching.[894] People come to hear (ἀκούω) and the result is that they ἐθεραπεύοντο.[895] So θεραπεύων-behaviour has to be the practical expression of Jesus' preaching and teaching message, behaviour that produces an effect: a change in thinking which in turn alters one's way of life.[896] In this way the verb θεραπεύω provides a practical expression for living the new commandment: in a medical context involving work and

---

883 For example, see Apps 2:1, **20**; 2:2, **26**; 4:1; 5:5, **7**.

884 See Apps 5:6, **40**; 5:7, **3**; and Epictetus 1.19 where θεραπεύω appears illustrating a wide range in meaning.

885 For a change in health: App. 4:1, **1-10**, **13-24**; for a change in behaviour: App. 5:7, **6**.

886 See Section One: chapters three and four.

887 See Apps 7:8 and 7:9. Cf. Apps 7:10, 7:11, 8:3, 8:4 and 9:2.

888 Cf. Apps 2:1, 2:2, 3:2.

889 The disciples: Mk 6.13; Lk 9.6

890 See App. 6:1.

891 For example, Mk. 6.5; Mk 10.1 cf. Mt 19.2; Mt 4.23, 9.35; Lk 5.15, 6.18. See Apps 7:1, 7:2, 7:3, 7:8.

892 Mk 3.1-6; Mt12.9-14; Lk 6.6-11, 13.10-17, (14.1-6)

893 See Lk 13.14 and cf. Jn 5.1-18.

894 For example, see Mt 4.23, 9.35, 12.22, 21.14; Lk 5.15, 6.6-11, 6.18 and cf. Mk 10.1; Mt 19.2

895 Lk 6.18

896 Lk 5.29-32

worry, time and energy; in a teaching context involving a change in one's thinking which in turn produces a change in one's way of life. Always the aspect of θεραπεύω is continuous.

The gospel authors tried to present Jesus as a healer *par excellence*, but when one studies the terms they used it becomes obvious that the healing they had in mind was primarily of a spiritual nature. In crowd scenes the emphasis is always spiritual, and even in specific healings there is the notion of discipleship, faith, and peace in the result.[897] Thus there is a strong element of persuasion in the verb θεραπεύω, so that it appears to describe conversion.[898] The result of 'conversion' is inclusion in the new community. And like the Homeric θεράπων, those 'converted' enjoyed "the psychological values and satisfactions that went with belonging".[899] Therefore it is a mistake to give a physical emphasis to the use of θεραπεύω in a spiritual and teaching context.

As the healing language under consideration has been most prominent in the synoptic authors, so an unexpected result of this study has been the obvious differences revealed in the interest, audience and proclamation of each synoptist. Despite the fact that there appears to be a general acceptance of the idea that Luke was the most interested in medical matters,[900] a study of the use of healing language shows that Mark has far more interest in things medical than Matthew or Luke. For example, it is Mark who provides the most professional case history of the epileptic boy,[901] it is Mark who mentions the medical practice of anointing with oil,[902] it is Mark who describes the medical practice of using saliva for eye complaints,[903] it is Mark who gives the most detail concerning the background of the haemorrhaging woman,[904] and it is Mark who tells the parents of the sick girl to give her something to eat.[905] As

---

897 For example, the Lukan women (8.2-3)

898 See above, chapter seven.

899 Finley (1954) 54-55

900 See, for example, the works of Hobart (1882); Ramsay (1908); Harnack (1911); Cadbury (1958) and (1969); Kelsey (1973); Wilkinson (1980) and Maddocks (1981).

901 Mk 9.14-29 (cf. Mt 17.14-20; Lk 9.37-43)

902 Mk 6.13

903 Mk 8.22-26. John (9.1-7) also mentions that Jesus made clay with spittle and anointed the eyes of the man born blind.

904 Mk 5.25-26: she had had a flow of blood for twelve years, she had suffered much under many doctors, she had spent all she had, she was no better but rather grew worse.

905 Mk 5.43. Wilcox (1989) 1, argues that this is "not a 'raising from the dead' - despite the fact that the three Evangelists who record the story all seem to

well, Mark has often been criticised for his use of Greek, and his penchant for the historic tense,[906] and yet it is Mark who carefully differentiates between the disciples' and Jesus' healing practices by using the imperfect tense to describe the disciples' actions,[907] and crowd effects,[908] and the aorist to describe Jesus' actions.[909] Therefore Mark is particular in his use of tense.

Matthew, rather than removing the so-called 'magical' element in Mark's healing stories,[910] has carefully categorised them,[911] describing different types of healing in different language,[912] even duplicating stories[913] and adding numbers in places.[914] In this way Matthew's choice of healing terms shows that he both knew and used Mark's material. Thus the gospel of Mark is prior to the gospel of Matthew. Indeed in *Matthew* the human element so obvious in Mark's parallel healing stories diminishes, as they become type-cast.[915] Matthew is very careful to differentiate be-

---

interpret it as such, but rather the lifting of the patient out of a coma, and one possibly due to hypoglycaemia of some sort". Wilcox bases his argument on the evidence for 'Talitha' being the name of the girl in her home-language; the comments of Jesus that she was in a 'deep sleep'; and his instruction to give her something to eat immediately (necessary treatment after arousal from a hypoglycaemic coma). This instruction seems a remarkably rational one, and directly contradicts Hull (1974) 75 who states: "Whatever the actual physical value of the advice given by Jesus to sufferers, it is never ostensibly rational, in striking contrast to the cures of Asclepius and Apollonius of Tyana, who sometimes prescribed exercise, bathing or diet".

906 Even as recently as Sanders and Davies (1989) 266, who state: "Mark is written in Greek, but no one would want to claim that it evinces literary pretensions. The limited vocabulary, repetition of phraseology, all-too-frequent use of *kai* (and), of participles, of the historic present, the Aramaisms, the Hebraisms and the Latinisms combine to show that this is a 'popular' not a 'literary' work".

907 Mk 6.13

908 Mk 6.56 (cf. Mt 14.36). But see Lk 6.17-19

909 Mk 1.34; 3.10; 6.5

910 Hull (1974) 144

911 See above, 123-124.

912 For general healing: θεραπεύω plus a general statement; for gentile *in absentia* specific healings requested in faith: ἰάομαι in the passive; for the touch of a patient made in faith: ἅπτομαι ... σῴζω; for Jesus' touch: ἅπτομαι, κρατέω. For a discussion see chapters seven, eight and nine.

913 Cf. Mt 9.27-31; Mt 20.29-34

914 Cf. Mk 10.46-52; Mt 20.29-34; Lk 18.35-43

915 For example, the background information given concerning the haemorrhaging woman, and the epileptic boy.

tween Jesus' and God's healing activity, choosing ἰάομαι in the passive to describe the intervention of God in the cases of gentile healings,[916] and θεραπεύω in the passive voice to describe the intervention of God in the healing of the epileptic boy.[917] Otherwise he uses θεραπεύω in the active voice to describe Jesus' behaviour, particularly with crowds.[918] Thus, although there is a commission at the end of Matthew's gospel to preach to the gentiles[919] (perhaps a later 'church' addition?), Matthew's choice of healing language illustrates an early gentile-Jewish controversy, in that Matthew appears anxious to 'explain' the healing of gentile patients. Thus Matthew's gospel appears to have been written originally for a primarily Jewish audience.[920]

Luke, in contrast, tries to appeal to people of both sexes of differing cultural and social origins.[921] His choice of stories,[922] and patients,[923] casts a wide net for reader-response, and the extra detail in many seems designed to elicit sympathy from the reader.[924] Many of these extra details, often ascribed to an interest in things medical,[925] actually elicit a sympathetic identification-response in the reader, and so invite the reader to participate in Luke's message. As well, Luke chooses characters of both sexes, of varying ages and stations in life, and in this way tries for universal appeal. Certainly his method has stood the test of time. Perhaps he was a physician, but, like the other synoptists his message emphasises spiritual healing. Certainly he emphasises mass events that seem to describe spiritual conversion.

---

916 Mt 8.5-13; 15.21-8

917 Mt 17.14-20

918 Mt 4.23, 4.24, 8.16, 9.35, 12.15, 12.22, 14.14, 15.30, 19.2, 21.14

919 Mt 28.16-20

920 This is not only obvious from healing stories. Beare (1981) 126 says of Matthew's version of the beatitudes: "All the beatitudes, and indeed the entire sermon, take it for granted that attainment of entrance to the kingdom of heaven is the supreme goal of life, and that there is no serious alternative. Such an assumption could only be made in a Jewish community."

921 See above, 132-134.

922 ibid.

923 ibid.

924 For example, the widow of Nain's 'only' son (Lk 7.12); Jairus' 'only' daughter (Lk 8.42).

925 For example, the information that the fever of Simon's mother-in-law was 'high' (Lk 4.38) makes a 'better' story by heightening the element of the miraculous; and the information that the 'right' hand of the man with the withered hand was the one affected (Lk 6.6) also heightens the miraculous effect of the story (if we assume that most of the population at that time was right-handed, as is the case now).

A study of healing language has revealed much about human nature and human striving for health and happiness. Before the advent of Christianity, the Greek god Asklepios initially provided help for physical problems,[926] but over the centuries Asklepios also came to fulfil a need for a personal 'Saviour',[927] and provided emotional,[928] psychological[929] and spiritual healing as well.[930] In this way he was very much a forerunner of and contemporary with Jesus of Nazareth. It is thus easy to see why Christian apologists attacked the cult of Asklepios with such vehemence.[931]

The healing language of both was similar, in that the same general healing terms were applied to healings of both traditions. However, while the same terms were used, the incidence of verb groups differs. The θεραπεύω ἰάομαι ὑγιαίνω word groups are popular in an inverse proportion in both traditions.[932] It is significant that the synoptists, particularly Mark and Matthew, describe Jesus' activities and behaviour with the verb θεραπεύω. In Asklepiadic literature as well as the Septuagint, this verb group more frequently describes human treatment or service,[933] whereas ἰάομαι describes the action of both Asklepios and the Septuagint god.[934] Thus both Mark and Matthew describe Jesus as a son of God, rather than God in human form.[935] It is Luke who describes Jesus' activ-

926 See Apps 2:1, 2:2, 3:2.

927 See Apps 2:4, 2:5, 5:6.

928 ibid.

929 ibid.

930 App. 5:6, 9 and 10.

931 Justin, *Apologia* 22.6; *Dialogus* 69.3; Origen, *Contra Celsum* 3.23; Ambrose, *De Virginibus* 3.176.7

932 The ὑγιαίνω and ἰάομαι word groups are more popular at asklepieia, while θεραπεύω occurs rarely (see Section One: chapters two, three and five). In the New Testament the reverse is true (cf. Section Two: chapters seven, eight and nine).

933 See Apps 3:2, 5:6, 6:1.

934 See Apps 2:1, 2:2, 3:2, 5:6, 6:1.

935 Despite Mk 1.1 (see above, 134). Metzger (1975) 73 comments thus on the inclusion of [υἱοῦ θεοῦ], category {C} within square brackets: "The absence of υἱοῦ θεοῦ in א* Θ 28^{c} *al* may be due to an oversight in copying, occasioned by the similarity of the *nomina sacra*. On the other hand, however, there was always a temptation (to which copyists often succumbed) to expand titles and quasi-titles of books. Since the combination of B D W *al* in support of υἱοῦ θεου is extremely strong, it was thought not advisable to omit the words altogether, yet because of the antiquity of the shorter reading and the possibility of scribal expansion, it was decided to enclose the words within square brackets." Mark's use of healing language would support the shorter reading.

ities with the pagan and Septuagint God-word,[936] and John who spells out the relationship in philosophical terms.[937]

Thus while θεραπεύω and ἰάομαι can overlap slightly in meaning they are not synonymous, and there is an aspectual quality implicit in each that is important for our understanding of them. As ἰάομαι is consistently the God-word in both traditions, so its aspect is usually aoristic: the action is instantaneous and complete.[938] In contrast, the aspect of θεραπεύω is imperfect: it describes an ongoing and growing reaction/effect, encompassing spiritual, emotional, psychological and physical factors. This activity involves both work and worry for the active agent as Euripides had earlier pointed out:

> It's better to be sick than nurse the sick.
> Sickness is single trouble for the sufferer:
> but nursing means vexation of the mind,
> and hard work for the hands besides.
> (κρεῖσσον δὲ νοσεῖν ἢ θεραπεύειν·
> τὸ μέν ἐστιν ἁπλοῦν, τῷ δὲ συνάπτει
> λύπη τε φρενῶν χερσίν τε πόνος.)[939]

This idea of 'work' and 'worry' is included in the gospel commission to θεραπεύειν, since this commission demands the nurturing of humans in a spiritual, emotional, psychological and physical sense. In this way the commission combines the continuous notions of work, comfort, care and service. However, a prerequisite for θεραπεύων-behaviour is the successful preaching and teaching of the healing word.[940] This healing λόγος demands the ignition of a continuing spark of recognition in the hearer to be effective, and requires that this recognition-process continue throughout life. In this way Jesus' λόγος produced a new way of living among those who heeded his word, a way of life designed to banish the πάθος of humankind. Thus in the synoptic gospels it is the spiritual aspect of θεραπεύω that is the most important: it is the healing word which strives to banish human anguish. As Epicurus had earlier stated:

---

936 See Apps 7:3, 8:1, 8:3 and 8:4.
937 Jn 1.1-18
938 Cf. Apps 2:1, 2:2, 3:2, 5:6, 6:1. Both Matthew (156-158) and Mark (156) use ἰάομαι in the same way.
939 Euripides, *Hippolytos* 186-188
940 "καὶ γὰρ οὔτε βοτάνη οὔτε μάλαγμα ἐθεράπευσεν αὐτους,
ἀλλὰ ὁ σός, Κύριε, λόγος ὁ πάντα ἰώμενος.
(For neither herb nor poultice healed them,
but it is your word, O Lord, which heals all humankind.)" Wisdom 16.12

> Vain is the word of that philosopher by which no human anguish is healed. For just as the art of medicine is no use unless it heals diseases of the body, neither is philosophy unless it banishes the anguish of the soul (κενὸς ἐκείνου φιλοσόφου λόγος ὑφ' οὗ μηδὲν πάθος ἀνθρώπου θεραπεύεται. ὥσπερ γὰρ ἰατρικῆς οὐδὲν ὄφελος εἰ μὴ τὰς νόσους τῶν σωμάτων θεραπεύει, οὕτως οὐδὲ φιλοσοφίας εἰ μὴ τὸ τῆς ψυχῆς ἐκβάλλει πάθος).[941]

Therefore, the meaning of θεραπεύω in the New Testament definitely incorporates the idea of healing, but this healing is primarily for the anguish of the soul, so that those who participate in and 'hear' the message experience a change in thinking (μετανοία), a repentance which leads to their inclusion in a spiritual community that brings peace (εἰρήνη).

941 Epicurus, (Porphyrius, *ad Marcellam* 31 34 10). See App. 3:5, **1**. The language used at Mt 8.16 is similar. Jesus threw out (ἐξέβαλεν) spirits with a word (λόγῳ), and healed (ἐθεράπευσεν) all those who were feeling poorly (πάντας τοὺς κακῶς ἔχοντας).

Bibliography

Primary

Aelius Aristides, (1968) *The civilizing power,* (ed J. H. Oliver) Transactions of the American Philosophical Society, New Series, 58, 1, Philadelphia.

(1973) *Aristides,* (trans. C. A. Behr) Loeb 1, London.

(1981) *The complete works,* (trans. C. A. Behr) vol. 2: Orations 17-53, Leiden.

(1986) *The complete works,* (trans. C. A. Behr) vol. 1: Orations 1-16, Leiden.

Aeschylus, (1960) *Agamemnon,* (ed J. D. Denniston and D. Page) Oxford.

(1964) *Aeschylus I: Oresteia,* (trans. R. Lattimore) Chicago

(1971) *Aeschylus II: Agamemnon, Libation Bearers, Eumenides, Fragments,* (trans. H. W. Smyth, ed H. Lloyd-Jones) Loeb 2, London.

Aristophanes, (1967) *Aristophanis Comoediae,* (ed F. W. Hall and W. M. Geldart) vol. 2, Oxford, reprint of 2nd edn (1942).

Aristotle, (1977) *Politics,* (trans. H. Rackham) Loeb 21, London.

Celsus, (1935) *De Medicina,* (trans. W. G. Spencer) Loeb 1, 2, 3, London.

Clement of Alexandria, (1979) *Clement of Alexandria,* (trans. G. W. Butterworth) Loeb, London.

Columella, (1979) *De Re Rustica,* (trans. E. S. Forster and E. H. Heffner) Loeb 3, London.

Diogenes Laertius, (1970) *Diogenes Laertius,* (trans. R. D. Hicks) Loeb 2, London.

Epictetus, (1967) *The discourses as reported by Arrian, the manual, and fragments,* (trans. W. A. Oldfather) Loeb 1, London.

Epicurus, (1964) *Epicurus : Letters, Principal Doctrines, and Vatican Sayings,* (trans. R. M. Geer) Indianapolis.

(1973) *Epicuro: Opere,* (ed G. Arrighetti) Torino.

Euripides, (1955) *Euripides I: Alcestis, The Medea, The Heracleidae, Hippolytus,* (trans. D. Grene), in ed D. Grene and R. Lattimore, *The Complete Greek Tragedies,* Chicago.

(1984) *Euripides: Hippolytus,* (ed J. Ferguson) Bristol.

Eusebius, (1973) *The Ecclesiastical History,* (trans. J. E. L. Oulton) Loeb 2, London.
(1980) *The Ecclesiastical History,* (trans. K. Lake) Loeb 1, London.
Galen, (1979) *Galen: On the natural faculties,* (trans. A. J. Brock) Loeb, London.
(1984a) *Galen: On respiration and the arteries,* (ed, trans. and commentary, D. J. Furley and J. S. Wilkie) Princeton.
(1984b) *Galen: On the doctrines of Hippocrates and Plato,* (ed., trans. and commentary, P. de Lacy) Part 1: Books 1-5, 3rd edn, Berlin.
(1984c) *Galen : On the doctrines of Hippocrates and Plato,* (ed., trans. and commentary, P. de Lacy) Part 2: Books 6-9, 2nd edn, Berlin.
Hermes Trismegistus, (1982) *Hermetica. The Ancient Greek and Latin Writings which contain religious or philosophic teachings ascribed to Hermes Trismegistus,* 1, (ed, trans. and notes, W. Scott) Colorado.
Herodas, (1904) *The Mimes of Herodas,* (ed J. A. Nairn) Oxford.
(1929) *Mime IV. Offerings and Sacrifices* in *Herodes, Cercidas and the Greek Choliambic Poets,* (ed and trans. A. D. Knox) Loeb, London.
Hippokrates, (1968) *Hippocrates III: On Wounds in the Head, In the Surgery, Fractures, Joints, Mochlichon,* (trans. E. T. Withington) Loeb 3, London.
(1972) *Hippocrates I: Ancient Medicine, Airs Waters Places, Epidemics I, III, Oath, Precepts, Nutriment,* (trans. W. H. S. Jones) Loeb 1, London.
(1979) *Hippocrates IV: Nature of Man, Regimen in Health, Humours, Aphorisms, Regimen I, II, III, IV,* (trans. W. H. S. Jones) Loeb 4, London.
(1981) *Hippocrates II: Prognostic, Regimen in Acute Diseases, The Sacred Disease, The Art, Breaths, Law, Decorum, Physician, Dentition,* (trans. W. H. S. Jones) Loeb 2, London.
(1988a) *Hippocrates V: Affections, Diseases I, II* (trans. P. Potter) Loeb 5, London.
(1988b) *Hippocrates VI: Diseases III, Internal Affections, Regimen in acute diseases (appendix),* (trans. P. Potter) Loeb 6, London.
(1990) *Hippocrates: Pseudepigraphic Writings,* (ed, trans., and with an introduction, W. D. Smith) Studies in Ancient Medicine vol. 2, Leiden.
Homer, (1947) *The Odyssey of Homer,* vol. 1 (ed W. B. Stanford) London.

(1961) *The Iliad of Homer,* (trans. R. Lattimore) Chicago.
(1977) *The Odyssey of Homer,* vol. 2 (ed W. B. Stanford) 2nd edn., London.
(1978) *The Iliad of Homer I-XII,* (ed M. M. Willcock) London.
(1984) *The Iliad of Homer XIII-XXIV,* (ed M. M. Willcock) London.
Inscriptions: (1892) *Inscriptiones Graecae* VII, *Inscriptiones Megaridis et Boeotiae,* Berlin.
(1913) *Inscriptiones Graecae* II/III^2 1, *Inscriptiones Atticae Euclidis anno posteriores,* Berlin.
(1929) *Inscriptiones Graecae* IV^2 1, *Inscriptiones Epidauri,* Berlin.
(1935a) *Inscriptiones Creticae* I, (ed M. Guarducci) Rome.
(1935b) *Inscriptiones Graecae* II/III^2 3, *Inscriptiones Atticae Euclidis anno posteriores,* Berlin.
(1950) *Supplementum Epigraphicum Graecum,* vol. 11, Leiden.
(1956) *Supplementum Epigraphicum Graecum,* vol. 13, Leiden.
(1957) *Supplementum Epigraphicum Graecum,* vol. 14, Leiden.
(1958) *Supplementum Epigraphicum Graecum,* vol. 15, Leiden.
(1962) *Supplementum Epigraphicum Graecum,* vol. 18, Leiden.
(1971) *Supplementum Epigraphicum Graecum,* vol. 25, Leiden.
Isocrates, (1968) *Isocrates,* (trans. L. van Hook) Loeb 3, London.
Josephus, (1966) *Josephus I: The Life,* (trans. H. St. J. Thackeray) Loeb 1, London.
(1967) *Josephus II: The Jewish War,* 1-3 (trans. H. St. J. Thackeray) Loeb 2, London.
(1968) *Josephus III: The Jewish War,* 4-7 (trans. H. St. J. Thackeray) Loeb 3, London.
(1977) *Josephus V: Jewish Antiquities,* 5-8 (trans. H. St. J. Thackeray and R. Marcus) Loeb 5, London.
(1978) *Josephus VI: Jewish Antiquities,* 9-11 (trans. R. Marcus) Loeb 6, London.
Marcus Aurelius, (1979) *Marcus Aurelius,* (trans. C. R. Haines) Loeb, London.
New Documents illustrating early Christianity, 1 (1981) *A review of the Greek inscriptions and papyri published in 1976,* (ed G. H. R. Horsley) North Ryde.
New Documents illustrating early Christianity, 2 (1982) *A review of the Greek inscriptions and papyri published in 1977,* (ed G. H. R. Horsley) North Ryde.
New Documents illustrating early Christianity, 3 (1983) *A review of the Greek inscriptions and papyri published in 1978,* (ed G. H. R. Horsley) North Ryde.

New Documents illustrating early Christianity, 4 (1987) *A review of the Greek inscriptions and papyri published in 1979*, (ed G. H. R. Horsley) North Ryde.
New Documents illustrating early Christianity, 5 (1989) *Linguistic Essays*, (ed G. H. R. Horsley) North Ryde.
New Documents illustrating early Christianity, 6 (1992) *A Review of the Greek Inscriptions and Papyri published in 1980-81*, (ed S. R. Llewelyn) North Ryde.
New Testament: (1975) *The Greek New Testament*, (ed K. Aland, M. Black, C. M. Martini, B. M. Metzger, and A. Wikgren) 3rd edn, United Bible Societies.
(1988) *Synopsis Quattuor Evangeliorum*, (ed K. Aland) 4th edn, Stuttgart.
Origen, (1965) *Contra Celsum*, (trans. H. Chadwick) Cambridge.
Pausanias, (1954) *Description of Greece*, (trans. W. H. S. Jones) Loeb 1, London.
Philo, (1967) *Philo*, (trans. F. H. Colson) Loeb 9, London.
(1971) *Philo*, (trans. F. H. Colson and G. H. Whitaker) Loeb 1, London.
Philostratus, (1969) *The Life of Apollonius of Tyana*, (trans. F. C. Conybeare) Loeb 1 and 2, London.
Plato, (1967) *Laws*, (trans. R. G. Bury) vol. 1, Loeb 10, London.
(1968) *Laws*, (trans. R. G. Bury) vol. 2, Loeb 11, London.
(1975) *Timaeus*, (trans. R. G. Bury) Loeb 9, London.
(1977) *Phaedo, Phaedrus*, (trans. H. N. Fowler) Loeb 1, London.
(1977) *Protagoras*, (trans. W. R. M. Lamb) Loeb 2, London.
Pliny, (1966) *Natural History*, (trans. W. H. S. Jones) Loeb 7, (Books 24-27) London.
(1969) *Natural History*, (trans. W. H. S. Jones) Loeb 6, (Books 20-23) London.
(1971) *Natural History*, (trans. D. E. Eichholz) Loeb 10, (Books 36-37) London.
(1975) *Natural History*, (trans. W. H. S. Jones) Loeb 8, (Books 28-32) London.
Septuagint: (1887) *The Old Testament in Greek according to the Septuagint*, vol. 1 (Genesis - 4 Kings), (ed H. B. Swete) Cambridge.
(1891) *The Old Testament in Greek according to the Septuagint*, vol. 2 (1 Chronicles - Tobit), (ed H. B. Swete) Cambridge.
(1894) *The Old Testament in Greek according to the Septuagint*, vol. 3 (Hosea - 4 Maccabees), (ed H. B. Swete) Cambridge.
Sophocles, (1893) *The Ajax*, (ed R. C. Jebb) London.
(1954) *Sophocles I: Oedipus the King, Oedipus at Colonus,*

Antigone, (trans. D. Grene) in ed D. Grene and R. Lattimore, *The Complete Greek Tragedies,* Chicago.
(1981) *Oedipus Tyrannus,* (ed R. C. Jebb) reprint, Bristol.
(1982) *Oedipus Rex,* (ed R. D. Dawe) Cambridge.
Soranus, (1956) *Soranus' Gynecology,* (ed and trans. O. Temkin) Baltimore.
Strabo, (1968) *The Geography of Strabo,* (trans. H. L. Jones) Loeb 4, London.
(1970) *The Geography of Strabo,* (trans. H. L. Jones) Loeb 6, London.
Tacitus, (1961) *The Annals of Tacitus,* (ed H. Furneaux) vol. 2, Oxford.
Thucydides, (1955) *Thucydidis Historiae,* (ed H. S. Jones and J. E. Powell) vol.1, Oxford, reprint of (1942).
(1965) *Thucydides Book VII,* (introduction and commentary, K. J. Dover) Oxford.
Tod, M. N. (1946) *A Selection of Greek Historical Inscriptions,* 1, Oxford.
(1948) *A Selection of Greek Historical Inscriptions,* 2, Oxford.
Xenophon (1965) *Xenophon: Memorabilia and Oeconomicus,* (trans. E. C. Marchant) Loeb, London.
(1968) *Xenophon V: Cyropaedia,* (trans. W. Miller) Loeb 5, London.

Secondary

Aleshire, S. B. (1989) *The Athenian Asklepieion. The people, their dedications, and the inventories,* Amsterdam.
Allbutt, T. C. (1921) *Greek Medicine in Rome,* London.
Alter, R. and Kermode, F., eds (1989) *The Literary Guide to the Bible,* London.
Armstrong, A. H. (1965) *An Introduction to Ancient Philosophy,*London.
ed (1967) *The Cambridge History of Later Greek and Early Medieval Philosophy,* Cambridge.
Arndt, W. F. and Gingrich, F. W. (1957) *A Greek-English Lexicon of the New Testament and Other Early Christian Literature,* Chicago.
Arnold, E. V. (1958) *Roman Stoicism,* London.
Austin, M. and Vidal-Naquet, P. (1977) *Economic and Social History of Ancient Greece,* London.

Baker, D. A. (1965-6) "The 'Gospel of Thomas' and the Syriac 'Liber Graduum'" *NTS* 12: 49-55.
Barclay, W. (1976) *The Gospels and Acts,* 2 vols, London.
Barr, A. (1938) *A Diagram of Synoptic Relationships,* Edinburgh.
Barr, J. (1962) *The Semantics of Biblical Language,* London.
Barrett, C. K. ed (1956) *The New Testament Background: Selected Documents,* London.
Bartsch, H. -W. ed (1972) *Kerygma and Myth. A Theological Debate,* (trans. R. H. Fuller) London.
Bauer, W. (1972) *Orthodoxy and Heresy in earliest Christianity,* London.
Beare, F. W. (1981) *The Gospel according to Matthew,* Oxford.
Best, E. and Wilson, R. McL., eds (1979) *Text and Interpretation: Studies in the New Testament presented to Matthew Black,* Cambridge.
Bettenson, H. ed (1963) *Documents of the Christian Church,* London.
Betz, H. D. (1986) *The Greek Magical Papyri in Translation including the Demotic Spells,* Chicago.
Bieler, L. (1976) *ΘΕΙΟΣ ΑΝΗΡ,* Darmstadt.
Billings, T. H. (1979) *The Platonism of Philo Judaeus,* New York.
Black, M. and Smalley, W. A., eds (1974) *On language, culture, and religion: in honor of Eugene A. Nida,* The Hague.
Blumenthal H. J. and Markus, R. A., eds (1981) *Neoplatonism and Early Christian Thought. Essays in honour of A. H. Armstrong,* London.
Boer, W. den (1979) *Private Morality in Greece and Rome. Some historical aspects,* Leiden.
Bonefas, S. (1989) "The Musical Inscription from Epidauros" *Hesperia* 58: 51-62.
Bowra, M. (1930) *Tradition and Design in the Iliad,* Oxford.
(1970) *Sophoclean Tragedy,* Oxford.
Brandon, S. G. F. (1973) *Religion in Ancient History. Studies in Ideas, Men and Events,* London.
Bréhier, E. (1965) *The Hellenistic and Roman Age,* (trans. W. Baskin) Chicago.
Bremer, J. M. (1981) "Greek Hymns" in Versnel (1981a) 193-215.
Bremmer, J. (1983) *The Early Greek Concept of the Soul,* New Jersey.
Bright, J. (1974) *A history of Israel,* 2nd edn, London.
Brock, A. J. (1929) *Greek Medicine. Being extracts illustrative of medical writers from Hippocrates to Galen,* London.

Brown, R. E. (1962-3) "The Gospel of Thomas and St John's Gospel" *NTS* 9: 155-177.
Bruce, F. F. ed (1986) *The International Bible Commentary,* rev. edn, Michigan.
Brunt, P. A. (1971) *Social Conflicts in the Roman Republic,* London.
Burdon, C. (1987) "Such a Fast God: True and False Disciples in Mark's Gospel" *Theology* 734, 90: 89-97.
Burford, A. (1969) *The Greek temple builders at Epidaurus,* Liverpool.
Bultmann, R. (1956) *Primitive Christianity in its Contemporary Setting,* (trans. R. H. Fuller) London.
(1963) *History of the Synoptic Tradition,* New York.
Burkert, W. (1979) *Structure and History in Greek Mythology and Ritual,* London.
(1985) *Greek Religion: Archaic and Classical,* Oxford.
Burton, R. W. B. (1980) *The Chorus in Sophocles' Tragedies,* Oxford.
Bury, J. B. (1958) *History of the Later Roman Empire,* 2 vols, New York.
Bury, J. B. and Meiggs, R. (1975) *A History of Greece. To the Death of Alexander the Great,* 4th edn, London.
Cadbury, H. J. (1958) *The making of Luke-Acts,* London, reprint of (1927) New York.
(1969) *The Style and Literary Method of Luke,* New York, reprint of (1920) Cambridge.
Caird, G. B. (1979) *The Gospel of St Luke,* Harmondsworth.
(1980) *The Language and Imagery of the Bible,* London.
Campbell, A. F. (1989) *The study companion to Old Testament literature,* Wilmington.
Castiglioni, A. (1947) *A History of Medicine,* (ed and trans. E. B. Krumbhaar) New York.
Castrén, P. ed (1989) *Ancient and Popular Healing,* Symposium on Ancient Medicine 4-10 October 1986, Athens.
Caton, R. (1900) *The Temples and Ritual of Asklepios at Epidauros and Athens,* London.
Cave, C. H. (1964-5) "The obedience of unclean spirits" *NTS* 10: 93-97.
Chadwick, H. (1981) *The Early Church,* Harmondsworth.
Clarke, H. W. (1967) *The Art of the Odyssey,* Englewood Cliffs.
Clarke, M. L. (1960) *The Roman Mind: Studies in the History of Thought from Cicero to Marcus Aurelius,* Cambridge.
Cohn-Haft, L. (1956) *The Public Physicians of Ancient Greece,* Smith College Studies in History 42, Massachusetts.

Cranfield, C. E. B. (1959) *The Gospel according to St Mark*, Cambridge.
Creed, J. M. (1960) *The Gospel according to St. Luke*, London.
Croke, B. and Harries, J., eds (1982) *Religious Conflict in Fourth-Century Rome; A Documentary Study*, Sydney.
Cushman, R. E. (1958) *Therapeia: Plato's conception of philosophy*, Chapel Hill.
Davids, P. H. (1982) *The Epistle of James*, Exeter.
Detienne, M. and Vernant, J.-P. (1989) *The Cuisine of Sacrifice among the Greeks*, (trans. P. Wissing) Chicago.
Dibelius, M. (1935) *From Tradition to Gospel*, New York.
(1981) *James*, (rev. H. Greeven, trans. M. A. Williams, *Der Brief des Jakobus*, ed H. Koester) Philadelphia.
Dihle, A. (1982) *The Theory of Will in Classical Antiquity*, Berkeley.
Dodd, C. H. (1971) *The Founder of Christianity*, London.
Dodds, E. R. (1951) *The Greeks and the Irrational*, Berkeley.
(1965) *Pagan and Christian in an Age of Anxiety. Some aspects of religious experience from Marcus Aurelius to Constantine*, Cambridge.
(1973) *The Ancient Concept of Progress and other Essays on Greek Literature and Belief*, Oxford.
Dorey, T. A. ed (1968) *Cicero*, London.
Douglas, A. E. (1968) *Cicero*, Oxford.
Drane, J. W. (1979) *Jesus and the four Gospels*, England.
Duculot, J. ed (1979) *Les Actes des Apôtres: Traditions, rédaction, théologie*, BETL, 48, Leuven.
Easterling, P. E. and Muir, J. V., eds (1985) *Greek Religion and Society*, Cambridge.
Ebeling, G. (1973) *Introduction to a Theological Theory of Language*, (trans. R. A. Wilson) Philadelphia.
Edelstein, E. and L. (1945) *Asclepius. A collection and interpretation of the testimonies*, 2 vols, Baltimore.
Edelstein, L. (1966) *The Meaning of Stoicism*, Massachusetts.
(1967) *Ancient Medicine. Selected Papers of Ludwig Edelstein*, (ed O. Temkin and C. L. Temkin, trans. C. L. Temkin) Baltimore.
Efird, J. M. (1980) *The New Testament Writings: History, Literature & Interpretation*, USA.
Ehrenberg, V. (1969) *The Greek State*, Oxford.
Farmer, W. R. (1964) *The Synoptic Problem*, New York.
ed (1983) *New Synoptic Studies*, Macon.

Farnell, L. R. (1907) *Cults of the Greek States*, vol. 4, Oxford.
(1921) *Greek Hero Cults and Ideas of Immortality*, Oxford.
(1926) *The Higher Aspects of Greek Religion*, London.
Farrington, B. (1947) *Head and Hand in Ancient Greece. Four studies in the social relations of thought*, London.
(1961) *Greek Science*, Harmondsworth.
Ferguson, W. S. (1907) "The Priests of Asklepios. A new method of dating Athenian archons" *Classical Philology* vol. 1, no. 5: 131-173.
Festugière, A. J. (1960) *Personal Religion among the Greeks*, Berkeley.
Filoramo, G. (1990) *A History of Gnosticism*, (trans. A. Alcock) Oxford.
Finegan, J. (1975) *Encountering New Testament Manuscripts. A Working Introduction to Textual Criticism*, London.
Finley, M. I. (1954) *The World of Odysseus*, New York.
(1985) *The Ancient Economy*, rev. edn, London.
Flacélière, R. (1965) *Greek Oracles*, London.
Foerster, W. (1972) *Gnosis. A Selection of Gnostic Texts*, (English translation ed R. McL. Wilson) vol. 1: *Patristic Evidence*, Oxford.
(1974) vol. 2: *Coptic and Mandean Sources*, Oxford.
Fox, R. L. (1986) *Pagans and Christians*, Harmondsworth.
Geach, P. T. (1977) *Providence and Evil*, (Stanton lectures 1971-2) Cambridge.
Geisler, N. L. (1982) *Miracles and Modern Thought*, with a response by R. C. Sproul, Texas.
Goar, R. J. (1972) *Cicero and the State Religion*, Amsterdam.
Golden, M. (1988) "Male chauvinists and pigs" *Echos du Monde Classique/Classical Views* 32, 7: 1-12.
Goodwin, W. W. (1965a) *A Greek Grammar*, London, reprint of (1894).
(1965b) *Syntax of the Moods and Tenses of the Greek Verb*, London.
Goulder, M. D. (1974) *Midrash and Lection in Matthew*, London.
Gourevitch, D. (1984) *Le Triangle Hippocratique Dans Le Monde Gréco-Romain. Le Malade, Sa Maladie et Son Médecin*, Rome.
Grandjouan, C. (1989) "Hellenistic Relief Molds from the Athenian Agora" (completed by E. Markson and S. I. Rotroff) *Hesperia* Suppl. 23.
Grant, M. (1960) *The world of Rome*, New York.
Grant, R. M. (1952) *Miracle and Natural Law in Graeco-Roman and Early Christian Thought*, Amsterdam.
(1959) *Gnosticism and Early Christianity*, New York.

Grant R. M. and Freedman, D. N. (1960) *The Secret Sayings of Jesus*, London.
Graves, R. (1965) *Greek Myths*, London.
Green, P. (1970) *Armada from Athens*, London.
(1974) *Alexander of Macedon*, Harmondsworth.
Griffin, J. (1980) *Homer on life and death*, Oxford.
Grmek, M. D. (1989) *Diseases in the ancient Greek world*, (trans. M. Muellner and L. Muellner) Baltimore.
Grube, G.M.A. (1951) "The Gods of Homer" *The Phoenix* 5: .
Gundry, R. H. (1982) *Matthew: A Commentary on His Literary and Theological Art*, Michigan.
Guthrie, W. K. C. (1961) "The Religion and Mythology of the Greeks" in *The Cambridge Ancient History Revised Edition of Volumes I and II*, vol. 2, ch. 40, Cambridge.
Hainsworth, J. B. (1969) "Homer," *Greece & Rome*, New Surveys in the Classics no. 3, Oxford.
Halliday, W. R. (1936) "On the Treatment of Disease in Antiquity" in *Greek Poetry and Life. Essays presented to Gilbert Murray*, Oxford: 277-294.
Hammond, N. G. L. (1967) *A History of Greece*, 2nd edn, Oxford.
Hands, A. R. (1968) *Charities and social aid in Greece and Rome*, London.
Hankinson, R. J. (1991) *Galen: On the therapeutic method*, (trans. with an introduction and commentary) 2 vols, Oxford.
Harnack, A. (1908) *The sayings of Jesus*, (trans. J. R. Wilkinson) New Testament Studies 2, Crown Theological Library vol. 23, London.
(1911) *Luke the Physician*, (trans. J. R. Wilkinson) New Testament Studies 1, Crown Theological Library vol. 20, London.
Hart, G. D. ed (1983) *Disease in Ancient Man*, Toronto.
Harvey, A. E. (1982) *Jesus and the Constraints of History*, London.
Hatch, E. and Redpath, H. A. (1897-1906) *A Concordance to the Septuagint and the Other Greek Versions of the Old Testament*, 3 vols, Oxford.
Hawkins, J. C. (1909) *Horae Synopticae: Contributions to the study of the Synoptic Problem*, Oxford.
Heer, C. de (1968) *ΜΑΚΑΡ–ΕΥΔΑΙΜΩΝ–ΟΛΒΙΟΣ–ΕΥΤΥΧΗΣ*, Perth.
Helmbold, A. (1964-5) "Translation problems in the Gospel of Philip" *NTS* 10: 90-93.
Henderson, I. (1963) *Myth in the New Testament*, Studies in Biblical Theology no. 7, London.

Hengel, M. (1974) *Judaism and Hellenism. Studies in their Encounter in Palestine during the Early Hellenistic Period*, London.
(1985) *Studies in the Gospel of Mark*, London.
(1986) *Earliest Christianity*, containing *Acts and the History of Earliest Christianity. Property and Riches in the Early Church*, (trans. J. Bowden) London.
Herzog, R. (1931) "Die Wunderheilungen von Epidaurus" *Philologus*, Suppl. 22, 3, Leipzig.
ed (1932) *Kos*, Berlin.
Hill, D. (1967) *Greek Words and Hebrew Meanings: Studies in the semantics of soteriological terms*, Cambridge.
Hobart, W. K. (1882) *The Medical Language of St. Luke*, Dublin.
Hollenbach, P. W. (1982) "The Conversion of Jesus: From Jesus the Baptizer to Jesus the Healer" *ANRW* II/25.1: 196-219.
Horsley, G. H. R. (1987) "Name Change as an indication of Religious Conversion in Antiquity" *Numen* 34: 1017.
Hubbe, R. O. (1959) "Decrees from the precinct of Asklepios at Athens" *Hesperia* 28: 169-201.
Huck, A. (1959) *Synopsis of the First Three Gospels*, Oxford.
Hull, J. M. (1974) *Hellenistic Magic and the Synoptic Tradition*, Studies in Biblical Theology Second Series 28, London.
Hyde, W. W. (1946) *Paganism to Christianity in the Roman Empire*, Philadelphia.
(1963) *Greek Religion and its Survivals*, New York.
Jackson, R. (1988) *Doctors and diseases in the Roman Empire*, London.
Jeremias, J. (1954) *The Parables of Jesus*, London.
(1966) *The Eucharistic Words of Jesus*, London.
(1967) *The Prayers of Jesus*, Studies in Biblical Theology, Second Series 6, London.
(1975) *New Testament Theology*, vol. 1: *The Proclamation of Jesus*, London.
Jones, A. H. M. (1957) *Athenian Democracy*, Oxford.
(1970) *Augustus*, London.
Judge, E. A. (1980) *The Conversion of Rome. Ancient Sources of Modern Social Tensions*, The Macquarie Ancient History Association, 1, North Ryde.
Kavvadias, P. (1891) *Fouilles d'Épidaure*, Athens.
(1900) *Το ἱερόν τοῦ 'Ασκληπιοῦ ἐν 'Επιδαυρῷ καί ἡ θεραπεία τῶν ἀσθενῶν*, Athens.
Kee, H. C. (1968) "The Terminology of Mark's Exorcism Stories" *NTS* 14: 232-246.

(1983) *Miracle in the Early Christian World*, New Haven.
(1986) *Medicine, Miracle and Magic in New Testament Times*, Monograph series/Society for New Testament Studies 55, Cambridge.
Kee, H. C., Young, F. W. and Froehlich, K. (1957) *Understanding the New Testament*, New Jersey.
Kee, H. C. and Young, F. W. (1971) *The Living World of the New Testament*, London.
Kelsey, M. T. (1973) *Healing and Christianity*, New York.
Kerényi, C. (1959) *Asklepios. Archetypal Image of the Physician's Existence*, (trans. R. Manheim) Bollingen Series, 65, vol. 3, New York.
Kirk, G. S. (1962) *The Songs of Homer*, Cambridge.
Kittel, G. *et al.*, ed (1964) *Theological Dictionary of the New Testament*, (ed and trans. G. W. Bromiley) vol 2, Δ–H, Michigan.
(1965) *Theological Dictionary of the New Testament*, (ed and trans. G. W. Bromiley) vol 3, Θ–K, Michigan.
(1971) *Theological Dictionary of the New Testament*, (ed and trans. G. W. Bromiley) vol 7, Σ, Michigan.
(1972) *Theological Dictionary of the New Testament*, (ed and trans. G. W. Bromiley) vol 8, T–Υ, Michigan.
(1974a) *Theological Dictionary of the New Testament*, (ed and trans. G. W. Bromiley) vol 1, A–Γ, Michigan.
(1974b) *Theological Dictionary of the New Testament*, (ed and trans. G. W. Bromiley) vol 9, Φ–Ω, Michigan.
(1977) *Theological Dictionary of the New Testament*, (ed and trans. G. W. Bromiley) vol 5, Ξ–Πα, Michigan.
Knox, B. M. W. (1971) *Oedipus at Thebes*, New York.
Kraemer, R. S. (1992) *Her Share of the Blessings*, Oxford.
Krug, A. (1985) *Medizin in der Antike*, Beck.
Laistner, M. L. W. (1951) *Christianity and Pagan Culture in the Later Roman Empire*, New York.
Lampe, G. W. H. (1961) *A Patristic Greek Lexicon*, Oxford.
Lang, M. (1977) *Cure and Cult in Ancient Corinth: A guide to the Asklepieion*, Princeton.
Leake, C. D. (1960) "The Asklepian myths revalued" *Communication au XVII Congres International d'Histoire de la Medicine* 1, Athens.
Leaney, A. R. C. (1958) *A commentary on the gospel according to St. Luke*, London.
Lesky, A. (1967) *Greek Tragedy*, (trans. H. A. Frankfort) London.
Lexicon Iconographicum Mythologiae Classicae II (1984) Zürich.

Liddell, H. G. and Scott, R., eds (1968) *A Greek-English Lexicon,* with a supplement, Oxford.
Lloyd, G. E. R. and Owen, G. E. L., eds (1978) *Aristotle on mind and the senses. Proceedings of the Seventh Symposium Aristotelicum,* Cambridge.
Lloyd, G. E. R. (1966) *Polarity and Analogy. Two types of argumentation in early Greek thought,* Cambridge.
(1970) *Early Greek Science: Thales to Aristotle,* London.
(1973) *Greek Science after Aristotle,* London.
(1975) "The Hippocratic Question" *The Classical Quarterly* New Series 25: 171-192.
(1979) *Magic, reason and experience. Studies in the origin and development of Greek science,* Cambridge.
(1983) *Science, folklore and ideology. Studies in the life sciences in Ancient Greece,* Cambridge.
Lloyd-Jones, H. (1971) *The justice of Zeus,* Berkeley.
Lonie, I. M. (1964a) "Erasistratus, The Erasistrateans, and Aristotle" *Bulletin of the History of Medicine* 38, 5: 426-443.
(1964b) "The ῎ΑΝΑΡΜΟΙ ῎ΟΓΚΟΙ of Heraclides of Pontus" *Phronesis* 9, 2: 156-164.
(1965a) "Medical Theory in Heraclides of Pontus" *Mnemosyne* 18: 126-143.
(1965b) "The Cnidian Treatises of the Corpus Hippocraticum" *The Classical Quarterly* 59 (New Series 15) 1: 1-30.
(1965c) "The Hippocratic Treatise περὶ διαίτης ὀξέων " *Sudhoffs Archiv* 49, 1: 50-79.
(1973) "The Paradoxical Text `On The Heart'" *Medical History* 17, 2: 1-34.
(1981) *The Hippocratic Treatises "On Generation", "On the nature of the child", "Diseases IV",* Berlin.
Louw, J. P. (1982) *Semantics of New Testament Greek,* Pennsylvania.
Luck, G. (1985) *Arcana Mundi. Magic and the Occult in the Greek and Roman Worlds,* A Collection of Ancient Texts Translated, Annotated and Introduced by Georg Luck, Baltimore.
Lyons, J. (1977) *Semantics,* vol. I, Cambridge.
MacMullen, R. (1966) *Enemies of the Roman Order: Treason, Unrest, and Alienation in the Empire,* Massachusetts.
(1981) *Paganism in the Roman Empire,* New Haven.
Macquarrie, J. (1969) *The Scope of Demythologising Bultmann and his Critics,* New York.
Maddocks, M. (1981) *The Christian Healing Ministry,* London.
Massey, L. F. (1989) *Women and the New Testament,* Jefferson.

Mayor, J. B. (1913) *The Epistle of St. James*, London.
McCown C. C. (1940) *The Search for the Real Jesus*, New York.
McDevitt, A. S. (1972) "Sophocles' praise of man in the Antigone" *Ramus* 1, 2: 152-164.
Meijer, P. A. (1981) "Philosophers, intellectuals and religion in Hellas" in Versnel (1981a) 216-264.
Merriam, A. C. (1885) "Aesculapia as Revealed by Inscriptions" *Gaillard's Medical Journal* 40, 5: 355-375.
Meritt, Wade-Gery, McGregor, eds (1950) *The Athenian Tribute Lists*, vol. 3, Princeton.
Metzger, B. M. (1975) *A textual commentary on the Greek New Testament*, London.
Mikalson, J. D. (1983) *Athenian Popular Religion*, Chapel Hill.
Mitropoulou, E. (1975) *Kneeling worshippers in Greek and Oriental literature and art*, Athens.
(1976a) *Five Contributions to the problems of Greek Reliefs*, Athens.
(1976b) *Horses' heads and snake in banquet reliefs and their meaning*, Athens.
(1977) *Corpus 1 Attic Votive Reliefs of the 6th and 5th centuries BC*, Athens.
Moloney, F. J. (1986) *The living voice of the Gospel: the Gospels today*, Blackburn.
(1991) "Narrative Criticism of the Gospels" *Pacifica* 4: 180-201.
(1992) *Beginning the good news: a narrative approach*, Homebush.
Montefiore, H. (1960-1) "A comparison of the parables of the Gospel according to Thomas and of the Synoptic Gospels" *NTS* 7: 220-248.
Moorsel, G. van (1955) *The Mysteries of Hermes Trismegistus. A phenomenologic study in the process of spiritualisation in the Corpus Hermeticum and Latin Asclepius*, Utrecht.
Mortley, R. (1981a) *Ancient Mysticism. Greek and Christian Mysticism, and some comparisons with Buddhism*, The Macquarie Ancient History Association, 2, North Ryde.
(1981b) *Womanhood. The feminine in Ancient Hellenism, Gnosticism, Christianity and Islam*, Sydney.
(1986) *From word to silence*, 2 vols, Bonn.
Moulton, J. H. and Milligan, G. (1930) *The Vocabulary of the Greek Testament illustrated from the papyri and other non-literary sources*, London.

Moulton, R. G. (1899) *The Literary Study of the Bible. An Account of the Leading Forms of Literature represented in the Sacred Writings,* Boston.
Mueller, M. (1984) *The Iliad,* London.
Murnaghan, S. (1987) *Disguise and Recognition in the Odyssey,* Princeton.
Nasr, R. T. ed (1980) *The Essentials of Linguistic Science,* Essex.
Neusner, J. ed (1975) *Christianity, Judaism and other Greco-Roman cults,* 4 vols, Leiden.
Nilsson, M. P. (1986) *Cults, Myths, Oracles, and Politics in Ancient Greece,* Göteborg.
Oliver, J. H. (1953) *The Ruling Power. A Study of the Roman Empire in the second century after Christ through the Roman Oration of Aelius Aristides,* Philadelphia.
Opstelten, J. C. (1952) *Sophocles and Greek Pessimism,* (trans. J. A. Ross) Amsterdam.
Pagels, E. (1981) *The Gnostic Gospels,* New York.
(1988) *Adam, Eve and the Serpent,* New York.
Palagia, O. and Clinton, K. (1986) "A Decree from the Athenian Asklepieion" *Hesperia* 55: 137-139.
Palmer, H. (1968) *The Logic of Gospel Criticism,* London.
Parker, R. (1983) *Miasma: pollution and purification in early Greek religion,* Oxford.
Paton, W. R. and Hicks, E. L. (1891) *The Inscriptions of Cos,* Oxford.
Peek, W. (1969) "Inschriften aus dem Asklepieion von Epidauros" *Philologisch-historische* 60, 2, Berlin.
(1972) "Neue Inschriften aus Epidauros" *Philologisch-historische* 63, 5, Berlin.
Perrin, N. (1969) *What is Redaction Criticism?* Philadelphia.
Phillips, E. D. (1973) *Greek Medicine,* London.
(1987) *Aspects of Greek Medicine,* Philadelphia.
Pinault, J. R. (1986) "How Hippocrates Cured the Plague" *J. Hist. Med. and Allied Sciences* 41: 52-75.
Pleket, H. W. (1981) "Religious history as the history of mentality: The 'believer' as servant of the deity in the Greek world" in Versnel (1981a) 152-192.
Quispel, G. (1958-9) "Some remarks on the Gospel of Thomas" *NTS* 5: 276-290.
(1965-6) "'The Gospel of Thomas' and the 'Gospel of the Hebrews'" *NTS* 12: 371-382.
Radt, W. (1984) *Pergamon,* Istanbul.
Ramsay, W. M. (1908) *Luke the Physician,* London.

Rawson, B. (1978) *The Politics of Friendship: Pompey and Cicero*, Sydney.
Reinach, S. (1884) "Les chiens dans le culte d'Esculapeius" *Revue Archeologique* 3rd Series, 4: 129-139.
Reitzenstein, R. (1978) *Hellenistic Mystery-Religions. Their basic ideas and significance*, (trans. J. E. Steely) Pittsburgh.
Rhodes, P. J. (1981) *Commentary on the Aristotelian Athenaion Politeia*, Oxford.
Rist, J. M. (1969) *Stoic Philosophy*, Cambridge.
(1977) *Plotinus: The Road to Reality*, Cambridge.
Robertson, A. T. (1934) *A Grammar of the Greek New Testament in the Light of Historical Research*, 6th edn, New York.
Robinson, J. A. T. (1976) *Redating the New Testament*, London.
(1985) *The priority of John*, London.
Robinson, J. M. ed (1971) *Essays in Honour of Rudolf Bultmann. The Future of Our Religious Past*, London.
(1981) *The Nag Hammadi Library*, San Francisco.
(1983) *A New Quest of the Historical Jesus and Other Essays*, Philadelphia.
Roetzel, C. J. (1987) *The World that Shaped the New Testament*, London.
Ropes, J. H. (1960) *The Synoptic Gospels*, Oxford.
Rose, H. J. (1946) *Ancient Greek Religion*, London.
Rostovtzeff, M. (1941) *The Social and Economic History of the Hellenistic World*, 3 vols, Oxford.
Rouse, W. H. D. (1976) *Greek Votive Offerings. An Essay in the History of Greek Religion*, Hildesheim.
Rudolph, K. (1987) *Gnosis: The Nature and History of Gnosticism*, San Francisco.
Salmon, E. T. (1974) *A history of the Roman World from 30 BC to AD 138*, 6th edn, London.
Salter, W. H. (1936) "The Evidence for Telepathy" in Thomson and Toynbee (1936) 261-277.
Sandbach, F. H. (1975) *The Stoics*, London.
Sanders, E. P. and Davies, M. (1989) *Studying the Synoptic Gospels*, London.
Saunders, R. (1991) "Matthew versus Mark - An early Jewish/ Gentile controversy" in *Newsletter* 12, Society for the Study of Early Christianity, North Ryde.
Schmitt, B. (1972) *Cicero Scepticus*, The Hague.
Schouten, J. (1967) *The Rod and Serpent of Asklepios. Symbol of Medicine*, (trans. M. E. Hollander) Amsterdam.

Schweitzer, A. (1948) *The Quest of the Historical Jesus,* (trans. W. Montgomery) New York.
Schweizer, E. (1981) *The Good News according to Mark,* London.
Scullard, H. H. (1963) *From the Gracchi to Nero,* London.
Shackleton Bailey, D. R. (1971) *Cicero,* London.
Sherwin-White, S. M. (1978) *Ancient Cos,* Göttingen.
Sidebottom, E. M. (1986) *James, Jude, 2 Peter,* (The New Century Bible Commentary) Grand Rapids.
Simboli, C. R. (1921) *Disease-Spirits and Divine Cures,* New York.
Simon, B. (1978) *Mind and Madness in Ancient Greece: The Classical Roots of Modern Psychiatry,* Ithaca.
Smith, M. (1973) *The Secret Gospel: The Discovery and Interpretation of the Secret Gospel according to Mark,* New York.
(1978) *Jesus the magician,* San Francisco.
Smith, R. C. and Lounibos, J. (1984) *Pagan and Christian anxiety: a response to E. R. Dodds,* Lanham.
Smith, W. D. (1979) *The Hippocratic Tradition,* Ithaca.
Snodgrass, K. R. (1975) "The parable of the wicked husbandmen: is the Gospel of Thomas version the original?" *NTS* 20: 142-144.
Snyder, G. F. (1985) *Ante Pacem: Archaeological Evidence of Church Life Before Constantine,* USA.
Stanford, W. B. (1963) *The Ulysses Theme,* 2nd edn, Oxford.
Stanton, G. N. (1989) *The Gospels and Jesus,* (Oxford Bible Series) Oxford.
Stead, G. C. (1964-5) "Translation problems in the Gospel of Philip" *NTS* 10: 90-93.
Stockton, D. (1971) *Cicero: A Political Biography,* Oxford.
Stoldt, H. H. (1980) *History and Criticism of the Marcan Hypothesis,* Macon.
Stone, M. (1980) *Scriptures, Sects, and Visions: A Profile of Judaism from Ezra to the Jewish Revolts,* Oxford.
Straten, F. T. van (1981) "Gifts for the gods" in Versnel (1981a) 65-151.
Streeter, B. H. (1930) *The Four Gospels,* rev. edn, London.
Taylor, C. H. (1961) "The Obstacles to Odysseus' Return: Identity and Consciousness in *The Odyssey*" *The Yale Review* 50: 569-580.
Temkin, O. (1973) *Galenism: Rise and Decline of a Medical Philosophy,* Ithaca.
(1991) *Hippocrates in a World of Pagans and Christians,* Baltimore.

Tiede, D. L. (1972) *The charismatic figure as miracle worker,* Montana.
Theissen, G. (1983) *The Miracle Stories of the Early Christian Tradition,* (trans. F. McDonagh, ed J. Riches) Philadelphia.
(1987) *The Shadow of the Galilean. The Quest of the historical Jesus in narrative form,* (trans. J. Bowden) London.
Thomson, J.A.K. and Toynbee, A.J. eds (1936) *Essays in honour of Gilbert Murray,* London.
Thompson, J. M. (1950) *The Synoptic Gospels,* London.
Throckmorton, B. H. (1979) *Gospel Parallels. A Synopsis of the First Three Gospels,* Tennessee.
Tomlinson, R. A. (1983) *Epidauros,* London.
Tracy, S. V. (1975) "The lettering of an Athenian mason" with an introduction "The study of lettering" by S. Dow, *Hesperia* Suppl. 15.
Trench, R. C. (1961) *Synonyms of the New Testament,* London.
Tyrrell, W. B. and Brown, F. S. (1991) *Athenian Myths and Institutions : Words in Action,* Oxford.
Ullmann, S. (1972) *Semantics. An Introduction to the Science of Meaning,* Oxford.
Unnik, W. C. van (1963-4) "Three notes on the 'Gospel of Philip'" *NTS* 10: 465-469.
Vaughan, A. C. (1919) *Madness in Greek Thought and Custom,* Baltimore.
Vermes, G. (1983) *Jesus the Jew. A Historian's Reading of the Gospels,* London.
Versnel, H. S. ed (1981a) *Faith Hope and Worship: Aspects of religious mentality in the ancient world,* Leiden.
Versnel, H. S. (1981b) "Religious mentality in ancient prayer" in Versnel (1981a) 1-64.
Waldock, A. J. A. (1951) *Sophocles The Dramatist,* Cambridge.
Walls, A. F. (1960-1) "The references to apostles in the Gospel of Thomas" *NTS* 7: 266-270.
Walton, A. (1894) *The Cult of Asklepios,* Cornell Studies in Classical Philology 3, New York.
Whitman, C. H. (1951) *Sophocles. A Study of Heroic Humanism,* Harvard.
Wilamowitz-Moellendorff, U. von (1886) "Isyllos von Epidauros" *Philologische* 9, Berlin.
(1931-2) *Der Glaube der Hellenen,* 2 vols, Berlin.
Wilcox, M. (1961) "Qumran eschatology: some observations on 1QS" *Australian Biblical Review* 9, 1-4: 37-42.
(1965) *The Semitisms of Acts,* Oxford.

(1970-1) "The denial-sequence in Mark XIV. 26-31, 66-72" *NTS* 17: 426-436.
(1972-3) "The Judas-tradition in Acts I. 15-26" *NTS* 19: 438-452.
(1975) "A foreword to the study of the speeches in Acts" in Neusner (1975) 1: 205-226.
(1975-6) "Peter and the rock: a fresh look at Matthew XVI. 17-19" *NTS* 22: 73-88.
(1977) "'Upon the tree' - Deut 21: 22-23 in the New Testament" *JBL* 96: 85-99.
(1977-8) "The 'prayer' of Jesus in John XI. 41b-42" *NTS* 24: 128-132.
(1979a) "On investigating the use of the Old Testament in the New Testament" in Best and Wilson (1979) 231-243.
(1979b) "The promise of the 'seed' in the New Testament and the Targumim" *JSNT* 5: 2-20.
(1979c) "Luke and the Bezan Text of Acts" in Duculot (1979) 447-455.
(1982) "Jesus in the Light of his Jewish Environment" *ANRW* II/25.1: 131-195.
(1984) "Semitisms in the New Testament" *ANRW* II/25.2: 978-1029.
(1989) "Jesus as Healer" (transcript of a lecture, incomplete, delivered at Macquarie University, North Ryde).
Wilkinson, J. (1980) *Health and Healing. Studies in New Testament Principles and Practice,* Edinburgh.
Wilson, R. McL. (1956-7) " The New Testament in the gnostic Gospel of Mary" *NTS* 3: 236-243.
(1958-9) "The coptic 'Gospel of Thomas'" *NTS* 5: 273-276.
(1959-60) "Some recent studies in Gnosticism" *NTS* 6: 32-44.
Winer, G. B. (1877) *A Treatise on the Grammar of New Testament Greek,* (trans. W. F. Moulton) Edinburgh.
Wisse, F. (1971) "The Nag Hammadi Library and the Heresiologists" *Vigiliae Christianae* 25: 205-223.
Woodhead, A. G. (1959) *The Study of Greek Inscriptions,* Cambridge.
Wrede, W. (1971) *The Messianic Secret,* Cambridge.
Young, D. (1967) "Never a Blotted Line? Formula and Premeditation in Homer and Hesiod" *Arion* 6: 279-324.
Young, D. G. (1968) *Three Odes of Pindar. A literary study of Pythian 2, Pythian 3, and Olympian 7,* Leiden.

Part Two
Appendices

Section One
The language of healing in the Greek world

Appendix 1 : 1
Greece and the Aegean

Appendix 1 : 2
Greece

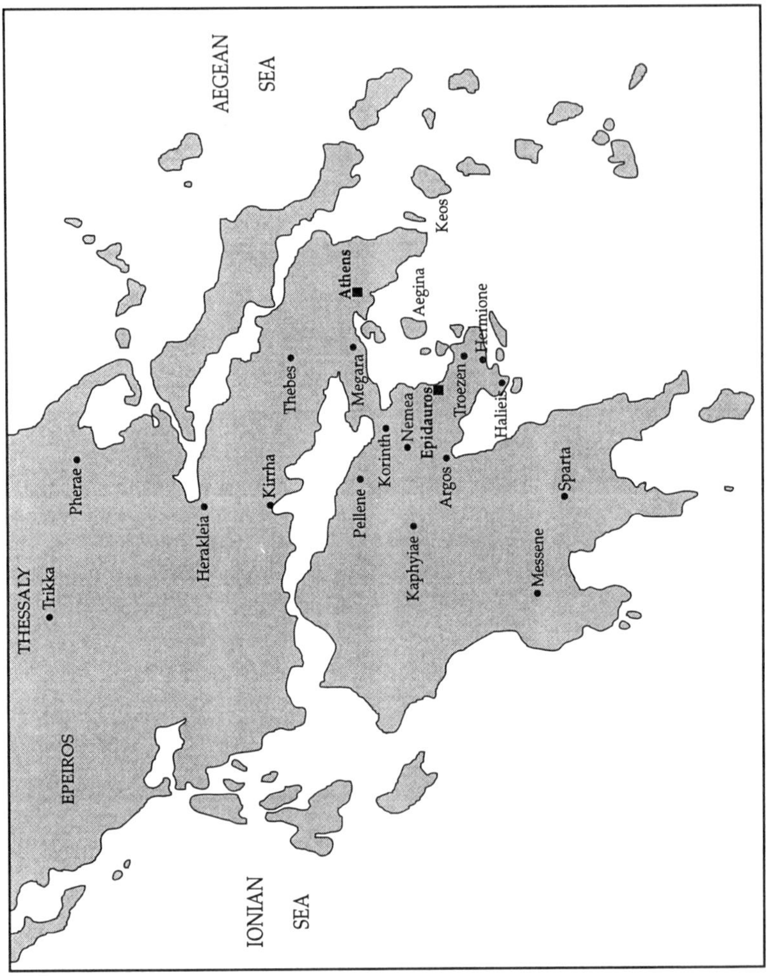

Appendix 2 : 1

Inscriptiones Graecae IV^2 1, no. 121 [2nd half of 4th c. BC]

Reference	Name origin gender age	Illness	Method	Words	Comment
Title	Θεός Τύχα [ἀγ]αθά [Ἰά]ματα τοῦ Ἀπόλλωνος καὶ τοῦ Ἀσκλαπιοῦ			God (and) Good Fortune Cures of Apollo and Asklepios	
1	Kleo of ? female, adult	5-year pregnancy	(i) name, description and duration of complaint (ii) abaton sleep (iii) result: birth of a son able to both wash himself and walk about. The boy was born outside the temple precincts, it being forbidden for either death or birth to occur within the enclosure. (see Pausanias 2.27.1) The inscription concludes with the words: he made her sound. (iv) description of offering	(iii) καὶ μιν ἔθηκε ὑγιῆ	The first inscription shows a basic formula of four steps: (i) identity of patient and nature of complaint (ii) sleep (iii) result, and (iv) comment about votive offering. These four steps will be used as the basis for an analysis of each inscription in the tables presented in Appendices 2:1 and 2:2.

2	Ithmonika of Pellene female, adult	(i) infertility (ii) 3-year pregnancy	i) name, description and duration of complaint Two visits: 1. *re* pregnancy (ii) sleep vision: conversation with Asklepios *re* possibility of pregnancy with a daughter. Asklepios asked if she had any further request, to which she gave a negative reply (iii) result: pregnancy 2. *re* birth (ii) sleep vision: conversation with Asklepios, about the further request *re* the birth, omitted before (iii) result: birth of a daughter outside the sacred precincts (see **1** above)	(ii) ὄψιν εἶδε· ἐδόκει (ii) ὄψ[ι]ν εἶδε· ἐδόκει	This patient required two visits to the god: the first *re* pregnancy, the second *re* giving birth. On both occasions the patient slept, and in her sleep had a vision of a conversation with Asklepios. This episode illustrates: (a) the need for specific requests, and (b) the god's sense of humour. Step (iv) omitted

3	? of ? male, adult	paralysed fingers	(i) unidentified man, but complaint precise: all fingers paralysed except one + a description of his incredulity and derision *re* cures and inscriptions (ii) sleep vision: (a) at a game of dice the god intervened and stretched out (ἐκτεῖναί) the man's fingers, after which the man was able to stretch them out himself, and (b) a conversation with the god about his incredulity, and a pronouncement *re* his future name (῎Απιστος)! (iii) result: when day came he departed sound	(i)+: θεωρῶν δὲ τοὺς ἐν τῶι ἱαρῶι | πίνακας ἀπίστει τοῖς ἰάμασιν καὶ ὑποδιέσυρε τὰ ἐπιγράμμα[[τ]]α (ii) ὄψιν εἶδε· ἐδόκει (iii) ἁμέρας δὲ γενομένας ὑγιὴς ἐξῆλθε	The motif of disbelief is here introduced, and dealt with, as in **4** below. But cf. *IG* IV^2 1, no. 122, 36 (App. 2:2, **36**) where Kaphisias is punished for his disbelief and derision, (although Asklepios relents and heals him) Step (iv) omitted

4	Ambrosia of Athens female, adult	blind in one eye	(i) name and nature of complaint + a description of her incredulity and derision *re* the healing of the blind and lame by seeing a dream (ἐνύπνιον) (ii) sleep vision: (a) conversation with the god that in return for her cure she should dedicate a silver pig (iv) to the temple as a memorial of her ignorance, and (b) surgery on the diseased eyeball, and application of a drug (iii) result: when day came she departed sound	(i)+: περιέρπουσα δὲ | [κατὰ τ]ὸ ἱαρὸν τῶν ἱαμάτων τινὰ διεγέλα ὡς ἀπίθανα καὶ ἀδύνα‖τα ἐόν]τα, χωλοὺς καὶ τυφλοὺ[ς] ὑγιεῖς γίνεσθαι ἐνύπνιον ἰδόν‖τας μό]νον (ii) ὄψιν εἶδε· ἐδόκει (ii) (b) ἀνσχίσσαι οὑ τὸν ὄπτιλλον τὸν νοσοῦντα και φάρμ[α|κόν τι ἐγχέ]αι· (iii) ἁμέρας δὲ γενομένας ὑγιὴς ἐξῆλθε	As above (**3**) the motif of disbelief and derision is introduced and dealt with, but cf. *IG* IV^2 1, no. 122, 36 (App. 2:2, **36**) where Kaphisias is punished for his disbelief and derision, (although Asklepios relents and heals him) Step (iv) included as part of step (ii)
5	? of ? male, boy	voiceless	(i) unidentified boy, mute, accompanied by his father + extra information about preliminary sacrifices, rites, and duties of temple servants, + a demand by the temple servant that the father promise to bring the thank-offering within one year (step iv), to which the boy replied, startling his father (ii) omitted (iii) result: after that he became well	(i)+: προεθύσατο καὶ | [ἐπόησε τὰ] νομιζόμενα . . . ὁ παῖς ὁ τῶι θεῶι πυρφορῶν (iv) ὁ δὲ πατὴρ ἐκπλαγεὶς (iii) καὶ ἐκ τούτου ὑγιὴς ἐγέ‖νετο	Step (iv) included as part of step (i), which also contains extra material about preliminary sacrifices, rites, and duties of temple servants. The role of the bystander is introduced, here exhibiting amazement: ἐκπλήσσω. The role of the bystander is also important in New Testament healing stories, and in accounts of Vespasian's healing miracles (Tacitus *Histories* 4. 81)

6	Pandaros of Thessaly male, adult	marks on forehead	(i) name and nature of complaint (ii) sleep vision: the god bandaged his marks and commanded that the headband be dedicated as an offering (iv) (iii) result: when he took off the headband his forehead was free of marks (iv) he dedicated the headband to the temple as instructed	(i) στίγματα (ii) ὄψιν εἶδε· ἐδόκει	This inscription provides the background for the following one, in which Pandaros' friend, Echedoros, is punished for not delivering the thankoffering entrusted to him, and for being untruthful when questioned about it
7	Echedoros of ? male, adult	liar	(i) name and nature of complaint, with additional information about his failure to deliver Pandaros' money to the temple at Epidauros (ii) sleep vision: (a) conversation with the god in which he was untruthful, and (b) the god's action in applying Pandaros' headband to his forehead, followed by the instructions to take off the headband after leaving the abaton, wash his face, and look at his reflection in the water (iii) his face retained its own marks, plus those of Pandaros	(ii) ὄψιν εἶδε· ἐδόκει	This is the first of two examples of punishment for failure to bring (promised?) thank-offerings. (Cf. *IG* IV^2 1, no. 122, 22, App. 2:2, **22**). Echedoros lied concerning the monetary offering for the temple entrusted to him by his friend Pandaros, and made an (empty ?) promise regarding his own offering. Thus this story concerns step (iv), a step vital to the continuing survival and growth of the sanctuary. (Cf. Acts 5. 1-11)

8	Euphanes of Epidauros male, boy	stone	(i) name and nature of complaint (ii) sleep vision: the god asked what his payment would be for a cure, to which the boy replied that he would give him ten dice, and the god laughed and promised to cure him (iii) result: when day came he departed sound	(ii) ἐνε[κά]θευδε· ἔδοξε "τί μοι δωσεῖς, αἴ τύ[κα ὑγιῆ ποιήσω;" . . . τὸν δὲ θεὸν γελά[σαντα (iii) ἀμέρας δὲ γενομένας ὑγιὴς ἐξῆλθε	Again the god's sense of humour is noted, (cf. **2**), and his ability to communicate with people of all ages
9	? of ? male, adult	total blindness, missing one eyeball	(i) unidentified adult male of unstated origin, nature of complaint amplified with anatomical details and details of the reaction of others: both eyes blind, but one missing the eyeball itself and having only the eyelids. Bystanders in the temple laughed at his silliness in thinking that he would recover his sight (ii) sleep vision: the god prepared some drug and, opening his eyes, poured it in (iii) when day came he departed seeing with both eyes	(ii) ὄψις ἐφάνη· ἐδόκει τὸν θεὸν ἑψῆσαί τι φά[ρμακον, ἔπε]ιτα διαγαγόντα τὰ βλέφα[ρα ἐγχέαι εἰς αὐτά (iii) ἀμέρ[ας δὲ γενομέν]ας βλέπων ἀμφοῖν ἐξῆλθε	Here the faith of the patient is contrasted with the disbelief and derision of bystanders

10	? of ? male, boy (porter)	broken goblet	(i) unidentified porter of unstated origin. Specific purpose of journey to the temple unstated. Problem: broken goblet, caused by a fall. Passer-by scoffed at porter's attempts to mend the goblet, saying that it was even beyond the power of Asklepios to do so (ii) omitted (iii) on arrival the goblet found to be entirely whole (iv) porter's master dedicated the goblet to the god	(i) τὸγ κώθωνα κατε[αγ]ότα (iii) ὑγιῆ τὸγ κώθωνα γεγενημέ|νον	Again a passer-by who expresses disbelief is shown to be ignorant. This is the only occasion in *IG* IV^2 1, 121-122, where an inanimate object is restored so that it is sound. The same word (ὑγιῆ) is used to describe the restoration of the goblet as is used in formulae to describe the restoration of people.
11	Aeschines of ? male, adult?	blindness	(i) name and description of cause of problem: when the suppliants were already asleep, Aeschines climbed a tree and tried to see into the abaton. He fell onto some fencing which injured his eyes, causing blindness (ii) temple sleep (iii) he became whole	(ii) ἐνε|κάθευδε (iii) καὶ ὑγιὴς ἐγένετο	
12	Euhippos of ? male, adult	spear point embedded in jaw	(i) name, origin unstated, battle wound: point of spear embedded in jaw for six years (ii) temple sleep during which the god extracted the spearhead and gave it to Euhippos (iii) when day came he departed healthy, holding the spearpoint in his hands	(iii) ἁμέρας | δὲ γενομένας ὑγιὴς ἐξῆρπε τὰν λόγχαν ἐν ταῖς χερσὶν ἔχων	

13	? of Torone male, adult	ingested leeches	(i) unidentified man from Torone, illness described as "leeches", + the cause of illness cited thus: he had swallowed them, having been tricked by his stepmother who had thrown them into a potion which he drank. (ii) dream: the god cut open his chest, took out the leeches, gave them to him, and stitched up his chest (iii) at daybreak he departed well, holding the leeches	(i) δεμελέας +: κατέπιε δ' αὐτὰ δολωθεὶς ὑπὸ ματρυιᾶς ἐγ κυ|κᾶνι ἐμβεβλημένας ἐκπιών (ii) οὗτος ἐγκαθεύδων ἐνύπνιον εἶδε· ἔδοξέ οἱ (iii) ἁμέρας δὲ γενομένας ἐξῆλθε τὰ θηρία ἐν ταῖς χερσὶν ἔχων καὶ ὑγιὴς ἐγένετο	(i) This occurrence of δεμελέας is the only citation of this word in Liddell and Scott (1968). Is this the first appearance of the wicked stepmother (ματρυιᾶς) in inscriptions? (Metaphorically a rocky coast is called μητρυιὰ νεῶν!)
14	? of ? male, adult	genital (kidney?) stone ('Ανὴρ ἐναἰδοίωι λίθον)	(i) unidentified man of unstated origin, illness described (ii) dream: he was lying with a handsome boy, and when he had a seminal discharge he ejected the stone, picked it up, and went out holding it in his hands (iii) implied in dream	(i) ἐν αἰδοίωι λίθον (ii) οὗτος ἐνύπνιον εἶδε· ἐδόκει (ii) cont. & (iii) ? ἐξῆλθε ἐν ταῖς χερσὶν ἔχων	

15	Hermodikos of Lampsakos male, adult	bodily paralysis	(i) name, origin and illness described (ii) temple sleep: the god healed him, and ordered him, upon leaving, to bring to the temple as large a stone as he could (iii) and (iv) the man brought the stone which "lies before the abaton"	(i) ἀκρατὴς τοῦ σώματος (ii) (iii) & (iv) τοῦτον ἐγκαθεύ|δοντα ἰάσατο καὶ ἐκελήσατο ἐξελθόντα λίθον ἐνεγκεῖν εἰς τὸ | ἱαρὸν ὁπόσσον δύναιτο μέγιστον· ὁ δὲ τὸμ πρὸ τοῦ ἀβάτου κείμε|νον ἤνικε	Cf. *IG* IV^2 1, no. 125 [3rd c. BC] (App. 2:3), an inscription dedicated by Hermodikos of Lampsakos, which seems to be the large stone referred to here. However there Hermodikos describes his illness as an abscess in the chest and paralysis of the hands. The dating is also an embarrassment.
16	Nikanor of ? male, adult	lameness	(i) name, origin unstated, illness described (ii) variation: while he was sitting wide-awake, a boy snatched his crutch from him and ran away (iii) Nikanor got up, pursued the boy and became well	(iii) καὶ ἐκ τούτου ὑγιὴς ἐγένετο	

17	? of ? male, adult	malignant sore in toe	(i) unidentified man of unstated origin; illness described, and healing agent: a serpent. (ii) & (iii) variation: during the day, the man was sitting outside on a seat, having been taken there by the temple servants (ὑπὸ τῶν θε|ραπόντων) when he fell asleep. As he was sleeping a snake came out of the abaton, healed his toe with its tongue, and went back to the abaton. However, the patient's vision was of a beautiful youth anointing his toe with a drug	(i) 'Ανὴρ δάκτυλον ἰάθη ὑπὸ ὄφιος (ii) & (iii) ὕπνου δέ νιν | λαβόντος ἐν τούτωι δράκων ἐκ τοῦ ἀβάτου ἐξελθὼν τὸν δάκτυλον | ἰάσατο τᾶι γλώσσαι καὶ τοῦτο ποιήσας εἰς τὸ ἄβατον ἀνεχώρησε | πάλιν. ἐξεγερθεὶς δὲ ὡς ἦς ὑγιής, ἔφα ὄψιν ἰδεῖν, δοκεῖν νεανίσ|κον εὐπρεπῆ τὰμ μορφὰν ἐπὶ τὸν δάκτυλον ἐπιπῆν φάρμακον	Cf. the Archinos relief, # 3369, National Archaeological Museum, Athens. See App. 3:1, **3**.
18	Alketas of Halieis male, adult	blindness	(i) name, origin and illness specified (ii) dream: the god approached and opened the man's eyes with his fingers, and he first saw the trees in the sanctuary (iii) at daybreak he departed sound	(ii) οὗτος τυφλὸς ἐὼν ἐνύπνιον εἶδε· ἐδόκει οἱ ὁ θεὸς ποτελθὼν τοῖς δα|κτύλοις διάγειν τὰ ὄμματα καὶ ἰδεῖν τὰ δένδρη πρᾶτον τὰ ἐν τῶι ἱαρῶι (iii) ἁμέρας δὲ γε|νομένας ὑγιὴς ἐξῆλθε	Cf. Jesus' healing of the blind man in Mark 8.22-26

19	Heraieus of Mytilene male, adult	baldness	(i) name, origin and nature of illness described. He was bald with an abundant beard, and ashamed because of the laughter of others (ii) temple sleep: the god anointed his head with some drug (iii) his hair grew	(ii) ἐνεκάθευδε. τὸν δὲ ὁ θεὸς χρίσας φαρμάκωι τὰν κεφαλὰν (iii) ἐπόησε | τρίχας ἔχειν	Although the complaint is described in physical terms, the patient suffered mental anguish because of the reaction of others
20	Lyson of Hermione male, boy	blindness	(i) name, origin and illness specified (ii) variation: while wide-awake he had his eyes cured by one of the dogs in the temple (iii) he went away healthy	(ii) & (iii) οὗ[τος] ὕπαρ ὑπὸ κυνὸς τῶν | κατὰ τὸ ἱαρὸν θε[ραπ]ευόμενος τοὺς ὀπτίλλους ὑγ[ιὴ]ς ἀπῆλθε	The boy goes away healthy after being treated by one of the temple dogs. The verb used is θεραπεύω. This verb appears again in *IG* IV^2 1, 122, 26 (see App. 2:2, **26**), again describing the treatment of a boy by one of the temple dogs.

Of the twenty cures recorded, 13 record the wholeness of the person (or object) when they depart from the sanctuary by using some form of ὑγιὴς. Otherwise their cure (or punishment) is precise: a daughter was born (**2**); stigmata vanished (**6**) or were increased (**7**); a man who had arrived blind, and with only one eyeball, departed seeing with both eyes (**9**); a man left holding his (genital?) stone (**14**); and a bald man's hair grew again (**19**). Two other general terms are used: Hermodikos (**15**) is healed: ἰάσατο. ἰάομαι is also used to describe the action of a serpent (ἰάθη . . . ἰάσατο) which heals the toe of a patient in the daytime, while he is sleeping in the grounds (**17**). However the man's dream differs from the reality: in his dream he saw a beautiful youth anointing his toe. The verb θεραπεύω occurs only once: to describe the action of a temple dog in treating a blind boy while he was wide-awake. The boy departs whole: ὑγ[ιὴ]ς (**20**).

Several themes emerge: the importance of votive offerings, the importance of honesty and humility, the importance of hope and trust. Healing methods are usually recounted as the patient's vision while he/she is sleeping, in a regular formula: "the patient slept and saw a vision/dream. And it seemed to him/her that ...". However **17** makes it obvious that a dream vision might not correspond to reality, even if the end result is the same. Dream visions can include conversations with the god, commands from the god, or actions by the god and his helpers, such as touching, surgery, application of drugs, or other actions. Patients can also be healed by temple serpents (**17**) or temple dogs (**20**).

Of the 20 inscriptions, 16 describe male patients (13 adult males and three boys), and 3 adult female patients. One incident records the restoration of a broken goblet (**10**). The goblet when mended is described as ὑγιῆ, and perhaps this use of the word provides us with a clue as to its meaning.

Of the 20 inscriptions, 19 describe a restoration to wholeness, while one describes a punishment (**8**). Echedoros receives stigmata in addition to the ones he already has because he fails to bring offerings entrusted to him, lies about them, and then makes an (empty?) promise about his own votive offering. His punishment serves as a warning to others. Disbelief and derision in the god's healing power is also noted and dealt with (**3 & 4**), both patients having a permanent reminder of their initial disbelief, as well as a successful healing outcome.

Appendix 2 : 2

Inscriptiones Graecae IV^2 1, no. 122 [2nd half of 4th c. BC]

Reference	Name origin gender age	Illness	Method	Words	Comment
21	Arata of Lacedaemon female, adult	dropsy	(i) identity and nature of illness (ii) mother's temple dream: surgical action by Asklepios who cut off her daughter's head and hung her upside down, allowing fluid matter to drain out, then took down the body and fitted the head back on the neck (iii) on her return home the mother found her daughter in good health	(iii) θυγατέρα ὑγιαίνουσαν	Mother fulfilled cult ritual on behalf of her daughter, who remained in Lacedaemon, but "saw" the same dream (τὸ αὐτὸ ἐνύπνιον ὡρακυῖαν), so healing can occur at a distance. Cf. Luke 7. 10, where the present participle of ὑγιαίνω occurs (as here) as the final description of the slave's health when the centurion returned home; and Luke 15. 27, where a slave tells of a father's joy because his son has returned home ὑγιαίνοντα
22	Hermon of Thasos male, adult	(1) blindness (2) blindness	1: (i) identity and nature of illness (ii) omitted (iii) he was healed (iv) he failed to bring the thank offerings, and the god made him blind again 2: (ii) he slept again in the temple (iii) he was made well	1 (iii) : ἰάσατο 1 (iv) : ἐπόησε τυφλὸν αὖθις 2 (iii) : ὑγιῆ κατέστασε	(1: iv): again (cf. *IG* IV^2 1, no. 121, 7, App. 2:1, 7) punishment is inflicted for failure to bring thank offerings, but (2): Hermon is given a second chance. Presumably he brought thank offerings on this occasion. It is curious that the inscription omits details here.

23	Aristagora of Troezen	tapeworm (in stomach)	(i) identity and nature of illness (ii) temple dream at Troezen: the sons of the god cut off her head, and, unable to put it back on, send a messenger to Asklepios at Epidauros asking him to come + at daybreak the priest sees (ὁρῆι) her head cut off from her body, (ii) cont. : at nightfall she saw a vision (ὄψιν): Asklepios had come from Epidauros, fastened her head onto her neck, cut open her belly, removed the tapeworm and stitched her up again (iii) after that she became well	(iii) καὶ ἐκ τούτου ὑγ[ι]ὴ]ς ἐγένετ[ο	This inscription (part [ii]) seems to imply, (a) that the healing practice of the sons of Asklepios is inferior to that of their father (cf. the synoptic account of the healing of the epileptic boy: Matthew 17. 14-20, Mark 9. 14-29, Luke 9. 37-43); (b) that Asklepios cannot be in both places at once; and, (c) that Epidauros is the most important healing sanctuary.
24	Aristokritos of Halieis male, boy	missing	(i) identity and nature of problem: the boy was lost and trapped (ii) father slept in abaton and saw a dream: the god led him to the place where his son was (iii) father quarried through the cliffs and found his son after seven days	(iii) ἀ[ν]ηῦρε τὸμ παῖ̣δα	Father fulfilled cult ritual on behalf of his son (cf. **21** above)

25	Sostrata of Pherae female, adult	pregnant with worms	(i) identity and nature of illness (ii) carried into the temple, but **no dream** (iii) on the way home, met by a man, who, after the problem had been explained, cut open her abdomen and removed two washbasins full of worms, stitched her up and made her well. (iv) Asklepios revealed his presence and asked her to send thank-offerings back to Epidauros	(iii) καὶ ποήσας ὑ[γιῆ] | τὰν γυναῖκα	This is an extraordinary thing to allow a stranger to do to a very sick person, who is undertaking an arduous journey. This story shows that Asklepios is not confined to practise within the temple precincts.
26	? of Aegina male, boy	neck growth	(i) unidentified boy from Aegina, description of illness (ii) omitted: no dream, but while he was awake, (iii) one of the temple dogs licked him and made him well	(iii) κύων τῶν ἱαρῶν ὑ[παρτ]ᾶι γλώσσαι ἐθεράπευσε | καὶ ὑγιῆ ἐπόη[σ]ε	Cf. *IG* IV^2 1, no. 121, 20 (App. 2:1, **20**) where a blind boy is treated by one of the temple dogs, and departs healthy. Again the verb used to describe the treatment given by the dog is θεραπεύω
27	? of ? male, adult	abdominal abscess	(i) unidentified man, origin unknown, illness described (ii) temple dream: temple servants gripped and bound the man, Asklepios cut open his belly and removed the abscess, stitched him up again, and released him (iii) he walked out sound, + the floor of the abaton was covered with blood	(iii) καὶ ἐ|κ τούτου ὑγιὴς ἐξῆ|λθ|ε, τὸ δὲ δάπεδον ἐν τῶι ἀβάτωι αἵματος κατά | πλεον ἧς	(iii) contains tangible evidence

28	Kleinatas of Thebes male, ?	lice	(i) identity and description of illness (ii) temple vision: Asklepios stripped him, stood him upright, naked, and brushed the lice from his body with a broom (iii) when day came he left the temple well	(iii) ἁμέρας δὲ γ[ε]νομένας ἐκ τοῦ ἀβάτου ὑγιὴς ἐξῆλθε	
29	Hagestratos of ? male, adult	headaches, and insomnia caused by headaches	(i) identity and description of illness (ii) abaton dream: the god cured (ἰασάμενος) his headaches, and taught him the lunge used in the pancratium (iii) when day came he departed well, and not long afterwards won in the pancratium at the Nemean games	(ii) ὁ θεὸς ἰασάμενος τὸ τᾶς κεφαλᾶς ἄλγος (iii) ἁμέρας δὲ γενη|θείσας ὑγιὴς ἐξῆλθε	(iii) contains tangible evidence
30	Gorgias of Herakleia male, adult	pus (arrow wound in lung)	(i) identity and description + of illness: in a battle he had been wounded by an arrow in the lung and for a year and a half had suppurated so badly that he filled 67 basins with pus (ii) temple vision: the god extracted the arrow (iii) when day came he departed well, holding the point of the arrow in his hands	(iii) ἁμέρας δὲ γενομένας ὑγιὴς ἐξῆλθε τὰν ἀκί|δα ἐν ταῖς χερσὶ φέρων	(iii) contains tangible evidence

31	Andromache of Arybbas in Epeiros female, adult	infertility	(i) identity, and description of problem (ii) temple dream: a handsome boy uncovered her, and then the god touched her with his hand (iii) a son was born to her	(ii) ἐδόκει αὐτᾶι π[α]ῖς τις ὡραῖ|ος ἀγκαλύψαι, μετὰ δὲ τοῦτο τὸν θεὸν ἅψασθαί οὑ τᾶι [χη]ρί· (iii) ἐκ δὲ τού|του τᾶι 'Ἀδρομάχαι υ[ἱ]ὸς ἐξ 'Αρύββα ἐγένετο	This is the only occasion Asklepios' healing touch is described in *IG* IV^2 1, nos. 121 and 122. The verb used is ἅπτομαι. ἅπτομαι is also the most frequently used synoptic word chosen to describe Jesus' healing touch. See Appendices 7:12 and 7:13
32	Antikrates of Knidos male, adult	blindness (spear wound in battle)	(i) identity, and description + of illness: in battle he had been hit by a spear in both eyes and had become blind, and the spear point was embedded in his face (ii) sleep vision: the god extracted the missile and inserted pupils into his eyelids (iii) when day came he walked out sound	(iii) ἁμέρας δὲ γενομένας ὑγιὴς ἐξῆλθ[ε]	

33	Thersandros of Halieis male, adult?	consumption	(i) identity and illness specified (ii) **no vision** (iii) was carried back to Halieis. While resting at home, a serpent from Epidauros, which had coiled itself around the axle of the wagon, descended and cured Thersandros. The city of Halieis, not knowing whether to keep the serpent, or return it to Epidauros, sent to Delphi for an oracle. The god decided they should keep the serpent, and set up a sanctuary of Asklepios at Halieis, make an image of him, and set it up in the temple there. (iv) the city erected a sanctuary and followed the rest of the god's commands.	(iii) ὁ δράκων ἀπὸ τᾶς ἁμά[ξα]ς καταβὰ[ς τ]ὸν Θέρσανδρον ἰάσατο	The verb chosen to describe the serpent's treatment is *ἰάομαι*, as at *IG* IV^2 1 no. 121, 17 (App. 2:1, **17**) The sanctuaries at Athens (*SEG* 25.226) and also at Rome (Livy, *Periocha* 11, *Ab Urbe Condita* 29.11.1) were established in the same manner: by the arrival of a temple snake from Epidauros
34	? of Troezen female, adult	infertility	(i) identity illegible, problem specified. (ii) temple dream: conversation with Asklepios about the preferred sex of her child (male). (iii) within a year a son was born to her	(iii) μετὰ δὲ τοῦ]το ἐ[ντὸς ἐνι] | αυτοῦ ἐγένετο αὐτᾶι υἱ[ός]	

35	? of Epidauros male, adult	lameness	(i) name unknown, origin and illness cited. (ii) sleep vision: the god broke his crutch and ordered him to get a ladder and climb as high as possible to the top of the sanctuary. The man tried, lost his courage, and rested on the cornice, gave up and came down little by little. Asklepios was angry at first, but then laughed at the man's cowardice. (iii) the man dared to do it after it was daylight, and walked out unhurt	(iii) δὲ ἀμ(έρας γενομένας ἐπιτελέσαι ἀσκηθὴς ἐ‖ξῆλθε (Herzog)	
36	Kaphisias of ? male, adult	crippled foot	(i) name specified, origin illegible, body part identified ++ his disbelief and derision of Asklepios' cures. When riding Kaphisias was injured and taken to the temple, where he entreated the god earnestly (ii) omitted (iii) the god made him well	(i) ++: Καφισί[ας – – – τὸμ πόδα. οὗτος τοῖς τοῦ 'Ασ‖κλαπιοῦ θεραπεύμασιν ἐπ[ιγελῶν "χωλούς,' ἔφα, "ἰάσασθαι ὁ θεὸς ψεύ]‖δεται λέγων· ὡς, εἰ δύναμιν ε[ἶχε, τί οὐ τὸν "Αφαιστον ἰάσατο'; ὁ δὲ θεὸς] . . . (iii) [. . . ὁ θεὸς ὑγιῆ ἐπόησε.]	The number of times ἰάομαι is used in this inscription is unusual. Both occurrences are supplied by Herzog, as is the final (common) formula containing ὑγιῆ.

37	Kleimenes of Argos male, adult	bodily paralysis	(i) name, origin, and illness cited (ii) abaton vision: the god wound a red woollen fillet around his body and led him for a bath to a cold lake. When he behaved in a cowardly fashion Asklepios said he would not heal those who were cowardly, but would do no harm to those who came to his temple full of hope, but would send them away well (iii) when he woke up he took a bath and walked out unhurt	(ii) δειλῶς] | δ' αὐτοῦ ἔθεν διακειμένου τὸν Ἀ[σκλαπιὸν οὐκ ἰασεῖσθαι τοὺς δει]λοὺς . . . ἀλλ' ὑγιῆ ἀποπ[εμψοῖ· . . . (iii) . . . ἐξεγερθεὶς δ' ἐλοῦτο καὶ ἀσ]κηθὴς ἐξῆλθε	Again ἰάομαι in this inscription is supplied by Herzog
38	Diaitos of Kur? (Kirrha?) male, adult	paralysis of knees	(i) name, origin and problem cited (ii) temple dream: the god ordered his servants to carry him outside and lie him down in front of the temple. After this the god drove his horses and chariot around him three times, trampled on him with his horses and the man gained instant control of his knees (iii) when day came he walked out sound	(iii) ἁμέρας δὲ γενομένας ὑγ[ιὴς ἐξῆλθε.]	
39	Agamede of Keos female, adult	infertility	(i) name, origin and problem cited (ii) temple dream: that a serpent lay on her belly (iii) five children were born to her	(ii) ἐδό]κει οἱ ἐν τῶι ὕπνωι δράκων ἐπὶ τᾶς γαστ[ρὸς κεῖσθαι· καὶ ἐκ τούτου] (iii) | παῖδές οἱ ἐγένοντο πέντε	

40	Timon of ? male, adult	wound under the eye	(i) name cited, origin illegible, problem cited (ii) temple dream: the god rubbed down a herb and poured it in his eye (iii) he became well	(iii) καὶ ὑγι]ὴς ἐγένετο	
41	Erasippe of Kaphyiae female, adult	worms	(i) name, origin and problem cited ++ stomach swollen, burning? and unable to keep anything inside (ii) temple dream: the god massaged her stomach, kissed her, and gave her a vomit inducing drug. She vomited and her dress was full of it (iii) when day came she saw her dress full of evil matter which she had vomited, and became well	(iii) ἁμέρας δὲ γ[ενομένας ἑώρη πᾶν] | τὸ λῶπουν μεστὸν ὧν ἐξήμεσε κακῶν, καὶ ἐκ το[ύτου ὑγιὴς ἐγένε]το	
42	Nikasibula of Messene female, adult	infertility	(i) name, origin and problem cited (ii) temple dream: the god approached her with a snake creeping behind him, and she had intercourse with the snake (iii) within a year she had two sons	(ii) ἐδόκει οἱ ὁ θεὸς δράκοντα μεθ[έρποντα ἵκειν] | φέρων παρ' αὐτάν, τούτωι δὲ συγγενέσθαι αὐτά· (iii) παῖδές οἱ ἐγένοντο εἰς ἐνιαυτὸν ἔρσενες δύ[ε	

43	? of Kios male, adult	gout	(i) name illegible, origin and complaint cited ++ while awake he walked towards a goose which bit his feet and made them bleed (ii) omitted (iii) by making the feet bleed the goose made him well	(iii) τούτου ὕπαρ χὰν ποτιπορευο[μένου δάκνων] | αὐτοῦ τοὺς πόδας καὶ ἐξαιμάσσων ὑγιῆ ἐπόη [σε]	

Of the 23 inscriptions recorded, 15 patients are males (including 2 boys). Of the 8 females, 4 seek help for infertility, 3 for worms, and 1 on behalf of her dropsical daughter. Serpents (**33**, **39**, **42**) figure in three accounts, a dog once (**26**), and a goose (**43**) once. Two men are punished, one for failing to bring votive offerings as promised (**22**), and one for laughing at accounts of Asklepios' cures (**36**), although both are healed when they are suitably repentant and remorseful. Parents request help on behalf of their children (**21** & **24**). Votive offerings are not so prominent on this stele, although tangible evidence of cures is offered: blood on the abaton floor (**27**), a dress full of vomit (**41**), basins full of worms (**25**), victory at the Nemean Games (**29**), an arrow point (**30**), a sanctuary established (**33**), babies are born (**34**, **39**, **42**).

ὑγιὴς again appears frequently as a part of a closing formula, ἰάομαι also appears, and θεραπεύω again describes only the treatment given by temple dogs to patients (both boys) who are wide awake. ἅπτομαι appears as the description of Asklepios' healing touch. Male children are preferred to female children by those who seek to become pregnant. Again dream visions include conversational encounters with the god, as well as actions taken by him : surgery, the preparation and administration of drugs, as well as psychological instructions (**35**), bizarre actions (**38**), and gymnastic instruction (**29**).

Appendix 2 : 3

Inscriptiones Graecae IV² 1, no. 125 [3rd c. BC]

Ἑρμόδικ[ος Λαμψακ]ηνός	Hermodikos of Lampsakos
σῆς ἀρετῆς [παράδειγμ]', Ἀσκληπιέ, | τόνδε ἀνέ[θηκα π]έτρον ἀειρά|μενος, πᾶσι[ν ὁρᾶν] φανερόν, | ὄψιν σῆς τέχνης· πρὶν γὰρ | σὰς εἰς χέρας ἐλθεῖν | ἔνπυος ὢν στῆθος χει|ρῶν τε ἀκρατής· σὺ δέ, | Παιάν, πείσάς με ἄρασθαι | τόνδε, ἄνοσον διάγειν.	As an example of your power, Asklepios, I have dedicated this rock which I lifted up, manifest for all to see, an evidence of your art. For before coming into your hands I had an abscess in my chest and was paralysed in my hands. But you, Paean, by ordering me to lift this rock,[1] made me live free from disease.

[1] See *IG* IV² 1, no. 121 [2nd half of 4th c. BC] 15, and App. 2:1, **15**.

Appendix 2 : 4

Inscriptiones Graecae IV² 1, no. 126 [*ca.* 160 AD]

Text and translation from Edelstein, E. and L. (1945) *Asclepius: A collection and interpretation of the testimonies*, Baltimore, 1: **T432** 247-8

Ἐπὶ ἱερέως Π. Αἰλ. Ἀντιόχου

Μ. Ἰούλιος Ἀπελλᾶς Ἰδριεὺς Μυλασεὺς μετεπέμφθην
ὑπὸ τοῦ θεοῦ, πολλάκις εἰς νόσους ἐνπίπτων καὶ ἀπεψί-
αις χρώμενος. κατὰ δὴ τὸν πλοῦν ἐν Αἰγείνῃ ἐκέλευσέν
με μὴ πολλὰ ὀργίζεσθαι. ἐπεὶ δὲ ἐγενόμην ἐν τῷ ἱερῷ, ἐ-
κέλευσεν ἐπὶ δύο ἡμέρας συνκαλύψασθαι τὴν κεφαλήν,
ἐν αἷς ὄμβροι ἐγένοντο, τυρὸν καὶ ἄρτον προλαβεῖν, σέλει-
να μετὰ θρίδακος, αὐτὸν δι' αὑτοῦ λοῦσθαι, δρόμῳ γυμνάζε-
σθαι, κιτρίου προλαμβάνειν τὰ ἄκρα, εἰς ὕδωρ ἀποβρέξαι, πρὸς
λα
ταῖς ἀκοαῖς ἐν βανείῳ προστρίβεσθαι τῷ τοίχωι, περιπάτῳ χρῆ-
σθαι ὑπερῴῳ, αἰώραις, ἁφῇ πηλώσασθαι, ἀνυπόδητον περι-
πατεῖν, πρὶν ἐνβῆναι ἐν τῶι βαλανείῳ εἰς τὸ θερμὸν ὕδωρ
οἶνον περιχέασθαι, μόνον λούσασθαι καὶ Ἀττικὴν δοῦναι
τῶι βαλανεῖ, κοινῇ θῦσαι Ἀσκληπιῷ, Ἠπιόνῃ, Ἐλευσεινίαις,

In the priesthood of Poplius Aelius Antiochus

I, Marcus Julius Apellas, an Idrian from Mylasa, was sent for by the god, for I was often falling into sickness and was suffering from dyspepsia. In the course of my journey, in Aegina, the god told me not to be so irritable. When I arrived at the temple, he told me for two days to keep my head covered, and for these two days it rained; to eat cheese and bread, celery with lettuce, to wash myself without help, to practise running, to take lemonpeels, to soak them in water, near the (spot of the) *akoai* in the bath to press against the wall, to take a walk in the upper portico, to take some passive exercise, to sprinkle myself with sand, to walk around barefoot, in the bathroom, before plunging into the hot water, to pour wine over myself, to bathe without help and to give an Attic drachma to the bath attendant, in common to offer sacrifice to Asclepius, Epione and the Eleusinian goddesses,

γάλα μετὰ μέλιτος προλαβεῖν· μιᾷ δὲ ἡμέρᾳ πιόντός μου γάλα μόνον, εἶπεν· 'μέλι ἔμβαλλε εἰς τὸ γάλα, ἵνα δύνηται διακόπτειν.' ἐπεὶ δὲ ἐδεήθην τοῦ θεοῦ θᾶττόν με ἀπολῦσαι, ᾤμην (ν)άπυϊ καὶ ἅλσὶν κεχρειμένος ὅλος ἐξιέναι κατὰ τὰς ἀκοὰς ἐκ τοῦ ἀβάτου, παιδάριον δὲ ἡγεῖσθαι θυμιατήριον ἔχον ἀτμίζον καὶ τὸν ἱερέα λέγειν 'τεθεράπευσαι, χρὴ δὲ ἀποδιδόναι τὰ ἴατρα.' καὶ ἐποίησα, ἃ εἶδον, καὶ χρείμενος μὲν τοῖς ἁλσὶ καὶ τῶι νάπυϊ ὑγρῶι ἤλγησα, λούμενος δὲ οὐκ ἤλγησα. ταῦτα ἐν ἐννέα ἡμέραις ἀφ' οὗ ἦλθον. ἥψατο δέ μου καὶ τῆς δεξιᾶς χιρὸς καὶ τοῦ μαστοῦ, τῇ δὲ ἑξῆς ἡμέρᾳ ἐπιθύοντός μου φλὸξ ἀναδραμοῦσα ἐπέφλευσε τὴν χεῖρα, ὡς καὶ φλυκταίνας ἐξανθῆσαι· μετ' ὀλίγον δὲ ὑγιὴς ἡ χεὶρ ἐγένετο. ἐπιμείναντί μοι ἄνηθον μετ' ἐλαίου χρήσασθαι πρὸς τὴν κεφαλαλγίαν εἶπεν. οὐ μὴν ἤλγουν τὴν κεφαλήν. συνέβη οὖν φιλολογήσαντί μοι συνπληρωθῆναι· χρησάμενος τῷ ἐλαίῳ ἀπηλάγην τῆς κεφαλαλγίας. ἀναγαργαρίζεσθαι ψυχρῷ πρὸς τὴν σταφυλὴν—καὶ γὰρ περὶ τούτου παρεκάλεσα τὸν θεὸν—τὸ αὐτὸ καὶ πρὸς παρίσθμια. ἐκέλευσεν δὲ καὶ ἀναγράψαι ταῦτα. χάριν εἰδὼς καὶ ὑγιὴς γενόμενος ἀπηλλάγην.

to take milk with honey. When one day I had drunk milk alone he said, "Put honey in the milk so that it can get through." When I asked of the god to relieve me more quickly I thought I walked out of the abaton near the (spot of the) *akoai* being anointed all over with mustard and salt, while a small boy was leading me holding a smoking censer, and the priest said: "You are cured but you must pay up the thank-offerings."

And I did what I had seen, and when I anointed myself with the salts and the moistened mustard I felt pains, but when I bathed I had no pain. That happened within nine days after I had come. He touched my right hand and also my breast. The following day as I was offering sacrifice the flame leapt up and scorched my hand, so that blisters appeared. Yet after a little the hand got well. As I stayed on he said I should use dill along with olive oil against my headaches. I usually did not suffer from headaches. But it happened that after I had studied, my head was congested. After I used the olive oil I got rid of the headache. To gargle with a cold gargle for the uvula-since about that too I had consulted the god- and the same also for the tonsils. He bade me also inscribe this. Full of gratitude I departed well.

Appendix 2 : 5

Inscriptiones Graecae IV^2 1, no. 126 [ca. 160 AD]

'Επὶ ἱερέως Π. Αἰλ. 'Αντιόχου : In the priesthood of Publius Aelius Antiochus

Name origin gender	Illness	Method	Words	Comment
Marcus Julius Apellas an Idrian adult male from Mylasa (see App. 1:1)	chronic ill health and suffering from dyspepsia πολλάκις εἰς νόσους ἐνπίπτων καὶ ἀπεψίαις χρώμενος	At Aegina: the god ordered me not to be so irritable At Epidauros: the god said to keep my head covered for two days (it rained for 2 days), to eat cheese and bread, celery with lettuce, to wash without help, to practise running, to take lemonpeels soaked in water, in the bath to press against the wall, to walk in the upper portico, to take passive exercise, to sprinkle myself with sand, to walk around barefoot, before plunging into a hot bath to pour wine over myself, to bathe without help and give an Attic drachma to the bath attendant, to offer sacrifice in common to Asklepios, Epione, and the Eleusinian goddesses, to take milk with honey ... (vision: the priest's instructions) ... He touched my right hand and also my breast ... the hand became sound (from blisters) ... He said to use dill with olive oil for headaches, to gargle with cold water for the uvula and tonsils	ἐκέλευσέν με μὴ πολλὰ ὀργίζεσθαι τεθεράπευσαι, χρὴ δὲ ἀποδιδόναι τὰ ἴατρα ἥψατο δέ μου καὶ τῆς δεξιᾶς χιρὸς καὶ τοῦ μαστοῦ ὑγιὴς ἡ χεὶρ ἐγένετο χάριν εἰδὼς καὶ ὑγιὴς γενόμενος ἀπηλλάγην	This patient came a long way, having been sent for (μετεπέμφθην) by the god. He seems to have almost a personal relationship with Asklepios: he comes at his command, stops at another of his sanctuaries on the way, where he is commanded not to be irritable, and after following instructions involving diet, exercise, independent action, payment, and religious obligations, he has the temerity to ask the god to hurry things along a bit! Asklepios therefore fulfils the role of advisor, physician and friend. Apellas stays at the sanctuary for an extended period (nine days, plus a further indeterminate period: ἐπιμείναντί μοι). He is careful to note that he has fulfilled all the commandments of the god, one of which was this particular inscription. The method of healing, i.e. the instructions for diet and exercise, are Hippokratic in character, and presuppose a patient with the wealth and leisuretime to be able to obey them.

Appendix 2 : 6

Inscriptiones Graecae IV^2 1, no. 127 [224 AD]

Text and translation from Edelstein, E. and L. (1945) *Asclepius: A collection and interpretation of the testimonies*, Baltimore, 1: **T424** 238

Τιβ. Κλ. Σευῆρος
Σινωπεὺς Ἀπόλ-
λωνι Μαλεάτᾳ καὶ
Σωτῆρι Ἀσκληπιῷ
κατ' ὄναρ, ὃν ὁ θεὸς
εἰάσατο ἐν τῷ ἐν-
κοιμητηρίῳ, χοι-
ράδας ἔχοντα ἐπ[ὶ]
τοῦ τραχή[λου] καὶ
καρκίνον [τ]ọ(ῦ ὠ)τός,
ἐπιστὰς ẹ[ν]αργῶς,
οἷος ἐστ – – – –.
ἐπὶ ἱερέω[ς] Μάρ.
Αὐρ. Πυ[θοδώρ]ου
ἔτους ἑ[κ]ạ[το]σ-
στοῦ πρώṭọυ.

Tib. Cl. Severus of Sinope to Apollo Maleatas and the Savior Asclepius according to a dream; him, the god healed in the sleeping hall of the temple, when he had scrofulous swellings in the glands of the neck and an ulcer of the ear, appearing to him clearly, as he is . . . under the priesthood of Marcus Aurelius Pythodorus. In the 101st year.

Appendix 3 : 1

1. Six worshippers (four adults and two children) facing Asklepios and his family: Asklepios, head of Epione or Hygieia?, two sons and three daughters (Athens, N.M. 1402)

2. The relief of the doctors (Athens, N.M. 1332)

Healing method

3. Votive relief of Archinos to Amphiaraos, representing scenes of the procedure of therapy of the patient Archinos who is the dedicator of the relief. As Archinos slept in the temple the snake licked him and he dreamt that the god treated him. He recovered and in gratitude offered this relief, showing himself in the three positions.

The eyes featured at the top of the relief are unique in Greek votive reliefs.
(400-350 BC) (from the sanctuary of Amphiaraos at Oropos) (Athens, N.M. 3369)

4. Asklepios in the act of healing (Piraeus Museum 405)

Healing method

5. Asklepios in the act of healing; extending his arm over the sick person (Attic relief, end of 5th century BC) (Athens, N.M. 1841)

6. Person at left lifts a patient onto a bed, helped by person at head of bed. Asklepios is bending over the bed; Hygieia stands behind him at right (Athens, N.M. 2373)

Healing method

7. Hygieia? standing at left, Asklepios seated with arm around a standing suppliant. Snake under throne (Athens, N.M. 1352)

8. Woman giving a patient a footbath (Athens, N.M. 1914)

The Athenian family

9. Votive relief from the asklepieion at Athens depicting an Athenian family (Athens, N.M. 1384)

10. (Athens, N.M. 1408)

The Athenian family

11. (Athens, N.M. 1345)

Sacrificial Offerings

12. Asklepios seated on right, Hygieia standing beside him. On the altar an offering of bread and fruit (Athens, N.M. 1335)

Sacrificial Offerings

13. Suppliants with sacrificial ox (Athens, N.M. 1429)

14. Asklepios seated, showing hands, staff and legs. Hygieia standing. Suppliants with sacrificial ram (Athens, N.M. 1333)

Anatomical votives

15. Anatomical votives of the late 5th to 4th centuries BC (Room of the Asklepieion) (Korinth Museum)

16. Relief depicting a varicose vein (Athens, N.M. 3526)

Appendix 3 : 2

The language of healing in inscriptions at Athens

Reference	Greek	Comment
1 *IG* II^2, no. 4388	Ἀκεσώ Ἰασώ Πανάκεια Ἠ[πιόνη]	Chosen because it names the wife of Asklepios (Epione), and three of their daughters (Akeso, Iaso, and Panakeia). See #1352, National Archaeological Museum, Athens; and cf. Aristophanes *Ploutos* 701-3. The three daughters personify 'cure'.
2 *IG* II^2, no. 4486	Ἀσκληπιῷ καὶ Ὑγείᾳ | καὶ τοῖς ἄλλοις θεοῖς | πᾶσι καὶ πάσαις κατὰ ὄ|νειρον . . . (1–4)	Chosen to illustrate the usual dedication at Athens. Asklepios, and his daughter, Hygieia, are generally named in inscriptions from the asklepieion, other gods being included in the general "and all the others", as here.
3 *IG* II^2, no. 772 [ca. 252-1 BC] (but dated 270-69 BC by Pritchett and Meritt)	. . . ἐπειδὴ πάτριόν ἐστιν τοῖς ἰατρο[ῖ]ς ὅσοι δημοσιεύουσιν θύειν τῶι Ἀσκ|ληπιῶι καὶ τεῖ Ὑγιείαι δὶς τοῦ ἐνιαυ|τοῦ ὑπέρ τε αὑτῶν καὶ τῶν σωμάτων ὧν ἕ|καστοι ἰάσαντο, . . . (9–13)	"...Whereas it is an ancestral custom of the physicians who are in the service of the state to sacrifice to Asclepius and to Hygieia twice each year in behalf of themselves and of the people whom they healed..." (Trans. Edelstein, in Edelstein [1945] 1: **T 552** 309) This illustrates the cordial and cooperative nature of the relationship between Asklepios and physicians. There does not seem to have been any competition between temple and civilian medicine.

4 *IG* II^2, no. 974 [137-6 BC]	. . . [. . . θύσας δὲ καὶ ὑπὲρ] | [τ]ῆς βουλῆς καὶ τοῦ δήμου καὶ παίδ[ων καὶ γυναικῶν καὶ καλλιερή]‖[σ]ας ἐν ἅπασιν ἀπήγγειλεν τεῖ βο[υλεῖ γεγονέναι τὰ ἱερὰ καλὰ καὶ] | σωτήρια· . . . (13–16) . . . [κ]αθ' ἑκάστην ἡμέραν γινομένας θε[ραπείας ἐν αἷς τοῖς θύουσιν] (24)	See Hubbe (1959) 169-201, especially 188-194, for a restoration of this decree, and a commentary. These lines have been chosen to illustrate the recording of sacrifices with good omens which had been made on behalf of the Boule, the demos, and children and wives. The sacrifices were καλὰ καὶ σωτήρια (15-16). Hubbe (1959) 193 *re* line 24 states: "θε[ραπείας was restored already by Koehler in the older Corpus. The word could refer to divine cures, but since this is not specifically stated, we are probably meant to understand it in the more general sense of *worship*". It would be extremely unlikely for this word to refer to divine cures, as at Athens it is used rarely, and usually means either *worship* or *service* in a religious context, or *treatment* in a medical context (see chapter three). Hubbe cites *IG* VII, no. 235, lines 21-22, from the Amphiaraion, for an occurrence of θεραπεύω in reference to divine healing (see below, **15**, and App. 3:6).
5 *IG* II^2, no. 4475a	ἡ βο[υλὴ] | Σωσικλῆν Ἡσιόδου Σφή[ττιον] | ἰαθέντα Ἀσκληπιῷ καὶ Ὑ[γιείαι] | προστάξαντος τοῦ [θεοῦ]	Chosen to illustrate the use of ἰάομαι (ἰαθέντα) to describe divine healing.
6 *IG* II^2, no. 4533 (*IG* IV^2, 1, no. 132)	. . . Παιήων . . . (1) . . . ὦ ἰώμενος . . . (30)	Chosen to illustrate some epithets of (i) Asklepios: Παιήων (line 1); and (ii) of his son Telesphoros: ἰώμενος (line 30) that are part of the healing vocabulary.
7 *IG* II^2, no. 4514 [2nd c. AD] (for the full inscription see Appendix 3:3)	. . . ἰασάμενος . . . (9) . . . σῶσόν με . . . (13) . . . ἰασάμενος . . . (14) . . . ὦ Παιὰν Ἀσκληπιέ . . . (22) . . . [ἰα]θεὶς . . . ἀνίατον . . . (23)	Chosen to illustrate the use of ἰάομαι and σῴζω, and the epithet Παιὰν.

8 *IG* II², no. 354 [328-7 BC]	. . . ἐπειδὴ δὲ Ἀνδροκλῆς ἱερ⟦εὺς λαχὼ⟧ν τ[ῶι Ἀσ]κληπιῶι ἐπιμελεῖται το[ῦ] | τε ἱεροῦ καὶ [τῶν] ἄλλων ὧν αὐτῶι οἱ νόμοι πρ|οστάττουσιν κ[αλ]ῶς καὶ εὐσεβῶς καὶ οἱ λαχ|όντες ἐπιμελητ[α]ὶ τῆς εὐκοσμίας τῆς περ[ὶ] | τὸ θέατρον ἀπέφη[να]ν αὐτὸν ἐν τῶι δήμω[ι χρ]⟦ήσιμον γεγονέναι α[ὐ]τοῖς περὶ τὴν ἐπ[ιμέλ]⟧ειαν τοῦ θεάτρου· . . . (13–19) . . . [ὁ ἱερεὺς γεγονέναι ἐν τοῖς] ἱεροῖς ἐ[φ' ὑγιεί]⟦αι καὶ σωτηρίαι τῆς βουλῆς κ]αὶ τοῦ [δήμου.] (43–4)	For a restoration, and a commentary, see Hubbe (1959) 171-174. Chosen to illustrate the use of ἐπιμελέομαι (lines 13 and 16; and its cognate form, lines 18-19) in the context of maintaining order. This decree shows that the priest of Asklepios was responsible for maintaining order in the adjacent theatre, as well as in the asklepieion. The decree also illustrates the contiguous use of the terms "health" and "safety" (ἐ[φ' ὑγιεί]⟦αι καὶ σωτηρίαι) in relation to the Boule and the demos.
9 *IG* II², no. 775 [244-3 BC]	. . . τοῖς ἱεροῖς ἐφ' ὑγιείαι κα[ὶ σωτηρίαι τῆς βουλῆς καὶ] | τοῦ δήμου καὶ παίδων καὶ γ[υναικῶν ⟦καὶ τοῦ βασιλέως⟧ (14–15)	For a restoration, and a commentary, see Hubbe (1959) 174-178. Chosen to illustrate the use of the terms "health" and "safety" (as above, **8**) in relation to the Boule and the demos, and children and wives.
10 *IG* II², no. 1019 [138-7 BC]	[ὁ ἱερεὺ]ς τοῦ Ἀσκληπιοῦ Λεωνίδη[ς Νικοκράτου | Φλυεὺς ἐμφανίζει τό τε τέμενος καὶ τὸν ναὸν καὶ πάντα τὰ ἐ]ν αὐτῶι θεραπείας καὶ ἐπι[σκευῆς δεό|μενα] (13–14)	For a commentary, see Hubbe (1959) 187-188. Chosen to illustrate the use of θεραπείας in the context of caring for sacred property, in an inscription where its presence is not restored (as in *IG* II², no. 974, **4** above), but certain.

11 *IG* II², no. 950 [165-4 BC]	. . . ἐπειδὴ ὁ ἱερεὺς τοῦ Ἀσκληπιοῦ | τοῦ ἐν ἄστει Πρωταγόρας Νικήτου Περγασῆθεν πρό|σοδον ποιησάμενος πρὸς τὴμ βουλὴν ἀπήγγελκεν | ἐν αἷς πεποίηται θυσίαις γεγονέναι τὰ ἱερὰ καλὰ | καὶ σωτήρια πᾶσιν Ἀθηναίοις καὶ τοῖς οἰκοῦσιν τὰς πό[[λ]ε̲ις τὰς Ἀθηναίων· ἐπιμεμέληται δὲ καὶ τῆς τοῦ ἱε[[ρ]ο̲ῦ̲ εὐκοσμίας καὶ τὰς θυσίας ἁπάσας τέθυκεν κατὰ [τὰ] | ψ̲η̲φ̲ί̲σματα· . . . (5–12) . . . ὅτι δοκεῖ τεῖ βουλεῖ | ἐπαινέσαι τὸν ἱερέα τοῦ Ἀσκληπιοῦ τοῦ ἐν ἄστει . . . (16–17)	For a restoration, and a commentary, see Hubbe (1959) 185-186. Chosen to illustrate : (i) the phrase τοῦ Ἀσκληπιοῦ | τοῦ ἐν ἄστει (lines 5-6, and line 17), used to identify the Athenian asklepieion, common in inscriptions and literature. (ii) the use of σωτήρια *re* πᾶσιν Ἀθηναίοις καὶ τοῖς οἰκοῦσιν τὰς πό[[λ]ε̲ις τὰς Ἀθηναίων· (iii) the use of ἐπιμελέομαι to describe the duties of the priest in maintaining order (cf. *IG* II², no. 354, **8** above).
12 *IG* II², no. 4538	– – ον Ἀσ[κληπιῷ ? – ἐπὶ] θεραπίᾳ – – – τῆς] νόσου κατ' ὄναρ – ἐκ] μεγάλη(ς) νόσο(υ) [σωθεῖσα] μετὰ τῶν ἰα[τρῶν] ἀνέθηκ(ε)ν	Chosen to illustrate a rare use of θεραπεία used in a medical context. Here it must refer to treatment that was successful ([σωθεῖσα]).
13 *IG* II², no. 975 + 1061 [2nd c. AD]	. . . [. . . θύσας δὲ καὶ ὑπὲρ τῆς βουλῆς] | καὶ τοῦ δήμου κα[ὶ παίδων καὶ γυναικῶν καὶ καλλιερήσας, ἐν ἅπα]|σιν ἀπήγγειλεν [γεγονέναι τὰ ἱερὰ καλὰ καὶ σωτήρια· . . .] . . . (8–10)	For a restoration, and a commentary, see Hubbe (1959) 195-198. Chosen to illustrate the formula "on behalf of the Boule and the demos and children and wives", and the desire for their "safety" (σωτήρια).

14 *IG* II^2, no. 976 [late 2nd c. AD]	. . . ἐπε[μελήθη δὲ] | καὶ τῆς στρώσεως τῆς κλί]νης καὶ τῆς [κοσμήσεως] | [τῆς τραπέζης καὶ τῆς πα]ννυχίδος· [θύσας δὲ καὶ τοῖς] | [Ἀσκληπιείοις τῶι Ἀσκληπ]ιῶι καὶ τ[ῆι Ὑγιείαι καὶ τοῖς] | [ἄλλοις θεοῖς οἷς πάτριον ἦ]ν ἐπε[μελήθη – – – (5–9)	For a restoration, and a commentary, see Hubbe (1959) 199-200. Chosen to illustrate the use of ἐπιμελέομαι, again in the context of the stewardship of sanctuary belongings.
15 *IG* VII, no. 235 lines 18-30	προσκαλεῖσθαι δὲ καὶ αὐθημερὸν περὶ τῶν ἐ|ν τοῖ ἱεροῖ ἀδικιῶν, ἂν δὲ ὁ ἀντίδικος μὴ συνχ|ωρεῖ, εἰς τὴν ὑστέρην ἡ δίκη τελείσθω. ἐπαρ|χὴν δὲ διδοῦν τὸμ μέλλοντα θεραπεύεσθαι ὑ|πὸ τοῦ θεοῦ μὴ ἔλαττον ἐννεοβόλου δοκίμου ἀργ|υρίου, καὶ ἐμβάλλειν εἰς τὸν θησαυρὸν παρε|όντος τοῦ νεωκόρου. κατεύχεσθαι δὲ τῶν ἱερῶν καὶ ἐπ|ὶ τὸν βωμὸν ἐπιτιθεῖν, ὅταν παρεῖ, τὸν ἱερέα, | ὅταν δὲ μὴ παρεῖ, τὸν θύοντα. καὶ τεῖ θυσίει α|ὐτὸν ἑαυτοῖ κατεύχεσθαι ἕκαστον, τῶν δὲ δη|μορίων τὸν ἱερέα, τῶν δὲ θυομένων ἐν τοῖ ἱε|ροῖ πάντων τὸ δέρμα [λαμβάνειν].	For the entire inscription see App. 3:6

Appendix 3 : 3

Inscriptiones Graecae II^2, no. 4514 [2nd c. AD]

Text and translation from Edelstein, E. and L. (1945) *Asclepius: A collection and interpretation of the testimonies,* Baltimore, 1: **T428** 242

Διοφάντου Σφηττίου	[Dedicated by] Diophantus of Sphettus.
Τάδε σοὶ ζάκορος φίλιος λέγω ᾿Ασκληπιέ, Λητοΐδου παῖ· πῶς χρύσεον ἐς δόμον ἵξομαι τὸν σόν, μάκαρ ὦ πεποθημένε, θεία κεφαλά, πόδας οὐκ ἔχων, οἷς τὸ πρὶν ἐς ἱερὸν ἤλυθον, εἰ μὴ σὺ πρόφρων ἐθέλοις ἐμὲ ἰασάμενος (π)άλιν εἰσάγειν, ὅππως σ᾿ ἐσίδω, τὸν ἐμὸν θεόν, τὸν φαιδρότερον χθονὸς εἰαρινᾶς;	I, a beloved temple attendant, say these things to you, Asclepius, son of Leto's child. How shall I come to your golden abode, O blessed longed-for, divine head, since I do not have the feet with which I formerly came to the shrine, unless by healing me you graciously wish to lead me there again so that I may look upon you, my god, brighter than the earth in springtime.
Τάδε σοὶ Διόφαντος ἐπεύχομαι· σῶσόν με, μάκαρ, σθεναρώτατε, ἰασάμενος ποδάγραν κακήν, πρὸς σοῦ πατρός, ᾧι μεγάλ᾿ εὔχομαι· οὐ γάρ τις ἐπιχθονίων βροτῶν τοιῶνδε πόροι λύσιν ἀλγέων. μόνος εἶ σύ, μάκαρ θεῖε, σθένων· σὲ γὰρ θεοὶ οἱ πανυπείροχοι δῶρον μέγα, τὸν φιλελήμονα, θνητοῖς ἔπορον, λύσιν ἀλγέων.	So I, Diophantus, pray you, save me, most powerful and blessed one, by healing my painful gout : in the name of your father, to whom I offer earnest prayer. For no mortal man may give release from such sufferings. Only you, blessed divine one, have the power. For the gods who are eminent above all gave you to mortal men as a great gift, the compassionate one, the deliverance from sufferings.
[Τρισμ]άκαρ, ὦ Παιὰν ᾿Ασκληπιέ, σῆς ὑπὸ τέχνης [ἰα]θεὶς Διόφαντος ἀνίατον κακὸν ἕλκος οὐκέτι καρκινόπους ἐσορώμενος οὐδ᾿ ἐπ᾿ ἀκάνθας ὡς ἀγρίας βαίνων, ἀλλ᾿ ἀρτίπος, ὥσπερ ὑπέστης.	Thrice-blessed Paeon Asclepius, by your skill Diophantus was healed of his painful incurable ailment; no longer does he appear crab-footed nor as if walking on cruel thorns, but sound of foot, just as you promised.

Appendix 3 : 4

Suidas, Lexicon, *s. v.* Δομνῖνος

Text and translation from Edelstein, E. and L. (1945) *Asclepius: A collection and interpretation of the testimonies*, Baltimore, 1: **T427** 240-241

. . . ἦν δὲ οὐδὲ τὴν ζωὴν ἄκρος οἷον ἀληθῶς φιλόσοφον εἰπεῖν· ὁ γὰρ Ἀθήνησιν Ἀσκληπιὸς τὴν αὐτὴν ἴασιν ἐχρησμῴδει Πλουτάρχῳ τε τῷ Ἀθηναίῳ καὶ τῷ Σύρῳ Δομνίνῳ, τούτῳ μὲν αἷμ' ἀποπτύοντι πολλάκις καὶ τοῦτο φέροντι τῆς νόσου τὸ ὄνομα, ἐκείνῳ δὲ οὐκ οἶδα ὅ τι νενοσηκότι. ἡ δὲ ἴασις ἦν ἐμπίπλασθαι χοιρείων κρεῶν. ὁ μὲν δὴ Πλούταρχος οὐκ ἠνέσχετο τῆς τοιαύτης ὑγιείας καίτοι οὐκ οὔσης αὐτῷ παρανόμου κατὰ τὰ πάτρια, ἀλλὰ διαναστὰς ἀπὸ τοῦ ὕπνου καὶ διαγκωνισάμενος ἐπὶ τοῦ σκίμποδος ἀποβλέπων εἰς τὸ ἄγαλμα τοῦ Ἀσκληπιοῦ (καὶ γὰρ ἐτύγχανεν ἐγκαθεύδων τῷ προδόμῳ τοῦ ἱεροῦ), 'ὦ δέσποτα,' ἔφη, 'τί δὲ ἂν προσέταξας Ἰουδαίῳ νοσοῦντι ταύτην τὴν νόσον; οὐ γὰρ ἂν καὶ ἐκείνῳ ἐμφορεῖσθαι χοιρείων κρεῶν ἐκέλευσας.' ταῦτα εἶπεν, ὁ δὲ Ἀσκληπιὸς αὐτίκα ἀπὸ τοῦ ἀγάλματος ἐμμελέστατον δή τινα φθόγγον, ἑτέραν ὑπεγράψατο θεραπείαν τῷ πάθει. Δομνῖνος δὲ οὐδὲ κατὰ θέμιν πεισθεὶς τῷ ὀνείρῳ, θέμιν τὴν Σύροις πάτριον, οὐδὲ παραδείγματι τῷ Πλουτάρχῳ χρησάμενος ἔφαγέ τε τότε καὶ ἤσθιεν ἀεὶ τῶν κρεῶν. λέγεται που μίαν εἰ διέλειπεν ἡμέραν ἄγευστος ἐπιτίθεσθαι τὸ πάθημα πάντως, ἕως ἐνεπλήσθη.

. . . [Domninus, 5th c. AD] was not perfect in his manner of life, so as to call him a true philosopher. For the Asclepius at Athens revealed the same cure for Plutarch the Athenian [ca. 400 AD] and for Domninus the Syrian, of whom the latter continually coughed up blood and had the sickness of this name, the former was ill with some disease, I know not what. The treatment prescribed was to keep sated with pork. Plutarch could not abide the health thus acquired although it was not contrary to his ancestral laws, but rising up from the dream and leaning on his elbow on the couch, he looked at the statue of Asclepius (for he happened to be sleeping in the vestibule of the shrine) and said, "My lord, what would you have prescribed to a Jew suffering this same illness, for certainly you would not bid him to take his fill of pork." Thus he spoke, and straightway Asclepius spoke from the statue in a very harmonious voice, prescribing another remedy for the illness. But Domninus, trusting the dream, even if it was not in accordance with the law - the ancestral law of the Syrians - and not availing himself of the example of Plutarch, ate of the meat at that time and ever after. It is said somewhere that if he omitted one day, fasting from the meat, the illness unfailingly returned, until he was sated with pork again.

Appendix 3 : 5

Epicurus

The text is from Epicurus (1973) *Epicuro: Opere,* (ed. G. Arrighetti) Torino.
References are numbered by numeral, and then as in the edition cited above, with the page number of that edition cited as well.
Translations are by R. M. Geer, in Epicurus (1964) for **4, 5, 6, 10, 11, 12, 15, 16**; and R. D. Hicks, in Diogenes Laertius (1970) for **2, 13, 14**; and C. R. Haines in Marcus Aurelius (1979) for **9**; while **1, 3, 7** and **8** are my own translation.

Reference	Greek	Translation/Comment
1: **[247]** 570, #64 Porphyrius (Pötscher) *ad Marcellam* 31 34 10	κενὸς ἐκείνου φιλοσόφου λόγος ὑφ' οὗ μηδὲν πάθος ἀνθρώπου θεραπεύεται. ὥσπερ γὰρ ἰατρικῆς οὐδὲν ὄφελος εἰ μὴ τὰς νόσους τῶν σωμάτων θεραπεύει, οὕτως οὐδὲ φιλοσοφίας εἰ μὴ τὸ τῆς ψυχῆς ἐκβάλλει πάθος	Vain is the word of that philosopher by which no human anguish is healed. For just as the art of medicine is no use unless it heals diseases of the body, neither is philosophy unless it banishes the anguish of the soul.
2: **[1] 121** b 29 *Vita Epicuri cum testamento*	χρηματίσεσθαι τε, ἀλλ' ἀπὸ μόνης σοφίας, ἀπορήσαντα. καὶ μόναρχον ἐν καιρῷ θεραπεύσειν.	If in need he will make money for himself, but only by his wisdom. And he will pay homage to a king, if necessary.
3: **[54]** 428 *Epistularum fragmenta* Plutarch *adversus Coloten* 1117d-e	πέμπε οὖν ἀπαρχὰς ἡμῖν εἰς τὴν τοῦ ἱεροῦ σώματος θεραπείαν ὑπέρ τε αὑτοῦ καὶ τέκνων· οὕτω γάρ μοι λέγειν ἐπέρχεται.	Therefore continue to send us the offerings of first-fruits for the care of our sacred person on behalf of both yourself and your children. For thus I am moved to speak.
4: **[6] 55** 151 *Gnomologium Vaticanum*	Θεραπευτέον τὰς συμφορὰς τῇ τῶν ἀπολλυμένων χάριτι καὶ τῷ γινώσκειν ὅτι οὐκ ἔστιν ἄπρακτον ποιῆσαι τὸ γεγονός	We should find solace for misfortune in the happy memory of things that are gone and in the knowledge that what has come to be cannot be undone.

5: **[6] 54** 151 *Gnomologium Vaticanum*	Οὐ προσποιεῖσθαι δεῖ φιλοσοφεῖν, ἀλλ' ὄντως φιλοσοφεῖν· οὐ γὰρ προσδεόμεθα τοῦ δοκεῖν ὑγιαίνειν, ἀλλὰ τοῦ κατ' ἀλήθειαν ὑγιαίνειν.	It is not the pretended but the real pursuit of philosophy that is needed; for we do not need to seem to enjoy good health, but to enjoy it in truth.
6: **[4] 122** 107 *Epistula ad Menoeceum*	Ἐπίκουρος Μενοικεῖ χαίρειν. Μήτε νέος τις ὢν μελλέτω φιλοσοφεῖν, μήτε γέρων ὑπάρχων κοπιάτω φιλοσοφῶν. οὔτε γὰρ ἄωρος οὐδείς ἐστιν οὔτε πάρωρος πρὸς τὸ κατὰ ψυχὴν ὑγιαῖνον.	Epicurus to Menoeceus, greeting. Let no young man delay the study of philosophy, and let no old man become weary of it; for it is never too early nor too late to care for the well-being of the soul.
7: **[40]** 421 Lucian *de lapsu salutantis* 6	Ἐπίκουρος . . . . . . ἐν ταῖς σπουδαιοτέραις ἐπιστολαῖς (εἰσὶ δὲ αὗται ὀλίγαι) καὶ ἐν ταῖς πρὸς τοὺς φίλους μάλιστα ὑγιαίνειν εὐθὺς ἐν ἀρχῇ προστάττει.	Epicurus . . . in the more serious letters (and the same are few), and in those to his friends especially, straightaway, in the beginning, ascribes good health (to them).
8: **[261]** 679 *Pap. Herc.* 176 5 XXIII Vo.	ἀ]φείγμεθα εἰς Λάμψακον ὑ– γιαίνοντες ἐγὼ καὶ Πυθο– κλῆς κα[ὶ Ἕρ]μαρχος καὶ Κτή– σιππος καὶ ἐκεῖ κατειλήφα– μεν ὑγ[ι]αίνοντας Θεμίσ– ταν καὶ τοὺς λοιποὺς φίλο[υ]ς· εὖ δὲ ποιεῖς καὶ εἰ σὺ ὑγι– αίνεις καὶ ἡ μ[ά]μμη [σ]ου καὶ πάπαι καὶ Μάτρω[ν]ι πάν– τα πείθῃ [ὥσπ]ερ καὶ ἔμ– προσθεν· εὖ γὰρ ἴσθι [. .]απια, ὅτι καὶ ἐγὼ καὶ ο[ἱ] λοιποὶ πάντες σε μέγα φιλοῦμεν ὅτι τούτοις πείθῃ πάντα α με· [ἥ]ξω γὰρ ο[. . . .]ατα[	A letter to a child, illustrating **7** above, and Epicurus' preoccupation with the "health" (1-2, 5, 7-8) of those around him. See (i) Diogenes Laertius (1970)*Epicurus* 10.10, where Epicurus' trips to Ionia are noted; and (ii) 10.14, where Diogenes Laertius states that in his correspondence Epicurus replaced the usual greeting (Χαίρειν), with wishes for welfare and right living (Εὖ πράττειν καὶ Σπουδαίως ζῆν) (Loeb 2). Although ὑγιαίνω is used here, this comment would argue for its referral to a way of living as well as to physical health.

9 : **[259]** 672 M. Aurelius 9.41	ὁ Ἐπίκουρος λέγει ὅτι ἐν τῇ νόσῳ οὐκ ἦσάν μοι αἱ ὁμιλίαι περὶ τῶν τοῦ σωματίου παθῶν οὐδὲ πρὸς τοὺς εἰσιόντας τοιαῦτά τινα, φησίν, ἐλάλουν· ἀλλὰ τὰ προηγούμενα φυσιολογῶν διετέλουν καὶ πρὸς αὐτῷ τούτῳ ὤν, πῶς ἡ διάνοια συμμεταλαμβάνουσα τῶν ἐν τῷ σαρκιδίῳ τοιούτων κινήσεων ἀταρακτῇ τὸ ἴδιον ἀγαθὸν τηροῦσα. οὐδὲ τοῖς ἰατροῖς ἐμπαρεῖχον, φησί, καταφρυάττεσθαι ὥς τις ποιοῦσιν ἀλλ' ὁ βίος ἤγετο εὖ καὶ καλῶς.	Listen to Epicurus where he says: "In my illness my talk was not of any bodily feelings, nor did I chatter about such things to those who came to see me, but I went on with my cardinal disquisitions on natural philosophy, dwelling especially on this point, how the mind, having perforce its share in such affections of the flesh, yet remains unperturbed, safeguarding its own proper good." "Nor did I"-he goes on- "let the physicians ride the high horse as if they were doing grand things, but my life went on well and happily."
10 : **[6] 37** 147 *Gnomologium Vaticanum*	Ἀσθενὴς ἡ φύσις ἐστὶ πρὸς τὸ κακόν, οὐ πρὸς τὸ ἀγαθόν· ἡδοναῖς μὲν γὰρ σῴζεται, ἀλγηδόσι δὲ διαλύεται.	When confronted by evil the soul is weak, but not when faced with good; for pleasures make the soul secure, but pains ruin it.
11 : **[6] 63** 153 *Gnomologium Vaticanum*	Ἔστι καὶ ἐν λεπτότητι καθαριότης, ἧς ὁ ἀνεπιλόγιστος παραπλήσιόν τι πάσχει τῷ δι' ἀοριστίαν ἐκπίπτοντι.	There is a limit in simple living. He who fails to heed this limit falls into an error as great as that of the man who gives way to extravagance.
12 : **[6] 64** 153 *Gnomologium Vaticanum*	Ἀκολουθεῖν δεῖ τὸν παρὰ τῶν ἄλλων ἔπαινον αὐτόματον, ἡμᾶς δὲ γενέσθαι περὶ τὴν ἡμῶν ἰατρείαν.	We should welcome praise from others, if it comes unsought, but we should be concerned with correcting ourselves.
13 : **[1] 120** b 29 *Vita Epicuri cum testamento*	[Τὸ δ' ἑξῆς] Δοκεῖ δ' αὐτοῖς ἁμαρτήματα ἄνισα εἶναι. καὶ τὴν ὑγίειαν τισὶ μὲν ἀγαθόν, τισὶ δὲ ἀδιάφορον. τὴν δὲ ἀνδρείαν φύσει μὴ γίνεσθαι, λογισμῷ δὲ τοῦ συμφέροντος. καὶ τὴν φιλίαν διὰ τὰς χρείας·	The school holds that sins are not all equal; that health is in some cases a good, in others a thing indifferent; that courage is not a natural gift but comes from calculation of expediency; and that friendship is prompted by our need.
14 : **[1] 138** 31 *Vita Epicuri cum testamento*	Διὰ δὲ τὴν ἡδονὴν καὶ τὰς ἀρετὰς αἱρεῖσθαι, οὐ δι' αὑτάς, ὥσπερ τὴν ἰατρικὴν διὰ τὴν ὑγίειαν, . . .	And we choose the virtues too on account of pleasure and not for their own sake, as we take medicine for the sake of health.

15: **[4] 128** 111 *Epistula ad Menoeceum*	τούτων γὰρ ἀπλανὴς θεωρία πᾶσαν αἵρεσιν καὶ φυγὴν ἐπανάγειν οἶδεν ἐπὶ τὴν τοῦ σώματος ὑγίειαν καὶ τὴν τῆς ψυχῆς ἀταραξίαν, ἐπεὶ τοῦτο τοῦ μακαρίως ζῆν ἐστι τέλος. τούτου γὰρ χάριν πάντα πράττομεν, ὅπως μήτε ἀλγῶμεν μήτε ταρβῶμεν.	The man who has a perfect knowledge of this (i.e. the necessary desires) will know how to make his every choice or rejection tend toward gaining health of body and peace of mind, since this is the final end of the blessed life. For to gain this end, namely freedom from pain and fear, we do everything.
16: **[4] 131** 115 *Epistula ad Menoeceum*	τὸ συνεθίζειν οὖν ἐν ταῖς ἁπλαῖς καὶ οὐ πολυτελέσι διαίταις καὶ ὑγιείας ἐστὶ συμπληρωτικὸν καὶ πρὸς τὰς ἀναγκαίας τοῦ βίου χρήσεις ἄοκνον ποιεῖ τὸν ἄνθρωπον καὶ τοῖς πολυτελέσιν ἐκ διαλειμμάτων προσερχομένοις κρεῖττον ἡμᾶς διατίθησι καὶ πρὸς τὴν τύχην ἀφόβους παρασκευάζει. Ὅταν οὖν λέγωμεν ἡδονὴν τέλος ὑπάρχειν, . . . , ἀλλὰ τὸ μήτε ἀλγεῖν κατὰ σῶμα μήτε ταράττεσθαι κατὰ ψυχήν.	To be accustomed to simple and plain living is conducive to health and makes a man ready for the necessary tasks of life. It also makes us more ready for the enjoyment of luxury if at intervals we chance to meet with it, and renders us fearless against fortune. . . but by pleasure we mean the state wherein the body is free from pain and the mind from anxiety.

Epicurus uses healing language in a variety of ways. The verb θεραπεύω (**1**, **2**, **4**) and the noun θεραπεία (**3**) appear illustrating different aspects of the sense of θεραπεύω: denoting *service* (**2**), *care/treatment?* (**3**), *comfort* (**4**) and *healing* (**1**). It is significant that the only instance where it must mean healing the healing agent is specified as the λόγος of the philosopher (**1**). It is this λόγος that heals the πάθος of mankind, and banishes the πάθος of his soul. (Cf. the NT exorcisms which feature Jesus driving out demons [ἐκβάλλω] with a word [λόγῳ].)

The verb ὑγιαίνω (**5**, **6**, **7**, **8**) appears equating the study of philosophy with the health of the soul (**6**), and in an analogy between true health and the true pursuit of philosophy (**5**). It also denotes physical health (**7**, **8**), but, given the depth of these friendships (Diogenes Laertius [1970] *Epicurus* 10. 10), and his use of language in correspondence (Diogenes Laertius [1970] *Epicurus* 10.14), it would be surprising if Epicurus does not include some reference to their way of life in these instances of ὑγιαίνω. The noun ὑγίεια (**13**, **14**, **15**, **16**) appears denoting physical health and is integral to Epicurus' idea of the blessed life, i.e. freedom from pain and fear (**15**, **16**).

Thus physical health is bound up with the health of the soul, in that pain is a distraction. To experience pleasure saves (σῴζεται) the soul, whereas pains ruin it and make it weak (**10**). This causes error and suffering (πάσχει [**11**]), which requires correction (ἰατρείαν [**12**]).

Appendix 3 : 6

Inscriptiones Graecae VII, no. 235

Θεοί. | Τὸν ἱερέα τοῦ Ἀμφιαράου φοιτᾶν εἰς τὸ ἱερὸ|ν ἐπειδὰν χειμὼν παρέλθει μέχρι ἀρότου ὥρ|ης, μὴ πλέον διαλείποντα ἢ τρεῖς ἡμέρας, καὶ | μένειν ἐν τοῖ ἱεροῖ μὴ ἔλαττον ἢ δέκα ἡμέρα|ς τοῦ μηνὸς ἑκ[ά]στο[υ], καὶ ἐπαναγκάζειν τὸν ν|εωκόρον τοῦ τε ἱεροῦ ἐπιμελεῖσθαι κατὰ τὸ|ν νόμον καὶ τῶν ἀφικνε(ο)μένων εἰς τὸ ἱερόν. [1–8]

ἂν δέ τις ἀδικεῖ ἐν τοῖ ἱεροῖ ἢ ξένος ἢ δημότ|ης, ζημιούτω ὁ ἱερεὺς μέχρι πέντε δραχμέων | κυρίως καὶ ἐνέχυρα λαμβανέτω τοῦ ἐξημιωμ|ένου· ἂν δ' ἐκτίνει τὸ ἀργύριον, παρεόντος τοῦ | ἱερέος ἐμβαλέτω εἰς τὸν θησαυρόν. δικάζει|ν δὲ τὸν ἱερέα ἄν τις ἰδίει ἀδικηθεῖ ἢ τῶν ξέ|νων ἢ τῶν δημοτέων ἐν τοῖ ἱεροῖ μέχρι τριῶν | δραχμέων· τὰ δὲ μέζονα ἡχοῖ ἑκάστοις αἱ δίκ|αι ἐν τοῖς νόμοις εἴρηται, ἐντοῦθα γινέσθων. [9–17]

προσκαλεῖσθαι δὲ καὶ αὐθημερὸν περὶ τῶν ἐ|ν τοῖ ἱεροῖ ἀδικιῶν, ἂν δὲ ὁ ἀντίδικος μὴ συνχ|ωρεῖ, εἰς τὴν ὑστέρην ἡ δίκη τελείσθω. ἐπαρ|χὴν δὲ διδοῦν τὸμ μέλλοντα θεραπεύεσθαι ὑ|πὸ τοῦ θεοῦ μὴ ἔλαττον ἐννεοβόλου δοκίμου ἀργ|υρίου, καὶ ἐμβάλλειν εἰς τὸν θησαυρὸν παρε|όντος τοῦ νεωκόρου. κατεύχεσθαι δὲ τῶν ἱερῶν καὶ ἐπ|ὶ τὸν βωμὸν ἐπιτιθεῖν, ὅταν παρεῖ, τὸν ἱερέα, | ὅταν δὲ μὴ παρεῖ, τὸν θύοντα. καὶ τεῖ θυσίει α|ὐτὸν ἑαυτοῖ κατεύχεσθαι ἕκαστον, τῶν δὲ δη|μορίων τὸν ἱερέα, τῶν δὲ θυομένων ἐν τοῖ ἱε|ροῖ πάντων τὸ δέρμα [λαμβάνειν]. θύειν δὲ ἐξ|εῖν ἅπαν ὅτι ἂν βούληται ἕκαστος, τῶν δὲ κρεῶ|ν μὴ εἶναι ἐκφορὴν ἔξω τοῦ τεμένος. τοῖ δὲ ἱε|ρεῖ διδοῦν τοὺς θύοντας ἀπὸτοῦ ἱερήου ἑκ|άστου τὸν ὦμον, πλὴν ὅταν ἡ ἑορτὴ εἶ· τότε δὲ ἀπ|ὸ τῶν δημορίων λαμβανέτω ὦμον ἀφ' ἑκάστου | τοῦ ἱερήου. ἐγκαθεύδειν δὲ τὸν δειόμενο|ν, πειθόμενον τοῖς νόμοις. τὸ ὄνομα τοῦ ἐγκαθεύδον|τος, ὅταν ἐμβάλλει τὸ ἀργύριον, γράφεσθαι τ|ὸν νεωκόρον καὶ αὐτοῦ καὶ τῆς πόλεος καὶ ἐκ|τιθεῖν ἐν τοῖ ἱεροῖ γράφοντα ἐν πετεύροι σ|κοπεῖν [τ]οῖ βουλομένοι· ἐν δὲ τοῖ κοιμητηρίο|ι καθεύδειν χωρὶς μὲν τοὺς ἄνδρας, χωρὶς | δὲ τὰς γυναῖκας, τοὺς μὲν ἄνδρας ἐν τοῖ πρὸ ἠ|οῦς τοῦ βωμοῦ, τὰς δὲ γυναῖκας ἐν τοῖ πρὸ ἑσπέ|ρης . . . . τὸ κοι|μητήριον τοὺς ἐν|καθεύδοντας. (18–48)

Appendix 4 : 1
Hippokrates

Text and translation from the Loeb Classical Library edition of *Hippocrates*, Volumes 1 (1972), 2 (1981), and 4 (1979), (trans. W.H.S.Jones); and Volume 3 (1968), (trans. E.T.Withington).

References are by numeral, Loeb volume number, title of work, and reference within that work.

Reference	**Text**	**Translation**
1 : 1 *Ancient Medicine* 9.29-36	οὕτω δὴ καὶ οἱ κακοί τε καὶ οἱ πλεῖστοι ἰητροί, ὅταν μὲν θεραπεύωσιν ἀνθρώπους μηδὲν δεινὸν ἔχοντας, ἐς οὓς ἄν τις τὰ μέγιστα ἐξαμαρτάνων οὐδὲν δεινὸν ἐργάσαιτο – πολλὰ δὲ τοιαῦτα νοσήματα καὶ πολλόν τι πλείω τῶν δεινῶν ἀνθρώποις συμβαίνει – ἐν μὲν τοῖσι τοιούτοις ἁμαρτάνοντες οὐ καταφανέες εἰσὶν τοῖσιν ἰδιώτῃσιν·	So also when bad physicians, who comprise the great majority, treat men who are suffering from no serious complaint, so that the greatest blunders would not affect them seriously - such illnesses occur very often, being far more common than serious disease - they are not shown up in their true colours to laymen if their errors are confined to such cases;
2 : 1 *Ancient Medicine* 15.1, 3-4	Ἀπορέω δ' ἔγωγε, . . . ποτὲ τρόπον θεραπεύσουσι τοὺς ἀνθρώπους . . .	I am at a loss to understand how those ... treat their patients ...
3 : 1 *Ancient Medicine* 20.1-4	Λέγουσι δέ τινες ἰητροὶ καὶ σοφισταί, ὡς οὐκ εἴη δυνατὸν ἰητρικὴν εἰδέναι ὅστις μὴ οἶδεν ὅ τί ἐστιν ἄνθρωπος. ἀλλὰ τοῦτο δεῖ καταμαθεῖν τὸν μέλλοντα ὀρθῶς θεραπεύσειν τοὺς ἀνθρώπους.	Certain physicians and philosophers assert that nobody can know medicine who is ignorant what a man is; he who would treat patients properly must, they say, learn this.
4 : 1 *Oath* 1-3, 29-32	Ὄμνυμι Ἀπόλλωνα ἰητρὸν καὶ Ἀσκληπιὸν καὶ Ὑγείαν καὶ Πανάκειαν καὶ θεοὺς πάντας τε καὶ πάσας, . . . ἃ δ' ἂν ἐν θεραπείῃ ἢ ἴδω ἢ ἀκούσω, ἢκαὶ ἄνευ θεραπείης κατὰ βίον ἀνθρώπων, ἃ μὴ χρή ποτε ἐκλαλεῖσθαι ἔξω, σιγήσομαι, ἄρρητα ἡγεύμενος εἶναι τὰ τοιαῦτα.	I swear by Apollo Physician, by Asclepius, by Health, by Panacea and by all the gods and goddesses ... And whatsoever I shall see or hear in the course of my profession, as well as outside my profession in my intercourse with men, if it be what should not be published abroad, I will never divulge, holding such things to be holy secrets.
5 : 4 *Aphorisms* 6.38	Ὁκόσοισι κρυπτοὶ καρκίνοι γίνονται, μὴ θεραπεύειν βέλτιον· θεραπευόμενοι γὰρ ἀπόλλυνται ταχέως, μὴ θεραπευόμενοι δὲ πολὺν χρόνον διατελέουσιν.	It is better to give no treatment in cases of hidden cancer; treatment causes speedy death, but to omit treatment is to prolong life.

6 : 4 *Aphorisms* 7.37	Ὁκόσοι αἷμα ἐμέουσιν, ἢν μὲν ἄνευ πυρετοῦ, σωτήριον· ἢν δὲ σὺν πυρετῷ, κακόν· θεραπεύειν δὲ τοῖσι στυπτικοῖσιν ἢ τοῖσι ψυκτικοῖσιν.	The vomiting of blood, if without fever, may be cured; if with fever, it is bad. Treat it with styptics or refrigerants.
7 : 2 *The Art* 4.1-14	Ἔστι μὲν οὖν μοι ἀρχὴ τοῦ λόγου ἣ καὶ ὁμολογηθήσεται παρὰ πᾶσιν· ὅτι μὲν ἔνιοι ἐξυγιαίνονται τῶν θεραπευομένων ὑπὸ ἰητρικῆς ὁμολογεῖται· ὅτι δὲ οὐ πάντες, ἐν τούτῳ ἤδη ψέγεται ἡ τέχνη, καὶ φασὶν οἱ τὰ χείρω λέγοντες διὰ τοὺς ἁλισκομένους ὑπὸ τῶν νοσημάτων τοὺς ἀποφεύγοντας αὐτὰ τύχῃ ἀποφεύγειν καὶ οὐ διὰ τὴν τέχνην. ἐγὼ δὲ οὐκ ἀποστερέω μὲν οὐδ' αὐτὸς τὴν τύχην ἔργου οὐδενός, ἡγεῦμαι δὲ τοῖσι μὲν κακῶς θεραπευομένοισι νοσήμασι τὰ πολλὰ τὴν ἀτυχίην ἕπεσθαι, τοῖσι δὲ εὖ τὴν εὐτυχίην. ἔπειτα δὲ καὶ πῶς οἷόν τ' ἐστὶ τοῖς ὑγιασθεῖσιν ἄλλο τι αἰτιήσασθαι ἢ τὴν τέχνην, εἴπερ χρώμενοι αὐτῇ καὶ ὑπουργέοντες ὑγιάσθησαν;	The beginning of my discourse is a point which will be conceded by all. It is conceded that of those treated by medicine some are healed. But because not all are healed the art is blamed, and those who malign it, because there are some who succumb to diseases, assert that those who escape do so through luck and not through the art. Now I, too, do not rob luck of any of its prerogatives, but I am nevertheless of opinion that when diseases are badly treated ill-luck generally follows, and good luck when they are treated well. Again, how is it possible for patients to attribute their recoveries to anything else except the art, seeing that it was by using it and serving it that they recovered?
8 : 2 *The Art* 5.1-11	Ἐρεῖ δὴ ὁ τἀναντία λέγων, ὅτι πολλοὶ ἤδη καὶ οὐ χρησάμενοι ἰητρῷ νοσέοντες ὑγιάσθησαν, καὶ ἐγὼ τῷ λόγῳ οὐκ ἀπιστέω· δοκεῖ δέ μοι οἷόν τε εἶναι καὶ ἰητρῷ μὴ χρωμένους ἰητρικῇ περιτυχεῖν, οὐ μὴν ὥστε εἰδέναι ὅ τι ὀρθὸν ἐν αὐτῇ ἔνι ἢ ὅ τι μὴ ὀρθόν, ἀλλ' ὥσει ἐπιτύχοιεν τοιαῦτα θεραπεύσαντες ἑωυτούς, ὁποῖά περ ἂν ἐθεραπεύθησαν εἰ καὶ ἰητροῖσιν ἐχρῶντο. καὶ τοῦτό γε τεκμήριον μέγα τῇ οὐσίῃ τῆς τέχνης, ὅτι ἐοῦσά τέ ἐστι καὶ μεγάλη, ὅπου γε φαίνονται καὶ οἱ μὴ νομίζοντες αὐτὴν εἶναι σῳζόμενοι δι' αὐτήν·	Now my opponent will object that in the past many, even without calling in a physician, have been cured of their sickness, and I agree that he is right. But I hold that it is possible to profit by the art of medicine even without calling in a physician, not indeed so as to know what is correct medical treatment and what is incorrect, but so as by chance to employ in self-treatment the same means as would have been employed had a physician actually been called in. And it is surely strong proof of the existence of the art, that it both exists and is powerful, if it is obvious that even those who do not believe in it recover through it.
9 : 2 *The Art* 7.13-17	οἱ μὲν γὰρ ὑγιαινούσῃ γνώμῃ μεθ' ὑγιαίνοντος σώματος ἐγχειρέουσι, λογισάμενοι τά τε παρεόντα, τῶν τε παροιχομένων τὰ ὁμοίως διατεθέντα τοῖσι παρεοῦσιν, ὥστε ποτὲ θεραπευθέντα εἰπεῖν ὡς ἀπήλλαξαν·	The physician sets about his task with healthy mind and healthy body, having considered the case and past cases of like characteristics to the present, so as to say how they were treated and cured.

10 : 2 *The Art*
11.1-3, 10-41

Οὐ γὰρ δὴ ὀφθαλμοῖσί γε ἰδόντι τούτων τῶν εἰρημένων οὐδενὶ οὐδὲν ἔστιν εἰδέναι· . . . ὅσα γὰρ τὴν τῶν ὀμμάτων ὄψιν ἐκφεύγει, ταῦτα τῇ τῆς γνώμης ὄψει κεκράτηται· καὶ ὅσα δὲ ἐν τῷ μὴ ταχὺ ὀφθῆναι οἱ νοσέοντες πάσχουσιν, οὐχ οἱ θεραπεύοντες αὐτοὺς αἴτιοι, ἀλλ' ἡ φύσις ἥ τε τοῦ νοσέοντος ἥ τε τοῦ νοσήματος· ὁ μὲν γάρ, ἐπεὶ οὐκ ἦν αὐτῷ ὄψει ἰδεῖν τὸ μοχθέον οὐδ' ἀκοῇ πυθέσθαι, λογισμῷ μετῄει. καὶ γὰρ δὴ καὶ ἃ πειρῶνται οἱ τὰ ἀφανέα νοσέοντες ἀπαγγέλλειν περὶ τῶν νοσημάτων τοῖσι θεραπεύουσιν, δοξάζοντες μᾶλλον ἢ εἰδότες ἀπαγγέλλουσιν· εἰ γὰρ ἠπίσταντο, οὐκ ἂν περιέπιπτον αὐτοῖσιν· τῆς γὰρ αὐτῆς συνέσιός ἐστιν ἥσπερ τὸ εἰδέναι τῶν νούσων τὰ αἴτια καὶ τὸ θεραπεύειν αὐτας ἐπίστασθαι πάσῃσι τῇσι θεραπείῃσιν αἳ κωλύουσι τὰ νοσήματα μεγαλύνεσθαι. ὅτε οὖν οὐδὲ ἐκ τῶν ἀπαγγελλομένων ἔστι τὴν ἀναμάρτητον σαφήνειαν ἀκοῦσαι, προσοπτέον τι καὶ ἄλλο τῷ θεραπεύοντι· ταύτης οὖν τῆς βραδυτῆτος οὐχ ἡ τέχνη, ἀλλ' ἡ φύσις αἰτίη τῶν σωμάτων· ἡ μὲν γὰρ αἰσθανομένη ἀξιοῖ θεραπεύειν, σκοπεῦσα ὅπως μὴ τόλμῃ μᾶλλον ἢ γνώμῃ, καὶ ῥαστώνῃ μᾶλλον ἢ βίῃ θεραπεύῃ· ἡ δ' ἢν μὲν διεξαρκέσῃ ἐς τὸ ὀφθῆναι, ἐξαρκέσει καὶ ἐς τὸ ὑγιανθῆναι· ἢν δ' ἐν ᾧ τοῦτο ὁρᾶται κρατηθῇ διὰ τὸ βραδέως αὐτὸν ἐπὶ τὸν θεραπεύσοντα ἐλθεῖν ἢ διὰ · τὸ τοῦ νοσήματος τάχος, οἰχήσεται. ἐξ ἴσου μὲν γὰρ ὁρμώμενον τῇ θεραπείῃ οὐκ ἔστι θᾶσσον, προλαβὸν δὲ θᾶσσον· προλαμβάνει δὲ διά τε τὴν τῶν σωμάτων στεγνότητα, ἐν ᾗ οὐκ ἐν εὐόπτῳ οἰκέουσιν αἱ νοῦσοι, διά τε τὴν τῶν καμνόντων ὀλιγωρίην· ἐπεὶ ἔοικε· οὐ λαμβανόμενοι γάρ, ἀλλ' εἰλημμένοι ὑπὸ τῶν νοσημάτων θέλουσι θεραπεύεσθαι.

Without doubt no man who sees only with his eyes can know anything of what has here been described ... for what escapes the eyesight is mastered by the eye of the mind, and the sufferings of patients due to their not being quickly observed are the fault, not of the medical attendants, but of the nature of the patient and of the disease. The attendant in fact, as he could neither see the trouble with his eyes nor learn it with his ears, tried to track it by reasoning. Indeed, even the attempted reports of their illnesses made to their attendants by sufferers from obscure diseases are the result of opinion, rather than of knowledge. If indeed they understood their diseases they would never have fallen into them, for the same intelligence is required to know the causes of diseases as to understand how to treat them with all the treatment that prevents illnesses from growing worse. Now when not even the reports afford perfectly reliable information , the attendant must look out for fresh light. For the delay thus caused not the art is to be blame, but the constitution of human bodies. For it is only when the art sees its way that it thinks it right to give treatment, considering how it may give it, not by daring but by judgment, not by violence but by gentleness. As to our human constitution, if it admits of being seen, it will also admit of being healed. But if, while the sight is being won, the body is mastered by slowness in calling in the attendant or by the rapidity of the disease, the patient will pass away. For if the disease and treatment start together, the disease will not win the race, but will if it start with an advantage, which advantage is due to the density of our bodies, in which diseases lurk unseen, and to the careless neglect of patients. This advantage is not to be wondered at, as it is only when diseases have established themselves, not while they are doing so, that patients are ready to submit to treatment.

11 : 4 *Regimen in Health* 9 (a fragment from the beginning of περὶ παθῶν [Littré, vi. 208])	Ἄνδρα δὲ χρή, ὅς ἐστι συνετός, λογισάμενον ὅτι τοῖσιν ἀνθρώποισι πλείστου ἄξιόν ἐστιν ἡ ὑγιείη, ἐπίστασθαι ἐκ τῆς ἑωυτοῦ γνώμης ἐν τῇσι νούσοισιν ὠφελεῖσθαι.	A wise man should consider that health is the greatest of human blessings, and learn how by his own thought to derive benefit in his illnesses.
12 : 4 *Regimen II* 59.1-5	Ἔμετοι ἰσχναίνουσι διὰ τὴν κένωσιν τῆς τροφῆς, οὐ μέντοι ξηραίνουσιν, ἢν μή τις τῇ ὑστεραίῃ θεραπεύῃ ὀρθῶς, ἀλλ' ὑγραίνουσι μᾶλλον διὰ τὴν πλήρωσιν καὶ διὰ τὴν σύντηξιν τῆς σαρκὸς τὴν ὑπὸ τοῦ πόνου·	Vomitings reduce through the evacuations of nourishment. They do not, however, dry, unless appropriate treatment be applied on the following day; they tend rather to moisten through the repletion and through the melting of flesh caused by the fatigue.
13 : 4 *Regimen II* 66	35-6: χρὴ δὲ τοὺς τοιούτους κόπους ὧδε θεραπεύειν 41-2: καὶ ἀλείφεσθαι τῷ ἐλαίῳ ἡσυχῇ πολὺν χρόνον 51: συμφέρει δὲ θεραπεύεσθαι ὧδε· 66: ἢν μή τις ἐκθεραπεύσῃ ὀρθῶς 78: ἡ θεραπείη . . .	35ff.: Pains of this sort (i.e. fatigue pains in untrained people) should be treated thus. Break up the collected humour by vapour baths, and by hot baths, and make firm the reduced flesh by gentle walks, in order to effect purgation, by restricted diet and by practices that cause leanness: it is beneficial to apply oil gently to the body for a long time, that the heating be not violent, to use sudorific unguents, and to lie on a soft bed.... 51: Beneficial treatment of such cases (i.e. fatigue pains in those in training) is as follows. Accustomed exercises ... hot baths ... 66: unless proper treatment be applied ... warm bath ... soft wine, well diluted ... food... 78: The treatment ...
14 : 4 *Regimen III* 71.19-23	ἀλλ' οὐ χρὴ προέσθαι τὸν φρονέοντα, ἀλλ' ὁκόταν ἐπιγνῷ τὰ πρῶτα, τῇσι θεραπείῃσιν ὥσπερ τὸν πρότερον ἐκθεραπευθῆναι, πλείονος δὲ χρόνου καὶ λιμοκτονίης δεῖται.	The wise man, however should not let things drift, but as soon as he recognises the first signs, he should carry out a cure by the same remedies as in the first case, although more time is required and strict abstinence from food.

15 : 4 *Regimen III* 75		1ff.: There also occurs the following kind of surfeit.... So first one should use warm, fermented bread, crumbling it into dark wine or into pork broth. Also fish boiled in acrid brine. Use also fleshy meats, such as pig's feet well boiled and fat roast pork, but be sparing of sucking-pig, and the flesh of puppies and kids. Vegetables should be leeks and onions, boiled and raw, boiled blite and the pumpkin. Drink should be undiluted, and no luncheon should be taken at first. There should be sleep after exercises, running in the double course, increased gradually, gentle wrestling with the body oiled, few baths, more anointings than usual, plenty of early-morning walks, but only short ones after dinner. Figs with food are good, and neat wine therewith.
	19-22 : ὕπνοισί τε ἀπὸ τῶν γυμνασίων, τοῖσί τε δρόμοισι καμπτοῖσιν, ἐξ ὀλίγου προσάγων, πάλῃ τε μαλακῇ ἐν ἐλαίῳ, λουτροῖσί τε ὀλίγοισι, χρίσμασι πλείοσι, . .	
	25-27 : ἐκ δὲ ταύτης τῆς θεραπείης καθίσταται τοῖσι μὲν θᾶσσον, τοῖσι δὲ βραδύτερον.	25-27: This treatment brings recovery, in some cases rapid, in others slower.
16 : 4 *Regimen III* 76.27-29	καὶ ἢν μὲν ἐν μηνὶ καθιστῆται, θεραπευέσθω τὸ λοιπὸν τοῖσι προσήκουσιν· ἢν δέ τι ὑπόλοιπον ᾖ, χρήσθω τῇ θεραπείῃ.	If recovery occur in a month, let the patient take hereafter the fitting treatment; but if the illness has not completely disappeared, let the patient continue the treatment.
17 : 4 *Regimen III* 78.16-17	χρὴ δὲ τοὺς τοιούτους ὧδε θεραπεύειν·	16ff.: Such persons (i.e. people out of training taking violent exercise) must be treated thus.... Reduce their food ... Running ... massage ... hand-wrestling ... long walks ... voice exercises ... for ten days ... increase food for six days ... an emetic ... increase food for four days ... after ten days an emetic ... normal food, exercises and walks...
18 : 4 *Regimen III* 82	43-44 : . . . ἢν δὲ μή, οὕτω θεραπευέσθω τὸν ἐπίλοιπον χρόνον.	43-44 : ... Otherwise, the same treatment should be continued for the rest of the time.

19 : 4 *Regimen IV* 88.1-18	Ἔχει δὲ περὶ τούτων ὧδε· ὁκόσα τῶν ἐνυπνίων τὰς ἡμερινὰς πρήξιας τοῦ ἀνθρώπου ἢ διανοίας ἐς τὴν εὐφρόνην ἀποδίδωσι κατὰ τρόπον γινομένας ὥσπερ τῆς ἡμέρας ἐπρήχθη ἢ ἐβουλεύθη ἐπὶ δικαίῳ πρήγματι, ταῦτα τῷ ἀνθρώπῳ ἀγαθά· ὑγιείην γὰρ σημαίνει, διότι ἡ ψυχὴ παραμένει τοῖσιν ἡμερινοῖσι βουλεύμασιν, οὔτε πλησμονῇ κρατηθεῖσα οὔτε κενώσει οὔτε ἄλλῳ οὐδενὶ ἔξωθεν προσπεσόντι. ὅταν δὲ πρὸς τὰς ἡμερινὰς πρήξιας ὑπεναντιῶται τὰ ἐνύπνια καὶ ἐγγίνηται περὶ αὐτῶν ἢ μάχη ἢ νίκη, σημαίνει τάραχον ἐν τῷ σώματι· καὶ ἢν μὲν ἰσχυρὴ ᾖ, ἰσχυρὸν τὸ κακόν, ἢν δὲ φαύλη, ἀσθενέστερον. περὶ μὲν οὖν τῆς πρήξιος εἴτ' ἀποτρέπειν δεῖ εἴτε μή, οὐ κρίνω· τὸ δὲ σῶμα θεραπεύεσθαι συμβουλεύω· πλησμονῆς γάρ τινος ἐγγενομένης ἀπόκρισίς τις γενομένη ἐτάραξε τὴν ψυχήν. . . .	1-18ff.: This is the truth of the matter. Such dreams as repeat in the night a man's actions or thoughts in the day-time, representing them as occurring naturally, just as they were done or planned during the day in a normal act-these are good for a man. They signify health, because the soul abides by the purposes of the day, and is overpowered neither by surfeit nor by depletion nor by any attack from without. But when dreams are contrary to the acts of the day, and there occurs about them some struggle or triumph, a disturbance in the body is indicated, a violent struggle meaning a violent mischief, a feeble struggle a less serious mischief. As to whether the act should be averted or not I do not decide, but I do advise treatment of the body. For a disturbance of the soul has been caused by a secretion arising from some surfeit that has occurred... emetic ... light diet ... long walks ...
20 : 4 *Regimen IV* 90.63	εὔχεσθαι δὲ Γῇ καὶ Ἑρμῇ καὶ ἥρωσιν.	Pray to Earth, Hermes and the Heroes.
21 : 2 *Decorum* 14	Ἐπιτηρεῖν δὲ χρὴ καὶ τὰς ἁμαρτίας τῶν καμνόντων, δι' ὧν πολλάκις διεψεύσαντο ἐν τοῖσι προσάρμασι τῶν προσφερομένων· ἐπεὶ τὰ μισητὰ ποτήματα οὐ λαμβάνοντες, ἢ φαρμακευόμενοι ἢ θεραπευόμενοι, ἀνηρέθησαν· καὶ αὐτῶν μὲν οὐ πρὸς ὁμολογίην τρέπεται τὸ ποιηθέν, τῷ δὲ ἰητρῷ τὴν αἰτίην προσῆψαν.	Keep a watch also on the faults of the patients, which often make them lie about the taking of things prescribed. For through not taking disagreeable drinks, purgative or other, they sometimes die. What they have done never results in a confession, but the blame is thrown upon the physician.
22 : 2 *Decorum* 6.14-16	. . . ἃ δὲ μετὰ χειρουργίης ἰώμενα, ἃ δὲ βοηθεόμενα, θεραπευόμενα ἢ διαιτώμενα. . .	... [Disease] sometimes being cured by surgery, sometimes being relieved, either through treatment or through regimen....
23 : 3 *On Fractures* 11.30-35	. . . ἢ ἐπ' ἄλλῳ νοσήματι ὑπτιασμοῦ χρονίου γενομένου, ὁμῶς καὶ τοῖσι τοιούτοισι χρόνια, καὶ ὀχλώδεα καὶ πολλάκις ἀναρρηγνύμενα, ἢν μὴ χρηστῇ μὲν μελέτῃ θεραπευθῇ, πολλῇ δὲ ἡσυχίῃ, ὥς τά γε σφακελίζοντα·	[Necrosis from other causes] ... or another malady involving prolonged rest on his back-all these necroses are equally chronic and troublesome, and often break out afresh if not treated with most skilful attention and long rest.

24 : 2 *The sacred disease* 1, 2, 3, 10.	1.1-10: Περὶ τῆς ἱερῆς νούσου καλεομένης ὧδ᾽ ἔχει. οὐδέν τί μοι δοκεῖ τῶν ἄλλων θειοτέρη εἶναι νούσων οὐδὲ ἱερωτέρη, ἀλλὰ φύσιν μὲν ἔχει καὶ πρόφασιν, οἱ δ᾽ ἄνθρωποι ἐνόμισαν θεῖόν τι πρῆγμα εἶναι ὑπὸ ἀπειρίης καὶ θαυμασιότητος, ὅτι οὐδὲν ἔοικεν ἑτέροισι· καὶ κατὰ μὲν τὴν ἀπορίην αὐτοῖσι τοῦ μὴ γινώσκειν τὸ θεῖον διασῴζεται, κατὰ δὲ τὴν εὐπορίην τοῦ τρόπου τῆς ἰήσιος ᾧ ἰῶνται, ἀπόλλυται, ὅτι καθαρμοῖσί τε ἰῶνται καὶ ἐπαοιδῇσιν.	1: I am about to discuss the disease called "sacred." It is not, in my opinion, any more divine or more sacred than other diseases, but has a natural cause, and its supposed divine origin is due to men's inexperience, and to their wonder at its peculiar character. Now while men continue to believe in its divine origin because they are at a loss to understand it, they really disprove its divinity by the facile method of healing which they adopt, consisting as it does of purifications and incantations....
	2.27-31: ταῦτα δὲ τοῦ θείου εἵνεκα προστιθέασιν, ὡς πλέον τι εἰδότες, καὶ ἄλλας προφάσιας λέγοντες, ὅπως, εἰ μὲν ὑγιὴς γένοιτο, αὐτῶν ἡ δόξα εἴη καὶ ἡ δεξιότης, εἰ δὲ ἀποθάνοι, ἐν ἀσφαλεῖ καθισταῖντο αὐτῶν αἱ ἀπολογίαι καὶ ἔχοιεν πρόφασιν ὡς οὐδὲν αἴτιοί εἰσιν, ἀλλ᾽ οἱ θεοί·	2: These observances they impose because of the divine origin of the disease, claiming superior knowledge and alleging other causes, so that, should the patient recover, the reputation for cleverness may be theirs; but should he die, they may have a sure fund of excuses, with the defence that they are not at all to blame, but the gods...
	3.1-12: Οὕτως οὖν ἔμοιγε δοκέουσιν οἵτινες τῷ τρόπῳ τούτῳ ἐγχειρέουσιν ἰῆσθαι ταῦτα τὰ νοσήματα οὔτε ἱερὰ νομίζειν εἶναι οὔτε θεῖα· ὅπου γὰρ ὑπὸ καθαρμῶν τοιούτων μετάστατα γίνεται καὶ ὑπὸ θεραπείης τοιῆσδε, τί κωλύει καὶ ὑφ᾽ ἑτέρων τεχνημάτων ὁμοίων τούτοισιν ἐπιγίνεσθαί τε τοῖσιν ἀνθρώποισι καὶ προσπίπτειν; ὥστε τὸ θεῖον μηκέτι αἴτιον εἶναι, ἀλλά τι ἀνθρώπινον. ὅστις γὰρ οἷός τε περικαθαίρων ἐστὶ καὶ μαγεύων ἀπάγειν τοιοῦτον πάθος, οὗτος κἂν ἐπάγοι ἕτερα τεχνησάμενος, καὶ ἐν τούτῳ τῷ λόγῳ τὸ θεῖον ἀπόλλυται.	3: Accordingly I hold that those who attempt in this manner to cure these diseases cannot consider them sacred or divine; for when they are removed by such purifications and by such treatment as this, there is nothing to prevent the production of attacks in men by devices that are similar. If so, something human is to blame, and not godhead. He who by purifications and magic can take away such an affection can also by similar means bring it on, so that by this argument the action of godhead is disproved.
	10.44: ταῦτα δὲ πάσχει πάντα, . . .	10.44: The patient suffers all these things ... i.e. (10.7-13) the patient becomes speechless and chokes; froth flows from the mouth; he gnashes his teeth and twists his hands; the eyes roll and intelligence fails, and in some cases excrement is discharged.

25 : 2 *The sacred disease* 11, 16, 21.	11.23-25: κίνδυνος δὲ συντραφῆναι καὶ συναυξηθῆναι, ἢν μὴ θεραπευθῶσι τοῖσιν ἐπιτηδείοισιν.	11: There is a risk however that the disease will be nourished and grow with the patient, unless appropriate remedies be used.
	16.42-46: οὕτως αὕτη ἡ νοῦσος γίνεται καὶ θάλλει ἀπὸ τῶν προσιόντων τε καὶ ἀπιόντων, καὶ οὐδέν ἐστιν ἀπορωτέρη τῶν ἄλλων οὔτε ἰῆσθαι οὔτε γνῶναι, οὐδὲ θειοτέρη ἢ αἱ ἄλλαι.	16: Thus this disease is born and grows from the things that come to the body and leave it, is no more troublesome to understand and cure than are others, and is no more divine than others are.
	21.22-26: ὅστις δὲ ἐπίσταται ἐν ἀνθρώποισι ξηρὸν καὶ ὑγρὸν ποιεῖν, καὶ ψυχρόν καὶ θερμόν, ὑπὸ διαίτης, οὗτος καὶ ταύτην τὴν νοῦσον ἰῷτο ἄν, εἰ τοὺς καιροὺς διαγινώσκοι τῶν συμφερόντων, ἄνευ καθαρμῶν καὶ μαγείης.	21: Whoever knows how to cause in men by regimen moist or dry, hot or cold, he can cure this disease also, if he distinguish the seasons for useful treatment, without having recourse to purifications and magic.
26 : 4 *Aphorisms* 7.87	Ὁκόσα φάρμακα οὐκ ἰῆται, σίδηρος ἰῆται· ὅσα σίδηρος οὐκ ἰῆται, πῦρ ἰῆται· ὅσα δὲ πῦρ οὐκ ἰῆται, ταῦτα χρὴ νομίζειν ἀνίατα.	Those diseases that medicines do not cure are cured by the knife. Those that the knife does not cure are cured by fire. Those that fire does not cure must be considered incurable.

Appendix 4 : 2

Decree conferring a gold crown on a physician, Xenotimos, for his services during an epidemic (Third century BC)

Text from Paton, W. R. and Hicks, E. L. (1891) *The Inscriptions of Cos,* Oxford, **5** 4-5
Translation from Hands, A. R. (1968)*Charities and social aid in Greece and Rome,* London, **D63** 202-3

Πραξιμένης εἶπε· ἐπειδὴ [Ξενότιμος Τι]μοξέ–
νου ἔν τε τοῖς πρότερον χρόνοις ἐ[πιμέλ]ειαν
ἐποιεῖτο τῶν πολιτᾶν κατὰ τὰν τέ[χ]ναν τὰν
ἰατρικὰν παρέχων αὐτὸς αὑ[τὸ]ν π[ρ]ό[θυμ]ον εἰς
τὰν σωτηρίαν τῶν νοσεύντ[ων, κ]αὶ [νῦ]ν ἐν[π]ετό[ν–
των πολλῶν ἄγ[αν ὀλεθρί]ων [ἀρρω]στ[η]μάτων,
καὶ τῶν ἰατρῶν τῶν [δαμ]οσ[ιεύν]των ἐν τᾷ πό–
λει ἀρρωστησάντων [διὰ] τὰς [κ]α[κο]παθίας τὰς
γενομένας περὶ αὐτοὺς δ[ιὰ] τὰν ἐπιμέλειαν ἃν
ἐ]ποιεῦ[ντο] τῶν καμνό[ντων], Ξενότιμος αὐτε–
π]ά[γγελτος] ἀεὶ τοῖς δεομένοις παρείχετο τὰν
βο[άθειαν φέρ]ειν προαιρεύμεν[ος] τοῖς ἀρρωσ–
τοῦσι πᾶσι τὰν ἄ]κ[εσι]ν, οὐδεμίαν [δὲ προτί]μασιν
πο[ιεύμενος], ἀλλ' ὁμοίως περὶ πάντα[ς τὸ]ς πολί–
τ]ας [σπουδ]άζων διέσῳσε πολλούς, [δεδ]όχθαι
τῷ δάμῳ ἐπαινέσαι Ξενότιμον Τιμοξένου καὶ
στεφανῶσαι χρυσῷ στεφάνῳ εὐνοίας ἕνεκεν
καὶ ἐπιμελείας ἅμ ποιεύμενος διατελεῖ τῶν πο–
λιτᾶν, ὁ δὲ ἱεροκᾶρυξ τοῖς Διονυσίοις ἀναγγει–
λάτ[ω], ὅτι ὁ δᾶμος στεφανοῖ Ξενότιμον Τιμοξέ–
νου ἀπὸ ἀργυρίου οὗ ἐκ τῶν νόμων πλείστου
κ]υρί[α] ἐστὶ ἁ ἐκκλησία χειροτονίᾳ μεγίσταν
δ]ωρ[ε]ὰν δόμεν εὐνοίας ἕνεκεν καὶ ἐπιμελείας
ἃν ἐπ]οιεῖ[το κ]ατ[ὰ τὰν ἰα]τρι[κὰ]ν τέχναν τῶν ἐν
τᾷ π]ό[λει – – – – – – – – – – – – – –]ων, ὅπως εἰδῶντι
πάντες ὅτι ὁ δᾶμ]ος [το]ὺς χρησίμους ὄντας κα[ὶ
εὐνοῦς τῶν π[ο]λιτᾶν καταξίω]ς τ – – – –

[Praximenes proposed]: Since Xenotimos, son of Timoxenos, in previous times took care of the citizens according to his medical skill, showing himself eager to save the sick and now, in face of the onset of many virulent diseases and the illness of the public doctors in the city resulting from the ill effects of their attendance upon their patients, he of his own volition has been unfailing of his help for those in need, taking it upon himself to provide a remedy for every illness, and allowing to no one undue favour but saving men's lives by his ready service of all men equally: it is resolved by the people to commend Xenotimos, son of Timoxenos, and to crown him with a golden crown, etc.

Appendix 4 : 3

Decree of Knossos in honour of a doctor from Kos (221-219 BC)

Text from *Inscriptiones Creticae* I, (1935) (ed M. Guarducci) Rome, **7** 62
Translation from Austin, M. M. (1981) *The Hellenistic world from Alexander to the Roman conquest*, Cambridge, **124** 217

Κνωσίων οἱ κόσμοι καὶ ἁ πόλις Κώιων τᾶι βωλᾶι καὶ τῶι δ–
άμωι χαίρειν. Ἐπειδὴ πρεσβευσάντων Γορτυνίων πρ–
ὸς ὑμὲ ὑπὲρ ἰατροῦ καὶ ὑμῶν φιλοτίμως σπευσάντων
καὶ ἀποστειλάντων αὐτοῖς Ἑρμίαν ἰατρόν, στάσιος δ–
ὲ γενομένας ἐγ Γόρτυνι καὶ ἐλθόντων ἁμίων κατ[ὰ
τὰν συμμαχίαν ἐς τὰμ μάχαν τ[ὰγ Γορτυνίοις γεν–
ομέναν] ἐν τᾶι πό[λει, συνέ]βα τινὰς τῶμ πολι[τᾶν καὶ τ–
ῶν ἄλλων τῶν συνελθόντων παρ' ἁμίων ἐπὶ [τὰμ μά–
χαν τραυματίας τε γενέσθαι καὶ πλείους ἐκ τ[ῶν
τραυμάτων ἀρωστίαις οὐ ταῖς τυχούσαις π[εριπε–
σεῖν, Ἑρμίας ὑπάρχων ἀγαθὸς ἀνὴρ τότε τε πᾶσ[αν σ–
πουδὰν ἐποήσατο ὑπὲρ ἁμίων καὶ διέσωσε αὐτο[ὺς ἐγ
μεγάλων κινδύνων ἔν τε τοῖς λοιποῖς ἀπροφα[σίστ–
ως διετέλει συναντῶν τοῖς παρακαλοῦσι [αὐτὸ–
ν, πάλιν τε γενομένας μάχας περὶ Φαιστὸν π[ολλ–
ῶν τραυματιᾶν γενομένων καὶ ὡσαύτως πολλ[ῶν κι–
νδυνευσάντων ἐν ταῖς ἀρωστίαις πᾶσαν [σπου–
δὰν ἐν ταῖς θεραπείαις ποιούμενος διέ[σωσε αὐτοὺς
ἐγ μεγάλων κινδύνων ἔν τε [τοῖς λοιποῖς παρέχων
αὑτὸν πρόθ]υμον τ[οῖς παρακαλοῦσι αὐτὸν – –
– –

The kosmoi and the city of Cnossus to the council and people of
Cos, greetings. Since, when the people of Gortyn sent an
embassy to you concerning a doctor, and you responded with
zealous eagerness by sending them Hermias the doctor, and
when there was a revolution /
at Gortyn and we came in accordance with our alliance to the
battle [which took place at Gortyn] in the [city] and it
happened that some of the citizens [and] of the others of our
own number who had come to [the] battle were wounded and
that many [fell] seriously ill from [their] /
wounds, Hermias being a good man showed them all his zeal
on our behalf and saved them [from] great dangers, and
otherwise he constantly gives assistance without stint to
those who call upon [him],/
and on another occasion when a battle took place near
Phaestus [many] were wounded and similarly many were in
danger because of their ailments, he displayed all his [zeal]
in looking after them and [saved them] from great dangers,
and [otherwise he shows /
himself helpful to those who call upon him . . .]

Appendix 4 : 4

Herodas IV

Text from Nairn, J. A. (1904) *The Mimes of Herodas*, Oxford, 44-57
Translation from Edelstein, E. and L.(1945) *Asclepius: A collection and interpretation of the testimonies*, Baltimore, 1: **T482** 272-277

Reference	Text	Translation
1 : 1-18 ΚΟΚΚΑΛΗ	Χαίρος ἄναξ Παίηον, ὃς μεδεῖς Τρίκκης, καὶ Κῶν γλυκῆαν κἠπίδαυρον ᾤκηκας, σὺν καὶ Κορωνὶς ἥ σ' ἔτικτε κὦπόλλων χαίροιεν, ἧς τε χειρὶ δεξιῇ ψαύεις Ὑγίεια, κὦνπερ οἵδε τίμιοι βωμοί, Πανάκη τε κἠπιώ τε κἰησὼ χαίροι χοἰ Λεωμέδοντος οἰκίην τε καὶ τείχη πέρσαντες, ἰητῆρες ἀγρίων νούσων, Ποπαλείριός τε καὶ Μαχάων χαιρόντων, χὤσοι θεοὶ σὴν ἑστίην κατοικεῦσιν καὶ θεαί, πάτερ Παίηον· ἵλεῳ δεῦτε τοῦ ἀλέκτορος τοῦδ' ὅντιν' οἰκίης τοίχων κήρυκα θύω, τἀπίδορπα δέξαισθε. οὐ γάρ τι πολλὴν οὐδ' ἕτοιμον ἀντλεῦμεν, ἐπεὶ τάχ' ἂν βοῦν ἢ νενημένην χοῖρον πολλῆς φορίνης, κοὐκ ἀλέκτορ', ἴητρα νούσων ἐποιεύμεσθα, τὰς ἀπέψησας ἐπ' ἠπίας σὺ χεῖρας, ὦ ἄναξ, τείνας.	Hail to thee, Lord Paieon, ruler of Tricca, who hast got as thine habitation sweet Cos and Epidaurus, hail to Coronis thy mother withal and Apollo; hail to her whom thou touchest with thy right hand, Hygieia, and those to whom belong these honoured altars, Panace and Epio and Iaso; hail ye twain which did sack the house and walls of Laomedon, healers of savage sicknesses, Podalirius and Machaon, and what gods and goddesses soever dwell by thine hearth, Father Paieon; come hither with your blessings and accept the aftercourse of this cock whom I sacrifice, herald of the walls of my house. For we draw no bounteous nor ready spring; else might we, perchance, with an ox or stuffed pig of much fatness and no humble cock, be paying the price of cure from diseases that thou didst wipe away, Lord, by laying on us thy gentle hands.

2 : 19-20 ΚΥΝΝΩ	ἐκ δεξιῆς τὸν πίνακα, Κοκκάλη, στῆσον τῆς Ὑγιείης.	Set the tablet, Coccale, on the right of Hygieia.
3 : 79-85 ΝΕΩΚΟΡΟΣ	κάλ' ὔμιν, ὦ γυναῖκες, ἐντελεώς τὰ ἱρὰ καὶ ἐς λῷον ἐμβλέποντα· μεζόνως οὔτις ἠρέσατο τὸν Παιήον' ἤπερ οὖν ὑμεῖς. – ἰὴ ἰὴ Παίηον, εὐμενὴς εἴης καλοῖς ἐπ' ἱροῖς ταῖσδε, κεἴ τινες τῶνδε ἔασ' ὀπυιηταί τε καὶ γενῆς ἆσσον. ἰὴ ἰὴ Παίηον· ὧδε ταῦτ' εἴη.	Your sacrifice is entirely favorable, ladies, with still better things in store; no one has appeased Paieon in greater sort than you. Glory, glory to thee, Paieon, mayst thou look with favor for fair offerings on these, and all that be their husbands or near of kin. Glory, glory, Paieon. So be it.
4 : 86-94 ΚΟΚΚΑΛΗ	εἴη γάρ, ὦ μέγιστε, χὐγιίῃ πολλῇ ἔλθοιμεν αὖτις μέζον' ἱρ' ἀγινεῦσαι σὺν ἀνδράσιν καὶ παισί. Κοττάλη, καλῶς τεμεῦσα μέμνεο τὸ σκελύδριον δοῦναι τῷ νεωκόρῳ τοὔρνιθος, ἔς τε τὴν τρώγλην τὸν πελανὸν ἔνθες τοῦ δράκοντος εὐφήμως, καὶ ψαιστὰ δεῦσον· τἄλλα δ' οἰκίης ἔδρῃ δαισόμεθα· καὶ ἐπὶ μὴ λάθῃ φέρειν, αὔτη. τῆς ὑγιίης λῶ.	So be it, Almighty, and may we come again in full health once more bringing larger offerings, and our husbands and children with us. Coccale, remember to carve the leg off the fowl carefully and give it to the sacristan, and put the mess into the mouth of the snake reverently, and souse the meat-offering. The rest we will eat at home; and remember to take it away.

Appendix 4 : 5

Inscriptiones Creticae IV, 168 [218BC, Gortyn, Crete (Pouilloux, Choix, No. 15)]

Translation from Hands, A. R. (1968) *Charities and social aid in Greece and Rome,* **D64** 203

The *kosmoi* of Gortyn and the city send greetings to the council and the people of Cos. Since Hermias, son of Emmenidas, having been elected by you and sent to us as a doctor, has made his stay among us worthy both of you who sent him and of himself, and also of ourselves who gave you the responsibility of the choice of doctor; and since he has been irreproachable in all his dealings with us and has completed his stay of five years, looking after the citizens and the rest of those dwelling at Gortyn, and has by the enthusiastic and earnest application of his skill and his other care saved many from great dangers, never failing in his energy; and since, when many allies were with us at the time when we were at war, he displayed the same care for them and saved them from great dangers, wishing to show his gratitude to our city, and now he has come to the assembly and has asked of us his return to his own home, we have agreed and have sent to accompany him Soarchos and Kydas of our own citizens, wishing to express our gratitude to him; and since it has seemed good to us to commend Hermias for his merits and goodwill towards the city and also to commend the Coans in that they sent to us a good doctor and a worthy man; in order that all may know that we understand how to show our gratitude, it was resolved by us to give citizenship to him and his descendants ...

Cf. Appendix 4:3, where the same doctor is honoured in a decree of Knossos, for his services during the war mentioned in this inscription.

Appendix 5 : 1

Inscriptio Pergamena [ed. R. Herzog, *Berl. Sitzber.*, 1934, pp. 753ff.]

Text and translation from Edelstein, E. and L. (1945)*Asclepius: A collection and interpretation of the testimonies,* Baltimore, 1: **T 596** 331-332

. . . .
[σωτὴρ . . . .]
[κληθεὶς ἐν νυξίν τε καὶ ἤμασι πολλ]άκι[ς ἦλθες]
[νούσοις ἀργαλέαις τρυομένω]ι κραδίην.
[εἰν ἁλὶ δὲ πρόφρων μου] κήδεαι οὐδὲ δ[αμῆναι]
[οὔποτέ με προδίδως] πήμασι λευγαλ[έοις],
[ἀλλ' ἀδεῶς μὲν πέμψας], ὅτε πλώοντά με Δ[ήλωι]
[ἴσχες ἄμ' Αἰγαῖον τ' οἶδ]μα καταστόρεσᾶς,
[ῥύσαο δ' αὖ ναυηγό]ν, ὅτε στροφάλιγγι βαρεί[ηι]
[κῦμα τρόπει μι]κρῆι στῆσας ὑφ' ἡμετέρηι,
[πρήυνας δ' ἀνέ]μους, ὅτ' ἐπ' ἀνδράσι μαίνετ' ἀ]ήτης]
[αἰνὴν ἀμ]φ' αὐτοῖς αἶσαν ἄγων θανάτου.
[ἐκ δ' ἀλέη]ς με σάωσᾶς ἀεικέος ἔκ τε ῥο[άων]
[χειμε]ρίων ποταμῶν ἔκ τ' ἀνέμοιο βίη[ς].
[αὐτὸς δ'] Αὐσονίων ἔταρον ποίησας ἀν[άκτων]
[καὶ κλέ]ος ἐκ πολίων ἐσθλὸν ἔνευσ[ας ἄγειν]
[εὐλογίηι ζ]αθέης Βειθυνίδος ἔνδοθι [χώρης]
[καὶ γῆν θεσπ]εσίην σὴν ἀνὰ Τευθρ[ανίην].
[ἀνθ' ὧν σὸν τιμ]ῶ τε καὶ ἅζομαι οὔν[ομα, Σῶτερ],
[κληίζω δέ σε] γῆς πε[ίρ]ατ[' ἐς ἡμεδαπῆς].

. . . Savior . . . .

Summoned night and day, you came to me many times when I was distressed in heart by painful illness. On the sea you kindly protected me, and you never let me be overcome by baneful calamities, but you conducted me safely when you steered my ship to Delos, smoothing the Aegean swell. Again, you rescued the shipwrecked when you made the waves in a powerful eddy rise under my little boat. You calmed the winds when the gale raged against men and surrounded them with the grim destiny of death. You saved me from the glaring heat and from the currents of the wintery rivers and from the violence of the wind. You made me a comrade of the Ausonian lords and graciously promised on account of my rhetoric to spread my good reputation from the cities within the sacred Bithynian land even to your divine land of Teuthrania. In gratitude for these kindnesses I revere and respect your name, Savior; I sing your praises to the ends of our [i.e., the Roman] Empire.

This hymn is ascribed to Aristides by Herzog.

Appendix 5 : 2

***Inscriptio Pergamena* [ed. M. Fränkel, *Inschriften von Pergamon* II, 1895, no. 264; Imperial time].**

Text and translation from Edelstein, E. and L. (1945)*Asclepius: A collection and interpretation of the testimonies,* Baltimore, 1: **T 513** 291

– – εἰσπορευέσθ]ω εἰς – – – – – – – – – – – – – – – – –	... let him enter into ...
– – – – – – ἡμέ]ρας δέκ[α] ἀποδέξετ(α) [ι – – – – – – – –	... he will have ten days ...
– – – – – – – – εἰσιὼν λουσάμενος, ἐὰ[ν – – – – – – –	... entering, after bathing, if ...
– – – – ἀπαλ]λάσσεσθαι περικαθαιρέ[τω – – – – – – – –	... to be set free, let him purify completely ...
– – – χιτῶ]νι λευκῶι καὶ [θ]είωι καὶ δ[άφνηι – – – – – –	... in a white chiton and with brimstone, and with laurel ...
– – – ται]νίας, ἃς περικ[α]θαιρέτω ω – – – – – – – – –	... with fillets which let him purify completely ...
– – – εἰσ]πορευέσθω πρὸς τὸν θεὸν τ – – – – – – – – –	... let him go toward the god ...
εἰς τὸ μ]έγα ἐνκοιμητήριον ὁ ἐγκο[ιμησόμενος – – – – – –	into the great incubation room, the incubant ...
– – – ἱερε]ίοις λευκοῖς ἁγνοῖς ἐλάας ἔ[ρνεσιν ἐστεμμένοις	...with pure white sacrificial victims garlanded with olive shoots
– – – μήτε δακτ]ύλιον μήτε ζώνην μ[ήτε – – – – – – – –	... neither seal-ring nor belt nor ...
– – – – – – – – – – – – ἀνυπ]ό[δ]ητο[ν – – – – – – – –	... barefoot ...
–	

Appendix 5 : 3

Inscriptio Pergamena [ed. M. Fränkel, *Inschriften von Pergamon* II, 1895, no. 251; 2nd c. BC ?].

Text and translation from Edelstein, E. and L. (1945)*Asclepius: A collection and interpretation of the testimonies*, Baltimore, 1: **T 491** 280-282

Ἐπὶ πρυτάνεως Καβείρου, μηνὸ(ς) Πανθείου
εἰκάδι· ἔγνω βουλὴ καὶ δῆμος γνώμηι
στρατηγῶν περὶ τῆς ἱερωσύνης τοῦ Ἀσκληπι[οῦ,
ὅπως ὑπάρχηι εἰς τὸν ἅπαντα χρόνον
Ἀσκληπιάδηι καὶ τοῖς ἀπογόνοις τοῖς
Ἀσκληπιάδου· τύχηι τῆι ἀγαθῆι· δεδόχθαι
τῆι βουλῆι καὶ τῶι δήμωι· τὴν μὲν ἱερωσύνην
τοῦ Ἀσκληπιοῦ καὶ τῶν ἄλλων θεῶν τῶν ἐν τῶ[ι
Ἀσκλη[πι]είωι ἱδρυμένων εἶναι Ἀσκληπιάδου
τοῦ [Ἀρχί]ου καὶ τῶν ἀπογόνων τῶν Ἀσκληπιάδου
εἰς ἅ[π]α[ντ]α [τ]ὸν χρόνον καὶ στεφανηφορεῖν αὐτῶν
ἀεὶ τὸν ἔχοντα τὴν ἱερωσύνην, λαμβάνειν δὲ
καὶ γέρα τῶν θυομένων ἱερείων ἐν τῶι ἱερῶι
πάντων σκέλος δεξιὸν καὶ τὰ δέρματα καὶ τἆλλ[α
τραπεζώματα πάντα τὰ παρατιθέμεν[α
. . . . σ[. . καρ]πεύεσθαι [δ]ὲ α[ὐ]τὸν καὶ τὸ ἱερ[ὸν
– –
– –
– – – – – – – ὑ[πάρ]χειν εἰς ἅπαν[τ]α [τ]ὸν χρό[νον.

In the magistracy of Cabeirus, on the 20th day of the month Pantheius: The Council and Demos on the motion of the generals decreed concerning the priesthood of Asclepius that it should belong to Asclepiades and to the descendants of Asclepiades for all time to come. With good fortune. Be it resolved by the Council and the Demos, that the priesthood of Asclepius and of the other gods who are residing in the Asclepieion shall belong to Asclepiades, the son of Archias, and to the descendants of Asclepiades for all time to come, and that he who among them at any particular time is holding the priesthood shall wear a crown, and that he shall take as a perquisite the right leg and the skin of all the sacrificial animals offered in the temple, and all the other offerings which are dedicated on the holy table along with them . . . and he shall enjoy the fruits and the holy . . . for all time to come.

εἶναι δ]ὲ καὶ ἀτέλειαν Ἀσκληπιάδηι πάντων
ὧν] ἡ πόλις κυρία, καὶ εἰς τὸ λοιπὸν
ἀ]εὶ τῶι τὸν στέφανον ἔχοντι, ἀναγορεύεσθαι δ[ὲ
εἰς προεδρίαν τὸν ἱερέα ἐν ἅπασι τοῖς ἀγῶσιν.
ἐπιμελεῖσθαι δὲ καὶ τῆς εὐκοσμίας τῆς κατὰ τὸ ἱερ[ὸν
πάσης τὸν ἱερέ[α] ὡς ἂν αὐτῶι δοκῆ[ι
καλῶς ἔχειν καὶ ὁσίως, κυριεύοντα τῶν ἱερῶν παίδων.
ὅπως δὲ ταῦτα εἰς τὸν ἅπαντα χρόνον διαμένηι
βέβαια (Ἀ)σκληπιάδηι καὶ τοῖς ἀπογόνοις τοῖς
Ἀσκληπιάδου, ἐπιτελεῖν ὁρκωμόσιον τὴν πόλιν
ἐν τῆι ἀγορᾶι ἐπὶ τοῦ Διὸς τοῦ σωτῆρος τῶι βωμῶι
καὶ ὀμόσαι τ(ὰ)ς τιμουχίας· ἦ μὴν ἐμμενεῖν ἐν οἷς
ἐψήφισται ἡ πόλις Ἀσκληπιάδηι καὶ τοῖς ἀπογόνοις
τοῖς Ἀσκληπιάδου. τοὺς δὲ στρατηγοὺς τοὺς ἐπ[ὶ
Καβείρου πρυτάνεως ἐπιμεληθῆναι, ὅπως
συντελεσθῇ ὁ ὅρκος καθάπερ γέγραπται.

And Asclepiades shall be exempted from all obligations that the city is entitled to impose, and likewise for all time to come shall he be exempted whoever wears the crown, and the priest shall be entitled to a front seat at all the games. And furthermore the priest shall have charge of the general good conduct within the sanctuary as it may seem right to him and fitting, and he shall have power over the temple servants. In order that this may be safeguarded for all time to come for Asclepiades and the descendants of Asclepiades, the city shall undertake a solemn oath in the Agora at the altar of Zeus Savior, and the officials shall swear to it: namely that the city shall abide by what it has decreed for Asclepiades and the descendants of Asclepiades. It shall be the duty of the generals of the magistracy of Cabeirus to see to it that the oath be fulfilled as it is written.

ἀναγράψαι δὲ αὐτοὺς καὶ τὸ ψήφισμα τόδ[ε
εἰς στήλας λιθίνας τρεῖς καὶ στῆσαι αὐτῶν
μίαν μὲν ἐν τῶι ἱερῶι τοῦ ᾿Ασκληπιοῦ ἐμ Περγάμῳ,
ἄλλην δὲ ἐν τῶι ἱερῶι τῆς ᾿Αθηνᾶς ἐν ἀκροπόλ[ει,
τὴ]ν δὲ τρίτην ἐμ Μυτιλήνηι ἐν τῶι ἱερῶι τοῦ
᾿Ασκλ]ηπιοῦ. ἐγγράψαι δὲ καὶ εἰς τοὺς νόμους
τοὺς τ]ῆς πόλεως τὸ ψήφισμα τόδε καὶ
χρήσθω]σαν αὐτῶι νόμωι κυρίωι εἰς ἅπαντα τὸν χρόνον.

They must inscribe this decree on three stone tablets and set up one of them in the sanctuary of Asclepius at Pergamon, the other one in the sanctuary of Athena on the Acropolis, the third one at Mytilene in the sanctuary of Asclepius. And they must list this decree among the laws of the city and must treat it as a regular law for all time to come.

Cf. **T491a** 282: *Inscriptiones Graecae*, II^2, no. 5045 [time of Hadrian] : Ἱερέως | ᾿Ασκληπιοῦ | Π[αί]ω(ν)ος ? [inscribed on front seat in the theater of Dionysus at Athens].

Appendix 5 : 4
Oribasius, *Collectiones Medicae* XLV. 30. 10-14

Text and translation from Edelstein, E. and L. (1945) *Asclepius: A collection and interpretation of the testimonies,* Baltimore, 1: **T 425** 238-239

Σπασμὸς δ' ἄρα καὶ ἡ ἐπιληψία· ταύτης οὖν τεταρταῖος πυρετὸς ἴαμά ἐστιν, ὥστε ἤν τε ὕστερον ἐπιγένηται, λύεται ἡ ἐπιληψία, ἤν τε πρόσθεν, οὐκ ἂν ἔτι τούτῳ τῷ ἀνθρώπῳ γένοιτο. ὅπως δὲ καὶ Τεύκρῳ τῷ Κυζικηνῷ ἔσχεν, εἰπεῖν ἄξιον· ἐπεὶ γὰρ ἥλω τῇ ἐπιληψίᾳ, ἧκε μὲν εἰς Πέργαμον παρὰ τὸν 'Ασκληπιόν, αἰτῶν λύσιν τῆς νόσου· ὁ δ' αὐτῷ φανεὶς εἰς λόγους ἀφικνεῖται, καὶ ἐρωτᾷ εἰ ἐθέλει τῶν παρόντων ἕτερα ἀλλάξασθαι. καὶ ὃς μάλιστα μὲν οὐκ ἐθέλειν ἔφη, ἀλλά τινα εὐθεῖαν ἀπαλλαγὴν σχεῖν τοῦ κακοῦ· εἰ δ' ἄρα, μὴ χείρω τὰ γενησόμενα εἶναι τῶν παρόντων. φήσαντος δὲ τοῦ θεοῦ ῥᾴω τε ἔσεσθαι καὶ παντὸς ἄλλου σαφέστερον θεραπεύσειν, οὕτω δὲ ὑφίσταται τὴν νόσον, καὶ αὐτῷ ἥκει τεταρταῖος πυρετός, καὶ τὸ ἀπὸ τοῦδε τῆς ἐπιληψίας ἐξάντης γίνεται.	Also epilepsy is a cramp; of this quartan fever, therefore, is a cure, so that if it supervenes afterwards epilepsy is broken up, while if it comes previously epilepsy does not befall that man any more. How it happened to Teucer, the Cyzicenean [*ca*. 100 AD], is worth telling: when he was afflicted with epilepsy he came to Pergamum to Asclepius, asking for liberation from the disease. The god appearing to him holds converse with him and asks if he wants to exchange his present disease against another one. And he said he surely did not want that but would rather get some immediate relief from the evil. But if at all, he wished that the future might not be worse than the present. When the god had said it would be easier and this would cure him more plainly than anything else, he [*sc*., Teucer] consents to the disease, and a quartan fever attacks him, and thereafter he is free from epilepsy.

The passage is taken from Rufus, a physician of the 1st century AD.

Appendix 5 : 5

Galen

The Greek text and translation of the following references is taken either from Edelstein, E. and L. (1945) *Asclepius: A collection and interpretation of the testimonies*, vol. 1, Baltimore; or the Loeb Classical Library edition of Galen (1979) *Galen: On the natural faculties* (trans. A. J. Brock) London.

References are by numeral, followed by either a testimony number (=T) (Edelstein), or Loeb page number.

Reference	Text	Translation
1 : T 803 *De Anatomicis Administrationibus* I. 2 [II, pp. 224-225 K.]	Ἐγὼ δὲ ἐν τῇ πατρίδι κατ' ἐκεῖνον ἔτι διέτριβον τὸν χρόνον, ὑπὸ Σατύρῳ παιδευόμενος, ἔτος ἤδη τέταρτον ἐπιδημοῦντι τῇ Περγάμῳ μετὰ Κοστουνίου Ῥουφίνου, κατασκευάζοντος ἡμῖν τὸν νεὼν τοῦ Διὸς Ἀσκληπιοῦ.	I [*sc.*, Galen] was still living in my native land at that time, receiving instruction from Satyrus who was then spending his fourth year in Pergamon with Costunius Rufinus who was building for us the temple of Zeus Asclepius.
2 : T 620 *De Compositione Medicamentorum Secundum Locos* Cp. 3 [XIII, pp. 271-272 K.]	Προσέθηκε δὲ τῷ Διὶ τὴν Πίσσαν, ὡς εἰώθασι πολλοὶ καὶ χωρὶς ποιητικῆς ἐν τῷ βίῳ λέγειν, μὰ τὸν ἐν Περγάμῳ Ἀσκληπιόν, μὰ τὴν ἐν Ἐφέσῳ Ἄρτεμιν . . .	He [*sc.*, Philo] added Pissa [i.e., Olympia] to the name of Zeus as many are wont, even apart from poetry, to say in everyday-life, "by Asclepius in Pergamon," "by Artemis in Ephesus" . . .
3 : T 595 *De Antidotis* I. 6 [XIV, p. 42K.]	Ἰλήκοις ὃς τήνδε μάκαρ τεκτήναο, Παιών, εἴτε σε Τρικκαῖοι, δαῖμον, ἔχουσι λόφοι, ἢ Ῥόδος ἢ Βουρίννα καὶ ἀγχιάλη Ἐπίδαυρος· ἰλήκοις, ἱλαρὴν δ' αἰὲν ἄνακτι δίδου παῖδα τεὴν Πανάκειαν. ὁ δ' εὐαγέεσσι θυηλαῖς ἱλάσεται τὴν σὴν αἰὲν ἀνωδυνίην.	Be gracious, blessed Paeon, you who fashioned this remedy, whether the Triccaean ridges hold you, O demigod, or Rhodes, or Cos and Epidaurus on the sea; be gracious, send your always gracious daughter, Panacea, to the emperor, who will propitiate you with pure sacrifices for the everlasting freedom from pain which you can grant.

4: T 458 *De Libris Propriis* Cp. 2 [II, p. 99 M.]	. . . τὸν πάτριον θεὸν Ἀσκληπιόν, οὗ καὶ θεραπευτὴν ἀπέφαινον ἐμαυτόν, ἐξ ὅτου με θανατικὴν διάθεσιν ἀποστήματος ἔχοντα διέσωσε . . .	. . . the ancestral god Asclepius of whom I declared myself to be a servant since he saved me when I had the deadly condition of an abscess . . .
5: T 459 *De Morborum Differentiis* Cp. 9 [VI, p. 869 K.]	Νικομάχῳ δὲ τῷ Σμυρναίῳ πᾶν ἀμέτρως ηὐξήθη τὸ σῶμα, καὶ οὐδὲ κινεῖν ἔτι δυνατὸς ἦν ἑαυτόν· ἀλλὰ τοῦτον μὲν ὁ Ἀσκληπιὸς ἰάσατο.	The whole body of Nicomachus of Smyrna swelled excessively and it was impossible for him to move himself. But this man Asclepius healed.
6: T 413 *De Sanitate Tuenda* I. 8. 19-21	Καὶ οὐκ ὀλίγους ἡμεῖς ἀνθρώπους νοσοῦντας ὅσα ἔτη διὰ τὸ τῆς ψυχῆς ἦθος ὑγιεινοὺς ἀπεδείξαμεν, ἐπανορθωσάμενοι τὴν ἀμετρίαν τῶν κινήσεων. οὐ σμικρὸς δὲ τοῦ λόγου μάρτυς καὶ ὁ πάτριος ἡμῶν θεὸς Ἀσκληπιός, οὐκ ὀλίγοις μὲν ᾠδάς τε γράφεσθαι καὶ μίμους γελοίων καὶ μέλη τινὰ ποιεῖν ἐπιτάξας, οἷς αἱ τοῦ θυμοειδοῦς κινήσεις σφοδρότεραι γενόμεναι θερμοτέραν τοῦ δέοντος ἀπειργάζοντο τὴν κρᾶσιν τοῦ σώματος, ἑτέροις δέ τισιν, οὐκ ὀλίγοις οὐδὲ τούτοις, κυνηγετεῖν καὶ ἱππάζεσθαι καὶ ὁπλομαχεῖν. εὐθὺς δὲ τούτοις διώρισε τό τε τῶν κυνηγεσίων εἶδος, οἷς τοῦτο προσέταξε, τό τε τῆς ὁπλίσεως, οἷς δι' ὅπλων ἐκέλευσε τὰ γυμνάσια ποιεῖσθαι. οὐ γὰρ μόνον ἐπεγείρειν αὐτῶν τὸ θυμοειδὲς ἐβουλήθη, ἄρρωστον ὑπάρχον, ἀλλὰ καὶ μέτρον ὡρίσατο τῇ τῶν γυμνασίων ἰδέᾳ.	And not a few men, however many years they were ill through the disposition of their souls, we have made healthy by correcting the disproportion of their emotions. No slight witness of the statement is also our ancestral god Asclepius who ordered not a few to have odes written as well as to compose comical mimes and certain songs (for the motions of their passions, having become more vehement, have made the temperature of the body warmer than it should be); and for others, these not a few either, he ordered hunting and horse riding and exercising in arms; and at the same time he appointed the kind of hunting for those whom he prescribed this; and the type of armor for those whom he enjoined to take exercise with armor. For he not only desired to awake the passion of these men because it was weak but also defined the measure by the form of exercises.

7 : T 401 *Commentarius in Hippocratis Epidemias* VI. iv, Sectio IV. 8 [XVIIb, p. 137 K.]	Οὕτω γέ τοι καὶ παρ' ἡμῖν ἐν Περγάμῳ τοὺς θεραπευομένους ὑπὸ τοῦ θεοῦ πειθομένους ὁρῶμεν αὐτῷ πεντεκαίδεκα πολλάκις ἡμέρας προστάξαντι μηδ' ὅλως πιεῖν, οἳ τῶν ἰατρῶν μηδενὶ προστάττοντι πείθονται. μεγάλην γὰρ ἔχει ῥοπὴν εἰς τὸ πάντα ποιῆσαι τὰ προσταττόμενα τὸ πεπεῖσθαι τὸν κάμνοντα βεβαίως ἀκολουθήσειν ὠφέλειαν ἀξιόλογον αὐτῷ.	Thus at any rate even among ourselves in Pergamum we see that those who are being treated by the god obey him when on many occasions he bids them not to drink at all for fifteen days, while they obey none of the physicians who give this prescription. For it has great influence on the patient's doing all which is prescribed if he has been firmly persuaded that a remarkable benefit to himself will ensue.
8 : T 436 *Subfiguratio Empirica* Cp. X, p. 78 [Deichgräber]	Ἄλλος δέ τις ἀνὴρ πλούσιος οὐχ ἡμεδαπὸς οὗτός γε, ἀλλ' ἐκ μέσης Θρᾴκης ἧκεν ὀνείρατος προτρέψαντος αὐτὸν εἰς τὴν Πέργαμον· εἶτα τοῦ θεοῦ προστάξαντος ὄναρ αὐτῷ πίνειν τε τοῦ διὰ τῶν ἐχιδνῶν φαρμάκου καθ' ἑκάστην ἡμέραν καὶ χρίειν ἔξωθεν τὸ σῶμα μετέπεσε τὸ πάθος οὐ μετὰ πολλὰς ἡμέρας εἰς λέπραν ἐθεραπεύθη τε πάλιν οἷς ὁ θεὸς ἐκέλευσε φαρμάκοις καὶ τοῦτο τὸ νόσημα.	Another wealthy man, this one not a native but from the interior of Thrace, came, because a dream had driven him, to Pergamum. Then a dream appeared to him, the god prescribing that he should drink every day of the drug produced from the vipers and should anoint the body from the outside. The disease after a few days turned into leprosy; and this disease, in turn, was cured by the drugs which the god commanded.
9 : Loeb, 64 *De naturalibus facultatibus* 1. 13 [2. 40 K.]	Τί δὴ τὸ κέρδος ἐκ τῶν τοιούτων δογμάτων εἰς τὰς θεραπείας ἐκτήσατο; μήτε νεφριτικόν τι νόσημα δύνασθαι θεραπεῦσαι μήτ' ἰκτερικὸν μήτε μελαγχολικόν, ἀλλὰ καὶ περὶ τοῦ πᾶσιν ἀνθρώποις οὐχ Ἱπποκράτει μόνον ὁμολογουμένου τοῦ καθαίρειν τῶν φαρμάκων . . .	And what profit did he [*sc.*, Asclepiades] derive from these opinions from the point of view of treatment? He neither was able to cure a kidney ailment, nor jaundice, nor a disease of black bile, nor would he agree with the view held not merely by Hippocrates but by all men regarding drugs . . .

10 : Loeb, 64
De naturalibus facultatibus
1. 13 [2. 41 K.]

Ἆρ' οὖν οὐ μαίνεσθαι νομιστέον αὐτὸν ἢ παντάπασιν ἄπειρον εἶναι τῶν ἔργων τῆς τέχνης; τίς γὰρ οὐκ οἶδεν, ὡς, εἰ μὲν φλέγματος ἀγωγὸν δοθείη φάρμακον τοῖς ἰκτεριῶσιν, οὐκ ἂν οὐδὲ τέτταρας κυάθους καθαρθεῖεν· οὕτω δ' οὐδ' εἰ τῶν ὑδραγωγῶν τι· χολαγωγῷ δὲ φαρμάκῳ πλεῖστον μὲν ἐκκενοῦται χολῆς, αὐτίκα δὲ καθαρὸς τοῖς οὕτω καθαρθεῖσιν ὁ χρὼς γίγνεται. πολλοὺς γοῦν ἡμεῖς μετὰ τὸ θεραπεῦσαι τὴν ἐν τῷ ἥπατι διάθεσιν ἅπαξ καθήραντες ἀπηλλάξαμεν τοῦ παθήματος. οὐ μὴν οὐδ' εἰ φλέγματος ἀγωγῷ καθαίροις φαρμάκῳ, πλέον ἄν τι διαπράξαιο.

Must we not, therefore, suppose that he [*sc*., Asclepiades] was either mad, or entirely unacquainted with practical medicine? For who does not know that if a drug for attracting phlegm be given in a case of jaundice it will not even evacuate four *cyathi*[1] of phlegm? Similarly also if one of the hydragogues be given. A cholagogue, on the other hand, clears away a great quantity of bile, and the skin of patients so treated at once becomes clear. I myself have, in many cases, after treating the liver condition, then removed the disease by means of a single purgation; whereas, if one had employed a drug for removing phlegm one would have done no good.

1 About 4 oz., or one-third of a pint.

11 : Loeb, 194-196
De naturalibus facultatibus
2. 9 [2. 126 K.]

As for the scientific proofs of all this, they are to be drawn from these principles of which I have already spoken - namely, that bodies act upon and are acted upon by each other in virtue of the Warm, Cold, Moist and Dry. And if one is speaking of any activity, whether it be exercised by vein, liver, arteries, heart, alimentary canal, or any part, one will be inevitably compelled to acknowledge that this activity depends upon the way in which the four qualities are blended. Thus I would like to ask the Erasistrateans why it is

τὸ γὰρ ὅτι περιστέλλεται μόνον αὐτὸ καθ' ἑαυτὸ γιγνώσκειν οὐδέπω χρηστόν, εἰ μὴ καὶ τὴν αἰτίαν εἰδείημεν· οὕτω γὰρ ἂν οἶμαι καὶ τὰ σφάλματα θεραπεύσαιμεν.

that the stomach contracts upon the food, and why the veins generate blood. There is no use in recognising the mere fact of contraction, without also knowing the cause; if we know this, we shall also be able to rectify the failures of function.

Appendix 5 : 6

Aelius Aristides

Text and translation from either Edelstein, E. and L. (1945) *Asclepius: A collection and interpretation of the testimonies*, vol. 1, Baltimore, or the Loeb Classical Library edition of Aristides (1973) *Aristides*, vol. 1, (trans. C. A. Behr) London.
References are by numeral, and either testimony number (=T) (Edelstein), title of work and reference within that work; or Loeb volume, page number, title of work and reference within that work.

Reference	Text	Translation
1 : T 282 *Or*. 38. 1	ἝΚλῦτε φίλοι, θεῖός μοι ἐνύπνιον ἦλθεν ὄνειρος,᾿ ἔφη αὐτὸ τὸ ὄναρ· . . . ἐχέτω δὴ καὶ τὸ ἐνύπνιον ὡς ὕπαρ καὶ τὸ δρώμενον ὡς ἡ πρόρρησις εἶχεν.	"Listen friends, a dream came to me, a vision sent from the gods," said the dream itself. . . . May the dream then become waking reality, and may the actual performance be like the prediction.
2 : T 282 *Or*. 38.19	Ἐπάνειμι δὲ ὅθεν ἐξέβην, ἐπὶ τοὺς ἀρχηγέτας τε καὶ τοὔνομα πρώτους λαβόντας τὸ τῶν Ἀσκληπιαδῶν. οἱ δὲ ἕως μὲν ἦσαν ἐν ἀνθρώποις, στρατείαις καὶ ὁμιλίαις καὶ γενέσει παίδων πρεπόντων αὐτοῖς καὶ συλλήβδην ἁπάσῃ τῇ πολιτικῇ δυνάμει τὰς πόλεις ὠφέλουν, οὐ μόνον τὰς τοῦ σώματος νόσους ἐξαιροῦντες, ἀλλὰ καὶ τὰ τῶν πόλεων νοσήματα ἰώμενοι, μᾶλλον δὲ οὐδ᾿ ἐγγίγνεσθαι τὴν ἀρχὴν ἐῶντες, ἀπ᾿ ἀμφοῖν σῴζοντες τοὺς ὑπηκόους, [καὶ] τῇ τέχνῃ τὴν ἀρχὴν ἀκόλουθον κατασκευασάμενοι.	Now I shall return to my starting-point, to the founders and those who first assumed the name Asclepiads. As long as they were dwelling among men, by participating in warfare and in community life, by begetting children worthy of themselves and in general by their whole political ability they helped the communities, alleviating not only the ailments of the body, but healing also the ills of the cities; or rather not even permitting evils of either kind to put in an appearance they saved their subjects from both and made their rule conform to their art.
3 : T 282 *Or*. 38.10	. . . τὸ δ᾿ ἁλῶναι τὴν Τροίαν καὶ παντάπασιν ἦλθεν εἰς αὐτοὺς τῇ τε ἄλλῃ καὶ (διὰ) τὴν Φιλοκτήτου νόσον, ἣν Ὀδυσσεὺς καὶ Ἀτρεῖδαι προκαταγνόντες ἀνίατον εἶναι Φιλοκτήτην οὐχὶ δικαίως ἐν Λήμνῳ κατέλιπον, οὗτοι δὲ δέκα ἔτεσιν αὐξηθεῖσαν ἰάσαντο.	. . . the fall of Troy, moreover, was entirely due to them, for other reasons and particularly on account of Philoctetes' ailment. Odysseus and the Atrides had wrongly assumed beforehand that it was incurable, and had unjustly left Philoctetes behind in Lemnos, but they [the Asclepiads] healed it even though it had been augmented by ten years.

4: T 282 *Or.* 38. 12	Ἀπόλλω τε γάρ φασιν οἱ ποιηταὶ τὴν Δῆλον φερομένην πρότερον στῆσαι κατὰ τοῦ πελάγους ἐρείσαντα, ἐπειδὴ πρῶτον ἐν αὐτῇ ἐγένετο, καὶ οὗτοι τῆς Μεροπίδος τότε ἐπιβάντες. προκρίναντες ἁπασῶν εἶναι καλλίστην, ὅσαι παραπλήσιαι μέγεθος, ἰάσαντό τε καὶ ἀπέφηναν ἐμβατὸν πᾶσιν Ἕλλησι καὶ βαρβάροις, πρότερον σφαλερὰν καὶ ὕποπτον οὖσαν, καὶ τὴν εὐδαιμονίαν κυρίαν τῇ νήσῳ κατέστησαν.	For the poets say that Apollo firmly fixed Delos - which formerly was floating around - anchoring it on the sea when he was born there; and they, when they first arrived in the land of the Meropes, judging it to be the most beautiful of all that were of similar size, cured it and made accessible to all, Greeks and barbarians alike, the land that formerly was dangerous and suspicious, and established the happiness proper to that island.
5: T 282 *Or.* 38. 21-22	Ἀμφιάραος μὲν γὰρ καὶ Τροφώνιος ἐν Βοιωτίᾳ καὶ Ἀμφίλοχος ἐν Αἰτωλίᾳ χρησμῳδοῦσί τε καὶ φαίνονται, οὗτοι δὲ πανταχοῦ τῆς γῆς διᾴττουσιν ὥσπερ ἀστέρες, περίπολοι κοινοὶ καὶ πρόδρομοι τοῦ πατρός. ὁσαχοῖ δὲ Ἀσκληπιῷ εἴσοδοι, καὶ τούτοις κλισιάδες τε [αὐτοῖς] ἀνεῖνται πανταχοῦ γῆς, καὶ διὰ πάντων ἡ κοινωνία τῷ πατρὶ σῴζεται νεῶν θυσιῶν παιάνων προσόδων ἔργων ἃ πράττουσιν. ὦ μακαριστοὶ μὲν ὑμεῖς τῶν ἄνω προγόνων ἐπ' ἀμφότερα, εὐδαίμονες δὲ τῶν ἀφ' ὑμῶν φύντων, ἔτι δὲ ὑμῶν τε αὐτῶν καὶ ἀδελφῶν, οἷς Ἰασώ τε καὶ Πανάκεια καὶ Αἴγλη σύνεστιν καὶ Ὑγίεια, ἡ πάντων ἀντίρροπος, Ἠπιόνης δὴ παῖδες ἐπώνυμοι·	For Amphiaraus and Trophonius give oracles and appear in Boeotia, Amphilochus in Aetolia; these, however, are darting all over the earth, like stars, being both the servants and the heralds of their father. Wherever Asclepius has admittance, the doors are open to them, too, everywhere on earth, and in every respect is the unity with their father preserved, in temples, sacrifices, paeans, processions, and other things which are performed. O, happy are you for your ancestors on both sides, blessed for those who have sprung from you, for yourselves and for your sisters, among whom are Iaso and Panacea and Aegle and Hygieia, who is worth as much as all the others, the famous children of Epione.
6: T 282 *Or.* 38. 24	ὑμεῖς δὲ τῇ ὑμετέρᾳ πραότητι καὶ φιλανθρωπίᾳ . . . θέντες αὐτὸν εἰς καλλίους, τῆς τε νόσου παύετε καὶ διδοίητε ὑγιείας τε ὅσον οἷς ἡ ψυχὴ βούλεται τὸ σῶμα ὑπακούειν, καὶ τὸ σύμπαν εἰπεῖν βίου ῥᾳστώνην.	You in your kindness and love of men . . . counting it [the speech?] among the finer ones, relieve me of my disease and grant me as much health as is necessary in order that the body may obey that which the soul wishes, and, to say it in one word, a life lived with ease.
7: T 400 *Or.* 52. 1	. . . δωδεκάτῳ δὲ ἀφ' οὗ πρῶτον ἔκαμον πολλὰ καὶ θαυμαστὰ ἐφοίτα φαντάσματα ἄγοντα εἰς Ἐπίδαυρον τὴν ἱερὰν τοῦ θεοῦ.	. . . in the twelfth [*sc.*, year] from the time when I first became ill many wondrous visions came repeatedly, leading [me] to Epidaurus, the holy city of the god.

8 : T 402 *Or.* 23. 15	Ἑστία γὰρ Ἀσκληπιοῦ τῆς Ἀσίας ἐνταῦθα ἱδρύθη . . .	For the hearth of Asclepius was established in this part of Asia Minor [*sc.*, in Pergamum].
9 : T 402 *Or.* 23. 17	οὐκοῦν οὐδὲ ἀλίμενα φῆσαι τις ἂν εἶναι τὰ τῇδε, ἀλλ' ἐκεῖνο ὀρθότατον καὶ δικαιότατον λέγειν, ὡς ἄρα οὗτος λιμένων ἁπάντων ὀχυρώτατος καὶ βεβαιότατος καὶ πλείστους δεχόμενος καὶ γαλήνῃ πλεῖστον προέχων, ἐν ᾧ πᾶσιν ἐξ Ἀσκληπιοῦ τὰ ἐπίγυια τῆς σωτηρίας ἤρτηται.	Therefore no one would say that these regions have no harbor, but most correctly and justly is it said that this is the most secure and steadfast of all ports, receiving the greatest number of people and affording the most in tranquillity. Here, the stern-cable of salvation for all is anchored in Asclepius.
10 : T 317 *Or.* 42. 4	Ἀσκληπιοῦ δυνάμεις μεγάλαι τε καὶ πολλαί, μᾶλλον δ' ἅπασαι, οὐχ ὅσον ὁ τῶν ἀνθρώπων βίος χωρεῖ. καὶ Διὸς Ἀσκληπιοῦ νεὼν οὐκ ἄλλως οἱ τῇδε ἱδρύσαντο·. . .οὗτός ἐσθ' ὁ τὸ πᾶν ἄγων καὶ νέμων σωτὴρ τῶν ὅλων καὶ φύλαξ τῶν ἀθανάτων, . . . σῴζων τά τε ὄντα ἀεὶ καὶ τὰ γιγνόμενα. εἰ δ' Ἀπόλλωνος παῖδα καὶ τρίτον ἀπὸ Διὸς νομίζομεν αὐτόν, αὖθις ⟨δ'⟩ αὖ καὶ συνάπτομεν τοῖς ὀνόμασιν, *– – – –* ἐπεί τοι καὶ αὐτὸν τὸν Δία γενέσθαι λέγουσίν ποτε, πάλιν δὲ αὐτὸν ἀποφαίνουσιν ὄντα τῶν ὄντων πατέρα καὶ ποιητήν.	Asclepius has great and many powers, or rather he has every power, and not alone that which concerns human life. And it is not by chance that the people here [*sc.*, at Pergamum] have built a temple of Zeus Asclepius . . . he is the one who guides and rules the universe, the savior of the whole and the guardian of the immortals . . . he who saves that which already exists and that which is in the state of becoming. But if we believe him to be the son of Apollo, and the third from Zeus, and if again we link him with these names *. . . *; since sometimes they maintain that even Zeus is born, and then again they show that he is the father and maker of everything. *Lacunam indicavit Keil*

11: T 317 *Or.* 42. 5	πάσας δὲ ἔχων ὁ θεὸς τὰς δυνάμεις διὰ πάντων ἄρα εὐεργετεῖν προείλετο τοὺς ἀνθρώπους ἑκάστῳ τὰ προσήκοντα ἀποδιδούς. μεγίστην δὲ καὶ κοινοτάτην εὐεργεσίαν εἰς ἅπαντας κατέθετο ἀθάνατον ποιήσας τὸ γένος τῇ διαδοχῇ, γάμους τε καὶ παίδων γενέσεις καὶ τροφῶν ἀφορμὰς καὶ πόρους διὰ τῆς ὑγιείας ἐργασάμενος. . . . κοινῷ τινι φαρμάκῳ πρὸς ἅπαντας πόνου καὶ πράξεις πάσας τῇ ὑγιείᾳ χρώμενος. ἰατρεῖα δ' εἰς τὸ μέσον κατεστήσατο, καὶ φιλοτεχνεῖν ἀνέθηκεν ἑαυτῷ νύκτα καὶ ἡμέραν ὑπὲρ εὐθυμίας τῶν αἰεὶ δεομένων τε καὶ δεησομένων.	The god having all powers has chosen to be men's benefactor in every respect, granting everyone that which is his due. The greatest and most common benefit, however, he bestowed upon all by making their race immortal through succession, by means of health bringing about marriage and the begetting of children and the procurement of the resources of nourishment. . . . using one common remedy for all pains and troubles, namely health. Furthermore he established places of treatment in their midst, and he took it upon himself to pursue his art night and day in order to bring cheer to whoever always are and will be in need of it.
12: T 317 *Or.* 42. 6	εἰσὶν οἵ φασιν ἀναστῆναι κείμενοι,ὁμολογούμενα δήπου λέγοντες καὶ πάλαι τῷ θεῷ μελετώμενα·	There are some who claim that they have risen after lying dead, stating something, to be sure, on which we all agree and which has been one of the old-established practices of the god.
13: T 317 *Or.* 42. 7	ἀλλὰ καὶ μέλη τοῦ σώματος αἰτιῶνταί τινες, καὶ ἄνδρες λέγω καὶ γυναῖκες, προνοίᾳ τοῦ θεοῦ γενέσθαι σφίσι, τῶν παρὰ τῆς φύσεως διαφθαρέντων, καὶ καταλέγουσιν ἄλλος ἄλλο τι, οἱ μὲν ἀπὸ στόματος οὑτωσὶ φράζοντες, οἱ δὲ ἐν τοῖς ἀναθήμασιν ἐξηγούμενοι· ἡμῖν τοίνυν οὐχὶ μέρος τοῦ σώνατος, ἀλλ' ἅπαν τὸ σῶμα συνθείς τε καὶ συμπήξας αὐτὸς ἔδωκε δωρεάν, ὥσπερ Προμηθεὺς τἀρχαῖα λέγεται συμπλάσαι τὸν ἄνθρωπον. πολλὰς ὀδύνας τε καὶ ἀλγηδόνας καὶ ἀπορίας μεθημερινάς τε καὶ νυκτερινὰς ἀφεῖλεν πολλοῖς, οὐ μὲν οὖν ἔχοι τις ἂν εἰπεῖν ὅσοις·	But also limbs of the body, some declare - I mean men and women alike - have been restored to them through the god's providence after they had been destroyed by nature, and they enumerate, one this, the other that, some of them expressing it by word of mouth, others by their votive offerings. Now for us, he has put together and fastened not part of the body, but the whole frame, and has given it to us as a present, just as of old Prometheus is said to have fashioned man. From many pains and sufferings and distresses, by day and by night, he has delivered many people; no one could tell how many.

14 : T 317 *Or.* 42. 8	καὶ μὴν τό γε παράδοξον πλεῖστον ἐν τοῖς ἰάμασι τοῦ θεοῦ, οἷον τὸν μὲν γύψου πίνειν, τὸν δὲ κωνείου, τὸν δὲ γυμνοῦσθαι καὶ λούειν ψυχρῷ, θέρμης οὐδόλως, ὡς ἄν τις δόξαι, δεόμενον. ἡμᾶς τοίνυν καὶ τοῦτον τὸν τρόπον τετίμηκεν, κατάρρους καὶ ψύξεις ποταμοῖς καὶ θαλάττῃ παύων, κατακλίσεις ἀπόρους ὁδῶν μήκεσιν ἰώμενος, τροφῆς δ' ἐνδείᾳ συνεχεῖ τὰς ἀμυθήτους καθάρσεις προστιθείς, ἀναπνεῖν δὲ ἀποροῦντι λέγειν καὶ γράφειν προστάττων, ὥστ' εἴ τι καὶ τοῖς οὕτω θεραπευθεῖσιν ἔπεστιν αὔχημα, μηδ' ἡμᾶς ἀμοίρους εἶναι τούτου.	And indeed it is the paradoxical which is paramount in the cures of the god, for example, one drinks chalk, another hemlock, another one is stripped of his clothes and takes cold ablutions when one would think him in need of warmth [?]. Now ourselves he has likewise distinguished in this way, stopping catarrhs and colds by baths in rivers and in the sea, healing us through long walks when we were helplessly bedridden, administering terrible cleansings on top of continuous abstinence from food, prescribing that I should speak and write when I could hardly breathe, so that if there is any cause for boasting for those who have been healed in such a way, we certainly have our share in this boast.
15 : T 317 *Or.* 42. 10	ἤδη τοίνυν τινῶν ἤκουσα λεγόντων ὡς αὐτοῖς πλέουσι καὶ θορυβουμένοις φανεὶς ὁ θεὸς χεῖρα ὤρεξεν, ἕτεροι δέ γε φήσουσιν ὡς πράγματα ἄττα κατώρθωσαν ὑποθήκαις ἀκολουθήσαντες τοῦ θεοῦ· οὐδὲ ταῦτα ἀκούειν μᾶλλον ἢ λέγειν ἔχομεν πεπειραμένοι.	Now I have heard some people saying that, when they were at sea and in the midst of a storm, the god appeared to them and stretched forth his hand; others again will tell how they settled their affairs following the advice of the god. Even these things we know not from hear-say, but we can talk about them from our own experience . . .
16 : T 317 *Or.* 42. 11	ἀλλὰ καὶ σοφίσματα πυκτικὰ πύκτῃ τινὶ τῶν ἐφ' ἡμῶν ἐγκαθεύδοντι προειπεῖν λέγεται τὸν θεόν, οἷς ἔδει χρησάμενον καταβαλεῖν τινα τῶν πάνυ λαμπρῶν ἀνταγωνιστῶν·	But it is said that the god revealed even boxing tricks to one of our contemporary boxers while he was asleep, by the use of which it is no wonder that he knocked out one of his outstanding competitors.
17 : T 804 *Or.* 39. 4	. . . ὅτι ἐν τῷ καλλίστῳ τῆς πάσης οἰκουμένης ἐστιν. ὃ γὰρ ἐξ ἁπάντων χωρίων εἵλετο ὁ θεὸς ὡς ὑγιεινότατον καὶ καθαρώτατον καὶ ὃ ταῖς εὐεργεσίαις ταῖς παρ' αὐτοῦ πεποίηκεν ἁπάντων ἐκφανέστατον, ἦ που σφόδρα τοῦτο κάλλιστόν ἐστι τῶν ἐν γῇ πάντων.	. . . the well is in the fairest spot on earth. For the place which the god selected from all places as the healthiest and the purest, the place which he has made most notable of all by the services performed there by himself, surely this place is the fairest of all there are on earth.

18: T 804 *Or.* 39. 5	ὃ δὲ θεὸς καὶ θεῶν ὁ πραότατός τε καὶ φιλανθρωπότατος προέχειν ἔκρινεν, πῶς ἡμῖν γε, καὶ ταῦτα τοῖς τούτου θεράπουσιν, ἄλλο τι λέγειν ἔνεστιν ἢ ὡς τοῦτ' ἔστι τὸ βέλτιστον;	In regard, then, to that which the god who is the gentlest and most manloving of the gods decided to prefer, how is it possible for us, particularly those of us who are his servants, to say anything except that this is the best?
19: T 804 *Or.* 39. 11	ἅτε γὰρ ὂν διάκονόν τε καὶ συνεργὸν τοῦ φιλανθρωποτάτου τῶν θεῶν ἑτοιμότατον πρὸς τὴν ὑπηρεσίαν καὶ αἰεὶ πλῆρές ἐστι, καὶ οὔτε ἐκεῖνος ἄγει σχολὴν ἄλλο τι πράττειν ἢ σῴζειν ἀνθρώπους καὶ τοῦτο μιμούμενον τὸν δεσπότην αἰεὶ πληροῖ τὴν τῶν δεομένων χρείαν, καὶ ἔστιν ὥσπερ ἄλλο τι θρέμμα ἢ δῶρον Ἀσκληπιοῦ	For, since the well is the servant and co-worker of the most manloving of the gods, it is always full and ready for service. And as the god has no leisure to do anything except to save men, so the well, imitating its master, always fills the need of those who require it and is a sort of nursling or gift of Asclepius . . .
20: T 804 *Or.* 39. 14	ὥσπερ γὰρ οἱ παῖδες οἱ τῶν ἰατρῶν τε καὶ θαυματοποιῶν γεγυμνασμένοι πρὸς τὰς διακονίας εἰσὶ καὶ συμπράττοντες ἐκπλήττουσι τοὺς θεωμένους καὶ χρωμένους, οὕτω τοῦ μεγάλου θαυματοποιοῦ καὶ πάντα ἐπὶ σωτηρίᾳ πράττοντος ἀνθρώπων εὕρημα τοῦτο καὶ κτῆμά ἐστι· συμπράττει δὴ πρὸς ἅπαντα αὐτῷ καὶ γίγνεται πολλοῖς ἀντὶ φαρμάκου.	For just as the servants of physicians and miracle-workers are trained to ministrations, and, working with their superiors, astonish those who behold them and ask their advice, so is this well the discovery and possession of the great miracle-worker who does everything for the salvation of men: it works with him in all matters and for many it takes the place of a drug.
21: T 804 *Or.* 39. 15	πολλοὶ μὲν γὰρ τούτῳ λουσάμενοι ὀφθαλμοὺς ἐκομίσαντο, πολλοὶ δὲ πιόντες στέρνον ἰάθησαν καὶ τὸ ἀναγκαῖον πνεῦμα ἀπέλαβον, τῶν δὲ πόδας ἐξώρθωσεν, τῶν δὲ ἄλλο τι· ἤδη δέ τις πιὼν ἐξ ἀφώνου φωνὴν ἀφῆκεν, ὥσπερ οἱ τῶν ἀπορρήτων ὑδάτων πιόντες μαντικοὶ γιγνόμενοι· τοῖς δὲ καὶ αὐτὸ τὸ ἀρύτεσθαι ἀντ' ἄλλης σωτηρίας καθέστηκεν. καὶ τοῖς τε δὴ νοσοῦσιν οὕτως ἀλεξιφάρμακον καὶ σωτήριόν ἐστιν καὶ τοῖς ὑγιαίνουσιν ἐνδιαιτωμένοις παντὸς ἄλλου χρῆσιν ὕδατος οὐκ ἄμεμπτον ποιεῖ.	For when bathed with it many recovered their eyesight, while many were cured of ailments of the chest and regained their necessary breath by drinking from it. In some cases it cured the feet, in others something else. One man upon drinking from it straightway recovered his voice after having been a mute, just as those who drink sacred waters become prophetic. For some the drawing of the water itself took the place of every other remedy. Furthermore, not only is it remedial and beneficial to the sick but even for those who enjoy health it makes the use of any other water improper.

22: T 804 *Or.* 39. 17	τὸ δὲ τῷ σῴζειν τοὺς χρωμένους, οὐ τῷ μηδένα αὐτοῦ ψαύειν, ἱερόν ἐστιν·	. . . this water is sacred because it saves those who use it and not because no one touches it.
23: T 411 *Or.* 49. 28	Αὖθις δὲ ἐκέλευσεν πρὸς ἄρτῳ φαγεῖν τοῦ αὐτοῦ τούτου φαρμάκου, καὶ ἔφαγον πρὸς τῷ τρίποδι τῷ ἱερῷ, ἀφορμήν τινα ταύτην ἀσφαλείας ποιούμενος.	Again, he gave me instructions to eat of this same drug together with wheat-bread, and I ate it near the holy tripod, thus making a beginning of my well-being.
24: Loeb 1, 294 *Or.* 2. 22	. . . μιᾶς δὲ οὔσης τῆς τοῦ σώματος θεραπείας δύο μόρια λέγω, τὴν μὲν γυμναστικήν, τὴν δὲ ἰατρικήν. . . . τεττάρων δὲ τούτων οὐσῶν καὶ ἀεὶ πρὸς τὸ βέλτιστον θεραπευουσῶν, τῶν μὲν τὸ σῶμα, τῶν δὲ τὴν ψυχήν, . . .	. . . I say there are two arts. That pertaining to the soul I call politics. That pertaining to the body, I cannot name as a unit. But although there is a single service of the body, I say that there are two parts of this, gymnastics and medicine. In politics, legislation is the opposite of gymnastics, justice the opposite of medicine. Each of these pairs has a community of interests, since they are concerned with the same thing; medicine with gymnastics, justice with legislation. Still they differ somewhat from one another. These are four in number and ever serve aiming at the best, the one the body, the other the soul.
25: Loeb 1, 318 *Or.* 2. 62	πολλοὶ γὰρ καὶ τῶν καμνόντων ὑγιεῖς γίγνονται οἱ μὲν ἀνθρωπίνῃ (τέχνῃ), οἱ δὲ θείᾳ μοίρᾳ. ὅσοι μὲν οὖν ἀνθρωπίνῃ τέχνῃ, ὑπὸ ἰατρῶν θεραπευόμενοι, ὅσοι δὲ θείᾳ μοίρᾳ, ἐπιθυμία αὐτοὺς ἄγει ἐπὶ τὸ ὀνῆσον·	"For many of the sick become well, some by human art, some by a divine portion. Those by human art, cured by doctors; those by a divine portion, desire leads to what will profit them. . . . "
26: Loeb 1, 318 *Or.* 2. 65	καὶ μὴν εἰ πολλοὶ τῶν καμνόντων ὑγιεῖς γίγνονται χωρὶς ἰατρῶν καὶ τέχνης, καὶ ταῦτ' οὐδ' ἐφ' ἑνὶ ἄλλῳ τῆς τῶν ἰατρῶν τέχνης οὔσης ἢ τῷ ποιεῖν ὑγιεῖς, . . .	Indeed, if many of the sick are cured without doctors and art, and at that while the art of doctors exists for no other purpose than to cure, . . .

27 : Loeb 1, 320 *Or*. 2. 67-68	ἀλλ' ὡς ἀληθῶς ὥσπερ οἱ θεομάντεις οἱ τοῖς τῶν πραγμάτων ἐπωνύμοις τετελεσμένοι παρ' αὐτῶν τῶν θεῶν ἔχω τὸ μάθημα, ὑφ' ὧν ἃ μηδεὶς ἰατρῶν μήτε οἶδεν ὅ τι χρὴ προσειπεῖν, οὐχ ὅπως ἰάσασθαι, μήτε εἶδεν ἐν ἀνθρώπου φύσει συμβάντα, ἄλλοτε ἄλλαις παραμυθίαις τε καὶ συμβουλαῖς ἐκ τοῦ θεοῦ διαφεύγων ζῶ παρὰ πᾶν τὸ ἐκ τῶν παρόντων εἰκός. πολλοὶ δ' ἔμοιγε καὶ ἄλλοι κοινωνοί τε καὶ μάρτυρές εἰσι τῶν λόγων, οὐ μόνον τῶν Ἑλλήνων, ἀλλὰ καὶ βαρβάρων, αἵ τ' ἐν Ἀσκληπιοῦ τῶν ἀεὶ διατριβόντων ἀγέλαι καὶ ὅσοι τῷ κατ' Αἴγυπτον θεῷ συνεγένοντο.	Truly just as the seers, initiated into the service of the Gods who have given their name to their specialty, I have knowledge from the gods themselves. Through their aid, contrary to the likelihood of the circumstances, I am alive, having escaped at different times through various kinds of consolation and advice on the part of the God from things which no doctor knew what to call, to say nothing of cure, nor had seen befall the nature of man. There are many others like me and they can bear witness to these tales, not only Greeks, but barbarians, both the flocks of those who dwell at times in the temple of Asclepius and all who attend upon the God of Egypt [*sc.*, Sarapis].
28 : Loeb 1, 320-322 *Or*. 2. 70-71	ἀλλὰ καὶ ὀνείρασι χρώμεθα οὐ προειδότες, οἶμαι, τῆς ἑσπέρας ὅ τι μέλλομεν ὄψεσθαι, καὶ τί χρὴ ποιήσαντας σωθῆναι γιγνώσκομεν, ἀγνοοῦντες μέχρις ἐκείνου τοῦ μέρους τῆς ὥρας, ἐν ᾧ παρὰ τῶν θεῶν ἧκεν τἀγαθόν, καὶ πάλιν γὰρ ὥσπερ ἐπᾴδων ἐν μέλει ταὐτὸν ἐρῶ, τέχνης οὐδὲ ὁτιοῦν ἐπαΐοντες οὐ μόνον περὶ τῶν ἡμῖν αὐτοῖς συμφερόντων, ἀλλὰ καὶ περὶ τῶν ἑτέροις ἔχομεν εἰπεῖν πολλάκις, ἂν δοκῇ τῷ θεῷ, ὥστε καὶ τοὺς ἰατροὺς οὐδὲν κωλύει φρίττειν, ἐπειδὰν ἀκούωσιν πολλὰ τῶν ἔργων. πότερ' οὖν τὰ ὀνείρατα ποιεῖ θεοῖς ἀνακεῖσθαι τὰ ἀνθρώπεια, ἢ τὸ θεοὺς ἀνθρώπων κήδεσθαι ποιεῖ καὶ δι' ὀνειράτων ἀνθρώπους σῴζεσθαι; ἐγὼ μὲν οἶμαι τοῦτο.	But we employ dreams, not knowing in advance of the evening, surely, what we are going to see, and we know what we must do to be saved, although we are in ignorance up to that minute in which the benefit has come from the Gods. For again as if singing a refrain, I shall repeat myself, knowing nothing of art, we can often speak not only about what is expedient for ourselves, but also for others, if the God approves, so that the doctors must shudder whenever they hear many of these practices. So do dreams cause a concern for man to be attributed to the Gods, or does the care of the Gods for mankind cause mankind to be saved through dreams? I think the latter.
29 : Loeb 1, 348 *Or*. 2. 114-115	ἀλλ' ἐπαλεῖψαι μὲν ταῦτα καὶ θεραπεῦσαι τῆς τέχνης εἶναι δοκεῖ, συστήσασθαι δ' ἐξ ἀρχῆς οὐδεμία οὕτω τέχνη ἂν εἴη δεινή. οὐκοῦν διακόνου καὶ θεραπαίνης τάξιν ἔχειν προσήκει τῇ τέχνῃ, τὴν φύσιν δ' ἐν σχήματι δεσποίνης ετάχθαι, εἰ μὴ καὶ τοὺς σκευοφόρους πρὸ τῶν ὁπλιτῶν τάττοιμεν ἄν. ἀλλ' οὐκ ἄξιον.	But to prepare and tend these seems to belong to art, but no art would be clever enough to compose these things to begin with. Therefore art ought to have the position of servant or maid; but nature to be put in the rank of mistress, unless we should place the sutlers before the infantry. But this is unfitting.

30 : Loeb 1, 366
Or. 2. 149-153

εἶεν. ὁ δὲ δὴ τῆς μὲν πείρας εἰς πίστιν ἰσχύσας καὶ τοῖς φαρμάκοις καὶ ταῖς διαίταις ἤδη χρώμενος τούτοις ἰατρός, ὅπως δ' ἕκαστος ἡμῶν ἔχει φύσεως ἢ συγκρίσεως ἀγνοῶν, ἆρ' οὐ στοχαζόμενος προσάγει πάνθ' ὅσα ἂν ποιῇ περὶ τὸν κάμνοντα ἀναφέρων εἰς τὸ εἰκός; ἐγὼ μὲν οἶμαι. [152]

By Zeus, take medicine, according to you, the opposite of justice and second ranking good for the body, and if you wish, gymnastics. Do they not conjecture at the nature of the body? Yes by Zeus, whether you say so or not. Or has the trainer foreseen right at the start the state of each of our bodies? Does he not learn by trial? Well! whenever he is training someone for the purpose which he is attempting, then like Apollo in Delphi, does he know the future and assert that he will make this man wholly and in every way free from these symptoms, either once and for all or for some length of time? Then either you think the trainer a madman, if he does not conjecture, or he himself will agree, if he is in his right senses, that he conjectures at what is best, but that he can predict and promise no such thing. Well then! this doctor who has achieved a credible experience and now employs these various drugs and regimens, but is ignorant of one's physical state or constitution, does he not apply all of his treatment for the sick person, by conjecturing and referring to probability? I think so. Or could any one of them say off-hand that by using these things this sick man will be free from all danger and have no trouble at all? Then they would not be so inferior to the God who holds Epidaurus, you would say, and indeed I at least agree. But they form a picture of one's particular physical state from many common characteristics, I think. But if they have privately attended any people, they conjecture according to their experience, selecting what will be expedient for each.

31: Loeb 1, 368 *Or*. 2. 154-156	ἀλλὰ μὴν τόν γε συντυχόντα καὶ δεηθέντα κελεύει θεραπεύειν ἡ τέχνη, κἂν ἐκ περάτων ἥκῃ τις ἀρτίως. τί οὖν δεῖ λοιπὸν ἢ στοχάζεσθαι; εἰ γὰρ μήτ' εἴσεται πάντας καὶ θεραπεύσει τὸν προσελθόντα, καὶ τοσοῦτον εἴσεται δήπου, μὴ πᾶσι δεῖν τῶν αὐτῶν, ὃ λέγω λείπεται. [155–156]	I say that the same things do not profit all bodies, either when they are sick or well. But just as they are not sick and well in the same way, so still more neither when they have the same diseases nor when they are healthy, will the doctors tell you the same things for all. But again it is impossible to classify the natures of all men. For just as all men differ in appearance from one another, so throughout every race each man is separate in the nature pervading his whole body. Indeed, a doctor's art commands him to treat whatever chance person has requested his aid, even if someone has just now come from the ends of the earth. What of necessity is left, other than conjecture? If he will not know all men and will treat whoever approaches him, and he will also know this much at any rate, that all do not need the same treatment, there is left what I say.
32: Loeb 1, 382 *Or*. 2. 185	. . .οὐχ ὥστε τὰς ἐκείνων ἐπιθυμίας θεραπεύειν, . . .	. . . not so as to serve their desires, . . .
33: Loeb 1, 382 *Or*. 2. 187	εἰ δ' ὑπείκειν αὐτοὺς τοῖς πλήθεσι φῂς καὶ ποιεῖν τὰ κελευόμενα, ἀλλ' οὐ κελεύειν, τὴν θεράπαιναν εἴληφας ἀντὶ τῆς δεσποίνης, καὶ τοὺς δημοσίους ψέγων δοκεῖς τοὺς ῥήτορας.	But if you say that they yield to the multitudes and do what they are commanded, but do not command, you have taken the servant-girl for the mistress, and in blaming the public slaves, you think you blame the orators.
34: Loeb 1, 384 *Or*. 2. 189	ἀλλ' οἶμαι συνίσασιν αὐτοῖς οὐ τὰς ἡδονὰς θεραπεύουσιν, ἀλλὰ τὰς ἐπιθυμίας σωφρονίζουσιν, οὐδὲ ὁρῶσιν εἰς τοὺς πολλούς, ἀλλὰ (τοῖς) πολλοῖς ὁρῶσιν εἰς τούτους, οὐδ' ἀρχομένοις ὑπὸ τῶν ἰδιωτῶν [ἑαυτοῖς], ἀλλ' ἄρχουσιν αὐτοῖς τῶν πολλῶν.	But I think they know in their hearts that they do not serve pleasures, but chastise desires, nor look to the multitude, but the multitude looks to them, nor are ruled by ordinary citizens, but themselves rule the multitude.

35 : Loeb 1, 388 *Or*. 2. 196	δήμου δὲ βουλήματα γνῶναι καὶ θεραπεῦσαι διὰ τέλους τίς μηχανή;	What method can be contrived to know and continuously serve the will of the people?
36 : Loeb 1, 388 *Or*. 2. 198	ὅταν γὰρ δέῃ μὲν διακονεῖν πολλοῖς, οὗτοι δ' ὦσι μὴ κατὰ ταὐτὰ γιγνώσκοντες, πᾶσι δὲ ἀμήχανον ἐκ τῶν αὐτῶν ταὐτὰ χαρίζεσθαι, πῶς ὁ ῥήτωρ θεραπεύσει τὰς ἐπιθυμίας αὐτῶν;	For whenever it is necessary to serve many people and they are not of the same opinion, and it is impossible to gratify all on the same subject in the same way, how will the orator serve their desires?
37 : Loeb 1, 446 *Or*. 2. 296	. . . ἢ πολὺ τοὐναντίον προτρέπων καὶ θεραπευτικὸν ἀξιῶν εἶναι ὅπως ὡς πλείστους τοὺς συμπράττοντας ἐπ' αὐτὸν ἔχοι·	Or is his encouragement far different, and does he deem it salutary that he raise as many fellow conspirators as possible against him?
38 : Loeb 1, 456-458 *Or*. 2. 309	οἱ μέν γέ που κόλακες οἱ μέγιστοι δήπου καὶ τελεώτατοι αὐτῶν (εἰσὶ τῶν τυράννων πάντῃ θεραπευταί·) εἰσὶ δ, οἶμαι, καὶ τῶν τυχόντων τινές· ὥσθ' ὅπερ δοῦλος πρὸς δεσπότην, τοῦτο κόλαξ πρὸς τύραννον συμβαίνει· οἱ δ' αὖ τύραννοι τοσοῦτον ἀπέχουσι τοῦ κολακεύειν ὥστε βίᾳ πάντας ὠθοῦσιν καὶ οὐδὲ τῶν μετρίων οὐδενός ἐστιν παρ' αὐτῶν τυχεῖν, μή τί γε δὴ τῆς ὑπὲρ τὸ προσῆκον θεραπείας·	As for flatterers, the greatest and most perfect of them are in every way the servants of tyrants; and some also, I think, of common men. Therefore as the slave is to the master, so it turns out to be that the flatterer is to the tyrant. On the other hand, tyrants are so far from being flatterers that they push everyone around by force, and it is impossible to get any moderate treatment from them, to say nothing about service beyond their duty.
39 : Loeb 1, 472 *Or*. 2. 326; phrase repeated in 327	καὶ ἱερῶν ἀθεραπευσίαν	. . . and the neglect of the temples, . . .

40 : Loeb 1, 528-530 *Or*. 2. 412	Εἰ δὲ δὴ καὶ κοινωνήσειέν τινι τῶν ἄλλων τεχνῶν καὶ δυνάμεων, Ἡράκλεις, ὡς οὐδ' εἰπεῖν ἔστιν ὡς ἐκφαίνει τὸ παρ' αὐτῆς. οἷον ἰατρὸς εἰ προσλάβοι ῥητορικήν, τῆς ἰατρικῆς αὐτῆς μάλιστα οὕτω τὴν χάριν εἴσεται. εἰ γὰρ προσέλθοι τὸ δύνασθαι πείθειν τοῖς ἄλλοις τοῖς ὑπάρχουσιν αὐτῷ κατὰ τὴν τέχνην, τί κωλύει προθεραπεύειν τὰ πολλὰ τῇ ῥητορικῇ, πρὶν τῶν τῆς ἰατρικῆς ὀργάνων ἅψασθαι, τῷ σοφωτάτῳ τῶν φαρμάκων, ἔφη τις, χρώμενον;	If it should make a common cause with some one of the other arts and faculties, Heracles! - It could not be expressed how it would be put into high relief its own contribution. For example, if a doctor would add oratory to his art, then he would particularly know the charm of medicine itself. For if the power to persuade should be added to the other means available to him in his art, why would he not give much preliminary treatment through oratory, before touching the instruments of medicine, using, as someone said, "the wisest of drugs?"
41 : Loeb 1, 62 *Or*. 1. 77	οὐ τοίνυν μόνον ταῖς ἄλλαις δωρεαῖς οὐδὲ τῇ τῶν καταφευγόντων δήπου θεραπείᾳ καὶ προστασίᾳ, οὐδ' οἷς, ὡς εἴπομεν, ηὔξησε τὸ Ἑλληνικὸν τῆς εἰς πάντας ἀρετῆς καὶ μεγαλοψυχίας ἐναργῆ δείγματα ἐξήνεγκεν ἡ πόλις ἡμῖν, ἀλλ' οὐδείς ἐστιν ἀγὼν ὅτου δεῆσαν ὤκνησεν, ἀλλ' ἀμείνων περὶ τοὺς δεηθέντας ἢ 'κεῖνοι συνεβούλοντο ἐγένετο.	The city not only has presented clear proofs to us of its virtue and generosity to all by its other gifts, and by its care and protection of those who sought refuge with it, and by the acts in which, as we said, it increased the Greek race, but there was no necessary contest which it shirked, but it behaved better toward those in need than they requested.
42 : Loeb 1, 124 *Or*. 1. 159	. . . διεκώλυσαν αὐτοὶ καὶ κατηνάγκασαν ὥσπερ παῖδας ἄκοντας ὑποστῆναι τῇ θεραπείᾳ πάντα πραγματευσάμενοι, τὸ μὲν πρῶτον ἐνδεχομένους μόλις φωνὴν πείθοντες, ἔπειτα, ὡς ἀπέραντον ἦν, ἀπροσδοκήτως περιθέντες τὰς ἀνάγκας καὶ συσκευάσαντες τὴν ναυμαχίαν, ὥστε πρὸς βίαν θαρρῆσαι.	. . . they [*sc.*, the Athenians] restrained them [*sc.*, the Greeks] and compelled them, like unwilling children, to submit to the cure, and they used every contrivance, first of all trying to persuade those who scarcely listened to their voice, and next when this was proving endless, unexpectedly forcing them to act and contriving the naval battle [*sc.*, Salamis], so that they were compelled to be courageous.
43 : Loeb 1, 178-180 *Or*. 1. 237	καὶ Φαρναβάζου κακῶς τὸ συμβὰν ἰωμένου καὶ τὴν ἵππον ἐπεισάγοντος . . .	And when Pharnabazus badly tried to remedy what had happened and introduced his cavalry . . .

44 : Loeb 1, 190 *Or*. 1. 255	ἐνόσησεν μὲν γὰρ τῇ τῶν πάντων ἀνθρώπων φύσει, ἰάθη δὲ τῇ ἑαυτῆς·	For in the nature of mankind the city was diseased, but it was cured by its own nature, . . .
	Cf. Oliver, J. H. (1968) "The civilizing power" *Transactions of the Americam Philosophical Society* New Series Volume 58, part 1, Philadelphia, 134, who comments thus on this passage: "'While the city fell ill by the nature of all mankind, she was cured by her own nature.' Plato, *Menexenus* 243e referred to the city falling ill (νοσῆσαι) with stasis and in 244a he says that what cured them was their real kinship which produces, not theoretically but actually, a firm group loyalty (φιλίαν βέβαιαν καὶ ὁμόφυλον). There is a play on the word φύσις = nature, which Aristides has used in section 29 [Loeb I, p. 30; *Or.* 1.29] in speaking of descent from the original stock. A contrast to the firm group loyalty of the Athenians lies in the stasis which characterizes the Jews and Christians according to Celsus (see Carl Andresen, *Logos und Nomos* . . . Berlin, 1955, IIB)."	
45 : Loeb 1, 192 *Or*. 1. 261	τὸ γοῦν Ἀργείων πλῆθος νοσοῦν ὕστερον ἰάσατο καὶ ἔργῳ καὶ λόγῳ·	Later it cured by its actions and counsel the masses of the Argives when they were sick with faction.
46 : Loeb 1, 222-224 *Or*. 1. 313	Διονυσίου γὰρ . . . εἰς νοῦν ἐμβαλομένου ἐπιθέσθαι τῇ Ἑλλάδι, τῷ μήκει τῶν πολέμων κεκακωμένῃ, καὶ τοῦτο μὲν τοὺς προσοίκους τοῖς Ἕλλησι βαρβάρους τεθεραπευκότος ἐκ πολλοῦ, τοῦτο δὲ τὸν Περσῶν βασιλέα καλοῦντος, . . .	When Dionysius . . . took up the idea of attacking Greece which had been injured by the length of its wars, and when he had long cultivated the friendship of the barbarian neighbours of the Greeks and was appealing to the king of the Persians for help, . . .
47 : Loeb 1, 236 *Or*. 1. 331	καὶ σιωπῶ τὸν Ἀλέξανδρον, ὡς ἀεὶ πρὸς αὐτὴν ἔσχεν θεραπευτικῶς.	And I omit the fact that Alexander was always solicitously disposed toward it [*sc*., Athens].

Appendix 5 : 7

Marcus Aurelius

Text and translation from the Loeb Classical Library edition of Marcus Aurelius (1979) *Marcus Aurelius*, (trans. C. R. Haines) London.

References are by numeral, and Loeb page number and reference within the work.

Reference	Text	Translation
1: Loeb, 36 2.13	Οὐδὲν ἀθλιώτερον τοῦ πάντα κύκλῳ ἐκπεριερχομένου, καὶ "τὰ νέρθεν γᾶς," φησίν, "ἐρευνῶντος," καὶ τὰ ἐν ταῖς ψυχαῖς τῶν πλησίον διὰ τεκμάρσεως ζητοῦντος, μὴ αἰσθομένου δέ, ὅτι ἀρκεῖ πρὸς μόνῳ τῷ ἔνδον ἑαυτοῦ δαίμονι εἶναι καὶ τοῦτον γνησίως θεραπεύειν. θεραπεία δὲ αὐτοῦ, καθαρὸν πάθους διατηρεῖν καὶ εἰκαιότητος καὶ δυσαρεστήσεως τῆς πρὸς τὰ ἐκ θεῶν καὶ ἀνθρώπων γινόμενα. τὰ μὲν γὰρ ἐκ θεῶν αἰδέσιμα δι' ἀρετήν· τὰ δὲ ἐξ ἀνθρώπων φίλα διὰ συγγένειαν, ἔστι δὲ ὅτε καὶ τρόπον τινὰ ἐλεεινὰ δι' ἄγνοιαν ἀγαθῶν καὶ κακῶν· οὐκ ἐλάττων ἡ πήρωσις αὕτη τῆς στερισκούσης τοῦ διακρίνειν τὰ λευκὰ καὶ μέλανα.	Nothing can be more miserable than the man who goes through the whole round of things, and, as the poet says, *pries into things beneath the earth* (Pindar, *Frag*. [see Plato, *Theaet*. 173E]), and would fain guess the thoughts in his neighbour's heart, while having no conception that he needs but to associate himself with the divine 'genius' in his bosom, and to serve it truly. And service of it is to keep it pure from passion and aimlessness and discontent with anything that proceeds from Gods or men. For that which proceeds from the Gods is worthy of reverence in that it is excellent; and that which proceeds from men, of love, in that they are akin, and, at times and in a manner, of compassion, in that they are ignorant of good and evil - a defect that is no less than the loss of power to distinguish between white and black.
2: Loeb, 60 3.13	Ὥσπερ οἱ ἰατροὶ ἀεὶ τὰ ὄργανα καὶ σιδήρια πρόχειρα ἔχουσι πρὸς τὰ αἰφνίδια τῶν θεραπευμάτων, οὕτω τὰ δόγματα σὺ ἕτοιμα ἔχε πρὸς τὸ τὰ θεῖα καὶ ἀνθρώπινα εἰδέναι, καὶ πᾶν καὶ τὸ μικρότατον οὕτω ποιεῖν, ὡς τῆς ἀμφοτερων πρὸς ἄλληλα συνδέσεως μεμνημένον. οὔτε γὰρ ἀνθρώπινόν τι ἄνευ τῆς ἐπὶ τὰ θεῖα συναναφορᾶς εὖ πράξεις οὔτε ἔμπαλιν.	Just as physicians always keep their lancets and instruments ready to their hands for emergency operations, so also do thou keep thine axioms ready for the diagnosis of things human and divine, and for the performing of every act, even the pettiest, with the fullest consciousness of the mutual ties between these two. For thou shalt never carry out well any human duty unless thou correlate it to the divine, nor the reverse.

3: Loeb, 122 5.28 Cf. Galen, *Comm.* iv. 9, *Epid.* vi. [xvii. B. 151] Matthew 18.15 Luke 4.23	Τῷ γράσωνι μήτι ὀργίζῃ; μήτι τῷ ὀζοστόμῳ ὀργίζῃ; τί σοι ποιήσει; τοιοῦτον στόμα ἔχει, τοιαύτας μάλας ἔχει· ἀνάγκη τοιαύτην ἀποφορὰν ἀπὸ τοιούτων γίνεσθαι. "Ἀλλ' ὁ ἄνθρωπος λόγον ἔχει, φησί, καὶ δύναται συννοεῖν ἐφιστάνων, τί πλημμελεῖ." εὖ σοι γένοιτο· τοιγαροῦν καὶ σὺ λόγον ἔχεις· κίνησον λογικῇ διαθέσει λογικὴν διάθεσιν, δεῖξον, ὑπόμνησον. εἰ γὰρ ἐπαίει, θεραπεύσεις καὶ οὐ χρεία ὀργῆς. Οὔτε τραγῳδὸς οὔτε πόρνη.	If a man's armpits are unpleasant, art thou angry with him? If he has foul breath? What would be the use? The man has such a mouth, he has such armpits. Some such effluvium was bound to come from such a source. *But the man has sense,* quotha! *With a little attention he could see wherein he offends.* I congratulate thee! Well, thou too hast sense. By a rational attitude, then, in thyself evoke a rational attitude in him, enlighten him, admonish him. If he listen, thou shalt cure him, and have no need of anger. Neither tragedian nor harlot.
4: Loeb, 134 6.12	Εἰ μητρυιάν τε ἅμα εἶχες καὶ μητέρα, ἐκείνην τ' ἂν ἐθεράπευες, καὶ ὅμως ἡ ἐπάνοδός σοι πρὸς τὴν μητέρα συνεχὴς ἐγίνετο. τοῦτό σοι νῦν ἐστιν ἡ αὐλὴ καὶ ἡ φιλοσοφία· ὧδε πολλάκις ἐπάνιθι καὶ προσαναπαύου ταύτῃ, δι' ἣν καὶ τὰ ἐκεῖ σοι ἀνεκτὰ φαίνεται καὶ σὺ ἐν αὐτοῖς ἀνεκτός.	Hadst thou at once a stepmother and a mother thou wouldst pay due service to the former, and yet thy constant recourse would be to thy mother. So hadst thou now the court and philosophy for stepmother and mother. Cease not then to come to the latter and take thy rest in her, whereby shall both thy court life seem more tolerable to thee, and thou to thy court life.
5: Loeb, 160 6.55	Εἰ κυβερνῶντα οἱ ναῦται ἢ ἰατρεύοντα οἱ κάμνοντες κακῶς ἔλεγον, ἄλλῳ τινὶ ἂν προσεῖχον ἢ πῶς αὐτὸς ἐνεργοίη τὸ τοῖς ἐμπλέουσι σωτήριον ἢ τὸ τοῖς θεραπευομένοις ὑγιεινόν;	If the sailors spoke ill of a steersman or the sick of a physician, what else would they have in mind but how the man should best effect the safety of the crew or the health of his patients?
6: Loeb, 330 12.16 Cf. Galen (above, **3**) Luke 4.23	Ὅτι ὁ μὴ θέλων τὸν φαῦλον ἁμαρτάνειν ὅμοιος τῷ μὴ θέλοντι τὴν συκῆν ὀπὸν ἐν τοῖς σύκοις φέρειν καὶ τὰ βρέφη κλαυθμυρίζεσθαι καὶ τὸν ἵππον χρεμετίζειν καὶ ὅσα ἄλλα ἀναγκαῖα. τί γὰρ πάθῃ τὴν ἕξιν ἔχων τοιαύτην: εἰ οὖν γοργὸς εἶ, ταύτην θεράπευσον.	Note that he who would not have the wicked do wrong is as one who would not have the fig-tree secrete acrid juice in its fruit, would not have babies cry, or the horse neigh, or have any other things be that must be. Why, what else can be expected from such a disposition? If then it chafes thee, cure the disposition.

7: Loeb, 4 1.6	Παρὰ Διογνήτου, τὸ ἀκενόσπουδον· καὶ τὸ ἀπιστητικὸν τοῖς ὑπὸ τῶν τερατευομένων καὶ γοήτων περὶ ἐπῳδῶν καὶ περὶ δαιμόνων ἀποπομπῆς καὶ τῶν τοιούτων λεγομένοις·	From Diognetus, not to be taken up with trifles; and not to give credence to the statements of miracle-mongers and wizards about incantations and the exorcizing of demons, and such-like marvels;
8: Loeb, 4 1.7	Παρὰ Ῥουστίκου, τὸ λαβεῖν φαντασίαν τοῦ χρήζειν διορθώσεως καὶ θεραπείας τοῦ ἤθους·	From Rusticus, to become aware of the fact that I needed amendment and training for my character;
9: Loeb, 20 1.17.4	Τὸ ἀδελφοῦ τοιούτου τυχεῖν δυναμένου μὲν διὰ ἤθους ἐπεγεῖραί με πρὸς ἐπιμέλειαν ἐμαυτοῦ, . . .	That it was my lot to have such a brother, capable by his character of stimulating me to watchful care over myself, . . .
10: Loeb, 22 1.17.6	Τὸ ἀντισχεῖν μοι τὸ σῶμα ἐπὶ τοσοῦτον ἐν τοιούτῳ βίῳ· τὸ μήτε Βενεδίκτης ἅψασθαι μήτε Θεοδότου, ἀλλὰ καὶ ὕστερον ἐν ἐρωτικοῖς πάθεσι γενόμενον ὑγιᾶναι·	That my body holds out so long in such a life as mine; that I did not touch Benedicta or Theodotus, but that even afterwards, when I did give way to amatory passions, I was cured of them;
11: Loeb, 24 1.17.8 Cf. Fronto, *ad Caes.*, 3.9; Artemidorus, *De Somniis*, 4.24; Pliny *N.H.*, 25.6	Τὸ δι' ὀνειράτων βοηθήματα δοθῆναι ἄλλα τε καὶ ὡς μὴ πτύειν αἷμα καὶ μὴ ἰλιγγιᾶν, καὶ τὸ τοῦ ἐν Καιήτῃ "ὥσπερ χρήσῃ·" ὅπως τε ἐπεθύμησα φιλοσοφίας, μὴ ἐμπεσεῖν εἴς τινα σοφιστήν, μηδὲ ἀποκαθίσαι ἐπὶ τοὺς συγγραφεῖς, ἢ συλλογισμοὺς ἀναλύειν, ἢ περὶ τὰ μετεωρολογικὰ καταγίνεσθαι. πάντα γὰρ ταῦτα 'θεῶν βοηθῶν καὶ τύχης δεῖταί (τινος).'	That by the agency of dreams I was given antidotes both of other kinds and against the spitting of blood and vertigo; and there is that response also at Caieta, *"as thou shalt use it."* And that, when I had set my heart on philosophy, I did not fall into the hands of a sophist, nor sat down at the author's desk, or became a solver of syllogisms, nor busied myself with physical phenomena. For all the above *the Gods as helpers and good fortune need.*

Section Two

The language of healing in the New Testament

Appendix 6 : 1

Greek healing language in the Septuagint: θεραπεύω and ἰάομαι

Text from *The Old Testament in Greek according to the Septuagint,* (ed. H. B. Swete) 3 vols.: 1 (1887) Genesis - 4 Kings; 2 (1891) 1 Chronicles - Tobit; 3 (1894) Hosea - 4 Maccabees; Cambridge.

Translations are (i) my own, or are based on (ii) the Revised Standard Version (1952) of *The Holy Bible*, London, or (iii) the expanded edition of the Revised Standard Version (1957) of *The Oxford Annotated Apocrypha,* (ed. B. M. Metzger) New York, where appropriate.

Reference	**Text**	**Translation/Comment**
1 Genesis 20.17	προσηύξατο δὲ Ἀβραὰμ πρὸς τὸν θεόν, καὶ ἰάσατο ὁ θεὸς τὸν Ἀβιμέλεχ καὶ τὴν γυναῖκα αὐτοῦ καὶ τὰς παιδίσκας αὐτοῦ, και ἔτεκον·	Abraham prayed to God, and God healed Abimelech, and his wife and his female slaves, and they bore children.
2 Exodus 15.26	καὶ εἶπεν Ἐὰν ἀκοῇ ἀκούσῃς τῆς φωνῆς Κυρίου τοῦ θεοῦ σου, καὶ τὰ ἀρεστὰ ἐναντίον αὐτοῦ ποιήσῃς, καὶ ἐνωτίσῃ ταῖς ἐντολαῖς αὐτοῦ, καὶ φυλάξῃς πάντα τὰ δικαιώματα αὐτοῦ, πᾶσαν νόσον ἣν ἐπήγαγον τοῖς Αἰγυπτίοις οὐκ ἐπάξω ἐπὶ σέ· ἐγὼ γάρ εἰμι Κύριος ὁ θεός σου ὁ ἰώμενός σε.	For I am the Lord your God, the one who heals you.
3 Leviticus 14.3	καὶ ἐξελεύσεται ὁ ἱερεὺς ἔξω τῆς παρεμβολῆς, καὶ ὄψεται ὁ ἱερεύς, καὶ ἰδοὺ ἰᾶται ἡ ἁφὴ τῆς λέπρας ἀπὸ τοῦ λεπροῦ.	and behold, the leprous disease in the leper is healed.
4 Leviticus 14.48	ἐὰν δὲ παραγενόμενος εἰσέλθῃ ὁ ἱερεὺς καὶ ἴδῃ, καὶ ἰδοὺ οὐ διαχύσει οὐ διαχεῖται ἡ ἁφὴ ἐν τῇ οἰκίᾳ μετὰ τὸ ἐξαλειφθῆναι τὴν οἰκίαν, καὶ καθαριεῖ ὁ ἱερεὺς τὴν οἰκίαν, ὅτι ἰάθη ἡ ἁφή.	because the disease is healed
5 Numbers 12.13	καὶ ἐβόησεν Μωυσῆς πρὸς Κύριον λέγων Ὁ θεός, δέομαί σου, ἴασαι αὐτήν.	And Moses cried out to the Lord saying, "O God, I beseech you, heal her."

6 Deuteronomy 28.27	πατάξαι σε Κύριος ἕλκει Αἰγυπτίῳ εἰς τὴν ἕδραν καὶ ψώρᾳ ἀγρίᾳ καὶ κνήφῃ, ὥστε μὴ δύνασθαί σε ἰαθῆναι.	The Lord will wound you with the boils of Egypt, and the ulcers and the scurvy and the itch, so that you cannot be healed.
7 Deuteronomy 28.35	πατάξαι σε Κύριος ἐν ἕλκει πονηρῷ ἐπὶ τὰ γόνατα καὶ ἐπὶ τὰς κνήμας, ὥστε μὴ δύνασθαί σε ἰαθῆναι, ἀπὸ ἴχνους τῶν ποδῶν σου ἕως τῆς κορυφῆς σου.	The Lord will wound you with grievous boils on the knees and on the legs so that you cannot be healed, from the soles of your feet to the crown of your head.
8 Deuteronomy 30.3	καὶ ἰάσηται Κύριος τὰς ἁμαρτίας σου· καὶ ἐλεησει σε, καὶ πάλιν συνάξει σε ἐκ πάντων τῶν ἐθνῶν εἰς οὓς διεσκόρπισέν σε Κύριος ἐκεῖ.	And the Lord will heal your mistakes; and he will pity you and will gather you again from all the peoples where the Lord has scattered you.
9 Deuteronomy 32.39	ἴδετε ἴδετε ὅτι ἐγώ εἰμι, καὶ οὐκ ἔστιν θεὸς πλὴν ἐμοῦ· ἐγὼ ἀποκτενῶ καὶ ζῆν ποιήσω· πατάξω, κἀγὼ ἰάσομαι, καὶ οὐκ ἔστιν ὃς ἐξελεῖται ἐκ τῶν χειρῶν μου.	Behold, see that I am, and that there is no god except me; I shall kill and I shall make alive; I shall wound and I shall heal, and there is no one who can deliver out of my hand.
10 1 Kings 6.3	καὶ εἶπαν Εἰ ἐξαποστέλλετε ὑμεῖς τὴν κιβωτὸν διαθήκης θεοῦ Κυρίου Ἰσραήλ, μὴ δὴ ἐξαποστείλητε αὐτὴν κενήν, ἀλλὰ ἀποδιδόντες ἀπόδοτε αὐτῇ τῆς βασάνου, καὶ τότε ἰαθήσεσθε, καὶ ἐξιλασθήσεται ὑμῖν·	. . . and then you will be healed . . .
11 2 Kings 19.24	Καὶ Μεμφιβόσθε υἱὸς υἱοῦ Σαοὺλ κατέβη εἰς ἀπαντὴν τοῦ βασιλέως, καὶ οὐκ ἐθεράπευσεν τοὺς πόδας αὐτοῦ οὐδὲ ὠνυχίσατο οὐδὲ ἐποίησεν τὸν μύστακα αὐτοῦ καὶ τὰ ἱμάτια αὐτοῦ οὐκ ἀπέπλυνεν ἀπὸ τῆς ἡμέρας ἧς ἀπῆλθεν ὁ βασιλεὺς ἕως τῆς ἡμέρας ἧς αὐτὸς παρεγένετο ἐν εἰρήνῃ.	. . . and he had not dressed his feet . . .

12 3 Kings 18.32 (B)	καὶ ᾠκοδόμησεν τοὺς λίθους ἐν ὀνόματι Κυρίου, καὶ ἰάσατο τὸ θυσιαστήριον τὸ κατεσκαμμένον, καὶ ἐποίησεν θάλασσαν χωροῦσαν δύο μετρητὰς σπέρματος κυκλόθεν τοῦ θυσιαστηρίου.	. . . and he (Elijah) repaired the altar that had been thrown down . . .
13 4 Kings 2.21-22	καὶ ἐξῆλθεν Ἐλεισαῖε εἰς τὴν διέξοδον τῶν ὑδάτων, καὶ ἔριψεν ἐκεῖ ἅλα καὶ εἶπεν Τάδε λέγει Κύριος Ἴαμαι τὰ ὕδατα ταῦτα· οὐκ ἔσται ἔτι ἐκεῖθεν θάνατος καὶ ἀτεκνουμένη. καὶ ἰάθησαν τὰ ὕδατα ἕως τῆς ἡμέρας ταύτης κατὰ τὸ ῥῆμα Ἐλεισαῖε ὃ ἐλάλησεν.	Elisha went out to the spring of water and threw salt in it and said, "Thus says the Lord, I have made the water wholesome, from it there will be neither death nor miscarriage." And the water was made wholesome until this day, according to the word which Elisha spoke.
14 4 Kings 9.15, 16-17	καὶ ἀπέστρεψεν Ἰωρὰμ ὁ βασιλεὺς ἰατρευθῆναι ἐν Ἰσραὴλ ἀπὸ τῶν πληγῶν ὧν ἔπαισαν αὐτὸν οἱ Σύροι ἐν τῷ πολεμεῖν αὐτοὺς μετὰ Ἀζαὴλ βασιλέως Συρίας . . . καὶ ἵππευσεν καὶ ἐπορεύθη Εἰού, καὶ κατέβη ἐν Ἰσραήλ, ὅτι Ἰωρὰμ βασιλεὺς Ἰσραὴλ ἐθεραπεύετο ἐν τῷ Ἰσραὴλ ἀπὸ τῶν τοξευμάτων ὧν κατετόξευσαν αὐτὸν οἱ Ἀραμιεὶν ἐν τῇ Ῥαμμὰθ ἐν τῷ πολέμῳ μετὰ Ἀζαὴλ βασιλέως Συρίας, ὅτι δυνατὸς καὶ ἀνὴρ δυνάμεως·	King Joram had returned to be medically treated in Israel from the wounds which the Syrians had inflicted in the war which he fought with Hazael, king of Syria . . . . . . King Joram was being nursed in Israel for arrow wounds . . . [Cf. Josephus *Jewish Antiquities*, 9.112]
15 4 Kings 20.5	Τάδε λέγει Κύριος ὁ θεὸς Δαυεὶδ τοῦ πατρός σου Ἤκουσα τῆς προσευχῆς σου, εἶδον τὰ δάκρυά σου· ἰδοὺ ἐγὼ ἰάσομαί σε, τῇ ἡμέρᾳ τῇ τρίτῃ ἀναβήσῃ εἰς οἶκον Κυρίου.	Thus says the Lord, the God of David your father, "I have heard your prayer, I have seen your tears; behold, I shall heal you; on the third day you will go up to the house of the Lord."
16 4 Kings 20.8	καὶ εἶπεν Ἐζεκίας πρὸς Ἠσαίαν Τί τὸ σημεῖον ὅτι ἰάσεται Κύριός με, καὶ ἀναβήσομαι εἰς οἶκον Κυρίου τῇ ἡμέρᾳ τῇ τρίτῃ;	And Hezekiah said to Isaiah, "What will be the sign that the Lord will heal me, and that I shall go up to the house of the Lord on the third day?"

17 2 Chronicles 6.30	καὶ σὺ εἰσακούσῃ ἐκ τοῦ οὐρανοῦ ἐξ ἑτοίμου κατοικητηρίου σου καὶ ἰάσῃ, καὶ δώσεις ἀνδρὶ κατὰ τὰς ὁδοὺς αὐτοῦ ὡς ἂν γνῷς τὴν καρδίαν αὐτοῦ, ὅτι μόνος γινώσκεις τὴν καρδίαν υἱῶν ἀνθρώπων·	And you will hear from heaven your dwelling place, and you will heal, and will give to a man according to his ways as you know his heart, because only you know the heart of the sons of men.
18 2 Chronicles 7.14	καὶ ἐὰν ἐντραπῇ ὁ λαός μου ἐφ' οὓς τὸ ὄνομά μου ἐπικέκληται ἐπ' αὐτούς, καὶ προσεύξωνται καὶ ζητήσωσιν τὸ πρόσωπόν μου, καὶ ἀποστρέψωσιν ἀπὸ τῶν ὁδῶν αὐτῶν τῶν πονηρῶν, καὶ ἐγὼ εἰσακούσομαι ἐκ τοῦ οὐρανοῦ καὶ ἵλεως ἔσομαι ταῖς ἁμαρτίαις αὐτῶν καὶ ἰάσομαι τὴν γῆν αὐτῶν.	If my people who are called by my name humble themselves, and pray and seek my face, and turn from their wicked ways, I shall hear from heaven and I shall deal graciously with their mistakes and I shall heal their land.
19 2 Chronicles 30.20	καὶ ἐπήκουσεν Κύριος τῷ Ἐζεκίᾳ, καὶ ἰάσατο τὸν λαόν.	And the Lord heard Hezekiah, and healed the people.
20 1 Esdras 1.4	καὶ νῦν λατρεύετε τῷ κυρίῳ θεῷ ὑμῶν, καὶ θεραπεύετε τὸ ἔθνος αὐτοῦ Ἰσραήλ, καὶ ἑτοιμάσατε κατὰ τὰς πατριὰς καὶ τὰς φυλὰς ὑμῶν κατὰ τὴν γραφὴν Δαυεὶδ βασιλέως Ἰσραὴλ καὶ κατὰ τὴν μεγαλειότητα Σαλωμὼν τοῦ υἱοῦ αὐτοῦ·	Now worship the Lord your God, and serve his people Israel, . . .
21 1 Esdras 2.17	καὶ νῦν γνωστὸν ἔστω τῷ κυρίῳ βασιλεῖ ὅτι Ἰουδαῖοι ἀναβάντες παρ' ὑμῶν πρὸς ἡμᾶς, ἐλθόντες εἰς Ἰερουσαλήμ, τὴν πόλιν τὴν ἀποστάτιν καὶ πονηρὰν οἰκοῦσιν, τάς τε ἀγορὰς αὐτῆς καὶ τὰ τείχη θεραπεύουσιν καὶ ναὸν ὑποβάλλονται.	And now let it be known to our lord the King that the Jews who came up from you to us have gone to Jerusalem, and are building that rebellious and wicked city, and are repairing both its market places and its walls, and are laying the temple foundations.

22 Psalm 6.3-5	ἐλέησόν με, Κύριε, ὅτι ἀσθενής εἰμι· ἴασαί με, ὅτι ἐταράχθη τὰ ὀστᾶ μου. καὶ ἡ ψυχή μου ἐταράχθη σφόδρα· καὶ σύ, Κύριε, ἕως πότε; ἐπίστρεψον, Κύριε, ῥῦσαι τὴν ψυχήν μου, σῶσόν με ἕνεκεν τοῦ ἐλέους σου.	Have mercy on me, O Lord, for I am ailing, heal me, for my bones are troubled. My soul also is sorely troubled. But you, O Lord, how long? Turn, O Lord, defend my soul, save me for the sake of your mercy.
23 Psalm 29(30).3-4	Κύριε ὁ θεός μου, ἐκέκραξα πρὸς σὲ καὶ ἰάσω με· Κύριε, ἀνήγαγες ἐξ ᾅδου τὴν ψυχήν μου, ἔσωσάς με ἀπὸ τῶν καταβαινόντων εἰς λάκκον.	O Lord my God, I cried out to you and you healed me, O Lord, you have brought up my soul from Hades, You have saved me from going down into the pit.
24 Psalm 40(41).4-5	Κύριος βοηθήσαι αὐτῷ ἐπὶ κλίνης ὀδύνης αὐτοῦ, ὅλην τὴν κοίτην αὐτοῦ ἔστρεψας ἐν τῇ ἀρρωστίᾳ αὐτοῦ. ἐγὼ εἶπα Κύριε, ἐλέησόν με· ἴασαι τὴν ψυχήν μου, ὅτι ἥμαρτόν σοι.	The Lord sustained him on his bed of pain, in his illness you changed all his bed. As for me, I said, "O Lord, have mercy on me; heal me, for I have sinned against you!"
25 Psalm 59(60).4-5	συνέσεισας τὴν γῆν καὶ συνετάραξας αὐτήν· ἴασαι τὰ συντρίμματα αὐτῆς, ὅτι ἐσαλεύθησαν, ἔδειξας τῷ λαῷ σου σκληρά, ἐπότισας ἡμᾶς οἶνον κατανύξεως.	You have made the land to quake and torn it open; heal its breaches, for they were made to totter. You have shown unpleasant things to your people, You have given the wine of stupefaction to us to drink.
26 Psalm 102(103).3	τὸν εὐιλατεύοντα πάσαις ταῖς ἀνομίαις σου, τὸν ἰώμενον πάσας τὰς νόσους σου·	the one forgiving all your lawless deeds, the one healing all your diseases.
27 Psalm 106(107).20	ἀπέστειλεν τὸν λόγον αὐτοῦ καὶ ἰάσατο αὐτούς, καὶ ἐρρύσατο αὐτοὺς ἐκ τῶν διαφθορῶν αὐτῶν.	he sent forth his word and healed them, and protected them from destruction.
28 Psalm 146(147).3	ὁ ἰώμενος τοὺς συντετριμμένους τὴν καρδίαν, καὶ δεσμεύων τὰ συντρίμματα αὐτῶν·	He heals the brokenhearted, and binds up their wounds.

29 Proverbs 12.18	εἰσὶν οἳ λέγοντες τιτρώσκουσιν μάχαιραι, γλῶσσαι δὲ σοφῶν ἰῶνται.	There are those whose words injure like sword thrusts, but the tongues of the wise bring healing.
30 Proverbs 14.19	ὀλισθήσουσιν κακοὶ ἔναντι ἀγαθῶν, καὶ ἀσεβεῖς θεραπεύσουσιν θύρας δικαίων.	The evil bow down before the good, the impious at the gates of the righteous.
31 Proverbs 18.9	ὁ μὴ ἰώμενος αὐτὸν ἐν τοῖς ἔργοις αὐτοῦ ἀδελφός ἐστιν τοῦ λυμαινομένου ἑαυτόν.	He who is slack in his work is a brother to him who destroys.
32 Proverbs (19).(6)	πολλοὶ θεραπεύουσιν πρόσωπα βασιλέων, πᾶς δὲ ὁ κακὸς γίνεται ὄνειδος ἀνδρί.	Many fawn before the face of kings while every evil man is a reproach to man.
33 Proverbs 26.18-19	ὥσπερ οἱ ἰώμενοι προβάλλουσιν λόγους εἰς ἀνθρώπους, ὁ δὲ ἀπαντήσας τῷ λόγῳ πρῶτος ὑποσκελισθήσεται· οὕτως πάντες οἱ ἐνεδρεύοντες τοὺς ἑαυτῶν φίλους, ὅταν δὲ ὁραθῶσιν, λέγουσιν ὅτι Παίζων ἔπραξα.	Just as healers hurl advice at men, and the one having met with the word first has been tripped up, so are all those who deceive their own friends whenever they see them, saying, "I was only joking!"
34 Proverbs 29.26	πολλοὶ θεραπεύουσιν πρόσωπα ἡγουμένων, παρὰ δὲ Κυρίου γίνεται τὸ δίκαιον ἀνδρί.	Many seek the favour of a ruler, but from the Lord a man gets justice.
35 Ecclesiastes 3.3	καιρὸς τοῦ ἀποκτεῖναι καὶ καιρὸς τοῦ ἰάσασθαι, καιρὸς τοῦ καθελεῖν καὶ καιρὸς τοῦ οἰκοδομεῖν	a time to kill and a time to heal, a time to break down, and a time to build up
36 Job 5.18	αὐτὸς γὰρ ἀλγεῖν ποιεῖ καὶ πάλιν ἀποκαθίστησιν· ἔπαισεν, καὶ αἱ χεῖρες αὐτοῦ ἰάσαντο.	For he sends suffering, but also restores; he has smitten, but his hands have also healed.
37 Job 12.21	ἐκχέων ἀτιμίαν ἐπ' ἄρχοντας, ταπεινοὺς δὲ ἰάσατο.	He pours contempt on princes, but healed the lowly.

38 Wisdom 10.9	σοφία δὲ τοὺς θεραπεύσαντας αὐτὴν ἐκ πόνων ἐρρύσατο	Wisdom rescued from trouble those who served her
39 Wisdom 16.10	τοὺς δὲ υἱούς σου οὐδὲ ἰοβόλων δρακόντων ἐνίκησαν ὀδόντες, τὸ ἔλεος γάρ σου ἀντιπαρῆλθεν καὶ ἰάσατο αὐτούς.	But your sons were not conquered even by the teeth of venomous serpents, for your mercy came to their help and healed them.
40 Wisdom 16.12	καὶ γὰρ οὔτε βοτάνη οὔτε μάλαγμα ἐθεράπευσεν αὐτους, ἀλλὰ ὁ σός, Κύριε, λόγος ὁ πάντα ἰώμενος.	For neither herb nor poultice healed them, but it is your word, O Lord, which heals all humankind.
41 Sirach 18.19-21	πρὶν ἢ λαλῆσαι μάνθανε, καὶ πρὸ ἀρρωστείας θεραπεύου· πρὸ κρίσεως ἐξέταζε σεαυτόν, καὶ ἐν ὥρᾳ ἐπισκοπῆς εὑρήσεις ἐξιλασμόν· πρὶν ἀρρωστῆσαί σε ταπεινώθητι, καὶ ἐν καιρῷ ἁμαρτημάτων δεῖξον ἐπιστροφήν.	Before you speak, learn, and before you fall ill, take care of your health. Before judgment, examine yourself, and in the hour of visitation you will find forgiveness. Before falling ill, humble yourself, and when you are on the point of sinning, turn back.
42 Sirach 32 (35).20	θεραπεύων ἐν εὐδοκίᾳ δεχθήσεται, καὶ ἡ δέησις αὐτοῦ ἕως νεφελῶν συνάψει·	He whose service is pleasing will be welcomed, and his prayer will reach to the clouds.

43 Sirach 38.1-8

1 Τίμα ἰατρὸν πρὸς τὰς χρείας τιμαῖς αὐτοῦ,
καὶ γὰρ αὐτὸν ἔκτισεν Κύριος·
2 παρὰ γὰρ Ὑψίστου ἐστὶν ἴασις,
καὶ παρὰ βασιλέως λήμψεται δόμα.
3 ἐπιστήμη ἰατροῦ ἀνυψώσει κεφαλὴν αὐτοῦ,
καὶ ἔναντι μεγιστάνων θαυμασθήσεται.
4 Κύριος ἔκτισεν ἐκ γῆς φάρμακα,
καὶ ἀνὴρ φρόνιμος οὐ προσοχθιεῖ αὐτοῖς.
5 οὐκ ἀπὸ ξύλου ἐγλυκάνθη ὕδωρ
εἰς τὸ γνωσθῆναι τὴν ἰσχὺν αὐτοῦ;
6 καὶ αὐτὸς ἔδωκεν ἀνθρώποις ἐπιστήμην
ἐνδοξάζεσθαι ἐν τοῖς θαυμασίοις αὐτοῦ·
7 ἐν αὐτοῖς ἐθεράπευσεν καὶ ἦρεν τὸν πόνον αὐτοῦ,
8 μυρεψὸς ἐν τούτοις ποιήσει μίγμα·
καὶ οὐ μὴ συντελέσῃ ἔργα αὐτοῦ,
καὶ εἰρήνη παρ' αὐτοῦ ἐστιν ἐπὶ προσώπου τῆς γῆς.

1 Honour the physician with honours according to your need of him,
for the Lord created him;
2 for healing comes from the Most High,
and he will receive a gift from the king.
3 The skill of a physician lifts up his head,
and in the presence of great men he is admired.
4 The Lord created medicines from the earth,
and a sensible man will not despise them.
5 Was not water made sweet with a tree
in order that his (its?) power might be known?
6 And he gave skill to men
that he (they?) might be glorified in his marvellous works.
7 By them he heals and takes away pain;
8 the pharmacist makes of them a compound.
His works will never be finished;
and from him health (peace?) is upon the face of the earth.

44 Sirach 38.9-15	9 τέκνον, ἐν ἀρρωστήματί σου μὴ παράβλεπε, ἀλλ' εὖξαι Κυρίῳ, καὶ αὐτὸς ἰάσεταί σε· 10 ἀπόστησον πλημμελίαν καὶ εὔθυνον χεῖρας, καὶ ἀπὸ πάσης ἁμαρτίας καθάρισον καρδίαν· 11 δὸς εὐωδίαν καὶ μνημόσυνον σεμιδάλεως, καὶ λίπανον προσφοράν, ὡς μὴ ὑπάρχων. 12 καὶ ἰατρῷ δὸς τόπον, καὶ γὰρ αὐτὸν ἔκτισεν Κύριος, καὶ μὴ ἀποστήτω σου, καὶ γὰρ αὐτοῦ χρεία. 13 ἔστιν καιρὸς ὅτε καὶ ἐν χερσὶν αὐτῶν εὐοδία· 14 καὶ γὰρ αὐτοὶ Κυρίου δεηθήσονται, ἵνα εὐοδώσῃ αὐτοῖς ἀνάπαυσιν καὶ ἴασιν χάριν ἐμβιώσεως. 15 ὁ ἁμαρτάνων ἔναντι τοῦ ποιήσαντος αὐτὸν ἐμπέσοι εἰς χεῖρας ἰατροῦ.	9 My child, when you are sick do not be negligent, but pray to the Lord, and he will heal you. 10 Give up your faults and direct your hands aright, and cleanse your heart from all sin. 11 Offer a sweet-smelling sacrifice, and a memorial portion of fine flour, and pour oil on your offering, as much as you can afford. 12 And give the physician his place, for the Lord created him; let him not leave you, for there is need of him. 13 There is a time when success lies in their hands, 14 for they too will pray to the Lord that he should grant them success in rest and gracious healing for the maintenance of life. 15 He who makes mistakes before his Maker may he fall into the hands of a physician!
45 Esther 1.1-3	ἔτους δευτέρου βασιλεύοντος 'Αρταξέρξου τοῦ μεγάλου βασιλέως τῇ μιᾷ τοῦ Νεισὰ ἐνύπνιον ἴδεν Μαρδοχαῖος ὁ τοῦ 'Ιαείρου τοῦ Σεμεείου τοῦ Κεισαίου ἐκ φυλῆς Βενιαμείν, ἄνθρωπος 'Ιουδαῖος οἰκῶν ἐν Σούσοις τῇ πόλει, ἄνθρωπος μέγας, θεραπεύων ἐν τῇ αὐλῇ τοῦ βασιλέως·	In the second year of the reign of Artaxerxes the Great, on the first day of Nisan, Mordecai the son of Jair, son of Shimei, son of Kish, of the tribe of Benjamin, had a dream. He was a Jew, dwelling in the city of Susa, a great man, serving in the court of the king.
46 Esther 2.19	ὁ δὲ Μαρδοχαῖος ἐθεράπευεν ἐν τῇ αὐλῇ.	Mordecai was serving in the court
47 Esther 6.10	εἶπεν δὲ ὁ βασιλεὺς τῷ 'Αμάν Καλῶς ἐλάλησας· οὕτως ποίησον τῷ Μαρδοχαίῳ τῷ 'Ιουδαίῳ τῷ θεραπεύοντι ἐν τῇ αὐλῇ, καὶ μὴ παραπεσάτω σου λόγος ὧν ἐλάλησας.	And the king said to Haman, "You have spoken well. Do you thus to Mordecai the Jew who serves in the court, and let not the word which you spoke go astray!"

48 Judith 11.17	ὅτι ἡ δούλη σου θεοσεβής ἐστιν, καὶ θεραπεύουσα νυκτὸς καὶ ἡμέρας τὸν θεὸν τοῦ οὐρανοῦ·	For your servant is religious, serving the God of heaven night and day
49 Tobit 1.7	τὴν δεκάτην ἐδίδουν τοῖς υἱοῖς Λευεὶ τοῖς θεραπεύουσιν εἰς Ἰερουσαλήμ,·	I would give a tenth to the sons of Levi who ministered at Jerusalem
50 Tobit 2.10 (א)	א: καὶ οὐκ ᾔδειν ὅτι στρουθία ἐν τῷ τοίχῳ ἐπάνω μού εἰσιν, καὶ ἐκάθισεν τὸ ἀφόδευμα αὐτῶν εἰς τοὺς ὀφθαλμούς μου θερμὸν καὶ ἐπήγαγεν λευκώματα. καὶ ἐπορευόμην πρὸς τοὺς ἰατροὺς θεραπευθῆναι, καὶ ὅσῳ ἐνεχρίοσάν με τὰ φάρμακα, τοσούτῳ μᾶλλον ἐξετυφλοῦντο οἱ ὀφθαλμοί μου τοῖς λευκώμασιν μέχρι τοῦ ἀποτυφλωθῆναι. καὶ ἤμην ἀδύνατος τοῖς ὀφθαλμοῖς ἔτη τέσσερα.	I did not know that there were sparrows on the wall above me, and their fresh droppings fell into my eyes and formed white films. I went to the physicians to be treated, and by as much as they anointed me with drugs, by that much more my eyes were blinded with white films until they were completely blinded. And I was unable to see for four years.
51 Tobit 3.17	καὶ ἀπεστάλη ἰάσασθαι τοὺς δύο, τοῦ Τωβεὶτ λεπίσαι τὰ λευκώματα, καὶ Σάρραν την τοῦ Ῥαγουὴλ δοῦναι Τωβίᾳ τῷ υἱῷ Τωβεὶτ γυναῖκα, καὶ δῆσαι Ἀσμώδαυν τὸ πονηρὸν δαιμόνιον, διότι Τωβίᾳ ἐπιβάλλει κληρονομῆσαι αὐτήν. א: καὶ ἀπεστάλη Ῥαφαὴλ ἰάσασθαι τοὺς δύο· Τωβείθ, ἀπολῦσαι τὰ λευκώματα ἀπὸ τῶν ὀφθαλμῶν αὐτοῦ ἵνα ἴδῃ τοῖς ὀφθαλμοῖς τὸ φῶς τοῦ θεοῦ . . .	He was sent to heal the two of them: to scale away the white films from Tobit's eyes; to give Sarah the daughter of Raguel in marriage to Tobias the son of Tobit, and to bind Asmodeus the evil demon, because Tobias was entitled to possess her. א: And Raphael was sent to heal the two of them: with respect to Tobit, to loose the white films from his eyes so that he might see with his eyes the light of God . . .
52 Tobit 5.10	א: καὶ ἀποκριθεὶς Τωβεὶθ εἶπεν αὐτῷ Τί μοι ἔτι ὑπάρχει χαίρειν; καὶ ἐγὼ ἄνθρωπος ἀδύνατος τοῖς ὀφθαλμοῖς καὶ οὐ βλέπω τὸ φῶς τοῦ οὐρανοῦ, ἀλλ' ἐν τῷ σκότει κεῖμαι ὥσπερ οἱ νεκροὶ οἱ μηκέτι θεωροῦντες τὸ φῶς· ζῶν ἐγὼ ἐν νεκροῖς εἰμι, φωνὴν ἀνθρώπων ἀκούω καὶ αὐτοὺς οὐ βλέπω. καὶ εἶπεν αὐτῷ Θάρσει, ἐγγὺς παρὰ τῷ θεῷ ἰάσασθαί σε· θάρσει.	In reply Tobit said to him, "Why do you continue to greet me? I am a man incompetent in my eyes and I do not see the light of heaven, but lie in darkness just like corpses who no longer see the light. Living I am in death, I hear the voice of men but I do not see them." And he said to him, "Have confidence that you will soon be healed by God! Have confidence!"

53 Tobit 6.9	ἡ δὲ χολὴ ἐνχρῖσαι ἄνθρωπον ὃς ἔχει λευκώματα ἐν τοῖς ὀφθαλμοῖς, καὶ ἰαθήσεται.	. . . and he will be healed.
	ℵ: καὶ ἡ χολὴ ἐνχρῖσαι ἀνθρώπου ὀφθαλμούς, οὗ λευκώματα ἀνέβησαν ἐπ᾽ αὐτῶν, ἐμφυσῆσαι ἐπ᾽ αὐτοὺς ἐπὶ τῶν λευκωμάτων, καὶ ὑγιαίνουσιν.	ℵ: . . . and they are healthy.
54 Tobit 12.3	ὅτι με ἀγίοχέν σοι ὑγιῆ, καὶ τὴν γυναῖκά μου ἐθεράπευσεν καὶ τὸ ἀργύριόν μου ἤνεγκεν, καὶ σὲ ὁμοίως ἐθεράπευσεν.	Because he has led me to you in health, and he healed my wife, and carried my money, and also healed you.
	ℵ: ἐμὲ ἀγίοχεν ὑγιαίνοντα, καὶ τὴν γυναῖκά μου ἐθεράπευσεν, καὶ τὸ ἀργύριον ἤνεγκεν μετ᾽ ἐμοῦ, καὶ σὲ ἐθεράπευσεν·	
55 Tobit 12.14	καὶ νῦν ἀπέστειλέν με ὁ θεὸς ἰάσασθαί σε καὶ τὴν νύμφην σου Σάρραν.	Now God sent me to heal you and your daughter-in-law Sarah.
	ℵ: τότε ἀπέσταλμαι ἐπὶ σὲ πειράσαι σε, καὶ ἅμα ἀπέσταλκέν με ὁ θεὸς ἰάσασθαι καὶ Σάρραν τὴν νύμφην σου.	ℵ: Then I was sent to you to test you, and at the same time God sent me to heal Sarah your daughter-in-law.
56 Hosea 5.13	καὶ εἶδεν Ἐφράιμ τὴν νόσον αὐτοῦ, καὶ Ἰούδας τὴν ὀδύνην αὐτοῦ· καὶ ἐπορεύθη Ἐφράιμ πρὸς Ἀσσυρίους καὶ ἀπέστειλεν πρέσβεις πρὸς βασιλέα Ἰαρείμ· καὶ οὗτος οὐκ ἠδυνάσθη ἰάσασθαι ὑμᾶς, καὶ οὐ μὴ διαπαύσῃ ἐξ ὑμῶν ὀδύνη.	Ephraim saw his sickness, and Judah his pain. And Ephraim went to Assyria, and sent ambassadors to the king. And he was unable to heal you, or relieve your pain.
57 Hosea 6.1-3	Ἐν θλίψει αὐτῶν ὀρθριοῦσι πρὸς μὲ λέγοντες Πορευθῶμεν καὶ ἐπιστρέψωμεν πρὸς Κύριον τὸν θεὸν ἡμῶν, ὅτι αὐτὸς ἥρπακεν καὶ ἰάσεται ἡμᾶς, πατάξει καὶ μοτώσει ἡμᾶς, ὑγιάσει ἡμᾶς μετὰ δύο ἡμέρας· ἐν τῇ ἡμέρᾳ τῇ τρίτῃ καὶ ἀναστησόμεθα, καὶ ζησόμεθα ἐνώπιον αὐτοῦ, καὶ γνωσόμεθα· διώξομεν τοῦ γνῶναι τὸν κύριον, . . .	In their distress they seek me saying, "Come, let us return to the Lord our God, because he has torn and will heal us; he has smitten, and will bind us up, and he will restore us after two days. On the third day we shall be raised up, and we shall live before him, and we shall understand. We shall seek knowledge of the Lord, . . .

58 Hosea 7.1	. . . ἐν τῷ ἐπιστρέφειν με τὴν αἰχμαλωσίαν τοῦ λαοῦ μου, ἐν τῷ ἰάσασθαί με τὸν Ἰσραὴλ	. . . When I would turn back the captivity of my people, when I would heal Israel, . . .
59 Hosea 11.3-4	καὶ ἐγὼ συνεπόδισα τὸν Ἐφράιμ, ἀνέλαβον αὐτὸν ἐπὶ τὸν βραχίονά μου· οὐκ ἔγνωσαν ὅτι ἴαμαι αὐτούς. ἐν διαφθορᾷ ἀνθρώπων, ἐξέτεινα αὐτοὺς ἐν δεσμοῖς ἀγαπήσεώς μου, καὶ ἔσομαι αὐτοῖς ὡς ῥαπίζων ἄνθρωπος ἐπὶ τὰς σιαγόνας αὐτοῦ· καὶ ἐπιβλέψομαι πρὸς αὐτόν, δυνήσομαι αὐτῷ.	And I taught Ephraim to walk, I took him up in my arms; but they did not know that I healed them. In humane cords, I led them out in the bands of my love, and I shall be to them as one who eases the yoke on his jaws. I shall watch over him, and empower him.
60 Hosea 14.5	ἰάσομαι τὰς κατοικίας αὐτῶν, ἀγαπήσω αὐτοὺς ὁμολόγως, ὅτι ἀπέστρεψεν τὴν ὀργήν μου ἀπ' αὐτοῦ.	I shall heal their dwellings, I shall certainly love them, because he has turned my anger from him.
61 Zechariah 11.16	διότι ἰδοὺ ἐξεγείρω ποιμένα ἐπὶ τὴν γῆν· τὸ ἐκλιμπάνον οὐ μὴ ἐπισκέψηται, καὶ τὸ ἐσκορπισμένον οὐ μὴ ζητήσῃ, καὶ τὸ συντετριμμένον οὐ μὴ ἰάσηται, καὶ τὸ ὁλόκληρον οὐ μὴ κατευθύνῃ, καὶ τὰ κρέα τῶν ἐκλεκτῶν καταφάγεται, καὶ τοὺς ἀστραγάλους αὐτῶν ἐκστρέψει.	For behold, I am raising up a shepherd in the land; one who does not care for the perishing or seek the wandering, heal the maimed or nourish the sound, but who devours the flesh of the fat ones, and tears their hooves.
62 Isaiah 6.10	ἐπαχύνθη γὰρ ἡ καρδία τοῦ λαοῦ τούτου, καὶ τοῖς ὠσὶν αὐτῶν βαρέως ἤκουσαν καὶ τοὺς ὀφθαλμοὺς ἐκάμμυσαν, μή ποτε ἴδωσιν τοῖς ὀφθαλμοῖς καὶ τοῖς ὠσὶν ἀκούσωσιν, καὶ τῇ καρδίᾳ συνῶσιν καὶ ἐπιστρέψωσιν, καὶ ἰάσομαι αὐτούς.	For the heart of this people was made fat, and their ears heavy, and they shut their eyes, lest they ever see with their eyes and hear with their ears, and understand in their heart and turn, and I shall heal them.
63 Isaiah 7.4	καὶ ἐρεῖς αὐτῷ Φύλαξαι τοῦ ἡσυχάσαι καὶ μὴ φοβοῦ, μηδὲ ἡ ψυχή σου ἀσθενείτω ἀπὸ τῶν δύο ξύλων τῶν δαλῶν τῶν καπνιζομένων τούτων· ὅταν γὰρ ὀργὴ τοῦ θυμοῦ μου γένηται, πάλιν ἰάσομαι.	. . . and say to him, "Beware and be quiet and do not fear, and do not let your heart be faint because of these two smouldering stumps of firebrands. For whenever the passion of my rage occurs, I shall heal again.

64 Isaiah 19.22	καὶ πατάξει Κύριος τοὺς Αἰγυπτίους πληγῇ, καὶ ἰάσεται αὐτοὺς ἰάσει, καὶ ἐπιστραφήσονται πρὸς Κύριον, καὶ εἰσακούσεται αὐτῶν καὶ ἰάσεται αὐτούς.	And the Lord will smite the Egyptians with a blow, and will heal them with a cure, and they will return to the Lord, and he will hear them and will heal them.
65 Isaiah 30.26	καὶ ἔσται τὸ φῶς τῆς σελήνης ὡς τὸ φῶς τοῦ ἡλίου, καὶ τὸ φῶς τοῦ ἡλίου ἔσται ἑπταπλάσιον, ἐν τῇ ἡμέρᾳ ὅταν ἰάσηται Κύριος τὸ σύντριμμα τοῦ λαοῦ αὐτοῦ, καὶ τὴν ὀδύνην τῆς πληγῆς σου ἰάσεται.	And the light of the moon will be as the light of the sun, and the light of the sun will be sevenfold, on the day when the Lord will heal the hurt of his people, and will heal the pain of his? blow.
66 Isaiah 53.5	αὐτὸς δὲ ἐτραυματίσθη διὰ τὰς ἁμαρτίας ἡμῶν, καὶ μεμαλάκισται διὰ τὰς ἀνομίας ἡμῶν· παιδία εἰρήνης ἡμῶν ἐπ' αὐτόν, τῷ μώλωπι αὐτοῦ ἡμεῖς ἰάθημεν.	He was wounded because of our transgressions, and bruised because of our lawlessnesses. Upon him is the nurturing of our wholeness, by his wound we are healed.
67 Isaiah 54.17	ἔστιν κληρονομία τοῖς θεραπεύουσιν Κύριον, καὶ ὑμεῖς ἔσεσθέ μοι δίκαιοι, λέγει Κύριος.	This is the heritage of the servants of the Lord, and you will be vindicated by me, says the Lord.
68 Isaiah 57.18-19	τὰς ὁδοὺς αὐτοῦ ἑόρακα, καὶ ἰασάμην αὐτὸν καὶ παρεκάλεσα αὐτόν, καὶ ἔδωκα αὐτῷ παράκλησιν ἀληθινήν, εἰρήνην ἐπ' εἰρήνην τοῖς μακρὰν καὶ τοῖς ἐγγὺς οὖσιν. καὶ εἶπεν Κύριος Ἰάσομαι αὐτούς·	I have seen his ways, and I have healed him and comforted him. And I gave to him true comfort. Peace upon peace I gave to those far and near. And the Lord said, I shall heal them.
69 Isaiah 61.1	Πνεῦμα Κυρίου ἐπ' ἐμέ, οὗ εἵνεκεν ἔχρισέν με εὐαγγελίσασθαι πτωχοῖς, ἀπέσταλκέν με ἰάσασθαι τοὺς συντετριμμένους τὴν καρδίαν, κηρῦξαι αἰχμαλώτοις ἄφεσιν καὶ τυφλοῖς ἀνάβλεψιν,	The spirit of the Lord is upon me, because the Lord has anointed me to bring good news to the poor. He has sent me to heal the broken-hearted, to proclaim liberty to the captives, and restoration of sight to the blind.
70 Jeremiah 3.22	ἐπιστράφητε, υἱοὶ ἐπιστρέφοντες, καὶ ἰάσομαι τὰ συντρίμματα ὑμῶν. ἰδοὺ δοῦλοι ἡμεῖς ἐσόμεθά σοι, ὅτι σὺ Κύριος ὁ θεὸς ἡμῶν εἶ.	Return, O faithless sons, and I shall heal your faithlessness. Behold we shall be your slaves, because you are the Lord our God.

71 Jeremiah 6.14	καὶ ἰῶντο τὸ σύντριμμα τοῦ λαοῦ μου, ἐξουθενοῦντες καὶ λέγοντες Εἰρήνη εἰρήνη· καὶ ποῦ ἐστιν εἰρήνη;	They heal the wounds of my people, disdainfully saying, "Peace, peace." But where is peace?
72 Jeremiah 15.18	ἵνα τί οἱ λυποῦντές με κατισχύουσίν μου; ἡ πληγή μου στερεά, πόθεν ἰαθήσομαι;	Why is my pain unceasing, my wound incurable? Whence shall I be healed?
73 Jeremiah 17.14-15	ἴασαί με, Κύριε, καὶ ἰαθήσομαι· σῶσόν με, καὶ σωθήσομαι, ὅτι καύχημά μου σὺ εἶ. ἰδοὺ αὐτοὶ λέγουσι πρὸς μέ Ποῦ εστιν ὁ λόγος Κυρίου; ἐλθάτω.	Heal me, O Lord, and I shall be healed. Save me, and I shall be saved, for you are my praise. Behold, they say to me, "Where is the word of the Lord? Let it come!"
74 Jeremiah 19.11	καὶ ἐρεῖς Τάδε λέγει Κύριος Οὕτως συντρίψω τὸν λαὸν τοῦτον καὶ τὴν πόλιν ταύτην καθὼς συντρίβεται ἄγγος ὀστράκινον, ὃ οὐ δυνήσεται ἰαθῆναι.	and you will say, "Thus says the Lord: So shall I break this people and this city, as one breaks a potter's vessel, one which will be unable to be mended. . . ."
75 Jeremiah 28 (51).8-9	καὶ ἄφνω ἔπεσεν Βαβυλὼν καὶ συνετρίβη. θρηνεῖτε αὐτήν, λάβετε ῥητίνην τῇ διαφθορᾷ αὐτῆς, εἴ πως ἰαθήσεται. ἰατρεύσαμεν τὴν Βαβυλῶνα, καὶ οὐκ ἰάθη·	Suddenly Babylon has fallen and been broken. Wail for her! Take balm for her pain; perhaps she will be healed. We would have healed Babylon, but she was not healed.
76 Lamentations 2.13	Τί μαρτυρήσω σοι ἢ τί ὁμοιώσω σοι, Θύγατερ Ἰερουσαλήμ; τίς σώσει καὶ παρακαλέσει σε, παρθένος θύγατερ Σειών; ὅτι ἐμεγαλύνθη ποτήριον συντριβῆς σου· τίς ἰάσεταί σε;	What shall I say for you, to what compare you, O Daughter of Jerusalem? Who will save and comfort you, O virgin daughter of Zion? For vast is the cup of your suffering. Who will heal you?

77 Letter of Jeremiah 25-26	ἄνευ ποδῶν ἐπ' ὤμοις φέρονται ἐνδεικνύμενοι τὴν ἑαυτῶν ἀτιμίαν τοῖς ἀνθρώποις, αἰσχύνονταί τε καὶ οἱ θεραπεύοντες αὐτά, διὰ τό, μή ποτε ἐπὶ τὴν γῆν πέσῃ, δι' αὐτῶν ἀνίστασθαι· μήτε ἐάν τις αὐτὸ ὀρθὸν στήσῃ, δι' ἑαυτοῦ κινηθήσεται, μήτε ἐὰν κλιθῇ, οὐ μὴ ὀρθωθῇ, ἀλλ' ὥσπερ νεκροῖς τὰ δῶρα αὐτοῖς παρατίθεται.	Having no feet they are carried on men's shoulders, revealing to mankind their worthlessness. And those who serve them are ashamed because through them these gods are made to stand, lest they fall to the ground. If any one sets one of them upright, it cannot move of itself; and if it is tipped over, it cannot straighten itself; but gifts are placed before them just as before the dead.
78 Letter of Jeremiah 38	τοῖς ἀπὸ τοῦ ὄρους λίθοις ὡμοιωμένοι εἰσὶν τὰ ξύλινα καὶ τὰ περίχρυσα καὶ τὰ περιάργυρα, οἱ δὲ θεραπεύοντες αὐτὰ καταισχυνθήσονται.	These things that are made of wood and overlaid in gold and silver are like stones from the mountain, and those who serve them will be put to shame.
79 Daniel (O′) 7.10	ποταμὸς πυρὸς ἕλκων, καὶ ἐξεπορεύετο κατὰ πρόσωπον αὐτοῦ ποταμὸς πυρός· χίλιαι χιλιάδες ἐθεράπευον αὐτὸν καὶ μύριαι μυριάδες παρειστήκεισαν αὐτῷ· καὶ κριτήριον ἐκάθισε καὶ βίβλοι ἠνεῴχθησαν.	A stream of fire issued and came forth from before him; a thousand thousands served him and ten thousand times ten thousand stood before him; the court sat in judgment and the books were opened.
	Cf. **Θ**: χίλιαι χιλιάδες ἐλειτούργουν αὐτῷ . . .	
80 4 Maccabees 3.10	ὁ δὲ βασιλεὺς ὡς μάλιστα διψῶν, καίπερ ἀφθόνους ἔχων πηγάς, οὐκ ἠδύνατο δι' αὐτῶν ἰάσασθαι τὴν δίψαν.	The king was extremely thirsty, and although springs were plentiful, he was unable to slake his thirst.

Appendix 6 : 2

Josephus

Text and translation from the Loeb Classical Library edition of *Josephus*, in 9 volumes: 1 (1966) *The Life*, (trans. H. St. J. Thackeray); 2 (1967) *The Jewish War*, 1-3 (trans. H. St. J. Thackeray); 3 (1968) *The Jewish War*, 4-7 (trans. H. St. J. Thackeray); 5 (1977) *Jewish Antiquities*, 5-8 (trans. H. St. J. Thackeray and R. Marcus); 6 (1978) *Jewish Antiquities*, 9-11 (trans. R. Marcus).

References are by numeral, title of work and reference within that work, and Loeb volume and page number.

Reference	Text	Translation
1 *War* 1.187 Loeb 2, 86	Ἀντίπατρος δὲ μετὰ τὴν Πομπηίου τελευτὴν μεταβὰς ἐθεράπευεν Καίσαρα	Antipater, on the death of Pompey, went over to his opponent and paid court to Caesar.
2 *War* 1.222 Loeb 2, 104	. . . ἐπέσχεν δὲ τὴν τούτου καὶ τὴν τῶν ἄλλων πόλεων ἀπώλειαν Ἀντίπατρος ταχέως ἑκατὸν ταλάντοις θεραπεύσας Κάσσιον.	. . . but Antipater saved both his life and the other cities from destruction, by hastily propitiating Cassius with a gift of a hundred talents.
3 *War* 1.242 Loeb 2, 112	πρὸς ἃ παρὼν Ἡρώδης καὶ τεθεραπευκὼς οὐκ ὀλίγοις Ἀντώνιον χρήμασιν οὕτως διέθηκεν, ὡς μηδὲ λόγου τῶν ἐχθρῶν ἀνασχέσθαι.	Herod thereupon appeared and by large bribes so wrought upon Antony that he refused his adversaries a hearing.
4 *War* 1.272 Loeb 2, 126	κατέχει δὲ καὶ ἄλλος λόγος, ὡς ἀνενέγκαι μὲν ἐκ τῆς τότε πληγῆς, πεμφθεὶς δ' ἰατρὸς ὑπ' Ἀντιγόνου θεραπεῦσαι δῆθεν αὐτὸν ἐμπλήσειεν τὸ τραῦμα δηλητηρίων φαρμάκων καὶ διαφθείρειεν αὐτόν.	According to another account, Phasael recovered from his self-inflicted blow, and a physician sent by Antigonus, ostensibly to attend him, injected noxious drugs into the wound and so killed him.
5 *War* 1.289 Loeb 2, 136	Ἀντίγονος δὲ πάλιν ἐλπίζων Πάρθους ἐπαμυνεῖν καὶ Σίλωνα τέως ἐθεράπευεν, ὡς μηδὲν ἐνοχλοίη πρὸ τῆς ἐλπίδος.	Antigonus, on his side, hoping for renewed assistance from the Parthians, meanwhile paid court to Silo, as he had to Ventidius, to prevent any trouble from him before his expectations were realized.
6 *War* 1.302 Loeb 2, 142	ἐπέτυχεν δὲ καὶ Ἀντίγονος παρὰ τῆς Σίλωνος δωροδοκίας ὑποδέξασθαι τοῦ στρατοῦ μοῖραν ἐν Λύδδοις θεραπεύων Ἀντώνιον.	Antigonus, on his side, to ingratiate himself with Antony, induced Silo by a bribe to billet a division of his troops in Lydda.

7 *War* 1.460 Loeb 2, 216	οὐ γὰρ τοσοῦτον εὐφρανεῖ τις τὸν παρ' ἡλικίαν θεραπευόμενον, ὅσον ὀδυνήσει τὸν ἀτιμούμενον.	. . . for in paying deference to any beyond the deserts of his age, you gratify him less than you grieve the one whom you slight.
8 *War* 1.462 Loeb 2, 218	τὸ δὲ θεῖον οὕτως τεθεραπεύκαμεν, ὥστ' ἂν ἐπὶ μήκιστον βίου προελθεῖν.	I have served the deity so faithfully that I may hope for the longest term of life.
9 *War* 1.463 Loeb 2, 218	ὁ δὴ τοὺς ἐμοὺς παῖδας θεραπεύων ἐπὶ τῇ ἐμῇ καταλύσει δώσει μοι καὶ περὶ ἐκείνων δίκας·	Whoever, then, pays court to my sons to bring about my downfall shall be punished by me for their sakes as well as my own.
10 *War* 1.464 Loeb 2, 218	εἴ γε μὴν ἕκαστος ἐνθυμηθείη τῶν προσιόντων, ὅτι χρηστὸς μὲν ὢν παρ' ἐμοῦ λήψεται τὴν ἀμοιβήν, στασιάζων δὲ καὶ παρὰ τῷ θεραπευομένῳ τὸ κακόηθες ἀνόνητον ἕξει, πάντας οἶμαι τὰ ἐμὰ φρονήσειν, τουτέστιν τὰ τῶν ἐμῶν υἱῶν·	If everyone who is brought into contact with my sons will but remember that, if he acts honourably he will win his reward from me, whereas if he promotes discord his malicious conduct will bring him no benefit even from the object of his flattery, then I think that all will have my inerests, in other words my sons' interest, at heart; . . .
11 *War* 1.474 Loeb 2, 222	πάντες μὲν οὖν ἐπὶ ταῖς ἐλπίσιν ἐθεράπευον Ἀντίπατρον ἤδη,	All persons, accordingly, now paid court to Antipater, . . .
12 *War* 1.507 Loeb 2, 240	ἐν γὰρ ταῖς βασιλείαις ὥσπερ ἐν μεγάλοις σώμασιν ἀεί τι μέρος φλεγμαίνειν ὑπὸ τοῦ βάρους, ὅπερ ἀποκόπτειν μὲν οὐ χρῆναι, θεραπεύειν δὲ πρᾳότερον.	. . . for in kingdoms, as in corpulent individuals, there was always some member becoming inflamed from the weight which it supported; yet what it needed was not amputation but some milder method of cure.
13 *War* 1.524 Loeb 2, 248	καὶ τὰς θεραπευθείσας πόλεις ἐπὶ τίσιν	and . . . the favouritism shown to particular cities
14 *War* 1.547 Loeb 2, 258	"κἀμέ," γὰρ ἔφη, "Τίρων οὗτος ἀνέπειθεν, ὅταν θεραπεύω τῷ ξυρῷ σε διαχειρίσασθαι, μεγάλας τέ μοι παρ' Ἀλεξάνδρου δωρεὰς ὑπισχνεῖτο."	"Me too," he cried, "this Tiro tried to induce to cut your throat with my razor when in attendance upon you, promising me a large reward from Alexander."

15 *War* 1.580 Loeb 2, 274-6	ἀλλ' ὁ μὲν παρ' ἐλπίδα σῴζεται, μετ' οὐ πολὺ δὲ νοσεῖ Φερώρας, εὑρίσκετο δὲ Ἡρώδης μετριώτερος καὶ γὰρ ἧκει πρὸς αὐτὸν καὶ συμπαθῶς ἐθεράπευεν. οὐ μὴν ὑπερίσχυσεν τοῦ πάθους· μετὰ γὰρ ἡμέρας ὀλίγας ἀποθνήσκει Φερώρας.	Herod, however, unexpectedly recovered, and not long after Pheroras himself fell sick; Herod thereupon displayed greater humanity, for he went to him and affectionately tended him. But he could not cope with the malady, and a few days later Pheroras expired.
16 *War* 1.658 Loeb 2, 312	θορύβου δὲ τῶν θεραπευόντων γενομένου πρὸς μὲν τὴν φωνὴν ἀνήνεγκεν, εἰς δὲ τὸ λοιπὸν ἀπογνοὺς τὴν σωτηρίαν	His attendants raising an uproar, their cries brought him to himself, but, now despairing of recovery . . . [This description of Herod's suffering and death (656-665) has parallels with the account of the death of his grandson Herod Agrippa I, "eaten of worms," in Acts 12.23. It is interesting that θεραπεύω refers to those nursing him (658), and θεραπεία (657) to different modes of treatment.]
17 *War* 2.4 Loeb 2, 324	ἐπένευσε δ' ἑτοίμως ἅπασι θεραπεύων τὸ πλῆθος.	To all these requests, in his desire to ingratiate himself with the people, he readily assented.
18 *War* 2.178 Loeb 2, 392	τοῦ δὲ μὴ προσδεξαμένου τὴν κατηγορίαν μένων ἐπὶ Ῥώμης τούς τε ἄλλους τῶν γνωρίμων ἐθεράπευεν καὶ μάλιστα τὸν Γερμανικοῦ παῖδα Γάιον, ἰδιώτην ἔτι ὄντα.	The emperor having declined to countenance the charge, Agrippa remained in Rome, paying court to various notabilities and in particular to Gaius, son of Germanicus, who was still a private citizen.
19 *War* 2.297 Loeb 2, 438	Ὁ δὲ δῆμος προδυσωπῆσαι τὴν ὁρμὴν αὐτοῦ βουλόμενος ὑπαντᾷ τοῖς στρατιώταις μετ' εὐφημίας καὶ τὸν Φλῶρον θεραπευτικῶς ἐκδέχεσθαι παρεσκευάσατο.	The citizens, anxious to forestall and make him ashamed of his intention, went to meet the troops with acclamations, and prepared to give Florus an obsequious reception.
20 *War* 2.350 Loeb 2, 458	θεραπεύειν γάρ, οὐκ ἐρεθίζειν χρὴ τὰς ἐξουσίας·	The powers that be should be conciliated by flattery, not irritated;

21 *War* 3.8 Loeb 2, 576	. . . πέμπει τὸν ἄνδρα ληψόμενον τὴν ἡγεμονίαν τῶν ἐπὶ Συρίας στρατευμάτων, πολλὰ πρὸς τὸ ἐπεῖγον οἷα κελεύουσιν αἱ ἀνάγκαι μειλιξάμενός τε καὶ προθεραπεύσας.	Nero sent this general to take command of the armies in Syria, lavishing upon him, at this urgent crisis, such soothing and flattering compliments as are called for by emergencies of this kind.
22 *War* 4.249 Loeb 3, 74	νῦν μὲν γὰρ οὐδὲ βουλομένοις διαλύσασθαι ῥᾴδιον, ὅτε Ῥωμαίους μὲν ὑπερόπτας πεποιηκεν ὑποχείριος ἡ Γαλιλαία, φέρει δ' αἰσχύνην ἡμῖν θανάτου χαλεπωτέραν τὸ θεραπεύειν αὐτοὺς ὄντας ἤδη πλησίον.	But now, even if we desired it, a reconciliation would be no easy matter, when their conquest of Galilee has made the Romans contemptuous, and to court them, now that they are at our doors, would bring upon us a disgrace even worse than death.
23 *War* 4.365 Loeb 3, 106	καὶ ὁ μὲν μηδ' ὅλως αὐτοῖς προσιὼν ὡς ὑπερήφανος, ὁ προσιὼν δὲ μετὰ παρρησίας ὡς καταφρονῶν, ὁ θεραπεύων δ' ὡς ἐπίβουλος ὑπωπτεύετο.	. . . the man who never approached them was suspected of pride; he who approached them with freedom, of treating them with contempt; he who courted them, of conspiracy. [Cf. Thucydides 3.82]
24 *War* 7.424 Loeb 3, 624	ποιήσειν δὲ τὰ δυνατὰ τοῦ βασιλέως ὁμολογήσαντος ἠξίωσεν ἐπιτρέπειν αὐτῷ νεών τε που τῆς Αἰγύπτου κατασκευάσασθαι καὶ τοῖς πατρίοις ἔθεσι θεραπεύειν τὸν θεόν·	The king having promised to do what was in his power, he asked permission to build a temple somewhere in Egypt and to worship God after the manner of his fathers; . . .
25 *Ant.*, 5.189 Loeb 5, 86	κατῴκει μὲν ἐν Ἱεριχοῦντι καὶ αὐτός, συνήθης δὲ γίνεται τῷ Ἐγλῶνι δωρεαῖς αὐτὸν θεραπεύων καὶ ὑπερχόμενος, ὡς διὰ τοῦτο καὶ τοῖς περὶ τὸν βασιλέα προσφιλῆ τυγχάνειν αὐτόν.	(Judes [Ehud]) . . . was also himself residing in Jericho; there he became familiar with Eglon, courting and cajoling him with presents, whereby moreover he endeared himself to those in waiting on the king.
26 *Ant.*, 6.18 Loeb 5, 174	ἐθεράπευον δὲ τὴν κιβωτὸν οἱ τούτου παῖδες, καὶ τῆς ἐπιμελείας ταύτης ἕως ἐτῶν εἴκοσι προέστησαν·	This man's sons tended the ark and had the charge of it for twenty years

27 *Ant.*, 6.21 Loeb 5, 174	ἀλλὰ γίνεσθε δίκαιοι, καὶ τὴν πονηρίαν ἐκβαλόντες τῶν ψυχῶν καὶ θεραπεύοντες αὐτάς,* ὅλαις ταῖς διανοίαις προστρέπεσθε τὸ θεῖον καὶ τιμῶντες διατελεῖτε· *=Loeb n. *d*: "Text a little doubtful: it has been proposed, by a slight change, to read 'and cultivating virtue' (ἀρετήν in place of αὐτάς)."	Nay, be ye righteous and, casting out wickedness from your souls and purging them,* turn with all your hearts to the Deity and persevere in honouring Him. [This emendation seems sensible, given Josephus' consistent use of θεραπεύω in the sense of 'to cultivate' and his rare use of the verb in a medical sense. However, if the verb θεραπεύω is understood in a spiritual, rather than a medical, sense the text makes perfect sense, and a better translation would then read 'and (spiritually) nurturing them'.]
28 *Ant.*, 6.341 Loeb 5, 338	φύσει τῶν ἀνθρώπων ἢ πρὸς τοὺς ἀγαθόν τι παρεσχημένους φιλοτιμουμένων, ἢ παρ' ὧν ἄν τι δύνωνται λαβεῖν ὄφελος τούτους προθεραπευόντων.	whereas men are by nature wont either to emulate those who have bestowed some kindness upon them or to be beforehand in flattering those from whom they may possibly receive some benefit.

29 *Ant.*, 8.45-49 Loeb 5, 594-6	παρέσχε δ' αὐτῷ μαθεῖν ὁ θεὸς καὶ τὴν κατὰ τῶν δαιμόνων τέχνην εἰς ὠφέλειαν καὶ θεραπείαν τοῖς ἀνθρώποις· ἐπῳδάς τε συνταξάμενος αἷς παρηγορεῖται τὰ νοσήματα καὶ τρόπους ἐξορκώσεων κατέλιπεν, οἷς οἱ ἐνδούμενοι τὰ δαιμόνια ὡς μηκέτ' ἐπανελθεῖν ἐκδιώκουσι. καὶ αὕτη μέχρι νῦν παρ' ἡμῖν ἡ θεραπεία πλεῖστον ἰσχύει· ἱστόρησα γάρ τινα Ἐλεάζαρον τῶν ὁμοφύλων Οὐεσπασιανοῦ παρόντος καὶ τῶν υἱῶν αὐτοῦ καὶ χιλιάρχων καὶ ἄλλου στρατιωτικοῦ πλήθους τοὺς ὑπὸ τῶν δαιμονίων λαμβανομένους ἀπολύοντα τούτων. ὁ δὲ τρόπος τῆς θεραπείας τοιοῦτος ἦν· προσφέρων ταῖς ῥισὶ τοῦ δαιμονιζομένου τὸν δακτύλιον ἔχοντα ὑπὸ τῇ σφραγῖδι ῥίζαν ἐξ ὧν ὑπέδειξε Σολομὼν ἔπειτα ἐξεῖλκεν ὀσφρομένῳ διὰ τῶν μυκτήρων τὸ δαιμόνιον, καὶ πεσόντος εὐθὺς τἀνθρώπου μηκέτ' εἰς αὐτὸν ἐπανήξειν* ὥρκου Σολομῶνός τε μεμνημένος καὶ τὰς ἐπῳδὰς ἃς συνέθηκεν ἐκεῖνος ἐπιλέγων. βουλόμενος δὲ πεῖσαι καὶ παραστῆσαι τοῖς παρατυγχάνουσιν ὁ Ἐλεάζαρος ὅτι ταύτην ἔχει τὴν ἰσχύν, ἐτίθει μικρὸν ἔμπροσθεν ἤτοι ποτήριον πλῆρες ὕδατος ἢ ποδόνιπτρον καὶ τῷ δαιμονίῳ προσέταττεν ἐξιόντι τἀνθρώπου ταῦτ' ἀνατρέψαι καὶ παρασχεῖν ἐπιγνῶναι τοῖς ὁρῶσιν ὅτι καταλέλοιπε τὸν ἄνθρωπον. γενομένου δὲ τούτου σαφὴς ἡ Σολομῶνος καθίστατο σύνεσις καὶ σοφία δι' ἥν, ἵνα γνῶσιν ἅπαντες αὐτοῦ τὸ μεγαλεῖον τῆς φύσεως καὶ τὸ θεοφιλὲς καὶ λάθῃ μηδένα τῶν ὑπὸ τὸν ἥλιον ἡ τοῦ βασιλέως περὶ πᾶν εἶδος ἀρετῆς ὑπερβολή, περὶ τούτων εἰπεῖν προήχθημεν. * [MSPE: ἐπανελθεῖν]	And God granted him (Solomon) knowledge of the art used against demons for the benefit and healing of men. He also composed incantations by which illnesses are relieved, and left behind forms of exorcisms with which those possessed by demons drive them out, never to return. And this kind of cure is of very great power among us to this day, for I have seen a certain Eleazar, a countryman of mine, in the presence of Vespasian, his sons, tribunes and a number of other soldiers, free men possessed by demons, and this was the manner of the cure: he put to the nose of the possessed man a ring which had under its seal one of the roots prescribed by Solomon, and then, as the man smelled it, drew out the demon through his nostrils, and, when the man at once fell down, adjured the demon never to come back into him, speaking Solomon's name and reciting the incantations which he had composed. Then, wishing to convince the bystanders and prove to them that he had this power, Eleazar placed a cup or footbasin full of water a little way off and commanded the demon, as it went out of the man, to overturn it and make known to the spectators that he had left the man. And when this was done, the understanding and wisdom of Solomon were clearly revealed, on account of which we have been induced to speak of these things, in order that all men may know the greatness of his nature and how God favoured him, and that no one under the sun may be ignorant of the king's surpassing virtue of every kind.

30 *Ant.*, 9.112 Loeb 6, 60	ὁ δὲ ἀθροίσας τὴν στρατιὰν ἔμελλεν ἐξορμᾶν ἐπὶ Ἰώραμον εἰς Ἰεζάρηλαν πόλιν, ἐν ᾗ, καθὼς προείπομεν, ἐθεραπεύετο τὴν πληγὴν ἣν ἔλαβε πρὸς τῇ Ἀραμάθης πολιορκίᾳ.	Then he collected the army and prepared to set out against Joram to the city of Jezarela, where, as we have said before,* he was being healed of the wound which he received in the siege of Aramathe. * 9.105 (Loeb 6, 56): ἐν δὲ τῇ πολιορκίᾳ τοξευθεὶς ὑπό τινος τῶν Σύρων οὐ καιρίως ἀνεχώρησεν εἰς Ἰεζαρήλην πόλιν ἰαθησόμενος ἐν αὐτῇ τὸ τραῦμα . . . [Josephus is faithful to the language of the Septuagint here. The purpose of Joram's journey was to be healed (ἰατρευθῆναι) but θεραπεύω is the verb chosen to describe Joram's medical (nursing) care (see App. 6:1, **14**).]
31 *Ant.*, 9.121 Loeb 6, 64	ὁ δ' ἐπιδιώξας καὶ καταλαβὼν ἔν τινι προσβάσει τοξεύσας ἔτρωσε, καταλιπὼν δὲ τὸ ἅρμα καὶ ἐπιβὰς ἵππῳ φεύγει τὸν Ἰηοῦν εἰς Μαγεδδὼ κἀκεῖ θεραπευόμενος μετ' ὀλίγον ἐκ τῆς πληγῆς τελευτᾷ.	But he pursued him closely and, overtaking him at a certain rise of ground, shot and wounded him; thereupon Ochozias abandoned his chariot and, mounting a horse, fled from Jehu to Mageddo, where, although he received treatment, he died from the wound shortly after.
32 *Ant.*, 11.62 Loeb 6, 342	ἐπέτρεψε δὲ καὶ τὴν χορηγίαν ἅπασαν καὶ τὴν ἱερὰν στολήν, ᾗ θεραπεύουσι τὸν θεὸν ὅ τε ἀρχιερεὺς καὶ οἱ ἱερεῖς, ἐκ τῶν ἰδίων γίνεσθαι	(He) allowed all the charges, including that of the sacred vestments in which the high priest and the priests worshipped God, to come out of his own treasury
33 *Life*, 404 Loeb 1, 148	μεταπεμψάμενος οὖν ἰατροὺς καὶ θεραπευθεὶς τὴν ἡμέραν ἐκείνην αὐτοῦ κατέμεινα πυρέξας, δόξαν τε τοῖς ἰατροῖς τῆς νυκτὸς εἰς Ταριχαίας μετεκομίσθην.	I sent for physicians and, after receiving their attention, remained there for that day in a feverish condition; at night, under medical advice, I was removed to Tarichaeae.
34 *Life*, 421 Loeb 1, 154	ὁ δ' εὐθὺς ἐκέλευσεν καθαιρεθέντας αὐτοὺς θεραπείας ἐπιμελεστάτης τυχεῖν. καὶ οἱ μὲν δύο τελευτῶσιν θεραπευόμενοι, ὁ δὲ τρίτος ἔζησεν.	He (Titus) gave orders immediately that they should be taken down and receive the most careful treatment. Two of them died in the physician's hands; the third survived.

Appendix 6 : 3

Philo

Text and translation from the Loeb Classical Library edition of Philo, (1941) *Philo*, (trans. F. H. Colson) Loeb 9, London. References are by numeral, title of work and reference within that work, and Loeb volume and page number.

Reference	Text	Translation/Comment
1 *Every good man is free*, 35 Loeb 9, 30	ἀλλ' ὅμως εἰσὶ δοῦλοι, δανείζοντες, ὠνούμενοι, προσόδους ἐκλεγόμενοι, θεραπευόμενοι.	Still all the same they are slaves though they lend, purchase, collect revenues and are much courted.
2 *Every good man is free*, 39 Loeb 9, 32	σημεῖον δέ· θεραπεύουσιν, ἱκετεύουσιν, εὐμένειαν ὡς παρὰ τύχης καὶ ἀγαθοῦ δαίμονος αἰτεῖσθαι γλίχονται	This is shown by the way in which their owners court them, supplicate them, eagerly beg their favours, as though they were praying to fortune or some good genius.
3 *Every good man is free*, 43 Loeb 9, 34	νεανικώτερον δ' ὁ τῶν Ἰουδαίων νομοθέτης προσυπερβάλλων, ἅτε γυμνῆς ὡς λόγος ἀσκητὴς φιλοσοφίας, τὸν ἔρωτι θείῳ κατεσχημένον καὶ τὸ ὂν μόνον θεραπεύοντα οὐκέτ' ἄνθρωπον ἀλλὰ θεὸν ἀπετόλμησεν εἰπεῖν·	The legislator of the Jews in a bolder spirit went to a further extreme and in the practice of his "naked" philosophy, as they call it, ventured to speak of him who was possessed by love of the divine and worshipped the Self-existent only, as having passed from a man into a god, . . .
4 *Every good man is free*, 75 Loeb 9, 54	λέγονταί τινες παρ' αὐτοῖς ὄνομα Ἐσσαῖοι, πλῆθος ὑπερτετρακισχίλιοι, κατ' ἐμὴν δόξαν-οὐκ ἀκριβεῖ τύπῳ διαλέκτου Ἑλληνικῆς-παρώνυμοι ὁσιότητος, ἐπειδὴ κἀν τοῖς μάλιστα θεραπευταὶ θεοῦ γεγόνασιν, οὐ ζῷα καταθύοντες, ἀλλ' ἱεροπρεπεῖς τὰς ἑαυτῶν διανοίας κατασκευάζειν ἀξιοῦντες.	. . . as it is said, certain persons, more than four thousand in number, called Essenes. Their name which is, I think, a variation, though the form of the Greek is inexact, of ὁσιότης (holiness), is given them, because they have shown themselves especially devout in the service of God, not by offering sacrifices of animals, but by resolving to sanctify their minds.

5 *The Contemplative Life*, 2 Loeb 9, 112-4	ἡ δὲ προαίρεσις τῶν φιλοσόφων εὐθὺς ἐμφαίνεται διὰ τῆς προσρήσεως· θεραπευταὶ γὰρ καὶ θεραπευτρίδες ἐτύμως καλοῦνται, ἤτοι παρόσον ἰατρικὴν ἐπαγγέλλονται κρείσσονα τῆς κατὰ πόλεις-ἡ μὲν γὰρ σώματα θεραπεύει μόνον, ἐκείνη δὲ καὶ ψυχὰς νόσοις κεκρατημένας χαλεπαῖς τε καὶ δυσιάτοις, ἃς ἐγκατέσκηψαν ἡδοναὶ καὶ ἐπιθυμίαι καὶ λῦπαι καὶ φόβοι πλεονεξίαι τε καὶ ἀφροσύναι καὶ ἀδικίαι καὶ τὸ τῶν ἄλλων παθῶν καὶ κακιῶν ἀνήνυτον πλῆθος-ἢ παρόσον ἐκ φύσεως καὶ τῶν ἱερῶν νόμων ἐπαιδεύθησαν θεραπεύειν τὸ ὄν, ὃ καὶ ἀγαθοῦ κρεῖττόν ἐστι καὶ ἑνὸς εἰλικρινέστερον καὶ μονάδος ἀρχεγονώτερον· οἷς τίνας συγκρίνειν ἄξιον τῶν ἐπαγγελλομένων εὐσέβειαν;	The vocation of these philosophers is at once made clear from their title of Therapeutae and Therapeutrides, a name derived fron θεραπεύω, either in the sense of "cure" because they profess an art of healing better than that current in the cities which cures only the bodies, while theirs treats also souls oppressed with grievous and well-nigh incurable diseases, inflicted by pleasures and desires and griefs and fears, by acts of covetousness, folly and injustice and the countless host of the other passions and vices: or else in the sense of "worship," because nature and the sacred laws have schooled them to worship the Self-existent who is better than the good, purer than the One and more primordial than the Monad. Who among those who profess piety deserve to be compared with these?
6 *The Contemplative Life*, 10-11 Loeb 9, 118	Ἀλλ' οὗτοι μέν, ἐπειδήπερ οὐ τοὺς ὁμοφύλους μόνον ἀλλὰ καὶ τοὺς πλησιάζοντας ἀναπιμπλᾶσι φλυαρίας, ἀθεράπευτοι διατελείτωσαν ὄψιν, τὴν ἀναγκαιοτάτην τῶν αἰσθήσεων, πεπηρωμένοι· λέγω δὲ οὐ τὴν σώματος, ἀλλὰ τὴν ψυχῆς, ᾗ τὸ ἀληθὲς καὶ τὸ ψεῦδος μόνη γνωρίζεται. τὸ δὲ θεραπευτικὸν γένος βλέπειν ἀεὶ προδιδασκόμενον* τῆς τοῦ ὄντος θέας ἐφιέσθω καὶ τὸν αἰσθητὸν ἥλιον ὑπερβαινέτω καὶ μηδέποτε τὴν τάξιν ταύτην λειπέτω πρὸς τελείαν ἀγουσαν εὐδαιμονίαν. * [mss.: προσδιδασκόμενον]	These indeed, since they infect not only their own compatriots but the peoples in their neighbourhood with their folly, must remain incurable, for they have lost the use of the most vital of the senses, sight. And by this I do not mean the sight of the body but of the soul, the sight which alone gives a knowledge of truth and falsehood. But it is well known that the Therapeutae, a people always taught from the first to use their sight, should desire the vision of the Existent and soar above the sun of our senses and never leave their place in this company which carries them on to perfect happiness.
7 *The Contemplative Life*, 22 Loeb 9, 124	οἱ δὲ πανταχόθεν ἄριστοι καθάπερ εἰς πατρίδα [θεραπευτῶν] ἀποικίαν στέλλονται πρός τι χωρίον ἐπιτηδειότατον, ὅπερ ἐστὶν ὑπὲρ λίμνης Μαρείας κείμενον ἐπὶ γεωλόφου χθαμαλωτέρου, σφόδρα εὐκαίρως, ἀσφαλείας τε ἕνεκα καὶ ἀέρος εὐκρασίας.	But the best of these votaries journey from every side to settle in a certain very suitable place which they regard as their fatherland. This place is situated above the Mareotic Lake on a somewhat low-lying hill very happily placed both because of its security and the pleasantly tempered air.

8 *The Contemplative Life*, 88 Loeb 9, 166	Τούτῳ μάλιστα ἀπεικονισθεὶς ὁ τῶν θεραπευτῶν καὶ θεραπευτρίδων, μέλεσιν ἀντήχοις καὶ ἀντιφώνοις πρὸς βαρὺν ἦχον τῶν ἀνδρῶν ὁ γυναικῶν ὀξὺς ἀνακιρνάμενος, ἐναρμόνιον συμφωνίαν ἀποτελεῖ καὶ μουσικὴν ὄντος· πάγκαλα μὲν τὰ νοήματα, πάγκαλοι δὲ αἱ λέξεις, σεμνοὶ δὲ οἱ χορευταί· τὸ δὲ τέλος καὶ τῶν νοημάτων καὶ τῶν λέξεων καὶ τῶν χορευτῶν εὐσέβεια.	It is on this model above all that the choir of the Therapeutae of either sex, note in response to note and voice to voice, the treble of the women blending with the bass of the men, create an harmonious concent, music in the truest sense. Lovely are the thoughts, lovely the words and worthy the reverence of the choristers, and the end and aim of thoughts, words and choristers alike is piety.
9 *The Contemplative Life*, 90 Loeb 9, 168	Θεραπευτῶν μὲν δὴ πέρι τοσαῦτα θεωρίαν ἀσπασαμένων φύσεως καὶ τῶν ἐν αὐτῇ καὶ ψυχῇ μόνῃ βιωσάντων, οὐρανοῦ μὲν καὶ κόσμου πολιτῶν, τῷ δὲ πατρὶ καὶ ποιητῇ τῶν ὅλων γνησίως συσταθέντων ὑπ' ἀρετῆς, ἥτις <θεοῦ> φιλίαν αὐτοῖς προυξένησεν οἰκειότατον γέρας καλοκἀγαθίας προσθεῖσα, πάσης ἄμεινον εὐτυχίας, ἐπ' αὐτὴν ἀκρότητα φθάνον εὐδαιμονίας.	So much then for the Therapeutae, who have taken to their hearts the contemplation of nature and what it has to teach, and have lived in the soul alone, citizens of Heaven and the world, presented to the Father and Maker of all by their faithful sponsor Virtue, who has procured for them God's friendship and added a gift going hand in hand with it, true excellence of life, a boon better than all good fortune and rising to the very summit of felicity.
10 *The eternity of the world*, 72 Loeb 9, 234	τὸν δὲ κόσμον εἴ τις νομίζει χρήσασθαί ποτε ταῖς τοιαύταις μεταβολαῖς, ἀθεραπεύτῳ μανίᾳ κεκρατημένος μὴ ἀγνοείτω·	Now if anyone thinks that the world has passed through such changes, he had better recognise that he is under the sway of a fatal delusion.
11 *Flaccus*, 9 Loeb 9, 308	εἴτε καὶ κακόνους ὢν τῷ διαδόχῳ διὰ τὸ τὴν τῶν γνησίων πρὸ τῆς τῶν θετῶν τεθεραπευκέναι μερίδα . . .	Or it may have been the ill-will he bore to his successor, since he had been a devoted partisan of the actual rather than the adopted children.
12 *Flaccus*, 108 Loeb 9, 360-1	Γίνεται δ' ὁ τρόπος αὐτῷ τῆς συλλήψεως τοιόσδε. ὑπέλαβεν ἤδη τὸν Γάιον περὶ ὧν ὕποπτος ἦν ἐξευμενίσθαι, τὰ μὲν ἐπιστολιμαίοις γράμμασιν, ἃ κολακείας ἦν ὑπέρμεστα, τὰ δὲ ἐν οἷς δημηγορῶν πολλάκις ἐθεράπευε λόγους θῶπας καὶ μακρὰς ῥήσεις πεπλασμένων ἐγκωμίων συνείρων, τὰ δὲ καὶ ἐκ τοῦ σφόδρα εὐδοκιμεῖν παρὰ τῷ πλείστῳ μέρει τῆς πόλεως.	The manner of his arrest was as follows. He supposed that Gaius had been by now propitiated as to the matters on which he was under suspicion, partly through his written dispatches, which overflowed with flattery, partly through the obsequiousness of his public harangues, in which he span together fawning words and long screeds of insincere encomium, partly again by the high esteem in which he was held by the chief part of the city.

Appendix 7 : 1

The language of healing in the synoptic gospels : *Matthew*

Reference	Agent	Greek word	Illnesses treated	Type, number, method	Patient profile, location, motive	Comments
Matt 4.23 (cf. Luke 6.17-19?)	Jesus	θεραπεύων	πᾶσαν νόσον καὶ πᾶσαν μαλακίαν	General: many; ?	ἐν τῷ λαῷ in the whole of Galilee	διδάσκων . . . κηρύσσων . . . θεραπεύων
Matt 4.24 (cf. Luke 6.17-19?)	Jesus	ἐθεράπευσεν	πάντας τοὺς κακῶς ἔχοντας, ποικίλαις νόσοις καὶ βασάνοις συνεχομένους, δαιμονιζομένους, καὶ σεληνιαζομένους, καὶ παραλυτικούς	General: many; ?	ὅλην τὴν Συρίαν πάντας τοὺς κακῶς ἔχοντας (all these brought for healing) Syria	
Matt 8.2-4 (cf. Mk 1.40-45; Lk 5.12-16. See also Lev.14.4; Lk 7.1)	Jesus	ἐκτείνας τὴν χεῖρα ἥψατο ... καθαρίσθητι ... ἐκαθαρίσθη	λεπρὸς	Specific: 1; touch & command	Leper came down from mountain & asked for healing	Three conditions: (i) silence, (ii) go to priest, (iii) offer gift which Moses commanded.
Matt 8.5-13 (cf. Lk 7.1-10; Jn 4.45-54)	Jesus	(ἰαθήσεται. . . θεραπεύσω) . . . ἰάθη	παραλυτικός	Specific: 1; word "Ὕπαγε, ὡς ἐπίστευσας γενηθήτω σοι	ὁ παῖς (servant /child) of centurion, who had faith & came on his behalf. Capernaum. (δοῦλος later used for slave /bond servant)	ἰάομαι used here to describe non-Jewish in-absentia healing, in answer to a parental request made in faith.
Matt 8.14-15. (cf. Mk 1.29-34; Lk 4.38-41)	Jesus	ἥψατο τῆς χειρὸς αὐτῆς	πυρέσσουσαν (fever)	Specific: 1; touch	Peter's mother-in-law. Peter's house. (compassion)	

Matt 8.16-17. (cf. Mk 1.32; Lk 4.40)	Jesus	ἐξέβαλεν ... λόγῳ ἐθεράπευσεν	δαιμονιζομένους πολλούς πάντας τοὺς κακῶς ἔχοντας	General: many; word ?	Many brought for healing; at Peter's house.	Prophecy fulfilment: Is. 53.4
Matt 8.28-34. (cf.Mk 5.1-20; Lk 8.26-39)	Jesus	Ὑπάγετε	δύο δαιμονιζόμενοι	Specific: 2; word	Two exceedingly fierce Gadarene men "met" Jesus. Note: (i) πρὸ καιροῦ, (ii) Jesus' speech with demons, (iii) their fear & recognition of Jesus.	City people afraid, asked Jesus to depart. He did.
Matt 9.2-8. (cf. Mk 2.1-12; Lk 5.17-26)	Jesus	θάρσει, τέκνον. ἐγερθεὶς ἆρόν ... καὶ ὕπαγε. ... καὶ ἐγερθεὶς ἀπῆλθεν	παραλυτικός	Specific: 1; word	Brought to Jesus; own city.	Dispute with scribes *re* blasphemy
Matt 9.12-13 (cf. Mk 2. 17; Lk 5.31-32)	ὁ δὲ ἀκούσας εἶπεν, Οὐ χρείαν ἔχουσιν οἱ ἰσχύοντες ἰατροῦ ἀλλ' οἱ κακῶς ἔχοντες. πορευθέντες δὲ μάθετε τί ἐστιν, Ἔλεος θέλω καὶ οὐ θυσίαν· οὐ γὰρ ἦλθον καλέσαι δικαίους ἀλλὰ ἁμαρτωλούς.					
Matt 9.18,23-6 (cf Mk 5.21-43; Lk 8.40-56)	Jesus	ἐκράτησε τῆς χειρὸς αὐτῆς	Ruler: "death"; Jesus:"sleep"	Specific: 1; touch	Ruler's daughter; Ruler's house; Jesus came to her at her father's request.	
Matt 9.20-22 (cf Mk 5.21-43; Lk 8. 40-56)	Jesus	Patient: ἥψατο; Jesus: θάρσει, θύγατερ· ἡ πίστις σου σέσωκέν σε.	γυνὴ αἱμορροοῦσα	Specific: 1; touch (& word)	Haemorrhaging woman approached Jesus in the crowd, and "touched" the border of his cloak.	Thought of woman: σωθήσομαι. Matthew's description: ἐσώθη.
Matt 9.27-31.	Jesus	ἥψατο . . . κατὰ τὴν πίστιν ὑμῶν γενηθήτω ὑμῖν	Blindness	Specific: 2; touch	Two blind men came to Jesus in faith	Jesus charged them with secrecy: ἐνεβριμήθη αὐτοῖς ... λεγων Ὁρᾶτε μηδεὶς γινωσκέτω.

Matt 9.32-34. (cf Lk 11.14)	Jesus	καὶ ἐκβληθέντος τοῦ δαιμονίου, ἐλάλησεν ὁ κωφός	κωφὸν δαιμονιζόμενον (dumbness, compounded by demonic possession)	Specific: 1; ?	Dumb demoniac "brought" to Jesus.	Pharisees' comment: "He casts out demons by the prince of demons."
Matt 9.35 (cf Mk 6.6; Lk 13.22)	Jesus	θεραπεύων	πᾶσαν νόσον καὶ πᾶσαν μαλακίαν	General: many; ?	While travelling through all the cities and villages.	διδάσκων, κηρύσσων, θεραπεύων.
Matt 10.1 (cf Mk 3.14 ?; Lk 9.1 ?)	ἔδωκεν αὐτοῖς ἐξουσίαν πνευμάτων ἀκαθάρτων ὥστε ἐκβάλλειν αὐτὰ καὶ θεραπεύειν πᾶσαν νόσον καὶ πᾶσαν μαλακίαν					Jesus gives "authority" to the disciples
Matt 10.8 (cf Mk 6.8 (7-13)?; Lk 9.3 (1-6)? See Mk 3.13-19; Lk 6.12-16)	ἀσθενοῦντας θεραπεύετε, νεκροὺς ἐγείρετε, λεπροὺς καθαρίζετε, δαιμόνια ἐκβάλλετε					Jesus gives instructions and advice to the disciples. (10.5-42)
Matt 11.5 (cf Lk 7.18-35)	Jesus lists his credentials for John: τυφλοὶ ἀναβλέπουσιν καὶ χωλοὶ περιπατοῦσιν, λεπροὶ καθαρίζονται καὶ κωφοὶ ἀκούουσιν, καὶ νεκροὶ ἐγείρονται καὶ πτωχοὶ εὐαγγελίζονται·					i.e.: help for the suffering
Matt 12.10-13 (cf Mk 3.1-6; Lk 6.6-11)	Jesus	(θεραπεῦσαι) . . . ἀπεκατεστάθη ὑγιὴς	χεῖρα . . . ξηράν (withered hand)	Specific: 1; word ("Εκτεινόν σου τὴν χεῖρά . . . καὶ ἀπεκατεστάθη ὑγιὴς)	Man in synagogue on Sabbath	Pharisees tried to trick Jesus on law *re* Sabbath: ὥστε ἔξεστιν τοῖς σάββασιν καλῶς ποιεῖν.

Matt 12.15-16	Jesus	καὶ ἐθεράπευσεν αὐτοὺς πάντας		General: many [ὄχλοι] πολλοί; ?	People followed Jesus when he withdrew from the synagogue	12.16: Jesus charged them with secrecy (ἐπετίμησεν αὐτοῖς)
Matt 12.22-24 (cf. Mk 3.20-30 ?; Lk 11.14-23; 12.10)	Jesus	καὶ ἐθεράπευσεν αὐτόν, ὥστε τὸν κωφὸν λαλεῖν καὶ βλέπειν	δαιμονιζόμενος τυφλὸς καὶ κωφός (possession, causing blindness and dumbness)	Specific: 1; ?	The afflicted man is brought to Jesus.	No mention of healing the demon, but note the following discussion with the Pharisees (12. 24-28 and ff.).
Matt 13.58	δυνάμεις πολλὰς: Wilkinson (1980) 22, includes this description in his table of miracles. In my opinion, the language used is not typical of Matthew's healing language, and therefore this description should be excluded.					
Matt 14.14 (cf. Mk 6.30-44; Lk 9.10-17; Jn 6.1-14)	Jesus	ἐσπλαγχνίσθη . . . ἐθεράπευσεν	τοὺς ἀρρώστους αὐτῶν	General: many; ?	πολὺν ὄχλον followed Jesus who was overcome by compassion	Immediately prior to the feeding of the 5,000.
Matt 14.13-21	The feeding of the 5,000					
Matt 14.35-36 (cf. Mk 6.53-6)	Jesus	διεσώθησαν	πάντας τοὺς κακῶς ἔχοντας . . . καὶ ὅσοι ἥψαντο διεσώθησαν	General: many; patients touched his cloak	Many came to Jesus and asked to touch the hem of his cloak. Faith of patients.	Immediately following Jesus' walking on water and the disciples' declaration: "Truly you are the son of God!"
Matt 15.21-28 (cf. Mk 7.24-30)	Jesus	ἰάθη	ἡ θυγάτηρ . . . κακῶς δαιμονίζεται	Specific: 1; word (in-absentia). ὦ γύναι, μεγάλη σου ἡ πίστις· γενηθήτω σοι ὡς θέλεις	Canaanite woman's badly demon-possessed daughter. Mother asked Jesus on daughter's behalf. Jesus motivated by mother's great faith.	ἰάομαι used here for non-Jewish in-absentia healing, in answer to a parental request made in faith.

Matt 15.29-31	Jesus	ἐθεράπευσεν	χωλούς, τυφλούς, κυλλούς, κωφούς, καὶ ἑτέρους πολλούς	General: many; ?	Great crowds (ὄχλοι πολλοὶ) brought them to Jesus. The result: ὥστε τὸν ὄχλον θαυμάσαι βλέποντας κωφοὺς λαλοῦντας, κυλλοὺς ὑγιεῖς, καὶ χωλοὺς περιπατοῦντας καὶ τυφλοὺς βλέποντας·	Impressive *re* numbers: reaction of crowd to glorify the god of Israel.
Matt 15.32-39	The feeding of the 4,000; motive: compassion (σπλαγχνίζομαι)					(cf. Mk 8.1-10)
Matt 16.13-20 (cf. Mk 8.27-30; Lk 9.18-21)	**Peter's declaration**					
Matt 17.14-20 (cf. Mk 9.14-29; Lk 9.37-43a)	Jesus	(καὶ οὐκ ἠδυνήθησαν αὐτὸν θεραπεῦσαι) (i.e. the disciples) . . . ἐπετίμησεν . . . ἐθεραπεύθη	σεληνιάζεται καὶ κακῶς πάσχει	Specific: 1; word (rebuke) ἐπετίμησεν ... καὶ ἐξῆλθεν ἀπ' αὐτοῦ το δαιμόνιον, ... ἐθεραπεύθη	Man's epileptic son. Father had gone to disciples, without result. Father came up from crowd, and knelt before Jesus. Note ms variation (insertion of v. 21): "But this kind never comes out except by prayer and fasting."	Note: J's chagrin, ms variation, θεραπεύω in the passive, linking of το δαιμόνιον with epilepsy, and rare use of πάσχω.
Matt 19.2	Jesus	ἐθεράπευσεν	?	General: great crowd; ?	A great crowd (ὄχλοι πολλοί) followed Jesus.	Very vague.
Matt 20. 29-34 (cf. Mk. 10.46-52; Lk. 18. 35-43)	Jesus	σπλαγχνισθεὶς . . . ἥψατο τῶν ὀμμάτων αὐτῶν	δύο τυφλοὶ (blindness)	Specific: 2; touch (ἥψατο), triggered by compassion (σπλαγχνισθεὶς).	Two blind men heard that Jesus was approaching, and came to him; Jesus motivated by compassion.	Straight away they could see, and followed him.
Matt 21.14	Jesus	ἐθεράπευσεν	τυφλοὶ καὶ χωλοὶ (the blind and lame)	General: ?; ?	The blind (plural) and lame (plural) in the temple came to Jesus.	Vague.

Appendix 7 : 2

The language of healing in the synoptic gospels : *Mark*

Reference	Agent	Greek word	Illnesses treated	Type, number, method	Patient profile, location, motive	Comments
Mark 1.23-28 (cf. Lk 4.31-37)	Jesus	ἐπετίμησεν	ἐν πνεύματι ἀκαθάρτῳ	Specific: 1; command: Φιμώθητι καὶ ἔξελθε ἐξ αὐτοῦ (1.25)	Demonic spirirt of man in synagogue recognised Jesus as the holy one of god, and cried out to him in fear: Τί ἡμῖν καὶ σοί, Ἰησοῦ Ναζαρηνέ; ἦλθες ἀπολέσαι ἡμᾶς; οἶδά σε τίς εἶ, ὁ ἅγιος τοῦ θεοῦ. (1.24)	Note recognition; and result: Jesus' reputation spread, wonder of people (1.26).
Mark 1.30-31 (cf. Mt 8.14-17; Lk 4.38-41)	Jesus	κρατήσας τῆς χειρός	πυρέσσουσα	Specific: 1; touch	Simon's mother-in-law; at his house.	καὶ ἀφῆκεν αὐτὴν ὁ πυρετός, καὶ διηκόνει αὐτοῖς
Mark 1.32-34 (cf. Mt 8.14-17; Lk 4.38-41)	Jesus	ἐθεράπευσεν ἐξέβαλεν	πολλοὺς κακῶς ἔχοντας ποικίλαις νόσοις (vague) δαιμόνια πολλὰ (demonic)	General: many; ?		Note: recognition of Jesus by demons, and his demand for secrecy.
Mark 1.39 (cf. Lk 4.42-44)	Jesus	ἐκβάλλων (τὰ δαιμόνια)	δαιμόνια (demons)	General: ?; ?	As Jesus encountered them (?); Galilee; part of his preaching mission.	Linked with κηρύσσων

Mark 1.40-45 (cf. Mt 8.1-4; Lk 5. 12-16)	Jesus	καθαρίσαι . . . καθαρίσθητι . . ἐκαθαρίσθη	λεπρὸς (leprosy)	Specific: 1; touch (ἐκτείνας τὴν χεῖρα αὐτοῦ ἥψατο) & command (καθαρίσθητι)	A leper came to Jesus and requested cleansing; Galilee; σπλαγχνισθεὶς. Note the combination of καθαίρω, σπλαγχνίζομαι, ἅπτομαι and ἐμβριμάομαι. Cf. Matt, who has command to secrecy, but not ἐμβριμάομαι here.	Request, command, description. Note secrecy command not kept.
Mark 2.1-12 (cf. Mt 9.1-8; Lk 5.17-26)	Jesus	Τέκνον, ἀφίενταί σου αἱ ἁμαρτίαι . . . ἔγειρε ἆρον . . . ὕπαγε	παραλυτικὸν	Specific: 1; word (command).	A paralytic, who was let down through the roof by his four friends. Jesus recognised their faith: καὶ ἰδὼν ὁ Ἰησοῦς τὴν πίστιν αὐτῶν λέγει τῷ παραλυτικῷ, Τέκνον, ἀφίενταί σου αἱ ἁμαρτίαι . . . ἔγειρε ἆρον. . . ὕπαγε. . . .	Note Jesus' conversation with the scribes *re* "authority" to forgive sins and heal.
Mark 2. 17 (cf. Mt 9.12-13; Lk 5.31-32)	καὶ ἀκούσας ὁ Ἰησοῦς λέγει αὐτοῖς (ὅτι) Οὐ χρείαν ἔχουσιν οἱ ἰσχύοντες ἰατροῦ ἀλλ' οἱ κακῶς ἔχοντες· οὐκ ἦλθον καλέσαι δικαίους ἀλλὰ ἁμαρτωλούς.					
Mark 3.1-6 (cf. Mt 12.9-14; Lk 6.6-11)	Jesus	(θεραπεύσει) Ἔκτεινον τὴν χεῖρα. καὶ ἐξέτεινεν, καὶ ἀπεκατεστάθη ἡ χεὶρ αὐτοῦ.	ἄνθρωπος ἐξηραμμένην ἔχων τὴν χεῖρα (a man with a withered hand)	Specific: 1; word (command)	Jesus approached a man with a withered hand, in the synagogue, on the sabbath, to show a different interpretation of the law regarding the sabbath.	Jesus' words: "Is it lawful on the sabbath to do good or to do harm, to save life or to kill? (ἀγαθὸν ποιῆσαι ἢ κακοποιῆσαι, ψυχὴν σῶσαι ἢ ἀποκτεῖναι; (3.4))"

Mark 3.10-12	Jesus	ἐθεράπευσεν	?	General: many (πολλούς); ? So that all who had diseases pressed upon him to touch him (ὥστε ἐπιπίπτειν αὐτῷ ἵνα αὐτοῦ ἅψωνται ὅσοι εἶχον μάστιγας) (3.10).	Jesus withdrew with his disciples to the sea, and a great multitude ... followed; ... from Galilee ... Judaea ... Jerusalem ... Idumea ... beyond the Jordan ... Tyre and Sidon.... And he told his disciples to have a boat ready for him because of the crowd, lest they should crush him; for he had healed many, so that all who had diseases pressed upon him to touch him. And whenever the unclean spirits beheld him, they fell down before him and cried out, "You are the Son of God." And he strictly ordered them not to make him known. (3.7-12)	Note 3.11 where the unclean spirits (τὰ πνεύματα τὰ ἀκάθαρτα) "recognise" Jesus, and 3.12 where Jesus ordered them (πολλὰ ἐπετίμα) not to make him known.
Mark 3.14-15	καὶ ἐποίησεν δώδεκα . . . ἵνα ὦσιν μετ' αὐτοῦ καὶ ἵνα ἀποστέλλῃ αὐτοὺς κηρύσσειν καὶ ἔχειν ἐξουσίαν ἐκβάλλειν τὰ δαιμόνια·					cf. Mark 1.38-39. The "12" for companionship, and commissioned to preach, and given authority to expel demons.

Mark 5.1-20 (cf. Mt 8. 28-34; Lk 8.26-39)	Jesus	ἔξελθε (5.8) . . . καὶ ἐπέτρεψεν αὐτοῖς (5.13)	ἄνθρωπος ἐν πνεύματι ἀκαθάρτῳ	Specific: 1; conversation ... command.	Gerasene demoniac approached Jesus and worshipped him.	Note demons' recognition of Jesus (5.7 cf. 1.24); and 5.19, where Jesus commands the healed man to spread the news.
Mark 5. 21-24, 34-43 (cf. Mt 9.18-26; Lk 8.40-56)	Jesus	καὶ κρατήσας τῆς χειρὸς . . . ἔγειρε	At father's request: on the point of death (ἐσχάτως ἔχει); before arrival at house: report of death (ἀπέθανεν), denied by Jesus (τὸ παιδίον οὐκ ἀπέθανεν ἀλλὰ καθεύδει).	Specific: 1; touch and command.	Daughter of Jairus, one of the rulers of the synagogue. At Jairus' home, after responding to her father's request.	Immediate (εὐθὺς) recovery, followed by Jesus' command for secrecy (διαστέλλομαι).
Mark 5. 25-34 (cf. Mt 9. 18-26; Lk 8. 40-56)	Jesus	ἥψατο τοῦ ἱματίου αὐτοῦ (27) . . .. ἴαται (29)	γυνὴ οὖσα ἐν ῥύσει αἵματος δώδεκα ἔτη	Specific: 1; her touch (and faith?)	Haemorrhaging woman approached Jesus in crowd, and touched his garment. ἔλεγεν γὰρ ὅτι Ἐὰν ἅψωμαι κἂν τῶν ἱματίων αὐτοῦ σωθήσομαι (5.28).. θυγάτηρ, ἡ πίστις σου σέσωκέν σε· ὕπαγε εἰς εἰρήνην, καὶ ἴσθι ὑγιὴς ἀπὸ τῆς μάστιγός σου (5.34)	Note the combination of ἅπτομαι, ἰάομαι (the only use of this verb in *Mark*), πίστις, σῴζω, εἰρήνη, ὑγιής and μάστιξ.

Mark 6. 1-6 (cf. Mt 13.53-58; Lk 4.16-30)	Jesus	ἐθεράπευσεν	ὀλίγοις ἀρρώστοις ἐπιθεὶς τὰς χεῖρας ἐθεράπευσεν (he laid his hands upon a few sick people and healed them)	General: few; touch	People at Nazareth. Because of their unbelief Jesus could do no mighty work there, except that he laid his hands upon a few sick people and healed them (6.5). (καὶ οὐκ ἐδύνατο ἐκεῖ ποιῆσαι οὐδεμίαν δύναμιν, εἰ μὴ ὀλίγοις ἀρρώστοις ἐπιθεὶς τὰς χεῖρας ἐθεράπευσεν.)	Jesus marvelled because of their unbelief (καὶ ἐθαύμαζεν διὰ τὴν ἀπιστίαν αὐτῶν (6.5)).
Mark 6. 7-13 (cf. Mt 10.1, 5-15; Lk 9. 1-6)	καὶ ἐδίδου αὐτοῖς ἐξουσίαν τῶν πνευμάτων τῶν ἀκαθάρτων (6.7)					
Mark 6.13 (cf. Lk 9.6)	The "12"	καὶ δαιμόνια πολλὰ ἐξέβαλλον, καὶ ἤλειφον ἐλαίῳ πολλοὺς ἀρρώστους καὶ ἐθεράπευον. (6.13)	The demonic and weak. 6.13: "And they began casting out many demons, and used to anoint with oil many who were weak and began healing them."	General: many; anointed with olive oil	Disciples went out and preached, and began healing, in response to Jesus' commission to do so. Cf. Matt, who does not report the disciples' success in healing, and Luke's condensation and generalisation of this passage (9.6). Cf. *GT* #14, for similar instructions to heal, and similar conditions. (When you go into any land and walk about in the districts, if they receive you, eat what they will set before you, and heal the sick among them.)	Note the imperfect ἐξέβαλλον, ἤλειφον, ἐθεράπευον to describe the disciples' healing activity, and their use of current medical practice in using oil. Cf. also Acts 28.8, where Publius fulfils the requirements concerning hospitality.

Mark 6.53-56 (cf. Mt 14.34-36)	Jesus	ἅψωνται, ἥψαντο . . . ἐσῴζοντο	τοὺς κακῶς ἔχοντας (6.55); τοὺς ἀσθενοῦντας (6.56): i.e. the ailing and the infirm.	General: many; patients' touching the fringe of Jesus' garment.	The people of Gennesaret brought the patients to Jesus, with the result that as many as touched him began (being made/to feel) whole. (καὶ ὅσοι ἂν ἥψαντο αὐτοῦ ἐσῴζοντο)	Note combination of ἅπτομαι and σῴζω, and especially the imperfect tense of σῴζω
Mark 7.24-30 (cf. Mt 15.21-28)	Jesus	Διὰ τοῦτον τὸν λόγον ὕπαγε, ἐξελήλυθεν ἐκ τῆς θυγατρός σου τὸ δαιμόνιον	πνεῦμα ἀκάθαρτον (unclean spirit of Syrophoenician woman's daughter)	Specific: 1; word.	Mother approached Jesus and asked him to cast out the demon from her daughter.	Healing in-absentia, in response to a non-Jewish parental request, made in faith.
Mark 7.31-37	Jesus	(Εφφαθα) ... Διανοίχθητι	κωφὸν καὶ μογιλάλον (deaf man with a speech impediment)	Specific: 1; touch and word. (After taking the man aside, Jesus put fingers in his ears, and, having spat, touched his tongue; then issued a command)	Near Decapolis in Galilee, the man was brought to Jesus with the request that Jesus lay his hands on him.	Note: instantaneous nature of the healing; the unusual method, and the detailed description of it, and the demand for secrecy (διαστέλλομαι) which wasn't fulfilled
Mark 8. 22-26	Jesus	πτύσας, ... ἐπιθεὶς τὰς χεῖρας αὐτῷ, ... ἐπέθηκεν ... ἀπεκατέστη	τυφλὸν (blindness)	Specific: 1; spit and touch	The blind man at Bethsaida was brought to Jesus so that Jesus might touch him (ἅψηται).	This is unusual, because it is a protracted healing.

Mark 8.29 (cf. Mt 16. 15-18; Lk 9.20)	**Peter's declaration**					
Mark 9.14-29 (cf. Mt 17.14-20; Lk 9.37-43a)	Jesus	ἐπιτιμάω ἐπιτάσσω ἐξέρχομαι κράτεω ἐγείρω	πνεῦμα ἄλαλον (9.17), πνεῦμα ἀκάθαρτον (9.25) (dumb spirit . . . unclean spirit) ἐπετίμησεν τῷ πνεύματι τῷ ἀκαθάρτῳ. . . ἐγὼ ἐπιτάσσω σοι ἔξελθε ... καὶ μηκέτι εἰσελθῃς (9.25) ἐξῆλθεν (9.26) κρατήσας τῆς χειρὸς αὐτοῦ ἤγειρεν αὐτόν, καὶ ἀνέστη (9.27).	Specific: 1; rebuke and command	The father brought his son to Jesus for healing, and, in his absence, the disciples had unsuccessfully tried to heal him. The Markan account gives an excellent description of a grandmal epileptic seizure. According to the father the boy had suffered similar attacks since childhood. See Wilkinson (1980) 61-9 for a modern medical discussion of this healing.	Good case history of epilepsy (cf. Hippokrates, *The Sacred Disease*, esp. 10). Note the synoptic differences. Cf. Mk 1.27, Lk 4.36, for other instances of the verb ἐπιτάσσω.
Mark 9. 38-41 (cf. Lk 9. 49-50)	Ἔφη αὐτῷ ὁ Ἰωάννης, Διδάσκαλε, εἴδομέν τινα ἐν τῷ ὀνόματί σου ἐκβάλλοντα δαιμόνια, καὶ ἐκωλύομεν αὐτόν, ὅτι οὐκ ἠκολούθει ἡμῖν. ὁ δὲ Ἰησοῦς εἶπεν, Μὴ κωλύετε αὐτόν, οὐδεὶς γάρ ἐστιν ὃς ποιήσει δύναμιν ἐπὶ τῷ ὀνόματί μου καὶ δυνήσεται ταχὺ κακολογῆσαί με· ὃς γὰρ οὐκ ἔστιν καθ' ἡμῶν, ὑπὲρ ἡμῶν ἐστιν. John said to him, "Teacher, we saw a man casting out demons in your name, and we tried preventing him, because he was not following us." But Jesus said, "Do not prevent him; for no one who does a mighty work in my name will be able soon after to speak evil of me. For he that is not against us is for us...."					This exorcist was obviously successful. Cf. Acts 19.13-20.
Mark 10.46-52 (cf. Mt 20.29-34; Lk 18. 35-43)	Jesus	Ὕπαγε, ἡ πίστις σου σέσωκέν σε. καὶ εὐθὺς ἀνέβλεψεν, καὶ ἠκολούθει αὐτῷ ἐν τῇ ὁδῷ .(10.52)	τυφλός	Specific: 1; word?	The blind beggar, Bartimaeus, son of Timaeus, called out to Jesus, as he was leaving Jericho.	Note the combination of πίστις, and σῴζω. Note also ἐπετίμων ... πολλοὶ (10.48)

Appendix 7 : 3

The language of healing in the synoptic gospels : *Luke*

Reference	Agent	Greek word	Illnesses treated	Type, number, method	Patient profile, location, motive	Comments
Luke 4. 23	Ἰατρέ, θεράπευσον σεαυτόν Physician, heal/treat yourself. (4.23-4: And he said to them, "Doubtless you will quote to me this proverb, 'Physician, heal/treat yourself; what we have heard you did at Capernaum, do also here in your own country.'" And he said,"Truly, I say to you, no prophet is acceptable in his own country....")					See App. 7:8 : θεραπεύω, and App. 8:3 : ἰατρός, for Lk 4.23. This saying of Jesus is most significant.
Luke 4.31-38 (cf. Mk 1.21-28)	Jesus	Φιμώθητι καὶ ἔξελθε ἀπ' αὐτοῦ	ἄνθρωπος ἔχων πνεῦμα δαιμονίου ἀκαθάρτου (a man with the spirit of an unclean demon) 4.36: Τίς ὁ λόγος οὗτος, ὅτι ἐν ἐξουσίᾳ καὶ δυνάμει ἐπιτάσσει τοῖς ἀκαθάρτοις πνεύμασιν, καὶ ἐξέρχονται:	Specific: 1; word (rebuke: ἐπετίμησεν αὐτῷ)	A man in the synagogue, on the sabbath, at Capernaum in Galilee, with the spirit of an unclean demon, "recognised" Jesus, and called out to him, proclaiming his identity.	Cf. Mk 1.24.
Luke 4. 38-39 (cf. Mt 8.14-15; Mk 1.29-31)	Jesus	(rebuke: ἐπετίμησεν τῷ πυρετῷ)	ἦν συνεχομένη πυρετῷ μεγάλῳ (she was in the grip of a high fever)	Specific: 1; word (rebuke: ἐπετίμησεν τῷ πυρετῷ)	Simon's mother-in-law, on the sabbath, in Simon's house in Galilee. Jesus was asked to (help) her.	

Luke 4.40 (cf. Mt 8.16; Mk 1.32-34)	Jesus	ὁ δὲ ἑνὶ ἑκάστῳ αὐτῶν τὰς χεῖρας ἐπιτιθεὶς ἐθεράπευεν αὐτούς	ἅπαντες ὅσοι εἶχον ἀσθενοῦντας νόσοις ποικίλαις	General: as many as were weak with various diseases; touch	At sunset, people brought those who were weak with various ailments to Jesus.	Luke is more specific with his account of healing method, than Matthew and Mark. Note the use of the imperfect tense of θεραπεύω.
Luke 4.41 (cf. Mt 8.16; Mk 1.32-34)	Jesus	ἐξήρχετο δὲ καὶ δαιμόνια ἀπὸ πολλῶν, κρ[αυγ]άζοντα καὶ λέγοντα ὅτι Σὺ εἶ ὁ υἱὸς τοῦ θεοῦ	δαιμόνια ἀπὸ πολλῶν (demons from many). "And demons also began coming out of many, crying out and saying 'You are the Son of God!'"	General: many; ? Jesus does "rebuke" the demons, after they "come out".	Demonic patients, same time and location as Lk 4.40 above. (Jesus rebukes and converses with the spirits: καὶ ἐπιτιμῶν οὐκ εἴα αὐτὰ λαλεῖν, ὅτι ᾔδεισαν τὸν Χριστὸν εἶναι.)	Luke is careful to differentiate these exorcisms from 4.40. Note his use of the imperfect tense, and his request for secrecy.
Luke 5.12-14 (cf. Mt 8.1-4; Mk 1.40-45)	Jesus	θέλω, καθαρίσθητι	ἀνὴρ πλήρης λέπρας (a man full of leprosy). Compare Matthew and Mark. It is Luke who records the extent of the man's leprosy.	Specific: 1; touch (ἐκτείνας τὴν χεῖρα ἥψατο αὐτοῦ)	A man full of leprosy, in one of the cities, approached Jesus and asked for cleansing.	Note the leper's instructions: to tell no-one (παρήγγειλεν αὐτῷ μηδενὶ εἰπεῖν); to fulfil the law. But people heard about it, and gathered for advice and healing. See 5.15-16.

Luke 5.15-16	Jesus	ἀκούειν καὶ θεραπεύεσθαι ἀπο τῶν ἀσθενειῶν αὐτῶν	ἀσθενειῶν : weaknesses?: mental, emotional, spiritual, physical? The inference is that it is Jesus' "message" that heals, and that this is a process. Hence the use of the present infinitives. Cf. Lk 6.17-19	General: great crowds (ὄχλοι πολλοὶ); ?: is the therapy in this case "listening" and "hearing"?	These people gathered because of the leper's cleansing (5.12-14).	It is typical of Luke that Jesus' response to this situation (crowding) is to withdraw to the wilderness to pray (5.16).
Luke 5.17-26 (cf. Mt 9.1-8; Mk 2. 1-12)	Jesus	καὶ δύναμις κυρίου ἦν εἰς τὸ ἰᾶσθαι αὐτόν (17) Ἄνθρωπε, ἀφέωνταί σοι αἱ ἁμαρτίαι σου (20) ἔγειρε ((24)	παραλελυμένος (paralysis)	Specific: 1; word and command	Men brought the paralysed man on a bed, which they let down through the tiles of the roof to be near Jesus. Jesus was motivated by their faith.	The language of the healing itself matter-of-fact. Incident more important as a basis for discussion concerning the forgiveness of sins.
Luke 5.31-32 (cf. Mt 9.9-13; Mk 2.13-17)	Οὐ χρείαν ἔχουσιν οἱ ὑγιαίνοντες ἰατροῦ ἀλλὰ οἱ κακῶς ἔχοντες· οὐκ ἐλήλυθα καλέσαι δικαίους ἀλλὰ ἁμαρτωλοὺς εἰς μετάνοιαν. (Those who are whole/healthy have no need of a physician, but those who are suffering. I have not come to call the righteous, but sinners [those who have missed the mark] to repentance).					

Luke 6.6-11 (cf. Mt 12.9-14; Mk 3. 1-6)	Jesus	(θεραπεύει) Ἔκτεινον τὴν χεῖρά σου ἀπεκατεστάθη ἡ χεὶρ αὐτοῦ	ἡ χεὶρ αὐτοῦ ἡ δεξιὰ ἦν ξηρά (a withered right hand)	Specific: 1; word.	A man with a withered right hand was in the synagogue on the sabbath. Jesus approached him because he wished to show the scribes and Pharisees the true meaning of the law concerning the sabbath.	It is again Luke who gives extra information: it was the right hand of the man that was withered. Note that θεραπεύει is used here when the scribes and Pharisees are wondering what Jesus will do. Cf. Mk 3.2; Mt 12.10
Luke 6.17-19 (cf. Mt 4.23-25; and, for the language, cf. also Lk 4.40; 5.15-16 and Acts 5.16)	Jesus	οἳ ἦλθον ἀκοῦσαι αὐτοῦ καὶ ἰαθῆναι ἐθεραπεύοντο ἐζήτουν ἅπτεσθαι ἰᾶτο πάντας	οἳ ἦλθον **ἀκοῦσαι** αὐτοῦ καὶ **ἰαθῆναι** ἀπὸ τῶν νόσων αὐτῶν· καὶ οἱ ἐνοχλούμενοι ἀπὸ πνευμάτων ἀκαθάρτων **ἐθεραπεύοντο**. καὶ πᾶς ὁ ὄχλος ἐζήτουν **ἅπτεσθαι** αὐτοῦ, ὅτι δύναμις παρ' αὐτοῦ ἐξήρχετο καὶ **ἰᾶτο** πάντας.	General: great crowd (ὄχλος πολὺς) of his disciples, and a great multitude of the people (πλῆθος πολὺ τοῦ λαοῦ): word and touch	A great crowd of disciples, and a great multitude of the people from the surrounding area: Judaea, Jerusalem, Tyre and Sidon, came to hear and be healed. (Cf. Lk 5.15-16) The therapy appears to be the "message" and the "touch" of Jesus.	θεραπεύω is used here in the imperfect passive to describe the healing of those troubled by unclean spirits. It is a healing process, as above at 4.40. Cf. also 5.15. In crowd situations, could it mean "one by one"?

Luke 7.1-10 (cf. Mt. 8.5-13; Jn. 4.43-54)	Jesus	διασώσῃ ἰαθήτω ὑγιαίνοντα	κακῶς ἔχων ἤμελλεν τελευτᾶν (he was ill, and about to die)	Specific: 1; ?word? (in absentia)	The δοῦλος (slave) of the centurion at Capernaum. The centurion sent Jewish elders to Jesus to request healing. Jesus marvelled at his faith. ἀλλὰ εἰπὲ λόγῳ, καὶ ἰαθήτω ὁ παῖς μου. (But say the word, and let my servant be healed.) Some mss cite ἰαθήσεται.	Note the differences in Matthew's language when describing this incident.
Luke 7.11-18	Jesus	ἐσπλαγχνίσθη ἐπ' αὐτῇ ἥψατο τῆς σορου ἐγέρθητι	τεθνηκὼς	Specific: 1; word	A man who had died, the only son of his mother, who was a widow, was being carried out of the town of Nain on a bier. Jesus, overcome with compassion (ἐσπλαγχνίσθη), "raised" the dead man.	Note the context: after the healing of the centurion's servant, and immediately prior to John the Baptist's question *re* identity.

Luke 7.21	Jesus	ἐθεράπευσεν πολλοὺς ἀπὸ νόσων καὶ μαστίγων καὶ πνευμάτων πονηρῶν, καὶ τυφλοῖς πολλοῖς ἐχαρίσατο βλέπειν	ἐν ἐκείνῃ τῇ ὥρᾳ ἐθεράπευσεν πολλοὺς ἀπὸ νόσων καὶ μαστίγων καὶ πνευμάτων πονηρῶν, καὶ τυφλοῖς πολλοῖς ἐχαρίσατο βλέπειν (in that hour he healed many of diseases and irritations and evil spirits, and gave sight to many who were blind)	General: many; ?	A general healing episode between the question from John the Baptist, and Jesus' answer to him. So far Luke has recounted stories concerning the healing of those possessed by unclean and evil spirits, fever, leprosy, paralysis, atrophy, death, blindness and unnamed diseases.	Note the context and θεραπεύω in another "general" episode.
Luke 7.22-23 (cf. Mt 11.4-6)	καὶ ἀποκριθεὶς εἶπεν αὐτοῖς, Πορευθέντες ἀπαγγείλατε Ἰωάννῃ ἃ εἴδετε καὶ ἠκούσατε· τυφλοὶ ἀναβλέπουσιν, χωλοὶ περιπατοῦσιν, λεπροὶ καθαρίζονται καὶ κωφοὶ ἀκούουσιν, νεκροὶ ἐγείρονται, πτωχοὶ εὐαγγελίζονται· καὶ μακάριός ἐστιν ὃς ἐὰν μὴ σκανδαλισθῇ ἐν ἐμοί. And in reply he said to them, "Tell John what you have seen and heard: the blind see again, the lame walk about, lepers are cleansed and the deaf hear, the dead are raised up, the poor hear good news; and blessed is he who takes no offence at me."					

Luke 8.2-3	Jesus	ἦσαν τεθεραπευμέναι	καὶ γυναῖκές τινες αἳ ἦσαν τεθεραπευμέναι ἀπὸ πνευμάτων πονηρῶν και ἀσθενειῶν. Μαρία ἡ καλουμένη Μαγδαληνή, ἀφ' ἧς δαιμόνια ἑπτὰ ἐξεληλύθει, καὶ Ἰωάννα γυνη Χουζᾶ ἐπιτρόπου Ἡρῴδου καὶ Σουσάννα καὶ ἕτεραι πολλαί, αἵτινες διηκόνουν αὐτοῖς ἐκ τῶν ὑπαρχόντων αὐταῖς.	General and specific. general: some women; specific: 3: Mary, Joanna and Susanna; ?	On a preaching tour with the 12 "and also some women who had been healed of evil spirits and illnesses: Mary, called Magdalene, from whom seven demons had gone out, and Joanna, the wife of Chuza, Herod's steward, and Susanna, and many others (women), who provided for them out of their means."	Note θεραπεύω in the pluperfect tense; the important social and economic information *re* the women, and that the women were part of the travelling group.
Luke 8.26-39 (cf. Mt 8. 28-34; Mk 5.1-20	Jesus	παρήγγειλεν ἐξελθεῖν (29) description: 8.36: ἐσώθη	τῷ πνεύματι τῷ ἀκαθάρτῳ (unclean spirit). Afterwards the man is described as "clothed and in his right mind" (ἱματισμένον καὶ σωφρονοῦντα).	Specific: 1; word	At the country of the Gerasenes, (opposite Galilee), a demonic man met Jesus, (recognition, fear, conversation), who cast the demons into a herd of swine, which perished. The locals were afraid, and asked Jesus to leave.	Jesus instructs this man to declare (διηγέομαι) what God had done for him.
Luke 8.40-42. 49-56 (cf. Mt. 9.18-26; Mk. 5.21-43)	Jesus	Μὴ φοβοῦ, μόνον πίστευσον, καὶ σωθήσεται (50) κρατήσας τῆς χειρὸς . . . ἔγειρε (54)	ἀπέθνῃσκεν (42) τέθνηκεν (49) οὐ γὰρ ἀπέθανεν ἀλλὰ καθεύδει (52) Jairus: dying; others: death; Jesus: not death, but sleep.	Specific: 1; touch and word	Parental request by Jairus, a ruler of the synagogue, for his only daughter, who was near death/dead.	Secrecy request by Jesus.

Luke 8.43-48 (cf. Mt 9.18-26; Mk 5.21-43)	Jesus	ἥψατο τοῦ κρασπέδου τοῦ ἱματίου . . . ὡς ἰάθη παραχρῆμα	γυνὴ οὖσα ἐν ῥύσει αἵματος ἀπὸ ἐτῶν δώδεκα . . . οὐκ ἴσχυσεν ἀπ' οὐδενὸς θεραπευθῆναι	Specific: 1; touch initiated by patient. She touched the fringe of his garment.	As Jesus walked in a crowd, a woman who had had a flow of blood for twelve years (and had spent all her living upon physicians (ἰατροῖς)), and could not be healed by anyone, touched the fringe of his garment, and the flow of blood ceased. When Jesus challenged those around him, she "confessed".	Jesus felt power (δύναμιν) go forth. He said: "Your faith has saved you; go in peace" (ἡ πίστις σου σέσωκέν σε· πορεύου εἰς εἰρήνην).
Luke 9.1-2, and see 1-5 (cf. Mt 10. 1-15; Mk 6. 7-12; GT # 14)	Συγκαλεσάμενος δὲ τοὺς δώδεκα ἔδωκεν αὐτοῖς δύναμιν καὶ ἐξουσίαν ἐπὶ πάντα τὰ δαιμόνια καὶ νόσους θεραπεύειν, καὶ ἀπέστειλεν αὐτοὺς κηρύσσειν τὴν βασιλείαν τοῦ θεοῦ καὶ ἰᾶσθαι [τοὺς ἀσθενεῖς] After calling the twelve together he gave them power and authority over all demons and to treat diseases, and he sent them out to preach the kingdom of God and to heal (the infirm).					Note the different language, & the contiguous use of ἰᾶσθαι and θεραπεύειν.
Luke 9.6 (cf. Mk 6.13)	The "12"	ἐξερχόμενοι δὲ διήρχοντο κατὰ τὰς κώμας εὐαγγελιζόμενοι καὶ θεραπεύοντες πανταχοῦ (And they departed and went through the villages, preaching the good news and treating the sick everywhere)		General: everywhere; ?	Luke's choice of present participles to describe the disciples' behaviour denotes a behavioural process. Note Jesus' instructions *re* food, equipment, money and lodgings for this trip.	Luke chooses θεραπεύω, not ἰάομαι, to describe the disciples' behaviour.
Luke 9.11 (cf. Mt. 14.13-21; Mk. 6.30-44; Jn 6.1-14)	Jesus	καὶ τοὺς χρείαν ἔχοντας θεραπείας ἰᾶτο	καὶ τοὺς χρείαν ἔχοντας θεραπείας (those in need of treatment)	General: those in need of treatment; ?	Luke links this episode with Jesus' preaching about the kingdom of God in a city called Bethsaida. It is immediately prior to Luke's account of the feeding of the 5,000.	Luke chooses ἰάομαι in the imperfect to describe Jesus' behaviour.

Luke 9.18-21 (cf. Mt 16.13-20; Mk 8.27-31)	εἶπεν δὲ αὐτοῖς, Ὑμεῖς δὲ τίνα με λέγετε εἶναι; Πέτρος δὲ ἀποκριθεὶς εἶπεν, Τὸν Χριστὸν τοῦ θεοῦ. And he said to them, "Who do you say that I am?" And Peter answered, "The Christ of God." (9.20)					**Peter's declaration.** Note the context.
Luke 9.37-43 (cf. Mt 17.14-18; Mk 9.14-27)	Jesus	ἐπετίμησεν τῷ πνεύματι τῷ ἀκαθάρτῳ ἰάσατο	πνεῦμα λαμβάνει αὐτόν, καὶ ἐξαίφνης κράζει, καὶ σπαράσσει αὐτὸν μετὰ ἀφροῦ καὶ μόγις ἀποχωρεῖ ἀπ' αὐτοῦ συντρῖβον αὐτόν (a spirit seizes him and he suddenly cries out; it convulses him with foam and scarcely leaves him alone, and shatters him).	Specific: 1; word (rebuke)	The father, in a crowd, requested Jesus to look upon his only child. The boy was seized by a spirit which the disciples were unable to expel (ἐκβάλλω). Jesus shows some exasperation: Ὦ γενεὰ ἄπιστος καὶ διεστραμμένη, ἕως πότε ἔσομαι πρὸς ὑμᾶς καὶ ἀνέξομαι ὑμῶν; (O faithless and perverse generation,how long shall I be with you and bear with you?)	Luke's medical information is curiously condensed here (cf. Mk 9.14-27). He gives social information: the boy is an only child (cf. Jairus' daughter, and the widow of Nain's son).
Luke 9.49-50 (cf. Mk 9.38-41)	Ἀποκριθεὶς δὲ Ἰωάννης εἶπεν, Ἐπιστάτα, εἴδομέν τινα ἐν τῷ ὀνόματί σου ἐκβάλλοντα δαιμόνια, καὶ ἐκωλύομεν αὐτὸν ὅτι οὐκ ἀκολουθεῖ μεθ' ἡμῶν. εἶπεν δὲ πρὸς αὐτὸν ὁ Ἰησοῦς, Μὴ κωλύετε, ὃς γὰρ οὐκ ἔστιν καθ' ὑμῶν ὑπὲρ ὑμῶν ἐστιν. And in reply John said, "Master, we saw a man casting out demons in your name, and we prevented him, because he does not follow with us." But Jesus said to him, "Do not prevent him; for he that is not against you is for you."					This exorcist was obviously successful. Cf. Acts 19.13-20.
Luke 10.1-20 (cf. GT #14)	καὶ εἰς ἣν ἂν πόλιν εἰσέρχησθε καὶ δέχωνται ὑμᾶς, ἐσθίετε τὰ παρατιθέμενα ὑμῖν, καὶ θεραπεύετε τοὺς ἐν αὐτῇ ἀσθενεῖς, καὶ λέγετε αὐτοῖς, Ἤγγικεν ἐφ' ὑμᾶς ἡ βασιλεία τοῦ θεοῦ Whenever you enter a town and they welcome you, eat what is set before you, and treat the sick people in it, and say to them, "The kingdom of God has come near to you." (10.8-9)					Jesus' commission to the "72" to go, and instructions re provisions, lodgings, healing, behaviour.

Luke 10.17	The "72"	τὰ δαιμόνια ὑποτάσσεται ἡμῖν ἐν τῷ ὀνόματί σου	Κύριε, καὶ τὰ δαιμόνια ὑποτάσσεται ἡμῖν ἐν τῷ ὀνόματί σου (Lord, even the demons obey us in your name)	General: ?; word?	The "72" return from their mission, and report back to Jesus.	
Luke 10.25-37 The parable of the good Samaritan	Jesus' story of the good Samaritan, who, overcome with compassion (ἐσπλαγχνίσθη) when he saw the wounded man, bound up his wounds, pouring over them a mixture of oil and wine (κατέδησεν τὰ τραύματα αὐτοῦ ἐπιχέων ἔλαιον καὶ οἶνον), and made arrangements for his care (ἐπιμελέομαι). This is an interesting parable because it mentions anointing the wounds with oil and wine. This was a common therapeutic practice in the ancient world. It had several functions. If the skin was broken it served as an antiseptic by providing an effective barrier against harmful bacteria, and as an emollient, preventing bandages sticking to the wound. As well, it was used extensively to treat skin disorders, and as the emollient agent for massage, particularly in the treatment of muscular complaints. (See Hippokrates *In the Surgery* 12; Celsus *De Medicina* 2.14.4) This raises the question: Did Jesus have medical knowledge? Note that θεραπεύω, the "normal" verb to describe medical treatment and nursing of this type does not appear in this story. Instead the verb ἐπιμελέομαι describes this behaviour. Luke's choice of language is significant.					The "good" man is an outcast, a Samaritan, who has a knowledge of current medical practice, as well as the capacity to feel compassion, the motivating emotion for many of Jesus' miracles.

Luke 11.14-16 (cf. Mt 12.22-30; Mk 3.20-27)	Jesus	ἐκβάλλων δὲ τοῦ δαιμονίου ἐξελθόντος	δαιμόνιον . . . κωφόν (dumb demon)	Specific: 1; ?	This incident occurs in a long teaching passage, after Jesus taught the disciples to pray, and told them the parable about asking and receiving. Luke uses this incident to set the scene for more of Jesus' teaching.	Note that the people do not question the miracle as such, but question Jesus' authority to perform such miracles.
Luke 13.10-17	Jesus	Γύναι, ἀπολέλυσαι τῆς ἀσθενείας σου, καὶ ἐπέθηκεν αὐτῇ τὰς χεῖρας· καὶ παραχρῆμα ἀνωρθώθη, καὶ ἐδόξαζεν τὸν θεόν. ("Woman, you are freed from your infirmity." And he laid his hands upon her, and immediately she was made straight, and she began glorifying God.) (ἐθεράπευσεν...θεραπεύεσθε)	γυνὴ πνεῦμα ἔχουσα ἀσθενείας ἔτη δεκαοκτώ, καὶ ἦν συγκύπτουσα καὶ μὴ δυναμένη ἀνακύψαι εἰς τὸ παντελές (a woman who had had a spirit of weakness for eighteen years, and was bent over and could not fully straighten herself). Wilkinson (1980) 74, diagnoses ankylosing spondylitis.	Specific: 1; word and touch	In the synagogue, on the sabbath. The ruler was displeased because Jesus ἐθεράπευσεν (14) on the sabbath. But Jesus states that the woman had been bound by Satan (16). Jesus definitely sees illness as the work of Satan. His battle with demonic forces, and his dualistic understanding of the cosmos is explicit. Again the language used to describe the ruler's idea of Jesus' activity on the Sabbath is θεραπεύω (cf. Lk 6.6-11; Mt 12.10; Mk 3.2)	See Wilkinson (1980) 70-80. A sabbath healing peculiar to Luke.

Luke 14.1-6	Jesus	(θεραπεῦσαι) καὶ ἐπιλαβόμενος ἰάσατο αὐτὸν καὶ ἀπέλυσεν (And taking him he healed him and let him go.)	ἀνθρωπός τις ἦν ὑδρωπικὸς (dropsy)	Specific: 1; ? touch?	On the sabbath, when Jesus went to dine with a Pharisaic ruler, the man was "there". Jesus justifies his action with a similar argument to the one he gave when he healed the bent woman (14.5 cf. 13.15-16).	A sabbath healing peculiar to Luke.
Luke 17.11-19	Jesus	ἐλέησον ἡμᾶς ἐκαθαρίσθησαν ἰάθη ἡ πίστις σου σέσωκέν σε (have mercy on us ... they were cleansed ... he was healed ... your faith has saved you)	δέκα λεπροὶ ἄνδρες (ten men who were lepers)	Specific: 10; word	On the way to Jerusalem, between Samaria and Galilee, 10 lepers asked Jesus to have mercy on them. All found they were cleansed when they followed Jesus' instructions to show themselves to the priests. One, a Samaritan, a foreigner (ἀλλογενὴς), returned to praise God and thank Jesus. Jesus told him his faith had "saved" him.	Note the linking of: ἐλέησόν, ἐκαθαρίσθησαν, ἰάθη, πίστις and σέσωκέν. The one leper who gave thanks was an outsider.

Luke 18.35-43 (cf. Mt 20.29-34; Mk 10.46-52)	Jesus	ἐλέησόν με ᾿Ανάβλεψον· ἡ πίστις σου σέσωκέν σε. καὶ παραχρῆμα ἀνέβλεψεν καὶ ἠκολούθει αὐτῷ, δοξάζων τὸν θεόν (have mercy on me ... "See again; your faith has saved you." And immediately he saw again, and began following him, praising God.)	τυφλός τις . . . ἐπαιτῶν (a blind man . . . begging)	Specific: 1; word	Near Jericho, a blind man, sitting by the roadside, begging, asked Jesus to have mercy on him.	Note the linking of: ἐλέησόν, Ανάβλεψον·, πίστις, and σέσωκέν. Note also the results: for the patient: discipleship; for the crowd: praise to God.
Luke 22.49-51	Jesus	καὶ ἁψάμενος τοῦ ὠτίου ἰάσατο αὐτον (and he touched his ear and healed him)	καὶ ἀφεῖλεν τὸ οὖς αὐτοῦ τὸ δεξιόν (and he cut off his right ear). Sword wound: severed ear.	Specific: 1; touch	At the Mount of Olives, a slave (δοῦλος) of the high priest, was struck with a sword by one of Jesus' companions.	No synoptic parallel, but cf. Mt 26.47-56; Mk 14.43-50; Jn 18.3-11.

Appendix 7 : 4

Peter's declaration

Gospel	**Matthew**	**Mark**	**Luke**
Total chapters	28	16	24
Reference	16.13-20	8.27-31	9.18-21
Context	After the feeding of the 4,000 (15.32-39), and Jesus' explanation of bread=teaching (16.1-12)	After the feeding of the 4,000 (8.1-10), Jesus' teaching (8.11-21) and the healing of a blind man (8.22-26)	After the feeding of the 5,000 (9.10-17)
Percentage in terms of space	57%	50%	37.5%
Percentage in terms of healing miracles	84% (21 before, 4 after)	89% (17 before, 2 after)	66.6% (18 before, 9 after)
Followed by:	-epileptic boy -crowd -two blind men -blind & lame in temple	-epileptic boy -blind Bartimaeus	-epileptic boy -exorcisms of other healer -exorcisms of the "72" -dumb demon -bent woman on sabbath -man with dropsy on sabbath -10 lepers -blind beggar -sword wound
Instruction	διεστείλατο . . . ἵνα μηδενὶ εἴπωσιν ὅτι αὐτός ἐστιν ὁ Χριστός (16.20)	καὶ ἐπετίμησεν αὐτοῖς ἵνα μηδενὶ λέγωσιν περὶ αὐτοῦ (8.30)	ὁ δὲ ἐπιτιμήσας αὐτοῖς παρήγγειλεν μηδενὶ λέγειν τοῦτο, εἰπὼν ὅτι Δεῖ τὸν υἱὸν τοῦ ἄθρώπου πολλὰ παθεῖν (9.21-22)
Comment	Note Matthew's embellishment		

Appendix 7 : 5

The incidence of healing in the synoptic gospels

(based on Appendices 7:1, 7:2, and 7:3)

1: Jesus

Gospel	Matthew	Mark	Luke
Jesus: general	11	5	7 (inc. 8.2-3)
Jesus: specific	14	13	18 (inc. 8.2-3)
Total	25	18	25

2: The "12", the "72", and one other in Jesus' name

Gospel	Matthew	Mark	Luke
The "12": general		1	1
The "72": general			1 (exorcism)
Other			1 (exorcism in Jesus' name: 9.49-50)
Total		1	3

3: Total healing episodes in the synoptic gospels

Gospel	Matthew	Mark	Luke
Total	25	19	27 (counting 8.2-3 as one episode, although it contains both general and specific information)

Appendix 7 : 6

Gender differentiation of specific healings

(based on Appendices 7:1, 7:2, and 7:3)

Gospel	**Matthew**	**Mark**	**Luke**
Peter's mother-in-law	8.14-15	1.29-31	4.38-39
Jairus' daughter	9.18-19, 23-26	5.21-24, 35-43	8.40-42, 49-56
Haemorrhaging woman	9.20-22	5.25-34	8.43-48
Syrophoenician girl	15.21-28	7.24-30	
Mary, Joanna, Susanna and others			8.2-3
Bent woman			13.10-17 [Note also that it is compassion for the mother that motivates Jesus to act in the case of the raising of the widow of Nain's son (Luke 7.11-18)]
Total female episodes	4	4	5
Total male episodes	10	9	13

Appendix 7 : 7

The synoptic portrayal of issues and antagonists

Reference	Issue	Antagonist	Comment
Mark 1.40-45	The healing of the leper: Jesus instructs the leper not to tell anyone, but to show himself to the priest, and make the offering that Moses commanded. i.e. Jesus commands the leper to fulfil Jewish law. (This is Mark's fifth healing: third specific ff. two general.)		
Mark 2.1-12	**1**: blasphemy/authority	some of the scribes	the healing of the paralytic who was let down through the roof. The issue according to the scribes was Jesus' blasphemy when he forgave sins; Jesus spoke of "authority" to do so.
Mark 2.15-17	**2**: eating companions	scribes of the Pharisees	altercation introduces Jesus' saying: "Those who are well have no need of a physician, but those who are sick; I came not to call the righteous, but sinners."
Mark 2.18-22	**3**: fasting	people	John's disciples & the Pharisees were fasting and "people" wondered why Jesus' disciples did not fast. Introduces the parables of the bridegroom, the patch, and the wine skin.
Mark 2.23-28	**4**: work on sabbath (plucking ears of grain)	Pharisees	One sabbath he (Jesus) was going through the grainfields; and as they made their way his disciples began to pluck ears of grain. And the Pharisees said to him, "Look, why are they doing what is not lawful on the sabbath?" -> Jesus' saying: "The sabbath was made for man, not man for the sabbath; so the Son of man is lord even of the sabbath." (NB: the Pharisees were walking with them.)
Mark 3.1-6	**5**: healing on sabbath	Pharisees	The man with the withered hand in the synagogue. Jesus' question: "Is it lawful on the sabbath to do good or to do harm, to save life (ψυχὴν σῶσαι) or to kill (ἀποκτεῖναι) ?" The result: the Pharisees held counsel with the Herodians against him, how to destroy him (ὅπως αὐτὸν ἀπολέσωσιν).

Mark 3.19-27	**6**: authority	scribes	scribes: "He is possessed by Beelzebul, and by the prince of demons he casts out demons."
Mark 7.1-23	**7**: washing & eating	Pharisees and scribes	introduces the sayings about man being defiled from within. Cf. GT #70, #89 (*NHL*)
Mark 8.11-13	**8**: demand for a sign	Pharisees	follows the feeding of the 4,000 and introduces Jesus' warning against the leaven of the Pharisees & of Herod.
Mark 10.2-12	**9**: divorce	Pharisees	Matthew's issue is similar, although his introduction (19.2) to this episode is strikingly different. In *Mark* this incident follows the general verse, "and crowds gathered to him again; and again, as his custom was, he began teaching them" (καὶ ὡς εἰώθει πάλιν ἐδίδασκεν αὐτούς (10.1)). Luke only touches on divorce in the context of adultery, in a large passage of ethical teaching (16.18).
Mark 11.15-28 ff	**10**: authority	chief priests & scribes & elders	following Jesus' triumphal entry to Jerusalem, the clearing out of the temple, & the fig tree, as Jesus was walking in the temple, the chief priests, scribes, & elders asked Jesus the source of his authority to "do these things" ('Εν ποίᾳ ἐξουσίᾳ ταῦτα ποιεῖς [11.28]). Jesus refuses to answer, but tells the parable of the wicked tenants.
Mark 12.13-17	**11**: taxes	Pharisees & Herodians	immediately following the previous episode, the Pharisees and some Herodians try to entrap him in his talk.
Mark 12.18-27	**12**: resurrection	Sadducees	immediately following the previous episode the Sadducees ask Jesus about teaching concerning the resurrection.
Mark 12.28-34	**13**: the first commandment	a scribe	immediately following the previous episode one of the scribes asked which was the first commandment of all. Although Jesus tells this scribe that he is not far from the kingdom of God, the story introduces the general warning against scribes, and the story of the widow's mite.

Mark 3.19-27	**6**: authority	scribes	scribes: "He is possessed by Beelzebul, and by the prince of demons he casts out demons."
Mark 7.1-23	**7**: washing & eating	Pharisees and scribes	introduces the sayings about man being defiled from within. Cf. GT #70, #89 (*NHL*)
Mark 8.11-13	**8**: demand for a sign	Pharisees	follows the feeding of the 4,000 and introduces Jesus' warning against the leaven of the Pharisees & of Herod.
Mark 10.2-12	**9**: divorce	Pharisees	Matthew's issue is similar, although his introduction (19.2) to this episode is strikingly different. In *Mark* this incident follows the general verse, "and crowds gathered to him again; and again, as his custom was, he began teaching them" (καὶ ὡς εἰώθει πάλιν ἐδίδασκεν αὐτούς (10.1)). Luke only touches on divorce in the context of adultery, in a large passage of ethical teaching (16.18).
Mark 11.15-28 ff	**10**: authority	chief priests & scribes & elders	following Jesus' triumphal entry to Jerusalem, the clearing out of the temple, & the fig tree, as Jesus was walking in the temple, the chief priests, scribes, & elders asked Jesus the source of his authority to "do these things" (ποίᾳ ἐξουσίᾳ ταῦτα ποιεῖς [11.28]). Jesus refuses to answer, but tells the parable of the wicked tenants.
Mark 12.13-17	**11**: taxes	Pharisees & Herodians	immediately following the previous episode, the Pharisees and some Herodians try to entrap him in his talk.
Mark 12.18-27	**12**: resurrection	Sadducees	immediately following the previous episode the Sadducees ask Jesus about teaching concerning the resurrection.
Mark 12.28-34	**13**: the first commandment	a scribe	immediately following the previous episode one of the scribes asked which was the first commandment of all. Although Jesus tells this scribe that he is not far from the kingdom of God, the story introduces the general warning against scribes, and the story of the widow's mite.

Mark introduces 13 disputes, of which only two involve the sabbath (2.23-28; 3.1-6). The first concerns "work," i.e. plucking ears of grain while walking through a grainfield; the next also seems to involve "work," which the Pharisees think of in terms of θεραπεύω. In both incidents Jesus raises questions of law, which the Pharisees cannot answer.			
Matthew 8.1-4	the healing of the leper: Jesus instructs him not to tell anybody, but to show himself to the priest and make the offering that Moses had commanded. (This is Matthew's first specific healing episode, following two general accounts.)		
Matthew 9.1-8	**1**: blasphemy/authority	some of the scribes	the healing of the paralytic. To the scribes, Jesus committed blasphemy by forgiving sins. But Jesus spoke of the "authority" to do so.
Matthew 9.9-13	**2**: eating companions	Pharisees	introduces Jesus' saying: "Those who are well have no need of a physician, but those who are sick. Go and learn what this means, 'I desire mercy, and not sacrifice.' For I came not to call the righteous, but sinners."
Matthew 9.14-17	**3**: fasting	John the Baptist's disciples	J B's disciples asked Jesus why they and the Pharisees fasted, but Jesus' disciples did not. Introduces the parables of the bridegroom, the patch, and the wineskin.
Matthew 12.1-8	**4**: work on sabbath	Pharisees	Jesus went through the grainfields on the sabbath; his disciples were hungry, and they began to pluck ears of grain and to eat -> Jesus' saying: "... if you had known what this means, 'I desire mercy, and not sacrifice,' you would not have condemned the guiltless. For the Son of man is lord of the sabbath." Matthew justifies the disciples' behaviour by adding that they were hungry, and plucked the grain to eat it. He also expands Jesus' saying.

Matthew 12.9-14	**5**: healing on sabbath	Pharisees	The man with the withered hand in the synagogue. The result: the Pharisees took counsel against him, how to destroy him (ὅπως αὐτὸν ἀπολέσωσιν). Matthew introduces the story of a sheep in a pit - and ends by: "it is lawful to do good." But the Pharisaic issue is of saving life (as in *Mark*), <u>not</u> doing good. Are both Mark (3.1-6) and Luke (6.6-11) more aware of the real issue here?
Matthew 12.24ff.	**6**: authority	Pharisees	Beelzebul ff. blind and dumb healing -> Jesus' teaching, which brings healing and sight (13. 14-15)
Matthew 15.1-20	**7**: washing & eating	Pharisees & scribes	introduces the sayings about man being defiled from within. Cf. GT #70, #89 (*NHL*) The disciples ask Jesus if he knew that the Pharisees were offended by his sayings. Jesus' reply: "Let them alone; they are blind guides. And if a blind man leads a blind man, both will fall into a pit."
Matthew 16.1-4	**8**: demand for a sign	Pharisees & Sadducees	follows the feeding of the 4,000 and introduces Jesus' warning about the teaching of the Pharisees and Sadducees (16.5-12)
Matthew 19.3-12	**9**: divorce	Pharisees	Matthew changes Mark's introduction to this episode from "and again, as his custom was, he began teaching (ἐδίδασκεν) them," to, "and large crowds followed him, and he healed them there" (καὶ ἐθεράπευσεν αὐτοὺς ἐκεῖ (19.2)). All synoptists make it clear that Jesus' teaching, preaching and healing formed an indissoluble unit of behaviour, but here one term - healing - is actually substituted for another - that of teaching.
Matthew 21.12-46	**10**: authority	chief priests & elders	following Jesus' triumphal entry into Jerusalem and the clearing out of the temple, Matthew introduces a general healing episode (21.14) before the incident of the fig tree. Then, while Jesus was teaching in the temple, the chief priests and elders asked the source of Jesus' authority. Matthew also introduces a parable (21.28-32).
Matthew 22.15-22	**11**: taxes	Pharisees & Herodians	The Pharisees took counsel how to entangle Jesus in his talk, and sent their disciples, along with the Herodians.

Matthew 22.23-33	**12**: resurrection	Sadducees	Immediately following the previous episode the Sadducees ask Jesus a question about teaching concerning the resurrection.
Matthew 22.34-46	**13**: the great commandment	Pharisee	Matthew changes Mark's "scribe" to a "Pharisee" who wished to test him by asking which was the great commandment in the law. The great commandment - "on these two commandments depend all the law and the prophets" - introduces the warning against the scribes and Pharisees, and the "woes" chapter (23), where Jesus denotes the Pharisees and scribes as "blind guides" (16,23), "blind fools" (17), and "blind men" (19), (cf. 13.14-15, where Jesus says he came to bring sight and healing). The great commandment is explained at Matthew 25.35-36: i.e. providing food for the hungry, drink for the thirsty, a welcome for strangers, clothing for the naked, and visiting those who are sick and in prison.
Matthew follows Mark's order in these disputes. The only sabbath disputes concern "work" (12.1-8) and "healing" (12.9-14). It would seem that healing involves the notion of work, and as θεραπεύω is the word chosen, it must involve a process that was understood by the Jews (and particularly the Pharisees) as work. Chapter 23.1-4 ff. makes it clear that Jesus was very concerned with the practical side of the law, and as his behaviour is consistently designated as preaching, teaching and θεραπεύων behaviour, this θεραπεύων behaviour has to be the practical result of his message. Thus to love one's neighbour (22.37-9) is to teach and preach Jesus' message by θεραπεύων action, action summed up in Jesus' description at 25. 36-37.			
Luke 5.12-14	The cleansing of the leper, and Jesus' instructions to fulfil Jewish law. (Luke's fifth healing: third specific, ff. two general episodes.)		
Luke 5.17-26	**1** (M1): blasphemy/authority	Pharisees & scribes (scribes = teachers of the law, v17 ?)	The healing of the paralytic. This is not a sabbath healing (the verb θεραπεύω is not used), and althought the power was with Jesus to heal (ἰᾶσθαι), the issue is not one of healing, but, in the eyes of the Pharisees, the blasphemy of forgiving sins, which Jesus turns into an issue of authority.
Luke 5.29-32	**2** (M2): eating companions	Pharisees & their scribes	altercation introduces Jesus' saying: "Those who are well have no need of a physician, but those who are sick; I have not come to call the righteous, but sinners to repentance (μετάνοιαν)."

Luke 5.33-39	**3** (M3+): fasting & prayer	"they" : Pharisees & their scribes? (5.30)	Luke introduces prayer as an issue in this story. "They" say, "The disciples of John fast often and offer prayers, and so do the disciples of the Pharisees, but yours eat and drink." Introduces the parables of the bridegroom, the patch, and the wine skin.
Luke 6.1-5	**4** (M4+): work on sabbath	Pharisees	disciples plucked and ate some ears of grain, rubbing them in their hands. But some of the Pharisees said, "Why are you doing what is not lawful to do on the sabbath?" -> Jesus' saying: "The Son of man is lord of the sabbath." Luke expands the story to explain the concept of "work" more clearly: he adds that the disciples rubbed the ears of grain in their hands.
Luke 6.6-11	**5** (M5): healing on sabbath	scribes & Pharisees	The man with the withered hand in the synagogue on another sabbath -> Jesus' question: "I ask you, is it lawful on the sabbath to do good or to do harm, to save life (ψυχὴν σῶσαι) or to destroy (ἀπολέσαι) it?" The result: they (scribes & Pharisees?) were filled with rage and discussed with one another what they might do (ποιήσαιεν) to Jesus.
Luke 7.29-30	"When they heard this all the people and the tax collectors justified God, having been baptised with the baptism of John; but the Pharisees and the lawyers rejected the purpose of God for themselves, not having been baptised by him." Matthew includes a similar saying to the chief priests and elders in his presentation of the issue of authority (21.32), but Luke is the only one who specifically mentions Pharisees and lawyers.		
Luke 7.36-50	**6**: authority, (uncleanness/ blasphemy)	Simon the Pharisee, and others (Pharisees?)	Mark (14.3-9), and Matthew (26.6-13), place a similar incident in the house of Simon the leper. In *Mark* and *Matthew* the issue is financial, and Pharisees are not involved. Here, Jesus is in a Pharisee's house, at table, at the Pharisee's invitation, and the Pharisee's name is Simon. Here the issue is uncleanness, blasphemy, and the authority to forgive sins.

Luke 10.25-37	**7** (M13+): the (great) commandment	lawyer	The great commandment introduced by a lawyer's question (designed to test Jesus): "What shall I do to inherit eternal life?" Jesus commands (28): "Do this, and you will live." Introduces the parable of the Good Samaritan as an example of love in action and of the type of recipient (neighbour). Jesus' command (37): "Go and do likewise!" The commands are all present imperatives: ποίει, Πορεύου, and ποίει.
Luke 11.14-26	**8** (M6,M8): authority/seeking a sign	some of them	Luke introduces the saying "But if it is by the finger of God that I cast out demons, then the kingdom of God has come upon you" (11.20) to this story about Beelzebul. Luke combines Mark's (and Matthew's) sixth and eighth issues here, but does not identify the antagonists as do Mark (scribes [6]; Pharisees [8]) and Matthew (Pharisees [6]; Pharisees and Sadducees [8]).
Luke 11.37-53; 12.1-3	**9** (M7, + M8's warning): washing	Pharisee	a Pharisee, having invited Jesus to dine in his home was astonished to see that he did not wash before eating. Introduces sayings about the outside *vs* the inside, and woes to both the Pharisees and lawyers. (Jesus is a very rude guest!) Luke reports that while the scribes & Pharisees began to pressJesus hard, in order to catch him out, Jesus began to warn his disciples against the teaching of the Pharisees.
Luke 13.10-17	**10**: healing on sabbath	ruler of the synagogue	The healing of the bent woman, a story peculiar to Luke. The ruler thinks of healing in terms of θεραπεύω, but Luke describes the healing itself in clinical terms.
Luke 13.31-32	The Pharisees warn Jesus that Herod wants to kill him. Peculiar to Luke.		
Luke 14.1-6	**11**: healing on sabbath	lawyers & Pharisees	while dining at (a ruling) Pharisee's house: man with dropsy. Jesus speaks in terms of θεραπεύω, but Luke uses ἰάομαι to describe the action.
Luke 15.1-2	**12**: welcomes & eats with sinners (cf. L2, L17)	Pharisees & scribes	Luke uses these verses as an introduction to the parables of the lost sheep, the lost coin, and the prodigal son.

Luke 16.14ff.	**13** (M9): money/divorce	Pharisees	Luke introduces money as an issue, and includes Mark's (and Matthew's) ninth issue, i.e. divorce, in the context of adultery, in a long passage of ethical teaching.
Luke 17.20-21	**14**: Kingdom of God	Pharisees	Luke introduces the saying: "The kingdom of God is in the midst of you."
Luke 18.9-14	**15**: humility		Jesus' story about the Pharisee and the sinner. This teaching is echoed in Matthew 6.5, but there the story criticises hypocrites. Pharisees are not specifically identified by Matthew, as they are by Luke.
Luke 18.18-30	**16**: discipleship	ruler	In Mark 10.17ff. this story is about a "man" (with possessions), in Matthew 19.16ff. a "young man" (with possessions). Luke makes this man a "ruler".
Luke 19.7	**17**: eating companions (cf. L2, L12)	"they"	Peculiar to Luke: the story of Zacchaeus the tax collector.
Luke 19.28-48, 20.1-18	**18** (M10): authority	chief priests & scribes, the principal men of the people, & elders	following Jesus' triumphal entry into Jerusalem and the clearing of the temple. Luke omits the incident of the fig tree (Mk & Mt), and the general healing episode (Mt). As in both *Mark* and *Matthew*, the issue is the source of Jesus' authority (20.2).
Luke 20.19-26	**19** (M11): taxes	scribes & chief priests	immediately following the preceding episode as in *Mark* and *Matthew*, but Luke changes the personnel of the antagonists from Pharisees & Herodians to scribes & chief priests. (Is this because Luke cannot imagine Pharisees & Herodians cooperating with each other?)
Luke 20.27-45	**20** (M12): resurrection	Sadducees	immediately following the previous episode, the Sadducees ask Jesus about teaching concerning the resurrection. Mark and Matthew follow this with the question concerning the great commandment, which Luke omits here, having included it at 10.25-37. Instead Luke introduces the warning against scribes which Mark introduces at 12.38 (35ff.), and Matthew at chapter 23 (22.41ff.).

Luke includes all thirteen issues raised by Mark (and Matthew), and generally follows Mark's order of events. The major exception to this pattern is Luke's placing of Mark's (and Matthew's) final issue (**13**: the great commandment) as a central issue in his work, and illustrating it with the parable of the Good Samaritan. Luke also includes his own special material (**6**, **10**, **11**, **12**, **14**, **15**, **16**). Luke appears to be far more interested than either Mark or Matthew in the disputes between Jesus and those interested in Jewish law, particularly the Pharisees. Jesus appears to know many Pharisees well, and to be on good terms with them. He is invited into their homes as a guest (7.36-50; 11.37-12.3; 14.1-6), and knows them well enough to be an extremely rude guest and get away with it! He appears to have some authority amongst them. Disputes invariably turn on an interpretation of the law, and appear to be an example of Pharisees engaging in disputes concerning matters of *halakhah*. Despite his disputes with them, it is the Pharisees who warn Jesus of Herod's intention to harm him (13.31). Thus it would appear that Jesus is (or was) one of them, i.e. a Pharisee who disagreed with contemporary Pharisaic interpretation of the law, and who thus differed from his peers in his understanding of what repentance (*μετάνοια*) involved. Thus his saying at 5.31-2 gains significance. In all disputes concerning sabbath healings Jesus' behaviour is perceived by his antagonists as θεραπεύων behaviour. This is significant, given Luke's knowledge of the Greek language, and his ability to use technical terms if required.

Appendix 7 : 8

New Testament healing words : θεραπεύω θεραπεία θεράπων

Reference	Form	Part of speech	Comment
Matthew 4.23	θεραπεύων	Present participle active: nom, sing, masc.	In a general healing episode, describing Jesus' behaviour, throughout Galilee. This is the first of Matthew's healing accounts, and the first of two instances of Matthew using θεραπεύω in this form. It is linked to διδάσκων and κηρύσσων, and refers to the treatment of the vague maladies πᾶσαν νόσον καὶ πᾶσαν μαλακίαν. The other occurs at 9.35, again in a general healing episode, describing Jesus' behaviour while travelling. The language used is identical. Thus θεραπεύω in the form in *Matthew* of a present participle is part of a formula describing Jesus' behaviour while travelling. No other NT author uses θεραπεύω in this form.
Matthew 4.24	ἐθεράπευσεν	Aorist indicative active: 3 sing.	The first of eight occurrences in *Matthew* of θεραπεύω in this form. (Cf. 8.16, 12.15, 12.22, 14.14, 15.30, 19.2, 21.14.) It accounts for half of Matthew's use of this verb. In every instance it describes Jesus' behaviour when people either "follow" him, or are "brought" to him. In seven of the eight instances (cf. 12.22) the language used to describe the maladies of the people who "follow", or are "brought" is vague and generalised. Here the illnesses are cited as: πάντας τοὺς κακῶς ἔχοντας, ποικίλαις νόσοις καὶ βασάνοις συνεχομένους; but δαιμονιζομένους, καὶ σεληνιαζομένους, καὶ παραλυτικούς are cited as well.
Matthew 8.7	θεραπεύσω	Future indicative active: 1 sing.	The only occurrence of this form in *Matthew*. It is Jesus' reply to the centurion's request (cf. Lk 7.1-10; Jn 4.45-54).
Matthew 8.16	ἐθεράπευσεν	Aorist indicative active: 3 sing.	In a general healing episode, describing Jesus' behaviour in a crowd situation, in Syria. The illnesses cited are vague: πάντας τοὺς κακῶς ἔχοντας. See comment on 4.24.
Matthew 9.35	θεραπεύων	Present participle active: nom, sing, masc.	In a general healing episode, while travelling. The language used is identical with that at 4.23. (See comment on 4.23.)

Matthew 10.1	θεραπεύειν	Present infinitive: active.	Jesus gives "authority" to the disciples to "heal" (treat?) πᾶσαν νόσον καὶ πᾶσαν μαλακίαν. (Cf. 4.23 and 9.35). It is a commission linked with ἐξουσίαν πνευμάτων ἀκαθάρτων, ὥστε ἐκβάλλειν αὐτὰ. (Cf. Lk 9.1). The present infinitive active of θεραπεύω only occurs twice in the NT; here, and at Luke 9.1.
Matthew 10.8	θεραπεύετε	Present imperative: active, 2 pl.	Jesus gives instructions to the disciples, to ἀσθενοῦντας θεραπεύετε, νεκροὺς ἐγείρετε, λεπροὺς καθαρίζετε, δαιμόνια ἐκβάλλετε. (Cf. Lk 10.9) The use of the present imperative in each instruction implies an ongoing commission. The present imperative active (2 pl.) occurs only twice in the NT; here, and at Luke 10.9.
Matthew 12.10	θεραπεῦσαι	Aorist infinitive: active.	This form of θεραπεύω occurs three times in the NT; here, at Matthew 17.16, and at Luke 14.3. The language here, and at Luke 14. 3, is similar. Both infinitives appear in the form of a question, concerning the legality of healing on the Sabbath. Here, the question is framed by the Pharisees; in *Luke* the question is asked of the lawyers and Pharisees by Jesus himself. At Matthew 17.16, the father of the epileptic boy is explaining to Jesus that the disciples were unable to heal his son.
Matthew 12.15	ἐθεράπευσεν	Aorist indicative active: 3 sing.	In a general healing episode, ailments unknown. These people followed Jesus when he withdrew from the synagogue. Jesus charged them with secrecy, to fulfil a prophecy, according to Matthew, (see 12.17-21). See also comment on 4.24.
Matthew 12.22	ἐθεράπευσεν	Aorist indicative active: 3 sing.	The only use by Matthew of θεραπεύω in this form in a specific healing episode. The man was brought to Jesus by unnamed persons. He was δαιμονιζόμενος τυφλὸς καὶ κωφός. This incident is used by Matthew as the catalyst for Jesus' teaching (12.23-50). It is obvious that his audience is both blind and dumb to the significance of his person and message. Therefore this healing takes on a symbolic significance. Jesus heals the blind and dumb demoniac, so that he can speak and see; Jesus treats his audience by preaching and teaching. Their therapy is to "hear" and "see" (i.e. understand) his message.

Matthew 14.14	ἐθεράπευσεν	Aorist indicative active: 3 sing.	Again in a general healing episode (see comment on 4.24). A great crowd had followed Jesus, who was overcome with compassion (ἐσπλαγχνίσθη), and treated the weak amongst them (τοὺς ἀρρώστους αὐτῶν). Again, the maladies treated are vague, and healing treatment is closely linked with Jesus' other actions: here the feeding of the 5,000.
Matthew 15.30	ἐθεράπευσεν	Aorist indicative active: 3 sing.	Again in a general healing episode (see comment on 4.24). Here some of the maladies treated are listed: χωλούς, τυφλούς, κυλλούς, κωφούς, καὶ ἑτέρους πολλούς; but, again, there are the vague and generalised "many others". As with other occurrences of this form, great crowds had brought the patients to Jesus. The reaction of the crowd was to glorify the god of Israel, a reaction stimulated by the great numbers involved in this healing account. As with the other healing miracles, this one symbolises Jesus' identity and purpose, and it is appropriate that the illnesses specified should be those who were lame, blind, crippled and mute (deaf too?).
Matthew 17.16	θεραπεῦσαι	Aorist infinitive: active.	The second and final occurrence of this form in *Matthew*. As in 12.10, it describes the thought or speech of someone other than Jesus. Here it is the father of the epileptic boy, explaining to Jesus that the disciples were unable to heal his son.
Matthew 17.18	ἐθεραπεύθη	Aorist indicative passive: 3 sing.	The only occurrence of θεραπεύω in the passive voice in *Matthew*. It is of immense significance. It is the first healing episode recounted by Matthew following Peter's declaration (16.13-20) of Jesus' identity. Matthew uses it to highlight Jesus' identity, just in case any reader might still be doubtful. The language used to describe the whole incident is unusual, and underlines its significance for Matthew. Jesus ἐπετίμησεν the demon (the only occasion in *Matthew* where a δαιμόνιον is specifically linked with epilepsy), just as he ἐπετίμησεν the winds and the sea (8.26). In both stories the disciples are chastised for their little faith (ὀλιγοπιστίαν). This is the only occasion where Matthew chooses to use ἐπιτιμάω in a healing story (but cf. Mk). It is also the only occasion where πάσχω appears in Matthew's language of healing: καὶ κακῶς πάσχει; one would expect ἔχει, in keeping with Matthew's normal usage (but note the ms variation).

Matthew 19.2	ἐθεράπευσεν	Aorist indicative active: 3 sing.	In a general healing episode, very vague as to its nature and extent: καὶ ἠκολούθησαν αὐτῷ ὄχλοι πολλοί, καὶ ἐθεράπευσεν αὐτοὺς ἐκεῖ. It is sandwiched between Jesus' teaching about forgiveness, and the Pharisees questions concerning the legality of divorce. One cannot help but wonder whether θεραπεύω in this instance implies listening, forgiving, and teaching treatment, especially as Matthew chooses to use ἐθεράπευσεν instead of ἐδίδασκεν which appears in the parallel episode in *Mark* (10.1).
Matthew 21.14	ἐθεράπευσεν	Aorist indicative active: 3 sing.	The final use of θεραπεύω by Matthew. It occurs in the temple just after Jesus has overturned the tables of the moneychangers and the seats of those who sold pigeons, and quoted the true purpose of the temple: to be called a house of prayer. It is significant that his next action is not described by Matthew as prayer, but as the healing of the lame and blind who approached him in the temple. Again one wonders how much listening, forgiving and teaching is implicit in the word θεραπεύω. Matthew is very fond of the word θεραπεύω. He chooses to use it more than any other gospel author to describe Jesus' behaviour, especially in crowd situations, where the crowds seek him out. However it is not very clear just what Matthew understood by the term. Certainly, English translations of "heal" appear quite inadequate in some instances, and even misleading.
Mark 1.34	ἐθεράπευσεν	Aorist indicative active: 3 sing.	Mark only uses θεραπεύω five times in his gospel, in three different forms. Like Matthew, he uses ἐθεράπευσεν to describe Jesus' behaviour in general terms, in crowd situations. In this instance his patients are πολλοὺς κακῶς ἔχοντας ποικίλαις νόσοις.
Mark 3.2	θεραπεύσει	Future indicative active: 3 sing.	This form of θεραπεύω only occurs once in *Mark*. It describes the thought of the Pharisees, who wonder whether Jesus will heal on the sabbath. Cf. Mt 12.10, Lk 6.7.
Mark 3.10	ἐθεράπευσεν	Aorist indicative active: 3 sing.	In a crowd situation, ailments unspecified, numbers cited as πολλοὺς.
Mark 6.5	ἐθεράπευσεν	Aorist indicative active: 3 sing.	At Nazareth, (cf. Mt 13.53-58; Lk 4.16-30). Ailments described as ἀρρώστοις, numbers as ὀλίγοις.

Mark 6.13	ἐθεράπευον	Imperfect indicative active: 3 pl.	This is a most interesting usage of θεραπεύω, and the only occasion Mark uses it in the imperfect tense. It describes the activity of the "12", in response to the preaching and exorcising commission given them by Jesus (Mk 3.14-15). The other activity of the "12" is also described in the imperfect tense (ἐξέβαλλον . . . ἤλειφον ἐλαίῳ). Mark is very careful in his choice of tense, implying ongoing and incompleted action by the "12" in response to their commission. He does not mention their preaching, and one wonders whether this is implicit in the meaning of θεραπεύω. It is also interesting to note their use of current medical practice in using oil.
Luke 4.23	θεράπευσον	Aorist imperative active: 2 sing.	Luke uses θεραπεύω fourteen times in his gospel, in thirteen different forms. This particular form does not occur elsewhere in the NT. Jesus uses this form, concerning himself, reflecting what he understands as doubt by the people of Nazareth about his identity: "Doubtless you will quote to me this proverb, 'Physician, heal/treat yourself ... ' " (Ἰατρέ, θεράπευσον σεαυτόν). What does this mean? Is Jesus referring to some physical disability, or is he just trying to overcome the genuine and natural disbelief shown by those who watched him grow up, and knew all his weaknesses and failings? (See App. 8:3 : ἰατρός Lk 4.23.)
Luke 4.40	ἐθεράπευεν	Imperfect indicative active: 3 sing.	This form of the imperfect occurs only once in *Luke*. Here it describes Jesus' behaviour in a crowd situation (cf. Mt 8.16; Mk 1.32-34). Jesus is treating those people brought to him, who were weak with various ailments. Luke is more specific in his account of healing method than either Matthew or Mark. He describes how Jesus laid his hands on each one of them, and began healing them. Is this the beginning of a healing process in each individual, or does it imply a "crowd" healing process occurring one-by-one, or both? There is a significant difference here in Luke's account, and a translation in the past tense, implying completed action, is misleading.

Luke 5.15	θεραπεύεσθαι	Present infinitive: passive.	The only occurrence of this form in *Luke*, and in the NT. Again Jesus is in a crowd situation. The people came "to listen and to be healed of their weaknesses". Weaknesses: mental, emotional, spiritual, physical? The inference here is that it is Jesus' "message" that heals, and that this is a process. Hence the use of the present infinitives: ἀκούειν, and θεραπεύεσθαι. His audience were "great crowds" (ὄχλοι πολλοὶ), and Luke does not mention any physical contact by Jesus, such as laying on of hands, as at 4.40. The therapy in this case seems to be "listening" and "hearing". (These people had gathered because of the leper's cleansing [5.12-14]).
Luke 6.7	θεραπεύει	Present indicative active: 3 sing.	The only occurrence of this form of θεραπεύω in *Luke*, and in the NT. It occurs in Luke's account of the sabbath healing of the man with a withered right hand (cf. Mt 12.9-14; Mk 3.1-6). As in *Matthew*, and *Mark*, θεραπεύω is used to describe how the Pharisees perceive Jesus' behaviour, although each gospel author uses a different form of θεραπεύω. Healing is by command, and Jesus sought out this patient in order to show the Pharisees the true meaning of the law regarding the sabbath. That θεραπεύω is used consistently by the synoptists to describe the Pharisees' perception of Jesus' behaviour on the sabbath indicates that there is the notion of process implicit in the meaning of the word.
Luke 6.18	ἐθεραπεύοντο	Imperfect indicative passive: 3 pl.	This form of θεραπεύω occurs only once in Luke's gospel, but is used again, twice, by Luke, in *Acts* (5.16, 28.9). Here Luke is careful to use θεραπεύω and ἰάομαι contiguously. Again it is a crowd situation. The people came to listen/hear (ἀκοῦσαι), and be healed (ἰαθῆναι). It was those who were troubled by unclean spirits who ἐθεραπεύοντο (passive verb). Again, the therapy appears to be the "message" of Jesus. (Cf. comment on ἰάομαι at App. 8:3 : Lk 6.18, 19.)

Luke 7.21	ἐθεράπευσεν	Aorist indicative active: 3 sing.	The first of only two occurrences of this form in *Luke* (cf. Mt 8x, and Mk 3x). It is used in a general healing episode, in a crowd situation, to describe the treatment of diseases (νόσων), illnesses / chronic irritations? (μαστίγων) and evil spirits (πνευμάτων πονηρῶν). The context is significant. This episode occurs between the question from John the Baptist concerning Jesus' identity, and Jesus' answer to him. That it describes a completed action is emphasised by Luke's use of ἐν ἐκείνῃ τῇ ὥρᾳ ἐθεράπευσεν.
Luke 8.2	ἦσαν τεθεραπευμέναι	Pluperfect indicative passive: 3 pl.	The only occurrenc of θεραπεύω in the pluperfect tense in the NT. It is part of a general healing episode with specific information. The use of the feminine participle, and the following very specific information concerning three of the women, including their names, and their contribution to the support of Jesus and his disciples, provides important social and economic information. The women had been healed of evil spirits and weaknesses (πνευμάτων πονηρῶν καὶ ἀσθενειῶν). The result was that they travelled with Jesus (on this occasion at least), and provided for Jesus and the disciples out of their means. The "cure" was discipleship, i.e. listening, understanding, and acting on Jesus' message. This was their cure, but would it have been seen as a cure by other than Jesus' followers?
Luke 8.43	θεραπευθῆναι	Aorist infinitive: passive.	The only occurrence of this form of θεραπεύω in the NT. It occurs in the story of the haemorrhaging woman (cf. Mt 9.20-22; Mk 5.25-34). Luke uses it to describe the inability of anyone to heal her; however the word he uses to describe Jesus' healing is ἰάθη. Again Luke uses θεραπεύω and ἰάομαι contiguously, and again the actions of other people and Jesus are compared (cf. Lk 9.6; 9.11). In this story Luke uses three healing verbs: θεραπεύω, ἰάομαι, and σῴζω. To describe the physicians' unsuccessful ongoing attempts at treatment he chooses θεραπεύω, to describe Jesus' instantaneous healing he chooses ἰάομαι, but Jesus sums up the result with the verb σῴζω : Θυγάτηρ, ἡ πίστις σου σέσωκέν σε· πορεύου εἰς εἰρήνην. The final result was the woman's salvation (cf. the Septuagint use of the Greek word εἰρήνη in a healing context: App. 6:1, **43**, **66**, **68**, **71**).

Luke 9.1	θεραπεύειν	Present infinitive: active.	This form of θεραπεύω occurs twice in the NT: here, and at Mt 10.1, where Jesus gives authority to his disciples. Again Luke uses θεραπεύω and ἰάομαι together: "After calling the twelve together he gave them power and authority over all demons and to treat diseases (νόσους θεραπεύειν), and he sent them out to preach the kingdom of God and to heal [the infirm] (ἰᾶσθαι [τοὺς ἀσθενεῖς])." It is significant that Luke has chosen present infinitives for θεραπεύω, and ἰάομαι, implying continuous treatment, and linked them with preaching (present infinitive) the kingdom of God. The inclusion of [τοὺς ἀσθενεῖς] after ἰᾶσθαι is disputed. One wonders then whether "to preach the kingdom of God" is to produce the natural and consummate effect of wholeness in those who hear and understand the message. However, Luke chooses the present participle of θεραπεύω to describe the disciples' behaviour in response to this commission (see comment on Lk 9.6). Certainly it would seem that here Luke means something akin to "nurse and nurture" by νόσους θεραπεύειν, rather than instantaneous healing.
Luke 9.6	θεραπεύοντες	Present participle active: nom., masc., pl.	The only occurrence of this form in the NT. Luke's choice of present participles (εὐαγγελιζόμενοι καὶ θεραπεύοντες) to describe the disciples' behaviour, in response to their commission, denotes a behavioural process. (Cf. Mark's use of θεραπεύω in the imperfect tense at Mk 6.13.) It is significant that θεραπεύω in a continuing tense is again linked with "telling the good news". Both sense forms belong together.
Luke 9.11	θεραπείας	Noun (θεραπεία): gen., sing., fem.	This noun occurs here in Luke's account of a general healing episode: after he (Jesus) welcomed them (the crowd) he began speaking to them of the kingdom of God, and those in need of treatment he began healing (καὶ ἀποδεξάμενος αὐτοὺς ἐλάλει αὐτοῖς περὶ τῆς βασιλείας τοῦ θεοῦ, καὶ τοὺς χρείαν ἔχοντας θεραπείας ἰᾶτο). This incident is immediately prior to Luke's account of the feeding of the 5,000. Again Luke uses θεραπεύω and ἰάομαι side-by-side; and is careful to use the imperfect tense of ἰάομαι to describe Jesus' behaviour; and again this behaviour is linked with Jesus' message.

Luke 10.9	θεραπεύετε	Present imperative active: 2 pl.	This form of θεραπεύω occurs twice in the NT; here, and at Mt 10.8. Both occur in Jesus' commission to his disciples, the twelve in *Matthew*, the seventy (two) here. It is significant that Luke chooses to use θεραπεύω here, and that the instructions Jesus gives to his disciples imply that the disciples are only to treat the infirm after they (the disciples) have been welcomed and fed, and that they are then to talk to the people about their experience of the nearness of the kingdom of God. There is implicit in these instructions the assumption that the disciples will remain in a village long enough for their behaviour to have a lasting effect on its inhabitants. They cannot do this without the hospitality of the villagers. Again θεραπεύω appears to imply the sense of "nurse and nurture", a time-consuming commitment, rather than an instantaneous action.
Luke 12.42	θεραπείας	Noun (θεραπεία): gen., sing., fem.	This word occurs in Luke's account of Jesus' reply to Peter, concerning the faithful and wise servant. It is the same form as at 9.11; but here means "household", rather than "treatment". However, the sense of nurturing is common to both uses of the word. Cf. Mt 24.45, where Matthew uses οἰκετείας in a parallel saying.
Luke 13.14	ἐθεράπευσεν	Aorist indicative active: 3 sing.	The second occasion of this form in *Luke*, (cf. 7.21), occurring in Luke's account of the healing of the crippled woman in the synagogue, on the sabbath. The verb θεραπεύω occurs twice in this story, both times in the thought and words of the ruler of the synagogue (cf. Mt 12.10; Mk 3.2; and Lk 6.6-11; and see below, 13.14), and describes the ruler's idea of Jesus' activity on the sabbath. He is outraged by this activity.
Luke 13.14	θεραπεύεσθε	Present imperative passive: 2 pl.	The only use of this form of θεραπεύω in the NT; used here by the ruler of the synagogue, commanding the people to be treated on any of the six days other than the sabbath. He understands healing treatment as work. Luke's description of this healing is precise: Jesus "... laid his hands on her, and immediately she was made straight...".

Luke 14.3	θεραπεῦσαι	Aorist infinitive: active.	The final use of θεραπεύω by Luke, and his only use of θεραπεύω in this form (cf. Mt 12.10; 17.16). It occurs in a question asked by Jesus of the lawyers and Pharisees as to whether it is lawful to heal/ treat on the sabbath, (cf. 13.14; 6.6-11; Mk 3.2; Mt 12.10), in Luke's account of the healing of the man with dropsy. Luke chooses to describe the actual healing with the aorist tense of ἰάομαι.
John 5.10	τεθεραπευμένῳ	Perfect participle passive: dat., masc., sing.	The only use by John of θεραπεύω. It occurs as a description of a man who had been healed by Jesus on the sabbath, when the Jews addressed him. John prefers to use ὑγιὴς to describe Jesus' language to the patient, and to describe the state of the man after Jesus had spoken to him.
Acts 4.14	τεθεραπευμένον	Perfect participle passive: acc., masc., sing.	Forms of the verb θεραπεύω are used five times in *Acts*. Here it is used to describe the perception of the man lame from birth, whom Peter had caused to walk (3.1-26,4.1-22), by the rulers, elders, and scribes; and the high priest and all who were of the high-priestly family. It is the only occurrence of this verb in this story. Luke chooses specific language to describe the healing itself: the man's feet and ankles were made strong (ἐστερεώθησαν), so that jumping up, he stood and began walking about (ἐξαλλόμενος ἔστη καὶ περιεπάτει), walking about and leaping and praising God (περιπατῶν καὶ ἁλλόμενος καὶ αἰνῶν τὸν θεόν). Peter later (3.16) describes the man as made strong (ἐστερέωσεν), and in perfect health (ὁλοκληρίαν); and when describing him to all the rulers, noted above, who saw him as τὸν τεθεραπευμένον (4.14), Peter describes him (4.9) as a man who has been saved (σέσωται). Later (4.22), Luke describes the incident as: τὸ σημεῖον τοῦτο τῆς ἰάσεως. Again, as in all four gospels, θεραπεύω is chosen to describe a person perceived as a patient by Jewish leaders. Elsewhere the healing language is precise (the miracle itself), or other words are chosen (σῴζω, ἰάομαι).

Acts 5.16	ἐθεραπεύοντο	Imperfect indicative passive: 3 pl.	In a general healing episode performed by Peter, and possibly other apostles (5.12-16). The context is important: it is sandwiched between the account of the deaths of Ananias and Sapphira (5.1-11), and the apostles' imprisonment by the Sadducees and their miraculous release by an angel (5.17-21, and ff.). It is appropriate that this general healing episode is introduced by a general statement concerning σημεῖα καὶ τέρατα πολλὰ. The preceding episode has injected an atmosphere of fear; this episode an element of magic (Peter's shadow, v.15). The patients were the infirm (τοὺς ἀσθενεῖς), and those afflicted with unclean spirits (ὀχλουμένους ὑπὸ πνευμάτων ἀκαθάρτων). They all began being healed (ἐθεραπεύοντο ἅπαντες). The context of this healing episode is highly unsatisfactory. The preceding is characterised by greed, violence and fear; the following by violence. The language is predictable: one expects the healing verb to be θεραπεύω in a crowd situation, and for patients who are infirm and troubled by unclean spirits. Given the context, it is not surprising that there were many troubled people about! Luke's use of the passive form is important: it implies the intervention of God. The whole chapter appears highly hellenised.
Acts 8.7	ἐθεραπεύθησαν	Aorist indicative passive: 3 pl.	In a general healing episode with Philip the central character, in Samaria. The people there "gave heed to what was said by Philip, when they heard him (ἐν τῷ ἀκούειν) and saw the signs (τὰ σημεῖα) which he did". The patients were those possessed by unclean spirits, the paralysed, and the lame. This episode occurs between the death of Stephen, and conversion of Simon. The use of the passive verb implies the intervention of God.
Acts 17.25	θεραπεύεται	Present indicative passive: 3 sing.	In a speech given by Paul, at Athens, about the nature of God: "nor is he cared for (θεραπεύεται) by human hands, as though he needed anything, since he himself gives life and breath and everything to all." Here the notion implied in θεραπεύω is definitely one of "nurturing", embracing the continuous ideas of serving, looking after, diagnosing and attending to needs.

Acts 28.9	ἐθεραπεύοντο	Imperfect indicative passive: 3 pl.	In a general healing episode with Paul as the central character, on the island of Malta. It follows immediately after a specific healing episode (28.7-8), where Paul healed (ἰάσατο) the father of Publius, who had been sick with fever and dysentery (πυρετοῖς καὶ δυσεντερίῳ). Paul healed him by prayer and putting his hands on him. Publius here fulfils the hospitality requirements laid down by Jesus as a prerequisite for healing in Matthew 10.8-14, and Luke 9.4-5. Thus the rest of the people who were infirm (ἔχοντες ἀσθενείας) came and began being healed (ἐθεραπεύοντο). Luke is careful to differentiate between θεραπεύω and ἰάομαι, ἰάομαι describing Paul's action (see App. 8:3, Acts 28.8), and θεραπεύω the intervention of God (passive verb) in a crowd scene.
Hebrews 3.5	θεράπων	Noun: nom., sing., masc.	The only occurrence of this word in the NT. It is used to describe Moses' relationship with God, as faithful servant (θεράπων), in contrast to Jesus' relationship with God as son (υἱὸς). As such θεράπων faithfully reflects its Homeric meaning and usage, when used to describe Patroklos' relationship to Achilleus, by Achilleus (*Iliad* 16.244), and by Patroklos (*Iliad* 23.89-90). Thus the notions of love and loyalty, nurture and service, are implicit in both Homeric and NT usage. (It is in the care of his θεράπων that Patroklos leaves Eurypylos, after attending to his wounds [*Iliad* 15.401-2].)
Revelation 13.3	ἐθεραπεύθη	Aorist indicative passive: 3 sing.	In a description of John's vision of the first beast. It had seemed to have a mortal wound on one of its heads, but the mortal woundhad been healed/treated (ἐθεραπεύθη).
Revelation 13.12	ἐθεραπεύθη	Aorist indicative passive: 3 sing.	In a second description of the first beast.
Revelation 22.2	θεραπείαν	Noun (θεραπεία): acc., sing., fem.	The noun occurs in a description of the tree of life, where the leaves of the tree are described as being for the treatment of the nations (καὶ τὰ φύλλα τοῦ ξύλου εἰς θεραπείαν τῶν ἐθνῶν).

θεραπεύω in verbal form occurs 43 times in the New Testament: in *Matthew* 16 times, in 7 forms; in *Mark* 5 times, in 3 forms; in *Luke* 14 times, in 13 forms; in *John* once; in *Acts* 5 times, in 5 forms; and in *Revelation* twice, in the same form. The noun θεραπεία occurs three times: twice in *Luke*; and once in *Revelation*. The noun form θεράπων occurs once only, in *Hebrews*. From this it is clear that Luke is the most comfortable of the synoptists with the Greek language, able to manipulate it at will.

When using θεραπεύω the synoptists prefer its aorist active, third person singular form: Matthew choosing this form eight times, Mark three times, and Luke twice. In *Matthew* this usage becomes a formula to describe Jesus' behaviour, and assumes the nature of an epithet in crowd situations.

Appendix 7 : 9

Incidence of θεραπεύω in the New Testament according to tense, voice and mood

Tense	Voice and Mood	Form	Reference	Comment
Present	Active participle	θεραπεύων	Matt 4.23; 9.35	a doublet, describing Jesus' behaviour while travelling
	Active participle	θεραπεύοντες	Luke 9.6	describing the healing activity of the disciples
	Active indicative	θεραπεύει	Luke 6.7	Pharisees' perception of Jesus' behaviour on sabbath
	Active imperative	θεραπεύετε	Matt 10.8; Luke 10.9	Jesus' behavioural instructions to the disciples
	Active infinitive	θεραπεύειν	Matt 10.1; Luke 9.1	description of the type of authority Jesus gave to the disciples
	Passive infinitive	θεραπεύεσθαι	Luke 5.15	description of the desire of the crowd which gathered after Jesus cleansed a leper (5.12-14). As is usual, this verb follows ἀκούειν; the maladies are τῶν ἀσθενειῶν.
	Passive imperative	θεραπεύεσθε	Luke 13.14	A directive issued by the ruler of the synagogue. The use of the passive voice is important for no agent is specified (although perhaps "God" is implied), and there is the implication that θεραπεύεσθε = ἐργάζεσθαι.
	Passive indicative	θεραπεύεται	Acts 17.25	The one instance of the use of the passive voice where the agent is specified, used here to describe the notion of service given to God by humans. In a speech given by Paul at Athens.
Imperfect	Active indicative	ἐθεράπευον	Mark 6.13	describing the healing activity of the disciples
	Active indicative	ἐθεράπευεν	Luke 4.40	describing the healing activity of Jesus in a crowd situation
	Passive indicative	ἐθεραπεύοντο	Luke 6.18; Acts 5.16; Acts 28.9	3rd person plural passive imperfect peculiar to Luke. No agent specified, although one implied in each instance. Luke 6.18: in a crowd situation where Jesus is present; a prelude to Luke's Beatitudes. Acts 5.16: a crowd situation where Peter is present (note the reference to Peter's shadow [5.15]); not in a 'we' passage. Acts 28.9: a crowd situation where Paul is present, immediately ff. Paul's healing of Publius' father, at Malta; in a 'we' passage.

Future	Active indicative	θεραπεύσω	Matt 8.7	Jesus' reply to the centurion's request. This supports the argument that Jesus was a Pharisee, (see Wilcox [1982] 131-195), as Jewish leaders, particularly Pharisees, think of healing activity in terms of θεραπεύω.
	Active indicative	θεραπεύσει	Mark 3.2	A description of the thought of the Pharisees, where they wonder whether Jesus will perform this activity on the sabbath.
Aorist	Active indicative	ἐθεράπευσεν	Matt 4.24, 8.16, 12.15, 12.22, 14.14, 15.30, 19.2, 21.14; Mark 1.34, 3.10, 6.5; Luke 7.21, 13.14	Is this a gnomic aorist? (See Wilcox, [1984] 1017.) In *Matthew*, and *Mark*, all instances describe Jesus' behaviour in a crowd situation. In *Luke*, the first reference is a description of Jesus' activity in a crowd situation, following his reply to John the Baptist's messengers; the second a description of the ruler's perception of Jesus' behaviour, in the synagogue, on the sabbath.
	Active infinitive	θεραπεῦσαι	Matt 12.10, 17.16; Luke 14.3	In Mt 12.10 and Lk 14.3, the infinitives appear in the form of a question concerning the legality of healing on the sabbath. In *Matthew* the question is framed by the Pharisees, in *Luke* the question is asked of the lawyers and Pharisees by Jesus himself. Thus both Jesus and the Pharisees (again) think of healing activity in terms of θεραπεύω. It is a controversial activity. See Wilcox,(1982) 131-195, but especially 182: "The purpose of this 'watching' or 'testing' would thus have been to check his fidelity and trustworthiness in matters of *halakhah* ...". Wilcox concludes that Jesus belonged to the Pharisaic movement and that (185): "the tension between him and the Pharisees thus probably arises out of his very nearness to them, its intensity reflecting the fact that he was viewed as representing one strand - a non-conforming one - within it." At Mt 17.16 the infinitive is used by the father of the epileptic boy when he explains that the disciples were unable to heal his son.

Aorist	Active imperative	θεράπευσον	Luke 4.23	Used by Jesus, in reference to himself, at Nazareth.
	Passive indicative	ἐθεραπεύθη	Matt 17.18; Rev 13.3,13.12	The only use by Matthew of the passive voice, describing the healing of the epileptic boy. In *Revelation*, both usages describe the beast's wound.
	Passive indicative	ἐθεραπεύθησαν	Acts 8.7	In a general healing episode, main character Philip, more precise ailments than usual. Not in a 'we' passage.
	Passive infinitive	θεραπευθῆναι	Luke 8.43	In the story of the haemorrhaging woman (cf. Mt 9.18-26; Mk 5.21-43). Luke uses it to describe the inability of anyone to heal her; however the word he uses to describe this healing is ἰάθη.
Perfect	Passive participle	τεθεραπευμένῳ	John 5.10	The only use by John of θεραπεύω, as a description of a man who had been healed by Jesus on the sabbath, when the Jews addressed him.
	Passive participle	τεθεραπευμένον	Acts 4.14	A description of the perception of the man lame from birth whom Peter had caused to walk (3.1-26,4.1-22), by the Jewish hierarchy.
Pluperfect	Passive indicative	ἦσαν τεθεραπευμέναι	Luke 8.2	Part of a general healing episode with specific information. Luke cites three women as being among those healed, and gives their names, illnesses (πνευμάτων πονηρῶν καὶ ἀσθενειῶν), and the name and occupation of the husband of one of them. He also adds that they contributed to the support of Jesus and his disciples out of their means, and travelled with them. Thus their "cure" was discipleship: listening, understanding, and acting on Jesus' message.

Incidence of θεραπεία and θεράπων in the New Testament

Noun (θεραπεία)	gen., sing., fem.	θεραπείας	Luke 9.11, 12.42	9.11: in an account of a general healing episode, immediately prior to Luke's account of the feeding of the 5,000. After Jesus welcomed them (the crowd) he began speaking to them of the kingdom of God, and those in need of treatment he began healing (καὶ τοὺς χρείαν ἔχοντας θεραπείας ἰᾶτο). 12.42: in Luke's account of Jesus' reply to Peter, concerning the wise and faithful servant, meaning "household" rather than "treatment". However, the sense of nurturing is common to both uses of the word. (Cf. Mt 24.25, where Matthew uses οἰκετείας in a parallel saying.)
	acc., sing., fem.	θεραπείαν	Revelation 22.2	In a description of the tree of life, where the leaves of the tree are described as being for the treatment of the nations.
Noun (θεράπων)	nom., sing., masc.	θεράπων	Hebrews 3.5	The only occurrence of this word in the NT. It is used to describe Moses' relationship with God, as faithful servant (θεράπων), in contrast to Jesus' relationship with God as son (υἱὸς). So θεράπων faithfully reflects its Homeric meaning and usage, when used to describe Patroklos' relationship to Achilleus, by Achilleus (*Iliad* 16.244), and by Patroklos (*Iliad* 23.89-90). Thus the notions of love and loyalty, nurture and service, are implicit in both Homeric and NT usage.

Appendix 7 : 10

New Testament healing words : διασῴζω σῴζω

(as they appear in healing stories and the synoptic crucifixion accounts)

Reference	Form	Part of speech	Comment
Matthew 8.25	The aorist imperative active (2 sing.) σῶσον occurs here, out of the mouths of the disciples, in Matthew's account of Jesus' calming of the storm at sea (8.23-27). Neither Mark (4.35-41) nor Luke (8.22-25) use σῴζω in this story. Matthew also puts this form into Peter's mouth (14.30), addressing Jesus, when he tries to walk on the water. In both these episodes σῴζω means to *rescue and preserve*, a meaning of σῴζω explicit in Homer, Aeschylus, Sophocles and Euripides (see Part One, Section One: chapters 1 and 3).		
Matthew 9.21	σωθήσομαι	Future indicative passive: 1 sing.	In the thoughts of the haemorrhaging woman, and linked with ἅπτομαι: Ἐὰν μόνον ἅψωμαι τοῦ ἱματίου αὐτοῦ σωθήσομαι.
Matthew 9.22	σέσωκεν	Perfect indicative active: 3 sing.	Out of the mouth of Jesus, to the haemorrhaging woman: ἡ πίστις σου σέσωκέν σε.
Matthew 9.22	ἐσώθη	Aorist indicative passive: 3 sing.	Matthew's summing up of this episode: καὶ ἐσώθη ἡ γυνὴ ἀπὸ τῆς ὥρας ἐκείνης.
Matthew 14.30	The aorist imperative active (2 sing.) σῶσόν occurs here, out of the mouth of Peter, addressing Jesus, when he tries to walk on the water. See above: 8.25. In classical Greek, σῴζω is often used in a nautical context (see Part One, Section One: chapters 1 and 3). Cf. also Acts 27.43 and 44, where Luke uses διασῴζω in a nautical context.		
Matthew 14.36	διεσώθησαν	Aorist indicative passive: 3 pl.	In a general healing episode immediately following the story of Jesus and Peter walking on the water (14. 25-32) and the disciples' declaration that Jesus was truly the son of God (14.33), a story that contained the aorist imperative of σῴζω, in Peter's plea for help (14.30, and cf. 8.25). Here, the men of the region brought those feeling ill (πάντας τοὺς κακῶς ἔχοντας) to Jesus. Again σῴζω is linked with ἅπτομαι. "They began asking him if they might only touch the hem of his cloak (καὶ παρεκάλουν αὐτὸν ἵνα μόνον ἅψωνται τοῦ κρασπέδου τοῦ ἱματίου αὐτοῦ·), and as many as touched (it) were healed (καὶ ὅσοι ἥψαντο διεσώθησαν)." There is no mention of teaching.

Matthew 15.21-28	In Matthew's account of the healing of the Canaanite woman's daughter, neither σῴζω nor θεραπεύω appear, nor does σῴζω appear in Matthew's account of the healing of the centurion's servant (8.5-13). Instead, ἰάομαι appears in both stories (see Part One, Section Two: chapter 8). The absence of σῴζω may be significant. Here the woman beseeches Jesus' help: Κύριε, βοήθει μοι (15.25), and, although Jesus comments on her faith (15.28), and the centurion's faith (8.10), σῴζω appears in neither story. (Cf. Jesus' words to the haemorrhaging woman (9.22). As we shall see, forms of πίστις like to accompany forms of σῴζω in healing (and other) stories, which makes Jesus' final comment here (γενηθήτω σοι ὡς θέλεις (15.28)), and to the centurion (ὡς ἐπίστευσας γενηθήτω σοι (8.13)), quite striking. It is another example of Matthew using different vocabulary for gentile healings performed at a distance, as a result of a gentile 'parental' request.		
† Matthew 27.40	Here, in Matthew's account of the crucifixion, the aorist imperative active: 2 sing. σῶσον comes out of the mouths of passers-by addressing Jesus, σῶσον σεαυτόν, as he hangs on the cross. (Cf. Mk 15.30)		
† Matthew 27.42	Also in the crucifixion scene, the aorist indicative active: 3 sing. ἔσωσεν, and the aorist infinitive active σῶσαι, come out of the mocking mouths of the chief priests, scribes, and elders, in the saying, "He saved others; he cannot save himself! ("Ἄλλους ἔσωσεν, ἑαυτὸν οὐ δύναται σῶσαι·)". In this context Matthew must be using σῴζω to mean to *rescue, save from death.*		
† Matthew 27.49	Also in the crucifixion scene, the future active participle, nom., sing., masc., σώσων, comes out of the mouths of other bystanders, who wonder whether Elijah will come to save Jesus. (Cf. Mk 15.36: Matthew has substituted σώσων for Mark's καθελεῖν.)		
Mark 3.4	σῶσαι	Aorist infinitive active	Out of Jesus' mouth in Mark's account of the sabbath healing of the man with the withered hand. Here Jesus asks the Pharisees whether it is lawful on the sabbath to do good or to do harm (ἀγαθὸν ποιῆσαι ἢ κακοποιῆσαι), to save life or to kill (ψυχὴν σῶσαι ἢ ἀποκτεῖναι). Cf. Mt 12.9-14 , Lk 6.6-11.
Mark 5.23	σωθῇ	Aorist subjunctive passive: 3 sing.	Out of Jairus' mouth to Jesus, requesting that Jesus come and lay hands on his daughter (ἵνα ἐλθὼν ἐπιθῇς τὰς χεῖρας αὐτῇ), in order that she might be healed and might live (ἵνα σωθῇ καὶ ζήσῃ).
Mark 5.28	σωθήσομαι	Future indicative passive: 1 sing.	Out of the mouth of the haemorrhaging woman. As in *Matthew* σῴζω is linked with ἅπτομαι (cf. Mt 9.21): Ἐὰν ἅψωμαι κἂν τῶν ἱματίων αὐτοῦ σωθήσομαι.
Mark 5.34	σέσωκέν	Perfect indicative active: 3 sing.	As in *Matthew* (9.22), out of the mouth of Jesus to the haemorrhaging woman: ἡ πίστις σου σέσωκέν σε.

Mark 6.56	ἐσῴζοντο	Imperfect indicative passive: 3 pl.	In an account of general healing episodes in the region of Gennesaret, immediately following Mark's account of the feeding of the 5,000 (6.30-44), and Jesus' walking on the water (6.45-52). Cf. Matthew's alterations to this story (14.22-33), and the role he assigns to Peter. The disciples in Mark's account are "astounded, for they did not understand about the loaves, but their hearts were hardened" (Mk. 6.51-2). Mark's use of the imperfect tense is deliberate and precise: the people began to bring sick people (τοὺς κακῶς ἔχοντας ... τοὺς ἀσθενοῦντας) to any place they heard he was (villages, cities, or country), and they asked him whether they might touch the hem of his cloak (ἵνα κἂν τοῦ κρασπέδου τοῦ ἱματίου αὐτοῦ ἅψωνται). And as many as touched him *on each occasion* (my italics) were healed (καὶ ὅσοι ἂν ἥψαντο αὐτοῦ ἐσῴζοντο).
Mark 10.52	σέσωκέν	Perfect indicative active: 3 sing.	Out of Jesus' mouth to blind Bartimaeus: ἡ πίστις σου σέσωκέν σε. The sequel: καὶ εὐθὺς ἀνέβλεψεν, καὶ ἠκολούθει αὐτῷ ἐν τῇ ὁδῷ : discipleship?
† Mark 15.30	Here, in Mark's account of the crucifixion, the aorist imperative active: 2 sing. σῶσον comes out of the mouths of passers-by addressing Jesus, σῶσον σεαυτόν, as he hangs on the cross.		
† Mark 15.31	Also in Mark's crucifixion account, the forms of the aorist indicative active: 3 sing. ἔσωσεν, and the aorist infinitive active σῶσαι, come out of the mouths of the chief priests and scribes who mock Jesus, saying: "He saved others; he cannot save himself! ("Ἄλλους ἔσωσεν, ἑαυτὸν οὐ δύναται σῶσαι·)". (Cf. Mt 27.42, where 'elders' are introduced to the scene.)		
Mark 16.16	⟦ σωθήσεται ⟧	Future indicative passive: 3 sing.	⟦ In the longer ending to Mark's gospel: "And he said to them, 'Go into all the world and preach the gospel to the whole creation. He who believes and has been baptised will be saved (ὁ πιστεύας καὶ βαπτισθεὶς σωθήσεται); but he who does not believe will be condemned. And these signs (σημεῖα) will accompany those who believe: in my name they will cast out demons (ἐν τῷ ὀνόματί μου δαιμόνια ἐκβαλοῦσιν); they will speak in new tongues; they will pick up serpents in their hands, and if they drink any deadly thing, it will not hurt them; they will lay their hands on the weak and they will feel well (ἐπὶ ἀρρώστους χεῖρας ἐπιθήσουσιν καὶ καλῶς ἕξουσιν)'" (16.15-18). σῴζω is only included here because it is linked to ὁ πιστεύας, as in the healing stories. ⟧

Luke 6.9	σῶσαι	Aorist infinitive active	Out of Jesus' mouth, in Luke's account of the sabbath healing of the man with the withered hand (6.6-11). Jesus is addressing the scribes and the Pharisees. He had gone up to the synagogue to teach (διδάσκειν). Here he asks "if it is lawful on the sabbath to do good or to do evil (εἰ ἔξεστιν τῷ σαββάτῳ ἀγαθοποιῆσαι ἢ κακοποιῆσαι), to save or to destroy life (ψυχὴν σῶσαι ἢ ἀπολέσαι)?" As in *Matthew*, and *Mark*, the Pharisees think of healing in terms of θεραπεύω.
Luke 7.3	διασώσῃ	Aorist subjunctive active: 3 sing.	In the reported speech of Jewish elders, asking Jesus to come and heal the servant (ἐρωτῶν αὐτὸν ὅπως ἐλθὼν διασώσῃ τὸν δοῦλον), in Luke's account of the healing of the centurion's servant (7.1-10). Matthew (8.5-13) does not use διασῴζω in his story, while John (4.47) chooses ἰάσηται. Later (Lk 7.9) Jesus comments on the centurion's faith (πίστιν), and the slave is found (7.10) to be healthy (ὑγιαίνοντα).
Luke 8.36	ἐσώθη	Aorist indicative passive: 3 sing.	In Luke's story of the healing of the Gerasene demoniac (8.26-39). Here the bystanders explain "how he who had been possessed with demons was healed (πῶς ἐσώθη ὁ δαιμονισθείς)". The result in the life of this man is discipleship: they found him "sitting at the feet of Jesus ... [He] ... begged that he might be with him; but he sent him away, saying, 'Return to your home, and declare how much God has done for you.' And he went away, proclaiming (κηρύσσων) throughout the whole city how much Jesus had done for him." (8.35, 38-39)
Luke 8.48	σέσωκέν	Perfect indicative active: 3 sing.	Out of the mouth of Jesus, in Luke's story of the haemorrhaging woman. As in *Mark*, and *Matthew*, Jesus says: ἡ πίστις σου σέσωκέν σε.
Luke 8.50	σωθήσεται	Future indicative passive: 3 sing.	Out of the mouth of Jesus to Jairus and his companion: "Don't be afraid! Only believe, and she will be healed (Μὴ φοβοῦ, μόνον πίστευσον, καὶ σωθήσεται)!"
Luke 17.19	σέσωκέν	Perfect indicative active: 3 sing.	Out of the mouth of Jesus to the leper (one of ten) who returned to thank Jesus, praising God. As to the haemorrhaging woman (8.48), and to the blind beggar (18.42), Jesus says: ἡ πίστις σου σέσωκέν σε.
Luke 18.42	σέσωκέν	Perfect indicative active: 3 sing.	Out of the mouth of Jesus to the blind beggar near Jericho: ἡ πίστις σου σέσωκέν σε. The result of the healing in this man's life was discipleship.

† Luke 23.35	In Luke's account of the crucifixion, the aorist indicative active: 3 sing. ἔσωσεν, and the aorist imperative active: 3 sing. σωσάτω, occur in a saying of the 'rulers' (cf. Mk 15.31; Mt 27.42), "He saved others; let him save himself, if he is the Christ of God, his Chosen One ("Ἄλλους ἔσωσεν, σωσάτω ἑαυτόν, εἰ οὗτός ἐστιν ὁ Χριστὸς τοῦ θεοῦ ὁ ἐκλεκτός)!"		
† Luke 23.37	Also in Luke's crucifixion account, the aorist imperative active: 2 sing. σῶσον, out of the mouths of the soldiers, who, mockingly, tell Jesus to σῶσον σεαυτόν! (Cf. Mk. 15.30; Mt. 27.40)		
† Luke 23.39	Also in Luke's crucifixion account, the aorist imperative active: 2 sing. σῶσον, out of the mouth of one of the criminals: "Save yourself and us (σῶσον σεαυτὸν καὶ ἡμᾶς)!"		
John 11.12	σωθήσεται	Future indicative passive: 3 sing.	Out of the mouths of the disciples to Jesus, after Jesus had told them that Lazarus was sleeping: εἰ κεκοίμηται σωθήσεται. The same form of σῴζω is used by Jesus, in Luke's account of the healing of Jairus' daughter (8.50).
Acts 4.9	σέσωται	Perfect indicative passive: 3 sing.	Out of Peter's mouth, describing the healed man to the Council, in the Lukan account of the healing of the lame man at the temple gate (3.1-4.31). Peter explains (4.10) that the man was healed in the name of Jesus Christ, that there isn't any salvation (ἡ σωτηρία) in anyone else (4.12), for there is no other name by which we must be saved (ᾧ δεῖ σωθῆναι ἡμᾶς (4.12)), and that (3.16) it was "his (Jesus') name, by faith in his name, [that] made this man strong ... and gave him perfect health (καὶ ἐπὶ τῇ πίστει τοῦ ὀνόματος αὐτοῦ τοῦτον ... ἐστερέωσεν... καὶ ἡ πίστις ... ἔδωκεν αὐτῷ τὴν ὁλοκληρίαν)". Luke includes almost the whole range of healing words in this story: σῴζω, θεραπεύω, ὑγιής, ἴασις, ὁλοκληρία, (δύναμις, σημεῖον). Peter's touch is described by πιάζω (3.7).
Acts 4.12	ἡ σωτηρία	Noun: nom., sing., fem.	Out of Peter's mouth, in the speech described above at Acts 4.9.
Acts 4.12	σωθῆναι	Aorist infinitive: passive	Out of Peter's mouth, in the speech described above at Acts 4.9.
Acts 14.9	σωθῆναι	Aorist infinitive: passive	In the Lukan account of Paul's healing of the man lame from birth. Paul saw that "he had faith to be made well (καὶ ἰδὼν ὅτι ἔχει πίστιν τοῦ σωθῆναι)." Thus the exploits of Peter and Paul seem to be balanced, in deed and in word. (However it is important to note that ἰάομαι is only used of Paul [Acts 28.8])

Acts 16.17	ὁδὸν σωτηρίας	Noun: gen., sing., fem.	Out of the mouth of the slave girl who had a spirit of divination, in the story of her healing. She shouted that Paul and his companions were proclaiming the way of salvation (καταγγέλλουσιν ὑμῖν ὁδὸν σωτηρίας).
Acts 16.30	σωθῶ	Aorist subjunctive passive: 1 sing.	As a result of the above healing, Paul and Silas were imprisoned. There the gaoler asks them "What must I do to be saved (τί με δεῖ ποιεῖν ἵνα σωθῶ;)?"
Acts 16.31	σωθήσῃ	Future indicative passive: 2 sing.	Paul's and Silas' answer to the gaoler's question: "Believe in the Lord Jesus, and you will be saved, you and your household (Πίστευσον ..., καὶ σωθήσῃ σὺ καὶ ὁ οἶκός σου)!" The result was that he believed (πεπιστευκὼς τῷ θεῷ (16.34)), and he and his family were baptised. Again πίστις is linked with σῴζω.
Acts 28.28	τοῦτο τὸ σωτήριον τοῦ θεοῦ	At the conclusion of *Acts*, Paul quotes the Septuagint (Isaiah 6.9-10; see App. 6:1, **62**) as the final justification for his mission to the gentiles. It was to bring spiritual understanding and perception, and spiritual healing; i.e. "this salvation of God (τοῦτο τὸ σωτήριον τοῦ θεοῦ)".	
James 5.15	σώσει	Future indicative active: 3 sing.	In a passage giving advice as to procedure in the case of suffering (prayer), happiness (praise), and weakness (prayer by church elders and anointing with oil in the name of the Lord). For, says James, "the prayer of faith will save the man laid low, and the Lord will raise him up; and if he has committed sins he will be forgiven (καὶ ἡ εὐχὴ τῆς πίστεως σώσει τὸν κάμνοντα, καὶ ἐγερεῖ αὐτὸν ὁ κύριος κἂν ἁμαρτίας ᾖ πεποιηκώς, ἀφεθήσεται αὐτῷ)." Again we see the close proximity of πίστις and σῴζω, and the emphasis on spiritual healing as a prerequisite for physical healing.
Matthew uses forms of σῴζω four times (9.21, 22, 22; 14.36) in two healing stories. Both incidents record the healing of those who touched Jesus' clothes, in faith. Jesus claims that it was the faith of the haemorrhaging woman which saved her: "ἡ πίστις σου σέσωκέν σε" (9.22). The faith of those at Gennesaret is also noted: "καὶ παρεκάλουν αὐτὸν ἵνα μόνον ἅψωνται τοῦ κρασπέδου τοῦ ἱματίου αὐτοῦ· καὶ ὅσοι ἥψαντο διεσώθησαν" (14.36). The thoughts of the haemorrhaging woman: "ἔλεγεν γὰρ ἐν ἑαυτῇ, Ἐὰν μόνον ἅψωμαι τοῦ ἱματίου αὐτοῦ σωθήσομαι" (9.21), echo the description of the crowd, in content and language. And like the man's demonic epileptic son, the centurion's "boy", and the Canaanite woman's daughter, the haemorrhaging woman was healed from the hour that Jesus spoke to her: "καὶ ἐσώθη ἡ γυνὴ ἀπὸ τῆς ὥρας ἐκείνης" (9.22). σῴζω then, in *Matthew*, records instantaneous healing of those who touched Jesus' clothes in faith. The verb chosen to describe that touch on each occasion is ἅπτομαι. In *Matthew* it is only Jesus who uses σῴζω in the active voice.			

Mark uses σῴζω on more occasions than Matthew. However, as in *Matthew* σῴζω is linked with ἅπτομαι in the story of the haemorrhaging woman, in (almost) identical language: "Ἐὰν ἅψωμαι κἂν τῶν ἱματίων αὐτοῦ σωθήσομαι" (5.28). Jesus' saying is identical: "ἡ πίστις σου σέσωκέν σε" (5.34). Like Matthew, Mark also uses σῴζω with ἅπτομαι to report the healing of crowds of people at Gennesaret (6.56), but he chooses the imperfect, rather than the aorist, to describe these events, implying a series of episodes over a period of time. Mark uses σῴζω on two other occasions, occasions where Matthew chooses to omit σῴζω. The first is in Mark's story of the sabbath healing of the man with the withered hand (3.4), where Jesus asks the Pharisees whether it is lawful on the sabbath to save life (ψυχὴν σῶσαι), or to kill, wording that it is retained by Luke (6.9). Mark also has Jesus repeat the saying, "ἡ πίστις σου σέσωκέν σε" to Bartimaeus (10.52), a saying preserved by Luke (18.42). In *Mark*, as in *Matthew*, it is only Jesus who uses σῴζω in the active voice.

Luke chooses to use σῴζω more than Mark, in more healing stories. As in *Mark*, Luke retains σῶσαι in the story of the sabbath healing of the man with the withered hand (6.9). Luke also retains Jesus' saying, "ἡ πίστις σου σέσωκέν σε", in the stories of the haemorrhaging woman (8.48), and the healing of the blind beggar near Jericho (18.42). However Luke also puts this saying into the mouth of Jesus, when he addresses the Samaritan leper, who returned to thank him for his health (17.19). Jewish elders also use διασῴζω, when they request Jesus' help on behalf of the centurion (7.3), and the bystanders explain how the Gerasene demoniac was healed in terms of σῴζω (8.36). Finally, Luke puts it into the mouth of Jesus, when he tells Jairus not to fear, only believe, and his daughter will be saved (σωθήσεται (8.50)). This same form of σῴζω comes out of the mouths of the disciples in John's only use of this word in a healing story (11.12), the raising of Lazarus. It is interesting that the same form is used by both Luke and John, in stories concerning "sleep" and "death".

Other Lukan uses of σῴζω in healing stories occur in three stories in *Acts*. The first three forms (4.9, 12, 12) come out of Peter's mouth in the Lukan account of the healing of the lame man. It is a story which emphasises the man's faith (3.16). The second story is the Lukan account of Paul's healing of the man lame from birth (14.9). Again faith is linked with σῴζω. Thus the exploits of Peter and Paul are balanced, in deed, and in word. The third story concerns the healing of the slave girl who had a spirit of divination, and its result (16.17, 30, 31).

The only other New Testament use of σῴζω in a (physical?) healing context, is at James 5.15, where James says that the prayer of faith will save the man laid low (ἡ εὐχὴ τῆς πίστεως σώσει τὸν κάμνοντα).

Thus, in New Testament healing stories, the verb σῴζω likes to appear in close proximity to a form of πίστις, and ἅπτομαι. All uses of σῴζω in direct speech, in the active voice in the healing stories in the gospels, come out of the mouth of Jesus.

Appendix 7 : 11

Incidence of διασῴζω σῴζω in New Testament healing stories according to tense, voice and mood

Tense	Voice and Mood	Form	Reference	Comment
Aorist	Active infinitive	σῶσαι	Mark 3.4 = Luke 6.9	Out of Jesus' mouth in the parallel accounts of the sabbath healing of the man with the withered hand. In *Mark* Jesus asks the Pharisees whether it is lawful on the sabbath to do good or to do harm (ἀγαθὸν ποιῆσαι ἢ κακοποιῆσαι), to save life or to kill (ψυχὴν σῶσαι ἢ ἀποκτεῖναι). In *Luke* Jesus asks the Pharisees and the scribes whether it is lawful on the sabbath ἀγαθοποιῆσαι ἢ κακοποιῆσαι, ψυχὴν σῶσαι ἢ ἀπολέσαι; (Cf. Mt 12.9-14) In all three synoptic gospels the Pharisees think of healing in terms of θεραπεύω. The use of σῴζω here is significant. Jesus equates this healing with saving life. Pharisaic law did allow the sabbath to be broken where there was a "threat to life" (see Wilcox [1982] 176).
	Active subjunctive	διασώσῃ	Luke 7.3	In the reported speech of Jewish elders, who ask Jesus to come and heal the centurion's servant. Matthew (8.5-13) does not use διασῴζω; John (4.47) chooses ἰάσηται. Luke makes Jesus comment on the centurion's faith (πίστιν 7.9), and then (7.10) chooses ὑγιαίνοντα to describe the servant's condition when the centurion returns.

Perfect	Active indicative	σέσωκέν	(i) Matt 9.22 = Mark 5.34 = Luke 8.48; (ii) Mark 10.52 = Luke 18.42, (cf. Matt 20.29-34); (iii) Luke 17.19	On all occasions, out of the mouth of Jesus, in the saying, "ἡ πίστις σου σέσωκέν σε" to people he has healed: (i) the haemorrhaging woman. (All three synoptist link σῴζω and ἅπτομαι in this story.) (ii) blind Bartimaeus (Mark), the blind beggar near Jericho (Luke). Both synoptists state discipleship as the result of this healing. However, cf. Matthew (<u>two</u> blind men, who also includes discipleship as the result) who omits Jesus' saying, and therefore σῴζω, but includes ἅπτομαι to describe Jesus' touch. (Cf. (i), where ἅπτομαι describes the woman's touch.) (iii) the Samaritan leper, one of ten lepers healed, who returned to thank Jesus, praising God, in a story peculiar to Luke. (Luke does not use ἅπτομαι.)
Future	Active indicative	σώσει	James 5.15	In a passage giving advice as to procedure in the case of suffering: prayer. For, says James, "the prayer of faith will save the man laid low (ἡ εὐχὴ τῆς πίστεως σώσει τὸν κάμνοντα)". Again σῴζω is linked with πίστις.
Imperfect	Passive indicative	ἐσῴζοντο	Mark 6.56	In an account of general healing episodes in the region of Gennesaret. The people there began bringing sick people (τοὺς κακῶς ἔχοντας ... τοὺς ἀσθενοῦντας) to any place where they heard Jesus was (villages, cities, or country), and they asked him whether they might touch the hem of his cloak (ἵνα κἂν τοῦ κρασπέδου τοῦ ἱματίου αὐτοῦ ἅψωνται). And as many as touched him *on each occasion* (my italics) were healed (καὶ ὅσοι ἂν ἥψαντο αὐτοῦ ἐσῴζοντο). Mark's choice of the imperfect tense, implying continuous action, is supported by his description of Jesus' movements. Again σῴζω is linked with ἅπτομαι. (Cf. Mt 14.36) As in *Matthew*, there is no mention of teaching, although this episode follows immediately after Mark's comment that the disciples "did not understand about the loaves (6.52)".

Aorist	Passive infinitive	σωθῆναι	Acts 4.12; Acts 14.9	In the Lukan accounts of Peter's and Paul's healing of separate lame men. 4.12: out of Peter's mouth in his speech to the council. 14.9: Paul saw that the man "had faith to be made well (ὅτι ἔχει πίστιν τοῦ σωθῆναι)."
	Passive indicative	ἐσώθη	Matt 9.22; Luke 8.36	Matthew uses this form to conclude his account of the healing of the haemorrhaging woman: καὶ ἐσώθη ἡ γυνὴ ἀπὸ τῆς ὥρας ἐκείνης. Luke puts this form into the mouths of bystanders who explain how the Gerasene demoniac was healed: πῶς ἐσώθη ὁ δαιμονισθείς. The result in the life of this man (as in the lives of the blind beggars, and the Samaritan leper) was discipleship.
	Passive indicative	διεσώθησαν	Matt 14.36	In a general healing episode at Gennesaret (cf. Mark 6. 56). Here the men of the region brought all those feeling ill (πάντας τοὺς κακῶς ἔχοντας) to Jesus. Again σῴζω is linked with ἅπτομαι. "They began asking him if they might only touch the hem of his cloak (καὶ παρεκάλουν αὐτὸν ἵνα μόνον ἅψωνται τοῦ κρασπέδου τοῦ ἱματίου αὐτοῦ), and as many as touched (it) were healed (καὶ ὅσοι ἥψαντο διεσώθησαν)." There is no mention of teaching.
	Passive subjunctive	σωθῶ	Acts 16.30	As a result of the healing of the slave girl, the imprisonment of Paul and Silas, and the earthquake, the gaoler asks "What must I do to be saved? (τί με δεῖ ποιεῖν ἵνα σωθῶ;)"
	Passive subjunctive	σωθῇ	Mark 5.23	In Jairus' speech to Jesus, requesting that Jesus come and lay hands on his daughter (ἵνα ἐλθὼν ἐπιθῇς τὰς χεῖρας αὐτῇ), in order that she might be healed and might live (ἵνα σωθῇ καὶ ζήσῃ).
Perfect	Passive indicative	σέσωται	Acts 4.9	Out of Peter's mouth, describing the healed man to the Council, in the Lukan account of the healing of the lame man at the temple gate.

Future	Passive indicative	σωθήσομαι	Matt 9.21 = Mark 5.28	In both *Matthew* and *Mark*, healing (σωθήσομαι) is here thought of by the haemorrhaging woman as being conditional on her touching (ἅψωμαι) Jesus' cloak.
	Passive indicative	σωθήσῃ	Acts 16.31	Paul's and Silas' answer to the gaoler's question (see Acts 16.30): "Believe ... , and you will be saved, you and your household! (Πίστευσον .. . . καὶ σωθήσῃ σὺ καὶ ὁ οἶκός σου)"
	Passive indicative	σωθήσεται	Luke 8.50; John 11.12	In *Luke*, out of the mouth of Jesus to Jairus: "Don't be afraid! Only believe, and she will be healed. (Μὴ φοβοῦ, μόνον πίστευσον, καὶ σωθήσεται)" In *John*, the only use of σῴζω in a Johannine healing story, out of the mouths of the disciples to Jesus, after Jesus had told them that Lazarus was sleeping: εἰ κεκοίμηται σωθήσεται.

All occurrences of σῴζω in direct speech in the active voice come out of the mouth of Jesus. Two other active forms occur: the first in the indirect speech of Jewish elders in the Lukan gospel story of the healing of the centurion's servant; the second in the an advisory passage in the letter of James. Otherwise all forms of σῴζω in healing stories occur in the passive voice. σῴζω likes to appear in close proximity to a form of πίστις, and/or ἅπτομαι.

Appendix 7 : 12

Incidence of ἅπτομαι in New Testament healing stories according to tense, voice and mood

Tense	Voice and Mood	Form	Reference	Comment
Present	Middle infinitive	ἅπτεσθαι	Luke 6.19	In a general healing episode, following the healing words ἀκοῦσαι ... ἰαθῆναι ... ἐθεραπεύοντο (6.18). Luke says that the whole crowd of people were seeking to touch (and keep on touching) Jesus, because power was radiating from him and healing them all (καὶ πᾶς ὁ ὄχλος ἐζήτουν ἅπτεσθαι αὐτοῦ, ὅτι δύναμις παρ' αὐτοῦ ἐξήρχετο καὶ ἰᾶτο πάντας). Luke is the only author to use the present tense in this context (and note his use of the present tense at Lk 18.15 and Lk 7.39).
Aorist	Middle indicative: 3 sing.	ἥψατο	(i) Mk 1.41 = Mt 8.3 = Lk 5.13 (ii) Mt 8.15 (iii) Mk 5.27 = Mt 9.20 = Lk 8.44; Mk 5.30 = Lk 8.46; Mk 5.31; Lk 8.47 (iv) Mk 7.33 (v) Mt 9.29=? (vi) Mt 20.34 (vii) Lk 7.14	(i) In the parallel account of the healing of the leper, describing Jesus' touch, a touch that rendered him ritually unclean. (ii) In Matthew's account of the healing of Peter's mother-in-law, describing Jesus' touch. (Cf. Mk 1.31: κρατήσας, and Lk 4.39: ἐπετίμησεν.) (iii) In the parallel account of the healing of the haemorrhaging woman, describing her touch (Mk 5.27, Mt 9.20, Lk 8.44), Jesus' question (Mk 5.30, Lk 8.46), the disciples' question (Mk 5.31), and the woman's confession (Lk 8.47). (iv) In Mark's account of the healing of the deaf-mute, describing Jesus' action (7.33), action that is also described: ἔβαλεν τοὺς δακτύλους αὐτοῦ εἰς τὰ ὦτα αὐτοῦ (7.33); but his touch is requested by the crowd thus: ἐπιθῇ αὐτῷ τὴν χεῖρα (7.32). (v) and (vi) In Matthew's two accounts of the healing of two blind men, describing Jesus' action on each occasion (9.29, 20.34). (vii) In Luke's story of the son of the widow of Nain, describing Jesus' touching of the bier (7.14).

Aorist	Middle indicative: 3 pl.	ἥψαντο	Mark 6.56 = Matt 14.36	In the parallel account of the general healing episode at Gennesaret, describing the actions of the crowd.
Aorist	Middle participle: nom., masc,. sing.	ὁ ἁψαμενός	(i) Luke 8.45 (ii) Luke 22.51	(i) In Jesus' question in the Lukan account of the healing of the haemorrhaging woman. (ii) In the Lukan account of the healing of temple slave at the Mount of Olives, describing Jesus' action.
Aorist	Middle subjunctive: 1 sing.	ἅψωμαι	Mark 5.28 = Matt 9.21	In the thought of the woman in the parallel account of the healing of the haemorrhaging woman.
Aorist	Middle subjunctive: 3 sing.	ἅψηται	Mark 8.22	In the reported speech of the people who brought the blind man to Jesus, and begged that Jesus might touch him. Jesus' touch is described thus: ἐπιλαβόμενος τῆς χειρὸς ... ἐπιθεὶς τὰς χεῖρας (8.23) ... πάλιν ἐπέθηκεν τὰς χεῖρας (8.25). The only other healing story in *Mark* where Jesus' actions are described ἐπιθεὶς τὰς χεῖρας is in his account of the general healing episode at Nazareth (6.5). Elsewhere this expression in *Mark* occurs only in healings requests (5.23; 7.32).
Aorist	Middle subjunctive: 3 pl.	ἅψωνται	Mark 6.56 = Matt 14.36	In the repeated requests of the crowd in the parallel accounts of the general healing episode at Gennesaret.

ἅπτομαι appears to be a synoptic word. (It does not feature in healing stories in *John* or *Acts*.) It appears 25 times in synoptic healing stories, and in four other significant places. It appears in *Mark* (ἅψηται (10.13)) and *Luke* (ἅπτηται (18.15)), in the parallel report that they brought children to Jesus, in order that he might touch them; at Matthew 17.7, describing Jesus' touch (ἁψάμενος) when he allayed the disciples' fear after the Transfiguration; and at Luke 7.39, where the Pharisees discuss the woman who anointed Jesus, and describe her touch in the present tense: ἅπτεται.

Of the 25 synoptic occurrences in healing stories, nine describe Jesus' touch (in the parallel accounts of the healing of the leper, the Matthaean account of Peter's mother-in-law, the Markan deaf mute, both Matthaean stories of the two blind men, the bier at Nain, the temple slave), ten the touch or thought of the haemorrhaging woman, four the touch of the crowd at Gennesaret, one the touch of a Lukan crowd (in a possibly parallel story), and one the request on behalf of a Markan blind man. Thus ἅπτομαι describes nine synoptic healing stories (the leper [synoptic], Peter's mother-in-law [Matthew], the haemorrhaging woman [synoptic], the Matthaean blind men, the Lukan widow's son, the Markan blind man, the Markan deaf-mute, the Lukan temple slave, and the crowd scenes in *Matthew*, *Mark*, and *Luke*); possibly eleven (if Matthew's blind men are taken as separate healing accounts, and if the Lukan crowd scene is separated from the Markan and Matthaean Gennesaret crowd scene). Of these, two (the haemorrhaging woman, the crowd at Gennesaret,) include a form of σῴζω, while only one other healing story includes σῴζω and a different touching (κρατέω) verb (the Markan and Matthaean story of Jairus' daughter).

Both occurrences of ἐμβριμάομαι occur in ἅπτομαι stories (the Markan leper, 1.43; andthe Matthaean blind men, 9.30). Similarly σπλαγχνίζομαι always occurs in "touching" healing stories, three times with ἅπτομαι (Mk 1.41; Mt 20.34; Lk 7.13), and once with κρατέω (Mk 9.22). Otherwise σπλαγχνίζομαι occurs in crowd scenes (Mt 9.36; 14.14).

Appendix 7 : 13

Incidence of ἅπτομαι κρατέω ἐπιτίθημι τὰς χεῖρας ἐπιτιμάω ἐμβριμάομαι σπλαγχνίζομαι in synoptic healing stories

Reference & story	ἅπτομαι	κρατέω	ἐπιτίθημι τὰς χεῖρας	ἐπιτιμάω	ἐμβριμάομαι σπλαγχνίζομαι	Other
Mark 1.23-28 unclean spirit in synagogue				ἐπετίμησεν (1.25) ... ἐπιτάσσει (1.27)		τοῖς ἀκαθάρτοις ἐπιτάσσει (1.27) ἡ ἀκοὴ (1.28)
Mark 1.30-31 Peter's mother-in-law		κρατήσας (1.31)				
Mark 1.32-34 general						ἐθεράπευσεν ... ἐξέβαλεν (1.34)
Mark 1.39 general demonic						κηρύσσων ... ἐκβάλλων (1.39)
Mark 1.40-45 leper	ἥψατο (1.41)				σπλαγχνισθεὶς (1.41) ἐμβριμησάμενος αὐτῷ (1.43)	καθαρίσαι (1.40) καθαρίσθητι (1.41) ἐκαθαρίσθη (1.42) ἐξέβαλεν αὐτόν (1.43)
Mark 2.1-12 paralytic						καὶ ἰδὼν ὁ Ἰησοῦς τὴν πίστιν αὐτῶν λέγει ... ἀφίενταί σου αἱ ἁμαρτίαι (2.5)
Mark 3.1-6 withered hand						θεραπεύσει (3.2) σῶσαι (3.4)
Mark 3.10-12 general	ἅψωνται (3.10)			ἐπετίμα (3.12) (secrecy request)		ἐθεράπευσεν (3.10)

Mark 5.1-20 Gerasene demoniac						ὁρκίζω (5.7) (used by demoniac addressing Jesus) ... κηρύσσειν (5.20)
Mark 5.21-24, 35-43 Jairus' daughter		κρατήσας (5.41)	ἐπιθῇς τὰς χεῖρας (5.23) (request)			σωθῇ ... ζήσῃ (5.23) πίστευε (5.36) ἐκβαλὼν (5.40) διεστείλατο (5.43) (secrecy request)
Mark 5.24-34 haemorrhaging woman	ἥψατο (5.27) ἅψωμαι(5.28) ἥψατο (5.30) ἥψατο (5.31)					σωθήσομαι (5.28) ἴαται (5.29) πίστις ... σέσωκέν (5.34) εἰρήνην ... ὑγιὴς (5.34)
Mark 6.1-6 general			ἐπιθεὶς τὰς χεῖρας (6.5)			οὐδεμίαν δύναμιν, εἰ μὴ ὀλίγοις ἀρρώστοις... ἐθεράπευσεν (6.5) ἀπιστίαν (6.6)
Mark 6.13 disciples: general						ἐξέβαλλον ... ἤλειφον ... ἐθεράπευον (6.13)
Mark 6.53-56 general: Gennesaret	ἅψωνται ... ἥψαντο (6.56)					ἐσῴζοντο (6.56)
Mark 7.24-30 Syro-Phoenician's daughter						ἐκβάλῃ (7.26) (request)
Mark 7.31-37 deaf mute	ἥψατο (7.33)		ἐπιθῇ αὐτῷ τὴν χεῖρα (7.32) (request)			διεστείλατο ... διεστέλλετο ... ἐκήρυσσον (7.36) (secrecy command)
Mark 8.22-26 blind man	ἅψηται (8.22)		ἐπιλαβόμενος τῆς χειρὸς (8.23)...ἐπιθεὶς τὰς χεῖρας (8.23) ... ἐπέθηκεν τὰς χεῖρας (8.25)			ἀπέστειλεν (8.26) (secrecy request)

Mark 9.14-29 epileptic boy		κρατήσας τῆς χειρὸς αὐτοῦ (9.27)		ἐπετίμησεν ... ἐπιτάσσω (9.25)	σπλαγχνισθεὶς (9.22)	πάντα δυνατὰ τῷ πιστεύοντι (9.23) Πιστεύω· βοήθει μου τῇ ἀπιστίᾳ (9.24) ἠδυνήθημεν ἐκβαλεῖν (9.28) ἐξελθεῖν ... προσευχῇ (9.29)
Mark 10.46-52 blind Bartimaeus				ἐπετίμων ... πολλοὶ(10.48)		πίστις ... σέσωκέν (10.52)
Matthew 4.23 general						διδάσκων ... κηρύσσων ... θεραπεύων
Matthew 4.24 general						ἐθεράπευσεν
Matthew 8.2-4 leper	ἐκτείνας τὴν χεῖρα ἥψατο αὐτοῦ (8.3)					καθαρίσαι (8.2)... καθαρίσθητι ... ἐκαθαρίσθη (8.3)
Matthew 8.5-13 centurion's boy						θεραπεύσω (8.7), ἰαθήσεται (8.8), τοσαύτην πίστιν (8.10), ὡς ἐπίστευσας (8.13), ἰάθη (8.13)
Matthew 8.14-15 Peter's mother-in-law	ἥψατο τῆς χειρὸς αὐτῆς (8.15)					
Matthew 8.16-17 demonic & general						ἐξέβαλεν ... λόγῳ (8.16) ... ἐθεράπευσεν (8.16)
Matthew 8.28-34 2 demonic Gadarenes						ἐκβάλλεις (8.31) (demons); Ὑπάγετε (8.32)
Matthew 9.2-8 paralytic						πίστιν (9.2) ... θάρσει (9.2)
Matthew 9.18, 23-26 Jairus' daughter		ἐκράτησεν τῆς χειρὸς αὐτῆς (9.25)	ἐπίθες τὴν χεῖρα (9.18) (request)			ζήσεται (9.18), ἐξεβλήθη ὁ ὄχλος (9.25)

Matthew 9.20-22 haemorrhaging woman	ἅψωμαι (9.21) ἥψατο (9.20)					σωθήσομαι (9.21) θάρσει ... πίστις ... σέσωκέν ... ἐσώθη (9.22)
Matthew 9.27-31 2 blind men	ἥψατο τῶν ὀφθαλμῶν (9.29)				ἐνεβριμήθη αὐτοῖς (9.30) (secrecy demand, disregarded 9.31)	Πιστεύετε... ; (9.28) κατὰ ... πίστιν (9.29)
Matthew 9.32-34 dumb demonic						ἐκβληθέντος (9.33) οἱ δὲ Φαρισαῖοι ἔλεγον, Ἐν τῷ ἄρχοντι τῶν δαιμονίων ἐκβάλλει τὰ δαιμόνια (9.34)
Matthew 9.35 general					ἐσπλαγχνίσθη (9.36) (crowd leaderless)	διδάσκων ... κηρύσσων ... θεραπεύων
Matthew 12.10-13 withered hand						θεραπεῦσαι (12.10) ὑγιὴς (12.13)
Matthew 12.15-16 general				ἐπετίμησεν (12.16) (secrecy command)		ἐθεράπευσεν (12.15)
Matthew 12.22-24 blind & dumb demonic						ἐθεράπευσεν (12.22) οἱ δὲ Φαρισαῖοι ... εἶπον ... ἐκβαλλει τὰ δαιμόνια ... ἐν τῷ Βεελζεβοὺλ ἄρχοντι τῶν δαιμονίων (12.24)
Matthew 14.14 general					ἐσπλαγχνίσθη (14.14)	ἐθεράπευσεν (14.14)
Matthew 14.35-36 general: Gennesaret	ἅψωνται ... ἥψαντο (14.36)					διεσώθησαν (14.36)
Matthew 15.21-28 Canaanite woman's demonic daughter						βοήθει μοι (15.25) πίστις ... ἰάθη (15.28)

Matthew 15.29-31 general						ἐθεράπευσεν (15.30) ὑγιεῖς (15.31)
Matthew 17.14-20 epileptic demonic				ἐπετίμησεν αὐτῷ (17.18)		θεραπεῦσαι (17.16) ἄπιστος (17.17) ἐθεραπεύθη (17.18) οἱ μαθηταὶ ... οὐκ ἠδυνήθημεν ἐκβαλεῖν αὐτό; (17.19) ὀλιγοπιστίαν (17.20)
Matthew 19.2 general						ἐθεράπευσεν
Matthew 20.29-34 2 blind men	ἥψατο τῶν ὀμμάτων (20.34)			ἐπετίμησεν (20.31) (crowd)	σπλαγχνισθεὶς (20.34)	
Matthew 21.14 general: blind and lame						ἐθεράπευσεν (21.14)
Luke 4.31-38 demonic in synagogue				ἐπετίμησεν αὐτῷ (4.35) ... ἐπιτάσσει (4.36)		διδάσκων (4.31) ἐξῆλθεν (4.35)
Luke 4.38-39 Simon's mother-in-law				ἐπιστὰς ... ἐπετίμησεν τῷ πυρετῷ (4.39)		
Luke 4.40 general: weak			ὁ δὲ ἑνὶ ἑκάστῳ αὐτῶν τὰς χεῖρας ἐπιτιθεὶς			ἐθεράπευεν αὐτούς
Luke 4.41 general: demonic				ἐπιτιμῶν silence (4.41)		ἐξήρχετο (4.41)
Luke 5.12-14 leper	ἐκτείνας τὴν χεῖρα ἥψατο αὐτοῦ (5.13)					καθαρίσθητι (5.13) παρήγγειλεν silence (5.14) -> ὁ λόγος (5.15)

Luke 5.15-16 general: infirm						ὁ λόγος -> ὄχλοι πολλοὶ ἀκούειν καὶ θεραπεύεσθαι ἀπὸ τῶν ἀσθενειῶν (5.15)
Luke 5.17-26 paralytic						διδάσκων ... καὶ δύναμις κυρίου ἦν εἰς τὸ ἰᾶσθαι (5.17) πίστιν (5.20)
Luke 6.6-11 withered hand						διδάσκειν (6.6) θεραπεύει (6.7) σῶσαι (6.9)
Luke 6.17-19 general: diseases & demonic	ἅπτεσθαι (6.19)					ἀκοῦσαι ... ἰαθῆναι ... ἐθεραπεύοντο (6.18) δύναμις ... ἰᾶτο (6.19)
Luke 7.1-10 centurion's slave						διασώσῃ (7.3) λόγῳ ... ἰαθήτω (7.7) τοσαύτην πίστιν (7.9) ὑγιαίνοντα (7.10)
Luke 7.11-18 widow's son at Nain	ἥψατο τῆς σοροῦ (7.14)				ἐσπλαγχνίσθη (7.13)	
Luke 7.21 general: diseases, demonic & blind						ἐθεράπευσεν
Luke 8.2-3 general & specific: diseases & demonic women						κηρύσσων καὶ εὐαγγελιζόμενος (8.1) αἳ ἦσαν τεθεραπευμέναι (8.2)
Luke 8.26-39 Gerasene demoniac						παρήγγειλεν (8.29) ἐξελθόντα (8.33) ἐσώθη (8.36) καὶ διηγοῦ ὅσα σοι ἐποίησεν ὁ θεός (8.39)
Luke 8.40-42,49-56 Jairus' daughter		κρατήσας τῆς χειρὸς (8.54)				Μὴ φοβοῦ, μόνον πίστευσον, καὶ σωθήσεται (8.50) παρήγγειλεν secrecy (8.56)

Luke 8.43-48 haemorrhaging woman	ἥψατο (8.44) ὁ ἁψάμενός (8.45) ἥψατο (8.46) & (8.47)					οὐδενὸς θεραπευθῆναι (8.43) ἰάθη (8.47) πίστις ... σέσωκέν ... πορεύου εἰς εἰρήνην (8.48)
Luke 9.6 disciples: general						εὐαγγελιζόμενοι καὶ θεραπεύοντες πανταχοῦ (9.6)
Luke 9.11 general						καὶ τοὺς χρείαν ἔχοντας θεραπείας ἰᾶτο (9.11)
Luke 9.37-43 epileptic demonic				ἐπετίμησεν ... τῷ πνεύματι τῷ ἀκαθάρτῳ (9.42)		ἵνα ἐκβάλωσιν αὐτό, καὶ οὐκ ἠδυνήθησαν (9.40) ἄπιστος (9.41) ἰάσατο (8.42)
Luke 10.17 "72": demonic						καὶ τὰ δαιμόνια ὑποτάσσεται ἡμῖν ἐν τῷ ὀνόματί σου (10.17)
Luke 11.14-16 dumb demonic						ἐκβάλλων δαιμόνιον...κωφόν... ἐξελθόντος (11.14) τινὲς :'Εν Βεελζεβοὺλ τῷ ἄρχοντι τῶν δαιμονίων ἐκβαλλει (11.15)
Luke 13.10-17 bent woman			ἐπέθηκεν αὐτῇ τὰς χεῖρας (13.13)			διδάσκων(13.10)... γυνὴ πνεῦμα ἔχουσα ἀσθενείας (13.11) ἐθεράπευσεν ... ἐργάζεσθαι ... θεραπεύεσθε (13.14)
Luke 14.1-6 man with dropsy						ἔξεστιν τῷ σαββάτῳ θεραπεῦσαι; (14.3) ἐπιλαβόμενος ἰάσατο (14.4)
Luke 17.11-19 10 lepers						ἐκαθαρίσθησαν (17.14) ἰάθη (17.15) ἐκαθαρίσθησαν (17.17) 'Αναστὰς πορεύου· ἡ πίστις σου σέσωκέν σε (17.19)
Luke 18.35-43 blind man				οἱ προάγοντες ἐπετίμων αὐτῷ ἵνα σιγήσῃ (18.39)		ἡ πίστις σου σέσωκέν σε (18.42)
Luke 22.47-53 temple slave	ἁψάμενος (22.51)					ἰάσατο (22.51)

Appendix 8 : 1
The language of healing in *Acts*

Reference	Agent	Greek word	Illnesses treated	Type, number, method	Patient profile, location, motive	Comments
Acts 3.1-26, 4.1-31	Peter (and John?)	ἐν τῷ ὀνόματι Ἰησοῦ Χριστοῦ τοῦ Ναζωραίου [ἔγειρε καὶ] περιπάτει. καὶ πιάσας αὐτὸν τῆς δεξιᾶς χειρὸς ἤγειρεν αὐτόν· παραχρῆμα δὲ ἐστερεώθησαν αἱ βάσεις αὐτοῦ καὶ τὰ σφυδρά (3.6-7)	τις ἀνὴρ χωλὸς ἐκ κοιλίας μητρὸς αὐτοῦ (3.2)	Specific: 1, word and touch. But Peter describes it as faith in Jesus' name: "And his name, by faith in his name, has made this man strong (ἐστερέωσεν)...and the faith which is through him has given this man this perfect health (τὴν ὁλοκληρίαν)." (3.16)	At Jerusalem, a man lame from birth, who was laid, daily, at the temple gate which was called Beautiful, to ask alms of the people (3.1-2). He was more than forty years old (4.22).	This healing is described in clinical language. Luke uses πιάζω to describe Peter's grip on the man, and then στερεόω to describe the state of his feet and ankles, after Peter had spoken to and touched him (3.7). His condition is given in the terms of a clinical case history: he was over forty (4.22), and had been lame from birth (3.2). Immediately (3.8) he was able to jump up (ἐξάλλομαι), and walk about (περιπατέω). Peter describes him (3.16) as being in perfect health (τὴν ὁλοκληρίαν), as "saved" (σέσωται), (4.9-10) as healthy/whole (ὑγιής). The Pharisees (4.14) see him as the man who had been treated (τὸν τεθεραπευμένον). Luke sums up the whole episode (4.22) as "this sign of healing": το σημεῖον τοῦτο τῆς ἰάσεως.
Acts 4.30	ἐν τῷ τὴν χεῖρά [σου] ἐκτείνειν σε εἰς ἴασιν καὶ σημεῖα καὶ τέρατα γίνεσθαι διὰ τοῦ ὀνόματος τοῦ ἁγίου παιδός σου Ἰησοῦ while you stretch out your hand to heal, and signs and wonders are performed through the name of your holy son Jesus					This passage occurs in the common prayer of Peter, John and their friends, following Peter's and John's release from custody. Their prayer is the sequel to the healing of the lame man, and its aftermath.

Acts 5.12-16	Apostles (and Peter's shadow?)	σημεῖα καὶ τέρατα πολλὰ. . . τοὺς ἀσθενεῖς . . . ἵνα ἐρχομένου Πέτρου κἂν ἡ σκιὰ ἐπισκιάσῃ τινὶ αὐτῶν . . . ἀσθενεῖς καὶ ὀχλουμένους ὑπὸ πνευμάτων ἀκαθάρτων, οἵτινες ἐθεραπεύοντο ἅπαντες (5.12, 15-16)	τοὺς ἀσθενεῖς . . . ἀσθενεῖς καὶ ὀχλουμένους ὑπὸ πνευμάτων ἀκαθάρτων (5.15-16)	General: ?, all; ? Peter's shadow, ?	At Jerusalem, the weak were brought into the streets, so "that as Peter came by at least his shadow might fall on some of them"; the weak and those troubled by unclean spirits from the towns around Jerusalem were also brought, and they were all being healed (passive verb).	This is the first of four general healing episodes described in *Acts*. The verb θεραπεύω occurs in three of them, here, at 8.7, and at 28.9. This episode occurs in an extraordinary chapter: between the accounts of the deaths of Ananias and Sapphira, and the release of the apostles from prison by an angel. It is appropriate that this episode should be introduced by a comment about σημεῖα καὶ τέρατα πολλὰ (5.12). There is an atmosphere of fear, introduced by the accounts of the deaths of Ananias and Sapphira. The mention of Peter's shadow intensifies this atmosphere, but we are not told whether Peter's shadow was effective as an agent of healing. The inference appears positive. As in the gospels the illnesses linked with θεραπεύω are infirmities and unclean spirits. The tenor of the episode is unusual: the context and the method hint at magical practices, and there is no mention of the good news.

Acts 8.6-8	Philip	τὰ σημεῖα ἃ ἐποίει. . . πνεύματα ἀκάθαρτα . . . ἐξήρχοντο,. . . . παραλελυμένοι καὶ χωλοὶ ἐθεραπεύθησαν (8.6,7)	πολλοὶ γὰρ τῶν ἐχόντων πνεύματα ἀκάθαρτα βοῶντα φωνῇ μεγάλῃ ἐξήρχοντο, πολλοὶ δὲ παραλελυμένοι καὶ χωλοὶ ἐθεραπεύθησαν (8.7)	General: many, preaching the word.	In a city of Samaria, unclean spirits began coming out of many who were possessed, crying with a loud voice; and many who were lame or paralysed were healed (passive verb).	Multitudes (οἱ ὄχλοι) with one accord gave heed to Philip, (who was proclaiming to them the Christ), when they heard him and saw the signs which he was doing: signs of healing (freeing those possessed by unclean spirits, and treating the lame and the paralysed). θεραπεύω is here used in conjunction with preaching (εὐαγγελιζόμενοι τὸν λόγον [8.4]), in a general healing episode. The illnesses cited are more specific than usual: the lame and the paralysed, rather than the infirm. Again, the episode is introduced by τὰ σημεῖα (8.6).

Acts 9.1-22	Ananias	Ἀνανίας . . . ἐπιθεὶς ἐπ' αὐτὸν τὰς χεῖρας εἶπεν, . . καὶ εὐθέως ἀπέπεσαν αὐτοῦ ἀπὸ τῶν ὀφθαλμῶν ὡς λεπίδες, ἀνέβλεψέν τε (9.17,18)	οὐδὲν ἔβλεπεν (9.8)	Specific: Saul, touch and word.	Saul, on the road to Damascus, saw a great light and heard a voice, with which he conversed. Blinded, he went to Damascus, where his sight was restored after Ananias lay his hands on him.	The language used to describe this incident is clinical. Saul (9.9) was unable to see (μὴ βλέπων), and explains later that this was because of the brightness of the light (22.11). Ananias was instructed (9.10-12) to lay hands on him, in order that he might see again (ἐπιθέντα αὐτῷ [τὰς] χεῖρας ὅπως ἀναβλέψῃ). When Ananias did this, Saul regained his sight (ἀνέβλεψέν), rose, was baptised (9.18), took food (9.19), and was strengthened (ἐνίσχυσεν). However Saul was to learn how much he was to suffer (παθεῖν) for the sake of the name of the Lord (9.16).
Acts 9.32-35	Peter	καὶ εἶπεν αὐτῷ ὁ Πέτρος, Αἰνέα, ἰᾶταί σε Ἰησοῦς Χριστός· ἀνάστηθι καὶ στρῶσον σεαυτῷ. καὶ εὐθέως ἀνέστη (9.34)	ἐξ ἐτῶν ὀκτὼ κατακείμενον ἐπὶ κραβάττου, ὃς ἦν παραλελυμένος (9.33)	Specific: Aeneas; word.	At Lydda, Peter found a man named Aeneas, who had been bedridden for eight years and was paralysed.	Luke chooses ἰάομαι in the present tense to describe the healing action in this story. The result of this healing (9.35) was that all the residents of Lydda and Sharon turned to the Lord (πάντες . . . ἐπέστρεψαν ἐπὶ τὸν κύριον).

Acts 9. 36-43	Peter	ὁ Πέτρος . . . προσηύξατο, καὶ . . . εἶπεν, . . . ἀνάστηθι (9.40)	ἀσθενήσασαν αὐτὴν ἀποθανεῖν (9.37)	Specific: Dorcas; prayer, followed by command.	At Joppa, a disciple (9.36), who was full of good works and acts of charity (αὕτη ἦν πλήρης ἔργων ἀγαθῶν καὶ ἐλεημοσυνῶν ὧν ἐποίει), became weak, and died. She was washed and laid out. Peter was sent for, came, prayed, and commanded her to rise. She (9.40) opened her eyes, and sat up (ἀνεκάθισεν). Peter (9.41) gave her his hand, lifted her up (ἀνέστησεν αὐτήν), and presented her alive (ζῶσαν).	Chapter 9 deals with conversion, using healing miracles to lend credibility to the message. First Saul (1-30) is blinded, healed, and baptised, with the result that the church was built up and was multiplied (31). Then Aeneas was healed (32-34), so that all the locals were converted (35). Finally, Dorcas was restored to life (36-41), with the result that many believed (42). Cf. 20.7-12, where Paul "raises" Eutychus, and a present participle of ζάω is chosen to describe his condition (20.12), as it is here of Dorcas (9.41).
Acts 10.38	Ἰησοῦν τὸν ἀπὸ Ναζαρέθ, ὡς ἔχρισεν αὐτὸν ὁ θεὸς πνεύματι ἁγίῳ καὶ δυνάμει, ὃς διῆλθεν εὐεργετῶν καὶ ἰώμενος πάντας τοὺς καταδυναστευομένους ὑπὸ τοῦ διαβόλου, ὅτι ὁ θεὸς ἦν μετ' αὐτοῦ God anointed Jesus of Nazareth with the holy spirit and with power; how he went about doing good and healing all that were oppressed by the devil, for God was with him.					This passage occurs in a speech given by Peter to the centurion, Cornelius, and Cornelius' kinsmen and close friends. Does this describe spiritual or physical healing? Note the use of ἰάομαι here, and that Jesus' clientele were those "oppressed by the devil". Many physical healings are described in these terms. Cf. Luke 13.10-17, especially 13.16.

Acts 10.42	καὶ παρήγγειλεν ἡμῖν κηρύξαι τῷ λαῷ καὶ διαμαρτύρασθαι ὅτι οὗτός ἐστιν ὁ ὡρισμένος ὑπὸ τοῦ θεοῦ κριτὴς ζώντων καὶ νεκρῶν And he commanded us to preach to the people, and to testify that he is the one ordained by God to be judge of the living and the dead					This passage occurs in the same speech as 9.38 (above), given by Peter. Compare the commission and instructions given to the disciples in the gospels, at Matthew (10.1-15), Mark (6.7-13), and Luke (9.1-5, 10.1-17). There is no mention of healing here.
Acts 14.8-11	Paul	ἰδὼν ὅτι ἔχει πίστιν τοῦ σωθῆναι . . . Ἀνάστηθι ἐπὶ τοὺς πόδας σου ὀρθός. καὶ ἥλατο καὶ περιεπάτει (14.9,10)	τις ἀνὴρ ἀδύνατος ἐν Λύστροις τοῖς ποσὶν ἐκάθητο, χωλὸς ἐκ κοιλίας μητρὸς αὐτοῦ, ὃς οὐδέποτε περιεπάτησεν (14.8)	Specific: 1, word (command)	At Lystra, a man was sitting who was unable to use his feet. He had been lame from birth, and had never walked. He listened to Paul, who saw (14.9) that he had the faith to be "saved" (σωθῆναι). Paul then commanded him to stand upright on his feet. The man sprang up and began walking around (14.10).	Paul's motivation in this case is the faith (πίστιν τοῦ σωθῆναι) of the man. As in the gospels πίστις is linked to σῴζω.

Acts 16.16-18	Paul	διαπονηθεὶς δὲ Παῦλος καὶ ἐπιστρέψας τῷ πνεύματι εἶπεν, Παραγγέλλω σοι ἐν ὀνόματι Ἰησοῦ Χριστοῦ ἐξελθεῖν ἀπ' αὐτῆς· καὶ ἐξῆλθεν αὐτῇ τῇ ὥρᾳ (16.18)	παιδίσκην τινὰ ἔχουσαν πνεῦμα πύθωνα ὑπαντῆσαι ἡμῖν, ἥτις ἐργασίαν πολλὴν παρεῖχεν τοῖς κυρίοις αὐτῆς μαντευομένη (16.16)	Specific: 1, word (command)	At Philippi, "we" (Paul and Silas, Timothy and Luke?) were met by a slave girl who had a spirit of divination (i.e. was a fortune teller), who brought much gain to her masters by fortune telling. She followed Paul and "us", and began crying (16.17) "These men are servants of the Most High God, who proclaim to you the way of salvation (ὁδὸν σωτηρίας)." Paul, annoyed (διαπονηθεὶς), commanded the spirit to come out of her in the name of Jesus Christ (16.18).	This episode is the catalyst for the imprisonment of Paul and Silas at Philippi, and the subsequent earthquake which unfastened their fetters and opened the prison doors, causing the gaoler's fear, conversion and baptism. (Note the instant obedience of the spirit.)

Acts 19.11 and ff.	Paul	Δυνάμεις τε οὐ τὰς τυχούσας ὁ θεὸς ἐποίει διὰ τῶν χειρῶν Παύλου, ὥστε καὶ ἐπὶ τοὺς ἀσθενοῦντας ἀποφέρεσθαι ἀπὸ τοῦ χρωτὸς αὐτοῦ σουδάρια ἢ σιμικίνθια καὶ ἀπαλλάσσεσθαι ἀπ' αὐτῶν τὰς νόσους, τά τε πνεύματα τὰ πονηρὰ ἐκπορεύεσθαι (19.11-12)	τοὺς ἀσθενοῦντας . . . τὰς νόσους, τά τε πνεύματα τὰ πονηρὰ (19.12)	General: ?; Paul's handkerchiefs and aprons.	At Ephesus (19.11), God began doing unusual (οὐ τὰς τυχούσας) miracles (δυνάμεις) by Paul's hands, unusual miracles of healing. Diseases (τὰς νόσους) and evil spirits (τά τε πνεύματα τὰ πονηρὰ) were leaving (ἀπαλλάσσεσθαι . . . ἐκπορεύεσθαι) those who were infirm (τοὺς ἀσθενοῦντας), when Paul's handkerchiefs and aprons were carried away (ἀποφέρεσθαι) from his skin (ἀπὸ τοῦ χρωτὸς) to them.	The tenses chosen to describe these episodes (imperfect indicative, present infinitives) imply that these events occurred on a regular basis during the two years that Paul was in Ephesus. The context is important: the account follows the arrival of the Holy Spirit at Ephesus (19.1-7) and the spreading of the word throughout Asia (19.8-10), and is prior to the story of the unsuccessful exorcisms of Sceva's seven sons. Thus these healing episodes are used to give credibility to Paul's preaching in Asia, inspiring fear (19.17), and the cessation of the practice of curious arts (τὰ περίεργα). Cf. Acts 5.12-16, where Peter's shadow appears to have the same effect as Paul's handkerchiefs and aprons.

Acts 19.13	Itinerant Jewish exorcists	Ὁρκίζω ὑμᾶς τὸν Ἰησοῦν ὃν Παῦλος κηρύσσει	τοὺς ἔχοντας τὰ πνεύματα τὰ πονηρὰ	General: ?; word (i.e. in the name of Jesus).	At Ephesus. This account immediately follows the account about Paul's handkerchiefs and aprons (19.11-12). We are not told whether some of the exorcists were successful - only that they "endeavoured (ἐπεχείρησαν)" to exorcise. The inference is that these Jewish exorcists were unsuccessful, exemplified by the following story (19.14-20) about Sceva's seven sons (See App. 8:2, Acts 19.14-20).	This account (and ff.) is contrary to the gospel accounts of exorcists working in Jesus' name (Mk 9.38-41; Lk 9.49-50). The Greek word chosen is ὁρκίζω, only used once in a gospel exorcism account (Mk 5.7), but the ὁρκίζω ὁρκόω family of words is found in the writings of Josephus (*Jewish Antiquities* 8.47 [see App. 6:2, **29**]), Lucian (*Philopseudes* 16), and the magical papyri (*PGM* 4.3019; 4.3045) when describing exorcisms. Luke's use of ἐπιχειρέω to describe the efforts of the exorcists, and the following story of Sceva's sons, both imply that these exorcists were unsuccessful. Therefore this incident will not be included in the tally of healing episodes in *Acts*.

Acts 20.7-12	Paul	καταβὰς δὲ ὁ Παῦλος ἐπέπεσεν αὐτῷ καὶ συμπεριλαβὼν (20.10)	νεκρός ? (20.9)	Specific: 1 (Eutychus), touch.	At Troas, while Paul was preaching in an upper room, a young man named Εὔτυχος (Goodluck!) fell asleep while sitting in the window, fell three storeys and was taken up dead (νεκρός). Paul (20.10) went down, fell upon him (ἐπέπεσεν αὐτῷ), and, embracing him (συμπεριλαβὼν), asserted that the lad's spirit was in him (ἡ γὰρ ψυχὴ αὐτοῦ ἐν αὐτῷ ἐστιν). Paul returned to the upper room where he continued his preaching until daybreak, when the lad was led away (20.12), alive (ζῶντα).	Paul appears to deny that the lad had died, although the inference here is that in the eyes of those who were present Paul had brought the boy back to life. Cf. the language used at 9.41 to describe Dorcas' state, where a participle of ζάω is used, as here at 20.12.

Acts 20.35	πάντα ὑπέδειξα ὑμῖν ὅτι οὕτως κοπιῶντας δεῖ ἀντιλαμβάνεσθαι τῶν ἀσθενούντων, μνημονεύειν τε τῶν λόγων τοῦ κυρίου Ἰησοῦ ὅτι αὐτὸς εἶπεν, Μακάριόν ἐστιν μᾶλλον διδόναι ἢ λαμβάνειν. In all things I have shown you that by so toiling one must help the infirm, remembering the words of the Lord Jesus, how he said, "It is more blessed to give than to receive."	This passage is the final sentence of a farewell speech (20.18-35) delivered by Paul to the elders of the church at Ephesus, describing his ministry at Ephesus. He does not mention healing, but does describe the infirm (τῶν ἀσθενούντων) as his clientele. His work there included serving the Lord by preaching and teaching, testimony and admonishment.
Acts 26.17-18	ἐγὼ ἀποστέλλω σε ἀνοῖξαι ὀφθαλμοὺς αὐτῶν, τοῦ ἐπιστρέψαι ἀπὸ σκότους εἰς φῶς καὶ τῆς ἐξουσίας τοῦ Σατανᾶ ἐπὶ τὸν θεόν, τοῦ λαβεῖν αὐτοὺς ἄφεσιν ἁμαρτιῶν καὶ κλῆρον ἐν τοῖς ἡγιασμένοις πίστει τῇ εἰς ἐμέ I send you to open their eyes, that they may turn from darkness to light and from the power of Satan to God, that they may receive forgiveness of sins and a place among those who are sanctified by faith in me	This passage is part of a speech delivered by Paul to Agrippa, telling of his conversion, and here quoting Jesus' commission to him to go to the gentiles. Again, there is no mention of a commission to heal physical ailments. The implication is that the commission is to bring spiritual wholeness.

Acts 28.7-8	Paul	προσευξάμενος ἐπιθεὶς τὰς χεῖρας αὐτῷ ἰάσατο αὐτόν (28.8)	πυρετοῖς καὶ δυσεντερίῳ συνεχόμενον κατακεῖσθαι (28.8)	Specific: 1 (Publius' father); prayer and laying on of hands.	At Malta, the chief man of the island, Publius, welcomed and entertained Paul and his companions ("us") for three days. Publius' father lay sick with fever and dysentery.	Publius fulfilled the hospitality requirements laid down by Jesus (Matthew 10.11-14; Mark 6.8-11; Luke 9.1-6, 10.4-9, esp. 8-9; GT #14), with the effect that Paul healed (ἰάσατο) his father of specific ailments, and then the remaining population who came to him began being healed (ἐθεραπεύοντο). (See below 28.9)
Acts 28.9	Paul	προσήρχοντο καὶ ἐθεραπεύοντο (28.9)	οἱ λοιποὶ οἱ ἐν τῇ νήσῳ ἔχοντες ἀσθενείας (28.9)	General: those left on the island who were infirm; ?	At Malta, after Publius' father was healed, the rest of the population who were infirm (ἔχοντες ἀσθενείας) came, and were treated (ἐθεραπεύοντο).	A general healing episode, no specific ailments cited. The use of the imperfect tense, linked with the treatment of those ἔχοντες ἀσθενείας is to be expected here. Cf 20.35, where the infirm (τῶν ἀσθενούντῶν) are described as Paul's (and, by implication, Jesus'/God's) clientele.

Appendix 8 : 2
The language of punishment in *Acts*

Reference	Agent	Greek word	Malady / Provocation	Type, number, method	Victim profile, location, motive	Comments
Acts 1.15-20	Story recounted by Peter	Οὗτος μὲν οὖν ἐκτήσατο χωρίον ἐκ μισθοῦ τῆς ἀδικίας, καὶ πρηνὴς γενόμενος ἐλάκησεν μέσος, καὶ ἐξεχύθη πάντα τὰ σπλάγχνα αὐτοῦ (1.18)	Ἰούδα τοῦ γενομένου ὁδηγοῦ τοῖς συλλαβοῦσιν Ἰησοῦν, ὅτι κατηριθμημένος ἦν ἐν ἡμῖν καὶ ἔλαχεν τὸν κλῆρον τῆς διακονίας ταύτης (1.16,17)	Specific: 1, Judas	At Jerusalem, one of Jesus' twelve disciples, Judas, who had acted as a guide to those who arrested Jesus, bought a field with the reward of his wickedness, and died there (1.16-18). Peter recounts this story for two reasons: to explain that scripture had to be fulfilled concerning Judas' death, and to appoint another disciple in his place (1.16,20).	There is still debate concerning the translation of πρηνὴς γενόμενος (1.18): either *falling headlong* or *swelling up* having been proposed. (See Arndt and Gingrich [1957] 707.) The result is the same: Judas burst open in the middle and his bowels gushed out (ἐλάκησεν μέσος, καὶ ἐξεχύθη πάντα τὰ σπλάγχνα αὐτοῦ). The effect was that all the inhabitants of Jerusalem heard about it, and the field became known as the Field of Blood (Ἀκελδαμάχ, τοῦτ' ἔστιν, Χωρίον Αἵματος (1.19)). According to Peter this was to fulfil scripture (1.16,20). However, the implication is that capital punishment has been carried out by a higher power, in a gruesome manner. The effect on the audience must be one of fear, even if tempered by a sense of justification in this case.

Acts 5.5	Peter	ἀκούων δὲ ὁ Ἀνανίας τοὺς λόγους τούτους πεσὼν ἐξέψυξεν· καὶ ἐγένετο φόβος μέγας ἐπὶ πάντας τοὺς ἀκούοντας (5.5)	οὐκ ἐψεύσω ἀνθρώποις ἀλλὰ τῷ θεῷ (5.4)	Specific: 1, Ananias	At Jerusalem, a man named Ananias with his wife Sapphira sold a piece of property, and with his wife's knowledge he kept back some of the proceeds, and brought only a part and laid it at the apostles' feet. But Peter said, "Ananias why has Satan filled your heart to lie to the Holy Spirit and to keep back part of the proceeds of the land? While it remained unsold, did it not remain your own? And after it was sold was it not at your disposal? How is it that you have contrived this deed in your heart? You have not lied to men but to God." (5.1-4)	The verb ἐκψύχω used to describe Ananias' death (5.5) is a medical term (Hippokrates *Morb*. 1.5), meaning *breathe one's last*. It occurs again at 5.10, describing Sapphira's death, and at 12.23, describing Herod's death. Here, the event inspires great fear (φόβος μέγας). The young men wrapped him up and carried him out and buried him (5.5-6). The context of this story is important. The author has just recounted (4.32-37) how the believers held everything in common, so that there was not a needy person among them. Apparently it became the practice of those who owned property to sell it and lay the proceeds before the apostles for distribution to the needy. One such person is identified: Joseph, a Levite, a native of Cyprus. Thus the death of Ananias acts as a twofold warning to the believers: to tell the whole truth, and to give up one's entire wealth for distribution.

Acts 5.10	Peter	ἔπεσεν δὲ παραχρῆμα πρὸς τοὺς πόδας αὐτοῦ καὶ ἐξέψυξεν (5.10)	ὁ δὲ Πέτρος πρὸς αὐτήν, Τί ὅτι συνεφωνήθη ὑμῖν πειράσαι τὸ πνεῦμα κυρίου; ἰδοὺ οἱ πόδες τῶν θαψάντων τὸν ἄνδρα σου ἐπὶ τῇ θύρᾳ καὶ ἐξοίσουσίν σε (5.9)	Specific: 1, Sapphira	At Jerusalem, about three hours after Ananias' death, his wife came in , not knowing what had happened. And Peter said to her, "Tell me whether you sold the land for so much." And she said , "Yes, for so much." But Peter said to her, "How is it that you have agreed together to tempt the spirit of the Lord? Behold, the feet of those that have buried your husband are at the door, and they will carry you out." (5.7-9)	The same word (ἐκψύχω) is chosen to describe Sapphira's death. When the young men came in they found her dead (νεκράν), and they carried her out and buried her beside her husband. And great fear (φόβος μέγας) came upon the whole church, and upon all who heard these things (5.10-11). The deaths of Ananias and Sapphira occur at the beginning of a chapter containing many signs and wonders (σημεῖα καὶ τέρατα πολλὰ (5.12)): the healing of those who were weak and troubled by unclean spirits (5.16); the implication that Peter's shadow possessed healing power (5.15); and the miraculous release of the imprisoned apostles (5.17-20). The atmosphere is charged with fear and awe, accompanied by violent events.

Acts 9.1-9	A light from heaven: Jesus	ἐξαίφνης τε αὐτὸν περιήστραψεν φῶς ἐκ τοῦ οὐρανοῦ, καὶ πεσὼν ἐπὶ τὴν γῆν ἤκουσεν φωνὴν λέγουσαν αὐτῷ . . . ἠγέρθη δὲ Σαῦλος ἀπὸ τῆς γῆς, ἀνεῳγμένων δὲ τῶν ὀφθαλμῶν αὐτοῦ οὐδὲν ἔβλεπεν· χειραγωγοῦντες δὲ αὐτὸν εἰσήγαγον εἰς Δαμασκόν. καὶ ἦν ἡμέρας τρεῖς μὴ βλέπων, καὶ οὐκ ἔφαγεν οὐδὲ ἔπιεν (9. 3-4, 8-9)	ὁ δὲ Σαῦλος, ἔτι ἐμπνέων ἀπειλῆς καὶ φόνου εἰς τοὺς μαθητὰς τοῦ κυρίου, προσελθὼν τῷ ἀρχιερεῖ ᾐτήσατο παρ' αὐτοῦ ἐπιστολὰς εἰς Δαμασκὸν πρὸς τὰς συναγωγάς, ὅπως ἐάν τινας εὕρῃ τῆς ὁδοῦ ὄντας, ἄνδρας τε καὶ γυναῖκας, δεδεμένους ἀγάγῃ εἰς Ἰερουσαλήμ (9.1-2)	Specific: 1, Saul	On the road from Jerusalem to Damascus, Saul, who had breathed threats and murder against the disciples, and who was travelling to Damascus with the express intention of finding and persecuting disciples there, fell to the ground when a light from heaven flashed about him. He conversed with a voice, and then was led, sightless, to Damascus, where he remained for three days, blind and without food and drink. There, the Lord (in a vision) told a disciple, Ananias, to heal him for "he is a chosen instrument ... to carry my name to the gentiles and kings and sons of Israel ... he must suffer (παθεῖν) for my name." Ananias lay hands on Saul who regained his sight, was baptised, took food, and was strengthened (9.1-19).	Saul's blinding and conversion produced amazement (ἐξίσταντο) in his audience (9.21), and his preaching activities built up the church so that "the church throughout all Judea and Galilee and Samaria had peace and was built up; and walking in the fear (τῷ φόβῳ) of the Lord and in the comfort (τῇ παρακλήσει) of the Holy Spirit it was multiplied (9.31)."

Acts 12.23	An angel of the Lord (12.23)	καὶ γενόμενος σκωληκόβρωτος ἐξέψυξεν (12.23)	ὁ δὲ δῆμος ἐπεφώνει, Θεοῦ φωνὴ καὶ οὐκ ἀνθρώπου. παραχρῆμα δὲ ἐπάταξεν αὐτὸν ἄγγελος κυρίου ἀνθ' ὧν οὐκ ἔδωκεν τὴν δόξαν τῷ θεῷ, καὶ γενόμενος σκωληκόβρωτος ἐξέψυξεν (12.22-23)	Specific: 1, Herod	Herod's death took place at Caesarea (12.19-23). He had long been an opponent of Jesus and his followers. This is an informative chapter, providing social details of imprisonment, and housing, as well as names of disciples of both sexes and degree: Mary, the mother of John Mark; Rhoda, her maid; James, the brother of John; Peter, Barnabas, Saul, and John Mark. Herod's death is gruesome, as is the death of Judas. Their crimes obviously warranted greater punishment than those of Ananias and Sapphira, although, ultimately, the end result was the same.	Herod's death is the final act of his history, given in chapter 12, which begins: "About that time Herod the king laid violent hands upon some who belonged to the church. He killed James the brother of John..." (12.1-2). He then imprisoned Peter, who was miraculously released by an angel of the Lord (12.3-19). But it is because he did not give God glory in front of the people of Tyre and Sidon that he was smitten by an angel of the Lord, and, eaten by worms, died (12.20-23). The effect of this gruesome death was that (12.24): "the word of God was growing and multiplying."

Acts 13.11	Paul (through the hand of the Lord)	καὶ νῦν ἰδοὺ χεὶρ κυρίου ἐπὶ σέ, καὶ ἔσῃ τυφλὸς μὴ βλέπων τὸν ἥλιον ἄχρι καιροῦ. παραχρῆμά τε ἔπεσεν ἐπ' αὐτὸν ἀχλὺς καὶ σκότος, καὶ περιάγων ἐζήτει χειραγωγούς (13.11)	Σαῦλος δέ, ὁ καὶ Παῦλος, πλησθεὶς πνεύματος ἁγίου ἀτενίσας εἰς αὐτὸν εἶπεν, Ὦ πλήρης παντὸς δόλου καὶ πάσης ῥᾳδιουργίας, υἱὲ διαβόλου, ἐχθρὲ πάσης δικαιοσύνης, οὐ παύσῃ διαστρέφων τὰς ὁδοὺς [τοῦ] κυρίου τὰς εὐθείας; (13.9-10)	Specific: Elymas the magician	At Paphos, on the island of Cyprus, Barnabas and Paul came across a Jewish false prophet, who sought to turn the proconsul, Sergius Paulus, from the faith (13.4-12). Paul, (by the hand of the Lord) temporarily blinded him. The effect was predictable: "Then the proconsul believed, when he saw what had occurred, for he was astonished (ἐκπλησσόμενος) at the teaching (τῇ διδαχῇ) of the Lord." (13.12)	No details are given as to the content of the teaching given by Paul and Barnabas. All that is given is the detail of a contest between Paul and Elymas, which Paul won by physically disabling his opponent.

Acts 19.14-20	The man in whom the evil spirit was (19.16)	καὶ ἐφαλόμενος ὁ ἄνθρωπος ἐπ' αὐτοὺς ἐν ᾧ ἦν τὸ πνεῦμα τὸ πονηρὸν κατακυριεύσας ἀμφοτέρων ἴσχυσεν κατ' αὐτῶν, ὥστε γυμνοὺς καὶ τετραυματισμένους ἐκφυγεῖν ἐκ τοῦ οἴκου ἐκείνου (19.16)	ἐπεχείρησαν δέ τινες καὶ τῶν περιερχομένων Ἰουδαίων ἐξορκιστῶν ὀνομάζειν ἐπὶ τοὺς ἔχοντας τὰ πνεύματα τὰ πονηρὰ τὸ ὄνομα τοῦ κυρίου Ἰησοῦ λέγοντες, Ὁρκίζω ὑμᾶς τὸν Ἰησοῦν ὃν Παῦλος κηρύσσει. ἦσαν δέ τινος Σκευᾶ Ἰουδαίου ἀρχιερέως ἑπτὰ υἱοὶ τοῦτο ποιοῦντες. ἀποκριθὲν δὲ τὸ πνεῦμα τὸ πονηρὸν εἶπεν αὐτοῖς, Τὸν [μὲν] Ἰησοῦν γινώσκω καὶ τὸν Παῦλον ἐπίσταμαι, ὑμεῖς δὲ τίνες ἐστέ; (19.13-15)	Specific: Sceva's (a Jewish high priest) seven sons	At Ephesus, itinerant Jewish exorcists undertook to pronounce the name of the Lord Jesus over those who had evil spirits (19.11-13). Seven sons of a Jewish high priest named Sceva were doing this. But the evil spirit answered them, "Jesus I know, and Paul I know; but who are you?" And the man in whom the evil spirit was leaped on them, mastered all of them, and overpowered them, so that they fled out of that house naked and wounded. (19.14-16)	This account is contrary to the gospel account of exorcists working in Jesus' name (Luke 9.49-50; Mark 9.38-41). The effect here is as expected: "And this became known to all residents of Ephesus, both Jews and Greeks; and fear fell upon them all; and the name of the Lord Jesus was extolled (19.17). Many also came divulging magic practices, and burning their books (19.18-19). Overall "the word of the Lord was growing and prevailing mightily." (19.20)

These seven examples of punishment balance the twelve healing miracles in *Acts*. Paul's blinding is the central story. All stories are specific, the victims being carefully identified in every case, either by name or parentage. As well the locations of the victims, and their histories and occupations are cited. There appears to be a formula in content and purpose. The effect in every instance (except Paul's) produces fear in those around, and as a result of this fear people "turn" to Jesus, and the church grows mightily. In this way the tenor of *Acts* and the gospels is very different.

Appendix 8 : 3

New Testament healing words : ἰάομαι ἴασις ἴαμα ἰατρός

Reference	Form	Part of speech	Comment
Matthew 8.8	ἰαθήσεται	Future indicative passive: 3 sing.	Matthew only uses verbal forms of ἰάομαι to report two healing stories. Both stories concern the in-absentia healing of non-Jewish patients, in answer to a parental request made in faith. The faith of the "parent" is stressed. Here ἰάομαι appears in the words of the centurion to Jesus: "But only say the word, and my boy (παῖς) will be healed (ἰαθήσεται)." παῖς can mean either "servant" or "son"; in either case, the centurion here is making a request as the head of the household, acting *in loco parentis*.
Matthew 8.13	ἰάθη	Aorist indicative passive: 3 sing.	Matthew uses ἰάομαι to sum up his account of the healing of the centurion's boy: "And his boy was healed (ἰάθη) in that very hour." It may be significant that Matthew chooses ἰάομαι to recount this story. The centurion, a member of the Roman occupying forces, would have been seen as an outsider by the Jewish people, as a truly genuine gentile. Matthew uses this story to allow Jesus to marvel at the man's faith, faith that he had not discovered in Israel (8.10). Even so, Jesus does not touch the man or his son (cf. Jairus' daughter: 9.18-19, 23-26), or the Canaanite woman or her daughter (15.21-28); both healings where ἰάομαι is used to describe the outcome. ἰάομαι has a long history in the Greek language of healing, in use since Homeric times. It is appropriate that Matthew should choose it to recount the healing of a gentile. Matthew has to stress the faith of the centurion to justify Jesus' involvement to his Jewish readers, and uses ἰάομαι in the passive to denote the intervention of God. In the Greek world ἰάομαι is the preferred verb to describe the action and intervention of the healing god, Asklepios (see Section One, Part One); ἰάομαι is also the preferred verb to describe the action and intervention of God in the Septuagint (see chapter six, Section Two, Part One, and App. 6:1).

Matthew 9.12	ἰατροῦ	Noun (ἰατρός): gen., sing., masc.	The only occurrence of the noun form ἰατρός in *Matthew*. It occurs in a saying of Jesus, given in reply to a question put to his disciples by the Pharisees, asking why Jesus ate with tax collectors and sinners. Jesus replied: οὐ χρείαν ἔχουσιν οἱ ἰσχύοντες ἰατροῦ ἀλλ' οἱ κακῶς ἔχοντες (those who are well have no need of a physician, but those who are ill [9.12]). Matthew had no choice in using this word. There is no other word for physician in Greek. Matthew's account of Jesus' saying is identical with Mark in this case, but it is important to note that he adds material, amongst which is a quotation from the Septuagint (Hosea 6.6), a typically Matthaean practice. Luke, in contrast, prefers to substitute ὑγιαίνοντες for ἰσχύοντες in Jesus' saying, a word that implies holistic health, rather than just physical well-being (cf. Mk 2.13-17; Lk 5.27-32).
Matthew 13.15 (cf. John 12.40, Acts 28.27, Isaiah 6.10 [App. 6:1, **62**])	ἰάσομαι	Future indicative middle: 1 sing.	In a quotation from the Septuagint (Isaiah 6.10), and repeated at John 12.40 and Acts 28.27. It is part of a most significant quotation (Isaiah 6.9-10), linking healing with seeing and hearing (and therefore understanding) God's message. Thus, in *Matthew*, it is Jesus' message that causes the blind to see, the deaf to hear, and that ultimately brings healing. It is obvious that Jesus is referring to spiritual sight, spiritual hearing, and spiritual health. He explains (13.16), that the eyes and ears of the disciples are blessed (μακάριοι), because they see and hear what many prophets and righteous men before them had longed to see and hear, but had not.

Matthew 15.28	ἰάθη	Aorist indicative passive: 3 sing.	As 8.13 above, Matthew uses ἰάομαι to describe the instantaneous, in-absentia healing of the child of a gentile. As in the earlier episode Jesus does not touch the parent or the child, and stresses the remarkable faith of the parent. The mother is a Canaanite, and therefore not only a member of a gentile nation, but a gentile nation with a long history of inciting Jewish enmity. The mother's importunity is the catalyst for a conversation between the mother and Jesus concerning the relative claims of the Jews and the gentiles on Jesus. Jesus is reluctant to act: he ignores her, and then questions her about her rights. When she asks only for the scraps (i.e. what the Jews themselves did not want) Jesus makes it clear that it is only her exceptional faith that causes healing. In both instances of gentile healing - the centurion's boy, and the Canaanite woman's daughter - Matthew takes pains to make Jesus' involvement and God's action (passive verb) intelligible and acceptable to his Jewish audience. It is significant that he uses ἰάομαι in both stories, and that in this story he has reworked the parallel version in *Mark* (7.24-30), using different language to describe the healing itself (Mark does not use ἰάομαι), and also to describe the mother (Mark defines the woman as a Syro-Phoenician, the more common gentile word for people of that region). Therefore Matthew's choice of language is a conscious decision, a decision that can only be explained if Matthew uses ἰάομαι in the passive to describe the intervention of God, and if ἰάομαι does not involve any ongoing treatment or association between Jesus and the patient.
Mark 2.17	ἰατροῦ	Noun (ἰατρός): gen., sing., masc.	The first of two occurrences of the noun ἰατρός in *Mark*. As in *Matthew* this form occurs in Jesus' answer to the question concerning his eating companions. Jesus replied: οὐ χρείαν ἔχουσιν οἱ ἰσχύοντες ἰατροῦ ἀλλ' οἱ κακῶς ἔχοντες (those who are well have no need of a physician, but those who are ill [2.17]). The language used is identical with Matthew 9.12. Cf. Mt 9.9-13; Lk 5.27-32, and above on Mt 9.12, below on Lk 5.31.

Mark 5.26	ἰατρῶν	Noun (ἰατρός): gen., pl., masc.	The second of Mark's uses of the noun ἰατρός, here in the story of the haemorrhaging woman. It is Mark who gives us the most detail concerning this woman's background: she had had a flow of blood for twelve years, she had suffered much under many doctors, she had spent all that she had, she was no better but rather grew worse (5.25-6). Matthew omits all but the fact that the woman had suffered from a haemorrhage for twelve years (Mt 9.20), while Luke compresses Mark's information to a comment that she had spent all her livelihood on physicians, unable to be treated by anyone (Lk 8. 43). In *Mark* the woman thinks of healing in terms of the verb σῴζω (5.28), but when the haemorrhage ceases, knows that she is healed (ὅτι ἴαται ἀπὸ τῆς μάστιγος [5.29]). Jesus sums up the result with a combination of σῴζω and ὑγιής : θυγάτηρ, ἡ πίστις σου σέσωκέν σε· ὕπαγε εἰς εἰρήνην καὶ ἴσθι ὑγιὴς ἀπὸ τῆς μάστιγός σου (5.34). Both σῴζω and ὑγιής imply more than just physical health and wellbeing, they include the notions of emotional, mental and spiritual wholeness as well.
Mark 5.29	ἴαται	Perfect indicative in passive sense: 3.sing.	The only occurrence of the verbal form of ἰάομαι in *Mark*, found here in the story of the haemorrhaging woman (see above, Mk 5.26). It occurs in the woman's thoughts concerning the state of her body, after she had touched Jesus' cloak (καὶ ἔγνω τῷ σώματι ὅτι ἴαται ἀπὸ τῆς μάστιγος [5.29]). The woman thinks in terms of σῴζω and ἰάομαι; Mark reports Jesus as using the terms σῴζω and ὑγιής. Mark's use of the perfect form of ἰάομαι makes it perfectly clear that, in this case, the woman is experiencing a present state, following a completed action. No more treatment is necessary. Jesus too makes it obvious that the action is completed: he knew that power had gone out from him (τὴν ἐξ αὐτοῦ δύναμιν ἐξελθοῦσαν [5.30]). Thus ἰάομαι in *Mark* (as in *Matthew*) describes instantaneous healing, as a result of the intervention of God, intervention brought about by faith so great it causes Jesus to comment. (It may be significant that this woman, like the centurion [Mt 8.5-13] and the Canaanite woman [Mt 15.21-8], was also an "outsider": her affliction would have excluded her from participating fully in Jewish spiritual life.)

Luke 4.23	Ἰατρέ	Noun (ἰατρός): voc., sing., masc.	The only occurrence of this form of ἰατρός in the NT. Jesus is in the synagogue at Nazareth, and has just read a passage from *Isaiah*, which he claims to fulfil (4.16-21). Jesus uses this form, concerning himself, reflecting what he understands as the doubt of the people of Nazareth about his identity (see App. 7:8: θεραπεύω Lk. 4.23). It is significant that he should designate himself as ἰατρός in this situation, and that he chooses the verb θεραπεύω to describe appropriate action. The OT passage does not catalogue physical healings but rather the commission to bring good news to the poor, to preach freedom/forgiveness to prisoners and the recovery of (spiritual?) sight to the blind, to set at liberty those who are oppressed, and to proclaim the favourable year of the Lord. It would seem that Jesus sees himself as a spiritual physician, commissioned to bring a message of hope, freedom, forgiveness, and spiritual insight. That he should feel that the community of his home town would see him as being in need of this sort of message/treatment himself is not surprising: he was poor and not among the leaders of the community, certainly not in a position of religious authority. It is the message outlined in the OT passage, read by Jesus in the synagogue, that forms the treatment, the healing message that is to be delivered by Jesus, the spiritual physician.
Luke 5.17	ἰᾶσθαι	Present infinitive middle (the same form as the perfect infinitive)	Luke uses this form of ἰάομαι twice, here, and at 9.2. Here it occurs in an introductory statement (καὶ δύναμις κυρίου ἦν εἰς τὸ ἰᾶσθαι αὐτόν) to the account of the healing of a paralytic (5.18-26). This healing allows Jesus to discuss his mission to forgive sins (heal) with the Pharisees and the teachers of the law.

Luke 5.31	ἰατροῦ	Noun (ἰατρός): gen., sing., masc.	As in *Matthew* (9.12), and *Mark* (2.17), this noun occurs in a saying of Jesus in reply to a question concerning his choice of eating companions. Luke however, changes the wording of the saying (wording that is identical in *Matthew* and *Mark*), substituting ὑγιαίνοντες for ἰσχύοντες in Jesus' saying, a word that implies holistic health, rather than just physical well-being. In Luke's version Jesus replied: οὐ χρείαν ἔχουσιν οἱ ὑγιαίοντες ἰατροῦ ἀλλὰ οἱ κακῶς ἔχοντες (those who are healthy have no need of a physician, but those who are ill [5.31]). Luke has several other differences, but, overall, his language in this story is closer to the Markan version than Matthew's. (Cf. Mt 9.9-13; Mk 2. 13-17; Lk 5. 27-32). Where Mark says that Levi rose and followed Jesus, Luke adds that <u>he left everything</u>, and rose and followed him. Mark does not describe the food, but Luke tells us that Levi made him <u>a great feast</u>. Where Mark has many tax collectors and sinners sitting with Jesus and his disciples, Luke has a large company of tax collectors and others reclining with them. Luke does add εἰς μετάνοιαν to Mark's and Matthew's version of Jesus' final saying: οὐ γὰρ ἦλθον καλέσαι δικαίους ἀλλὰ ἁμαρτωλοὺς (I have not come to call the righteous but sinners [Mk 2.17; Mt 9.13]), so that Jesus' final saying on the question of his companions is: οὐκ ἐλήλυθα καλέσαι δικαίους ἀλλὰ ἁμαρτωλοὺς εἰς μετάνοιαν (I have not come to call the righteous but sinners (those who have missed the mark) <u>to repentance</u> (i.e. to return [to God] [5.32]).
Luke 6.18	ἰαθῆναι	Aorist infinitive passive	The only occurrence of this form of ἰάομαι in the NT. Here it occurs in a general healing episode, where a great crowd of people came to hear Jesus, and to be healed of their diseases (οἳ ἦλθον ἀκοῦσαι αὐτοῦ καὶ ἰαθῆναι ἀπὸ τῶν νόσων αὐτῶν). Again healing is linked with hearing the message, and the intervention of God (passive verb).

Luke 6.19	ἰᾶτο	Imperfect indicative middle: 3 sing.	Luke uses this form of ἰάομαι twice, here and at 9.11. Both are crowd situations. It is significant that Luke chooses the imperfect tense to describe these episodes. Here he differentiates between ἰάομαι and θεραπεύω, although, again, both are in the imperfect tense. He chooses θεραπεύω in the passive voice for those troubled by unclean spirits (οἱ ἐνοχλούμενοι ἀπὸ πνευμάτων ἀκαθάρτων ἐθεραπεύοντο), whereas ἰάομαι is reserved for the crowd seeking to touch him (καὶ πᾶς ὁ ὄχλος ἐζήτουν ἅπτεσθαι αὐτοῦ, ὅτι δύναμις παρ' αὐτοῦ ἐξήρχετο καὶ ἰᾶτο πάντας). Healing is not instantaneous, but rather a process, especially in crowd situations. Perhaps the imperfect tense, in crowd situations, might also imply that Jesus began healing/treating people one-by-one. It would seem that people troubled by unclean spirits were treated by hearing the message, whereas those seeking to touch Jesus were being healed by that touch.
Luke 7.7	ἰαθήτω	Aorist imperative passive: 3 sing.	The only occasion this form of ἰάομαι occurs in the NT. Luke puts it in the mouth of the centurion when he asks Jesus to heal his slave (δοῦλος). However, there is a manuscript variation, some citing ἰαθήσεται, as in the parallel story at Matthew 8.8. Luke sums up the result of this request by describing the condition of the slave as ὑγιαίνοντα (7.10).
Luke 8.43	{D} [ἰατροῖς]	Noun (ἰατρός): dat., pl., masc.	This noun (in square brackets) occurs in the story of the haemorrhaging woman, in a passage which describes how the woman had spent her livelihood on physicians, but she had been unable to treated (θεραπευθῆναι). Metzger (1975) 145, reports a divergence of opinion as to whether the text ἰατροῖς προσαναλώσασα ὅλον τὸν βίον should be retained, on the grounds that it looks "like a digest of Mk. 5.26", and that there is early evidence for the shorter text. However, the condensation and substitution of language appears typical of Luke. Accordingly the clause has been allowed to remain in the text, enclosed within square brackets, designated as category {D}. The woman's haemorrhage ceased after she touched the fringe of Jesus' cloak, so that she later declared how she had been immediately healed (ὡς ἰάθη παραχρῆμα (8.47)). But Jesus sums up her healing in terms of σῴζω : "Daughter, your faith has saved you; go in peace." (Θυγάτηρ, ἡ πίστις σου σέσωκέν σε; πορεύου εἰς εἰρήνην (8.48))

Luke 8.47	ἰάθη	Aorist indicative passive: 3 sing.	In Luke's version of the story of the haemorrhaging woman, when she declares how she had been healed. She reports instantaneous healing, when she had touched the fringe of Jesus' cloak.
Luke 9.2	ἰᾶσθαι	Present infinitive middle (the same form as the perfect infinitive)	In Luke's account of Jesus' commission to the twelve to preach the kingdom of God and to heal [the infirm] (ἰᾶσθαι (τοὺς ἀσθενεῖς)), after giving them authority and power over all demons and to treat diseases (νόσους θεραπεύειν). It is significant that Luke has chosen the present tense for all these infinitives, implying continuous action; and linked ἰᾶσθαι with preaching (κηρύσσειν) the kingdom of God. The inclusion of (τοὺς ἀσθενεῖς) after ἰᾶσθαι is disputed. One wonders then whether "to preach the kingdom of God" is to produce the natural and consummate effect of wholeness in those who hear and understand the message. However, Luke chooses the present participle of θεραπεύω to describe the disciples' behaviour in response to this commission (see comment on Lk 9.6, Apps 7:3, 7:8, 7:9).
Luke 9.11	ἰᾶτο	Imperfect indicative middle: 3 sing.	In a general healing episode describing Jesus' behaviour in a crowd situation. Luke chooses the imperfect tense: after he (Jesus) welcomed them (the crowd) he began speaking to them of the kingdom of God, and those in need of treatment he began healing (καὶ ἀποδεξάμενος αὐτοὺς ἐλάλει αὐτοῖς περὶ τῆς βασιλείας τοῦ θεοῦ, καὶ τοὺς χρείαν ἔχοντας θεραπείας ἰᾶτο). This incident is immediately prior to Luke's account of the feeding of the 5,000. Again Luke uses θεραπεύω and ἰάομαι contiguously; and is careful to use the imperfect tense of ἰάομαι to describe Jesus' behaviour; and again this behaviour is linked with Jesus' message.
Luke 9.42	ἰάσατο	Aorist indicative middle: 3 sing.	In Luke's version of the healing of the epileptic boy (cf. Mt 17.14-18; Mk 9. 14-27). All synoptic gospels emphasise the significance of this healing by placing it after Peter's declaration of Jesus' identity, and his transfiguration. Luke is curiously condensed; it is Mark who gives the more clinical case history (see Apps 5:2 and 7:8). However, Luke does say that the boy was the man's only child (cf. Jairus' daughter, and the widow of Nain's son). All three synoptists use this healing to portray Jesus' chagrin at the disciples' lack of faith. Luke is the only synoptist to choose ἰάομαι to describe Jesus' action, an action that clearly shows Jesus' superiority in the healing sphere.

Luke 13.32	ἰάσεις	Noun (ἴασις): acc., pl., fem.	This noun occurs in a saying of Jesus, in answer to the Pharisees' warning to him that Herod wanted to kill him. Jesus said: "Go and tell that fox, 'Behold, I cast out demons and bring healings (ἰάσεις ἀποτελῶ) to completion today and tomorrow, and on the third day I finish my course....'" It is curious that Luke chooses the present tense for all three verbs (ἐκβάλλω, ἀποτελω, τελειοῦμαι), and that this passage occurs in a teaching passage (13.22-35), between the sabbath healings of the bent woman (13.10-17), and the man with dropsy (14.1-6). Again healing is inextricably bound up with Jesus' message: in this case unspecified processes of healing (nearing completion), and the casting out of demons.
Luke 14.4	ἰάσατο	Aorist indicative middle: 3 sing.	As a description of Jesus' action, when he heals the man with dropsy on the sabbath. Luke again uses θεραπεύω and ἰάομαι in the same story, choosing θεραπεύω to describe the Pharisees' questioning of Jesus' probable course of action, and ἰάομαι to describe the action itself.
Luke 17.15	ἰάθη	Aorist indicative passive: 3 sing.	In Luke's story of the ten lepers who were cleansed (ἐκαθαρίσθησαν). One of them, seeing that he was healed (ἰδὼν ὅτι ἰάθη), returned to thank Jesus, praising God. Thus ἰάθη describes the man's perception of himself. This story has parallels with the haemorrhaging woman, who has the same perception of herself (Lk 8.47), and to whom Jesus makes the same comment: "Your faith has saved you (ἡ πίστις σου σέσωκέν σε)." Jesus describes their healing in terms of σῴζω.
Luke 22.51	ἰάσατο	Aorist indicative middle: 3 sing.	In Luke's account of Jesus' action at the Mount of Olives, when Jesus healed the right ear of the high priest's slave. The slave had been struck with a sword by one of Jesus' companions.

John 4.47	ἰάσηται	Aorist subjunctive middle: 3 sing.	In the reported speech of the official (βασιλικὸς) who asked Jesus to heal his son (καὶ ἠρώτα ἵνα καταβῇ καὶ ἰάσηται αὐτοῦ τὸν υἱόν). Cf. Mt 8.5-13; Lk 7.1-10. Jesus uses the verb ζάω to describe the boy's return to health. This is the first healing reported in *John*, and the second sign (σημεῖον). It appears at the end of a non-Jewish chapter: after the story of the Samaritan woman at the well, Jesus' declaration of identity (4.26), and the belief of the Samaritans. The boy's fever left him at the seventh hour, the hour at which the father spoke to Jesus. (The number seven has symbolic significance for John.) An *in absentia* healing: Jesus does not touch the patient, or the father. See Robinson (1985) 69, n. 158, for an interesting discussion concerning the identity of the father.
John 5.13	ἰαθεὶς	Aorist participle passive: nom., sing., masc.	As a description of the man whom Jesus chose to heal by the Beth-zatha pool, in Jerusalem, on the sabbath. John uses both θεραπεύω (5.10) and ἰάομαι (5.13) to describe the man in his narrative, while in direct speech Jesus uses ὑγιής (5.6), as does the man himself in reported speech (5.15). This healing is highly symbolic: the man had been ill for 38 years (Israel wandered in the wilderness for 38 years). That all three healing words are used is significant: the aspects of nurture, cure and wholeness are thus combined. This man appears to be symbolic of Israel, in that both were in a spiritual wilderness.
John 12.40 (cf. Matthew 13.15, Acts 28.27, Isaiah 6.10 [App. 6:1, **62**])	ἰάσομαι	Future indicative middle: 1 sing.	In a quotation from the Septuagint (Isaiah 6.10). A more accurate version of the entire Septuagint passage also appears at Matthew 13.15 and Acts 28.27. It is part of a most significant quotation (Isaiah 6.9-10), linking healing with seeing and hearing (and therefore understanding) God's message. Thus, in the NT, it is Jesus' message that causes the blind to see, the deaf to hear, and that ultimately brings healing. John uses this quotation in a passage explaining why people did not recognise Jesus' identity.

Acts 4.22	ἰάσεως	Noun (ἴασις): gen., sing., fem.	This form of the noun ἰάσις occurs as the summing up - this sign of healing (τὸ σημεῖον τοῦτο τῆς ἰάσεως) - of the first healing episode recorded in Acts (3.1-4.31). The actual account of the healing is described in clinical language: πιάζω is used to describe Peter's grip on the man; στερεόω to describe the state of his feet and ankles, after Peter had spoken to and touched him (3.7). His condition is given in the terms of a clinical case history: he was over forty (4.22), and had been lame from birth (3.2). Immediately (3.8) he was able to jump up (ἐξάλλομαι), and walk about (περιπατέω). Peter describes him (3.16) as being in perfect health (τὴν ὁλοκληρίαν), and (4.9) as "saved" (σέσωται). The Pharisees (4.14) see him as the man who had been treated (τὸν τεθεραπευμένον).
Acts 4.30	ἴασιν	Noun (ἴασις): acc., sing., fem.	In a corporate prayer (4.24-30) that describes the place and function of Jesus in the history of creation. Again the "message" and "healing" are linked.
Acts 9.34	ἰᾶταί	Present indicative middle: 3 sing.	In Peter's speech to the bedridden Aeneas: "Jesus Christ heals you..." (ἰᾶταί σε Ἰησοῦς Χριστός).
Acts 10.38	ἰώμενος	Present participle middle: nom., sing., masc.	In a description of Jesus in a speech given by Peter to the centurion, Cornelius, and Cornelius' kinsmen and close friends: " he (Jesus) went about doing good and healing all that were oppressed by the devil, for God was with him ..." (ὃς διῆλθεν εὐεργετῶν καὶ ἰώμενος πάντας τοὺς καταδυναστευομένους ὑπὸ τοῦ διαβόλου, ὅτι ὁ θεὸς ἦν μετ' αὐτοῦ). At first glance this appears to refer to spiritual healing only, Jesus' clientele being described as "those oppressed by the devil". However Luke describes physical healings in this manner also. See Luke 13.10-17, especially 13.16. (Cf. Wisdom 16.12; App 6:1, **40**)

Acts 28.8	ἰάσατο	Aorist indicative middle: 3 sing.	As a description of the effect of Paul's treatment of Publius' father at Malta. Paul, after praying, "placed his hands on him and healed him ..." (ἐπιθεὶς τὰς χεῖρας αὐτῷ ἰάσατο αὐτόν). Publius had fulfilled the hospitality requirements laid down by Jesus (Matthew 10.11-14; Mark 6.8-11; Luke 9.1-6, 10.4-9, esp. 8-9; GT #14), with the effect that Paul healed his father of specific ailments (fever and dysentery). This is the only occurrence in the NT of the use of ἰάομαι to describe the healing action of anyone other than Jesus (or God). This is significant, especially when compared with the use of θεραπεύω in Acts 28.9.
Acts 28.27 (cf. Matthew 13.15, John 12.40, Isaiah 6.10 [App. 6:1, **62**])	ἰάσομαι	Future indicative middle: 1 sing.	The final use of ἰάομαι in *Acts*. Paul quotes the Septuagint (Isaiah 6.9-10) as the final justification for his mission to the gentiles. Healing here is spiritual healing, incorporating spiritual understanding and perception, which, according to Paul, is the "salvation of God" (τὸ σωτήριον τοῦ θεοῦ (28.28)).
Hebrews 12.13	ἰαθῇ	Aorist subjunctive passive: 3 sing.	In a passage extolling the benefits of God's discipline, referring to spiritual healing.
James 5.16	ἰαθῆτε	Aorist subjunctive passive: 2 pl.	In a passage in James' letter giving advice as to procedure in the case of suffering (prayer), happiness (praise), and infirmity (prayer by church elders and anointing with oil in the name of the Lord). For, says James, "the prayer of faith will save (σώσει) the sick man (τὸν κάμνοντα), and the Lord will raise him up (ἐγερεῖ); and if he has committed sins he will be forgiven. Therefore confess your sins to one another, and pray for one another, that you may be healed (ὅπως ἰαθῆτε). The prayer of a righteous man has great power in its effects" (5.15-16). Thus spiritual healing is a prerequisite for physical healing.
1 Peter 2.24	ἰάθητε	Aorist indicative passive: 2 pl.	In Peter's call to be submissive, even as Christ was. He argues that "by his wounds you have been healed" (οὗ τῷ μώλωπι ἰάθητε). Again, this reference is to spiritual healing.
1 Corinthians 12.9	ἰαμάτων	Noun (ἴαμα): gen., pl., neut.	This form of the noun ἴαμα occurs three times in Paul's first letter to the Corinthians, in each case referring to the spiritual gifts of healing.

1 Cor. 12.28	ἰαμάτων	Noun (ἴαμα): gen., pl., neut.	Paul's second reference to the spiritual gifts of healing.
1 Cor. 12.30	ἰαμάτων	Noun (ἴαμα): gen., pl., neut.	Paul's third reference to the spiritual gifts of healing.
Colossians 4.14	Λουκᾶς ὁ ἰατρὸς	Noun: nom., sing., masc.	Paul not only designates Luke as ἰατρὸς, he also designates him ἀγαπητὸς, thus measuring his esteem for Luke, as well as identifying him by his profession. After a study of the language of healing it comes as no surprise to find that Paul designates Luke as Λουκᾶς ὁ ἰατρὸς. But if Luke is a physician, what does that make Mark? For while it is Luke who includes a greater number of healing stories (although in these he emphasises social information) it is Mark who gives the most clinical case histories (see Mark 5.25-34; 9.14-29), and who describes the disciples' healing practices in medical terms (Mark 6.13).

ἰάομαι occurs 26 times in verbal form in the New Testament. Of these 26, 15 are Lukan usages (gospel 11, *Acts* 4), 4 Matthaean, 3 Johannine, and 1 Markan. ἰάομαι also appears once in *Hebrews*, and in the letters of Peter and James.

Each synoptist uses ἰάομαι in different ways. Mark uses ἰάομαι for a woman's self-perception (5.29), while Matthew reserves it for instantaneous in-absentia gentile healings, which occur as a result of parental requests made in faith (8.8, 8.13, 15.28). Luke is fond of the verb, using it far more than any other author, in a variety of forms. Luke uses ἰάομαι and θεραπεύω contiguously, but does reserve θεραπεύω for Jewish thought and conversation, and as the subject of Pharisaic controversy.

John uses ἰάομαι sparingingly, preferring to use a range of healing verbs.

Other New Testament authors use ἰάομαι in a teaching context, referring to right doctrine, or correct Christian practice.

Appendix 8 : 4

Incidence of ἰάομαι in the New Testament according to tense, voice and mood

Tense	Voice and Mood	Form	Reference	Comment
Present	Middle indicative	ἰᾶταί	Acts 9.34	Peter's speech to Aeneas *re* Jesus
	Middle participle	ἰώμενος	Acts 10.38	Peter's speech to Cornelius the centurion, and Cornelius' kinsmen and close friends *re* Jesus
	Middle infinitive	ἰᾶσθαι	Luke 5.17, 9.2	**5.17:** in an introductory statement (καὶ δύναμις κυρίου ἦν εἰς τὸ ἰᾶσθαι αὐτόν) to the account of the healing of the paralytic (5.18-26). This healing allows Jesus to discuss his mission to forgive sins (heal) with the Pharisees and the teachers of the law. **9.2:** in Luke's account of Jesus' commission to the twelve to preach the kingdom of God and to heal [the infirm] (ἰᾶσθαι τοὺς ἀσθενεῖς), after giving them authority and power over all demons and to treat diseases (νόσους θεραπεύειν).
Imperfect	Middle indicative	ἰᾶτο	Luke 6.19, 9.11	Both Lukan usages describing crowd scenes where Jesus was the central figure. **6.19:** ἰᾶτο for those "touching", whereas those with unclean spirits ἐθεραπεύοντο; **9.11:** before the feeding of the 5,000, those in need of θεραπείας ἰᾶτο.

Future	Middle indicative	ἰάσομαι	Matthew 13.15; John 12.40; Acts 28.27; (cf. App. 6:1, **62**)	In all three cases this form occurs in a quotation from the Septuagint (Isaiah 6.10). It is part of a most significant quotation (Isaiah 6.9-10), linking healing with seeing and hearing (and therefore understanding) God's message (see App. 6:1, **62**). Thus, in *Matthew*, it is Jesus' message that causes the blind to see, the deaf to hear, and that ultimately brings healing. It is obvious that Jesus is referring to spiritual sight, spiritual hearing, and spiritual health. He explains (13.16), that the eyes and ears of the disciples are blessed (μακάριοι), because they see and hear what many prophets and righteous men before them had longed to see and hear, but had not. John uses this quotation in a passage explaining why people did not recognise Jesus' identity, while Luke, in Acts 28.27, has Paul quote the Septuagint as the final justification for his mission to the gentiles. Again, "healing" is understood as spiritual healing, incorporating spiritual understanding and perception, which, according to Paul, is the "salvation of God" (τὸ σωτήριον τοῦ θεοῦ (28.28)).
	Passive indicative	ἰαθήσεται	Matthew 8.8	out of the mouth of the centurion to Jesus: "But only say the word, and my boy (παῖς) will be healed (ἰαθήσεται)." In *Matthew* Jesus only once uses the verb ἰάομαι(13.15), (when quoting the Septuagint), never in thought or conversation. In conversation Matthew chooses to put this verb only into gentile mouths (as here), or to describe gentile healings (8.13, 15.28).
Aorist	Middle indicative	ἰάσατο	Luke 9.42, 14.4, 22.51; Acts 28.8	**9.42:** in Luke's version of the healing of the epileptic boy. **14.4:** as a description of Jesus' action, when he healed the man with dropsy on the sabbath. **22.51:** as a description of Jesus' action at the Mount of Olives, when he healed the right ear of the high priest's slave, who had been struck with a sword by one of Jesus' companions. **Acts 28.8:** as a description of Paul's treatment of Publius' father at Malta.

	Middle subjunctive	ἰάσηται	John 4.47	in the reported speech of the official (βασιλικὸς) who asks Jesus to heal his son. Jesus uses the verb ζάω to describe the boy's return to health. This is the first healing reported in *John* and the second sign (σημεῖον). It appears at the end of a non-Jewish chapter. An *in absentia* healing: Jesus does not touch the patient, or the father.
	Passive infinitive	ἰαθῆναι	Luke 6.18	in a general healing episode, where a great crowd of people came to hear Jesus, and to be healed of their diseases (οἳ ἦλθον ἀκοῦσαι αὐτοῦ καὶ ἰαθῆναι ἀπὸ τῶν νόσων αὐτῶν).
	Passive indicative	ἰάθη	Matthew 8.13, 15.28; Luke 8.47, 17.15	**Matt. 8.13:** as a final description of the instantaneous healing of the centurion's boy. **Matt. 15.28:** as a final description of the instantaneous healing of the Canaanite woman's daughter. **Luke 8.47:** in Luke's version of the story of the haemorrhaging woman, when she declares how she had been immediately healed. **Luke 17.15:** in Luke's story of the ten lepers, describing the leper's perception of himself.
	Passive indicative	ἰάθητε	1 Peter 2.24	in Peter's letter to the Jews of the Dispersion, in a call to be submissive, even as Christ was. The author argues that "by his wounds you have been healed" (οὗ τῷ μώλωπι ἰάθητε), a reference to spiritual healing.
	Passive imperative	ἰαθήτω	Luke 7.7	out of the mouth of the centurion when he asks Jesus to heal his slave (δοῦλος). There is a manuscript variation, some citing ἰαθήσεται, as at Matthew 8.8. Luke sums up the result of this request by describing the condition of the slave as ὑγιαίνοντα (7.10).
	Passive participle	ἰαθεὶς	John 5.13	in a description of the man whom Jesus chose to heal by the Beth-zatha pool, in Jerusalem, on the sabbath. John uses both θεραπεύω (5.10) and ἰάομαι (5.13) to describe the man in his narrative, while in direct speech Jesus uses ὑγιής (5.6), as does the man himself in reported speech (5.15).
	Passive subjunctive	ἰαθῇ	Hebrews 12.13	in a homily, exhorting right living to "make straight paths for your feet, so that what is lame may not be disabled but rather be healed."

	Passive subjunctive	ἰαθῆτε	James 5.16	in James' letter to the Jews of the Dispersion, giving advice as to procedure in the case of suffering (prayer), happiness (praise), and infirmity (prayer by church elders and anointing with oil in the name of the Lord) so "that you may be healed" (ὅπως ἰαθῆτε). James makes it clear that spiritual healing is a prerequisite for physical healing.
Perfect	Indicative in passive sense	ἴαται	Mark 5.29	the only occurrence of the verbal form of ἰάομαι in *Mark*, found here in the story of the haemorrhaging woman, in her thoughts concerning the state of her body, after she had touched Jesus' cloak. The woman thinks in terms of σῴζω and ἰάομαι; Mark reports Jesus as using the terms σῴζω and ὑγιής. Both σῴζω and ὑγιής imply more than just physical health and wellbeing, they include the notions of emotional, mental and spiritual wholeness as well. Mark's use of the perfect form of ἰάομαι makes it perfectly clear that, in this case, the woman is experiencing a present state, following a completed action. No more treatment is necessary. Thus ἰάομαι in *Mark*, as in *Matthew*, describes instantaneous healing, as a result of faith, faith so great it causes Jesus to comment. However Matthew does not use ἰάομαι in his account of this healing, reserving it for the description of gentile healings. (But note that this woman was ritually unclean when she touched Jesus' cloak. Cf. also Luke: ἰάθη for the haemorrhaging woman [8.47] and the leper [17.15]. Is there a link between the "unclean" and the "gentile" in Jewish thought?)

Incidence of ἴασις, ἴαμα, and ἰατρός in the New Testament

Noun (ἴασις)	acc., sing., fem.	ἴασιν	Acts 4.30	In a prayer to God, requesting opportunities to speak openly "while thou stretchest out thy hand to heal, and signs and wonders are performed through the name of the holy servant Jesus."
	gen., sing., fem.	ἰάσεως	Acts 4.22	The summing up - this sign of healing (τὸ σημεῖον τοῦτο τῆς ἰάσεως) - of the first healing episode recorded in *Acts* (3.1-4.31).
	acc., pl., fem.	ἰάσεις	Luke 13.32	In a saying of Jesus, in answer to the Pharisees' warning to him that Herod wanted to kill him: "Behold, I cast out demons and bring healings (ἰάσεις ἀποτελῶ) to completion ..."
Noun (ἴαμα)	gen., pl., neut.	ἰαμάτων	1 Corinthians 12.9, 12.28, 12.30	In Paul's first letter to the Corinthians, in each case referring to the spiritual gifts of healing.
Noun (ἰατρὸς)	nom., sing., masc.	ἰατρὸς	Colossians 4.14	Paul's designation of Luke as ἰατρὸς and ἀγαπητὸς.
	voc., sing., masc.	Ἰατρέ	Luke 4.23	A Lukan self-designation by Jesus.
	gen., sing., masc.	ἰατροῦ	Matthew 9.12; Mark 2.17; Luke 5.31	In a saying of Jesus in reply to a question concerning his choice of eating companions in all three synoptic gospels.
	gen., pl., masc.	ἰατρῶν	Mark 5.26	In Mark's story of the haemorrhaging woman.
	dat., pl., masc.	[ἰατροῖς]	Luke 8.43	In Luke's story of the haemorrhaging woman.

Appendix 9 : 1

The language of healing in the gospel according to John

Reference	Agent	Greek word	Illnesses treated	Type, number, method	Patient profile, location, motive	Comments
John 4.46-54 the second σημεῖον (cf. Mt 8.5-13; Lk 7.1-10)	Jesus	καὶ ἰάσηται αὐτοῦ τὸν υἱόν	ἠσθένει . . . ἤμελλεν γὰρ ἀποθνήσκειν	Specific: 1; word	The official's (βασιλικὸς) son, at Capernaum, healed at the father's request. A healing *in absentia*; Jesus does not touch the patient. The father believes. Could this be Chuza? See Robinson (1985) 69, n. 158. (But Chuza is a Herodian, not a gentile.)	This first healing (and second sign) appears at the end of ch. 4 in a non-Jewish chapter; after the story of the Samaritan woman at the well, Jesus' declaration of identity (4.26), and the belief of the Samaritans. Is the 7th hour significant? There is not the same emphasis on the gentile-Jewish controversy in John's account, which is apparent in the synoptic parallels, particularly *Matthew*, although John does choose to use ἰάομαι.

John 5.1-15	Jesus	θέλεις ὑγιὴς γενέσθαι; do you want to be healthy? (6) Ἔγειρε ἆρον τὸν κράβαττόν σου καὶ περιπάτει Take up your pallet and walk about (8) καὶ εὐθέως ἐγένετο ὑγιὴς ὁ ἄνθρωπος, καὶ ἦρεν τὸν κράβαττον αὐτοῦ καὶ περιεπάτει and immediately the man was whole, and took up his pallet and began to walk about(9) Ἴδε ὑγιὴς γέγονας· μηκέτι ἁμάρτανε, ἵνα μὴ χεῖρόν σοί τι γένηται Behold, you are whole! Sin no longer lest something worse happen to you! (14)	τριάκοντα [καὶ] ὀκτὼ ἔτη ἔχων ἐν τῇ ἀσθενείᾳ αὐτοῦ (5) ill for thirty eight years	Specific: 1; word	A man who had been sick for 38 years, was lying by the Beth-zatha pool, in Jerusalem, on the sabbath. Jesus saw him, asked if he wanted to be whole (ὑγιὴς), commanded him to get up, and pick up his pallet. Later, in the temple he told the man to sin no more, lest something worse happen to him (14). Jesus saw the wholeness /health of humankind as his and his father's work all the time, even (or especially?) on the sabbath. This man appears to be symbolic of Israel, in that both were in a spiritual wilderness.	Note the mss variants at vv.4,5. There were many other sick people there. Did Jesus choose him because he had been ill for 38 years? (The people of Israel wandered for 38 years unable to reach the promised land). Did Jesus choose to do this because it was the sabbath? Jesus said my father is working still, and I am working (ἐργάζομαι). Cf. 9.4 where to work for Jesus: ἐργάζεσθαι. His work on the sabbath was the cause of the Jews wanting to kill him. He broke the sabbath and called God his father, making himself equal with God. Jesus refers to this miracle at 7.23: ἐμοὶ χολᾶτε ὅτι ὅλον ἄνθρωπον ὑγιῆ ἐποίησα ἐν σαββάτῳ;

John 6.2	Jesus	τὰ σημεῖα ἃ ἐποίει ἐπὶ τῶν ἀσθενούντων (the signs which he was doing on the infirm)	τῶν ἀσθενούντων (the infirm)	General: ?, the infirm (τῶν ἀσθενούντων) ?	After this (teaching, following the two previous healing miracles,) Jesus went to the other side of the Sea of Galilee, which is the Sea of Tiberias. And a great crowd followed him, because they saw the signs which he was doing on the infirm (6.1-2). The feeding of the 5,000 follows (6.5-14): another "sign".	This may or may not be a description of a separate healing episode. The use of the imperfect tense to describe Jesus' behaviour would argue for an habitual pattern of behaviour on Jesus' part, and therefore that this is a separate general healing episode, recording Jesus' general behaviour, and not just a reference to the two previous specific healing episodes. The two previous healings occur one after the other, then Jesus (5.19-47) explains the parallels between his and his father's work. He explains the miracles thus: "these very works which I am doing (ποιῶ), bear me witness that the father has sent me" (αὐτὰ τὰ ἔργα ἃ ποιῶ, μαρτυρεῖ περὶ ἐμοῦ ὅτι ὁ πατήρ με ἀπέσταλκεν 5.36)
John 9.1-41	Jesus	ἐπέχρισεν . . . καὶ ἦλθεν βλέπων (9.5, 7)	τυφλὸν ἐκ γενετῆς (blindness from birth)	Specific: 1; spat, clay, anointed eyes, told to wash and come back	Jerusalem; on the sabbath; Jesus saw a man blind from birth.	Jesus said, "For judgment I came into this world, that those who do not see may see, and that those who see may become blind." (Εἰς κρίμα ἐγὼ εἰς τὸν κόσμον τοῦτον ἦλθον, ἵνα οἱ μὴ βλέποντες βλέπωσιν καὶ οἱ βλέποντες τυφλοὶ γένωνται) (9.39). This healing is symbolic of Jesus' purpose: to bring spiritual sight. That it is on the sabbath is also significant; Jesus deliberately tries to incite Jewish enmity.

John 11.1-57	Jesus	Λάζαρε, δεῦρο ἔξω . . . Λύσατε αὐτὸν καὶ ἄφετε αὐτὸν ὑπάγειν (11.43, 44)	ἀσθενῶν . . . Λάζαρος ἀπέθανεν . . . αὐτὸν τέσσαρας ἤδη ἡμέρας ἔχοντα ἐν τῷ μνημείῳ (11.1, 14, 17)	Specific: 1 (Lazarus); word (command)	Mary and Martha told Jesus of Lazarus' illness. Jesus deliberately delayed going to Bethany, so that Lazarus had been in his tomb four days by the time Jesus arrived.	This healing is the catalyst for Jesus' triumphal entry into Jerusalem, and the Jewish plot to kill him. It is symbolic that the catalyst for the crucifixion and Jesus' death (and resurrection) should be his restoring to life of someone else.

John uses ring compositon to record his selection of healing miracles. There are five healings: four specific and one general. The general episode occurs in the middle. The first and the last specific episodes both deal with death, and are in response to a family request, made in faith. The second and fourth specific healings are both of patients chosen by Jesus, on the sabbath, and are highly symbolic. Both represent spiritual ignorance.

Appendix 9 : 2

New Testament healing words : ὑγιαίνω ὑγιής

Reference	Form	Part of speech	Comment
Matthew 12.13	ὑγιὴς	Adjective: nom., sing., fem.	In Matthew's account of the healing of the man with the withered hand, as a description of the man's hand, after Jesus had spoken to him. It was whole/sound/healthy like the other (ὑγιὴς ὡς ἡ ἄλλη).
Matthew 15.31	ὑγιεῖς	Adjective: acc., pl., masc.	In a description of a general healing episode, qualifying κυλλοὺς (the maimed/crippled).
Mark 5.34	ὑγιὴς	Adjective: nom., sing., fem.	The only use of ὑγιὴς occurring in *Mark*, in the story of the haemorrhaging woman. It is part of a command from Jesus, following a statement from him that the woman's faith had saved her: θυγάτηρ, ἡ πίστις σου σέσωκέν σε· ὕπαγε εἰς εἰρήνην καὶ ἴσθι ὑγιὴς ἀπὸ τῆς μάστιγός σου (5.34). The word ὑγιὴς implies much more than physical health; it implies emotional, mental and spiritual health as well. Jesus' command: Go (and keep going) in peace, and be (always) healthy (whole) ....
Luke 5.31	ὑγιαίνοντες	Present participle active: nom., pl., masc.	The present participle of ὑγιαίνω occurs as a noun, οἱ ὑγιαίνοντες, in a saying which Luke attributes to Jesus. Jesus contrasts οἱ ὑγιαίνοντες (δικαίους) with οἱ κακῶς ἔχοτες (ἁμαρτωλοὺς), implying that his task was that of a spiritual physician (ἰατροῦ).
Luke 7.10	ὑγιαίνοντα	Present participle active: acc., sing., masc.	The present participle of ὑγιαίνω occurs as the final description of the centurion's slave in Luke's account of this story. The earlier healing words are spoken by the centurion. He uses διασῴζω, when asking the Jewish elders to request Jesus' help, and later ἰάομαι, in a message sent through his friends. Jesus does not take any action, other than to marvel at the man's faith, faith that he had not found in Israel. However, those sent out to talk to Jesus find the slave ὑγιαίνοντα when they return to the house. The slave had been ill, and about to die (κακῶς ἔχων ἤμελλεν τελευτᾶν [7.2]).

Luke 15.27	*ὑγιαίνοντα*	Present participle active: acc., sing., masc.	In Luke's parable of the lost son. Here, a slave tells of the father's joy because he has received his son *ὑγιαίνοντα*, i.e. safe and sound. Later, the father attempts to explain his joy to his other son, explaining that his brother who was dead (νεκρὸς) and lost (ἀπολωλὼς), has now lived (ἔζησεν), and been found (εὑρέθη). ζάω and νεκρὸς are similarly contrasted in Acts 20.7-12, where Luke recounts the story of Paul's treatment of Eutychus.
{A} **John** 5.4	{A} ὑγιὴς	Adjective: nom., sing., masc.	According to Metzger (1975) 209, verse 4 is a gloss, category {A}. Therefore the occurrence of ὑγιὴς in it will be disregarded when citing incidence and meaning of the *ὑγιαίνω* ὑγιής family of words.
John 5.6	ὑγιὴς	Adjective: nom., sing., masc.	All six occurrences of ὑγιής in John's gospel refer to the one healing story, that of the man beside the Beth-zatha pool in Jerusalem. Here Jesus asks the sick man (τις ἄνθρωπος . . . ἔχων ἐν τῇ ἀσθενείᾳ) "Do you want to be healthy/whole?" (Θέλεις ὑγιὴς γενέσθαι;)
John 5.9	ὑγιὴς	Adjective: nom., sing., masc.	As a description of the man after Jesus had commanded him to get up and pick up his pallet (*καὶ* εὐθέως *ἐγένετο* ὑγιὴς ὁ ἄθρωπος).
John 5.11	ὑγιῆ	Adjective: acc., sing., masc.	In the speech of the man, as he describes to the Jews what had happened to him , and why he was carrying his pallet on the sabbath. He described Jesus as "the man who made me whole" (Ὁ ποιήσας με ὑγιῆ).
John 5.14	ὑγιὴς	Adjective: nom., sing., masc.	In a speech of Jesus to the man: "Behold! You are whole!" (Ἴδε ὑγιὴς *γέγονας*). Jesus goes on to tell him to sin no more, lest something worse befall him.
John 5.15	ὑγιῆ	Adjective: acc., sing., masc.	In the reported speech of the man who had been healed, when he identifies Jesus to the Jews as the man who made him healthy/whole (ὅτι Ἰησοῦς ἐστιν ὁ ποιήσας *αὐτὸν* ὑγιῆ [5.15]). In this case the man appears to be symbolic of Israel: he had been sick for 38 years, (the people of Israel wandered for 38 years unable to reach the promised land). It is significant that Jesus chose the sabbath to perform this healing - his justification that he was working just as his father was still working (Ὁ πατήρ μου ἕως ἄρτι ἐργάζεται, κἀγὼ ἐργάζομαι [5.17]).

John 7.23	ὑγιῆ	Adjective: acc., sing., masc.	The final use of ὑγιής in John's gospel, and again referring to the healing of the man at the Beth-zatha pool. Here Jesus uses it himself, when talking with the Jews. He asks them: "Are you angry with me because I made a man wholly healthy on the sabbath?" (ἐμοὶ χολᾶτε ὅτι ὅλον ἄνθρωπον ὑγιῆ ἐποίησα ἐν σαββάτῳ;) There is no mention of healing in relation to the body only, as the RSV translation reads. Rather, the language stresses that it is the whole man that is ὑγιής. This stress is unusual. Jesus uses it to point out the right judgment (τὴν δικαίαν κρίσιν) of his actions to his accusers. That Jesus sought out this particular healing, and this particular confrontation, seems obvious. John underlines its significance by reserving his use of ὑγιής for this healing alone. ὑγιής must describe holistic health, i.e. total mental, emotional, physical and spiritual well-being.
Acts 4.10	ὑγιής	Adjective: nom., sing., masc.	In Peter's reply to the rulers, elders, scribes, and those of high-priestly family, concerning the healing of the man lame from birth (Acts 3.1-26, 4.1-31). In this speech (4.8-12) Peter describes the man in terms of σῴζω, and ὑγιής. Earlier (3.16), Peter had described him as enjoying perfect health (τὴν ὁλοκληρίαν). All these words convey holistic health.
1 Timothy 1.10	τῇ ὑγιαινούσῃ διδασκαλίᾳ	Present participle active (adjectival): dat., sing., fem.	All four instances of ὑγιαίνω in *1* and *2 Timothy* occur in the form of an adjectival participle qualifying διδασκαλία or λόγος. Here, it occurs qualifying διδασκαλία in an explanatory exposition on the use of the law, i.e. that the law is laid down for anything contrary to sound doctrine (τῇ ὑγιαινούσῃ διδασκαλίᾳ), according to the glorious gospel of the blessed God (κατὰ τὸ εὐαγγέλιον τῆς δόξης τοῦ μακαρίου θεοῦ).
1 Timothy 6.3	ὑγιαίνουσιν λόγοις	Present participle active (adjectival): dat., pl., masc.	Here ὑγιαίνουσιν qualifies λόγοις, words attributed to Jesus, and linked to teaching which is pious (τῇ κατ' εὐσέβειαν διδασκαλία). Thus ὑγιαίνω as an adjectival participle in *1 Timothy* implies pious teaching, teaching which is in accordance with the writer's interpretation of the teaching of Jesus.
2 Timothy 1.13	ὑγιαινόντων λόγων	Present participle active (adjectival): gen., pl., masc.	Here ὑγιαινόντων again qualifies λόγων in a command from the writer to "keep the example of the sound words which you have heard from me in faith and in the love which is in Christ Jesus". Cf. Titus 1.9,13, where ὑγιαίνω and faith are linked.

2 Timothy 4.3	τῆς ὑγιαινούσης διδασκαλίας	Present participle active (adjectival): gen., sing., fem.	In this, the final usage of ὑγιαίνω in *1* and *2 Timothy*, the writer warns that the time is coming when people will not endure sound teaching (τῆς ὑγιαινούσης διδασκαλίας), but will turn away from the truth, and wander into myths (4.3-4). Thus ὑγιαίνω, used as an adjectival participle in *1* and *2 Timothy*, implies pious teaching, teaching that is is accordance with the writer's interpretation of Jesus' gospel.
Titus 1.9	τῇ διδασκαλίᾳ τῇ ὑγιαινούσῃ	Present participle active (adjectival): dat., sing., fem.	Here, the writer expounds on the qualities necessary in a bishop (ἐπίσκοπος). "He must hold firm to the believing word (πιστοῦ λόγου), as taught, so that he may be able to speak words of encouragement in sound teaching (ἵνα δυνατὸς ᾖ καὶ παρακαλεῖν ἐν τῇ διδασκαλίᾳ τῇ ὑγιαινούσῃ), and refute those who contradict it."
Titus1.13	ἵνα ὑγιαίνωσιν ἐν τῇ πίστει	Present subjunctive active : 3 pl., in a final clause expressing purpose.	Again, the writer orders Titus to "rebuke them sharply, that they may be sound in the faith." (δι' ἣν αἰτίαν ἔλεγχε αὐτοὺς ἀποτόμως, ἵνα ὑγιαίνωσιν ἐν τῇ πίστει)
Titus 2.1	τῇ ὑγιαινούσῃ διδασκαλίᾳ	Present participle active (adjectival): dat., sing., fem.	Again, the writer commands Titus to "utter what befits sound sound teaching." (Σὺ δὲ λάλει ἃ πρέπει τῇ ὑγιαινούσῃ διδασκαλίᾳ)
Titus 2.8	λόγον ὑγιῆ ἀκατάγνωστον	Adjective: acc., sing., masc., qualifying λόγον.	In a catalogue of the qualities of good teaching: "sound argument that cannot be censured". Thus, to the writer, the words ὑγιαίνω and ὑγιής imply soundness, i.e. truth that springs out of faith.
3 John 2	ὑγιαίνειν	Present infinitive: active	The last occurrence of ὑγιαίνω in the NT. It occurs in the opening salutation of the third letter of John to Gaius: "Beloved, I pray concerning all things that you are prospering and healthy, just as your soul prospers."
Of the 22 occurrences of this family of words, 19 are adjectival. Matthew uses ὑγιής in a physical sense, to describe sound limbs, which had formerly been maimed (12.13, 15.31), while Mark uses it only once, in a holistic sense, in Jesus' command to the haemorrhaging woman (5.34). Luke uses ὑγιαίνω three times in his gospel, in participial form, to mean holistic health (5.31, 7.10, 15.27); and ὑγιής once in *Acts* in a holistic sense (4.10). John uses ὑγιής six times, in a holistic sense, in one healing story (5.6-23). The present infinitive ὑγιαίνειν is also used in a holistic sense by the author of *3 John* (2). Elsewhere (1 Timothy 1.10, 6.3; 2 Timothy 1.13. 4.3; Titus 1.9, 1.13, 2.1, 2.8) forms of ὑγιαίνω always refer to sound teaching, sound doctrine, and sound faith.			

Acknowledgements

I am grateful to Professor Hermann Kienast and Martin Schäfer of the German Archaeological Institute at Athens for their help in supplying the following photographs:

Plate 2: Votive relief of Asklepios (Athens, N.M. 173) (Neg. Nr.: N.M. 398)
Plate 3: Asklepios of Mounychia (Athens, N.M. 258) (Neg. Nr.: 89/70)
Plate 4: Votive relief of an Athenian family (Athens, N.M. 1384) (Neg. Nr.: N.M. 6245)
Plate 5: Statue of Hippokrates (Kos Museum 32) (Neg. Nr.: 72/164)
Plate 7: Head of a statue of the goddess Hygieia (Athens, N.M. 3602) (Neg. Nr.: N.M. 4688)

Appendix 3:1

1: Relief of Asklepios and his family (Athens, N.M. 1402) (Neg. Nr.: N.M. 4656)
2: The relief of the doctors (Athens, N.M. 1332) (Neg. Nr.: N.M. 642)
3: Relief of Archinos to Amphiaraos (Athens, N.M. 3369) (Neg. Nr.: N.M. 3312)
4: Relief of Asklepios in the act of healing (Piraeus Museum 405) (Neg. Nr.: 93/245)
5: Relief of Asklepios in the act of healing (Athens, N.M. 1841) (Neg. Nr.: N.M. 1186)
6: Relief of healing activity (Athens, N.M. 2373) (Neg. Nr.: N.M. 6256)
7: Relief of Asklepios seated (Athens, N.M. 1352) (Neg. Nr.: N.M. 6345)
8: Relief of woman giving a patient a footbath (Athens, N.M. 1914) (Neg. Nr.: N.M. 5594)
9: Relief of an Athenian family (Athens, N.M. 1384) (Neg. Nr.: N.M. 6245)
10: Relief of an Athenian family (Athens, N.M. 1408) (Neg. Nr.: N.M. 6362)
11: Relief of an Athenian family (Athens, N.M. 1345)(Neg. Nr.: N.M. 6342)
12: Relief of Asklepios, Hygieia, and offering (Athens, N.M. 1335) (Neg. Nr.: N.M. 6330)
13: Relief of suppliants with sacrificial ox (Athens, N.M. 1429) (Neg. Nr.: 93/341)
14: Relief of suppliants with sacrificial ram (Athens, N.M. 1333) (Neg. Nr.: N.M. 6246)
16: Relief depicting a varicose vein (Athens, N.M. 3526)(Neg. Nr.: ATH.V. 47)

I also owe acknowledgement to Dr Nancy Bookidis of the American School of Classical Studies at Athens, Korinth Excavations, for her help in supplying a photograph of anatomical votives of the late 5th to 4th centuries BC from the Room of the Asklepieion at Korinth Museum (Figure 15).

Index

Abimelech, 107
Achilleus, 2-6, 9-12, 154
Aelius Aristides, 93-101
Aeneas, 165
Aeschylus, 49 n.350, 52, 55-56
Agamede, 8
ailments:
  abscess, 24, 27, 86,87
  anguish, 56, 58, 62, 228
  baldness, 24, 28, 32
  blindness, 23, 25, 30-31, 34, 37, 45, 109, 114, 121, 131-132, 134, 144, 159, 182-185, 187-189, 196-199, 202
  conception/pregnancy, 25, 26, 29
  consumption, 24
  cripple, 132, 204
  deafness, 121, 131-132, 159, 196, 198, 202
  death, 2-7, 9, 15, 49, 52, 65, 73, 82, 101, 109, 117, 132, 141, 186-187, 190
  demonic, 126-127, 130, 132, 134, 171, 188, 201, 210, 212-203
  dropsy, 25, 162-163, 171
  dumb (voice), 5, 24, 132, 134, 143, 196, 198, 202
  epilepsy, 77-79, 89 n.668,131-132, 134, 144, 157, 162, 188, 200-201, 224, 226
  fever, 73, 122, 131, 134, 141, 164, 173, 200
  gout, 24, 30, 32
  haemorrhage, 122, 131, 134, 156, 166-167, 182-185, 188-189, 196-197, 203, 208, 219, 221, 224
  headache, 24, 35
  insomnia, 35
  lameness, 24, 28, 32, 37, 121, 142, 149, 171, 174, 185, 187-188, 190, 201, 205
  leeches, 24, 27, 31
  leprosy, 121, 131, 134, 148, 167, 182, 184-185, 187, 189, 191-192, 194-197, 210
  lice, 24, 28
  maimed, 131-132, 134, 204, 208
  paralysis, 23, 131, 134, 142
  sores, 24
  stigmata, 31
  tumour, 24
  withered, 122-123, 132, 149-150, 182, 189, 204
  worms, 25, 27, 31
  wounds, 8-13, 24, 26, 28, 37, 52, 80, 81, 106-107, 110, 117, 128, 134, 175, 215
Akeso, 16
Ambrosia, 26, 28
Ananias, 141, 202
Antikrates, 22
Apollo, 1, 4-9, 11-14, 19, 21-22, 45, 69, 71, 83, 94, 104
Arata, 27, 33
Aristophanes, 16, 43-45
Artaxerxes, 111
Bartimaeus, 183, 189
Canaanite, 157-158, 188, 198, 219

Celsus, 128 n.216
centurion, 146, 156-158, 164, 167, 188, 190, 192, 198, 207, 219
Cheiron, 9, 10, 12, 14
Delphi, 20, 33
Dorcas, 165
Echedoros, 22, 33-34
Elijah, 106
Elisha, 106
Epicurus, 57-59, 218, 228
Epione, 16, 67
Euripides, 52-53, 57, 228
Eutychus, 207
Galen, 85-89
Gerasene demoniac, 187, 190
Hagestratos, 24 n.154
healing agents:
  dog, 29-30, 32, 34-35, 37, 39
  goose, 29-30, 32, 35, 37
  serpent/snake, 29-30, 34-35, 37, 45, 68
healing method:
  conversation, 25-26, 33, 35, 38
  conversion, 139, 141, 161, 165, 173, 178, 184, 188, 191, 193, 218, 220, 224, 226
  counselling, 34
  diet, 38, 75, 78
  dream (vision), 25, 27-30, 33, 35, 37, 45, 75, 86-87, 92, 95-96, 111, 164
  drug, 25, 29, 87, 95, 99, 109-110, 116
  exercise, 38, 75, 78, 87, 95
  exorcism, 118, 145, 194, 201, 213
  finger, 28, 199, 199 n.678
  massage, 75, 128
  medicine, 8-13, 21, 30, 45, 59, 66, 69, 71-74, 78, 86-88, 98-99, 109-111, 125
  oil, 127-130, 175, 213, 215, 224
  prayer, 6-7, 60, 70, 75, 85-86, 96, 104-105, 108, 111, 129, 141, 163, 172, 175-176, 184, 186, 190, 193, 208
  psychological, 34, 39, 58, 62, 83, 93, 227-228
  saliva, 30, 35, 45, 198 n.674, 224
  surgery, 10, 25-27, 33, 76, 81
  touch, 8, 25, 28, 35, 38-39, 43-44, 69, 99, 123-124, 131, 137, 156, 160-161, 166, 171, 173, 180-181, 183-185, 188-189, 193-202, 222
  treatment, 109-111, 116-119, 128-131, 136, 139, 142, 144, 151, 153, 156, 158, 161, 173, 191, 207, 215, 220, 222-123, 227
healing motive:
  compassion, 105, 123-124, 131, 133, 141, 193, 198
healing (Sabbath), 149-151, 162-163, 171, 178, 182, 189, 204, 222-223
healing result: peace, 106-107, 166-167, 229
Heraieus, 22
Hermias, 80-81, 309
Hermodikos 22, 26, 33, 275
Hermon, 22, 32, 34
Herod, 116-117
Herod Antipas, 123
Herodas, 66-71
Herzog, 34-35, 69-70
Hesiod, 16
Hippokrates, 71, 72, 77, 109, 129, 162, 215
Hippokratic Corpus, 71-83
Hippokratic medicine, 10, 38, 62-63, 69, 71-83, 86

Homer, 124, 154, 164, 221-222, 224
humour, 25
Hygieia, 16, 44, 46
Iaso, 16, 44, 67
inscriptions, 16-17, 19, 21-22, 26, 29-31, 33-41, 46-9, 51, 54, 58, 61-63, 65, 79, 81-84, 100, 203-204, 221
Jairus, 122, 186, 190, 194, 200, 222
Joanna, 123, 133
Joram, 111
Josephus,115-119
Kavvadias, 21
Kleimenes, 28, 33, 35
Kleinatas, 22
Korinth, 23, 85
Lazarus, 185-186, 190
Lyson, 30
Machaon, 9-10, 12, 14, 16, 67, 93, 97
Marcus Aurelius, 38, 58, 89-93, 101
Marcus Julius Apellas, 38-39, 101, 276-278
Marinos, 59-60
Origen, 16
Paiëon, 8, 11-12, 67, 69, 104
Panakeia, 16, 44, 67, 71
Pandaros, 22, 26
Patroklos, 2, 6, 10-12, 58, 154
Pausanias, 21
Philo of Alexandria, 112-115
philosophy, 57-62, 112, 228-229
physician, 9-13, 16, 21, 45-47, 51, 60-62, 65, 71-73, 78-79, 81, 84-91, 97-100, 107, 109-111, 116, 123, 133, 147-149, 166, 168-170, 206, 218, 226
see also: Hermias, Hippokrates, Galen, Rufus of Ephesus, Xenotimos
pilgrimage, 18, 20
Pindar, 16
Plato, 16, 71
Pliny, 65, 70
Podaleirios, 9-12, 14, 16, 67, 93, 97
prayer 6, 7, 60, 70, 75, 85-86, 96
Proclus, 60
Publius, 141-142, 163-164, 202
punishment 4, 5, 31, 34, 452-458
Raphael, 106, 109-110
Rome, 8, 65, 85, 89, 93, 115
Rufus of Ephesus, 89 n.668, 318
Samaritan, 123, 128, 167, 173, 184, 187, 189, 195, 214-216
Sapphira, 141
Saul, 165
Septuagint, 103-112
slave, 134, 163, 168, 173, 196, 207
Sophocles, 5, 52, 56
Sostrata, 22, 26, 27, 36
Strabo, 20, 66
Suidas, 59, 61
Syro-Phoenician, 158
Thersandros, 29, 33
Thucydides, 50-55
Tobit, 109-110
Trikka, 9, 14, 18, 62, 67
votive, 16, 22, 26, 30, 33-34, 38, 40-43, 46, 67, 69
Xenophon, 50-52, 65
Xenotimos, 80-81, 308
Zeus, 2-6, 8, 11, 13, 15, 55, 86, 93-94